A TO... FOR THE MAN—

"Perhaps no single man did so much to swing American support behind British secret warfare in the horrifying two years when the United States remained officially neutral and Europe lay at Hitler's feet."
— General William J. Donovan, OSS

"When the full story can be told, I am quite certain that your contribution will be among the foremost in having brought victory."
— J. Edgar Hoover, in a letter to Sir William Stephenson

". . . It was—the greatest Anglo-American intelligence enterprise in history. Stephenson's personal contacts were such that he got the willing services of talented men and women from every field of human endeavor, of every nationality."
— Sir Noel Coward

"Stephenson and Donovan carried out the single outstanding intelligence coup of the Second World War when they delayed the Nazi invasion of Russia."
— Winston Churchill, in a private message to Franklin D. Roosevelt

. . . AND THE BOOK!

"FASCINATING . . . GRIPPING . . . Tells of the sinking of the **Bismarck,** the U-boat war, troubles with Latin America, guerrilla operations like the assassination of Heydrich, the development of the A-bomb, North Africa, Dieppe, D-Day—in fact, the entire course of the war seen from a different slant: that of the undercover man."
—**Boston Sunday Globe**

"The histories of World War II will have to be revised in light of the remarkable revelations made in this book . . . the narrative is crammed with astonishing stories. Can you imagine Leslie Howard, Greta Garbo and Noel Coward as secret agents. All of them— and others equally surprising—served their cause silently."
—**Cincinnati Post**

"DETAILED AND PRECISELY DOCU- MENTED . . . an intriguing story of secret actions against the backdrop of great events."
—**Washington Post**

"A SPLENDID BOOK. RICH IN INFOR- MATION . . . PROFOUND IN ITS IMPLI- CATIONS FOR TODAY."
—**San Francisco Chronicle**

"A MAN CALLED INTREPID IS ONE OF THE MOST SIGNIFICANT BOOKS OF OUR TIME . . . the detailed story of men and women—many who occupy unmarked graves in Europe—who enlisted in a cold and lonely cause, often dropped by aircraft into enemy territories, and who built an intelligence network that saved the free world . . . a book which kept me immobile until dawn-light . . . I THINK I SHALL NEVER FORGET MUCH OF IT."

—Los Angeles Herald-Examiner

"A book masterfully coordinated and filled with fascinating detail . . . a pulsing portrait of an unusually fascinating character . . . thank God he was there when we needed him."

—Hartford Courant

"The heroes and villains of the piece are every bit as heroic and villainous as those created fictionally, from the bloody Reinhard Heydrich, the butcher of Prague, to the woman code-named Cynthia, who exploited her beauty and sexual attraction with breathtaking results . . . AN ADVENTURE STORY OF MONUMENTAL PROPORTIONS . . . A HISTORICAL DOCUMENT OF MAJOR SIGNIFICANCE."

—NBC News and Information Service

ICELAND

EUROPE BEFORE 1938

0   300
Miles

NORWAY

SWEDEN

FINLAND

Oslo

Stockholm

Helsinki

ESTON

NORTH

SEA

DENMARK

LATV

LITHUA

EAST
PRUSSIA

IRELAND

Dublin

GREAT
BRITAIN

London

NETHERLANDS

Berlin

POLAN

War

ATLANTIC

OCEAN

BELGIUM

Paris

GERMANY

Prague

CZECHOSLOVAKIA

AUSTRIA

HUNGARY

R

SWITZ.

FRANCE

ITALY

Belgrade

YUGOSLAVIA

PORTUGAL

Madrid

SPAIN

Balearic Is.

Corsica

Sardinia

Rome

ALBANIA

GREE

Athe

Tangier

SP.
MOROCCO

Algiers

Tunis

Sicily

MOROCCO

ALGERIA

TUNISIA

MEDITERR

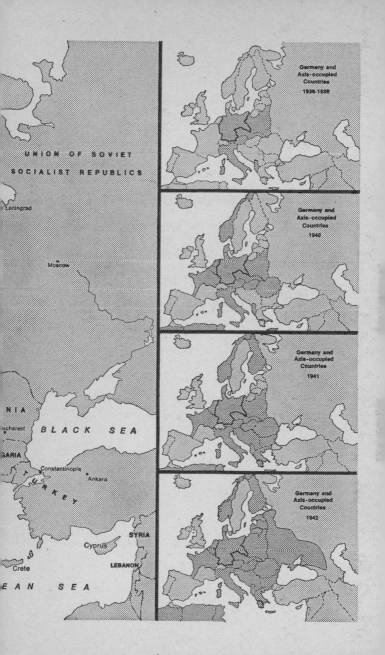

UNION OF SOVIET

SOCIALIST REPUBLICS

Leningrad

Moscow

NIA

Bucharest

GARIA

Constantinople

TURKEY

Ankara

BLACK SEA

Cyprus

SYRIA

Crete

LEBANON

EAN SEA

Germany and
Axis-occupied
Countries
1938-1939

Germany and
Axis-occupied
Countries
1940

Germany and
Axis-occupied
Countries
1941

Germany and
Axis-occupied
Countries
1942

MICHAEL YORK

BARBARA HERSHEY

and

DAVID NIVEN

as

A MAN CALLED INTREPID

A MAN CALLED INTREPID

THE SECRET WAR

William Stevenson

*For Carolyn —
An intrepid lady!
love —
Tom*

BALLANTINE BOOKS · NEW YORK

Copyright © 1976 by William Stevenson

All rights reserved. No part of this publication may be reproduced or transmitted in any form or by any means, electronic
or mechanical, including photocopy, recording, or any information storage and retrieval system, without permission in writing
from Harcourt Brace Jovanovich. Published in the United
States by Ballantine Books, a division of Random House, Inc.,
New York, and simultaneously in Canada by Random House
of Canada, Limited, Toronto, Canada.

Library of Congress Catalog Card Number: 75-30730

ISBN 0-345-29352-5

This edition published by arrangement with
Harcourt Brace Jovanovich

Manufactured in the United States of America

First Ballantine Books Edition: January 1977
Eleventh Printing: June 1980

First Canadian Printing: April 1977
Third Canadian Printing: September 1978

With love and admiration for
Mary French Simmons,
of Springfield, Tennessee,
in recognition of her
courage and devotion,
and who, as Lady Stephenson,
made Intrepid possible

CONTENTS

POINT OF DEPARTURE

A FOREWORD BY INTREPID

PRESIDENT FRANKLIN DELANO Roosevelt supported a secret war against tyranny for two years when the United States was formally at peace. Then, attacked without warning, the United States replaced the staid costume of diplomacy for the combat fatigues of war. The enemy—Nazi Germany, Imperial Japan, Fascist Italy, and their puppets—was at last out in the open. But the secret war continued in secrecy.

For cogent reasons, the fundamental facts of that hidden activity have never been fully revealed. The complete facts have been known to few; some have not been committed to any documents; the written records have been totally inaccessible; and for thirty-five years they were under the rigid restraint of Britain's Official Secrets Act. Even now, a few matters must remain undisclosed for reasons that, of course, will *not* be obvious. But in terms of history—what really happened and why—nothing significant need now be concealed.

In 1940, supplied all but daily with evidence that Hitler's scheme of world domination by terror, deceit, and conquest was undeniably underway, Roosevelt recognized that the defeat of embattled Britain would be prologue to an ultimate attack upon the United States. Intelligence was given to him by me or through me as Winston Churchill's secret envoy and as chief of British Security Coordination. BSC, the innocuous-sounding organization with headquarters in New York, was, in fact, the hub for all branches of British intelligence. Roosevelt was acutely aware that America, psychologically isolated since World War I and relying wistfully upon geographical insularity, was woefully unprepared to meet or counter the onslaught of newly developed military, propaganda, and espionage techniques. He desperately needed time to alert his nation and to arm it without plummeting into war. Churchill was in far more desperate need of arms and supplies to grant severely battered Britain even a modest hope of resistance and a slim chance of survival. Only a leader who could extend his vision of national self-interest to the belief that a union of free people was the real defense against totalitarian aggressors would wager on Britain at such unattractive odds. Roosevelt was such a rare gambler.

With Japan's attack on Pearl Harbor and, within a few days, Hitler's declaration of war against the United States, all diplomatic sham abruptly ceased. Military and naval operations, however covert their planning and launching, became dramatically public upon execution, frequently reported in eyewitness accounts by daring war correspondents. But the secret war, burgeoning in intricacy to immense proportion and purpose, remained by its very nature obscure and unknown. With few exceptions, the crucial events have remained so.

After all these years, why tell about them now? In my view, there are compelling arguments for disclosure.

In the most personal sense, I consider this account a tribute to the gallant women and men of many nations who volunteered to fight in unconventional ways. They assumed frightful risks, had no protection or privilege of uniform, carried the responsibility of countless lives in the solitary missions they accepted on trust, and often were forced to make lonely decisions that could mean merciless death to their families and countrymen. Many of these agents and resistance fighters lie in unmarked or unknown graves. Relatively few have gained recognition beyond mention in confidential archives. Most of those who survived returned to peaceful pursuits, unable to receive honors or rewards. Those who are named in this narrative are but a few of the vast hidden army to whom the free world owes a debt that cannot be repaid.

But there are less personal, more acute reasons for these disclosures.

With the surrender of the shattered Axis Powers in 1945, BSC dismantled its labyrinthine apparatus and silently passed out of existence. Its furious life had seen the tide of battle turn from near-fatal defeat to overwhelming victory. The Grand Alliance had prevailed in a fiery test. The Holocaust provided eleven million ghostly voices deafeningly raised against the malignancy of modern barbarism. The wreckage of London, Berlin, Hiroshima, and other landmarks of civilization stood as massive reminder of the monstrosity of the new concept of war that recognized no noncombatants, neither the infant, the infirm, nor the helpless. Yet the incipient United Nations promised an international commitment to comity and reason. And the imminent ordeal of Nuremberg seemed to signal the long-sought awakening of world conscience and the recognition of responsibility for crimes against humanity. We looked with yearning upon a planet in the springtime of safe coexistence.

The weapon of secret warfare, so terrifyingly effective, forged out of necessity in the crucible of combat, had no place in the pastures of peace. To my profound relief, INTREPID ceased to be the code name for the chief of an intelligence network. I closed the books on BSC, never, I hoped, to open them again.

Perhaps it was foolhardy to suppose that in real life we could undo what had been done, cancel our knowledge of evil, uninvent our weapons, stow away what remained in some safe hiding place. With the devastation of World War II still grimly visible, its stench hardly gone from the air, the community of nations started to fragment, its members splitting into factions, resorting to threats and, finally, to violence and to war. The certainty of peace had proved little more than a fragile dream. "And so the great democracies triumphed," Sir Winston Churchill wrote later. "And so were able to resume the follies that had nearly cost them their life."

Prophetic as he was, Churchill did not foresee the awesome extremes to which these follies would extend: diplomacy negotiated within a balance of nuclear terror; resistance tactics translated into guidelines for fanatics and terrorists; intelligence agencies evolving technologically to a level where they could threaten the very principles of the nations they were created to defend. One way or another, such dragon's teeth were sown in the secret activities of World War II. Questions of utmost gravity emerged: Were crucial events being maneuvered by elite secret power groups? Were self-aggrandizing careerists cynically displacing principle among those entrusted with the stewardship of intelligence? What had happened over three decades to an altruistic force that had played so pivotal a role in saving a free world from annihilation or slavery? In the name of sanity, the past now had to be seen clearly. The time had come to open the books.

Barriers stood in the way of so simple-appearing a task. A treasury of misinformation had already been gathered and widely distributed in the decades since the war. Much of this came from commercial exploiters who sought popularity at the expense of any semblance of truth. But many serious efforts, backed by exhausting (although hardly exhaustive) research, produced incomplete, thus unintentionally inaccurate reportage. Zealously preserved secrecy naturally thwarted the most dedicated investigator. And, ironically, some of the deliberately false concoctions we created to mislead our adversaries were still generally accepted as genuine. (If truth was not served by that, vanity surely was!) Adventure and sensationalism frequently were fictively injected into accounts that, were the real facts known, would have been infinitely more intriguing. Enforced silence prevented the correction of or even mild comment on these misrepresentations. Could these entrenched misconceptions and undenied speculations now be exploded?

The BSC Papers cover an enormous and complex sweep of events. The writer and historian Cornelius Ryan had been asked to consider a chronicle of the secret war and had consulted the papers of the U.S. Office of Strategic Services, the American equivalent of BSC. Ryan reported in the New York *Times* of September 17, 1972: "Stepping even briefly into that mysterious world was enough to convince me of the awesome task awaiting the historian. . . . Because of the many faces of intelligence itself, to reach the truth, to separate fact from fiction, the historian might well need as many trained researchers as there were operatives in the OSS."

Fortunately, BSC historians had consolidated their own papers to provide a summary "to be consulted," I wrote at the time, "if future need should arise for secret activities of this kind." These papers consisted of many thick volumes and exhibits, covering five years of intense activity and thousands of operations across the world.

While this summary eased somewhat the task that fell to William Stevenson, my friend and former colleague, it did not lift from his shoulders the staggering burdens of investigation and selection from such vast records. He is a painstaking researcher and drew on many other sources. Our shared interests made it inevitable that he should produce this chronicle. Yet he is too strong-willed and independent to borrow my views. (Despite the similarity of our names, we are not related.) I played no part in his selection of the material. I have read the manuscript and vouch for its authenticity. I willingly answered all the author's many and probing questions, for they are part of the larger question that must be answered now and in the future: *Will the democracies consent to their own survival?*

We failed to face that critical question prior to 1939. Not one of the democracies honestly confronted the obvious threats to its survival. They would not unite, rearm, or consider sacrifices for individual or collective security. There were those who argued that the sacrifices were not necessary. Today, parallel arguments are heard, similar responses given.

We are rightly repelled by secrecy; it is a potential threat to democratic principle and free government. Yet we would delude ourselves if we should forget that secrecy was for a time virtually our only defense. It served not only to achieve victory, but also to save lives in that perilous pursuit.

The weapons of secrecy have no place in an ideal world. But we live in a world of undeclared hostilities in which such weapons are constantly used against us and could, unless countered, leave us unprepared again, this time for an onslaught of magnitude that staggers the imagination. And while it may seem unnecessary to stress so obvious a point, the weapons of secrecy are rendered ineffective if we remove the secrecy. One of the conditions of democracy is freedom of information. It would be infinitely preferable to know exactly how our intelligence agencies function, and why, and where. But this information, once made public, disarms us.

So there is the conundrum: How can we wield the weapons of secrecy without damage to ourselves? How can we preserve secrecy without endangering constitutional law and individual guarantees of freedom?

Perhaps the story of BSC can help. It is common knowledge now that enemy codes were broken; that secret cadres were created within the enemy camps; that new technology was put at the service of agents and guerrillas. Equally true but possibly not so evident, is an important characteristic of BSC—it consisted of volunteer civilians convinced that individual liberty lies at the root of human progress. We were amateurs steeped in the traditions of freethinking individuals. Sometimes I wonder how we managed to win, considering the conflicts of opinion within our ranks. And then I conclude that success was possible because we were of sound but independent mind. Harsh decisions were made in agony; Roosevelt surely killed himself in the process, and isolated agents had to weigh singlehanded actions against the reprisals that would be taken against their kinsmen. Battles were won because we had advance knowledge of enemy plans, could influence those plans, and could anticipate enemy actions by methods heretofore concealed. Other struggles, no less decisive, were finally won by the resistance armies, a name for the people in occupied lands who loved freedom and, quite simply, were willing to fight for it against any odds.

When the history of World War II is revised in the light of the secret war, this may be the most striking element: the great engines of destruction did not determine the outcome. The invincibility of free people and the ingenuity of free minds did. I believe this as I believe today that the spirit of human resistance refuses to be crushed by mere technology.

Perhaps a day will dawn when tyrants can no longer threaten the liberty of any people, when the function of all nations, however varied their ideologies, will be to enhance life, not to control it. If such a condition is possible, it is in a future too far distant to foresee. Until that safer, better day, the democracies will avoid disaster, and possibly total destruction, only by maintaining their defenses.

Among the increasingly intricate arsenals across the world, intelligence is an essential weapon, perhaps the most important. But it is, being secret, the most dangerous. Safeguards to prevent its abuse must be devised, revised, and rigidly applied. But, as in all enterprise, the character and wisdom of those to whom it is entrusted will be decisive. In the integrity of that guardianship lies the hope of free people to endure and prevail.

It has been claimed that human progress depends on challenge, that individuals and nations have the need to believe in causes and struggle for them. Some theorists have extended this application of instinctual behavior to account for the periodic wholesale slaughters we call "war." The merit of such concepts is a matter for study by psychologists and historians. What seems poignantly evident to me is that humankind already has awesome enemies to engage—poverty, disease, and ignorance, for example—and in such common cause there is reward and glory enough for all.

Sir William Stephenson

Bermuda

A BREAK IN THE
SILENCE

A HISTORICAL NOTE

FROM NEW YORK, while the United States was at peace
and at war, Britain ran the most intricate integrated
intelligence and secret-operations organization in history. Could such activity be kept secret?

I had been twenty years in the professional secret-
intelligence service when in 1940 London sent me to
British Security Coordination headquarters in New
York to help maintain that secrecy. BSC networks
were manned by amateurs, and it was thought that
my special experience was required there. Such concern proved unwarranted. The British Secret Intelligence Service had been rendered useless in Europe
when our professional agents were cut down almost
in a single stroke after conventional armed resistance
to the Nazis ended on the Continent and Hitler entered Paris. But the amateurs who flocked to replace the professionals were well able to take care of
themselves.

I was soon requested to draft a blueprint for an
American intelligence agency, the equivalent of BSC
and based on these British wartime improvisations.
"Intrepid" did it himself—further demonstration that

secret options in the free world can be handled exceedingly well by men and women who have acquired their skill and proved their integrity in successful civilian careers.

Detailed tables of organization were disclosed to Washington. I have prepared for this book a simplified version of one of them, which portrays the main lines of command and, more particularly, clarifies the extraordinary relationship Intrepid maintained in utmost secrecy between the President of the United States and the Prime Minister of Great Britain.

With headquarters at Rockefeller Center, thousands of our agents and experts passed under the statue of Atlas on Fifth Avenue, yet their identities and activities remained effectively masked. But as an increasing number of Americans also passed Atlas and entered the crammed BSC offices, the probability of exposure increased substantially. To our astonishment, the secret endured.

Then, in the 1960's, the outer wrapping of protection, designed back in 1940, was suddenly stripped away. BSC's and Intrepid's operations were partially revealed, defined principally as playing a supporting role in the American effort to frustrate Nazi subversion in the Western hemisphere. The fact that this fractional truth did not leak out until 1962 is a striking tribute to the discretion of many outstanding Americans who, knowing some or most of BSC's and Intrepid's full activities and purposes, nonetheless recognized that silence had to be maintained if the liberty of the democracies was to be successfully defended against increasing totalitarian stratagems of every sort.

In 1962, I was working on a study of Soviet imperialism when a special watchdog committee of the Ministry of Defense and the Foreign Office in London discussed the wisdom of a partial leak. This took the form of a book, *The Quiet Canadian* (*Room 3603* in the U.S.), by the distinguished historian H. Montgomery Hyde, himself a most resourceful BSC officer. I was able to demonstrate that I had been given instructions by "higher authority" to disclose certain matters. These matters were, of course, a carefully limited disclosure of BSC's "secret" role. In no way did it reveal the full extent of the organization's prime purposes or most sensitive activities.

Essential secrecy was thus preserved for a further ten years. In 1972, the author of this book, William Stevenson, after many and long discussions with Intrepid, suggested to me that more was to be gained than lost by full disclosure. I could not have agreed more. The story of BSC was that of a great Anglo-American enterprise that began when President Roosevelt and his like-minded colleagues saved the British Isles from Nazi occupation despite the United States then being technically at peace. In 1972, Moscow, through its many secret agencies, was again mounting a formidable campaign in the United States with the purpose of isolating this single great power that might again save the democracies from their own follies. It was time, I felt, to remind ourselves that much as we may deplore the use of secrecy, it was secrecy that saved us only a generation ago. Now, the Central Intelligence Agency had become the chief target of those who would summarily disarm us and who would, citing real or alleged abuses by the agency, "throw the baby out with the bath water" and rob us of the essential means of preventive defense secured at such cost during the Second World War.

As one of BSC's historians, I readily agreed to place my own papers at the author's disposal. Among these were the organizational tables that led to the birth of General William Donovan's OSS. Intrepid was the midwife of OSS, and the reader can see for himself how it all began in a fierce struggle to save individual freedom.

I can now disclose that the reason for the break in the silence about BSC in 1962 was the escape to the Soviet Union of Kim Philby, the brilliant Communist agent who had infiltrated the British secret service; who, by the end of the Second World War, was directing the anti-Communist section; and who was the leading contender to become the chief of that fabled service. We knew that Philby took with him the knowledge of BSC's existence, but we also knew that he was not aware of the full and far-reaching purpose of Intrepid's organization. Thus just enough of the truth was revealed for publication to blunt the effect of any disclosures that Philby or his supporters might reveal. But ten years later, in 1972, we knew also that the Russians had learned rather more and might use this information to bludgeon our friends, to distort history, and to hurt United States and Canadian relations with Britain. Full disclosure at last was the answer to this threat and to the demands of history. Hence this book.

Charles Howard Ellis

Eastbourne, Sussex

Colonel C. H. ("Dick") Ellis, CMG, CBE, OBE, U.S. Legion of Merit, served as a British secret agent in Egypt, India, Persia, Russia, Afghanistan, and held British consular posts in Turkey, the Balkans, Germany, and Asia between the wars. He convinced Churchill at the end of World War II to pay a veiled but public tribute to INTREPID's BSC teams in these words: "We may feel sure that nothing of which we have any knowledge or record has ever been done by mortal men which surpasses the splendour and daring of their feats of arms." President Harry Truman, making Ellis an officer of the Legion of Merit, wrote: "He gave unreservedly of his talent and wealth of information toward the development of certain of our intelligence organizations and methods. His enthusiastic interest, superior foresight and diplomacy were responsible in large measure for the success of highly important operations."

BRITISH SECURITY COORDINATION CHART

A simplified version of one of the charts disclosed to Franklin D. Roosevelt when the concept of the Office of Strategic Services was first considered

PRESIDENT OF THE UNITED STATES

PRIME MINISTER OF GREAT BRITAIN

BRITISH FOREIGN OFFICE

BRITISH HOME OFFICE

BRITISH SECURITY COORDINATION (NEW YORK)

BRITISH WAR CABINET

JOINT INTELLIGENCE COMMITTEE

SECRET INTELLIGENCE SERVICE (MI-6 or SIS)
Espionage in foreign countries; counterpart of MI-5

MI-5
Counterespionage on British territory

SPECIAL OPERATIONS EXECUTIVE (SOE)
Undercover action, sabotage, subversion, underground propaganda

ASSISTANT CHIEF OF SECRET SERVICE

DEPUTY CHIEF OF SECRET SERVICE

OTHER SECTIONS AND SUBSECTIONS

IBERIAN SUBSECTION*
Spain and Portugal: neutral territory intelligence

SECTION V*
Counterintelligence in the United States & foreign countries

SECTION IX
Operations against political subversion

OTHER SECTIONS AND SUBSECTIONS

*Kim Philby was posted to these sections during the critical years of the war. After the war, he rose in the intelligence service and appeared likely to be its chief.

SIGNIFICANT DATES

Winston Churchill appointed First Lord of the Admiralty

• 1911 •
October 25

Franklin D. Roosevelt appointed Assistant Secretary of the Navy

• 1913 •
March 17

William Stephenson joins Royal Canadian Engineers after outbreak of World War I

• 1914 •
August 4

William Donovan sent by the Rockefeller Foundation's American War Relief Commission to investigate conditions in war-torn Europe

• 1916 •
March

First meeting of Stephenson and Donovan in England

April/May

Stephenson in France as fighter pilot with No. 73 Squadron, Royal Flying Corps

September

United States enters World War I

• 1917 •
April 6

Germany collapses; Churchill's "Thirty-Year Armistice" begins

• 1918 •
November 11

Adolf Hitler appointed Chancellor of Germany

• 1933 •
January 30

Stephenson witnesses Nazi "burning of the books"

May 20

| Allies land in North Africa (TORCH) | November 8 |
| | |

• 1943 •

| Operations begun for destruction of German heavy-water sources for atomic research | February |
| Atomic scientist Niels Bohr is flown to Britain to join U.S.-British atomic-bomb program | October 7 |

• 1944 •

| Allies land in Normandy | June 6 |
| Rockets hit London | June/September |

• 1945 •

Roosevelt dies	April 12
Hitler commits suicide	April 30
Germany surrenders unconditionally	May 8
Atomic bomb dropped on Hiroshima	August 6
Japan surrenders	August 14
INTREPID and BSC depart headquarters in New York	August/December
President Harry Truman disbands OSS	September 20

Part
One

IN TIME OF PEACE

"A wise man in time of peace prepares for war."
—Horace, *Satires*

1

A BRASH YOUNG man named Winston Churchill was on the North American lecture circuit at the turn of the century, retelling the story of guerrillas in South Africa and his own escape from one of their "camps of concentration." His audiences were disappointingly small. Nobody could have foreseen that Churchill was describing some of the grimmer features of future conflict: unconventional warfare, political terrorism, and concentration camps.

In January 1901 he left the United States for Canada. On the twenty-second he reached Winnipeg, and found it draped in black. Queen Victoria was dead. The British Empire had crossed a watershed. Churchill wrote home to his American mother in England that "this city far away among the snows . . . began to hang its head."

A five-year-old boy in the crowds mourning the death of the distant monarch was Billy Stephenson. His father had been killed in South Africa, and the news had reached him a few days earlier, on his birthday. Shivering on the snow-banked sidewalks on the day of Churchill's arrival in Winnipeg, he thought his dead father must have been a great hero to deserve such attention.

Stephenson's boyhood could not have been more different from that of the two partners he would have at a later critical moment in history: Winston Churchill and Franklin Delano Roosevelt. He had more in common with his future comrade in secret warfare William J. Donovan, then living on the United States side of the frontier.

Stephenson was self-reliant early in life. He was

3

three years old when his father went to fight in Africa with the Manitoba Transvaal Contingent. The boy grew up on the prairies of western Canada, where the long and bitter winters shaped and polished the character of the settlers. His own family had pioneer blood that went back for generations.

Great-grandpa Donald had migrated from Aberdeen in Scotland way back in 1780. He married another Scot, Jean Campbell. They had a son, William Victor, who married Christine Breckman. Her forebears had come from Norway. Billy was born in 1896, on January 11, the coldest day in recorded history in that bleak part of the American continent.

He devoured books. One of his earlier memories was reading "What hath God wrought!"—the words signaled in 1844 by Samuel F. B. Morse, who developed the first successful telegraph in the United States and the most commonly used telegraphic code. Billy's middle name was Samuel in honor of the great Morse. Morse influenced not only Billy Stephenson, but also, in a manner the youth could not imagine, the man he would become.

The boy grew up in Point Douglas, near Winnipeg, dividing his time between Argyle High School and the lumber mill started by his father.

"He was restless and inquisitive," recalled an Argyle teacher, Jean Moffatt. "A bookworm, we always thought, except he loved boxing. A wee fellow, but a real one for a fight. Of course, y'see, he was the man o' the house from the time he was a toddler."

In his early teens, Stephenson experimented with electricity, steam engines, kites, and crude airplanes. He rigged his own Morse telegraph, a transmitter and receiver, and tapped out messages to ships on the Great Lakes. He knew the call signs of all the stations within reach and he worked out his own code, an improvement on the *Secret Vocabulary Adapted For Use To Morse's Electromagnetic Telegraph,* published by Morse's legal representative, Francis O. J. Smith, for the benefit of commercial users of the telegraph system in the mid-nineteenth century. Later, when asked about his education, he would look blank. "I got it like everyone else. From books."

4

He went straight from high school into World War I. His final school report stated: "High powers of concentration when his interest is aroused. Strong sense of duty. Good sport. Will be greatly missed."

The British decision to go to war against Germany in 1914 brought volunteers from the United States and Canada, attracted often by the promise of adventure. Stephenson was sent straight to the trenches with the Royal Canadian Engineers. Before his nineteenth birthday, he was commissioned in the field. Men fell in such numbers that he was advanced to captain within the year. He suffered the trauma of a poison-gas attack and saw men die in convulsion or lose sight and mind. For twenty months he knew the misery of the foot soldier. Then, crippled in another gas attack, he was sent back to England as "disabled for life."

Another strand of the far-distant future then appeared. In the third summer of the war, William Donovan was completing a survey of the conflict for the Rockefeller-sponsored American War Relief Commission in the hope of limiting the carnage. Donovan was thirty-three, a successful New York lawyer, and a shrewd investigator. He was appalled by what he found. Great armies embraced and heaved and pulled without shifting ground, locked in lingering death.

"One of the 'veterans' from this nightmare was this twenty-year-old Canadian," Donovan said later in notes for a biographer.* "I felt an old man, wickedly well-fed, against this skinny kid. But when he started to talk, I paid attention. I had asked a couple of routine questions. His answers were concise and perceptive. At our first meeting, in 1916, we discovered a shared background that overcame the gulf between those already fighting the war and us Americans, still out of it. I'd been a member of Canadian rowing teams near my home in Buffalo. Each week at the Crystal Rowing Club in Ontario, I'd argued with Canadians about the American Republic's rejection of monarchy and Canada's device for keeping a British king without taking orders from London.

* Whitney Shepardson, first London chief of the Office of Strategic Services in World War II, later president of the CIA-funded Free Europe Committee, 1953–56.

"Stephenson understood our American style that was taken, in England in the midst of a bloodbath, for brash vulgarity. And I had some understanding of why the English who survived the front lines were close-mouthed. Stephenson was willing to translate the horror into facts and figures for me.

"He combined compassion and shrewdness in assessing German military and psychological weakness. He said Germany must lose in the end because she was fighting for bad reasons. He seemed terribly young to be a captain until he reeled off his observations. He didn't see the war as an accident of history complicated by lunacy at the top. He was certainly not in love with war. He said someone had to fight this evil. He refused to dismiss as propaganda the reports of German atrocities. He wanted to get back to the front. The doctors said his lungs would never stand up to more fighting in the trenches.

"So he decided to fly. He wangled a transfer to the Royal Flying Corps. They didn't ask questions. Men were getting killed faster than recruits came in. He fudged his medical history and nobody looked too close. After five hours' instruction, he was a fully-fledged combat pilot. It was an indication of how desperately the Allies needed pilots."

Stephenson reported for duty with No. 73 Squadron of the Royal Flying Corps. His adjutant was another Canadian, Thomas Drew-Brook, who would work for him and Donovan in World War II. Drew-Brook was aghast when he saw this new pilot, with the complexion of an invalid. Stephenson had turned down a safe and honorable job as a staff captain to become a temporary acting second lieutenant in what was widely regarded as the "Suicide Service," and he brushed aside Drew-Brook's objections that he was too sick for combat. "If I was heading for an early grave," he said, "I wanted to dig it myself." Instead, he won the Distinguished Flying Cross "for conspicuous gallantry and skill in attacking enemy troops and transports from low altitudes." He became noted for "valuable and accurate information on enemy movements." His score in downing enemy aircraft climbed. He was awarded the Military Cross for stampeding

6

enemy transport, destroying enemy scouts, and "when flying low and observing an open [German] staff car, attacking it with such success that it was seen lying upside down in a ditch." The citation offered the highest possible tribute to an airman in those days of the infantryman's travail: "He is always there when the troops need him."

A taste for individual combat and a talent for keeping a mental record of everything he saw made a rare combination. As one of 73 Squadron's two flight commanders, he could not indulge in lone-wolf sorties while on designated patrols. So he assigned himself to solitary missions in his own time and went looking for trouble. An obvious target was the Red Baron, Manfred von Richthofen. Stephenson analyzed enemy strategy and decided that the Baron's brother, Lothar, was the more damaging flier. The Red Baron went after spectacular but sometimes easy victories. Lothar was more interested in effective destruction than in personal glory. For every two of the Red Baron's victims, Lothar might destroy one undramatic but more dangerous observation balloon. Stephenson committed this view to a paper stating an argument for hot pursuit of enemy pilots like Lothar.

His report caught the attention of the spitfire of a man who then dominated British intelligence. Admiral Sir Reginald ("Blinker") Hall had advanced the art of secret warfare in the second decade of the century. The nickname "Blinker" referred to a twitch that made one eye flash like a Navy signal lamp. Hall refused to be restricted by his title of Director of Naval Intelligence, and operated beyond maritime horizons. He had served that other rebel against orthodoxy Winston Churchill, when he was First Lord of the Admiralty before the war began. Churchill's obstinacy brought him into direct conflict with his more politically astute colleagues, and in 1915 he was forced to quit the post. By then, Hall had no further need for protection. He had expanded into every field of espionage. Scotland Yard, investigating a spy case in London, would discover him on the scene. The Secret Intelligence Service became resigned to the fact that a likely recruit in some foreign port would turn out to be Hall's man. Nobody challenged Admiral Hall as a poacher; too many were indebted to him. He maintained as a cover that the staff in his unassuming quarters, in a backwater of the Admiralty known as Room 40, were only concerned with plotting the movements of enemy warships.

By 1917, Blinker Hall had won respect even among his critics by intercepting and deciphering a telegram that he believed would bring America into the war: the Zimmermann Telegram, dispatched from Berlin to the Imperial German Minister in Mexico. No single cryptanalysis, it would be said for years to come, had such enormous consequences. Hall's code breakers held history in their hands, and the memory of it would sustain the Admiral through discouraging times.

Stephenson's cool appraisal of enemy aviation, in a period when combat in the sky was regarded as chivalrous jousting between young daredevils, pleased Hall. The leather-skinned Admiral studied the fuzzy-cheeked aviator's record, noting that Stephenson was already skilled in what Hall regarded as the heart of future secret intelligence—wireless traffic. Stephenson had also proposed to file and cross-index weaknesses in enemy aircraft and manpower, for swift reference. He thought the Germans had vulnerabilities in character that should be exploited. Decoys could be used to lure pilots into dogfights far from their own lines so that they would be distracted by the fear of running out of fuel. This was not the game according to the rules of chivalry, thought Hall, who was no great sport himself when it came to war.

Having advocated the elimination of key enemy fliers, Stephenson practiced what he preached. He went after Lothar von Richthofen, and almost won himself the red ("presumed dead") label in Admiral Hall's card index.

Lothar kept to a section of the Western Front where British bombers operated during the German offensive of March 21, 1918. Stephenson was leading all three flights of 73 Squadron as part of the bomber escort. "We were joined at 16,000 feet by Bristol fighters of 62 and 22 Squadrons," he recalled later. "Tommy Drew-Brook was attacked by a Fokker Tripe

8

Red with black lines about four inches wide in a wavy pattern on both sides, down the length of the fuselage. Tommy was below me and to port. I did a diving turn and opened fire at about eighty yards." The Fokker made an Immelmann turn, gaining height and reversing direction. Stephenson recognized the style of Lothar. "We span, dived, looped and tried every trick to get in the finalizing burst. My Camel had two Vickers firing through the prop, and it was the more maneuverable aircraft, too. So it was no discredit to Lothar that I fought him down to hedge-hopping and into a clump of trees. He wasn't killed, but he never flew again—except as a passenger."

A fellow aviator in that operation was the American writer Arch Whitehouse, who recorded Stephenson's career as an air ace: "The air war that began over Flanders was new. It bred a new kind of warrior. No airman contributed so much to the English-speaking cause as Stephenson." Whitehouse was given a rare glimpse of Bill Stephenson's inner self—something that evaded observers throughout the years—when he got from Stephenson some verse written to cheer him up during a bad patch:

Why, flier shearing the rare strata of air
Knowing the awakening of speed shared
   by no bird
Why, when the whole ocean of resilient air
   is yours
Stoop to consider the cramped earth? . . .
Note with aloof and precise observation
   gestations in opening mushrooms of
The crude flame and expelled dust
That foul the floor of your cage.
And remember that you alone
Can escape through the single door
Open to Heaven.

The lines ended with a note to Whitehouse: "In other words, cheer up! We're all on borrowed time."

Flying a lone patrol on July 28, 1918, Stephenson spotted a lumbering French reconnaissance plane in difficulties. Seven Fokker D-VIIs were maneuvering

9

to attack. He broke up the formation, but a French observer, in the confusion, fired a burst into Stephenson's Camel. He was hit in the leg and crashed behind the lines. Wounded again in the same leg by a German gunner, he was taken prisoner.

He made several abortive escapes. "They were not well planned," he said later. "But I wanted to get back to the squadron. The air war seemed crucial. The Germans were near collapse but they still had good aircraft and pilots in reserve. Anyone on our side with firsthand experience of them was still needed."

The Germans also realized that each veteran Allied aviator was worth a dozen new American or British war planes. Stephenson was put under close guard at Holzminden, a maximum-security prison where important captives were held. The camp commandant, Hans Niemayer, vented his hatred for Anglo-Saxons in private beatings and public taunts. "He was a German who had lived before the war in Milwaukee and returned to fight for the Kaiser," Stephenson said later. "He was proud of his Americanisms. One day he lined us up because he'd uncovered an escape plan. 'You think I don't know what's going on!' he yelled. 'But I tell you, I know damn-all!' "

Stephenson nursed his injured leg and exaggerated his handicaps to persuade the guards that he could not escape. A week after entering camp, he had plotted its layout. He knew the weak points in the perimeter fence; the distance to the nearest village where he could shelter and change his clothes; and how far to Allied lines. He got this information by disguising his contempt for his captors and extracting what he could from casual contacts, even though it meant listening in seemingly friendly silence to Niemayer. By October 1918, less than three months after being first captured, he was ready for the final attempt.

Stephenson had been permitted to work in the kitchen. Bit by bit, he acquired utensils from which he fashioned wire cutters, a crude knife, and a simple compass. When he was ready to break out, he stole Niemayer's family portrait from the commandant's office as an insult, "so that he would have no illusions about our relationship." With the photograph stuffed under a stolen German Army greatcoat, he was away to freedom an hour before dawn.

He reached Allied lines within three days, and characteristically submitted a detailed report, this one on enemy prison camps.

A copy of the report went to Room 40 where Admiral Blinker Hall was tagging the handful of youngsters he wanted to coach for a new world of secret intelligence. The problem was that Stephenson was too well known. He had a record of twenty-six aircraft shot down in the comparatively short flying career that followed combat experience in the trenches. He had the French Legion of Honor and Croix de Guerre with Palm to add to his other medals. He was known as "Captain Machine-Gun" in the ring, where he had won the interservice lightweight world boxing championship on the same program as Gene Tunney, who had won the heavyweight title for the U.S. Marines. Tunney turned professional and became undefeated world champion, enjoying an influence that would later help Stephenson's work in World War II, for the two men became business partners and life-long friends. In 1918, Hall was about to withdraw behind the scene, where he would manipulate intelligence affairs for the next twenty-five years. He thought it best to have Stephenson transferred to the neutral zone of test-flying foreign warplanes. "As Chief Test Pilot at the Royal Flying Corps Reconstruction Center," the Admiral wrote him later, "you flew more different types of international aircraft than any other pilot known to me."

Stephenson did not share the easygoing attitude of the sportsmen fliers who romanticized aerial warfare. In his account of the first war, written privately for Hall, he noted that the Royal Flying Corps had initially gone into combat with fewer than fifty aircraft, under the command of a cavalry general who had got off his horse and learned to fly at the age of forty-nine. His chief of staff had been a Boer War veteran who literally floated around for years in balloons. Each pilot had to ferry to France his own plane, carrying a small stove, soup cubes, and field

11

glasses. Maps were provided by Monsieur Michelin, whose tire companies gave away automobile guides. All the aircraft were cannibalized; undercarriages designed for Morane Parasols were twisted to fit on BE8s; engines built for Farmans were shoehorned into the mountings of RE2s. Gunners qualified if they could load a cavalry carbine, drop metal darts onto German heads, and did not mind filling their large jacket pockets with rocks to fling at enemy aircraft. Technology had advanced under the pressure of war, but Stephenson was afraid that in a long period of truce the Allies would fall behind and find themselves ill-prepared to confront a more militarily advanced enemy.

He was still test-flying when he became entranced by the whole range of new ideas associated with aviation, as Hall guessed he would. He had a mathematical mind that his flying reflected. A cool application of tested principles could get a pilot out of tight spots. Even the seemingly harum-scarum Flying Corps recognized this in a requiem sung at mess parties:

> *He died in an hour and a quarter*
> *And this was the reason he died;*
> *He'd forgotten the fact that iota*
> *Was the maximum angle of glide.*

Not only did Stephenson know that if you lifted the nose an iota beyond the angle of glide in a dead-engine landing, you were finished, but also he suggested a new wing design that improved the gliding angle. His boisterous colleagues, feeling they had already made their covenant with death, tended to think only of each day. They were regarded with condescension by regular officers of the older established services, but not by Admiral Hall. He had picked out an older man, William Wiseman, gassed in the same German offensive that disabled Stephenson, and had sent him to Washington as chief of the British Secret Intelligence Service in the U.S. for the balance of World War I.

There was no public information on the British Secret Intelligence Service in those days. The operating

12

budget was buried from sight. The Official Secrets Act was applied with such rigor that Sir Compton Mackenzie, an honorable man with an immense following as a writer, was prosecuted and severely punished for a vague postwar account of his work in SIS. Such an attitude had persisted for centuries. Only occasionally were prominent names mentioned in connection with the secret services of the monarch: Cardinal Wolsey, Walsingham, Thurloe, and Rudyard Kipling. Wiseman's name came into public print because he had functioned in the United States, where it was not easy to conceal these things. A good deal of fun was poked at intelligence chiefs disguised behind initials. Much emphasis was laid upon the constipated nature of an agency that allegedly drew recruits from a small privileged class and the old-boy net. The ridicule was a welcome smoke screen. Stephenson met none of the fictional criteria but he met the real requirements, including the courage of a man of imagination who can visualize the bloody and painful consequences of his own actions.

2

"MY LORD! THERE are most uncommon creatures here among those who have this vast and appalling War-job—men about whom our great-grandchildren will read in their school histories; but of them all, the most extraordinary is this naval officer—of whom, probably, they'll never hear." Thus wrote U.S. Ambassador Walter H. Page in London to President Woodrow Wilson in 1916, referring to Admiral Blinker Hall. Hall did not think the end of the fighting meant an end to danger. Modern weapons and new methods of mass communication produced new possibilities for tyrants. His warnings, like those of others, were swept

13

away in the postwar wave of revulsion to war and disenchantment with military leaders.

In New York, the crowds turned out to cheer the 69th Regiment as it paraded down Fifth Avenue, with Colonel William Donovan marching on foot at the head of his men. His regiment had earned the title "The Fighting Irish," and their chief was famous as "Wild Bill." In explanation of his decision not to ride on horseback, as tradition required, he said: "If it was good enough to go on foot through Europe, it's good enough now." At the end of the day, in the empty silence of Camp Mills, where the regiment had been quartered before going to war, he wept. "I can't forget the men we left behind," he told his brother, Father Vincent Donovan.

"The most tragic thing about the war was not that it made so many dead men, but that it destroyed the tragedy of death," wrote the American poet John Peale Bishop. "Not only did the young suffer in the war, but so did every abstraction that would have sustained and given dignity to their suffering."

A future prime minister of Britain, Harold Macmillan, returned to the university city of Oxford, found it full of ghosts, and later wrote the words that spoke for a lost generation: "Bitterness ate into our hearts at the easy way many elders seemed to take up again and play with undiminished zest the game of politics."

The game of politics demanded the dismantling of the war machine. The public wanted it so. Military budgets were slashed. Aviation in England was returned to private enterprise. Test pilots were out of jobs. Stephenson was put through Oxford and the forerunner of Cranwell Aeronautical College, where he concentrated on Admiral Hall's favorite subject, radio communications. Stephenson went back to Canada with a private vision of a new world in which science would bring order and peace.

His ideas got a cool reception. He sought Canadian backing for popular broadcasting. This seemed an inevitable consequence of wartime developments in radio. But he was a stripling of twenty-three. On the home front he had to take his place in line as if still a child, although he had outlived his allotted span in the war, where each day after the age of twenty was a bonus. He was hired by the University of Manitoba to teach math and science while he studied the province's experiments in public broadcasting. "I had a guilt feeling that I should have died with the others," he recalled. "Being still alive, I had an obligation to justify my survival."

Among his notes appeared fragments of verse. One, from Wordsworth, indicates his frame of mind:

> Who is the happy Warrior . . .
> That every man in arms would wish to be?
> —It is the generous spirit . . .
> Who, doomed to go in company with Pain,
> And Fear, and Bloodshed . . .
> Turns his necessity to glorious gain. . . .
> And in himself possess his own desire . . .
> And therefore does not stoop, nor lie in wait
> For wealth, or honors, or for worldly state . . .
> And, through the heat of conflict, keeps the law
> In calmness made, and sees what he foresaw.

Stephenson never in his life publicly displayed his romanticism. It was, however, typical of the mood of those who survived a certain kind of individual combat. A few oldsters understood this sentiment and were willing to tap the energies it released.

Admiral Hall sent word that Stephenson should return to London in the early 1920s. Hall had retired into the shadows. The British intelligence community had been drastically reduced, and Hall tried to keep it alive through groups of civilians in politics, international affairs, and scientific development. He regarded Stephenson as "a brilliant mathematician who, like the American pioneers, can see no limit to his horizons . . . a most rare combination of the man of action and of imagination." Believing that the interception of enemy communications and cryptanalysis were the foundation of good modern intelligence, Hall built up contacts in industry, commerce, and the universities, where he could tap resources of intellect. The modern science of cryptology had grown from humble beginnings: the invention of telegraphy. Stephenson had demonstrated an inventive genius of his own in the field. Now he learned that while he had been fighting in France, other battles had been conducted by scholars who had applied academic discipline and logic to break down German codes and who could pinpoint the exact disposition of U-boats and Zeppelins by snatching orders out of the ether. Others analyzed general radio traffic to gain an insight into enemy thinking: a craft in itself, so that those who became skilled in "traffic analysis" were regarded by Hall as far too valuable to be lost in the postwar defense cuts. There was not yet a profession called "cryptanalysis," and those who were good at solving coded mysteries were found in departments of classical history, mathematics, and even dead languages. These formed a tiny unpaid nucleus. Around them, Hall gathered likely young fellows who could make it in the commercial world.

Stephenson found himself talking to British radio manufacturers about the Canadian pioneer venture in government-run broadcasting. He was convinced that public broadcasting services could be a powerful instrument for good or evil, and his views were shared by a former fellow pilot, Gladstone Murray, an air ace who became aviation correspondent for the London *Daily Express*, owned by another Canadian, Lord Beaverbrook. The three of them produced a case for the formation of a British Broadcasting Company. It was financed, like the Winnipeg station, by government license. The BBC was later incorporated to function without interference by the ruling political party. It created a national audience of millions and a market for builders of radio equipment. Thus it ensured research and development in Admiral Hall's field. It also gave work to talented individuals like Murray, who became BBC publicity director—an appointment that would prove useful in the next war.

"There wasn't a lot of money available in those days," Stephenson said later. "What counted was encouragement and being able to find enthusiastic coworkers. Whatever lesson the war taught me about personal survival were overshadowed by a conviction that our society had to defend itself against sudden attack or we'd have another world war. H. G. Wells became a good friend and adviser. The public knew him as a historian and prophet in fiction. Few knew about his passionate belief that in the science-fiction wars to come, our first line of defense would be information, rapidly conveyed. We'd both learned to distrust an elite class that claimed the privilege of leadership in good times and then, having led the people into calamity, let them fight their own way out."

Stephenson wrote papers on what he called "Television," the method of transmitting moving pictures by radio waves. Why not make it a practical reality? He worked on mathematical equations to prove pictures could be transmitted as easily as sound. He bought an interest in two electronics firms in England, contributing ideas and labor to make up for what he lacked in ready cash. General Radio and Cox-Cavendish were in the forefront of new developments in radio and electrical equipment. At the age of twenty-six he was marketing thousands of small home receiving sets for BBC listeners in the British Isles. His life was one of fiendish activity in spartan quarters. Lord Northcliffe, owner of the *Daily Mail,* backed his experiments in the conversion of light into electric current. In December 1922 that newspaper published the first photograph transmitted by radio. It hailed the event as "a revolution in communications" and the inventor as "a brilliant young scientist."

He was now drawn into a circle of scientists gathered by Winston Churchill, through his personal force of character, around the person of Professor Frederick Lindemann, later Lord Cherwell, but always "the Prof" to Churchill and Stephenson. It was the Prof who began sounding the alarm about German militarism and its revival in an atmosphere of pseudo-scientific racism. Germany was also leaping forward in science and military technology. Stephenson's own ideas were stimulated by the revolutionary theory that gravitation bends light, propounded by Albert Einstein, who had been part of resurgent Germany's intellectual establishment. The Prof and a secret British defense committee kept in touch with the physicist, and also encouraged

17

research in Britain on splitting the atom. The problem was always one of funds. There was popular hostility to government-financed research and development of arms. Men like Churchill were political outcasts for warning that preparation was the only guarantee against another "unnecessary war."

His secret defense committee was held together by little else than a common sense of purpose, to discourage tyrants by a display of armed readiness. One of its concealed accomplishments in the 1920s was the development of Larynx, a "catapult-bomb"—in effect, a guided missile that foreshadowed the rockets Hitler aimed later at London. Whatever was done, however, depended upon the interplay of industrial scientists. They attracted refugee scientists from Germany; and the best were given moral support by Churchill's followers.

Stephenson brought into his business such a man, Charles Proteus Steinmetz, a Jewish scientist whose socialist views were so strong that he had been forced to leave Germany years earlier. "Steiny was a mathematical genius. He calculated laws to prove the feasibility of inventions that even today seem pretty advanced," said Stephenson fifty years later. "He had already covered a wide range of electronics before the end of the nineteenth century. At the age of fifty-seven he found himself working in the United States for a large corporation whose policies stifled his creative powers. I knew his work, heard of his discontent, and offered him freedom in my own labs."

Their first encounter was described by writer Roald Dahl: "The first impression of Stephenson was a small man of immense power. Nothing indecisive about him at all. There was bound to be trepidation and fear because you were right in the lion's den. But when you got to know him better, you understood his immense capabilities. He worked hard, he played around with his businesses and his scientific things, he coupled them up and made fortunes with apparently no trouble at all. Even Steiny could never stretch this man to his full mental capacity. He just accommodated every new idea, digested everything, and created out of what he absorbed."

18

Stephenson was still a man of action. He continued to hold his title of amateur lightweight boxing champion until he retired in 1928, still undefeated, when he became owner of Britain's National Sporting Club. Steinmetz confronted him with a different kind of challenge, demanding days and nights of concentrated mental labor. Once, in pursuit of the laser beam, half a century before its practical application, Stephenson was still at work as dawn broke. "Steiny peered at my sheets of figures and said, 'Beeell, you are slowing down!' Then he studied my calculus and blamed the sloppy work on my heavy smoking. Not lack of sleep. Too many cigarettes! So I threw down my last cigarette and never smoked again."

Another refugee scientist, Chaim Weizmann, entered Stephenson's circle. This tall, princely figure first appeared on the English scene in 1903. He had left his home in the Jewish Pale near Pinsk to study chemistry in Europe. He was drawn to London for reasons shared with many Jewish scientists, which he summarized in a letter to his fiancée: "If we are to get help from any quarter, it will be England which, I don't doubt, will help us in Palestine. . . . This [London] is the hub of the world and really, you sense the breathing of a giant." In 1916, Weizmann had perfected a new process for making acetone, which eased a critical explosives shortage. This brought him in touch with Churchill and other English statesmen. They encouraged his dream of a Jewish dominion in which Jewish creative energies would combine with British improvisation. By the 1920s he had become president of the Zionist Organization and was known as "the uncrowned king of the Jews."

From Steinmetz and Weizmann, Stephenson learned more than scientific innovation. "They opened my mind to new concepts," he said later. "Steiny taught me German with a guttural Hebrew accent. Weizmann foresaw an age of small and independent nations whose first line of defense would be knowledge. They both believed science would produce weapons to enable small communities to put up impregnable defenses when danger threatened—like the porcupine raising its quills. And all would depend on early warning."

Stephenson saw such an early-warning system as a co-ordinated intelligence service. Admiral Blinker Hall was the man who might accomplish it. Hall was now Churchill's personal intelligence chief. But Churchill's political fortunes were in decline. There was no British intelligence service faintly resembling those intriguing versions of popular fiction. Instead, there were a few undervalued professionals and some amateurs who began to arrange themselves around Stephenson. And there was the small underpaid, overworked, and ill-appreciated British Secret Intelligence Service, which commanded official recognition and little else.

3

AN AMERICAN EQUIVALENT to the British Secret Intelligence Service did not exist at all. There was the United States Army's Signal Intelligence Service, charged with the interception and solving of enemy communications in wartime; and there was that relic of the war, an organization for intercepting foreign communications, known as the Black Chamber. It was supposed to be "a permanent organization for code and cipher investigation and attack." But the times were peculiar. Those who warned against the threat of war were warmongers. Those who sensed the menace in and tried to penetrate the secrets of the new totalitarians were sneaks. Those who peered too closely into closed societies were Peeping Toms. "Gentlemen do not read each other's mail," pontificated Henry L. Stimson after he became Secretary of State in 1929. The Black Chamber shifted its quarters from a fashionable town house at 3 East 38th Street in New York City to an old brownstone at 141 East 37th, like a genteel family going down in the world.

Bill Donovan, who, like Admiral Hall, believed that

a free society could survive only with efficient intelligence services, had been sent to Siberia in 1919 to assess the beleaguered White Russians. He applied a rule of good intelligence: his report must be free from personal prejudice. He reported from revolution-torn Russia to the State Department that anti-Communist forces were corrupt and divided. "We can prevent a shooting war," he wrote, "only if we take the initiative to win the subversive war."

He went back to Europe in 1920 on a private fact-finding mission financed by the Rockefeller Foundation, and again he returned with reports that did not support wishful thinkers. His carefully documented notes on Germany dwelt upon the dangerous mood of self-pity induced by the notion that German leaders had never actually surrendered and were therefore still unbeaten. This conflicted with American public opinion, summarized by William Wiseman, nearing the end of his appointment in Washington as British intelligence chief. "We should be wary," Wiseman had written to London, "of the American inclination to thrust responsibility for the war upon the Kaiser and what is termed the Military Party. Americans believe the rest of Germany has been an unwilling tool in the hands of military masters. If Germany was to repudiate the Kaiser and become a Republic, there would be an enormous reaction in America in her favour and she might be received again very much like the Prodigal Son."

Donovan noted the popularity of the German military caste, its determination to rearm, and the opportunities offered to fanatics promising to lead the people out of the economic chaos they were suffering. His reporting methods were described as "anticipating in an uncanny way the functions of a future American intelligence agency" by his biographer, Corey Ford. Donovan had also anticipated Churchill, who was soon saying publicly what Donovan reported privately to a few concerned Americans. "My mind is obsessed with the terrible Germany we saw and felt in action during the years 1914 to 1918," said Churchill. "I see Germany again possessed of all her martial

21

power while we, the Allies, who so narrowly survived, gape in idleness and bewilderment."

In the fortress prison of Landsberg, a new German hero conducted meetings of the National Socialist movement and dictated a book that cast a shadow across the years ahead. Adolf Hitler's autobiography expressed hatred for the Jews, denounced the Bolsheviks, and offered a disturbingly perceptive study of mass propaganda. It was called *Mein Kampf* (My Struggle). Hitler began it in 1922. Two years later, having failed to seize power in a Putsch, he served a jail sentence for high treason and finished his political testament. It summoned into existence a new kind of man: *der Führer,* who would command a new barbaric civilization.

Even in prison, Hitler commanded obedience. The warders cried *"Heil Hitler!"* on entering his cell. When he met a new jailer, he fixed the unfortunate man with blazing eyes. Those subjected to his manic stare agreed that it pierced them to the soul. The prison mailmen staggered to his cell with gifts from all over Germany: wine, fruit, flowers, chocolates, rich cakes, expensive meats, an abundance of luxuries while hardship stalked the streets. Hitler's chosen henchmen occupied other cells. He had secretaries and a valet. He lunched in a communal hall with fellow Nazis. And thus he finished *Mein Kampf,* a blueprint for total destruction of existing society and conquest of the world.

Meanwhile, Stephenson crossed the Atlantic again in search of business partners, scientific brains, and opportunities to expand his interests. Radio led him into recorded sound and movies, where he was experimenting, like many others, with the marvels of sound-on-film and "talking pictures." He was ready to move into the automobile industry. Henry Ford's assumed monopoly of it had been badly shaken by news that a rival, Chevrolet, had surpassed the Model T in sales. There was a stampede for radio sets and the first products of the embryo electronics industry. Those who were smitten by jazz were pouring money into records by George Gershwin and Paul Whiteman. Stephenson saw opportunity in all these fields. He went to New York, seeking business partners in 1924, the year that John D. Rockefeller, Sr., was found to have paid only $124,266 in taxes, whereas his son paid $7,435,169, and the year Charles Dawes presented Germany with a reparations bill that would bankrupt the new republic and smooth Hitler's rise to power.

Stephenson saw magnificent opportunities for applying American technology to comparatively backward Europe, and ways to develop mass markets in the United States for the products of British inventiveness. United Europe, too, could provide the kind of market that produced large sales and money to finance new ideas.

On the voyage back to England, he met a pretty young girl from Tennessee: Mary French Simmons. She had never traveled so far from home before, but she knew a great deal about the world. She noticed that the small, restless Canadian kept aloof from their fellow passengers and she concluded that he was shy. He seemed interested in reading dull-looking textbooks, although he answered politely when she questioned him about Europe.

"This Mr. Churchill speaks of a United Europe which could accomplish what the United States has done in wealth and industry," she said. "Is it possible?"

Stephenson smiled, and she noticed how it transformed his whole appearance. "There was a chance of that," he said, "two or three years ago. Now—I'm not so sure."

"Why is that?"

"For one thing, Mr. Churchill lives quietly in the country, painting visions on canvas. The men who could lead the United States and a United Europe together don't seem to have much of a following. . . ."

"Who is this man Mussolini?"

Stephenson surrendered to her polite interrogation. By the end of the voyage, he had only one question to ask in return: would Mary marry him. On Sunday, August 31, 1924, the New York *Times* carried the photograph of an uncommonly handsome girl under the headline AMERICAN GIRL WEDS CANADIAN SCIENTIST.

In Germany, the first chapters of *Mein Kampf*

were being smuggled out of Hitler's well-furnished cell. By the end of the year, the future Nazi dictator had been released "for good behavior." The *Berliner Tageblatt* wrote: "Never before has a court more openly denied the foundation upon which it rests and upon which every modern state is built." The thugs had bludgeoned justice. Europe united was a dream that would become a nightmare.

 4

IN THAT SAME year of 1924, Stephenson received from Cipher Machines, at 2 Steglitserstrasse, Berlin, the offer of a "secret writing mechanism to frustrate inquisitive competitors." This was Enigma, harmless enough in its commercial form. It resembled a clumsy great typewriter. Anything typed on its large keyboard passed through a ciphering system and emerged in a scrambled form that would mystify an unauthorized observer.

It seemed to Stephenson that Enigma could be electrified and remodeled into a compact machine. Unknown to him, this is what German intelligence thought, too. By the time Hitler had strong-armed his way to power, a different, and highly secret, Enigma would lie at the heart of Nazi cipher systems.

Stephenson played around with the design of the first Enigma and then forgot about it. In those breathless years from 1924 until 1933, when Hitler became Chancellor of a new Germany, much happened to distract this young man who had made his first million before he was thirty. His friendship with Frederick Lindemann, "the Prof," allowed him to prod Churchill out of a prolonged mood of depression. The Prof feared that Germany was developing new weapons and would destroy her old enemies when Hitler was ready. Stephenson fed those fears with facts.

Churchill seemed in 1933 to be "politically dead," in Harold Nicolson's words. "He is just a great round white face . . . incredibly aged. . . . His spirits also have declined and he sighs that he has lost his old fighting power."

But Churchill was not out of the battle. He had spent twenty years in governments formed by both major political parties. His detractors said this was proof of instability. His admirers saluted his stamina. He had held more ministerial posts than any man in England. Stephenson's firsthand reports of what was really happening in Germany now stirred Churchill. With the Prof to lean upon, the seemingly old man made a little-known journey. It took him into the nooks and crannies of Germany, from which he re-returned alarmed and angry. This near-forgotten German tour would later explain Churchill's ruthless pursuit of Hitler's destruction and the Prof's mobilization of air power to destroy the nation that spawned Nazism. They had glimpsed, in 1933, the possibility of a German atomic bomb and a dictatorship mad enough to use it.

There was a bonfire of books at Berlin University that same year. Stephenson watched students fling into the flames the works of Freud, Mann, H. G. Wells, Proust, and Einstein. Already, the Führer was dictating how the Third Reich should think. "The National Socialist German Workers' Party," decreed Hitler, "constitutes the only political party." In the burning of the books, Stephenson saw the forging of a weapon hard to define: thought control. He was asked by Churchill to seek out more facts and figures on secret German arms, details that would shatter British and American complacency. Thought control defied such analysis, though H. G. Wells had tried. Hitler had invented the Big Lie, said Wells. "It will be believed if repeated enough." The Big Lie spread like a gas that poisoned the minds of foreign observers as well as Germans disposed to trust one man's claim to infallibility.

"The Big Lie takes many forms. It can win

bloodless victories for Germany if our leaders are soft-headed. Hitler means to conquer the world," Stephenson wrote privately to Churchill. "But he will not attack his next victim until he has undermined him first, and digested the previous victim. Europe is rotten with indecision, and corrupted by hopes of making separate deals with the Nazis. Germany's final enemies are in North America. Hitler will try first to sap our courage by winning friends there."

Stephenson was pursued by Alfred Rosenberg, the pasty-faced fanatic who dressed Hitler's ugly intentions in pseudo-scientific disguise. There would come a day when Rosenberg choked while Hitler told him how the Jews were to be exterminated. In 1933, Rosenberg was still the self-deluded Nazi theoretician, earnestly preaching an anti-Bolshevik gospel to foreign visitors.

Rosenberg failed to see Stephenson's horror at the violence already visible in Germany. A dangerous arrogance blinded Nazi leaders to the reactions of such a foreigner. What Rosenberg did perceive was Stephenson's control of the biggest film and recording studios outside Hollywood, and his influence in the world of entertainment—a prime Nazi propaganda target. Furthermore, Stephenson conducted business all over the world. He was modernizing coal in Rumania. He led technical missions to help countries like India. His steel and cement companies were the largest outside the United States. The German cartels would love to plug into such a network.

Nazi intrigues led to the rediscovery of Enigma. The cipher machine had been modernized and put into limited German service, its presence noted by American engineers of the International Telephone and Telegraph Company. ITT was becoming involved in German arms manufacture, after talks with Hitler in 1933. The founder of ITT, Colonel Sosthenes Behn, set up German subsidiaries to take advantage of Nazi promises that foreign investors would get preferential treatment and the guarantee of huge global markets later.

A report on these advantageous terms was sent to Stephenson. One of his companies made equipment for ITT's British subsidiary. He found an opportunity to talk with ITT engineers, who were now in an unusual position to examine the German communications systems. They commented on the large amount of coded traffic. It seemed to result from Hitler's use of a coding machine for Nazi party business.

ITT's German interests were handled by Dr. Gerhard Alois Westrick. The German banker Kurt von Schroeder joined the directors of ITT subsidiaries. Both men caught Stephenson's attention—and would hold it for other reasons for a long time. Schroeder was on his way to becoming Gestapo treasurer and a general in the SS security service. Westrick was a partner of Heinrich Albert, a German propagandist in the United States, and would become an adversary when Stephenson tried to break up Nazi cartels in the Western Hemisphere. Sometimes it was wiser to leave these partnerships alone. In ITT's case, whatever benefit was obtained by the Nazis from American expertise had to be balanced against intelligence gathered by its technicians. The irony was that in those days this intelligence roused more interest in Enigma among Stephenson's colleagues in London than it could in Washington.

Several observers in different parts of the world must have guessed Enigma's importance at the same time. In the U.S., the Radio Intelligence Division of the Federal Communications Commission was peering into Nazi secret-radio traffic. RID was the American counterpart of the British Radio Security Service (RSS). Each worked under the handicap of official displeasure and justified operations by claiming only to watch for pirate radio stations that broke the law, usually by transmitting without government license.

In 1934, when Stephenson discussed Enigma with American friends, a Federal Communications Act became law in which Section 605 prohibited wiretaps and the interception of messages between foreign countries and the United States. The prohibition reflected the mood of the authorities in both countries and made it difficult for worried citizens to exchange information between countries—even if it did concern their mutual survival.

Enigma gleamed briefly on their horizon and vanished again. Within the armed forces of the United States and Britain, there were inadequately paid specialists who might have locked onto the secret more firmly if there had been official channels through which to compare notes. Instead, there were informal groups of men and women who were convinced war was coming. To say so, however, was "unpatriotic." Nobody in his right senses wanted war in a period of severe economic depression. There was a widespread belief in Britian and the United States that the manufacture of arms was in the hands of "Merchants of Death." Stephenson and his friends on both sides of the Atlantic had to resort to an almost conspiratorial style to avoid the label. They were becoming reluctant detectives, obliged to get the facts of German rearmament before they could prepare to defend their own people.

There was no financial inducement for Stephenson to chase ghosts like Enigma or to pry into Nazi secrets. Yet everything he touched not only turned to gold, but also involved technical developments that would transform warfare. He was building planes at a time when no British government would put money into military aircraft. His fellow flight-commander from 73 Squadron A. H. Orlebar won the coveted aeronautical trophy, the Schneider Cup, in the plane that sired the Spitfire. The designer, Reginald Mitchell, was dying; Stephenson encouraged him sufficiently that he fought pain and despair to complete the graceful fighter in time to defend Britain against invasion. The inventor of the jet, Frank Whittle, remembered his relief at discovering Stephenson, after the Royal Air Force had rejected his revolutionary concept of flight without propellers. Fortunately, such developments could be financed by Stephenson's Electric and General Industrial Trust. Stephenson listened to Whittle's proposals, sat silent for several minutes, then put his finger on the problem with characteristic brevity.

"He said we'd need a new alloy for the high-speed turbine blades," Whittle recalled. "Then he found it."

There were cautionary voices who had a more subtle influence on Stephenson: George Bernard Shaw,

George Orwell, and foreign correspondents whose horror stories from Germany were often suppressed by their own publishers. Stephenson had lost his dearest friend, Steinmetz, who died suddenly but whose voice persisted in a period of confusion. On visits to Germany, Stephenson "felt Steiny at my elbow, setting me straight. Everything I did was tangling with the knowledge that we were going to have to fight Hitler and his perversion of Darwin's theory of survival of the fittest."

The fight against Hitler finally began at home. In Britain and North America, small movements resisted further compromise with Hitler. In London, "Churchill's activists" were drawn from all sections of society. Their voice in Parliament was Churchill, but the public ignored his warnings. These were what he called the "Wilderness Years." He was branded a warmonger for writing that "when Hitler began, Germany lay prostrate at the feet of the Allies—Hitler may yet see the day when what is left of Europe will be prostrate at the feet of the Germans." In articles for the few newspapers that tolerated his opinions, he learned to modify his statements. "We shall be worse off if we get too far ahead of public opinion," he told Focus, anticipating what an American president would tell his own advisers when pressed to fight Nazism.

Focus was one of those informal groups pulled together by Admiral Blinker Hall. They consisted of men and women who saw war as inevitable, but whose views ran counter to British policy. Some came from the British Secret Intelligence Service itself, whose servants were bound to obey the government of the day. If that government chose to belittle the danger of war, what was a loyal intelligence officer to do? It was an offense even to utter the initials of any department of intelligence, let alone complain to the press. The problem was partly solved by an unobtrusive figure moving between the Directorate of Military Intelligence and these civilian-professional groups meeting in their clubs and company board rooms. He was Desmond Morton, a modest major who would eventually organize an Allied Committee of Resistance to rally civilians against Hitler inside Nazi territories. Major Morton's experience in organizing resistance within Britain in the mid-1930s offered lessons for the future.

Morton later told a story that caught the flavor of those days: "Our man in Dublin concluded that the chief of German intelligence in southern Ireland was a thug living in Bray. Some of our gentlemen hit him with a rubber truncheon one night, bundled him into a dinghy and rowed him out to one of His Majesty's submarines. When it reached England, there emerged from the lockers into which he'd been thrust, the bloody and bloody-minded features of the chief of British Naval Intelligence for southern Ireland . . ."

Morton was Special Assistant to Churchill in 1935, assigned to "discover the plans for the manufacture of arms and war stores abroad." He was to prepare a shadow organization that in wartime would answer to Parliament as a Ministry of Economic Warfare, secretly responsible for sabotage and assassination. Neither Churchill nor Morton had parliamentary authority. Their support came from the King, that higher authority whose intervention was permissible in times of crisis although it could be challenged. This traditional arrangement, by which the monarchy and the funds set aside for royal functions could be used to protect those acting secretly to defend national interests, was and still is little understood. It was to prove vital in the secret wars to come. Meanwhile, it allowed Morton to shuttle between groups like Focus, Electra, and the XYZ Committee; informal gatherings of men who had respectable reasons for traveling abroad, including adventurers and explorers like Ian and Peter Fleming. (Peter had just walked across Tibet from China to India and was speculating on methods of "strategic deception" if war with Germany broke out again.)

Stephenson's business office, in St. James's Street, off Piccadilly, had become the London base of an alliance with Washington between like-minded men. Through this channel came a report in 1935 that the Japanese Navy was sharing its version of Enigma with the Japanese Foreign Office.

A working partnership developed unofficially

through Stephenson. The U.S. Army's Signal Intelligence Service and the U.S Navy's equivalent were forbidden to exchange information with the British. But much was possible by word of mouth. Stephenson, with business reasons for talking with key figures, could arrange co-operation in a way that might be embarrassing if documented on paper. To many senior officers and a few politicians, it was clear that Germany and Japan were moving into an ominous stage preceding naked aggression: concealment. Their diplomatic and military traffic was protected by unfathomable ciphers. Part of the method of breaking such codes was to gather quantities of coded messages: the bigger the volume, the better the chance of detecting a pattern that would lead to a solution. With help from Canada, which was part of the Western Hemisphere but also a confidant of Britain, the old Allies could pool the results of their unofficial eavesdropping. Their clandestine method of co-operation provided useful experience for the hard times to come.

Stephenson, anything but a conspirator, was obliged to seek anonymity. "The less anyone knows about the personal life of an intelligence chief, the better" was an unwritten law. Stephenson was becoming chief of a private intelligence agency. All record of his activities was erased from the newspapers after 1935. Clippings about him began to disappear from newspaper files.

Still, he was in the public eye. This seeming contradiction had a purpose. If war came, such men would be scrutinized by enemy intelligence working through many channels, but largely dependent upon newspaper files. Stephenson's activities were part of the process of building up contacts abroad in preparation for secret warfare. He had just won the prestigious King's Cup air race when printed accounts of his past began to vanish. He won it with a machine designed and built in his own General Aircraft factory. This attracted the interest of Hitler's Air Force chiefs. They had worked on other British and American airmen, appealing to sportsmanship and a shared passion for flying.

Again Stephenson listened. It must have been an

odd spectacle. In London, his friends tore up his past. In Germany, he gently interrogated Hitler's men with little more than a smile and cocked eyebrow.

"At one conference," he reported, "a description was given of 'blitzkrieg.' . . . Dive bombers and tanks would spearhead each offensive, followed by troops in fast carriers. The Nazi war machine would rely on lightning victories, in turn dependent on the swift redirection of mechanized units by means of radio. It follows that blitzkrieg can succeed only by transmission of top-secret orders through the ether in unbreakable codes."

German chieftains talked so frankly because they took professional pride in their efficiency. Some hoped to overawe any potential opposition. Others used the sly justification that Germany was destined to destroy the ultimate and universal enemy: Bolshevik Russia.

Did Nazi Germany plan to invade Russia, then? The answer was yes, according to Albert Kesselring. The man destined to direct the bombing of London told Stephenson how German armored divisions would strike into Russia. "The secret will be speed . . . speed . . . speed!" Kesselring thumped the table to emphasize each word. "Fast as lightning! Blitzkrieg! Lightning war."

"How would your Air Force get support, so far ahead of the armies?" Stephenson asked General Erhard Milch, State Secretary for Air, who replied: "The dive bombers will form a flying artillery, directed to work in harmony with ground forces through good radio communications. You, a radio expert, must appreciate that for the first time in history, this coordination of forces is possible. The Air Force will not repair units. Tanks and planes will be disposable. The real secret is speed—speed of attack through speed of communications."

To Churchill, Stephenson reported that the weak link in the German armor would be communications. "If we can read their signals, we can anticipate their actions."

Stephenson was launched on a search for the modernized Enigma cipher machine, without knowing it.

5

WHENEVER HE FLEW from Berlin to London, Stephenson was angrily aware that the official German airline carried pilots and navigators of the shadow Nazi Air Force who were familiarizing themselves with their future target. In London, Parliament droned on, oblivious to the treachery being prepared in the skies above, intent only upon pacifying Hitler. Those who saw the danger hid themselves in Churchill's shadow Ministry of Economic Warfare, still informal and secret and unacknowledged. The difference between this clandestine British ministry and the shadow German Air Force was pathetic. The bomber crews had official German support and scarcely bothered to hide their preparations. Not only did Churchill's ministry run counter to official British policy, but also Churchill was himself a political leper.

Support had to come from outside. Where better, Stephenson argued, than the United States? The U.S. Navy had established a Mid-Pacific Strategic Direction-Finding Net, whose purpose was to locate Japanese units by tracking their radio transmissions. It would net coded Japanese traffic that then could be added to what was acquired by British monitors in India and Asia. The Japanese were making increasing use of their own versions of Enigma, and the Americans were at work on the Japanese machine-produced ciphers.

Small though these American preparations might seem, they could be traced back to a large truth. Churchill had courage but no visible power. In the White House there was a man possessed of the courage so conspicuously absent in Westminster. That man was Franklin Delano Roosevelt.

Hitler would later sneer that Roosevelt became president "when I became Chancellor. . . . This tortuous-minded Jew was born to riches. I knew squalor and harsh poverty." FDR was not, of course, Jewish. Nor did he seek pity. He was recognized by his magnificent head and his confident grin. He commanded such personal devotion that, for instance, press photographers loyally avoided showing the heavy braces that encumbered his withered legs. In 1933, President Roosevelt had written to Britain's socialist Prime Minister, Ramsay MacDonald: "I am concerned with events in Germany. An insane rush to further armaments is infinitely more dangerous than any number of other squabbles."

FDR was anything but a warmonger. But, like Churchill, he was forced to look danger squarely in the face. He relied for disinterested reports on foreign dangers upon Bill Donovan, who traveled abroad using vaguely defined legal interests as an excuse. Donovan had returned to law practice after a fling at politics, and was now established at 2 Wall Street. "If Bill Donovan had been a Democrat," said Roosevelt at a class reunion at Columbia Law School, "he'd be in my place today."

Donovan bore the same relationship to FDR that Stephenson bore to Churchill. There was mutual respect and trust. Donovan, knowing war, hated it. His investigation of the Bolshevik Revolution in Russia had been followed by discreet visits to Hitler. At home, Donovan enforced antitrust legislation for the Justice Department in such a way that the big corporations respected his fair play as well as his incorruptibility. He knew, in consequence, a great deal about the corporate structure of international firms controlled or influenced by the Nazis. It was inevitable that Stephenson would renew their brief World War I acquaintanceship. Donovan was the logical American to discuss how Nazi intelligence proposed to use dummy U.S. subsidiaries. Donovan was also a friend of the director of U.S. Naval Intelligence, Rear Admiral Walter S. Anderson, and Stephenson was the protégé of a British admiral, Blinker Hall. Though open cooperation between the two navies was restricted by political considerations, and the U.S. government continued to deplore the interception of communications on ethical grounds, nonetheless, it was impossible to stop Americans peering into the expanding world of codes and cryptology. Roosevelt did not intend to stop them. The field of cryptanalysis had an aura of sorcery, but the basis was highly scientific. Stephenson had a natural interest as a scientist, experience in signals transmission since childhood, and a talent for abstract mathematics that would be needed in meeting the challenge of Enigma. The existence of the cipher machine in its new Japanese and Nazi garb was vaguely understood. Stephenson's knowledge was welcome on both sides of the Atlantic. Interest in Enigma was a minor note in the overture to calamity.

Donovan agreed that dictatorship was made vulnerable by dependence on secrecy. "The soft area in a totalitarian state is the security system," he said. "So much has to be kept secret that machinery to process information is cumbersome. A dictator is apt to think he functions in a totally secure environment and he gets careless." Nazi Germany was forging a military machine that relied on secret communications, the weak link in Hitler's armor.

"I was delighted someone on the American side had come to this conclusion," Stephenson was to recall. "It laid the foundations of our partnership and put emphasis on the vital area of secret warfare. There could be no story about wartime intelligence that was not the story of Donovan and his activities before the outbreak of war. It was understood without anything being spelled out that Big Bill was the President's personal agent."

The two Bills saw the world in similar terms. Neither took pleasure in military affairs. Donovan never saw himself as a military hero, though General Douglas MacArthur was to describe him as "the most determined, resourceful and gallant soldier I have ever known in my life." Donovan replied that "I know too much about war to glory in it. But wars are made by politicians who neglect to prepare for it."

While the Americans groped for the secret of the Japanese version of Enigma, the British gathered evidence of Enigma variations in Nazi Germany. In

35

1937, Stephenson learned through his contacts in the German communications industry that Enigma was serving the Nazi party's own secret intelligence. It had come under the control of a few men with all the powers of spying, police interrogation, and execution. One of these men was Reinhard Tristam Eugen Heydrich.

"The most sophisticated apparatus for conveying top-secret orders was at the service of Nazi propaganda and terror," Stephenson noted. "The power of a totalitarian regime rested on propaganda and terror. Heydrich had made a study of the Russian OGPU, the Soviet secret security service. He then engineered the Red Army purges carried out by Stalin. The Russian dictator believed his own armed forces were infiltrated by German agents as a consequence of a secret treaty by which the two countries helped each other rearm.* Secrecy bred suspicion, which bred more secrecy, until the Soviet Union was so paranoid it became vulnerable to every hint of conspiracy. Late in 1936, Heydrich had thirty-two documents forged to play on Stalin's sick suspicions and make him decapitate his own armed forces. The Nazi forgeries were incredibly successful. More than half the Russian officer corps, some 35,000 experienced men, were executed or banished.** The Soviet Chief of Staff, Marshal Tukhachevsky, was depicted as having been in regular correspondence with German military commanders. All the letters were Nazi forgeries. But Stalin took them as proof that

---

* The Treaty of Rapallo was signed between Germany and Russia behind the backs of twenty-eight other nations attending the Genoa Conference, which failed miserably in an attempt to bring about the reconstruction of Europe in 1922. Had Genoa succeeded, many political commentators considered that there might perhaps have been no Ruhr, no Hitler, no World War II.

** Stephenson's intelligence summary concluded that the forged papers led to shooting or imprisonment for three out of five Soviet marshals, fourteen of sixteen military commanders in chief, all Russian Navy admirals of Ranks I and II, sixty of sixty-seven commanding generals, 136 of 199 divisional commanders, and 221 of 397 brigade commanders. All eleven deputy defense commissars and seventy-five out of eighty members of the Supreme War Soviet were liquidated.

36

even Tukhachevsky was spying for Germany. It was a most devastating and clever end to the Russo-German military agreement, and it left the Soviet Union in absolutely no condition to fight a major war with Hitler."

Heydrich, the architect of this triumph in Nazi deceptive operations, was Stephenson's opponent in the developing battle of wits. He was tall, blond, clear-eyed, and handsome. He played down his part-Jewish origins, and was driven by a personal and unlimited vindictiveness that had nothing to do with Nazi ideology. "His cold eyes glinted with icy pleasure when he gave directions for a Jewish family of shop-keepers, discovered by the Gestapo in a minor infringement of the law, to be murdered by whipping and strangulation," reported one of Heydrich's own intelligence rivals, Walter Schellenburg. "His schizophrenic hatred of his Jewish ancestry led to monstrous actions against Judaism in general. He was ambivalent even in sex. Simply to win advancement, he married the daughter of a secret sponsor of Germany's rearmament and close friend of Admiral Wilhelm Canaris."

Admiral Canaris was the name that always sprang to mind in connection with Germany's foreign-intelligence operations. Like Admiral Hall in Britain and Admiral Anderson in America, he commanded naval resources for espionage that could be expanded into foreign and political affairs without civilian interference. Although Heydrich had been kicked out of the German Navy for "dishonorable conduct" when a youngster, Canaris continued to groom him for a career in intelligence.

Stephenson awoke with a jolt to the full significance of this Nazi spy whose usefulness to Hitler had seemed to be mainly in cheating Allied watchdogs enforcing the Treaty of Versailles. Later, when the Allied Control Commission prepared to inspect German factories to see if Germany adhered to the treaty's arms limitations, it was Heydrich who warned the managers. If the Commission arrived at Krupp's, in Essen, it was to see household articles come off the assembly line instead of the guns and ammunition of a few hours earlier.

These deceptions were spotted by Stephenson because he could look into the records as a bona fide businessman representing, among other things, new industries created by discoveries in synthetic materials, prefabricated construction methods, and propulsion technology. As owner of the Pressed Steel Company in Britain, he negotiated with German United Steel and thus found that this conglomerate made howitzers as well as hairpins. He saw where tanks were hidden among the blueprints for tractors. Submarines were now constructed in prefabricated sections in Finland, Holland, and Spain, where the separate bits would not be recognized.

Heydrich was identified with the authors of such schemes, and with that typical Nazi weapon the Stuka dive bomber, which struck terror when it fell upon its victims. The Stuka's scream was intended to destroy morale already undermined by bombs. Typically, the plane combined propaganda and terror. One required the other. The Stuka was unthinkable, and those who might have resisted Hitler preferred not to think about it. Stephenson's reports failed to budge British leaders who wished to believe that the Stuka factories were making lawn mowers.

What Stephenson saw was reinforced by what he was told by Germans like Fritz Thyssen. The German steel king poured a fortune into Nazi party coffers, and then in 1938 lost control of Hitler. Hoping to separate the Führer from the Nazi movement, Thyssen sought sympathy abroad and unwittingly betrayed crucial information, including a clue to the greatest secret of all. Hundreds of new, portable versions of a cipher machine were being built to Heydrich's specifications in a factory near Berlin. This proved to be the new Enigma, for carrying the top-secret signals that would guide the massive Nazi war machine. It would be the nervous system of Germany's blitzkrieg.

Heydrich was in charge. His stature was to become, in secret warfare, greater than any rival within the Nazi camp. Knowing this in advance made it possible to study Hitler's chief thug and most malevolent practitioner of the politics of terror. This knowledge would prove as valuable as the discovery that the new portable Enigma was very different from the original. The machine had a keyboard like a typewriter. The keys were linked electrically through a system of drums. The relationship between the drums could be changed swiftly in a multitude of ways. The sender of a message would hit the keys as if typing routinely. The machine switched each letter to a different one. The operator might press A, and Z would be transmitted. The receiving Enigma, its drums adjusted to the prearranged setting, would respond by translating Z back into A. Anyone intercepting the signals between the two stations would pick up gobbledygook. This elaborate system seemed foolproof. Not only was the portable Enigma itself a mystery, but so also were the schedules for setting the drums.

The advantage in intercepting the signals and making sense of them would be incalculable. In the wars of rapid and surprise movement envisaged by the Germans, armadas of aircraft and tanks and troops could strike without warning. Their first aim would be to occupy vast areas before effective resistance could be mounted. Once some territory or an entire country had been occupied, it was likely that fighting would end with Hitler dictating terms. Possession would become the law. The success of blitzkrieg would depend on total secrecy and swift communications. Unless the secret signals were intercepted and solved, there would be no effective defense against blitzkrieg.

Stephenson estimated it would take a month for one combination of the drums to be solved by a team of brilliant mathematicians. The Greek name, Enigma, meant puzzle. No puzzle had been invented of greater complexity. The job of capturing a machine would be only a beginning. Day and night, a vast number of experts would have to concentrate to determine the specific settings of the originating cipher drums. Stephenson came back to London distressed and frustrated. Little was being done to penetrate these Nazi secrets. Only Hall's band of volunteers still worked at code-breaking. Working against similar odds with greater success, the U.S. Navy was making headway in analyzing the Japanese version of Enigma and in the development of its own ship-borne coding machines. In January 1938, the U.S. Navy's Director of War Plans, Captain R. E. Ingersoll, was sent to London to co-ordinate work against the potential enemy's ciphers. But Britain's Prime Minister of the time, Neville Chamberlain, was not much interested in American apprehensions. He was busy brooding on "Russians stealthily and cunningly pulling all strings to get us involved in war with Germany," as he confided to his diary on March 20, 1938. (His notes were quoted later by Sir K. Fielding in *The Life of Neville Chamberlain*.) Chamberlain added, with unconscious irony, "Our Secret Service doesn't spend all its time looking out of the window." Its preoccupation with Russia made Ingersoll's secret mission unpopular. Furthermore, Chamberlain's naval friends were not impressed with proposals for carrying coding machines on warships, and their disinterest ensured that the Royal Navy went into World War II without equipment that was by then standard with the U.S. Navy. Worst of all, press publicity made it seem that Ingersoll's consultations were a breach of the ban against Anglo-American co-operation. Incredibly, Ingersoll returned to Washington with nothing accomplished in the one field where preparation would have saved Britain from near-catastrophe. He did accomplish much by informal means; and became commander in chief of the U.S. Atlantic Fleet at a critical time, thanks to the fundamental good sense of regular naval officers on both sides who risked offending their political masters.

In September 1938, Hitler was fed another bloodless victory at Munich. The screaming Stukas were not even needed to strike terror in Chamberlain. Hitler caustically sketched a symbol for the sellout: Chamberlain's rolled umbrella broken across the German sword. Munich was to become the historic crossroad where the words "Chamberlain" and "appeasement" merged. And the independence of Czechoslovakia vanished.

The terms of the agreement between Adolf Hitler and Neville Chamberlain were studied by a retiring but exceedingly honest man, Alfred Duff Cooper.

He was First Lord of the Admiralty, loyal to his prime minister, incapable of subterfuge, and the kind of Englishman upon whose sense of fair play the Führer had counted in his policy of deceit. Duff Cooper read the terms of the Munich agreement. "I said to myself," he wrote later, "if these are accepted, it will be the end of all decency in the conduct of public affairs in the world."

Then he resigned.

Duff Cooper's action represented an attitude that was alien to Hitler's experience. Men did not resign in protest in the Nazi world. They risked losing everything. They stood to gain nothing. Sensible German insiders kept quiet and hung on to their jobs. In England this was not always so. There were resignations during this period; none perhaps as significant as that of Duff Cooper. He was an intimate of Admiral Hall. Quite soon, the post he vacated as First Lord of the Admiralty was filled by Churchill. Meanwhile, Duff Cooper set about organizing the groups of men and women who were amateurs in intelligence but professionals in business, science, and the arts. With Blinker Hall's help, he paved the way for secret intelligence operations once war broke out.

"I have given up an office that I loved, work in which I was deeply interested and a staff of which any man might be proud," Duff Cooper said in 1938. "I have given up the privilege of serving as lieutenant to a leader whom I still regard with the deepest admiration and affection. I have ruined, perhaps, my political career. But that is a little matter. I have retained something which is to me of great value—I can still walk about the world with my head erect."

Much was lost at Munich. The Nazis could now harness some of Europe's largest arsenals, and the Czech chemical industry was an immense prize. Stephenson recited the list of economic victories, speaking at a weekly luncheon chaired by Churchill, who sat with head bowed. Later, Stephenson was drawn aside.

"We not only betrayed our Czech friends," Churchill growled, "we gave that guttersnipe new slingshots."

41

Stephenson nodded. "Hitler now has the means to perfect the blitzkrieg."

"Czech brains—?"

"Their own Nazis will equip Germany with the new coding machine from mass-assembly lines."

"Can we get one?" Churchill demanded.

"Skoda is said to be making them."

"The sinews of war have become whispers in the ether." Churchill took Stephenson by the arm. "If you recover the whispers, I'll find the interpreters of what they say."

A professor of mathematics brought together the men and women who would interpret Enigma if it came their way. The professor was at this private luncheon, attended by civilians who became the core of Stephenson's secret intelligence. Occasionally the luncheons attracted sympathizers from the United States. One was President Roosevelt's "Elder Statesman," Bernard Baruch. The American millionaire was a powerful ally because of his skepticism about Nazi self-justifications. Baruch recalled Stephenson at these gatherings: "He was very serious, frightening even. He could think seven stages ahead of you. It was terrifying to watch. If he was absorbing information, not a muscle in his face moved, nor did his eyes shift around as you would expect from someone reflecting. He looked straight ahead, a sort of chess champion seeing three possibilities for a mate in five and debating which to choose. When he spoke, he cut clean through the matter. Never wasted a word."

What Stephenson said after the Czech disaster was that war was coming, the United States would be in it, and "you might as well work with us now."

At Baruch's suggestion, Roosevelt chose Canada for the setting of a little-known speech. At Queens University, in Kingston, Ontario, he said: "We in the Americas are no longer a faraway continent to which the eddies of controversies beyond the seas could bring no interest or no harm. . . . The vast amount of our resources, the vigor of our commerce and the strength of our men have made us vital factors in world peace whether we choose it or not." To the Canadian Prime Minister, Mackenzie King, in early

1939, he added in privacy: "Our frontier is on the Rhine."

Stephenson received word from Ottawa of this implied commitment. "FDR sees the Atlantic Ocean as no barrier, but, rather, a highway," he advised Churchill.

This was the time to mobilize powerful influences in Churchill's support from across that ocean. Churchill was never more isolated in his own country than now, never more unpopular, never more divorced from orthodox sources of political power. Ironically, the strong right arm he needed was being provided by none other than the President of the United States.

In April 1939, Roosevelt appealed to Hitler and Mussolini to give a ten-year guarantee of nonaggression to thirty-one nations. Hitler replied in a sarcastic speech to the Reichstag: "Mr. Roosevelt! I fully understand that the vastness of your country and the immense wealth of your nation allow you to feel responsible for the history of the whole world. I, sir, am placed in a much more modest and smaller sphere. I have re-established the historic unity of German living space and, Mr. Roosevelt, I have endeavored to attain all this without spilling blood." It was a speech described by Hitler's biographer Joachim Fest as "a moral declaration of war."

"It was all Roosevelt needed to settle in his own mind the morality of supporting those who resisted fascism," said Stephenson later. "He had made his gesture and Hitler had ranted and raved in derision. After this, the President was one of us."

6

PRESIDENT ROOSEVELT'S SUPPORT for Churchill's rebels must have begun almost unthinkingly. Hitler was set upon a monstrous course that seemed sure to bring disaster. Yet many in the United States, struggling with the Depression and disenchanted with the quarrels of Europe, saw only the economic success of Nazi Germany and not its evil roots.

"Germany must have markets for her goods or die," wrote an American military attaché in Berlin. "And Germany will not die." He found it understandable that this dynamic new Germany should demand more space. Hitler's interpretation of living space, *Lebensraum*, was less innocent than might appear to foreign admirers. His real intentions emerged in a four-hour harangue to his military chiefs and the ministers of war and foreign affairs. This was reported, apparently verbatim, by an official German archivist, Colonel Friedrich Hossbach.

Hitler talked about the "solid racial nucleus" of German Aryans, who must breed selectively and prosper on resources now held by "inferior tribes." The German Empire was "a spatially coherent" concept of a world governed by Nazi supermen. There would be a series of lightning military campaigns. Each expansion of German dominions would create a new need for still more expansion. The British Empire was 450 million people "governed by 45 million who will have to be removed." The final obstacle would be the United States, led by "the Jew-loving Roosevelt."

This program was condensed to 50,000 words in the summary from Hossbach, who was also Hitler's military adjutant. It reached Stephenson through Germans horrified by the network of intelligence agencies

44

directed by Heydrich, allegedly created for the security of the state but in practice employed against those who might oppose Hitler.

The report reached Churchill and Roosevelt about a month after Hitler's briefing, which took place on November 5, 1937. The sources had to be protected, and neither Churchill nor the President could risk betraying their knowledge. Instead, Roosevelt quietly arranged for the transfer from Prague to Berlin of Sam Edison Woods, a forty-five-year-old Texas engineer-turned-diplomat. Woods had the talents of Stephenson: wide knowledge of industrial techniques and finance, an ability to listen, a sympathetic understanding of people in many walks of life, and devotion to the old virtues. Woods had been commercial attaché for three years in Czechoslovakia before moving to Berlin to serve in the same capacity. He reported directly to the President on such undiplomatic and noncommercial matters as German progress in atomic science and submarine warfare.

Woods confirmed that Heydrich was a major customer for the new Enigma coding machines, mass-produced on the Czech border near Poland. Several factories by 1938 were assembling parts of what was dubbed the "Heydrich-Enigma." The British, through their Polish Secret Service contacts, nurtured by a Scot named Gubbins, located a Polish engineer working at the Czech border site who was willing to try to reconstruct a cipher machine from memory. He was brought to Paris, where some of the world's best cryptographers worked for French intelligence. Two of Stephenson's men examined the mock-up of the Heydrich-Enigma. They returned with the startling news that it resembled a machine registered in Washington under U.S. Patent 1,657,411. However, it was based on the original Enigma built fourteen years before. The Pole had recalled parts common to all models. He knew none of the specifics that might help the cipher experts. There was only one solution: steal a production model.

A British intelligence mission was sent to Warsaw early in 1939. Mystery still surrounds it. The operation, like many others, was conducted in defiance of official British appeasement policy. The Warsaw mission was led by an unusual man-at-arms, the Scot named Gubbins, otherwise known as Colonel Colin Gubbins, of the Royal Artillery, who had been working for some time in a shabby office near Stephenson's St. James's Street headquarters. Gubbins dressed immaculately, wore a red carnation in his buttonhole, and carried kidskin gloves. One acquaintance remembered him as "an amiable, rather vague sort of chap with no particular talents and some sort of desk job in the War Office." His middle name was McVeagh, and deep in his ancestry had been planted the instincts of a buccaneer. Years of practice had taught him to conceal this, along with fluency in Slavic languages and a most curious record of travel that one did not associate with officers of the regular army. He was producing handbooks for an underground British guerrilla army. Some of the books were printed on rice paper, to be chewed and swallowed if the owner was caught by the German occupation troops that Gubbins expected to see marching through London any day if Churchill's warnings continued to be ignored by those in power. He had written three of the books himself. They were *The Art of Guerrilla Warfare, Partisan Leader's Guide,* and *The Housewife's ABC of Home-Made Explosives.* They scooped Mao Tse-tung and North Vietnam's unconventional-warfare guides by several years.

Gubbins had written, in a War Office memo in 1938, "The coming war with Germany will have to be fought by irregular or guerrilla forces at all possible points." It was a revolutionary statement, against the grain for many professional soldiers. They played their war games according to the rules. There was nothing in those rules about using women and children to manufacture weapons out of everyday articles, or to form partisan units to fight behind the lines, as proposed by Gubbins, who had witnessed in revolutionary Russia and Asia the power of the peasants when united behind an idea and the promise of freedom. His instructions for blowing up enemy tanks by filling bottles with gasoline and rags became known later, when the Russians adopted them, as "Molotov cocktails." By designing

46

these deadly toys, he was blowing up the hallowed and traditional attitude that war was the business of professionals. Another rebel against this orthodoxy, Basil Liddell Hart, had the bitter experience of seeing his ideas rejected by British Army colleagues and adopted instead as the foundation of German blitzkriegs. Liddell Hart joined one of Stephenson's intelligence groups, while newspaper cartoonists continued to depict the typical British officer as a stick-in-the-mud Colonel Blimp.

Gubbins, however unorthodox, was still a member of the British Intelligence Directorate. He came under Prime Minister Chamberlain's orders. Chamberlain seemed to think that by yielding to Hitler's demands, he could satisfy them. Gubbins was convinced that yielding to such demands did not terminate hostility, but excited it. The conflict was resolved by the fact that directors of British intelligence are confirmed in their appointment by the Crown. Their jobs are "within the gift of the Monarch" by long tradition. This untidy British arrangement baffles Americans accustomed to constitutional legalities. A story is still told in Washington to clarify British eccentricities for U.S. intelligence chiefs. King George VI once asked "the Chief of the Secret Service" for classified information. The Chief replied: "I must answer that my lips are sealed." The King said: "Suppose I ordered 'Off with your head'?" The Chief replied: "In that case, Sir, I would lose my head with the lips still sealed." This familylike atmosphere, developed over centuries, gives British monarchs head-of-the-family privileges that are nonetheless open to challenge. That atmosphere depended upon mutual trust between senior members of the family in 1938. It may have seemed medieval then, but it has proved relevant to today's ideological warfare with its confusions of loyalty.

Those backing Gubbins were formidable, if eccentric. They had a trained eye, exotic experience, a common sense so uncommon as to seem lunatic. Through their friends at Scotland Yard, some knew the practitioners of crime—illusionists who propagated themselves into all forms of the human comedy with the aid of masks, false faces, hallucinations, and the tricks of magicians—

47

useful to know in times of trouble. They were also successful at transforming themselves into Colonel Blimps—bumbling, slightly stupid, fighting the next war with the lessons of the last. They saw Poland as the potential victim of Hitler's greed and that of Stalin, too.

When Gubbins returned there in early 1939, he discussed resistance with his old comrades in the Polish Secret Service. It was known that Heydrich had paved the road for Hitler's entry into Austria and Czechoslovakia, and Heydrich was reported to be preparing even more elaborate deceptions to justify a German invasion of Poland.

This was the time of general betrayal. Hitler and Stalin were feeling their way toward a pact, though sworn fundamentally to destroy each other. There had been hints of this pact in the diplomatic traffic that the British were already intercepting through the cryptographers of the Government Code and Cipher School, known irreverently as the Golf, Cheese and Chess Society, quartered at that time near Victoria Station in London. Gubbins warned the Polish Secret Service that their country was to be crushed between these two dictatorships. Then Hitler would bring his frontiers right up to those of the Soviet Union, the mortal enemy he planned to liquidate.

Gubbins's men flew back to London from Warsaw on August 22 with a companion and a prize that would remain secret for another thirty-five years. The very next day, the Nazi-Soviet Pact burst upon an astonished world. It sealed Poland's fate. But Gubbins was already on his way to Warsaw again. One of his colleagues, Eric Bailey, a legendary secret agent himself, commented to Stephenson later: "It seemed madness." Only Stephenson and one or two others knew that, crazy or not, Gubbins had to do it. The coming world war might be won or lost in consequence.

"The Second World War began with wirelessed intelligence," said Stephenson later. "Heydrich was the evil genius. It was a significant fact that the Nazi blitz was launched by coded orders, based on deceit we could not expose, directed by Heydrich. His orders were carried on the new Enigmas. Had we been able to recover those orders, our political leaders might have understood the depth of Nazi wickedness.

"It was made to appear that Polish troops attacked a German radio station early that morning of September 1, 1939. German forces thereupon fired on Polish-occupied points in the Free City of Danzig in 'self-defense.' . . .

"The so-called Polish aggressors were inmates from German concentration camps, taken by Heydrich and dressed in Polish uniforms, then given fatal injections. A few survived to tell the story. They knew they were doomed when they were told to get into foreign uniforms—it's hard to dress a corpse. They were trucked to the frontier and injected with lethal Skophedal. Then they were spread out and riddled with bullets.

"The code name given these men was CANNED GOODS. That was Heydrich's touch. Until he died, he boasted that he started the Second World War."

Heydrich's ruse worked. The New York *Times* reported that regular Polish Army troops took part in an attack on German positions and that this was the signal for a general offensive by Polish forces. The lie confused the British—bound by treaty to help Poland if she was attacked first—long enough to make intervention too late. The role of Heydrich and his weapons of deceit, terror, and lying propaganda was to give German armed forces time to consolidate the positions they gained in sudden movements of suprise.

Churchill dined at the Savoy Grill in London that night. "He looked tired and old," said Stephenson. "All his warnings were proving sound. But the hour seemed late for this solitary man, shunned by much of society, weighed down by grief."

The Duke of Westminster had been celebrating with Nazi-minded friends. The two parties collided. The Duke was rich, anti-Semitic, and an admirer of the powerful—and of Hitler. The Duke came yapping at the old man he regarded as the pariah of a twilight society, calling Churchill a Jew-lover who had conspired against Germany and now saw the consequences.

Churchill stood with head sunk until the drunken tirade ended. The Duke swept off. Churchill leaned on the arm of his daughter Mary. "This country is like a family," he muttered, quoting George Orwell, "with the wrong members in control."

Even as he spoke, other members of that confused family were working on the prize from Poland—a captured Heydrich-Enigma—in a clay field at the very heart of England.

—————————————— 7

BRITAIN WAS IN no condition to stop Hitler. Paradoxically, having missed a better time and place to stop Nazism, Chamberlain chose this time to warn the beast which had fattened during the wasted years on cheap victories. Unless German troops withdrew from Poland, he told Hitler, "we shall be in a state of war." Britain was honoring pledges made to Poland only days before, but the country was far from ready. Churchill noted: "Here was a decision at last, taken at the worst possible moment and on the least satisfactory ground, which must surely lead to the slaughter of tens of millions of people." Even the news of the German invasion of Poland had been broken first to the British by the Americans, wrote U.S. Ambassador Joseph P. Kennedy in a letter to his Secretary of State, Cordell Hull.

The gifted amateurs of intelligence had the possibility—and it was still no more than that—of reading high-grade German ciphers. A few dedicated code breakers in England, analyzing messages in the basic German diplomatic code, had learned to guess what Hitler planned to do before he did it. They were not yet receiving any serious attention from the Chamberlain clique.

The amateurs also helped a few obscure and badly paid civil servants of the Government Code and Cipher School. Two days after the Duke of Westminster bullied a downcast and defeated Churchill, the same Churchill was maneuvered back into the Admiralty as First Lord after a quarter-century's absence. A signal flashed through the Home Fleet: "Winston's back!" Churchill, while still serving irresolute leaders, now had the power to move great fleets over the oceans. He was also war lord in a field where Britain was mentally prepared—secret operations. From his Admiralty post he commanded weapons of intelligence. As companion, he had Admiral Sir Hugh Sinclair, known as "C," chief of the Secret Intelligence Service, and appointed by the King. Churchill and C were secure in the knowledge that they must act to help the King defend his peoples—against government policy, if necessary, although conflict was best avoided by forgetting to mention all that went on. They omitted mention of the strangely named Government Code and Cipher School.

The GCCS listened to messages between German units whose mobility made them dependent on radio rather than landlines. These messages, it was apparent, were sent in ever-changing gobbledygook over stations transmitting at low strength. So the traffic had to be picked up by extremely sensitive "ears," transposed from cipher to plain German, then translated and analyzed.

A small army of "brains" had to be formed; an army too large to keep in London, where it would be vulnerable to bombs and public scrutiny. The nucleus had long existed—a few bright men who once worked in Room 40 breaking the Zimmermann Telegram. They had been preserved through the twenty-year armistice by Admiral Blinker Hall, aided and abetted by C, who went about his business in a bowler hat too small for his head, and who was reported to turn his chair and face the wall when a stranger approached his meager office. C had a hard time adjusting to the high spirits and schoolboy whimsies of the newcomers to the GCCS. In August 1939, they were bundled off, kit and caboodle, to a place as ugly as its name: Bletchley.

There was no apparent reason for this sudden move, apart from C's preference for keeping scholars, solvers of crossword puzzles, mathematicians, linguists, and classical dons at arm's length. Bletchley was known for its brick kilns and possibly the grubbiest railway yards in the islands. It lay in a shallow basin in Buckinghamshire. No other place in England, it was said, was farther from the sea—all of sixty miles from the nearest possible invasion beach. A sample of the Heydrich-Enigma had been standing there for several days when the Golf, Cheese and Chess Society, in gray flannels and tweed skirts, descended upon the bemused inhabitants of the tiny market town, which was henceforth a nerve center of the secret wars.

Where had the Nazi coding machine come from? And why Bletchley?

When Stephenson had returned from Germany in 1933 with independent confirmation of the new portable Enigma, the task of trying to build a replica was assigned to a taciturn little Scot who had been a professor of German before working in Room 40. He was Alastair Denniston and he typified veterans of World War I Naval Intelligence, kept together through the hard years when spies of fiction lived like kings but the authentic British agent lived on little save a sense of serving his King. The few full-time agents based on foreign stations were drawn from regular Service officers, shipping clerks, explorers, bank managers. Few had private incomes or had gone to the "right" schools, despite the legends. They were men like C. H. ("Dick") Ellis, an Australian who started out as a musician and advanced his schooling through scholarships before winding up as an Army officer, out of uniform, in Russia. They were men like Eric Bailey, who had marched into Tibet with the first Western mission there; had explored alone the borderlands of Central Asia and India; had, with a price on his head, outwitted the Soviet Security Police; and had given his name to a celebrated Himalayan blue poppy.

Denniston looked more like an adventurer of the mind. And in 1938, with little to go upon, he had attempted the Mount Everest of intellectual challenges: the reconstruction of a top-secret Nazi cipher system possibly based on some unknown modifications of an old commercial coding mechanism. After the failure of the Polish engineer's mock-up, Stephenson, using his knowledge of electronic transmission and cipher machines, provided more specifications and tracked down a German SS unit in the Danzig area where Poland's Secret Service could hope to recover cipher books. The new Enigmas were being delivered to frontier units, and in early 1939 a military truck containing one was ambushed. Polish agents staged an accident in which fire destroyed the evidence. German investigators assumed that some charred bits of coils, springs, and rotos were the remains of the real Enigma. Ironically, the box that contained the battery model had been deliberately made of wood to facilitate destruction if the operator faced capture. Thus it was made easier for the hijackers to fake loss by fire.

The real Enigma, taken to Warsaw, was somewhat larger than an old-fashioned portable Underwood typewriter. During Colin Gubbins's mission to Warsaw early in 1939, it had been placed in one of those large leather bags then in general use among world travelers—a bulky affair with brass locks and reassuring leather straps to hold it together, and plastered with worn hotel and steamship stickers. This impressive bag was left beside the piles of luggage in the foyer of Warsaw's old Bristol Hotel, a watering hole favored by crusty colonels and their ladies. Among the Bristol's patrons was Alastair Denniston, who was then in his fifties. He had flown there with a steamship bag identical to the one now holding the stolen Enigma. The bags were casually shuffled, and Denniston left at once with his prize, exchanged for some dirty shirts and some weighty but otherwise dispensable books.

It was a week before Germany attacked Poland, and Denniston's prize was the greatest gift any nation could give another. The Polish Secret Service had helped capture it and work out some of the Nazi methods of using it. The gesture of passing this knowledge and the machine to the British was that of a warrior flinging his sword to an ally before he fell. It more than compensated Britain for signing the Anglo-Polish Treaty three days later, on August 25, committing Britain to make war on Germany if she invaded Poland: a promise regarded as foolish, ill-timed, and impractical by postwar historians.

The bag with its enigmatic cargo was flown to London and from there to the privacy of the Duke of Bedford's estate, some sixty miles away. It was Gubbins's close ties with the Polish Secret Service that had made possible this extraordinary moment.

So strong was Gubbins's sense of obligation and comradeship that he was already leading a thirty-man team straight back into Poland—"a journey carried out in the face of considerable diplomatic difficulties," a fellow intelligence officer, Carton de Wiart, wrote later. In fact, the British Foreign Office, in its self-righteous disapproval of espionage, refused to help. Gubbins and the team were trapped inside Poland after the invasion. The incident was one indication of British official attitudes. To avoid any more bureaucratic lunacies, the Heydrich-Enigma was smuggled up to the Duke's estate. Close by was Bletchley Park, once a Roman encampment, later granted to Bishop Geoffrey by William the Conqueror after the Battle of Hastings. The mansion on this historic piece of land dated back a mere sixty years. It was a red-brick Victorian monstrosity, but it was also just about the last place anyone would expect to find the keys to Hitler's day-by-day decisions and the enemy's inner secrets.

Hidden in the rolling farmland all about were webs of radio aerials, already spread to net the faint murmurings of distant transmitters. At the center of each web were groups of experienced ships' radio operators to supplement the few C employed. Stephenson, who had never forgotten his schoolboy exchanges with the Morse operators on Great Lakes freighters, regarded seagoing radiomen as among the world's best. They were accustomed to discomfort and to working in close quarters alone. They could hang onto the faint signals of a moving station surrounded by the clutter of other transmissions drifting across the wave bands. At sea, they had to recognize quickly the "fist" of the particular operator they might seek, detecting subtle characteristics in the way he worked his key that amounted to an individual signature. They had a sense for danger, important when later their transmissions guided the

54

secret armies in Nazi Europe. Between the wars, thousands of such ships' operators were kept on a special reserve list in anticipation of a conflict fought in darkness. Admiral Hall had long ago worked out his plans to mobilize these men without alarming the enemy.

The stolen Heydrich-Enigma was probably the most guarded mystery in Britain. The growing band of eavesdroppers proposed to behave in a manner shocking to those in power who shared Henry L. Stimson's view that "gentlemen do not read each other's mail." The task facing Bletchley was formidable enough without harassment from London. Teams would pluck out of the ether the faintest of enemy murmurings. Others would puzzle over the groups of meaningless figures and letters. Still others would attempt to test all the possible settings on the captured Heydrich-Enigma until the flow of messages for any particular day made sense—knowing the Germans altered the settings at the originating station as frequently as every eight hours.

There was a brief panic when the Nazis betrayed knowledge that something unusual might be happening. In a propaganda broadcast, the British traitor known as Lord Haw-Haw, William Joyce, followed his familiar opening—"Germany calling"—with a description of the small town. The British responded by spreading stories that the BBC was erecting some local broadcasting aerials. More to be feared than Nazi detection was the mentality of government leaders in London who stoutly refused to bomb Germany while the Nazi Air Force was engaged in Poland. In vain, Gubbins and his "agricultural mission" tried to convince London from their position inside the shattered country that Poles were being deliberately terrorized, their children and churches singled out for attack. Chamberlain's men were hypnotized by vague hints of peace and compromises from Berlin. Then silence fell over Poland. Gubbins's team and the Polish Secret Service were out of touch, lost in conquered Nazi territory, bringing home to Bletchley the urgent need to build an underground network of communications in Europe as well as to intercept the enemy's signals.

In the mansion at Bletchley Park, a priesthood of dons waited on the Heydrich-Enigma. Within their reach might be a coup greater by far than the interception of the Zimmermann Telegram. With perseverance and luck, they hoped to read Hitler's orders to his generals, their replies, their orders to subordinates, the field commanders' reports on each fighting unit's capacity in the immediate future, the positions of enemy warships, names of personnel and posts, requests for men and material—an almost hourly picture of the enemy's ability to strike, where and how and when. The Golf, Cheese and Chess Society could not know that it had only 150 days to solve the riddle before Hitler smashed his way to the English Channel.

8

"IN SOME MYSTERIOUS way, Hitler was expected by French and British leaders to wear himself out on the plains of Poland. Neville Chamberlain did everything not to antagonize the enemy," remembered Stephenson. "President Roosevelt was afraid Chamberlain might negotiate peace. There was not much the President could do to support those resisting both Chamberlain and Hitler. American public opinion was the target of Nazi propaganda guns, no less than Warsaw had been the target of Nazi bombs. And American opinion was against us."

So Roosevelt wrote an astonishing invitation to Churchill to bare his breast in private and confidential communications. A correspondence began on September 11, 1939, unique between the chief of state of a neutral power and an unrecognized foreign leader. The President acknowledged that although Churchill might be without power in Parliament, as First Lord of the Admiralty he was directing the secret warriors. The replies, during the next 150 days, called "the Phony War," were signed "Naval Person" and went to POTUS, the President of the United States.

The period was known as the Phony War because the Anglo-French alliance seemed to dodge any real engagement with the enemy, while behind the scenes there were disturbing signs of peace negotiations with Hitler. Those who believed that the enemy used these peace overtures to gain time were forced to behave like conspirators in preparing for the inevitable German onslaught. If the President wanted to join these secret warriors, it would help if they gave him ammunition to fight Nazi and isolationist influences in the U.S. Here was another reason for Bletchley to get results. If the British needed advance notice of Hitler's military moves, Roosevelt also needed inside information to convince his doubting service chiefs of Germany's ambitions and Britain's worthiness as an ally.

Churchill therefore wanted to put Stephenson at the President's side right away as director of British secret intelligence and as a practitioner of covert diplomacy. Stephenson could then prepare a base in the United States for over-all direction of secret warfare if Britain fell, as seemed likely if the appeasers stayed in control. But Stephenson had his own order of priorities. Solving the Enigma riddle came first. If that were done in time, guerrilla warfare inside Britain might be unnecessary.

A beautiful and secretive woman who prized her privacy gave him a clue. Greta Garbo was one of the many actors and actresses who, working in his studios, became his close friends. The Swedish actress had reported high-level Nazi sympathizers in Stockholm. The neutral port was ideal for German intelligence operations. Were the Germans using Heydrich-Enigma in foreign stations?

His commercial operations were now interwoven with intelligence. The top-secret Economic Pressure

57

on Germany Committee had always known that Stephenson's business interests would be at the disposal of British warmakers. In addition, all profits were to help defense. Commercial representatives abroad could be used as sources of intelligence. Industrial secrets would be shared ungrudgingly. This gave Stephenson more strength behind the scenes. He used it to mount the first intelligence operation in the new style. The Committee was the forerunner of the British wartime ministry devoted to blowing up, flooding, disrupting, wrecking, and in other ways neutralizing or stealing enemy resources. Churchill called it "the Ministry of Ungentlemanly Warfare." It was hidden in Desmond Morton's shadow Ministry of Economic Warfare, which had been organizing during the previous four years, when Churchill seemed beaten.

"There was more to Stephenson's mission for the Committee than met the eye," said Ian Fleming, who had been plucked out of newspaper work and the business world to join the Director of Naval Intelligence. The future creator of James Bond was known then only as "17F," a designation picked at random to conceal his real duties. Fleming said later: "Stephenson's cover story was that he had to go to Sweden on business. He had commercial interests there. The secondary cover, for intelligence types who needed to know his movements, was that he would destroy the source and the supply lines of iron ore which Germany's steel industries depended upon."

Arguments about the wisdom of risking Stephenson shuttled back and forth between Churchill and other secret-warfare chiefs. Then, in October 1939, Colin Gubbins made good his escape from conquered Poland. He had slipped into Rumania and from there traveled through the Balkans to the Mideast. He brought with him the nucleus of a Polish secret army. Otherwise, he had nothing but bad news.

Commander Fleming reported: "The rape of Poland by *both* Hitler and Stalin meant that the two greatest totalitarian states in the world were in partnership against us. And what were we? A group of small islands led by Chamberlain nervously biting his thumb. The news from Poland was that a secret additional protocol to the Stalin-Hitler pact had assigned spheres of influence splitting the world between them.

"Now we learned there was a distinct possibility of the physicists joining forces under the swastika *and* the hammer-and-sickle to split the atom too.

"This was not a wild nightmare. Until Stalin's purge of the Red Army, Russia and Germany worked closely on new weapons. A few months before Germany and Russia carved Poland between them, the Kaiser Wilhelm Institute in Berlin bombarded the uranium atom and split it—nuclear fission! The Russians were concentrating their energies on the same task. If they could make a pact with the Nazis and then denounce us in Britain as warmongers, we had to face the danger that they could complete the turnaround in science too."

Stephenson pointed out that atomic research required heavy water, a sinister and eerie term for that peculiar substance with the doubled hydrogen nucleus that was a neutron slower in uranium fission. The source of heavy water for German experiments was Norway.

"Deny it to the Germans and we stop that line of progress," he told Churchill.

"And then—?"

"One of the greatest atomic scientists is within Hitler's grasp. Niels Bohr has split the uranium atom with a release of energy a million times more powerful than the same quantity of high explosive. He did it in his Copenhagen laboratory."

Churchill nodded. "If we know this, so do the Russians."

"Exactly. It's a tossup if Hitler or Stalin takes over Scandinavia."

The northern regions were a powerful magnet by the winter of 1939 as Stephenson prepared to conduct his own intelligence operations there.

"He managed it very skilfully," Ian Fleming recalled. "He knew Churchill had already questioned the Secretary for Air . . . *'What danger is there, pray, that atomic bombs might fall on London?'* These demands from the First Lord were always brash and brief. They

59

had to be answered at once. They were known as Churchill's 'prayers' and they put lesser men on the defensive. Bill Stephenson simply used them so he could go on the offensive.

"Bill knew, too, that in this same month—October 1939—his colleague Alexander Sachs, the New York financier and mathematician, had got to President Roosevelt with a letter from Albert Einstein and other atomic scientists warning that the dictators could build the new bombs. Roosevelt had taken action and informed Churchill.

"So Bill held some winning cards. He thought the Norwegian heavy-water plant would have to be destroyed by 'schoolboy adventurers' raised by Churchill. . . . The Striking Companies. He could undertake an offensive-intelligence operation to demonstrate British resolve to fight the war, despite Chamberlain. He badly wanted to prevent the Germans getting the atom scientist, Professor Bohr. And he had a pretty good idea where to get code books that would help the Golf, Cheese and Chess Society solve Enigma. His target was Stockholm in neutral Sweden. From there, he could move in any direction and set up a network free from bureaucratic control here in London."

At the end of November, Russia invaded Finland. This put the adjoining territories of Norway and Sweden in double jeopardy. Hitler might have another secret protocol with Stalin. Or he might move first in anticipation of the Soviet Red Armies. Either way, Scandinavia was in grave danger.

On December 16, 1939, Churchill issued another "prayer," requiring Naval Intelligence support for STRIKE OX. Vital supplies for Nazi Germany "must be prevented from leaving by methods which will be neither diplomatic nor military."

STRIKE OX was named after Oxeloesund, an ice-free port about sixty miles southwest of Stockholm. The supplies for Nazi Germany were tons of Swedish iron ore, which, if interrupted, would leave Hitler with only enough stockpiled to keep the Ruhr steel industry going for another nine months. This was a seemingly valid argument for sabotaging the port's loading ramps and cranes; Nazi intelligence, if this idea was let slip, would believe it. But when Churchill spoke of stopping certain vital supplies, he and a very small circle of scientists knew that heavy water also traveled this route from Norway to Germany and might reach Russia, too. Only 150 miles across the Baltic Sea from Oxeloesund were the Baltic states of Estonia and Latvia, recently absorbed by the Soviet Union. To the northeast, Red Armies battled the Finns.

A sense of impending doom invaded England that Christmas of 1939, despite some jeers and criticism from the United States that the Chamberlain government was merely playing at war. King George VI broadcast a strangely haunting message, ending: "I said to the man at the gate of the Year—'Give me a light that I may tread safely into the unknown.' And he replied, 'Go out into the darkness and put your hand into the hand of God. That shall be to you better than light, and safer than a known way.' . . . May that Almighty Hand guide and uphold us all."

Stephenson spent the first Christmas of the war awaiting delivery in Stockholm of packages of plastic explosive wrapped in forty-pound bundles. The new explosive material resembled modeling clay, to be delivered to the studio of a Swedish sculptor. Then Swedish counterespionage picked up reports that Stephenson was on a sabotage mission. Walter Lindquist, its chief, filed a report that duly reached German agents: this forty-three-year-old Canadian industrialist had plans to destroy the port installations owned by his old friend Axel Axelson Johnson, a major stockholder in iron-ore mines and owner of the railroad from the mines to the port of Oxeloesund, whose docks and loading equipment also belonged to him. It seemed hardly likely to them that Johnson, however sympathetic to Britain, would help blow up his own properties.

The truth was that Johnson, as he told Stephenson, "felt he had the right to liquidate his own holdings in his own way." His mines produced an iron ore high in phosphorus and therefore essential to the German Bessemer process of making high-grade steel. Stephenson had studied the German process in visiting the United Steel Works, whose president was Hitler's former financial backer, the disenchanted Fritz Thyssen.

To German agents, this seemed to explain the presence of Stephenson. The destruction of Oxeloesund's facilities would strike a blow at the weak point in the Nazi arms industry. It would jar neutrals like Sweden. It would make all the Fritz Thyssens think twice about their loyalty, already wavering. Thyssen himself was in Switzerland and thinking of changing sides.

Then the secondary cover story for STRIKE OX spread along the intelligence grapevines. As a decoy, it proved so successful that to this day it persists in espionage tales, embellished with stories of how a British secret agent assigned to guard Stephenson accidentally fired his revolver in the hotel room, and how some explosives were stored under the British Legation.

This was pure deception. The melodrama reached its intended climax. Sweden's King Gustav V was frightened into urging King George VI of England to "halt this madness." In London, Lord Halifax, then Foreign Secretary, was informed. Halifax, hoping that peace could be negotiated if Britain did nothing to further annoy Hitler, thundered that STRIKE OX was "an unprecedented violation of international law."

King George kept quiet. This misleadingly modest man, who had stepped so hesitantly into the shoes of his brother, erstwhile King Edward VIII, was an active participant in Britain's clandestine warfare. He was in confidential correspondence with that other Scandinavian monarch, made of sterner stuff, King Christian X, of Denmark. Christian was the royal patron of Niels Bohr, who refused to move to exile in England, although he had acquired much of his knowledge of nuclear physics there.

The sabotage mission being conspicuously canceled, Stephenson was left in peace. He had legitimate reasons to visit his Swedish associates and friends of Greta Garbo. As a member of the Stephenson-Churchill group, she provided introductions and carried messages. When Stephenson called on her royal admirers, he was quietly arranging escape routes—especially for Professor Bohr, unaware of the threat hanging over Copenhagen, three months away from Nazi occupation.

German and pro-Nazi Swedish security agents were satisfied that Stephenson's operations were wrecked. They continued to watch Alexander Rickman, the British sabotage expert who came to Stockholm with Stephenson, and whose deliberate indiscretions convinced the enemy that Stephenson was attending to business before returning home. Other false trails were laid by Axel Axelson Johnson, who not only controlled essential resources and transport facilities, but also owned a daily newspaper, whose reporters spread extra tidbits among their police contacts.

Into this cloud of misinformation, Stephenson quietly vanished.

9

STRIKE OX MISDIRECTED German attention, allowing Stephenson to reinforce a network of friendly Swedes. They had a cryptologic bureau that systematically broke the codes of their neighbors. Some of their work on German communications was important to Bletchley, frantically seeking pieces to the Enigma puzzle.

The Swedes were also making tactical use of radio intelligence, an unconscious rehearsal of what would shortly happen in Britain. A big, easygoing professor of mathematics, Dr. Arne Beurling, had decoded Russian plans to invade Finland. The Russian invasion was launched on the last day of November in 1939, and Moscow fully expected to force terms on Finland before the end of the year. Instead, the giant was outwitted and outmaneuvered by Field Marshal Baron Carl Mannerheim. A warning to Helsinki enabled his tiny 175,000-man army to harass and delay a million Red Army troops, who then lost the vital element of surprise. Mannerheim was receiving, almost hour by hour, from Sweden an accurate account of the Russian's every move. The math teacher in Stockholm had simply decoded messages between the Russian fighting units and their headquarters, then forwarded them to Mannerheim.

Stephenson, equipped with false papers, crossed the narrow Gulf of Bothnia to join Mannerheim, who was holding a line some fifty miles from Leningrad in what was then Finnish territory, the Karlian Isthmus. By the first week of 1940, Finland's "Skiing Ghosts" were inflicting heavy casualties, arriving at the right place at the right time by courtesy of Sweden's code breakers.

In the end, the sheer weight of Russia forced Finland to stop fighting. Stephenson crossed back into Sweden at a point where the Arctic Circle bisects the border. He had learned some valuable lessons. Mannerheim's brilliant generalship was possible because of his tactical use of intelligence. Finland might have halted the Russians if promises of military aid from Washington had been fulfilled. Soon Britain would face a similar assault from Germany—possibly backed by Russia. When that crisis came, American aid must be committed, not stuck in Congress, as it had been in Finland's tragic case.

Stephenson headed now toward the source of German experiments in atomic science—the Norwegian heavy-water plant. On the way, he stopped at the Gallivare iron mines in Sweden. Mindful of Sweden's neutrality, he was discreet in discussing how the mines could be sabotaged. "I can speak only of industrial 'accidents,'" he told Swedish contacts. "If you have access to insurance-company files, you will see detailed studies of the weak point in any manufacturing process or mining procedure. Insurance companies stand to lose fortunes from an accident, and so they employ experts to figure out every possible way that things can go wrong. Their reports are guidebooks for saboteurs."

Next, on the train to the Norwegian port of Narvik,

he rendezvoused with Professor Leif Tronstad, the chemical engineer who was familiar with the layout of the Norsk Hydro Electric plant. Norsk Hydro was the world's only commercial producer of heavy water. Its total output was sought by I. G. Farben, the German industrial colossus whose products ranged from poison gases to time bombs. I. G. Farben was a large investor in the Norwegian atomic plant. To Tronstad, whose future collaboration was vital to Stephenson's plans, the Canadian confided "the convincing and frightening news" uncovered two months previously by the British Uranium Committee that atomic energy might be used in an explosive. He added cautiously that Norway, a sovereign and neutral nation, would hardly want warlike actions thrust upon her, with the two unpredictable giants, Russia and Germany, wrestling closer.

"The Russians may have their eye on Hydro," said Tronstad. "The Germans certainly have. But how can we be sure that your own industrial interests won't make use of these—" He gestured with the blueprints he carried in a satchel.

"You'll have to take my word for it," said Stephenson, looking him in the eye.

Tronstad was in his mid-thirties, some ten years younger. He studied the Canadian thoughtfully and saw, he said later, "a tough little man with rather a large head, very fine features, and eyes that changed color with the light. When he shook hands, he had a grip like iron. Otherwise, you wouldn't suspect *physical* strength. He struck me as an intellectual who'd got into this by accident."

Tronstad handed over a copy of the Norsk Hydro plant layout. It produced deuterium oxide, heavy water that weighed eleven percent more than normal water, and was the favored "moderator" to control an atomic reaction.

"If the Germans capture the plant, we may have to destroy it," said Tronstad.

"In the meantime—"

"Ah," sighed the Norwegian.

"In the meantime, your own Norwegian cod-liver oil loosens the bowels. A cup of it, dropped into an electrolytic tube, won't be noticed until the process is re-started in Germany. The presence of the oil will seem like an accident, but of course it will make the stuff useless as a moderator."

Before the train reached Narvik, the chemical engineer dropped off. When they met again, it would be in Scotland, on the eve of a suicidal expedition against German atomic scientists.

Stephenson returned to Britain aboard a submarine that collected him near Narvik shortly before Germany struck at Norway. Hitler's invasion had been blamed on the British Navy's aggressive behavior in Norwegian coastal waters on orders from Churchill, still at the Admiralty. It is true that Norway's coastal waters were used by German supply ships evading the British blockade. But Churchill had the waters mined because he possessed the incommunicable knowledge that Norwegian heavy water was vital to Germany's search for an atomic bomb. His attempt to disrupt shipments was the best that could be done in circumstances that included a nervous British government still terrified of provoking the enemy.

On the night of April 8, the German High Command had learned of Churchill's mine-laying expedition and sent out decoys to divert the British Home Fleet and the 1st and 2nd British Cruiser Squadrons. The British suffered heavy naval losses in battles away from the main thrust of a German invasion fleet. Norway was conquered almost before the British recovered their wits. That disaster eventually shook Chamberlain loose from Parliament and made way for a new aggressive-minded regime. It marked the beginning of the end of the Phony War.

While German scientists, hard on the heels of German invasion troops, moved into the Norsk heavy-water plant, their colleagues surrounded the nuclear-fission laboratories in Copenhagen and restricted the movements of Niels Bohr. Bohr, only days earlier, had been put in touch with the new British intelligence network in Sweden.

Stephenson reported in London on what had been accomplished and warned that Britain would be foolish to rely on Germany exhausting herself in a struggle with Russia. The Russians had learned from their misadventures in Finland that they were far from ready for a major war. The theme found its way into a column by George Orwell, writing in the *New English Weekly*: "The plan laid down in *Mein Kampf* was to smash Russia first, with the implied intention of smashing England afterwards. Now, as it has turned out, England has to be dealt with first, because Russia was the more easily bribed [by the Russo-German pact]. . . . Russia's turn will come when England is out of the picture."

10

"BETTER LOSE A battle than lose a source of secret intelligence" was Stephenson's advice to Churchill in the twilight months between Germany's invasion of Poland and the moment when British appeasement ended. That moment was not far away. A political crisis in London was brewing with the loss of Denmark and Norway.

The Nazi preparations to move into these two countries had been detected at Bletchley Park. The code breakers in the Victorian mansion could sense, from the change in the volume and source of ciphered traffic, the slow shift of attention. "We seemed to be pygmies around a monster," a section chief reported later. "We felt the tremor of a nerve, the flexing of a muscle, and then the great head moving toward a new prey."

Such hints were hardly enough for British battle commanders to act upon. Churchill understood Bletchley's intuitions. But he was not yet prime minister. The stolen Heydrich-Enigma was wrapped in secrecy and was not yet producing specific information.

Churchill's state of mind is revealed in memos that were not declassified until more than thirty years later. He feared Hitler's cat-paws who masqueraded as neutral "peace envoys." One was the Swedish businessman Birger Dahlerus, who had been flown back and forth between Berlin and London shortly before the invasion of Poland as an unofficial mediator for Hermann Göring, the Nazi Air Force chief. Dahlerus delayed Britain's declaration of war by two days, by relaying the German Air Minister's warning that Poland would betray the British at the last moment. Göring had reinforced this allegation by producing copies of Polish diplomatic cables that Germany had intercepted and decoded. By placing an emphasis here, deleting a passage there, the Nazi leader made it appear that Poland was sabotaging every German move toward negotiation. This German deception was conveyed by the Swede to the British Foreign Office, which incredibly, paid it serious attention. Chamberlain's appeasement-minded clique welcomed any excuse for postponing a bloodbath. But long after Poland fell, Churchill and his followers had to face the fact that the peace envoys still flew in and out of London in early 1940, had access to Chamberlain and his advisers, and might pick up information that would tell the Germans that their own coding systems were compromised. In one of his confidential memos, Churchill condemned self-designated peacemakers for leaking information that was vital to the defense of an embattled and poorly armed nation. "The King of Sweden's intrusion as a peacemaker," he wrote in one such comment, "when he is so absolutely in the German's grip . . . is singularly distasteful."

Other Swedes made a priceless contribution to Bletchley. They recovered German code books that gave a further clue to the manner in which Enigma was being used. As the mystery unfolded, so the population at the Park grew. Nissen huts of corrugated steel dotted the lawns like segments of a gigantic worm. Inside lived and worked the bright young things swept out of classrooms, banks, museums, and universities. Most were aged between seventeen and thirty-five. There was a sprinkling of oldsters who had analyzed the mechanism of Enigma. The nearby monitors gave them increasingly accurate "fixes" on German radio transmitters. How and when the enemy set the drums on his own Enigma coding machines was unknown. The aim was to find a routine way of duplicating in Bletchley the enemy's continual readjustment of these drums. The size of the challenge was mind-boggling, because there were several different German networks of Enigmas. Each network operated its own schedule.

By April 1940, progress had been made toward systematic examination of the coded German traffic. Enigma must be duplicated with copies from Stephenson's electronics labs. Teams of code breakers could then work separately on the duplicates. The work required mathematical minds. One lady professor had an aptitude for juggling the current mystery in her mind and arriving at sudden solutions. She was moved to the hut nearest the mansion so that if she woke in the middle of the night—which she did with increasing frequency—she could rush over to the Watch on duty and impart her latest inspiration. Speed was essential. On her first flash of revelation, she flung herself into the blackness of the rural countryside and tripped over a sunken wall, built to keep out cattle but designed to preserve the view. The lady went headfirst into the adjacent duck pond, struggled out, and made a dramatic entry at the mansion, bursting upon the Midnight Watch with weeds and water, and creating the effect of a fevered genius in disarray. She was still muttering the magic incantation that aroused her from slumber—the call sign of a particular German sending station. Once identified, it enabled others to work on the code, because they could assume that certain technical jargon would occur frequently in the text. A trail was marked in luminous paint in case new brain waves hit the professor, henceforth known as "the Lady of the Lake."

Churchill ordered a full-scale mobilization of all human resources. The Enigma system was producing out of the enemy camp a stream of mostly unreadable messages. Yet enough was often deduced by Bletchley to make a guess at German intentions. It was apparent that a massive redirection of blitzkrieg forces was underway, aimed at England by way of France and the Low Countries. Stewart Menzies, a former Life Guards officer and veteran of the permanent Secret Intelligence Service, had replaced Admiral Sinclair as "C." He decided that Bletchley's products, spotty though they might be, had better become the subject of a special policy agreement. If there was any risk of jeopardizing Bletchley by taking action on the basis of advance knowledge of enemy intentions, the secret must be kept. The breaking of codes through analyzing the text and searching for terms that might be expected to recur was only part of the code breakers' art. However, it was a function that lent itself to mechanical computation. Until some form of computer could be devised, Bletchley depended on human brains.

Prime Minister Neville Chamberlain was never told what Bletchely had within its grasp. Nor was the sinister significance of the heavy water in Norway ever explained. It was not a question of distrusting him. Chamberlain was an honorable man. But he had demonstrated, once more, his inability to judge events when he declared, five days before the Germans scored their lightning victories in Norway and Denmark, that "Hitler has missed the bus." He remained ignorant until the day he died of the atomic sword of Damocles suspended above his head—in the very same region where Hitler not only caught the bus, but was now driving it.

Meanwhile, Churchill debated with Stephenson the wisdom of consulting the Americans. He had ordered that no stone be left unturned to get Bletchley the staff and equipment it needed. There was a story, later, that during a visit to the Park, he gazed with some astonishment at the motley crowd of civilians and said finally: "I said leave no stone unturned to get the people you require. I did not think you would take me so literally."

He had not been able to use Bletchley to forestall German adventures in Scandinavia. Even now, he could not do much about the coming Nazi onslaught through Western Europe. If Bletchley's possibilities were to be fully exploited, American help must be obtained, in both brains and technology. That meant a direct approach to President Roosevelt, whom Churchill trusted. Thus the Prime Minister of Great Britain, so long as he was appeasement-minded Neville Chamberlain, was not taken into the confidence of the various intelligence groups, consisting now mostly of gifted amateurs, who were known in general as "The Baker Street Irregulars," after the amateurs who aided Sherlock Holmes. Like the methods of the great detective, their approach was unorthodox. They were reticent with their own Prime Minister, but agreed to confide in the President of the United States.

"We put the fate of Britain in Roosevelt's hands when we made that decision," said Stephenson later.

President Roosevelt paved the way for this momentous decision. He had invited the King and Queen of England to Washington the previous summer, before war broke out. He had asked the King and Queen, Eleanor Roosevelt wrote in her diary, "believing that we might all soon be engaged in a life and death struggle, in which Britain would be our first line of defense. . . ."

George VI recorded his talks with the President in notes that, read today, seem even more significant than when they were shown to Stephenson. The notes were carried in a dispatch box that never left the King's side throughout the war. They were later deposited in the Royal Archives. He summarized their talks on June 12, 1939, a good two months before war broke out in Europe: "The President . . . was very frank. . . . He gave me all the information in these notes either in answer to my questions, or he volunteered it. . . ."

King George then described FDR's *"ideas in case of War."* The President would lead U.S. public opinion by defining the economic price Americans would have to pay if Hitler conquered Europe. FDR then gave the King precise details on U.S. plans to defend its coasts. "He showed me his naval patrols in greater detail about which he is terribly keen," the King noted. "If he saw a U boat he would sink her at once & wait for the consequences.

"If London was bombed U.S. would come in."

The King set such store by these statements from the President that British intelligence chiefs were advised to go on the assumption that Roosevelt was "part of the family." Would the President have behaved differently if George VI had not made that brief visit to the White House? George was an exceedingly mild and self-effacing individual, but Roosevelt glimpsed a quality of pride and obstinacy that expressed the character of the islanders. It had surfaced briefly in the simple presentation of the British case that the King made to the U.S. Ambassador, Joseph P. Kennedy, a few days after Britain declared war on Germany. Kennedy, on September 9, 1939, had warned the King that England would bankrupt herself in this new war, and should get out while she still could. Three days later, George penned a letter to Kennedy that was remarkably frank. In it, the King wrote: "England, my country . . . is part of Europe. . . . We stand on the threshold of we know not what. Misery & suffering of War we know. But what of the future? The British mind is made up. I leave it at that."

11

IF THE FIRST Bletchley recoveries were garbled, their import was becoming clearer by the day. The summer would be bright with blood. Stephenson must convey, verbally, to President Roosevelt the sources of alarm and the need for American co-operation in perfecting the Bletchley duplication and understanding of the German Enigma system.

To get authority in the sullen spring of 1940, he went over Prime Minister Chamberlain's head to King George VI, with Churchill as intermediary. The

King was the ultimate authority in secret-intelligence matters. He made the top intelligence appointments. The British had worked out their own system of checks and balances to prevent the monarch abusing such power—and to prevent a governing party exploiting secret agencies to serve its own ends.

"If the Nazis set up a puppet government in Britain," Churchill said in explaining his seeking royal authority, "I could be accused of disclosing confidential material to a foreign state for having confided in Mr. Roosevelt."

"Then I lose my head at Traitor's Gate, too," replied the King.

George VI also wanted it made clear that no question would arise of a royal exodus to the United States if the Germans invaded. He would neither run away nor collaborate. His was an important decision. Those Britons who might resort to guerrilla warfare —and they were already being organized under the cover of "Auxiliary Units"—might be condemned by a Nazi government in London as traitors liable to execution. By declaring themselves loyal to a non-collaborating king, and not bound to obey a collaborationist government, they could appeal to the general population for support in resisting the Germans and the puppet authorities.

"If this question of loyalty had been clarified in occupied countries," Stephenson said later, "there would have been fewer collaborators. The local bureaucracy, the civil servants of an occupied country, were needed by the Nazis to run routine daily affairs. Wherever Germany conquered, Hitler insisted that the petty bureaucrat's allegiance automatically passed to whatever puppet held the rubber stamp. This King, commanding the higher loyalty of each citizen, could make it possible for his subjects to resist the enemy and work with 'a foreign state'—that is, the Americans— without being called traitors. The Nazis would shoot them as traitors anyway. *But what counted was that they should not feel like traitors.*"

Churchill, still disliked by many members of a so-called ruling class, needed and got the King's approval. He could reassure the contingency planners of secret

73

warfare that the lines of authority flowed up to the Palace, a precaution against betrayal by any government in power.

There were now many names for the groups clustered together to wage secret warfare. The general term "Baker Street Irregulars" was to become used by those in the know. Code names and slang disguised the truth from enemies abroad and at home. One Baker Street leader was that veteran of guerrilla operations Colin Gubbins. After his escape from Poland, he had made a desperate attempt in Norway to organize an armed resistance to German invaders there. By April 1940, he was back in London, determined at least to prevent Britain's betrayal.

Gubbins had been raised in the tradition of *noblesse oblige*. To him, Britain had an obligation to keep her word, to make sacrifices, to suffer pain, or to die to save the less fortunate. Britain should bankrupt herself before letting down others. He was appalled by any prospect of seeing these ideals abandoned.

Gubbins saw the spirit of resistance as the most powerful force in Europe, if properly inspired and directed. In London, that April, he detected the scent of fear that spread like a fog across the English Channel, the fear already instilled in weak and even treacherous politicians ready to collaborate with barbaric conquerors. He knew what it was like to stand helpless before bullies, to see hostages tortured and shot as a means of keeping control through terror. More important than guns and dynamite was helping the victims to straighten their backs, and Gubbins was determined to build a force of resistance fighters throughout the occupied countries. He had left behind, in Poland and Norway, the nucleus of secret armies based upon the stubborn courage of ordinary men and women. What he needed was the means to coordinate their operations and give them moral and physical support.

In the little time left between the Nazi conquest of Norway and Hitler's impending offensives across Western Europe, Gubbins's tailored figure was to be seen marching briskly between sandbagged buildings in the elegant backwaters of Mayfair and Piccadilly, up rickety stairs to dingy offices, or vanishing through the porticos of London's clubland near St. James's Place, where sentry boxes traditionally contained toy-like Guardsmen in scarlet tunics and top-heavy black bearskin busbies.

Now, in place of the royal paraphernalia, there were optimistic old men with armbands announcing AIR RAID WARDEN and with little buckets of sand and shovels to smother fire bombs. Elderly ladies brewed tea at Hyde Park Gate for the creaking ancients who drilled with broomsticks on Rotten Row. Along the banks of the River Thames, bare-kneed Boy Scouts with fish nets watched and waited for drifting experimental mines, in a guerrilla-warfare exercise about which they were sworn to secrecy.

For some, secrecy was the watchword of the hour. Chamberlain lingered in Parliament, a stone's throw from Gubbins's temporary quarters in St. Ermin's Hotel, on Caxton Street. "That particular prime minister should have resigned months earlier," wrote Iain Macleod, a courageous political leader and sometime editor of the *Spectator*. "Neville Chamberlain forced farsighted patriots to *hide* their preparations to defend their homes and carry the war back into Nazidom."

Randolph Churchill, son of Winston, destined for parachuting on special-intelligence operations, wrote later: "We had reached the point of bugging potential traitors and enemies. Joe Kennedy, the American Ambassador, came under electronic surveillance."

At Scotland Yard there were ugly reports that confidential material was leaking from the U.S. Embassy. Yet Kennedy was popular among the Prime Minister's cronies. The evidence of something wrong came from intercepted diplomatic messages, and it was too early to take action.

In this atmosphere of muddle and suspicion, Stephenson moved carefully. "I couldn't have blamed Roosevelt for wondering if Britain could be saved from herself, let alone from the enemy."

It was this shared outrage and apprehension that put Colin Gubbins in line to run the Baker Street Irregulars. He was with Stephenson at a dinner given by exiled Polish statesmen in London. Also present was the man who would answer in Parliament for the actions of the still unofficial Ministry of Economic Warfare, Hugh Dalton. He represented a left-wing Labour party faction that rebelled against appeasement. "I suddenly realized that here were the men to lead the Irregulars," Dalton recalled later. "Gubbins, at that dinner, described his chagrin in Poland where the people seeing him said 'Thank God for the British' when they should have been damning us. He told how the British Treasury squabbled about who would pay for transport to get 120 Hawker Hurricane fighters to the Polish Air Force. . . . Then Stephenson said it was time we learned to fight with the gloves off, the knee in the groin, the stab in the dark. Well, I knew him as a great amateur sportsman. Not an unkind bone in his body. And I thought: If these chaps want dirty tricks, things *are* in a bad way."

The training of Irregulars and future officers of secret armies was removed from direct War Office control.

"You'll be training gangsters," Gubbins was told by those of his colleagues who knew about the plan. "How can a professional soldier like yourself do it?"

Gubbins could do it because he had seen in Poland the consequences of halfhearted measures. Despite all his efforts to provide eyewitness proof of Nazi terrorism in Poland, the hope had lingered in some circles that a deal could be made with Hitler's powerful henchman Hermann Göring, whose Air Force had carried out the systematic terror raids against Poland's helpless civilians. Gubbins had watched those raids. While still trapped in Poland, he had dispatched one of his men through the lines with evidence of German atrocities. The courier, Captain "Tommy" Davies, was refused help by the British Legation in Latvia when he reached there. Davies found a boat to take him to Sweden. When his own Legation heard of his plans, it even telegraphed ahead to warn the British Embassy in Stockholm against protecting this "spy" and antagonizing the Swedes. The message was sent in clear language, endangering Davies, who had quickly realized that he was an inconvenient eyewitness to the Nazi brutality that Chamberlain's group would rather not know about.

Even with these bitter memories, the Baker Street Irregulars dared not push too hard. As planners of secret warfare, they vowed "to do those things which assisted in the execution of His Majesty's Government policy but which could not be acknowledged," as their Oath of Secrecy had it. The emphasis was on loyalty to the King, obedience to the Crown. Since Gubbins's return from Poland, a new German Governor-General had started to eliminate all "unnecessary" Poles, and to reduce the rest to slavery. During this first winter, Polish intellectuals, aristocrats, officers, priests, and Jews were being murdered. Yet, in the face of proof that Hitler was studiously acting out the wild dreams of *Mein Kampf,* Chamberlain continued to hope for the best.

The Swedish "peace envoy," Dahlerus, fed these hopes. Nothing should be done, he told Chamberlain, to provoke the Führer. Then the British could later make a deal with other Nazi leaders and isolate the little madman. Dahlerus came to London with such frequency that Halifax voiced the fear that "his visits, which cannot be kept secret, will inevitably cause misunderstanding."

The visits were not misunderstood by Churchill's rebels. They knew the truth about the Swedish "businessman." They knew his job was to gull British leaders until their hesitancy turned them into easy prey. The fact was that Dahlerus was in the power of the Nazi Air Minister, Göring, because his wife owned large estates inside the Third Reich which could be confiscated by a stroke of the pen. Göring had so far taken care that Mrs. Dahlerus retained her valuable properties in return for her husband's co-operation. During his "peace missions," Dahlerus carried the plea from the King of Sweden to the King of England to "stop Stephenson" sabotaging Swedish supplies to Germany.

Such peacemongers exercised more influence than was recognized at the time. It was a well-kept secret throughout the war that Prime Minister Chamberlain considered that there was a possibility of replacing Hitler with Göring. "This was to be achieved by relaxing British pressure on Germany," Stephenson recalled later. "Of course, Hitler and Göring were working together in this maneuver. They played on the weak-minded and simpletons, using intermediaries like Dahlerus to persuade us that if we were soft on Germany, there was a good chance that Nazism would be soft on us.

"Chamberlain really thought Göring might take over Germany in a transitional government. The longer he played with this idea, the longer Britain avoided a direct confrontation. That suited Hitler.

"But the peacemongers served another purpose by waking up a few hardheaded leaders in Britain and America to the realities of a war like none other. It was a way of treachery, with weapons of lies and deceit. The final and biggest battlefield was to be America. If Hitler could keep it 'neutral on his side,' using the Dahlerus-style strategy, he could conquer the world."

12

IN MID-APRIL when wind and rain swept through the bleak brickyards of Bletchley, the townsfolk noticed fewer academics bicycling along the winding streets. Up at the Park, odd scraps of intelligence were coming in to hold the scholars' attention. Other cryptanalytic teams were breaking low-grade codes, locating enemy units, and interpreting information gleaned from diplomatic dispatches.

The search for answers to Enigma was a frantic race against time. The other teams had detected fresh movements of the blitzkrieg forces. But high-grade German military orders were fed exclusively now through the enemy's hundreds of portable Enigmas. The most brilliant mathematicians could not work fast enough on intercepts by using the technique of first discovering what symbols appeared most frequently. A computer would make the calculations in a fraction of the time. This seems elementary today. Then, it occurred to few; and among those few, not many were aware that it could be done electronically.

Stephenson was convinced a computer for Enigma could be mass-produced in the United States. The prototype of such a computer had been made. What he wanted was a series of computers linked to banks of Enigma duplicates. In this way, the intercepted enemy ciphers might be handled hour by hour to get answers in time to make the right countermoves.

Meanwhile, other Bletchleyites mapped the new German distribution of forces. Two mighty air armadas, Luftflotte II and Luftflotte III, with 3,000 warplanes, were shifting to bases in an arc westward. German armored units, paratroop and infantry groups drew up in positions from which to strike across the rest of free Europe on the way to the English Channel.

Britain was stripped almost naked of home defenses. She had sent an expeditionary force, with front-line air cover, to France at the outbreak of war in 1939, and now these forces were in great jeopardy. It was cold comfort to be forewarned of Hitler's next offensives. Even if British and French commanders had believed some educated guesses from Bletchley, they were not equipped physically or mentally to move quickly to block Hitler. The lack of preparation under sick and ineffective leaders was described by George Orwell in *England Your England*:

After 1934 it was known that Germany was rearming. After 1936 everyone with eyes in his head knew that war was coming. After Munich it was merely a question of how soon the war would begin. In September 1939 war broke out. *Eight months later* it was discovered that, so far as equipment went, the British army was barely beyond the standard of 1918. We saw our soldiers fighting their way desperately to the coast, with one aeroplane against three, with rifles against tanks, with bayonets against tommy-guns. There were not even enough revolvers to supply all the officers. After a year of war the regular army was still short of 300,000 tin hats. There had even, previously, been a shortage of uniforms—this in one of the greatest woollen-goods producing countries in the world!

With that record, why should the British be bailed out by an American president? Roosevelt would risk political suicide.

"We need Rockefellers and Rothschilds," grumbled Churchill. "We need gold. Do you know we have *none?*" He was talking to his intelligence chiefs in Room 39 beneath his office as First Lord. Near him was the desk of Commander Ian Fleming and the baize door of the Director of Naval Intelligence. The tall westerly windows were crisscrossed with sticky tape to reduce splinters from bomb blast. Through the diamonds he could see the garden of No. 10 Downing Street, the Prime Minister's house, which seemed to Churchill still a million miles away. Room 39 was known as "the Zoo," because of its apparent untidiness and the peculiarities of its unconventional inhabitants. Around its marble fireplace and iron coal scuttles gathered those odd and dedicated men for whom there never had been a Phony War.

"We need," Churchill concluded after a dissertation on American politics that sounded like the rehearsal of a speech, "to fire up the boilers of the greatest engine in history. Tell them we have the guts. We'll fight." He turned away. "With God's help, America may escape the trials and tribulations that lie ahead . . . provided we can survive here in England."

"I can find the Rockefellers and they'll support us," said Stephenson. "We can offer our secret intelligence in return for help. It has to be done at the President's level. There have been intelligence breakthroughs in the United States that would advance our own efforts. The President would have to authorize disclosure. There are the means to produce, in America, the sophisticated equipment we need for intelligence weapons. The President can be told what that equipment is needed for, so that we don't have to explain the purpose to the manufacturers. But the President will have to be sure that our intelligence reports are accurate."

Admiral Hall, technically in retirement, looked down. Having devised the means to convince Americans in World War I that the Zimmermann Telegram was genuine—without giving away the secret of the cryptographers' existence—he could speak with authority: "The real source must be disguised from everyone not directly involved."

Churchill broke in. "We must make an exception with Mr. Roosevelt. To him, and to him alone, the truth should be confided . . . . Our daily intelligence summaries should be delivered to him through the FBI."

The U.S. Federal Bureau of Investigation, however, had not been in alliance with the regular British Secret Intelligence Service since the outbreak of war in Europe. The links were cut when politicians and the State Department became aware of them. If the news of restored British-FBI links should ever leak out, America's neutrality would look distinctly bent, and every isolationist in that country would join a campaign blaming Roosevelt. Foreign intelligence in those days was a sinister concept to most Americans. The thought of being caught hand in glove with the British SIS would shake the diplomats, none more so than Ambassador Kennedy. Yet it was Kennedy's Embassy that provided Stephenson with another argument for renewed covert American co-operation.

Kennedy had just revisited the United States on a vacation that the British Foreign Office thought might be in preparation for a campaign to win the presidency from Roosevelt. The platform on which Kennedy would fight, the British suspected, would include a policy of staying out of the war. Kennedy had used his visit to tell his fellow Americans, in public statements, that Hitler would win the war against the British and that the conflict involved no moral issues. He was back now in London, conscious of British disapproval and a new instruction from the Foreign Office to all government departments warning them to confide nothing to the American Ambassador. This reversed the previous policy of giving senior Embassy staff confidential information in an effort to show good faith.

On the day Stephenson left for his secret rendezvous with the President, Scotland Yard took the first reluctant step in an investigation into pro-Nazi activities by someone in the United States Embassy in London.

Stephenson flew on a Canadian passport in a military aircraft by the hazardous northern route through Labrador to Montreal. This was the fastest passage, avoiding fuel stops near enemy observation points. He bypassed the usual formalities, escorted by agents of Canada's MI-2, a branch of Military Intelligence, and plain-clothes men of the royal Canadian Mounted Police. He was in Washington within twenty-four hours of leaving London.

What Stephenson had to say to the President was so confidential, so shattering in its implications, that nothing could be placed on the record without risk of political chain reaction.

The British government had examined the claim that the fission of uranium atoms had been achieved in Berlin by Otto Hahn and Fritz Strassmann. German interest in Norway's heavy-water supplies was proof that Nazi funds must be supporting research into all the possible approaches to the control of a nuclear chain reaction. And in March 1940, the so-called Frisch-Peierls paper informed British defense chiefs that it was possible to construct an atomic bomb using the isotope U-235.

Stephenson communicated British conclusions, based on independent investigations, to Roosevelt, who had been prepared for such news by men like Albert Einstein, who had written confidentially to the President six months earlier that "extremely powerful bombs of a new type" could be constructed. Einstein suggested that the President should appoint a personal aide to keep in touch with physicists working on chain reactions.

That contact, Stephenson made it clear, would have to be extended to Britain, where atomic research was proceeding in London, Oxford, Cambridge, and Liverpool. If Nazi Germany captured these centers, Nazi progress toward a bomb might take a giant leap forward. British work in the field was thought to be well ahead of any competition, and there was no provision as yet for routine Anglo-American co-operation. The real danger, instead, was that Germany might reap the deadly harvest.

This was the first bombshell. Stephenson had others. He told the President of the progress at Bletchley toward breaking the German code system. He laid bare the complexities of Britain's wartime secret intelligence, the Baker Street Irregulars, the determination to wage war against Nazism no matter what deals might be considered by appeasement-minded Britons. Churchill was the leader of these men and women who would resist Hitler and muster secret armies in Europe, even within a Nazi-occupied Britain. The chief weapons were their resources of secret intelligence and guerrilla-warfare techniques.

"Guerrillas?" asked the President.

"They will get us back into Europe," said Stephenson.

"How?"

Stephenson picked up an orange. "If I were a worm and wanted to get into this orange, I would go on walking around it until I found a hole. I might have to walk around it until the orange went rotten and a hole appeared. But I would get into this orange in the end—provided I did not starve first."

In that moment of inspiration, Stephenson hit upon a description of British strategy that Churchill would later use in reminding Americans that supplies were the key to that strategy. "If we do not starve first . . . we shall get back into Europe."

Roosevelt grasped the point at once on that day in early spring of 1940. The supplies, at that date, were required by British intelligence irregulars who were not yet sure who their leader would be, but who took their lead from Churchill.

Within hours, a meeting had been arranged for Stephenson with John Edgar Hoover, the Director of the Federal Bureau of Investigation. With him, Stephenson discussed the investigation of the U.S. Embassy. This vexing matter would be solved discreetly, but it illustrated the need to re-establish British secret-intelligence liaison. Hoover said he could not sanction British employment of agents in the United States, if that was what Stephenson had in mind. The State Department, for one thing, insisted that any form of collaboration would infringe U.S. neutrality. "I cannot contravene this policy without direct presidential sanction."

"And if I get it?" asked Stephenson.

The face hardened into the mold familiar to newspapers. "Then we'll do business directly. Just myself and you. Nobody else gets in the act. Not State, not anyone."

Hoover was then forty-five years of age, a year older than Stephenson. It was the beginning of a long and stormy relationship. Hoover knew he was dealing with his equal when Stephenson told him: "You will be getting presidential sanction."

The President's instructions followed hard on Stephenson's words. In London, Stephenson reported to Churchill: "The President has laid down the secret ruling for the closest possible marriage between the FBI and British Intelligence. The fact that this co-operation was agreed upon is striking evidence of President Roosevelt's clarity of vision. The fact that it has to be kept secret even from the State Department is a measure of the strength of American neutrality. It is an essential first step toward combatting enemy operations but it is insufficient to meet the demands of the situation. The Nazis in America are already well organized and well entrenched. They realise the extent of British dependence on American material aid, and so direct their subversive propaganda toward buttressing the wall of traditional isolationism by which the President is encompassed."

On Monday, May 20, 1940, Special Branch detectives took the grave decision to enter the Gloucester Place apartment of a twenty-eight-year-old diplomat of the U.S. Embassy, a cipher clerk named Tyler Gatewood Kent. Copies of 1,500 pieces of correspondence labeled "top secret" and cabled between Whitehall and the White House were recovered. They included the coded messages between Naval Person and POTUS, the gist of which had been in Hitler's hands within days of transmission. When confronted, Kent claimed he wanted to thwart President Roosevelt's "secret and unconstitutional plot with Churchill to sneak the United States into the war."

The case was broken with Roosevelt's prior knowledge. He now had to wait for the results of the investigation. Ambassador Kennedy's behavior had raised such serious doubts that Roosevelt felt he could with full justification now authorize "the closest possible marriage between the FBI and the British Secret Intelligence Service." This, of course, had much wider implications, including the contribution of German radio transmissions intercepted by U.S. monitors. Although these messages were in code, they greatly increased the volume of material put before Bletchley's cryptanalysts, giving them more opportunities to detect recurrent names, call signs, and technical jargon from which deductions could be made. In this way the full range of Enigma Codes might be uncovered. In return, it was understood that the British would share their findings with their American partner. The shotgun wedding brought the United States and Britain closer in the waging of secret warfare. But how had Joseph P. Kennedy landed in a web of suspicion?

13

GERMAN DIPLOMATIC DISPATCHES had been intercepted and read by the small team in the British Government Code and Cipher School even before it moved to Bletchley. Among these dispatches were those of the German Ambassador to Italy. He seemed to be reporting matters that passed between the British Admiralty's First Lord, Churchill, and President Roosevelt.

So far as the eavesdroppers knew, Churchill and Roosevelt were strangers. It seemed that the German Ambassador must be faking inside knowledge, inventing spies and informers for whom he could claim expenses.

The intercepts went to the British Foreign Office with other routine material. Nobody who saw the reports was aware of the Churchill-Roosevelt exchanges in the names of Naval Person and POTUS. They agreed that the resourceful gentleman in Rome was writing lucrative fiction.

Then Stephenson saw the Rome reports while reading "recoveries" from low-grade German communications in codes already broken by the British. He checked them, hoping to find fresh clues to the Enigma system. He recognized the Rome intercepts to be fair summaries of what Churchill was confiding to Roosevelt. How could the German Ambassador in Italy possibly know?

Stephenson launched an investigation as the snows of winter melted into the spring of 1940. The Rome intercepts seemed a bit remote to other security men in London, overburdened with crises at home. Stephenson persisted. Glancing over the record of United States Embassy activities, he saw that Churchill relied more and more on it for the transmission in State Department code of his messages to the President.

Ambassador Kennedy seemed an odd go-between. He had been appointed to the plum London job in 1937. Ever since, he had drifted closer to Neville Chamberlain, and to notorious appeasers and members of the British aristocracy with pro-Nazi views. After Chamberlain's surrender at Munich, Kennedy had even claimed "credit" for saving the peace by influencing Chamberlain to trust Hitler.

In the last year of peace, Kennedy had announced that war was inevitable. Britain would inevitably suffer defeat. Churchill had tried to undo any harm caused by such statements. One way was to direct his correspondence with Roosevelt through the Embassy, in the hope that Kennedy might read and be thereby instructed. Another way was to talk with as many influential American visitors as possible, usually at private dinner parties where Churchill took the chair.

Stephenson had been at one such affair when Walter Lippmann was the target.

"Suppose Ambassador Kennedy is correct in his tragic utterances?" Churchill demanded. "I for one would lay down my life in combat rather than, in fear of defeat, surrender to the menace of these most sinister men. It will be for you, for the Americans, to preserve and to maintain the great heritage of the English-speaking peoples. It will be for you to think imperially, which means to think of something higher and more vast than one's own national interests. . . ."

Kennedy never could believe that such idealism was genuine. He later said to Churchill: "O for Christ's sake, stop trying to make this a holy war—you're fighting for your life as an Empire." He had consistently explained away Germany's step-by-step conquest of Europe. His conversations with the German Ambassador in London were reported almost verbatim back to Berlin. These dispatches, too, had been intercepted and decoded by the British, who learned with growing anger that he was telling the Germans how anxious Chamberlain was to reach a settlement, encouraging Hitler to ask for more. On June 15, 1938, the German Ambassador had telegraphed this version of Kennedy's views on the subject of the Jews: "He said Germany was hurting her own cause, not so much because we want to get rid of the Jews but rather by the way we set out to accomplish this purpose with such a lot of noise. At home in Boston, for instance, Kennedy said there were clubs to which no Jews had been admitted in fifty years . . . people simply avoided making a fuss about it. He himself understood our policy on Jews completely."

The misgivings about Kennedy could not be conveyed safely to Prime Minister Chamberlain, who was impressed by reports of German invincibility. The Ambassador had even brought Charles Lindbergh to London with frightening stories of Germany's overwhelming superiority in air power. Chamberlain listened. The Czech Minister in London, Jan Masaryk, recorded that Kennedy assured him there was no question of his country being "cut up or sold out," just before German tanks moved into the rest of Czechoslovakia in March 1939. The New York *Post* reported that Kennedy was identified with "the Germanophile clique" and sprinkled his conversations with anti-Roosevelt, defeatist, and profascist comments. The *Post* reprinted an article by the London writer Claud Cockburn: "Kennedy goes so far as to insinuate that the democratic policy of the United States is a Jewish production."

Kennedy's performance seemed incredible. Yet much of what he saw and heard in England led him to suppose that the leadership was sympathetic to German aspirations. Even Japan's incursions into China were treated understandingly. The London *Times* ran a letter on its editorial page explaining a Japanese raid on a Shanghai suburb: "Such loss of life as has occurred among the Chinese civilian population (many of whom were soldiers in disguise) has been unavoidable or accidental, and, we are convinced, is regretted by no one more than the Japanese."

Kennedy had domestic political reasons, too, for taking the line he did. "He owes his position to the fact that he represents a Catholic, Irish, anti-English group in America which must not be offended if President Roosevelt is to be re-elected in November," Stephenson noted. "Mr Kennedy therefore must exhibit the attitudes of the East Coast Irish, and isolationist groups loosely termed America Firsters."

America Firsters refused to be dragged into Europe's wars by the perfidious British. The Chicago *Tribune* raised an old specter when it cautioned Kennedy against "playing the role of office-boy of empire" and reminded its readers of Walter Hines Page, the American Ambassador in London during World War I, accused by his enemies of betraying his country because he had helped the British to bring the United States into the conflict. "To do a Walter Hines Page" had become synonymous with being suckered by the British, and Ambassador Kennedy was very much aware of the danger to his own political ambitions of seeming to fall into that trap.

A few days after the British declared war in September 1939, Kennedy had given a farewell dinner for his nine children before packing them off home. He toasted the Germans, who "would badly thrash the British." Evidently someone who was there made a report, for it began a series of wartime accounts in the Foreign Office file labeled "Kennediana," not to be opened for another thirty-five years. The file alleged that he was, in his utterances at least, a danger to Britain and a boost to Nazi morale. He joined his children in Boston the following Christmas and he seemed to go out of his way to predict disaster. When he returned to London in March 1940 he was linked with the appeasers, including the British Chancellor of the Exchequer, John Simon, who told Kennedy that he and his confreres would advocate peace but would be yelled down "by those warmongers around Churchill." So long as men like Simon were in and Churchill was out, little could be done to change Kennedy's defeatist influence.

When Stephenson made his first secret journey to Washington, he could at first tell the President only that the communications with London were not secure. There was some kind of leak inside the United States Embassy. Beyond that, he could say nothing.

"But in May 1940, Hitler forced the struggle between Churchill's men and the appeasers into the open," Stephenson noted later. "The Nazis launched sudden and savage attacks on Belgium and the Netherlands, making an end run around the French, who were still gazing placidly across the Rhine from the Maginot Line. The bulk of British fighting strength was in danger of being trapped in continental Europe. The support of the people for Churchill rose in a great swell of anger."

The nation turned to Churchill. He was the rebel whose political ambitions were curiously restrained. His wife, when asked before the war if he might become prime minister, had said: "Only if some great disaster were to sweep the country and no one could wish for that."

Stephenson continued: "It was the socialists who sensed disaster and put him in. The Labour Party Executive was prepared to join a coalition government, the traditional response to danger, but only if Churchill led it. Oddly enough, he continued to be mistaken for a diehard reactionary. Even dear Eleanor Roosevelt wrote that 'he knows the day of traditional class leadership is over, but the old feeling ties him to the old way and down at the bottom he is fighting for that with courage and the best qualities that the old order produced.' But Churchill knew well enough that the old order was changing and sought to use its best qualities to fight new dangers. The dictators fought with unfamiliar weapons; and not the least dangerous of these was their exploitation of democracy's weaknesses, including a kind of innocent good will."

In Britain, the rebels against complacency swept aside those who were guilty of this innocent good will.

"We got rid of the Better-Notters," wrote Hugh Dalton, given his head as Minister of Economic Warfare. "We hired the War-Wagers just in time."

Some old-guard civil servants whispered that Dalton would run a "Ministry of Ungentlemanly Warfare." They feared it would become a monster with concealed and unaccountable funds, dangerous and unorthodox weapons, and free to cause political mayhem abroad, even to the extent of political assassination. That, of course, was what Churchill anticipated; but he felt confident that he could curb any wilder impulses. Ministry headquarters in Berkeley Square quietly sucked in poets and professors, sportsmen and journalists, and others not already equipped with cloak and dagger. One recruit was Eric Maschwitz, who composed the wartime song "A Nightingale Sang in Berkeley Square." Those who really occupied Berkeley Square adopted the song as their theme.

Churchill's eleventh-hour rise to power has been described as a miracle that saved the free world. That Churchill might prove a disaster, however, was the view of Alexander Cadogan, the head of the Foreign Office. Others shared his misgivings. It needs to be remembered that such civil servants had never allowed private doubts to influence their actions. The first Earl of Cadogan had been Director of Intelligence to

90

Churchill's illustrious ancestor the Duke of Marlborough. On the eve of battle, Marlborough seemingly insulted Cadogan by throwing down his glove. That night, Marlborough said he wished to site a battery of guns where he had thrown down the gauntlet. "It's there now," replied Cadogan, who had understood what looked to the generals like an insulting act. "Nothing disturbed his fidelity to his chief or the mutual comprehension between them," commented Churchill.

Beside him, when he took over, were secret-warfare chiefs whose mutual comprehension was never more needed. Europe was vanishing into the darkness of a tyranny without precedent. The art of the guerrilla offered some faint hope of rising resistance, something better than the degrading and demoralizing prospect of a mere struggle to keep alive. Human endurance and ingenuity were to be pitted against military authority pursuing a scheme of racial purification that depended upon the extermination of "inferiors," the enslavement of others, selective breeding, and the worship of a new kind of superman.

It was not by chance that the vulnerabilities of this Nazi authority were being exposed at Bletchley. Jewish intellectuals and refugees from persecution were among those who began a routine to recover some coded German signals fed through the Enigma chain. A procedure was established that helped the Duty Watch to fasten upon the particular code—that is, the arrangement of Enigma drums—being used by a specific German network (the Air Force in Norway, for example) before the senders switched to another code. An elaborate system of telegraph and telephone lines between Bletchley and service chiefs in London was brought into operation and made secure against accidental betrayal by interception if sent via radio.

The change in Britain's leadership had produced a surge of confidence. In code-breaking, the consequences of the sudden lift in morale were spectacular. Mental blocks dissolved. A mechanical contrivance was built that reduced the work of the mathematicians. It would be some time before the enemy's secrets were laid bare by retrieving the German High Command's orders on a reasonably regular basis. But there was a sense of a breakthrough, sufficient for Stephenson to propose that intelligence distilled from this source be labeled "Top-secret Ultra." Under this label would be filed only that intelligence which came from Bletchley and sources so highly confidential that no more than selected segments could be communicated to battle commanders, and then often in disguised form. ULTRA reports would be confided to the smallest possible number of British leaders, to reduce the risk of a leak, and to one other: the President of the United States.

14

IN PARLIAMENT, NEVILLE CHAMBERLAIN was confronted by a member pointing a finger and quoting Cromwell: "You have sat too long here. . . . In the name of God, go!"

Churchill became prime minister on May 10, 1940, a few days before Hitler's armies swept to the English Channel in a series of blitzkriegs. "At long last," Churchill was to write later, "I could act with full authority in all directions." One of his first orders was to bring together the work of separate agencies concerned with the U.S. Embassy leaks. The gravity of the case could be judged by the priority given to it during this time of greatest danger. On the day the police came for Tyler Gatewood Kent, the American cipher clerk, British naval officers met in deep galleries carved into the cliffs of Dover and peered doubtfully across the English Channel. Could a fleet of sailing craft and rusty coasters be scraped together to rescue the British Expeditionary Force encircled by German armored forces in Flanders? In the War Office, a Military Intelligence tape machine rapped out a message that seemed to reflect the incoherence of events:

HOTLERS TROOPS OVERRUN LUXEMBOURG. . . .
HOTLER PROCLAIMS FALL OF BELGIUM AND HOL-
LAND. HOTLER SAYS HE WILL CRUSH BRITAIN.

There was a pause and then the machine stuttered
again.

CORRECTION. FOR HOTLER READ HITLER AND THE
MEANING WILL BECOME APPARENT.

Stephenson scanned the wire copy and then, back
in London briefly, meditated on the Tyler Kent case.
It stank of treachery. He hoped none of it extended to
other members of Ambassador Kennedy's staff.

The decoded messages to Berlin that first aroused
suspicion had been dispatched from the German Ambassador to Rome, Hans Mackensen. Intelligence
sources reported that Mackensen got his information
from an Italian attaché in London, the Duke of Del
Monte. Scotland Yard reported that the Duke of Del
Monte patronized a tearoom in London owned by a
former Tsarist Russian admiral, whose daughter,
Anna Wolkoff, was popular among anti-Semitic pro-
Nazi groups. Among her admirers was the same Duke
of Westminster who had attacked Churchill in the
Savoy. Anna Wolkoff had been followed by counterespionage agents whose job was made easier by the trail
she left of sticky-backed labels declaring: "This is
a Jew's War." These British agents were concerned
with England's fifth column, a term coined four years
before, during the Spanish Civil War, when it was
said that the four columns of insurgents marching
upon Madrid had a "fifth column" of sympathizers
inside the city ready to betray it.

A watch had also been kept on Anna's apartment by
MI-5, a branch of Military Intelligence then responsible for counterespionage, because she was listed as a
member of the Right Club, which distributed pro-
Nazi, anti-Jewish propaganda. Only now, when MI-
5's report was put beside the results of other
investigations, did it become evident that Anna was a
link in the chain between the Embassy and Berlin.
She was visited often at night by a U.S. Embassy code

clerk. He was Tyler Kent, who handled the secret cables dispatched to Washington in the State Department's Gray Code, said to be unbreakable.

Had Kent been acting on his own, inside the Embassy? Anna Wolkoff's background revealed a long history of collaboration with pro-Nazi diplomats. She wrote letters containing information to be used in propaganda broadcasts from Berlin by the British traitor William Joyce, Lord Haw-Haw. She was the source of material wirelessed to Rumania, through another diplomatic channel, to be sent on to Berlin. She was the means by which Kent passed on the contents of the Churchill-Roosevelt cables to the Italian attaché, who sent them to the German Ambassador in Rome.

All of these pieces had been in different hands. Put together, they completed a broad picture.

Even during the week before Kent's arrest, a sensitive message from Churchill was duplicated along the London-Rome-Berlin chain. He had cabled Roosevelt that Britain and France had passed from being Hitler's hateful "victors of Versailles" to the lowly level of being defeated in battle and divided. The Führer must have enjoyed reading: "TO POTUS: The scene has darkened swiftly. . . . The small countries are simply smashed up, one by one, like matchwood. We must expect, though it is not yet certain, that Mussolini will hurry in to share the loot of civilization. We expect to be attacked here ourselves, both from the air and by parachute and airborne troops, in the near future. . . . You may have a completely subjugated Nazified Europe established with astonishing swiftness, and the weight may be more than we can bear. All I ask now is that you should proclaim nonbelligerency, which would mean that you would help us with everything short of actually engaging armed forces." It was signed "Former Naval Person."

In another message, the details were given of the heavy losses Britain had suffered among warships. There followed a full disclosure of Britain's urgent need for forty or fifty outdated American destroyers.

It was the last time Hitler got such cheering news handed him on this silver plate. Stephenson was deeply involved in negotiations for the loan of the American ships. He recognized that the intercept was almost word for word Churchill's coded plea. There was no further doubt about the origin of the leak, which was the U.S. code clerk and not Ambassador Kennedy.

The Ambassador then had to disown his own man. Standing in the Kennedy house near Kensington Palace on the evening of the raid on Kent's apartment, he agreed to Lord Halifax's proposal that Kent should be dismissed from the U.S. Foreign Service so that British authorities could take legal action. Kennedy telephoned President Roosevelt that night to report "our most secret code has become useless. Just when France is collapsing, the United States has to suspend its confidential communications with diplomatic missions throughout the world." He added that if the United States had been at war, he would have recommended that Kent be shot as a traitor.

The trial of Tyler Kent and Anna Wolkoff was conducted in secrecy. They were sentenced to prison terms on charges of communicating confidential documents that might help the enemy. The case was hushed up because of its many implications, not the least being that Kent justified his actions on patriotic grounds and felt that it was Roosevelt who was guilty of treason. Kent was a well-educated young man, a career diplomat with an unusual amount of experience abroad. No matter how angrily Kennedy condemned him now, many Americans shared his isolationist feelings.

Ambassador Kennedy had said that Kent's activities compromised all American diplomatic communications. He did not know that Stephenson had made arrangements in Washington to bring an alternative system into operation. President Roosevelt's instruction to J. Edgar Hoover to form the closest possible alliance with Stephenson's intelligence clients had been followed on the American side as swiftly as the FBI's resources would allow. Everyone had been waiting for the day Churchill would take command. From now onward, Ambassador Kennedy would be bypassed. New channels of communication would open up between the Baker Street Irregulars and their companions in the United States.

These rebels on both sides of the Atlantic moved

cautiously. They feared betrayal by men in much higher positions than Tyler Kent's—uninformed men who would justify their actions in the name of patriotism, too. Ironically, the British, who were at least in the midst of war, had the most reason to tread warily. Kennedy's good friend Neville Chamberlain had been deposed, but his foreign secretary, Lord Halifax, was still active. Even while Churchill was moving into the post of prime minister, Halifax was anticipating the consequences of a French collapse. He commended a peace proposal "that will get us better terms now than we might get in three months' time." Mussolini had offered to negotiate a settlement with the Nazis without affecting Britain's independence, provided Fascist Italy could have the island of Malta and free play in the Mediterranean. If Britain would display a reasonable attitude and allow Germany and Italy to share the Middle East and Africa, peace could be secured.

Halifax and Chamberlain tried repeatedly to have this proposal endorsed by the British War Cabinet. "Had they collaborated, it would not have been long before our anti-Nazi activities became anti-British," said Stephenson.

The latest peace offer had originated in Rome while the German Ambassador was enciphering the last piece of information to leak from the U.S. Embassy in London: Roosevelt's frank explanation of his difficulty in letting Churchill have the forty or fifty antiquated destroyers. Stephenson now argued forcibly for the secure and co-ordinated intelligence alliance that would bring together those who opposed Nazism, no matter what their nationality, using the Tyler Kent investigation to make his case. Ambassador Kennedy had been cleared of any responsibility for the leak, but his testimony before a closed hearing of the House and Senate committees on Military Affairs put him in the same category as Halifax. That testimony was given shortly before Stephenson's first flying visit to Washington. In it, Kennedy was emphatic that Nazi Germany could not be beaten. He had recorded his view that Churchill was scheming and unscrupulous and "willing to blow up the American Embassy and say it was the Germans, if that would get the Americans in."

Churchill had leaned over backward to avoid impetuous actions that might alarm or antagonize the Americans. Events now forced his hand. The Prime Minister of France, Paul Reynaud, telephoned to say in English: "We have been defeated. We are beaten. We have lost the battle."

If Britain could hang on for a few weeks, if Roosevelt were not turned out of the White House by the defeatists, if the United States would provide arms at least for the secret armies (beginning with those auxiliary units preparing to conduct partisan warfare, if necessary, against the Nazis in Britain), there was still hope for freedom. To the Baker Street Irregulars, Churchill issued the orders to prepare for guerrilla operations. A body was to be created "to coordinate all action by way of subversion and sabotage,—To *Set Europe Ablaze.*"

Official action was delayed two months while Stephenson explained the proposal to President Roosevelt, for a blazing Europe might include an occupied Britain whose guerrillas would take direction from New York.

What seemed in April an academic question was now a probability. Stephenson had not exaggerated when he told the President that it would take Hitler little time to subjugate his unprepared neighbors, and the forces of freedom a long time to liberate them. "The Führer is not just a lunatic," Stephenson had said. "He's an evil genius. The weapons in his armory are like nothing in history. His propaganda is sophisticated. His control of the people is technologically clever. He has torn up the military textbooks and written his own. His strategy is to spread terror, fear, and mutual suspicion.

"There will be a period of occupation when we shall have to keep up the morale of those who are not taken to the death and slave camps, and build up an intelligence system so that we can identify the enemy's weak points. We'll have to fall back upon human resources and trust that these are superior to machines."

Part
Two

FIGHT ON

"Fight on, my men, Sir Andrew sayes,
A little ime hurt, but yett not slaine,
Ile but lye downe and bleede awhile,
And then ile rise and fight againe"

—*The Ballad of Sir Andrew Barton*

15

THE GERMAN ARMIES were flooding across France. There was every indication that the French would sign a separate peace. Then Germany would occupy Paris and the industrial centers, tolerating a "neutral" French administration in the south.

Churchill shuttled between England and France in his desperate attempts to shore up Allied morale, and was shattered to discover it was Reynaud's mistress who was really influencing decisions. The Countess Hélène de Portes had sapped whatever courage remained in the French Premier as she lay crying hysterically on his bed, pleading only to be left alone.

Stephenson flew with Churchill on one of the five grueling journeys made by the new Prime Minister, pitchforked in his mid-sixties into the role of war lord while his armies tried to escape from the enemy's trap. Every available vessel capable of crossing the English Channel formed an almost continuous stream between Dover and the bombed beaches of Dunkirk. In Paris, Reynaud knew nothing of the evacuation. He nodded numbly when Churchill, who seemed to him a pink little old man with wispy hair and frail artistic hands, said: "Better that the last of us should fall fighting than to linger on as slaves."

Churchill stumped up and down Reynaud's bedroom. There was "the great probability that Hitler will rule the world," he said. "We must think together of how to strike and strike again, no matter what the cost nor how long the trials ahead." He faced the French Premier and then sat down heavily. His changing moods raced like clouds across his baby face. He was

101

in turn sulky, tearful, and violent. None of it did any good. Reynaud in reply chanted the pace of Hitler's victories: Poland in twenty-six days, Norway in twenty-eight days, Denmark in twenty-four hours, Holland in five days, and Luxembourg in twelve hours. He turned sad luminous eyes on Churchill. "Belgium is finished. Now France . . ."

Back in London, Churchill told Parliament: "We have but one aim, and one single irrevocable purpose. We are resolved to destroy Hitler and every vestige of the Nazi regime. From this, nothing will turn us—nothing. We will never parley, we will never negotiate. . . . We shall never surrender." He spoke while his commanders counted their losses. Britain was virtually defenseless. Her expeditionary forces had left their weapons in conquered France. But the London tabloid *Daily Mirror* proclaimed in banner headlines: BLOODY MARVELOUS. Instead of only 50,000 troops, the makeshift fleet had evacuated 338,226 fighting men. It was called "the Miracle of Dunkirk." Churchill swiftly reminded his people that "we have suffered a catastrophic defeat."

He served warning that Hitler's weapons of subversion and bribery would fail, and hinted at the preparations of the Baker Street Irregulars by the promise that "if this Island or a large part of it were subjugated and starving," the struggle would continue until "the New World, with all its power and might, steps forth to the rescue and the liberation of the old."

Six days later, President Roosevelt publicly replied. "We will pursue two obvious and simultaneous courses: we will extend to the opponents of force the material resources of this nation; and at the same time we will harness and speed up the use of those resources in order that we in America may have equipment and training equal to the task of any emergency. . . ." He took an enormous personal risk in openly committing the United States in the face of domestic antiwar feeling.

"This was his first tremendous decision—to back the seemingly hopeless cause of Britain when everyone thought it was already lost," Stephenson recalled later. He understood the President's difficulties better than most British leaders.

Noel Coward, who had been snatched out of Paris from under German guns, glimpsed the short, slight Canadian at one of the curious cloak-and-dagger offices that overnight sprang up around Queen Anne's Gate in London. Coward had been working with French intelligence. "When the roof fell in," he said, "I suddenly realized we'd been playing games. One idea was to drop leaflets on Berlin. They would carry slogans like 'See—the Führer cannot stop Allied bombers!' It seemed quite pathetic when I got back to England. I thought—O dear, they'll be twiddling their thumbs here, too, until the tanks reach Westminster. I had to go to St. Ermin's Hotel in Caxton Street, very appropriately positioned between the House of Lords and Victoria Railway Station. I had to meet a contact in the foyer. I waited in this squalid place and eventually a man said 'Follow me.' I thought we'd go back into the street to some secret address. Instead, he wheeled me round and into an elevator. It was only labeled to go up three floors. To my absolute astonishment it went to the fourth instead. An immense fellow guarded the place, all scrunched up inside a porter's uniform and looking very uncomfortable. I found out later his name was Cornelius.

"Well this was the—ah, the Special Operations Executive. What we called later the Baker Street Irregulars. Some chap was saying President Roosevelt wanted us to do his fighting. And Little Bill was there, very calm, with those sort of hooded eyes watching everything. And all he said was—'We could have done with Roosevelt here these past few years.' "

Stephenson was engaged at this time in hot controversy about the future handling of ULTRA's reports from Bletchley. ULTRA covered many sources on intelligence but its principal product came from the daily deciphering of German orders coded through Enigma machines. Informed comments and analyses accompanied these decoded interceptions. There were fears that the Germans were torturing Polish and French prisoners who knew about the captured Heydrich-

Enigma. About a dozen senior intelligence officers in Warsaw and Paris had at least some knowledge of the British prize and might disclose it, inadvertently or under severe interrogation. If the Germans discovered that Enigma was already in British hands, they had only to switch to another system to destroy most of ULTRA's usefulness. (Official postwar investigations were to prove that nobody revealed the secret, placing British and Americans in the debt of those who never talked—a debt that in the light of events must seem irredeemable.)

With everyone on tenterhooks, Stephenson had the unenviable task of arguing for further disclosures to the Americans, thus increasing the risk of warning the enemy.

ULTRA was still stabbing in the dark. Bletchley cryptographers were coping with dozens of different Enigma ciphers or sets of couplings in use at the same time. For example, the German repair-and-maintenance network in Occupied Denmark would transmit daily routine orders on an Enigma cipher different from that in use by German U-boats in the Atlantic. Furthermore, the Germans had many variations of high-grade ciphers. At Bletchley, it was necessary to work out the order of priority in which these intercepted messages should be processed, lest a truly significant and urgent order be set aside while the specialists tackled something that would prove to be of minor importance. Even the word "specialists" is misleading. They were still learning on the job. What some achieved was a filing system that, as it grew, became invaluable. Out of the mass of material that did get decoded, indexers underlined what struck them as key words, transferred these to files, and cross-indexed them. This ever-expanding library led to sudden revelations. An intelligence officer plowing through a routine message might strike a word—perhaps the name of a solid-fuel propellant—that rang a bell. Seeking the word in records, he might find an earlier reference to the propellant in connection with weapon experiments. The propellant was being shipped to Denmark. This suggested either a new test range or the introduction of the new weapon into naval service in certain vessels thought to be based in Denmark. This detective work depended upon that initial moment of word association, which is why Bletchley clung to scholars with encyclopedic memories.

There was an awful element of chance in all this. Though Stephenson knew some of the work could be done mechanically, Britain still did not have such equipment. Meanwhile, the batteries of human brains had to be enlarged again. Why not keep American experts on tap? Not friendly professors in faraway cities, but American intelligence officers moved to Bletchley and available twenty-four hours a day. A revolutionary concept, it seemed. If ULTRA was vital to survival, sharing it with Americans would be an act of trust. Roosevelt knew, as quickly as Churchill, whatever British intelligence deduced about German intentions. But the President was an exception. Should the burden of such knowledge be placed on neutral officers? "Is there even such a creature as a professional American intelligence officer outside their service agencies?" demanded one hostile British admiral. "If American academics are brought in, will they submit to the harsh discipline of secrecy and its accompanying hardships of isolation?"

Stephenson argued for the acquisition of American brains while planning to solve mechanically the cipher and index problems that drained Bletchley's human energies. He proposed that British Tabulating be the cover for a computer to be called "Colossus." Smaller and better versions would then be constructed in the United States with expert British aid. Computers were something new. Computers powered electrically were unknown. He had International Business Machines in mind as the U.S. manufacturer. How was IBM to be kept in ignorance of the true purpose? The computers were called, in conversation, *"bombes,"* from French intelligence terminology, a sad echo of the days —now abruptly ended—when Paris was a center of cryptological research. The first British-built models were assembled near Bletchley, but it soon became apparent that production must take place away from enemy bombers, in the United States, where improvements could be made with the help of American mathematicians.

With France and presumably the rest of Europe cut off, what sources would there be for other intelligence officers? Stephenson could think only of the Americas. The neutrals of Latin America and the United States included millions of migrants whose first language would be that of a country occupied by the enemy. More important, these "hyphenated Americans" would have firsthand knowledge of local territories, Nazi-run factories and mines. They would know who could be trusted to help create secret units within the occupied countries. They would have to be trained out of sight, and without breaking neutrality laws. The obvious place was the Canadian wilderness.

These considerations kept Stephenson busy in May of 1940. It was the month marking the end of the Phony War. To all outward appearances, Britain had been taken by surprise. The Baker Street Irregulars, the guerrilla-warfare experts, and the intelligence chiefs were obliged to receive in silence the jeers about British muddle and unpreparedness.

"We were squeezing into a week what normally took a year," Stephenson said later. "We swept aside the dangerous rigidity of bureaucracy, the thumb-twiddlers and military dinosaurs. I daresay we made some enemies. . . ." He had hoped for a conventional fighting command for himself. He was forty-four, but danger seemed to lend him the energy of youth. Churchill asked him to a private dinner. The manner of invitation was cordial, casual, and discreet. "My dear Bill—We have matters to discuss. Pray come as you are, to the Beaver's, seven tonight. WC."

It was a fine evening, with the washed-blue skies that come in late May and early June. He decided to walk, to take his time, perhaps to divert past the sandbagged colossus that was the BBC, already a radio beacon of hope for millions under Nazi rule. He hummed the opening bars of Beethoven's Fifth Symphony, translating the rhythm into Morse code. Dot-dot-dot-dash . . . V. A stirring composition. It would make a dramatic signal. V—for Victory. A prelude to BBC broadcasts in every European language.

106

The signature of secret armies. The leaders would listen for it and rally to the V symbol. Dot-dot-dot-dash . . . He'd mention the idea to Churchill.

He passed the Yorkshire Grey, an old drinking house favored by American correspondents. It carried a sign on the door, quoting Queen Victoria: "Please understand there is no pessimism in this house and we are not interested in the possibilities of defeat. They do not exist."

A barrage balloon wobbled out of Regent's Park. It contained just enough gas to give it the drooping look of an exhausted elephant. Such balloons rose when an air raid was anticipated, their cables forming a steel mesh for blundering bombers. A patrol of Boy Scouts stood outside the divisional police station in Mayfair. On their bicycles, they would carry messages between posts whenever communications were knocked out by bombs.

"Adversity," Stephenson mused, "suits the British. They like their roads to be crooked, their trains slow, their phone lines crossed. In peace, they're in permanent resistance to authority. In war, they breathe a sigh of relief at getting back to normal. In solitude they feel happiest. In isolation they go back to being islanders."

The little man walked as if he had springs in his feet. The shimmer of young foliage painted with delicate green the sooty trunks of London trees. A flower girl on Portland Place called out: "Cheer up, mate, you ain't dead 'til yer buried!" With sunlight shining from time to time through the billowing clouds, he made his way down Regent Street and turned into a lane between the grimy buttressed buildings leading to Stornoway House, a forbidding mansion.

Churchill met him at the door and took the newcomer, still clutching a nosegay he had purchased, by the arm. "Dinner first. Then talk."

The laird of Stornoway was host—Lord Beaverbrook, another pugnacious little Canadian. Among the chiefs of war at the table were Frenchmen about to fly back to what remained of their country, and Hugh ("Boom") Trenchard, who had preserved the Royal Air Force during the muddleheaded years of appeasement. For him, a struggle for mastery of the sky lay ahead. His best fighter aircraft had been squandered over France, and he thought privately that he could not resist a full-scale German attack in the air for more than forty-eight hours.

The French listened glumly. Churchill, who had once sketched "The Timetable of a Nightmare," projecting a German advance upon London, now forecast a conflict of unutterable brutality, with women and children drawn in, and torture and treachery as weapons. "Whatever you may do," Churchill declared to the French, "we shall fight on forever and ever and ever."

Stephenson sat mostly silent. When he did speak, he seemed to have anticipated Churchill. He compressed an idea with the brevity of an ancient. The older man bubbled with schoolboy enthusiasm. Words were food and drink to Churchill, and sentences had a habit of reappearing in carefully composed speeches—"We shall fight on forever and ever and ever. . . ."

When port and cigars began to circulate, Churchill rose and beckoned Stephenson to join him alone beside the heavily draped windows. "Winston started by pointing a finger directly at me. 'You know what you must do. We have discussed it so fully from all angles, there is a complete fusion of minds. You are appointed my personal representative. You will be backed by all the resources at my command.' "

Stephenson was being given extraordinary independence and power. He was to direct His Majesty's Secret Intelligence Services and a great deal more. He was to move against the enemy wherever and whenever he saw fit, to take action through covert diplomacy or clandestine agencies without seeking prior approval from the War Cabinet. He would be protected only to the degree that the purpose of his movement would be known to very few.

This was not at all what Stephenson had wanted. He was, however, best qualified to build, in America, the invisible fortress that would sustain resistance to Hitler. The logic was inescapable. Britain now depended upon an appeal to the romantic imagination that in the past had saved her from seemingly certain disaster. Of weapons there were almost none. Hitler was preparing to transform Berlin into the colossal capital of the world. "He has a good chance of conquering the world," said Churchill. "All he needs is that a small island capitulate. Tell the President that!"

There was no official title at first for the new organization. Those in the know called it "BSC." The use of code names, initials, and homely phrases like "the firm" or "our friends" made conversation possible in awkward circumstances. The Baker Street Irregulars had become a club. Under the pressure of war, there was little time to check credentials. You had to assume that a member of the club had passed muster, subscribed to certain ideals, and played by the rules. The Baker Street Club was the handiest jargon. BSC became dignified as British Security Coordination only when it was obliged later to register with the U.S. State Department. It sounded harmless.

It sounds anything but harmless today. BSC rigged its headquarters in New York in haste. The invasion of Britain seemed imminent. Stephenson's mandate, when it was finally defined, ran to hundreds of pages, covering activities that ranged from operations against Americans helping Britain's enemies, to policing U.S. ports, to supervising the overthrow of a pro-Nazi government. BSC conducted guerrilla warfare from secret headquarters in the privileged sanctuary of neutral U.S. soil. The first priority was to secure arms and U.S. naval protection where possible. Stephenson's mandate assumed Britain might be conquered and Roosevelt would let the secret-warfare chiefs continue the fight from U.S. bases, linked with anti-Nazi guerrillas in British redoubts.

German plans to invade Britain, and in time to control an empire that girdled the globe, were reported by Bletchley as ULTRA became more efficient. ULTRA had demonstrated its effectiveness when British expeditionary forces escaped through Dunkirk. Roosevelt knew this, and must have been influenced thereby to tolerate Stephenson's operations when they might have become politically embarrassing to the White House.

ULTRA'S part in the miracle of Dunkirk was not central. Its usefulness in this period was in impressing on Roosevelt the fact that the British still had wit and cunning to make up for what they lacked in arms.

Hitler and his commanders failed to crush British forces trapped in Europe because DYNAMO, as the evacuation of Dunkirk was code-named, took them by surprise. Historians later puzzled and argued over the mystery of why the Führer let the British escape, when the destruction of their armies would have led to an easy victory over Britain, with incalculable consequences.

The real explanation is that the Bletchley code breakers, by a combination of familiarity with German military thinking, ULTRA'S still incomplete retrieval of orders, and analysis of other German signals, were able to guess German intentions and even to predict some German operations prior to the fall of France. Thus, during most of May, Vice-Admiral Bertram Ramsay was mobilizing 848 captains among fishermen, yachtsmen, merchant seamen, and Royal Navy officers for DYNAMO. Ramsay ensured that every ship, no matter how small, would get stores, fuel, provisions, and charts to cross the twenty-four miles from Dover to Dunkirk, to which the British expeditionary forces were told to withdraw. The rest was up to each captain.

DYNAMO surprised the Germans because it seemed impossible that the British could improvise such an evacuation in the midst of a blitzkrieg. Furthermore, Hitler knew that Chamberlain and Halifax wanted Britain to sue for peace. But Chamberlain was no longer prime minister. Halifax was hanging on as foreign secretary in name only. Nevertheless, the Chamberlain-Halifax proposals to end the war continued to tantalize the Führer as late as May 28, 1940 (according to the secret British War Cabinet report of that date, disclosed in 1971). Hitler assumed that the Chamberlain-Halifax appeasers still dominated British policy. On June 4, when German forces finally bore down in great numbers upon the dwindling Dunkirk perimeter, Hitler realized that he had been outwitted on the battlefield and misled politically. He thereupon ordered the destruction of the Royal Air Force as a prelude to the invasion of Britain. His party comrade Hermann Göring judged that his Luftwaffe would take four days to knock Britain's Fighter Command out of the air.

There was a pause in the German onslaught after Dunkirk. Historians may write that it occurred because Hitler still hoped to negotiate a settlement with Britain. President Roosevelt knew better, because he was getting, through the FBI, from Bletchley, a regular summary of what German military formations were actually doing. Troops were being concentrated in ports from Norway to France, air divisions were moved to bases that brought all England within bombing range. The long lists of German personnel postings alone confirmed that Hitler meant what he was saying in private, but overheard, directions to his commanders: Britain is to be occupied.

During this lull, Stephenson proceeded to build up BSC. New York was to be the hub because it was the commercial and communications center of the free world. From it, all forms of secret warfare could be directed, not only against the enemy in occupied territories, but also against Nazi fifth columns in the Americas, where the next attacks could be expected. Secret-warfare specialists and inventions that could be developed with the speed and in the quantity possible only in America began to flow from Britain to the United States. If Britain fell, New York would become the new source of moral and physical support for secret armies that in the early stages would have no contact with one another. And if Britain did not fall, New York would still be needed as the nerve center of resistance.

Historians may have later decided that peace was in the air during that lull. But even without the facts imparted by ULTRA, ordinary people in Britain knew otherwise. Ironically, England was enjoying an unusually beautiful summer. Rebecca West, whose special knowledge of the Balkans drew her into the

111

company of Baker Street Irregulars, described the mood in *Black Lamb and Grey Falcon:* "Under the unstained heaven of that perfect summer, curiously starred with the silver elephantines of the balloon barrage, the people sat on the seats among the roses [in Regent's Park] . . . their faces white. Some of them walked among the rose-beds, with a special earnestness looking down on the bright flowers and inhaling the scent, as if to say, 'That is what roses are like, that is how they smell. We must remember that, down in the darkness.' . . . Most of these people believed, and rightly, that they were presently to be subjected to a form of attack more horrible than had ever before been directed against the common man. Let nobody belittle them by pretending they were fearless. Not being as the ox and the ass, they were horribly afraid. But their pale lips did not part to say the words that would have given them security and dishonour."

16

"THE MANOEUVRE WHICH brings an ally into the field is as serviceable as that which wins a great battle," Churchill had written in his autobiographical account of World War I. As prime minister in the second, he added that the man to bring in the Americans must be fearless. He paused. "Dauntless?" He searched for the right word while Stephenson waited. "You must be—*intrepid!*"

Churchill felt strongly about code names. They should be neither flamboyant nor trivial. He put up with the flippancy of the Baker Street Irregulars because "the Germans would never think us such idiots as to proclaim the title in the actual address." Of course, in a way, Baker Street was not the real address. It sheltered those agencies in London charged with the task of rebuilding intelligence networks and creating guerrilla armies in Europe. But BSC was in New York, the junction box through which would pass all Allied secrets. BSC records were kept under the label INTREPID from the day Stephenson arrived back in New York posing as a passport control officer. This humble title was acceptable to the FBI, knowing it to be a traditional cover for British intelligence chiefs abroad.

The new passport control officer's immediate concerns included getting American help in developing the one weapon with which the British hoped to save themselves and, perhaps, civilization: communications. ULTRA was part of that weapon. To lead from defensive to offensive use of that weapon, enemy orders must be intercepted and analyzed swiftly, and orders to guerrilla units must be transmitted swiftly, all with absolute secrecy. Churchill acknowledged in June 1940 that most of this fighting would be conducted by guerrillas, special agents, revolutionaries, and saboteurs. Their operations would have to be orchestrated by radio. Wireless communication was the new factor in warfare that not only enabled the Germans to conduct blitzkriegs, but also could be used against the Germans to co-ordinate irregular actions. "The completely defensive habit of mind which has ruined the French must not be allowed to ruin all our initiative," Churchill wrote in a confidential memo. "How wonderful it would be if the Germans could be made to wonder where they were going to be struck next, instead of forcing us to try to wall in the Island and roof it over!"

Stephenson plunged straight into the wireless war when he got back to New York on June 21, 1940, the day after Churchill told a secret session of Parliament that the fall of France was the prelude to invasion: "Steady continuous bombing, probably rising to great intensity must be the regular condition of our life. It will be a test of our nerve against theirs." In case German bombing should destroy the secret devices being perfected in Britain, copies were dispatched to New York. They included new methods

113

of radio-location; in return for them, the Americans were asked to co-operate in Stephenson's effort to provide Bletchley with information on U-boats derived from U.S. radio-detection stations.

But this was only a beginning. Before Americans played their secret role in guerrilla operations and before the battles of Britain and the Atlantic, Stephenson found himself grappling with the enemy inside the United States. It was a dirty underside to the war, unexpected, and subsequently underestimated by those who chronicled the drama unfolding across the English Channel. It was the first of many guerrilla skirmishes fought on American soil. Defeat for the British here would have spelled defeat for Britain.

The Wednesday after Stephenson returned, the Nazi military victories in Europe were celebrated in a private suite at the Waldorf Astoria Hotel in Manhattan. The host was an agent of SS intelligence chief Reinhard Heydrich. The guests were prominent Americans, millionaires and industrialists who were being urged to "cut off supplies to Britain."

This advice came from Dr. Gerhard Alois Westrick, a German intelligence agent masquerading as a German trade official. Westrick served several Nazi masters, but his ultimate chief was Heydrich. He threw the Waldorf Astoria party in his capacity, he said, of an international business lawyer. "Britain will be polished off in three months," he advised his guests. "Then the prospects for American trade with the New German Empire will be beyond your wildest dreams." Stephenson knew Westrick as the Nazi representative who had done business years earlier with Colonel Sosthenes Behn, the American chief executive of International Telephone and Telegraph, who had been involved in producing weapons for the Germans and counter-weapons for the British. Behn attended Westrick's party, along with other American contacts with large financial interests in Germany and territories now falling under the Nazi shadow. James D. Mooney, chief of overseas operations for General Motors, was expected to pressure Roosevelt into suspending help for Britain so that the Germans would allow GM to continue business in Europe. Edsel Ford and his millionaire friend from Pennsylvania, Ralph Beaver Strassburger, had large financial investments in Germany and property in France they wished to protect from Göring's greedy treasure-hunting eyes. Executives from other U.S. corporations were supposedly susceptible to the argument that Nazi Germany had virtually won the war. This did not seem an unlikely proposition on the day of Westrick's celebration party: June 26, 1940. It was the day the War Cabinet in London received intelligence that the German invasion would be preceded by heavy bombing and use of "a new weapon." This was also the day that the British Ambassador in Washington, Lord Lothian, reported, "in a distressing telegram," a wave of pessimism in the United States that might affect the President's attempts to provide help, because it seemed most Americans regarded the defeat of Britain as inevitable. It was the day German troops prepared for the successful invasion of two of the British Channel Isles, Jersey and Guernsey, replacing the Union Jack with the Swastika.

The appalling situation in Britain haunted Stephenson as he studied an account of the German's victory party with American tycoons in the Waldorf Astoria. A message from Churchill advised caution and cool handling of the new threat. Another, also from the Prime Minister, was passed to Lothian: "Your mood should be bland and phlegmatic. No one is downhearted here."

One prominent figure at the German victory celebration was Torkild Rieber, of Texaco, whose tankers eluded the British blockade. The company had already been warned, at Roosevelt's instigation, about violations of the Neutrality Law. But Rieber had set up an elaborate scheme for shipping oil and petroleum products through neutral ports in South America. With the Germans now preparing to turn the English Channel into what Churchill thought would become "a river of blood," other industrialists were eager to learn from Texaco how to do more business with Hitler.

Not all industrialists were as eager as the bumptious Westrick supposed. Had he done his homework, he would have spotted telltale signs of a strong anti-

Nazi lobby. Nelson Rockefeller, for example, whose Standard Oil representative had been invited, was giving Stephenson discreet support and had recently lectured his executives on the political responsibilities of international corporations. Also in Stephenson's private army of Irregulars was the same James D. Mooney who had attended the Waldorf Astoria party. He reported to Stephenson as STALLFORTH. "American corporations are being offered trade monopolies inside the new Nazi empire," he said. "In return, American industrialists are asked to refuse to join any rearmament program."

A publicity spotlight was turned on Westrick by other friends of Stephenson. One of them was Frank Knox, Secretary of the Navy and owner of the Chicago *Daily News.* Another was Clare Boothe Luce, wife of the publisher of *Time* and *Life.* Helen Ogden Reid, of the New York *Herald Tribune,* was still another. They had been, at one time or another, guests of Mary Stephenson, now house-hunting in New York. It was not difficult to pass along the fact that a Nazi official was posing as a private citizen in order to pursue fifth-column activities. Big headlines about Westrick's real background forced the State Department to send him on his way. This particular threat had been removed with breath-taking speed. So much was telescoped within each twenty-four-hour day that Stephenson would say later: "Day and night followed one upon another unnoticed. You couldn't measure time by the clock. It was like being back in the lab with Steiny."

To keep the White House in secure and continuous contact with Whitehall, a confidential agent of Roosevelt's own choosing would have to be taken into the secret heart of Britain and given the freedom to measure morale and scrutinize the new and aggressive leadership. Many Americans would object to a presidential "spy" who might short-circuit diplomatic and political channels. Many in Britain would object to disclosing to a neutral the secrets that were their only defense.

"The right man will have to combine integrity and discretion, compassion and resolve," Stephenson wrote in a personal memo. "He will be going from a wealthy and self-indulgent society to one of austerity and the immediate prospect of annihilation, and he will need a great capacity to tolerate the short-tempered brusqueness of exhausted men at war."

Stephenson's choice was already made. William Joseph Donovan had a law office at 2 Wall Street, handy to the Passport Control Office. The PCO in New York's financial and shipping district was too cramped for what Stephenson had to do, but it was initially convenient. His aides, sent down from Canada in the guise of salesmen, were already de-bugging premises he had earmarked at the Dorset Hotel, Hampshire House, and Rockefeller Center. Stephenson had long ago envisioned this expansion. He had ambitious plans for Donovan, too.

17

ON THE FACE of it, Donovan would seem poorly qualified to work with Britain in any sensitive capacity. He was a Catholic of Irish descent, and a Republican who might seem also to represent all that was anathema to a Democratic administration. But Roosevelt trusted him and had already sent him on personal intelligence missions abroad. He was, in Stephenson's opinion, just the man to be taken into Britain's confidence. It was an unparalleled display of faith at a time when another Irish Catholic, Joseph P. Kennedy, created such cold hostility. Kennedy, quickly recovering from the scandal of his Embassy's leaky security, was now complaining that the President circumvented him altogether.

There were a number of matters about which Stephenson was empowered to tell Donovan. A great deal he knew already, for he had never been really out of touch with Stephenson since the World War I mission to England when the Canadian had given him such a vivid picture of battlefield realities. He knew Stephenson had arranged the emotionally charged and unprecedented visit by the British King and Queen the previous year, when Eleanor Roosevelt had written in her column, "They were returning to face a war," and when Father Charles Coughlin had said to his huge radio audience that the royal couple were "pawns to nullify American policy of no foreign entanglements." Donovan was aware that the President's wife carried in her purse a prayer given to her by Stephenson:

> *Dear Lord*
> *Lest I continue*
> *My complacent way*
> *Help me to remember*
> *Somewhere out there*
> *A man died for me today*
> *—As long as there be war*
> *I then must*
> *Ask and answer*
> *Am I worth dying for?*

That prayer reflected Stephenson's emotional response to what was happening in Europe. He talked little about these feelings, Donovan recalled in later years. Instead, Stephenson assembled a formidable number of documents that proved beyond doubt that Germany was committed to the most gruesome policies of mass murder and enslavement. Orders issued as far back as 1933 laid down the basis on which human beings were to be graded in accordance with Hitler's theories of racial purity. German "educational" films showed how doctors should select infants by measuring them against charts for the correct color of hair and eyes, the proper length and shape of nose and skull, and why it was important to discard children of inferior quality. The purification of the Germanic race, and in time the purification of all humanity, was the Nazis' declared aim. Carefully selected Germans were to mate and produce purebred

118

infants. In conquered territories, a system had been devised for picking out the few children deemed worthy of "Germanization." The rest were to be given limited educations—enough to make them useful laborers—or left to die. Nazi proposals for populating the globe with German supermen were not matters of conjecture. Stephenson produced the written orders, the propaganda films, the textbooks and bureaucratic forms by which the world was to be purified with Teutonic thoroughness, because he believed this gave the Nazis their drive; this was their ambition, this was their aim. Everything else—military campaigns, battles won or lost—was secondary to the great overriding impulse to purge the human race of "impure blood."

This explained his relentlessness. He feared this German fanaticism. He feared where it might lead if the Nazis should develop new weapons.

From Britain, Stephenson had brought "the first memorandum in any country which foretold with scientific conviction the practical possibility of a bomb and the horrors it would bring."* These fateful notes raised the specter of a German empire using the immense resources of Europe to build an atomic bomb. Only a totalitarian state, it was thought, could mobilize the huge industrial capacity, labor, and raw materials necessary to produce "the ultimate weapon." The memorandum was the product of years of British scientific research and espionage. All information on the matter should be restricted to the smallest possible circle, Stephenson had said. "If Germany conquers Britain, the way is clear for development of this weapon with which Hitler can blackmail the rest of the world. The Fuehrer has under his control the *doyen* of nuclear physicists, Niels Bohr, in Occupied Denmark. While Hitler remains preoccupied with military adventures, he may overlook this opportunity. Give him respite," Stephenson concluded, "and he will make this new weapon of horror."

"We've gone some distance in that direction our-

* From an official report, *Britain and Atomic Energy, 1939–1945,* by Margaret Gowing, later published by Macmillan, London.

119

selves," Donovan said to Stephenson when he read the scientific report known now as the Frisch-Peierls Paper. "But Hitler's got the power to mobilize men and material which neither of us have. If he conquers Britain, he'll capture the best brains in the business."

"Then we agree?"

"Of course," said Donovan, surprised.

He was a large man, fifty-seven years old to Stephenson's forty-four, and twice his size. They referred to each other as "Big Bill" and "Little Bill." They were strolling in New York, and paused by Trinity churchyard at the corner of Broadway and Wall Street. Stephenson nodded toward a 1794 tombstone. "There's our biggest need."

Big Bill Donovan peered between the rails at a cipher engraved on the stone. The grim admonition "Remember Death" was transcribed into a simple code of the sort often seen on old tombs.

Donovan said: "If unbreakable ciphers and safe communications are what you've got in mind, you'll need automation, cipher clerks, space, and transmitters—but where and how?"

"Here. Using staff *recruited* in Canada. With FBI help."

"And Hoover?"

"The FBI's backing us."

Donovan always remembered that moment standing by the churchyard dating back to the time a British monarch once tried to keep his American colonies by force. It was then he glimpsed the magnitude of the task ahead and the delicate political balance he would have to maintain.

A signal from INTREPID reached C in London on July 15, 1940:

COLONEL WILLIAM J DONOVAN PERSONALLY REPRESENTING PRESIDENT LEFT YESTERDAY BY CLIPPER. . . . UNITED STATES EMBASSY NOT REPEAT NOT BEING INFORMED. . . .

The reason for keeping Donovan's journey secret from the Embassy was Kennedy's continuing defeatism. He had written Roosevelt: "England is fighting for her possessions. They are not fighting Hitler. . . . They will spend every hour figuring how to get us in." And he warned American businessmen that Britain was broke and lacked even gold to pay for arms.

To King George VI, Stephenson sent another message, under the traditional cover marked: "For Your Eyes Only." It said:

DONOVAN BY VIRTUE OF HIS VERY INDEPENDENCE OF THOUGHT AND ACTION INEVITABLY HAS HIS CRITICS BUT NONE WILL DENY CREDIT THAT IS HIS DUE FOR REACHING CORRECT APPRAISAL OF INTERNATIONAL SITUATION. THE AMERICAN GOVERNMENT IS DEBATING TWO ALTERNATIVE COURSES OF ACTION. ONE WOULD KEEP BRITAIN IN THE WAR WITH SUPPLIES NOW DESPERATELY NEEDED. OTHER IS TO GIVE BRITAIN UP FOR LOST. DONOVAN IS PRESIDENT'S MOST TRUSTED PERSONAL ADVISOR DESPITE POLITICAL DIFFERENCES AND I URGE YOU TO BARE YOUR BREAST TO HIM.

Donovan reached London by way of Lisbon in the role of a bluff American businessman. Within hours he was talking with the King, who handed him the latest ULTRA recovery from the Enigma-enciphered directive issued the previous day, Tuesday, July 16, by Hitler: "Since England, in spite of her hopeless military situation, shows no sign of being ready to come to an understanding, I have decided to prepare a landing operation against England . . . to eliminate England as a base for the prosecution of the war against Germany." The British intelligence report concluded that the main enemy sea-borne assault would be aimed at suitable beaches on the east and south coasts, while paratroops might be dropped on the scale of 15,000 in a single day in areas like East Anglia and Kent. But Hitler was demanding first that "the English Air Force must be so reduced morally and physically that it is unable to deliver any significant attack against the German crossing."

The first stage of the Battle of Britain was being

fought overhead. The King joked about Buckingham Palace providing a conspicuous target. One bomb did miss the King and Queen by a few hundred feet. It became apparent to Donovan that these monarchs had no plans to run away.

A mild Marxist professor, J. B. S. Haldane, experimented on the River Thames with floating mines which were "detonated when the action of the water dissolves the retaining pin—a cough drop." Professor Haldane's assistants were schoolboys, who gleefully explained to Donovan how these improvised gadgets would blow up German barges. In crumbling English mansions, Donovan listened to leggy girls in tweed skirts teach the techniques of Gestapo interrogation. But he also met Englishmen who were sharply critical of romantic versions of their plight: men like George Orwell, who attacked the Ruling Class in an essay of that title, quoting what he called a piece of Shakespeare bombast: "Come the four corners of the world in arms / And we shall shock them: / Naught shall make us rue / If England to herself do rest but true." All very well, said Orwell, but the country would not be true to herself until she produced a revolution. The heirs of Nelson and Cromwell were not in the House of Lords, but in fields and streets, the factories and the armed forces, in the four-ale bar and the suburban back garden. "And at present they are still kept under by a generation of ghosts—the ladies in their Rolls-Royces, the company directors still fiddling their way around wartime laws. . . . Compared with the task of bringing the real England to the surface, even the winning of the war, necessary though it is, is secondary."

Three days after Hitler formally decided to "eliminate England," the real England found its voice. Churchill informed the War Cabinet of the creation of a body "to coordinate all action by way of subversion and sabotage against the enemy." The body was described for the record as Special Operations Executive, otherwise known as the Baker Street Irregulars. The identity of British Security Coordination was not disclosed until the United States came into the war; its headquarters in New York was never officially acknowledged.

Bill Donovan's presence in London for this secret declaration of unconventional warfare was, of course, essential. The President's agent had to see that BSC in New York was the fountainhead of all armed resistance that would be conducted in an offensive spirit. To the general public, it looked as if Britain could do nothing but absorb the punishment handed out by Hitler until the defenses collapsed.

The supreme trial had begun on July 10, which, unknown to the victims at the time, marked the opening of the Battle of Britain. The defending forces consisted of Hurricane and Spitfire single-engine fighters, which the Germans hoped to wear down in daily air battles. The main German assault on British Fighter Command was scheduled for August 10, according to Bletchley analysts. Hitler set the date of invasion for September 15 and called it OPERATION SEALION.

During these anxious days, Donovan talked to the Irregulars about underground warfare. He met Colin Gubbins, whom he knew as the author of the study written two years before based on the argument that "the coming war with Germany will have to be fought by irregular or guerrilla forces." Gubbins was now in charge of training saboteurs, agents, and the leaders of secret armies. His Irregulars worked behind a facade of commercial offices between Westminster and Soho. Some of their recruits were drawn from 20,000 Poles who had escaped from France; and the Dutch, Free French, Norwegians, and Belgians who had slipped across the narrow seas to continue the struggle against Nazism. Their instructors had been on secret missions to Russia and China. They had studied guerrilla warfare from the Boer War in South Africa to the Civil War in Spain, and Mao Tse-tung's Long March from Shanghai to Yennan.

The countryside was sprinkled with old mansions earmarked as schools for spies. There were agencies for political warfare and special operations. Something new, called "black" propaganda, was defined by its director as "the only answer to a lie."

"But there's only one answer to a lie," said Donovan. "And that's the truth."

"Yes, yes, yes. The truth. Exactly. Even if you have to bend it a little."

The truth-bender was a newspaper executive. Prominent bankers ran departments of economic warfare. A professor of ancient history, seconded to the cipher school, confessed that he was completely defeated in his attempts to thread a path through the shrubbery of cloak and dagger. "Some of my dear colleagues," he muttered darkly, "will be lost in that maze for years to come."

On the weekend following Donovan's arrival, Hitler's "final peace offer" was broadcast to Britain: "I consider myself in a position to make this appeal since I am not the vanquished seeking favors, but the victor speaking in the name of reason."

Within the hour, an insulting reply hit Berlin. It was delivered, without the British government even being consulted, by a newspaperman. Hitler's grandiose offer of peace was not even discussed by Churchill's War Cabinet, which had dispersed for the unshakable ritual of a weekend in the country. The vulgar nose-thumbing reply was left to Sefton Delmer, of Lord Beaverbrook's London *Daily Express,* who ran a center of propaganda dirty tricks at the Duke of Bedford's Woburn Abbey, ten miles east of Bletchley Park. When Delmer sat before a microphone that night of Friday, July 19, he had no authority—and neither had the British Broadcasting Corporation—to respond to Hilter's speech. In idiomatic German he spoke directly to the Führer: "Let me tell you what we here in Britain think of this appeal to what you are pleased to call our reason and commonsense. Herr Fuehrer and Reichskanzler, we hurl it right back at you. Right back into your evil-smelling teeth."

Nobody at the BBC questioned the sentiment. The final insult to Hitler was that the British government had not even troubled to discuss his peace offer. All Hitler could do was mutter back the threat of "an exceptionally daring undertaking"; meaning invasion.

Donovan made friends with a young English girl who typified this defiance of Hitler. She was Joan Bright, a stenographer who became a key figure in Allied war-making although her salary never rose to more than the equivalent of twenty dollars a week. She typified the adventurous, emotionally stable, selfless youngsters attracted to dangerous work without the reward or encouragement of public acclaim. From her mid-teens, she had sought whatever experience and knowledge she found stimulating, taking secretarial jobs in remote parts of the world and thus giving herself an unorthodox education. A year before the war, a friend told her of "work that might interest you." She was to stand inside St. James's Park Underground station at 11:00 A.M. on a certain day wearing a pink carnation. She would be approached by a woman. She went, was duly picked up, found herself taken by a circuitous route that constantly changed direction to the office of a colonel, who, warning her of tortures to come if caught, required her to sign the Official Secrets Act, and then explained that on leaving the building she must avoid certain street characters visible from his window. If such lurking observers identified her with intelligence, her name would go on the German Black List of those to be exterminated when Britain fell.

Donovan was aware that the Tyler Kent case had sharpened suspicions within this armed camp. Counter-espionage experts described to him how the American Embassy leak was plugged. A start had been made with the Double Cross System, by which German agents came under British control so that the next enemy infiltrator and his controllers could be led down the wrong path. "Wrong for them, right for us," murmured one Oxford don in charge of double agents.

A broadcasting station was being set up near Bletchley to beam very strange programs indeed into Germany, concocted by an anti-Nazi Berliner, Paul Sanders, once a writer of detective stories, now a British Army corporal. Sanders invented a conspiracy among German generals against Hitler. Then he created an imaginary network of radio stations run by the rebels. His transmitter near Bletchley was to operate in such a way that it seemed to be located inside Germany. The broadcasts were to be irregular, using different call signs, designed to excite Nazi watchdogs. Corporal

Sanders had a cast of characters led by "Der Chef," an imaginary German general in charge of this fictitious conspiracy. "By constantly changing transmission times and frequencies, we hope to keep a good part of the Gestapo busy chasing shadows," Sanders told Donovan. "We might even get some good Nazis arrested."

Such dirty tricks were inventive, certainly, but Donovan wondered if British ingenuity was enough. The German Air Force was attacking ships in the English Channel to lure British fighters into aerial battles, hoping the RAF would lose not only precious aircraft but also pilots. The pattern was set by an engagement on July 10 in which six RAF Hurricanes found themselves grossly outnumbered by long-range Messerschmitt 110s and short-range 109s escorting Dornier bombers. The skirmish drew other RAF squadrons into the fight, and into battle with other decoys. Over 600 British sorties were flown that day, twice the daily average during the Dunkirk withdrawal. The wear and tear rose in the days that followed. The Germans would lunge at relatively unimportant targets, which the RAF felt compelled to defend. Teasing attacks on ships were carried out by German dive bombers, while swift and deadly fighters waited up-sun to fall upon the British drawn into range. "We never had time to gain height before we were attacked," reported the chief of RAF Fighter Command, Air Marshal Hugh Dowding.

But inventiveness was paying off, Donovan discovered. Told about a scientist who "started work on a death-ray in 1934," Donovan expected a crank. Instead, he met Robert Watson-Watt, who had worked with Stephenson in that year on the rudimentary system later called "radar." At Stephenson's request, Watson-Watt risked arrest just before the Nazi invasion of Poland to travel through Germany looking for signs of parallel work in radar detection. By the time of the Battle of Britain, radar stations along England's coasts worked closely with a sophisticated system of fighter direction and control. Radar and visual information were fed into the central control rooms buried in the countryside. British fighters were then directed onto enemy formations. With practice, less and less time was wasted in the air, with a consequent saving in frayed nerves, engine wear, and fuel.

The Germans had no radar at this time and were puzzled by a growing British discrimination between feints and real attacks. There was another explanation for this skill. ULTRA was beginning to develop confidence in its ability to read and interpret orders to the German Air Force. This information was not vital to RAF victory, but together with radar it demonstrated that mechanized barbarism could be outwitted.

"I've always believed in the superiority of mind over matter," Watson-Watt told Donovan. "But, by God, we suffered from some witless leaders before the war. Stephenson and private enterprise helped me in the 1920s. Bill understood what I was doing because it was close to his own work with the rudiments of television. By the 1930s, he was able to get me secret support. If I'd relied on the British government, there'd have been no radar and no Spitfires."

On the tenth day of Donovan's journey, the London newspapers reprinted an editorial from the New York *Times*:

It is twelve o'clock in London. . . . Is the tongue of Chaucer, of Shakespeare, of Milton, of the King James version of the Scriptures, of Keats, of Shelley, to be hereafter, in the British Isles, the dialect of an enslaved race?

Let us try to see clearly. We have to look back a good many centuries to find the beginnings of English liberty. We see it as a rough and obstinate growth, heaving the rich soil under the oaks of lordly estates, breaking out in Wat Tyler's time and in Cromwell's and in the day of the Second James, forcing through the Reform Act, never perfected, never giving up. . . .

It is twelve o'clock in London. Not twelve o'clock for empire—there is no empire any more. Not twelve o'clock from the old "Dominion over Palm and Pine." Twelve o'clock for the common people of England, out of whom England's greatest souls have always come. Twelve o'clock for all that they are and have been, for all those things

127

which make life worth living for free men . . . We know little, and for a time shall know little, of this unparalleled spectacle of the nation rising as by a single impulse.

The rising, on the face of it, was one of spirits more than arms. There was a Home Guard of a million civilians, with 20,000 sporting guns to repel the invaders. Churchill reckoned that the available ammunition provided one bullet for every 2,000 Germans, judging by the size of Nazi forces committed to the invasion. Some fifty Lee-Enfield rifles had been unearthed behind the stage at Drury Lane, and a clutch of Indian mutiny rifles, circa 1857, was found in Manchester Zoo. The American Committee for the Defense of British Homes shipped 160 crates of shotguns and pistols to be shared among civilians. "The loss of these rifles would be a disaster of the first order," said Churchill to the naval commander who had to protect this pitiful shipment from U-boats.

Two weeks after arriving in Britain, Donovan wrote a note to Stephenson:

The defenders share a total of 786 field guns, 167 anti-tank guns, and 259 inadequate tanks, enough for two divisions against the forty German divisions waiting across the Channel. There are just over a thousand pilots left in the RAF, shredded by meat-grinding air attacks. The Royal Navy looks like a fleet of old bath tubs riddled with holes. The loss of destroyers in evacuating the troops from Dunkirk leaves the navy in no shape to stop an invasion. I have seen the *Orders Concerning the Organization and Function of the Military Government of England* instructing the German gauleiters on the liquidation of all intellectuals and all Jews. This is to be done under the direction of the former dean of political science at Berlin University, Dr. Franz Six. All other Englishmen between 17 and 45 are to be deported to Germany as slaves. The SS is to select mates from among its finest men to impregnate Englishwomen and breed a new race.

128

The two British islands of Guernsey and Jersey were now occupied. Hitler had English soil under his boots for the first time since he was a poor student in Liverpool before World War I. Few knew about Hitler's sojourn in the largest shipping center in the British Empire. He celebrated the capture of the Channel Islands on his fifty-second birthday, more than a quarter-century after his first glimpse of this maritime power. From these islands, Hitler intended to dispatch SS officers charged with the task of establishing liquidation centers in London, Bristol, Birmingham, Manchester, and Edinburgh. Special arrangements were specified in the Military Government Orders for Liverpool, where the selection of victims was to be especially harsh. Hitler, clearly, had not forgotten Liverpool.*

Yet Churchill directed the Irregulars to "Set Europe Ablaze." Baker Street maps of Europe were plastered with code names that represented great expectations and small realities. TROJAN and HORSE looked like a web centered on Paris but amounted to nothing more formidable than an agent and his radio operator still waiting in England to go. A printer from Leighton Buzzard, drawn into the nearby Bletchley web, protested that he could not produce edible editions ("to be swallowed if captured") of *The Partisans' Guide* on his flatbed press. The Ministry of Agriculture dis-

---

* Hitler's little-known sojourn in England between November 1912 and April 1913 is authenticated by BSC documents and an unpublished account by Bridget Elizabeth Hitler, "My Brother-in-law Adolf." Hitler's brother Alois married the actress Bridget Elizabeth Dowling in London in 1910. They lived at 120 Upper Stanhope Street, Texteth Park, Liverpool, and ran a small restaurant nearby. When the son of Alois, William Patrick Hitler, moved to New York in 1940, he disclosed details of the Liverpool period, taken from his mother's diaries and letters, before himself adopting another name. He was known to BSC as PEARL. His usefulness as a souce of information on the Führer was limited, but as a link with Hitler's brief life in England, he added a curious footnote to history. BSC records suggest that Adolf Hitler spent much of his time watching the flow of sea traffic through Liverpool to the four corners of the British Empire, undoubtedly impressed by this evidence of maritime power.

tributed pamphlets on wartime vegetable-growing, in which were concealed tips on blowing up invaders tramping through the fields of Hereford and Hertfordshire.

Each hamlet had its own guerrilla detachment and tunnels so well concealed that some villagers remained unaware of them thirty years later. Donovan was taken into the secret by that extraordinary product of another age Colonel Eric Bailey, the explorer and former British agent in Central Asia (whose collection of rare butterflies later went to the Metropolitan Museum of Art in New York). Bailey was nearing his sixtieth year but refused to recognize this. He ran his own guerrilla unit as if he were still His Majesty's Envoy Extraordinary and Minister Plenipotentiary at the Court of Nepal, his last official post, off in the Himalayas, where he had once conducted military expeditions. Bailey knew better than to question Donovan's appearance in his village, accompanied by a British general. The party repaired to Bailey's observation post near the Norfolk coast.

"Suppose you spotted enemy paratroopers here," said the general, "and Germans landing on the beaches over here. What would you do?"

Bailey peered down the hillside. "How many? Precisely where? Moving in what direction?" He peppered the general with questions, to which the dignitary replied with improvised details.

"Well," said Bailey, "I'd order my chaps back there to do such-and-such, and then our fellows back in the woods to move thus-and-thus. . . ."

"But how would you get the orders away?" demanded the general. "You've no radio and you're exposed up here, so you can't very well use signals."

"I've already got the orders away," Bailey replied. He lifted a sack lining his observation trench, revealing the end of a pipe. The pipe ran underground to his signal office under the village church. While the general talked, Bailey had scribbled notes he inserted into old tennis balls and rolled down the pipe. It was his communications system.

Donovan and Bailey became friends. Later, Bailey moved to New York to work for Stephenson as a

King's Messenger, carrying BSC's confidential papers around the world. "He sighed for the simpler days," Donovan would recall. "Rolling tennis balls down drainpipes, waiting to stick a German with a pitchfork, struck him as healthier than being stuffed into the gun turret of a bomber to be ferried back and forth."

Bailey wanted to get into the offensive side of operations. His ideas for industrial sabotage were also deadly simple. But he was up against stiff competition. Gubbins had collected some real geniuses in Baker Street. "Insurance adjustors, for instance," he told Donovan. "Clever blighters. In peacetime, they deal with claims for damages from factories. So they know what puts a machine out of action—fast. For example, the weak link in the chain of certain manufacturing processes may be the sulphuric-acid factories. You can knock one out with a well-placed hammer! You drive it through one of the gigantic clay vats holding the acid. The clay cracks. And in wartime, those vats are irreplaceable."

All this, too, captured Donovan's imagination. But was there enough time? On the last day of July, a secret session of the House of Commons was warned by Churchill that a dreadful month lay ahead: "Hitler may try to bomb and gas the country before landing. Italy and Japan will snarl and snap like jackals."

The very next day, another powerful nation bared its teeth. The Soviet Union accused Britain of prolonging the war by spurning Hitler's peace offers. This attack, from Foreign Minister Molotov, opening the seventh session of the USSR's Supreme Council, meant more than Russian moral support for Germany. It carried a message for all members of the Communist parties in Britain and America. Wherever Communists manipulated the workers—loading ships in U.S. ports for the dangerous supply runs to Britain, in American factories beginning to produce weapons, even in Britain's own vital industries—there would be strikes and go-slow campaigns and a betrayal of men dying at sea and in the air.

This brought Donovan's Irish temper to a boil. He prided himself upon hiding it; his value to Roosevelt was built on iron self-control. There had been a moment when he thought he should call on Kennedy at the U.S. Embassy. Now, unsure about keeping his temper in check, he let the temptation pass. "Joe's joined the knockers and the kickers," he told Stephenson. The Ambassador deplored the fact that Americans in London had formed the 1st American squadron of the RAF and wore British Home Guard uniforms with red eagles for shoulder flashes. And Kennedy's dispatches, becoming more defeatist than ever, matched those of Ambassador William Bullitt in France, who believed the physical and moral defeat of the French had been so complete that "they accept the fate of becoming a province of Nazi Germany [and] hope England will be rapidly and completely defeated." Just to make the British feel better about the desertions and betrayals, the French General Léon Huntziger told German General Walther von Brauchitsch: "France is fighting with Germany against Britain."

Despite Donovan's discretion, Kennedy soon learned of the presence in his bailiwick of the President's special agent. "Kennedy was furious at the intrusion and did his best to sabotage the mission," said a British Foreign Office historian, Nicholas Bethell, after the files were opened for the first time thirty-three years later. "Even the British diplomatic world knew nothing about Donovan when he arrived." Kennedy tried to limit Donovan's contacts, not knowing what powerful patrons stood behind him, by making it appear that Donovan was writing articles for U.S. publications—an ingenious move, because stringent British censorship would place Donovan at a disadvantage. Foreign journalists were regarded as a potential source of security leaks.

Lord Halifax, then still Foreign Secretary, wrote: "The U.S. Ambassador is somewhat embarrassed by [Donovan's] presence here and regards him as a newspaperman employed by Colonel Knox for his own newspaper [the Chicago *Daily News*]. It would seem therefore out of the question to treat him as a high official of the U.S. Government."

Donovan was due to report back to the White

132

House early in August. He lingered on, feeling something in common with people for whom the luxury and trappings of normal life were abruptly gone. Joan Bright, the girl in the middle of it all, later described, in *The Inner Circle,* "the relief to feel responsible, within one's own limitations, for one's own salvation. We hugged London to our beating hearts. London was ours from the hour the blacked-out night hid its beauty until the morning siren signalled the coming day. . . ."

Donovan found Bright at the heart of a labyrinth of tunnels under Whitehall, known as "The Hole in the Ground." The maze of underground rooms had been dungeons where fusty old documents were stored. At the bottom of a spiral staircase was the War Room where Churchill held forth. He usually sat in a wooden chair at the head of the conference table. When Donovan visited, he bumped into the Prime Minister balancing a food tray in the subterranean canteen, followed by the Chief of the Imperial General Staff. Churchill was in his "boilersuit," which zipped down the front and made him look like a large Teddy Bear. The corridors were lit by candles stuck in lanterns. The walls were damp. Ugly tubes snaked through the labyrinth, emitting odd pings and whistles whenever a message cannister propelled by compressed air whizzed at thirty miles an hour from one government post to another.

Amid the banging and hollow whistles of the tubes sat Joan Bright, keeping tabs on the Joint Planning Staff and the Joint Intelligence Committee. Above The Hole, enemy bombers were less than one hour's flying time from the crag at Felsennest, from which Hitler said he would direct his invasion. In The Hole, Bright and her "secret ladies"—girl secretaries with high security clearances—giggled over the Führer's rumored plan to terrify the islanders with "war crocodiles," which would carry 200 armed men in each concrete belly as they crawled along the bottom of the English Channel.

Their counterplans, however, looked pathetic by contrast. They seemed to be little more than neatly handwritten notes on file cards in Bright's index to the future prosecution of an aggressive war. Cards for Major Strategy had an orange edge; most of Europe was blue; the Iberian Peninsula, Africa, and Latin America were pale pink; and there was no edging at all for Asia.

The world in her shoe-box file was easily condensed. A/SPEC.OPS/1: Planning for Irregular and Subversive Activities; B/FOES/1: Formation of Future Operations (Enemy) Section; C/COMB.OPS/1: Landing Craft . . . The whole tone was belligerent. Nothing here about evacuating the Home Fleet to American bases. Instead, the colored eight-by-five inch cards referred to assaults and captures, demolitions and attacks, and future military expeditions to places not marked on the 1901 Navy League map behind Churchill's chair. One card was labeled B/SOE/1: Formation of Special Operations Executive. This referred to the red file labeled INTREPID and a red-bordered card calling for *"a reign of terror conducted by specially trained agents and fortified by espionage and intelligence so that the lives of German troops in Occupied Europe be made an intense torment."*

All this in a shoe box, thought Donovan. Was it reality? He said later to Stephenson: "In those dungeons under Whitehall, you step into a Shakespearean play with stage directions like 'Army Heard in Distance, Sound of Trumpets. . . .' You know there isn't an army, but it's hard to be sure, down there in the theatre."

Reality was a wooden signpost outside War Lord Churchill's conference room. Four cards could be put into a slot: COLD, SUNNY, FINE, WINDY. For the men and women who worked in The Hole, rain was an academic question when they were sometimes there for weeks on end without ever coming up. More often the signpost informed the troglodytes of the degree of aerial bombing above. For all its impressive superstructure and reinforced tunneling, The Hole would collapse under a direct hit or a near-miss.

Donovan was kept informed of Hitler's progress with OPERATION SEALION through the German orders plucked out of thin air by the ULTRA teams. Now, on the Thursday that Russia joined in kicking an apparently fallen Britain, the Führer issued Directive No. 17: "Establish the necessary conditions for the final conquest of England." The German Air Force was to overpower the RAF before the invasion. "I reserve to myself," Hitler added, "the right to decide on terror tactics. . . ."

None of this seemed to strike terror among Donovan's new friends. Instead, they showed him a device to turn the landing beaches into blazing infernos. The secrecy surrounding the weapon was such that many historians have since thought the whole thing was a British deception. Donovan's biographer, Corey Ford, wrote of "ingenious British propaganda devices, including the carefully planted rumor that a system of underwater pipelines could turn every beach and cove into a sea of flaming oil." The system did exist and led to Pluto, the Pipe Line under the Ocean, which would eventually carry oil from Britain to Allied forces storming Hitler's Fortress Europe. But it was first conceived as a deterrent.

"Stephenson proposed a Petroleum Warfare Department and flame-throwing weapons," Donovan was told. "PWD laid perforated pipelines out to sea and along the coast. The whole system could be ignited when the Germans landed. Churchill loved the scheme because he was convinced Hitler had a superstitious dread of fire."

When Donovan reluctantly left, the Germans had launched the mass bomber raids that were a prelude to invasion. He was convinced the British would pit ingenuity against invasion, even if they had to retreat underground for years to come. Back in Washington, he reported to Roosevelt that American aid should be accelerated and increased because "here is the first line of our own defense. If the British are reduced to guerrilla campaigns against a Nazi occupation, it will take Americans a generation to regain a foothold in Europe. And from what I have learned here about Nazi fifth-column methods, we in America by then may find it's too late to save ourselves."

Ambassador Kennedy reported that Britain was done. German air raids had employed only a fraction of the vast armadas that Charles Lindbergh had described to him in such graphic detail. When the real blitz got underway, London would be razed. He would endure a month of bombing, Kennedy announced, and then leave.

The Foreign Office expert on U.S. affairs, Professor North Whitehead, wrote mildly that "it looks as if he was thoroughly frightened and has gone to pieces. If his 'foreign policy' prevails, we will be left alone to be torn apart, piece by piece."

18

"I'M YOUR BIGGEST undercover agent," President Roosevelt said to Bill Stephenson after a frank disclosure of what a puppet British government might do to preserve the islanders from Hitler's worst excesses. The President was scarcely joking. The barbarians had overrun much of civilized Europe since he had ordered the FBI to join with British intelligence to work against Nazi subversion. Now, in early July 1940, the same logic propelled him another giant step toward deep involvement.

The secret alliance had seemed necessary when the British and French empires stood shoulder to shoulder. Now one empire had collapsed. Paris was stamped with the crooked cross. And Prime Minister Churchill was privately warning that he could not answer for his successors if Britain were occupied. She might become part of a united Nazi Europe whose combined fleets would control the oceans and put a Nazi gun at American heads.

The distant British garrison under Churchill might survive if life lines to America remained open. Roosevelt knew this. Could he convince his own people? The life lines to England were under constant U-boat attack. Convoys were betrayed by German agents in

U.S. ports. Stephenson was creating a police force to guard the cargoes of supplies and arms piling up in those ports, but he wanted more help from U.S. radio-detection stations to hunt enemy submarines. "Foreign police on American soil and Americans in a foreign conflict" was the way the President's enemies would portray these developments. Still, London's demands on BSC continued to grow, and Stephenson tried to meet them, his organization expanding in every direction.

"My secret legs" was Roosevelt's wistful description of Donovan. The President, trapped in his wheelchair, had less flattering names for ex-Prime Minister Chamberlain and those who still dealt with Hitler. He knew them, through Stephenson, as the Better-Notters. What was happening in Britain might foreshadow events in the United States—the War-Wagers in London had won power in time to see the war being apparently lost.

Roosevelt hoped such pessimism was ill-founded, but some of his own military advisers, though contemptuous of Britain's Better-Notters, admired Germany's military efficiency. Their views were shared by such private counselors as William Allen White. "What an avalanche of blunders Great Britain has let loose upon the democracies of the world!" he had written. "The old British lion looks mangy, sore-eyed. . . . He can't even roar." When the Better-Notters were thrown out by the British, however, White began campaigning for aid to Britain, because this would buy time for Americans to prepare for the inevitable attack upon themselves.

A Better-Notter had been British ambassador to Washington since the start of the war. He was Lord Lothian, whose family motto was *Sero Sed Serio* (Late but in Earnest). He had actually arrived several months late, long after his appointment was announced. He was a relic of the Cliveden Set, which thought Hitler's greed could be satisfied on scraps. Lothian had the grace to let Stephenson pursue his covert diplomacy, asking only that formal agreements go through the Embassy. Otherwise, he was bypassed as efficiently as Ambassador Kennedy was in London.

The undiplomatic question that had to be asked the President was would he run for a third term.

If Britain had sued for peace that summer, as might have happened had the Chamberlain appeasers won the day, "nothing would have made Roosevelt face another campaign," Stephenson had advised Churchill. "But FDR knew we depended on him as much as America depended on us. He was the single factor weighing the scales in our favor. If he seemed to be running as our candidate, the isolationists would accuse him of delivering the United States back into the British Empire. Then he would lose, and so would we." Stephenson believes FDR made the decision to run because Churchill was resolved to fight on. The evidence of British resourcefulness was to be seen in the mounting success of ULTRA and Bletchley's service to the White House. But some of Churchill's pressure on the President evoked a sharp warning from Stephenson: "All democratic governments in the run-up to an election are obliged to go to the country on a ticket of peace, no matter what the grim truth. Exercise patience. Recognize the basic good sense, generosity and instinct for doing the right thing that prevails among Americans."

This was difficult counsel to give. "It required real courage," said Lord Louis Mountbatten, the King's cousin. "He had to tell the British to be patient when we needed urgent action, and urge action on Americans who wanted any excuse to be patient."

Stephenson showed physical courage, too. "It gave the FBI the shudders and had to be kept from the President," said Ian Fleming, who had heard directly from J. Edgar Hoover about one incident. "A British seaman was selling information on convoys. Little Bill tracked down the traitor after seeing the decoded recoveries from a Nazi transmitter in New York. The signals told U-boats where to intercept British ships with the most militarily valuable cargoes. Bill went out that afternoon and was back in his office by nightfall. The FBI man on the case said to him: 'Someone ought to give the treacherous son of a bitch the chop.'

"Bill glanced down at his right hand. He lifted it

138

and chopped at an angle against the hardwood surface of his desk.

" 'I already have,' he said.

"The FBI thought he was joking, until the man was found dead in the basement of an apartment building."

Fleming's comment was: "There was overwhelming evidence against the seaman. Killing him quickly perhaps saved hundreds of sailors' lives and precious supplies. It did him a favor, too, saving a long journey to an English trial; and after many proceedings, the hangman's rope. Saved his Majesty's Government a lot of time and money, too." However, the Under-Secretary of State, Sumner Welles, later wrote that the zeal of British intelligence sometimes seemed excessive; and Stephenson tried to save the U.S. authorities any embarrassment from such incidents.* He had far too much at stake to jeopardize relations with the President.

Their first formal meeting was conducted in the presence of the British Ambassador and was confined to the shopping list of destroyers, aircraft, guns, steel, and ammunition desperately needed to replace the supplies the British had abandoned in Europe. Then Roosevelt and Stephenson were left alone to discuss British Security Coordination. The debacle of Dunkirk had shaken even FDR's confidence in the British. His misgivings were not in any way relieved by the continuing prophecies of doom from his Ambassador in London, and Bill Donovan was not ready yet to report. FDR was cheered, however, by Stephenson's description of "the cold chill that ran down the spines of the staff at 10 Downing Street when they heard Churchill was to become prime minister." Plans were well underway for guerrilla warfare if Britain should be occupied; and this secret army would link up with European partisans. If London fell, direction would come from BSC, now combining what were known officially as British Secret Intelligence Service, Special

* In *Seven Major Decisions,* Sumner Welles described reaction to "so flagrant a violation of American sovereignty" when British intelligence rounded up alleged deserters from ships in Baltimore.

Operations Executive, and Security Executive, all quartered in New York.

Stephenson was already known as a modest but forceful industrialist. There was a risk that he was also known in Washington as chief of British secret intelligence, reporting directly to Churchill. Obviously, he could not be identified as a confidant of President Roosevelt.

The President's own concern was evident in a letter he wrote to the Governor-General of Canada. Lord Tweedsmuir, better known as the writer of spy thrillers John Buchan, had proposed to visit Roosevelt at Hyde Park to discuss the use of Canada as the meeting and training ground for secret intelligence and other forms of "un-neutral" collaboration. The President discouraged this notion: "The first [reason] is that you could not 'slip down inconspicuously.' . . . The second reason is that . . . I am at the moment saying nothing, seeing nothing and hearing nothing."

Stephenson's meetings with Roosevelt were, therefore, discreet and kept to a minimum. His recollection of the first encounters was impressionistic: the speed and efficiency of the White House staff, the sudden meeting in the Oval Room with the familiar figure; hearing the warm, aristocratic voice; seeing the heavy head cocked to one side before a tray of half-consumed scrambled eggs and coffee placed beside the President's swivel chair; the cluttered desk alongside; and the adjacent door leading into the small private bedroom. FDR had the presence of a man in great office. Since Stephenson carried within himself another kind of authority, which Roosevelt acknowledged, there was none of the usual lighthearted banter. The President, his large frame informally clad, his sunken eyes sharp and inquiring, towered, even in the chair. Sometimes the eyes twinkled, and a bleak smile broke through.

Roosevelt wished to be given the flavor of Churchill the War Lord. Stephenson said: "There has never been such a rapid transformation of opinion as in the first twenty-three days between Winston's appointment and Dunkirk, nor such a swift acceleration in the tempo of business. The whole machinery of government is working at a pace and with an intensity of purpose unlike anything before. His leadership produces a new sense of unbeatability as well as urgency. Decisions taken in these first few days are of utmost consequence to the free world. They are supported only by the most slender resources spread all over the map. The War Cabinet is under terrific strain. The paperwork alone requires each minister to read the equivalent to two Victorian novels a day. There's no time for clashes of personality within this small group."

Roosevelt, sounding wistful, quoted from Shakespeare's *King Henry V:* "He which hath no stomach to this fight, Let him depart. . . . But we in it shall be remembered; We few, we happy few, we band of brothers; For he today that sheds his blood with me Shall be my brother. . . ." A few weeks later, he heard the words echoed in Churchill's tribute to RAF pilots who fought the Battle of Britain.

When ULTRA retrieved Hitler's invasion plans and their cover name, SEALION, Churchill prepared a speech. The penciled notes were shown to Roosevelt. As usual, Churchill had broken down key sentences into blank verse, and one phrase was this:

> . . . *essence of defence*
> *is to attack the enemy upon us*
> *leap at his throat*
> *and keep the grip until the life is out of him.*

In this way, offering the President glimpses of the War Lord at work, knowing that Big Bill Donovan would see the realities and state his own novel arguments, Stephenson opposed conventional American military detachment. Britain needed the fifty mothballed destroyers. Stephenson argued that they would at least assure the survival of the British Isles as bases for launching guerrilla raids against Hitler, even if the islanders were forced to retreat into caves and underground battle stations.

The notion of Churchill's followers leaping at an invader's throat and keeping the grip "until the life is out of him" captured the President's imagination. So, too, the picture of The Hole, which Stephenson described as resembling the quarters of a battleship, where Churchill met with his War Cabinet. For a Navy buff like Roosevelt, appeals from Former Naval Person in such surroundings were hard to resist.

And appeals there were. "If we are cut off, if we lose the war at sea, nothing else will count!" Churchill cried. The Battle of the Atlantic, the cruelest and most long-drawn-out of any campaign, was crucial. After France fell, the Germans had been able to throw into that battle even their small short-range 250-ton U-boats, usually confined to the Baltic and the North Sea. French ports now serviced the submarines; torpedoes were trucked to them from Paris. French naval officer had let slip the secrets of asdic (named after an Allied Anti-Submarine Detection Investigation Committee). U-boat commanders, now knowing asdic's limitations, became bolder. Italy's declaration of war against Britain on June 10, when the defeat of France was inevitable, had jeopardized the Mediterranean shipping routes to Britain's eastern bases and added to the U-boats' over-all mobility. The number of German submarines and raiders in the Atlantic rose dramatically, twenty-two percent, in that month of June, and the numbers of British ships sunk rose tenfold. Furthermore, the Germans had broken the British naval codes; it would be another two months before London found out why the enemy betrayed such an uncanny foreknowledge of naval dispositions. ULTRA had not yet broken the German U-boat codes for their Enigma cipher machines.

American seamen were moved by the spectacle of a seagoing nation's lifeblood draining into the cold gray wastes. Out of 145,000 British merchant seamen who sailed the Atlantic in this perilous time, 32,000 died. They were civilians who went back to sea because they were sailors and thought they should. Others in Washington might fret over legalities, but British seamen recorded acts of American generosity that often went far beyond the frontiers of friendly neutrality. Royal Navy war diaries were full of stories reflecting the U.S. Navy's unofficial readiness to help.

Among the Americans who saw themselves as War-Wagers was the Pulitzer Prize-winning playwright

Robert Sherwood, destined to collaborate closely with Stephenson. Sherwood had gained fame as an antiwar writer. But with the evidence of Nazi evil before him, he confessed sadly that war was not the worst tragedy. In that grim summer of 1940, he was promoting aid for Britain when he was tackled by Harry Hopkins, who was to become the President's ambassador-at-large.

"What are you warmongers plotting now?" Hopkins demanded.

Sherwood replied that he was helping Stephenson get fifty old American destroyers. Hopkins protested that, with an election coming up, such public demands embarrassed Roosevelt. The playwright shrugged and said some of his colleagues were persuading Roosevelt's rivals to adopt the proposal, too. Anyway, it was in line with the President's general policy.

"What do you know about his policy?" snapped Hopkins. "You know this country is neutral."

Sherwood told Stephenson later that he was shaken by evidence that someone so close to the President should be a narrow-minded isolationist.

Hopkins remarked further, in curt terms, "The whole country's isolationist except for a few pro-British fanatics like you. If the President gave up fifty destroyers, how d'you suppose he'd keep the confidence of the people?"

Sherwood answered hotly: "You don't give the people credit for sense. They're a damn-sight more anti-Nazi than you think. It's time Roosevelt plucked up courage to speak frankly the way he's done before."

A sudden grin spread over Hopkins's lean face. "Then why waste your breath shouting at me? Say these things to the people yourself."

President Roosevelt was afraid he might defeat his own ends by outstripping public opinion. Tom Driberg, a British journalist and politician, saw this when he reported on "a notoriously pro-Nazi outfit called America First. . . . I went to a rally at which Charles Lindbergh spoke, in Madison Square Garden. It was as hysterical as any Hitler mob, but much more unpleasant. They sang *America First, Last and*

143

Always but could not sing *God Bless America* because it was written by a Jew. . . . Reading the full text of Lindbergh's speech, I realized that—the war having been on for a year, France and much else of civilization enslaved, London bombed, the march to the death camps underway—it contained no word of even mild disapproval of Hitler."

Other Americans held firmly to an opposite view. Admiral William Standley, who had been Chief of Naval Operations during Roosevelt's first term, put his name to a manifesto recognizing "the fact and the logic of the situation by declaring that a state of war exists between this country and Germany." Groups that supported Churchill were attacked by isolationist leaders with large followings. Father Coughlin said: "Sneakingly, subversively and un-Americanly hiding behind sanctimonious stuffed shirts, these men form the most dangerous fifth column. . . . They are the Judas Iscariots within the Apostolic college of our nation." Coughlin had sometimes used Joseph P. Kennedy as a channel to the President before Kennedy went to London as ambassador. Now Coughlin had drifted into fascism, enthusiasm for the corporate state, and a noisy anti-Semitism that so worried some influential American Jewish leaders that they feared to voice pro-British sentiments. In contrast, it was the son of a prominent Jewish banker who did more than almost any single man to further Stephenson's campaign for help, especially for the fifty destroyers. He was Henry Morgenthau, Jr., who joined the War-Wagers with gusto.

Morgenthau, a long-time neighbor of Roosevelt, had been unswervingly loyal to him since the outbreak of World War I. He worked in the state administration when Roosevelt became governor of New York, then followed his friend to the White House. As Secretary of the Treasury, he was the best ally Stephenson could have found, for he wielded direct power as an official and greater indirect influence as a trusted counselor to the President. He did his best to make sure that the Stephenson-Roosevelt relationship was never exposed, directing formal arrangements through the proper diplomatic channels or by way of a British Purchasing Mission run by another Canadian within the growing complex of Stephenson's organization in New York.

"After the Purchasing Mission opened shop at 15 Broad Street," Morgenthau said later, "swarms of salesmen from the garment district flocked to it, offering samples of women's underwear. It did no harm and reinforced the impression of open buying." The head of the mission was Arthur Purvis, "the leading Canadian industrialist, a man of the highest integrity, with no enemies and indeed no critics," in the words of John Buchan, then Governor-General of Canada. Purvis was to provide the surface gloss on Stephenson's economic endeavors until he was killed the following year in an air crash on the transatlantic run, which had become the unpublicized means of shuttling important cargoes quickly between the secret allies.

Morgenthau discussed with Stephenson the dire implications of the delay in getting help to Finland during the Russian invasion. The President had described the Soviet attack as "this dreadful rape," and it was estimated that ninety-eight percent of the American people shared his outrage. But the legality of transferring or selling surplus arms to the Finns had been argued between the State, War, Navy, and Treasury departments until the day the Russians finally broke the Mannerheim Line, when the Senate finally passed a totally useless bill for nonmilitary financial help.

Direct sales to Britain were regarded as illegal although Stephenson's American friends unearthed old bits of legislation to show how to circumvent the Neutrality Law, originally passed in 1936 to prevent the United States getting into war as it had in 1917. "It was purely retroactive," commented Stephenson, "but it effectively tied Roosevelt's hands." On the morning that the evacuation of Dunkirk was finished, Edward Stettinius had resigned as chairman of United States Steel to begin work on a plan to get the most urgently required arms to Britain. He was an old and trusted friend of Stephenson. Though he might be faulted for his impetuous declarations in public, he had a flair for dramatic action and anticipated Churchill's so-called beer-bottle speech. The new Prime Minister, promising to fight the German invaders with everything to hand, added in an aside what sounded like "with bloody beer bottles if necessary." Stettinius wrote later: "As the Prime Minister spoke, stack after stack of guns for the defenders of Britain were being moved from America's arsenals. . . . Word had been flashed all along the line to give them right of way." The legality that cleared the line was Attorney General Robert Jackson's opinion that arms owned by the U.S. government could be sold without advertisement by the Secretary of War under a 1919 statute still in force.

The fifty destroyers presented a different problem, and Churchill, unwilling to acknowledge the constitutional difficulties of handing them over, maintained an unrelenting pressure. He was worried, too, by propaganda that Germany would find collaborators in Britain. This could persuade Americans that the loan of destroyers might benefit the Germans in the long run. The stories of pro-Nazi forces in Britain came from all sides, including the Communists. The Russian Ambassador in London, Ivan Maisky, was always looking for evidence of pro-Nazi sentiment. Stephenson recalled a scene shortly after Dunkirk when the Soviet Union had been once again critical of Britain for prolonging the war.

"Now that France has fallen," said Maisky, "what will be your general strategy?"

Churchill drew on his cigar. "My general strategy, sir? My general strategy will be to last out the next three months."

The Russian Ambassador had caught whispers of doubt among gossiping London diplomats. Charles Ritchie, a future Canadian ambassador to Washington, wrote at this time in his diary, later published as *The Siren Years: Undiplomatic Diaries 1937–1945:* "Winston Churchill is an old pirate and if things go wrong people will find out and will turn on him and he will end in disgrace and they will forget that he is the only thing that kept England—so far—from a Vichy Government." Ritchie, serving in London, ad-

146

mired Churchill's dismissal of defeatists in high places.

Behind the bold front, Churchill himself had misgivings. "In the event of a Nazi conquest," he wrote to Mackenzie King, "I cannot tell what policy might be adopted by a pro-German administration such as would be undoubtedly set up." He suggested King impress this upon the President and all Americans who had not considered what would happen if the British Navy were captured.

The British fleet would be the "sole remaining bargaining counter with Germany" available to British collaborators who might take control, Churchill warned in another message to Roosevelt. "Excuse me, Mr. President, for putting this nightmare bluntly. Evidently I could not answer for my successors, who in utter despair and helplessness might well have to accommodate themselves to the German will." He argued that the loan of the fifty American destroyers would enable the British Navy to prevent such a capitulation.

After three more British destroyers were badly damaged, Churchill put the case in the most despairing terms. The sympathetic U.S. Naval Attaché, Alan Kirk, had already reported from London that the situation was growing desperate as German invasion troops assembled in the newly captured ports, "amassing every kind of small craft and ship. . . . The urgent need for destroyers to combat invasion is obvious. . . . The Royal Navy is down to about one hundred destroyers on all stations." Churchill voiced a possibility that Captain Kirk shrank from putting on paper. If the invasion succeeded, said Churchill, "a pro-German government would certainly be called into being to make peace. It might present to a shattered or a starving nation an almost irresistible case for entire submission to the Nazi will." Churchill cabled Roosevelt on June 15:

THE FATE OF THE BRITISH FLEET WOULD BE DECISIVE ON THE FUTURE OF THE UNITED STATES BECAUSE IF IT WERE JOINED TO THE FLEETS OF JAPAN, FRANCE AND ITALY AND THE GREAT RESOURCES OF GERMAN INDUSTRY, OVERWHELM-

ING SEA POWER WILL BE IN HITLER'S HANDS.
. . . IF WE GO DOWN, YOU MAY HAVE A UNITED
STATES OF EUROPE UNDER THE NAZI COMMAND
FAR MORE NUMEROUS, FAR STRONGER, FAR BET-
TER ARMED THAN THE NEW WORLD.

Stephenson was working now with a team he had
pulled together of American legal and commercial
brains. With Big Bill Donovan's firsthand reports from
London, they helped in the President's search for the
formula that would release the destroyers. It involved
trading bases for American arms, for there was nothing else with which Britain could pay. By August
1940 she was close to bankruptcy.

When Donovan flew back to Washington with his
assessment of British reliability, the country's resources of gold and dollars were almost exhausted.
One-third of the British Army's budget, for instance,
had been shot on purchase of a single type of special
American shell. Yet there was a logical, equitable argument. Donovan believed the bases could be traded
for destroyers if presented as a bargain struck in defense of the United States. He believed the deal
should be pushed through swiftly. In the previous two
weeks, 135,000 tons of ships had been lost and twenty
percent of the total British fighter aircraft strength had
been destroyed in combat. The old four-funnel destroyers, ill-equipped though they might be for modern
fleet actions, would help cut down these unacceptable
shipping losses and would escort cargoes of new aircraft now being dispatched through Canada.

Stephenson cabled to Churchill on August 8:

DONOVAN GREATLY IMPRESSED BY VISIT AND RE-
CEPTION. HAS STRONGLY URGED OUR CASE RE
DESTROYERS. . . . IS DOING MUCH TO COMBAT
DEFEATIST ATTITUDE WASHINGTON BY STATING
POSITIVELY AND CONVINCINGLY THAT WE SHALL
WIN.

But the very next day, Göring began to mass German bombers for what he regarded as the real Battle
of Britain—the systematic destruction of fighter bases

in England. The attacks that followed were to reduce British reserves of pilots and aircraft to dangerously low numbers while simultaneously knocking out Fighter Command airfields and the radar stations that the Germans now vaguely realized must be playing some role in the dogfights filling the clear blue skies of this benevolent summer.

Roosevelt's faith in Stephenson's assertion that "we shall win" was badly shaken. The President followed each stage of the savage fighting in British skies, knowing that the RAF was not able to make best use of its two most secret weapons: radar and ULTRA. Five coastal radar stations had been bombed on the first day of the new German attacks. ULTRA's recovery of enemy orders was not yet swift and complete enough for British fighter pilots to be sure how to handle the new threat.

On Thursday, August 15, more Luftwaffe bombers and fighters were launched against England than at any previous time. Luftflotte 5 struck from Norway at the north of England. Luftflotten 2 and 3 hurled formations once again across the Channel. The Germans were convinced that the RAF had lost so many fighters that it could not handle attacks in both north and south. Actual losses in aircraft on both sides were difficult to assess in the heat of battle, but Churchill's War Cabinet had just completed a study of "pilot wastage" that projected the loss of young fighter pilots at the rate of 746 a month, a disastrously high figure.

A typical incident on this Thursday was the encounter between twelve Spitfires and 105 enemy bombers approaching the Northumberland coast. The bombers split into two groups. One was intercepted by Hurricanes rushed into the air by pilots supposedly snatching a rest on a northern airfield. The other German group lost eight aircraft while bombing a northern base. In the south, RAF squadrons frantically tried to split up German attacks on vital airfields; and aircraft were fighting, retiring, fighting again—with all the RAF's twenty-two squadrons fully engaged. The Germans flew nearly 1,800 sorties; the RAF almost 1,000. The British rate of "pilot wastage" rose astronomically. One Spitfire staggered back to base, the dying pilot grimly keeping control until certain the aircraft was safely down. The need to save machines was as great as the demand for more pilots. Knowing the growing crisis in the RAF's loss of pilots, some Germans machine-gunned those who bailed out as they helplessly dangled from their parachutes.

On this day, Churchill went to the Operations Room of 11 Group, Fighter Command, and stared in unaccustomed silence at the gigantic map table. Every squadron was engaged. No fighters remained in reserve. Still the enemy's aircraft could be seen moving, wave after wave, across the Channel. Even the taciturn Chief of General Staff, Hastings Ismay, describing the scene, said: "I was sick with fear. Churchill said: 'Don't speak to me. . . . I have never been so moved.' There were tears in his eyes."

Later, Churchill rose heavily in the House of Commons. Harold Nicolson reported: "He did not try to arouse enthusiasm, only give guidance." It was then that he spoke the words that fixed for all time the role of the pilots who held back the invaders: "Never in the field of human conflict was so much owed by so many to so few."

The words were directed as much to Roosevelt as they were to Churchill's own people. The Prime Minister regarded the RAF's Fighter Command as a typically British institution: the pilots were mainly reservists, young men at a university or training for a learned profession. They invented new tactics day by day with fellow volunteers from the United States and the Commonwealth. One pilot in ten was an escapee from Poland. (The Poles were doing in the air what their comrades would have to do, without the glamour, in the secret armies of resistance.)

Churchill regarded this struggle in the skies as crucial to his campaign to win American help. He described to Parliament, that day when both sides in the aerial conflict had fallen back in temporary exhaustion, America's own needs in air and naval defense, and announced that "without being asked or offered any inducement" the British proposed to place suitable facilities at America's disposal. This was the first hint of the destroyer deal. There would have to be some "mixing up" of British and American organizations. This Anglo-American mixing-up process, said Churchill, would not be stopped: "Like the Mississippi, it just keeps rolling along. Let it roll. Let it roll on—full flood, inexorable, irresistible, benignant, to broader lands and better days."

The mixing-up process, already underway, was Stephenson's job. The day after Churchill's vision of an Atlantic alliance rolling along, Stephenson cabled him:

DONOVAN BELIEVES YOU WILL HAVE WITHIN A FEW DAYS VERY FAVOURABLE NEWS. . . . THINKS HE HAS RESTORED CONFIDENCE AS TO BRITAIN'S DETERMINATION AND ABILITY TO RESIST.

Two days later, he was able to cable:

MOST IMMEDIATE. FIFTY DESTROYERS AGREED LAST NIGHT . . . FORTY-FOUR ARE IN COMMISSION FOR DELIVERY. . . .

Shaking out the mothballs from these antique vessels was the symbol of Roosevelt's commitment, and gave the British a tremendous lift, although few realized that the destroyers marked another step forward in secret matters. Now the British could operate from the United States all their different secret-intelligence agencies and undercover operations, so that even a German occupation of Britain need not impede the prosecution of the shadow wars fought by secret armies. For the first time in the four centuries of British espionage, there was a central agency to bring together the manifold strands so that one man could survey the global scene. Having this central agency on neutral soil was of inestimable value. New York was an ideal center of communications. It was not harassed by the enemy, or subject to bombing, or impeded by wartime shortages and restrictions. Experts could work on specific problems in relative calm, their conclusions dispatched to London by way of mechanical coding machines perfected by Stephenson's own team of inventors.

The organization, even prior to its official birth, had grown grotesquely in size and shape. Some respectable title had to be given it before Americans began to ask awkward questions. Here was an invisible man directing four major British intelligence departments—SOE, SIS, Security Executive, and now MI–5—plus a communications-intelligence web whose threads ran in every direction abroad, and a secret police force on American soil. To gloss over this unprecedented situation, an organization, British Security Coordination, was registered with the State Department with the following official explanation:

> Consequent on the large scale and vital interests of the British Government in connection with the purchasing and shipment of munitions and war matériel from the United States, coupled with the presence in this country of a number of official British missions, a variety of security problems have been created [and] call for very close and friendly collaboration between the authorities of the two countries. . . . With a view to coordinating the liaison between the various British missions and the United States authorities in all security matters arising from the present abnormal circumstances, an organization bearing the title *Security Coordination* has been formed under the control of a Director of Security Coordination, assisted by headquarters staff.

Stephenson's name was never mentioned. Even in 1971, more than thirty years later, a former Assistant Secretary of State, Spruille Braden, named BSC's director in his memoirs, *Diplomats and Demagogues,* with evident hesitation: "General Donovan asked if I wanted to meet the head of British intelligence. I assented and Donovan said: 'All right, Mr. So-and-So will call you.' I later learned that Mr. So-and-So had a quite different name."

There was no need for Braden's discretion in the 1970s. INTREPID's identity had been revealed by then.

But in 1940 there was every reason for caution. Hitler was sure that the Nazis could conquer America by propaganda. One of Stephenson's jobs was to counter that propaganda. Paradoxically, if he was caught in that role, or in any violation of American sovereignty, he would contribute to the propaganda against Britain.

And Nazi propaganda was not merely a war of words. It was a strategy of terror. The blood purges, the pogroms, the Black Mass in worship of force at Nuremberg, the concentration camps, the fifth columns operating openly behind the frontiers of Germany's next victims were demonstrations of Nazi boasts and threats leading to action. Civilians were driven to hysterical flight by fifth columnists in one European country after another; but there was cause for their panic, and force backed up the propaganda. Stukas dive-bombed the women and children who choked the roads. Nazi propaganda was as good as its word. The Germans really were supermen, and it was folly to resist.

Hitler intended that message to deflate Americans. Fear, he hoped, would encourage isolationism. Later, he planned there would be a repetition of those events in the Americas.

Churchill did not think that Anglo-Americans were in any less danger of self-betrayal than Europeans. He was blunt about the risk of a pro-Nazi puppet regime in London. And he gave Stephenson the task of outfoxing the Nazis in America. BSC was to give direction to those who would rather fight than surrender. The next step was to create an American intelligence agency on the larger scale that American resourcefulness warranted.

"Britain was a nursery bed of ideas," said Stephenson. "But the seeds had to be transplanted. This was true of intelligence and all our new weapons of destruction."

19

"THE MOST VALUABLE cargo ever brought to our shores" was the description given by the U.S. Office of Scientific Research and Development to the incredible bundle of secrets dispatched on August 14, 1940, by Winston Churchill. The custodian of this cargo was Tizard the Wizard, as he was known to the Royal Air Force. In Washington, he went by the rakish but quite misleading name of "Whizzbang," an effective disguise, because in reality Sir Henry Tizard was a gentle soul who had been Scientific Advisor to the Chief of Air Staff. In the middle of the Battle of Britain, he was told to take confidential information to Washington rather than have it fall into enemy hands after ULTRA had revealed Hitler's invasion plans, which depended upon the air battles then in progress.

"Tizard called me in Washington from the Shoreham," Stephenson said later. "He was housed in an apartment so stuffed with blueprints, scientific data, models, and working plans packed in wooden crates that you could barely maneuver. When I went over to discuss certain arrangements, he shocked me by saying: 'An officer of the FBI has just telephoned asking when I can see him to make arrangements to place my luggage in secure hands.'

"I phoned Hoover at once. He said he knew nothing about it and would 'drive right over.' We discovered the call came from some person unknown to and certainly unconnected with the FBI. I sent one of my own security men, John Hart, of the Royal Canadian Mounted Police, to keep both Tizard and his cargo under surveillance.

"Later, Sam Foxforth, who was chief of the FBI office in New York City, told me headquarters had checked the discs of the routinely monitored telephone calls by German Embassy staff and friends. They'd traced the call that had gone to Tizard. It had come from a Nazi agent who spoke with a convincing American accent."

The German attempt to hijack the Wizard's tricks was alarming proof of the enemy's vigilance. Stephenson had urged Churchill to trade secrets for aid. The British Uranium Committee had the theory to make an atomic bomb: TUBE ALLOYS was the cover name for the project. Radar, jet engines, chemical weapons, and a "magic black box," which was to be the most effective of the new weapons invented in Britain, were also offered either in blueprint form, in models, or in research documents.

The "magic black box" was the cavity magnetron. It generated short-wave-length electronic beams and made possible the centimetric radar that was small enough to fit into destroyers and aircraft. The device was eventually manufactured in the United States in such numbers that it turned the tide in the struggle against the U-boat. The exploitation of this electronic valve, which the Wizard had transported in a commonplace black metal box purchased hurriedly from the Army and Navy Stores, near Victoria Station, led to countless benefits. With it came films of new weapons in action, and papers on proximity fuses, rocket defense of ships, multiple pompoms, and other examples of Britain's most forward thinking.

"The President scraped the bottom of the American barrel for half a million rifles, eighty thousand machine guns, shells, bombs, TNT, and aircraft in return," Stephenson recorded later. "He got us Flying Fortresses, having them secretly *pushed* over the frontier into Canada because this way their delivery was less likely to draw hostile attention. He was getting us hundreds of thousands of tons of metals for British arsenals, all done in what Bob Sherwood called a 'damn-the-torpedoes' spirit when men close to the White House were shouting that this represented suicide for Roosevelt and possibly for the nation, and amid cries that Britain was finished and all this material would fall into Hitler's hands!"

Roosevelt had no delusions about Britain's condition. He got from BSC the Bletchley readings of the Nazi mind, showing that waves of German bombers would try to complete the destruction of RAF defenses by mid-September. The timetable called for occupation of all southern England by the end of the month and a victory march through London in early October. Hitler had 1,900 bombers and 1,100 fighter aircraft to hurl against 350 bombers and 700 fighters. During the final month of the Battle of Britain, the Wizard and Stephenson put into safekeeping in Washington all the "lightweight / high-value" secrets that Hitler would have within his grasp if he reached London.

Intercepted German military orders confirmed that if the islands resisted, and invasion was either repelled or postponed, Hitler was still committed to an attack upon Russia. With the President's approval, Stephenson and Donovan concocted a counterplan to delay fatally the march on Moscow: a plan that would further strain American neutrality.

First, the Battle of Britain had still to be won. Stephenson flew back in the week after the invasion alert, code-named CROMWELL, had been sounded, on Saturday, September 7. Intercepted signals showed that enemy squadrons were bedeviled with servicing problems. The repair-and-supply units, as Stephenson had foreseen when listening to Nazi boasts about blitzkrieg tactics, were inadequate. Consequently, only three-quarters of the 3,000 warplanes arrayed against England were ready for operations at any one time. This was vital intelligence for the defending RAF squadrons.

On September 15, ULTRA revealed a statistical picture of preparations to invade Britain, by piecing together orders to individual military units. Vast preparations were being made on Belgian and Dutch fields for the loading and fast turnaround of troop-carrying planes, based on the assumption that the RAF would be no longer capable of putting up opposition. Invasion was expected momentarily.

"Churchill drove over from Chequers to Number 11 Fighter Group Headquarters," said Stephenson. "It covered most of southeast England with only twenty-five squadrons. Commanding was Keith Park,

156

the air vice marshal whose decisions had kept one step ahead of the enemy the past five weeks. Keith had spent all morning fighting off the heaviest waves to reach England. Winston was feeling talkative and kept asking questions. The tension mounted all afternoon. The red lights, each indicating a squadron in action, were coming up one after another. Now every fighter in every squadron was either fighting or gulping fuel for another go. Winston asked, 'What other reserves have we?'

"Keith said there were none. And then Winston understood. The RAF had reached its limit. Unless a miracle happened, Germany had the mastery of the skies, which was Hitler's prerequisite for invasion."

Part of the miracle was Bletchley's analysis of German orders. It told Park that he could gamble all his fighters. The enemy, too, had reached the end of his resources. Churchill went home for his afternoon nap. He was emotionally exhausted and slept for three hours. When he awoke, John Martin, his private secretary, came in with the familiar budget of disastrous news. "However," he ended, "all is redeemed in the air. We have shot down one hundred and eighty-five for a loss of forty."

President Roosevelt heard this account with more than ordinary interest. The basic German cipher machine, Enigma, which had been rebuilt in England to serve ULTRA's organization, was also duplicated in Japan. American cryptanalysts had built an apparatus like the Japanese version and called it "Purple." By September 1940, the U.S Army's Signal Intelligence Service had completed the Purple solution, and the resulting recovery of Japanese ciphers was code-named from this point onward MAGIC. What held the President's attention was the apparent flow and flexibility of British secret intelligence based on interception and decipherment, for which there was not yet an American counterpart.

Roosevelt was recovering from a false alarm he had passed along to Stephenson just before his latest fast trip to Britain. On Monday, September 23, Churchill warned his ministers that an invasion attempt seemed imminent. The German High Command had confirmed OPERATION SEALION. What Churchill did not tell the War Cabinet was that on the previous day he had received an urgent message from the President through Stephenson. The Americans had irrefutable evidence that the German invasion was to start at 3:00 P.M. "It doesn't say," wrote the head of the Foreign Office, Alexander Cadogan, "whether it's departure Calais at 3 or arrive Dover!"

Churchill had phoned his Secretary of State for War, Anthony Eden, who was home for the weekend in Kent. Eden expressed polite interest in Roosevelt's "conjecture." Churchill said testily that this was not a matter of conjecture. Would Mr. Eden kindly walk down to the cliffs and see if anyone was coming? The War Minister grumpily thrust his way through the damp wind into sight of the Channel. The sea was choppy, the waves blown into spindrift. He phoned Churchill back: "If the Germans try to cross in weather like this; they'll arrive excessively seasick."

The days passed with no invasion. Confidence in the President was not shaken, however. He had been right in his original warning of an invasion—but it was an invasion by the Japanese into French Indochina. A cipher clerk had confused the code names for two different places.

The President was "getting the hang of it," noted Stephenson, who had arranged that some of Churchill's routine questions to BSC should be summarized to give FDR a sense of the pressures on the Prime Minister. One typical day's barrage of memos was impressive. "Do the Americans know of the Knickebein beacon?* There's a new guidance system for

---

* On June 12, 1940, a cryptogram was plucked out of German radio transmissions. Bletchley decoded it as follows: "Knickebein Cleves established. . . ." It threw the first light on documents found on a captured German bomber referring to a Knickebein radio-navigation system. Churchill formed a unit at once to check these beacons. Direction-finding vans and old aircraft tracked the guidance beams. Whenever the beacons were switched on, they naturally pointed at the German targets for that night. Deductions from this source had more to do with British anticipation of night raids than any other single intelligence operation, and came under the ULTRA label.

German bombers. What progress in getting the American bomb-sight? There are reports of a German plan to drop poison-gas bombs. Can rumors be sent through American pipelines suggesting there's a secret weapon the British will use in retaliation," The range of topics was bewildering and indicative of wide knowledge, a fertile mind, and an energy beyond belief in a man past his mid-sixties. Stephenson's replies bounced back with equal rapidity—from "French patriots are being processed here for training as agents" to "Wendell Willkie opposes the war but is open to reason." Glancing over the thousands of messages, knowing what fears and disasters pressed upon the Prime Minister, Stephenson admitted later that he had never felt more alive and well as when he was being stretched by these demands. Nothing was forgotten. If the highly secret Norden bombsight was refused to Britain on the grounds that the American device, fitted on RAF bombers, might fall into enemy hands, then proof was found that German intelligence had already stolen the blueprints from the U.S. manufacturer. By the end of the "Spitfire Summer," White House and Whitehall were learning to work together on pooled intelligence.

There would always be political dangers inherent in this co-operation. Secret knowledge could be used to get rid of awkward opponents. There was a strong temptation to do this in the case of Ambassador Kennedy.

"My God!" Churchill roared after one of Kennedy's teetotal sermons. "You make me feel I should go around in sack-cloth and ashes!" Kennedy, for his part, told the President that Churchill "is loaded with brandy from ten in the morning." Kennedy had been described by the British Foreign Office as a possible future president, and already he threatened to throw his weight into the scales against Roosevelt. If someone else moved into the White House after the elections in November, what would happen to the Wizard's scientific secrets and all the carefully nurtured apparatus labeled INTREPID in New York?

Lord Beaverbrook, responsible for the herculean effort of aircraft production that put Spitfires into

RAF hands only just in time, kept up a relationship with Kennedy while reporting to Stephenson on the diplomat's activities. Beaverbrook made no apology for his actions later. "My son was shooting down Germans in the air," he said. "I was obliged to be ruthless on the ground." He had made up his mind to "shoot down Kennedy" after Donovan's midsummer visit, which ended with the Beaver cabling Big Bill on his arrival in Washington: YOU ARE LIKE UNTO RIVERS OF WATER IN A DRY PLACE.

Although Beaverbrook and Stephenson had a lot in common—they were both Canadians raised in a strict Scottish Presbyterian code, self-made millionaires, and strong-willed—the press baron was not noted for reticence. Beaverbrook described Ambassador Kennedy's final weeks to Stephenson in these words: "We loyally hushed up the betrayal of U S Embassy communications. But Kennedy was soon back at it. He wanted an unconditional guarantee that we send the whole British fleet to American ports in the likely event of our surrender. To the very last, he was worried about money. The British should be made to pay cash for arms. British-owned securities in the United States should be taken over and sold to raise the money. He feared Roosevelt was holding private conversations with you, so nothing would get on record about the President's blank-check arrangements for unsecured British credit. When Churchill said we shall defend our island whatever the cost may be, Kennedy warned Washington: 'Remember all speeches are being made in beautiful sunshiny weather.' Even Russian Ambassador Ivan Maisky was astonished at Kennedy's state of panic, and is commenting acidly upon 'Capitalist Kennedy seeking personal concessions on imports of Haig & Haig whisky and Gordon's Gin, for which he holds exclusive distribution rights in the United States, in exchange for his help in obtaining American supplies, a crude form of blackmail.' The London *Spectator* thinks there seem to be plenty of eminent persons in the United States to give isolationist advice without the Ambassador, knowing our ordeal, joining their number."

Beaverbrook said bluntly that Kennedy's presence

threatened the strategy settled upon to carry Britain through the period when "we shall be losing the war in a conventional sense until mid-1941. Hitler has put off the invasion until Spring 1941 and that gives us six months to launch psychological counter-offensives—small secret warfare campaigns designed to play on what we know of the Fuehrer's temperament.

"Hitler cannot stand opposition. Our hopes rest upon inciting him to lunatic actions. He must *see* the insults offered his supermen by barefoot peasants. It will be good for our morale too, knowing we are defeated but still striking back.

"These plans depend on keeping the right man in the White House. Kennedy claims he can put 25 million Catholic votes behind Wendell Willkie to throw Roosevelt out."

Foreign Minister Lord Halifax, now committed to the total-war concept, reported Kennedy as having said he had arranged widespread publication of an article by himself in the United States five days before the presidential election: "Kennedy gave me to understand it would be an indictment of President Roosevelt's administration. . . ."

Beaverbrook sent Stephenson a detailed report of the Ambassador's conversations in which compromising statements were made. The report was submitted to FDR at once. Stephenson described the scene: "I sat back and watched FDR across his cluttered desk. He had a way of reading, tilting the sheet from side to side. You could tell when he was angry by small signs. On this occasion the sign was the sudden acceleration in the tilting of the sheet. Then he folded the sheet very calmly, very slowly, and he tore it just as slowly and calmly into very tiny pieces which he dropped into a wastebasket. And then, in front of me, he drafted a cable to Kennedy which said in essence:

THE LIQUOR TRADE IN BOSTON IS NOW CHALLENGING AND THE GIRLS OF HOLLYWOOD MORE . . FASCINATING STOP I EXPECT YOU BACK HERE BY SATURDAY.

Lyndon B. Johnson later said he was with the President when Kennedy arrived in New York and telephoned on Sunday, October 27. "Ah, Joe, old friend, it is so good to hear your voice. . . ." When Roosevelt replaced the telephone, he drew his forefinger razor-fashion across his throat, Johnson later recalled.

The Kennedys dined with the Roosevelts that evening. Two days later, Joseph P. Kennedy spoke on nationwide radio. A startled public learned he now believed "Franklin D. Roosevelt should be reelected President." He told a press conference: "I never made anti-British statements or said, on or off the record, that I do not expect Britain to win the war." British historian Nicholas Bethell wrote: "How Roosevelt contrived the transformation is a mystery." And so it remained until the BSC Papers disclosed that the President had been supplied with enough evidence of Kennedy's disloyalty that the Ambassador, when shown it, saw discretion to be the better part of valor.

"If Kennedy had been recalled sooner," said Stephenson later, "he would have campaigned against FDR with a fair chance of winning. We delayed him in London as best we could until he could do the least harm back in the States."

Kennedy's London was being torn apart by a new campaign of terror bombing. Just when the German Air Force seemed likely to swamp RAF Fighter Command, the attacks were switched from vital bases to England's open cities. Hitler stopped bombing fighter airfields and bombed London instead. It was a turning point in the Battle of Britain; and a decisive factor in making Kennedy get out of the smoking capital despite the efforts of society and the bureaucracy to detain him.

The Chief Diplomatic Advisor to Churchill, doubtless under stress from the nightly bombing, indulged in an undiplomatic comment that went into the sealed Kennediana file. Robert Vansittart wrote: "Mr. Kennedy is a very foul specimen of a double-crosser and defeatist. He thinks of nothing but his own pocket. I hope that this war will at least see the elimination of his type." It may seem unfair to exhume this bitter note, years later, but it does give deeper meaning to the generous amends made after the war by President John F. Kennedy when he proclaimed Churchill an honorary citizen of the United States for his leadership "in the dark days and darker nights when Britain stood alone—and most men save Englishmen despaired of England's life."

20

ON THE NIGHT of November 5, 1940, a few days after he won election to a third term, Roosevelt met his neighbors at Hyde Park. During the recent campaign, his chief opponent, Wendell Willkie, had warned that a third term would mean "dictatorship and war." FDR had responded that American boys "are not going to be sent into any foreign wars." Now he was, as a placard outside his door proclaimed, SAFE ON THIRD. What was Roosevelt going to do? Keep his pledge about foreign wars? Or continue to enlarge his extensive and secret commitments to Britain?

The questions were asked in The Hole, 3,000 miles away. Bombers had dumped fresh loads of fire and destruction on London. Dawn crept through the ruins. Churchill sat thirty-five feet below ground, tossing another cigar butt over his shoulder in the cheerful expectation that it would land in the bucket of sand behind him. In front of him was the red ULTRA box, with signals retrieved by Bletchley.

One signal shocked and sickened him. Evidently the terror bombing of London did not satisfy Hitler. Raids were to be directed at other centers of population. The danger of invasion had been lifted for the moment, but Churchill saw great crises ahead.

The Prime Minister had not dared speak before. "But now," he wrote to Roosevelt, "I feel you will not mind my saying that I prayed for your success. . . .

Things are afoot which will be remembered as long as the English language is spoken in any quarter of the globe. . . ."

The President had hardly read this message when he learned of the new horror. Bletchley was discovering ahead of time which civilian targets Hitler planned to strike next. Churchill and his War Cabinet had to decide which was more important: to warn the families marked for punishment or protect the secrets of Bletchley's growing apparatus for divining Nazi intentions.

Their agony had begun more than two months earlier, during the airfield-attack phase. A German bomber, by miscalculation, released a string of bombs that struck Buckingham Palace and nearby homes. The RAF scraped the barrel for aircraft that might reach as far as Berlin, and on the night of August 25, bombed the German capital as a warning. Hitler, enraged because his people had been promised that nothing like this could possibly happen, ordered reprisals —the change to the bombing of cities. It was tragic for British civilians, but gave their Fighter Command time to repair bases and patch up pilots and planes.

The German targets were, of course, coded. However, it was possible to guess the location of a target by studying the Knickebein beams that guided the bombers. These were not always switched on until thirty minutes before the German raiders took off. Then the British hastily notified ambulance and fire-fighting units, concealing the real source of their knowledge by giving credit to radar, aerial reconnaissance, and ground observers.

Occasionally, German orders did give the real name of a proposed target. This happened a few days after Roosevelt's re-election, by which time he was familiar with the moral dilemmas faced by Churchill. One reason for this was the presence in Bletchley of America's greatest cryptologist, William Friedman. He and his U.S. Army team, at work on the Japanese version of Enigma, having developed the equivalent of ULTRA in their own laboratories, had been toiling hand in glove with the British since the August exchange of highly secret weapons and intelligence devices. Of all the confidential matters surrounding Stephenson's new headquarters in New York, this was one of the most astounding. Like so much else, it remained unpublicized and unknown to all but a few. *"Inexplicable* is how securely the work has been held for 35 years," commented another American who worked at Bletchley, Washington *Post* columnist Alfred Friendly, when the first accounts of ULTRA were published in 1974. Stephenson had earlier argued for the permanent attachment of American specialists to Bletchley Park, and once he had gathered all the intelligence threads together at BSC in New York, this co-operation had begun.

In the second week of November in 1940, Bletchley obtained the German order to destroy Coventry. The name came through in plain text. Coventry was forty miles northwest of Bletchley, and some of Friedman's English colleagues had families billeted in the doomed city. Yet they could say nothing. Nearby, too, was the 300-year-old mansion where the first successful Whittle jet-engine blueprints were to be copied for safekeeping in America. Brownsover Hall, center of jet research, was undefended, to avoid drawing German attention to it.

The name of the target was in Churchill's hands within minutes of Hitler's decision. The Führer meant to annihilate nonmilitary targets in his attempt to crush civilian resistance. If the Prime Minister evacuated Coventry, as he so desperately wished to do, he would tell the enemy that he knew their plans. The value of Bletchley and all that ULTRA implied for the future would be lost. If the citizens were not warned, thousands would die or suffer.

Churchill chose wormwood, and did not warn them, beyond the customary alerting of fire-fighting and ambulance services, normal procedure in areas that might be logically assumed to have appeared on the German list of targets for the night. The Germans struck on schedule: November 14. The raid was so devastating that Berlin boasted that every town in England would be "Coventryized."

Roosevelt discussed with Stephenson the issues raised by knowing too much. "War is forcing us more and more to play God," he said. "I don't know what I should have done. . . ."

Coventry was a foretaste of the dreadful dilemmas imposed by the need to conceal secret knowledge. When so much had to be sacrificed to conceal sources, it was unthinkable that individuals should ask for public acknowledgment of their Bletchley labors. This lesson was remarked by William Friedman. Long after the war, he wrote a discreet tribute to his tutor at Bletchley, Alastair Denniston. Like so many others in British intelligence, Denniston could not be rewarded even financially, for fear of arousing curiosity, and he had to go back to teaching in his old age. Friedman wrote a letter to Denniston's daughter, nicknamed "Y" because she was an unknown quantity before her birth. "Your father was a great man in whose debt all English-speaking people will remain for a very long time, if not forever. That so few should know exactly what he did . . . is the sad part."

Silence was imposed on Roosevelt for the same reasons. After his re-election, he appeared to lose interest in the war. In fact, he was involving the nation more deeply than ever.

The President was being made privy to haunting secrets. He was moving cautiously toward the inevitable, deeply touched by Stephenson's disclosures. He learned of the torment of the commander of the young Battle of Britain pilots, Hugh Dowding. A row broke over the Air Chief Marshal's head when his junior commanders criticized his refusal to send up more fighters to meet the early swarms of German bombers. The youngsters were not aware that the enemy had been trying to draw them into battle in the wrong place at the wrong time; nor could they be told that Hitler's deceptive intentions were understood by Dowding through the Bletchley interpretation of intercepted signals. The incessant strain, heartache at the loss of those pilots he had often called "my sons," carried him to the verge of a nervous breakdown. In later years, he spoke of his communion with the dead pilots in a spirit world. He was an acutely sensitive man, almost dumb with shyness in any social gathering, who wrote in his diaries about his responsibility for sending the flower of youth into seemingly suicidal combats where the rewards were fearful facial burns, mutilation, death. The criticisms scarred him. But he carried to the grave the secrets of Bletchley and ULTRA that caused him to follow so difficult a policy, although they would have vindicated him.

Sharing these secrets with the President and with his carefully selected specialists had been a grave decision for Stephenson. In doing so, he felt he was preparing America for grim leadership in a world new to weapons that could condemn innocents to the gas chamber or cities to atomic destruction. Already it was becoming apparent that decisions taken to sabotage Nazi industry or to assassinate a Nazi leader could trigger consequences as awesome as any massacre in history.

There was no turning back. Just before Coventry, the wires had hummed between Washington and London over formation of the Axis, the formal linkage of Berlin with Rome and Tokyo.

"Can we get military staff and joint-intelligence talks underway with the Americans?" Churchill had asked.

"If it gets out that the President agreed to discussion of Anglo-American global strategy there will be renewed charges of warmongering," Stephenson replied.

Now, the election out of the way, Roosevelt was preparing for these strategy talks. To all appearances, he was basking aboard the U.S.S. *Tuscaloosa* in the Caribbean sun. In fact, he was studying a 4,000-word letter from Churchill, delivered by seaplane on December 9. It was a study of war from the North Sea to Singapore and dealt in great sweep and detail with the dangers and problems. One was Britain's financial position: dollar balances that had been on an imperial scale before the war were now gone, including the holdings in America of individual Britons. Britain could not survive if supplies had to be paid for, cash on the barrelhead. "I believe you will agree," wrote Churchill, "that it would be wrong in principle and mutually disadvantageous in effect if at the height of this struggle Great Britain were to be divested of all saleable assets, so that after the victory is won with our blood, civilisation saved, and the time gained for the United States to be armed against all eventualities, we should stand stripped to the bone."

Churchill had consulted Stephenson about this letter: "The most important I ever wrote." The Prime Minister seemed to his intelligence chief to be strained, irritable, and restlessly prodding for action. The letter was a masterly survey, yet it did not mention the one area in which Churchill was able to hit back at his evasive enemies: secret warfare. History records the results of the letter's overt proposals and appeals, from Lend-Lease to what Stephenson called "a common-law alliance."* History does not record, because what then was secret has remained so until now, how the decision to let Coventry burn so moved the President that he initiated a flurry of actions, most of them directed to the training, support, and expansion of guerrilla forces in Europe. A stream of special emissaries crisscrossed the Atlantic, ostensibly performing ambassadorial roles. Averell Harriman took over a mission in London to expedite military aid, reporting to Ambassador-at-large Harry Hopkins through Navy communications, though his mission was housed in the U.S. Embassy. Such surface activity concealed an even greater traffic on behalf of clandestine services, for FDR now felt he shared with Churchill the awesome burden of Coventry's destruction.

Help in disguise was on its way within forty-eight hours of the arrival of Churchill's letter. The President's special agent Bill Donovan was once again dispatched to look into Britain's immediate needs. Stephenson cabled to Churchill:

IMPOSSIBLE OVER-EMPHASIZE IMPORTANCE OF DONOVAN MISSION. HE CAN PLAY A GREAT AND PERHAPS VITAL ROLE. IT MAY NOT BE CONSISTENT WITH ORTHODOX DIPLOMACY NOR CONFINED TO ITS CHANNELS. . . .

---

* Robert Sherwood, as presidential aide, quoted the definition of a common-law marriage as applying perfectly to this alliance: an agreement between a man and a woman to enter into the marriage relation without ecclesiastic or civil ceremony, and not recognized in many jurisdictions ("such as Congress," Sherwood added to Stephenson). He was attached to BSC at the time.

Donovan was leaving on a mission comparable to that of Stephenson in STRIKE OX. The cable deliberately echoed Churchill's description of that earlier operation as "using methods neither diplomatic nor military."

Meanwhile, the President wondered if he could make some open gesture to hearten the islanders.

"What could be better than sending Mr. Wendell Willkie, your opponent in the recent bitter elections?" Stephenson suggested.

Roosevelt liked the idea. He was working on his third inaugural address when Willkie called before leaving for London. Tugging some of his personal stationery out of a drawer, the President wrote a passage from Longfellow as a message for the embattled Prime Minister. Churchill, seeing at once its significance and its value in boosting morale, read it before an assembly of the burghers of the City of London between bombing raids:

> Sail on, O Ship of State!
> Sail on, O Union, strong and great!
> Humanity with all its fears,
> With all the hopes of future years,
> Is hanging breathless on thy fate!

Roosevelt did not fear death for himself. His balance seemed to derive from having come to terms with death. What he feared was some misstep that might condemn humanity. He wanted to reassure and encourage Britain, but he dare not expose himself to political attacks that might destroy his plans. The swiftly expanding British intelligence operations in New York would have to take responsibility for concealing Anglo-American staff talks beginning in January 1941. What Roosevelt had been preparing was a conference that would provide the United States with the greatest degree of strategic preparedness ever achieved before entering war. He was drawing on British expertise, believing his commanders too big-minded to resent it. He had Stephenson's organization throw an invisible shield around the talks—with FBI cooperation. But playing second fiddle was not in director J. Edgar Hoover's nature.

21

"IF THESE PRECEDENTS are to stand unimpeached and to provide sanctions for the continued conduct of American affairs, the Constitution may be nullified by the President," wrote the American historian Charles A. Beard in *President Roosevelt and the Coming of the War, 1941,* an indictment of Roosevelt's "binding agreements" with Britain before Pearl Harbor.

"If the isolationists had known the full extent of the secret alliance between the United States and Britain," Robert Sherwood commented to Stephenson in the winter of 1940, "their demands for the President's impeachment would have rumbled like thunder through the land."

American-British staff talks opened in Washington in January 1941 with warnings from General George C. Marshall and Admiral Harold R. Stark that utmost secrecy must prevail. If their plans had fallen into Axis hands, no great harm would have resulted. Had they leaked to the press and Congress, American preparation for war might have been wrecked. "Utmost secrecy" meant preventing any premature disclosure to the American public. "Roosevelt never overlooked the fact that his actions might lead to his immediate or eventual impeachment," Sherwood wrote later, in *Roosevelt and Hopkins.*

ABC-1 was "the common-law alliance" suggested almost six months earlier by Stephenson when he reported the disastrous consequences of Dunkirk to the President. The name meant American-British Conference Number One, suggesting more to follow.

The British military men who came over for the conference were high-ranking officers in ill-fitting civilian suits. Within three months, these "low-level talks" produced operational war plans on a global scale. The policy was established that the Nazi threat should take priority over any military aggression by Japan. For the British, this was a major diplomatic victory that passed unnoticed and uncelebrated because it took place in the shadowy world occupied by Stephenson. He found it odd to sit in the austere battleship-gray offices of the old Navy Building for another session of Anglo-American talks on war when the New York *Times* for that morning had reported shrill Lend-Lease arguments in Congress, so far removed from what was being discussed behind locked doors. After one conference with the U.S. War Plans Division, he heard Marshall, the Army Chief of Staff, tell a Senate committee there was "absolutely no intention that America should enter the war." Nonetheless, that day's secret discussions centered on a projected American army of five million troops within two years. Marshall dared not disclose this. Nor could the President announce a "Germany first" policy.

Perhaps as many as a score of Americans and a tiny group of British service chiefs knew about these talks on global strategy. The task of keeping that knowledge secret fell on Stephenson's shoulders. It was a necessarily strange state of affairs. The President's dissembling was undignified. The lies did small justice to Congress. "Germany first" was a policy before the U.S. was at war. If there were no ABC-1, and no agreement on priorities, a surprise attack by Japan would swing the whole inadequate and ill-prepared American war machine to face east, significantly relieving the pressure on Germany. If Germany seized the French fleet, directed the affairs of Vichy France, controlled the raw materials of Eastern Europe, and continued to draw on Russian resources, Hitler would continue to conquer nations, then continents, with world domination a terrifyingly real possibility; he would have the time and resources to construct the atomic bomb already within his reach. Such cold logic could be safely presented only at those secret meetings.

"The Germans wanted the Americans to focus on Japan to give Hitler time to finish his initial schedule

171

of conquest, and to make sure that when Japan did advance, she wouldn't advance too far beyond Southeast Asia," Stephenson noted later.

The plans drawn up at ABC-1 were "gentlemen's agreements." There were no secret treaties. Operations directed by BSC from Rockefeller Center were at all times liable to be halted. The Manhattan headquarters were still a makeshift combination of borrowed offices, improvised coding machines, and filing systems that would have baffled an outsider. It was a twilight period, during which Walter Lippmann in his column expressed the widely held, glum opinion that when hard issues of war and peace come up for decision, "the executive and judicial departments, with their civil servants and technicians, lose their power to decide."

During the conference, British officers asked Secretary of War Stimson why his country still held back when the free world's survival hung in the balance. Stimson nodded toward the White House. "Take the question there," he said. "That's where you'll find the greatest isolationist of them all."

The answer the President gave Stephenson was, "I cannot bring a divided nation into war. I learned that from the First World War. I felt the same urgency then that your people feel now. But Wilson taught me a lesson. I am going to be sure, very sure, that if the United States publicly enters the war, it will enter united."

He might have added: "Secretly, we're in it now."

The dictators were sure that the President was incapable of action. This appeared in German diplomatic and military message traffic recovered by Bletchley. General Friedrich von Boetticher, the German military and air attaché in Washington, reported to Berlin that a pro-German military establishment dominated America. He told Hitler that Roosevelt and the State Department were outflanked by what he called the *Generalstab,* suggesting a parallel with the monolithic German military establishment. His favorite phrase was "the Jewish wire-pullers." These he blamed in February 1941 for Lend-Lease. Neither this nor the transfer of destroyers to Britain was to be regarded, he said, as posing any significant political or military threat. Hitler, hearing only what he wished to hear, was assured that the American *Generalstab* believed in Germany's lightning victories and counted Britain out. American intervention was out of the question. The trickle of American aid was only to gag the howling little minority of "Jew-lovers."

Hitler ordered an intensification of campaigns to "Nazify" these sympathetic Americans of Boetticher's fancy, to build up agencies in the Western Hemisphere for political and economic infiltration, and in strongly pro-German regions of South America to reinforce bases for military action.

General Raymond Lee, during a tenure in London as American military attaché, recorded the British dilemma in dealing with doubts about London's ability to survive. Lee's primary task was to provide a running commentary on British military fitness and to provide liaison for secret contacts. His reports to Washington also provided Stephenson with a welcome guide to how an independent and shrewd observer saw the changing situation. Lee sensed it was only a question of time before he would be helping the American counterpart to BSC to build a base in London. Operations born in secrecy in New York would be fulfilled in Europe, but he could not divine when or how.

Nelson Rockefeller had persuaded Roosevelt to let him start a new agency in the unguarded vastness of South America—"our soft under-belly," Lee called it—where Stephenson operated a network, hampered by shortages of equipment and money. This new Office of the Coordinator of Inter-American Affairs acted covertly on information from BSC on Nazi sympathizers in sensitive jobs. Millions of Rockefeller dollars went into various schemes to discredit, depose, or in other ways damage the pawns of Axis conspirators in South America. The FBI and the State Department were at loggerheads over who had jurisdiction in the region; it was easier for Rockefeller to show personal initiative and foot the bill than settle an argument about counterespionage in foreign lands. This also protected FDR's public stance of noninvolvement until Americans would demand to go to war.

Hoover was right to feel uneasy. The surreptitious scope of the Coordinator, worked out by Rockefeller with Stephenson, foreshadowed the global agency under Donovan. But Hoover now got some experience in the President's methods of inserting the thin end of a wedge.

In early 1941, Hoover saw yet another sign in advertisements appearing in Canadian newspapers. A typical "Help Wanted" notice appeared in the Toronto *Telegram:*

TO WORK FOR BRITAIN

A department of the British Government in New York City requires several young women, fully competent in secretarial work and of matriculation or better educational standing. The chief need is for expert file clerks and for typists and stenographers. . . . Those selected can expect to serve for the duration of the war. . . .

Hoover knew what this meant. Canadians were being recruited for BSC's overt operations to get around a ban on American citizens working for belligerents in a foreign war. Hoover was publicized as the world's most powerful policeman, but now he was being forced to turn a blind eye when the laws were bent. His personal vanity and professional pride were naturally involved. "The price of Hoover's cooperation was always conditioned by his overwhelming ambition for the FBI," noted the BSC Papers. "He wanted to retain a monopoly of liaison with BSC and this became progressively less possible."

To expand the FBI into an international agency like the British secret services, Hoover needed backing by Congress, and this was not forthcoming. He had no legal right to employ agents outside the United States. He directed FBI agents in Latin America secretly, took elaborate precautions against the State Department finding out, maintaining his own FBI liaison office midway between Rockefeller's Coordinator suite and BSC in Rockefeller Center. How this worked in practice was described later by a double agent known as TRICYCLE, actually a Yugoslav named Dusko Popov. "I walked slowly to Rockefeller Center, running a check on a possible tail. Inside, I spotted my contact scanning the directory. I followed him into an elevator and at the twenty-ninth floor we got out, neither speaking. He circled the floor and pressed an UP button but let the first elevator pass. Then he pressed again. This time a civilian in the cage nodded slightly and we rode to the forty-fourth floor where I was now recognized and escorted to the FBI."* TRICYCLE had just arrived back from Europe by way of South America, and his reports were of consequence to all three groups. Others who dealt with FBI agents, especially the Canadian security men, had nothing but praise for their discretion, efficiency, and willingness to admit ignorance of what were then new and startling espionage techniques.

A substantially different picture was given by a Baker Street Irregular who turned out to be one of the Soviet Union's top-ranking spies, Kim Philby. He wrote in *My Silent War:*

> Stephenson's activity in the United States was regarded sourly enough by J. Edgar Hoover. The implication that the FBI was not capable of dealing with sabotage on American soil was wounding to a man of his raging vanity. He was incensed when Stephenson's strong boys beat up or intoxicated the crews of ships loading Axis supplies. But the real reason for his suspicious resentment, which he never lost, was that Stephenson was playing politics in his own yard, and playing them pretty well. Hoover foresaw that the creation of Bill Donovan's OSS would involve him in endless jurisdictional disputes. The new office would compete with the FBI for Federal funds. It would destroy his monopoly of the investigative field. The creation and survival of the new OSS organization was to be the only serious defeat suffered by Hoover in his political career—and his career

* *Spy/Counterspy: The Master Intelligence Agent of the Second World War.*

has been all politics. He never forgave Stephenson for the part he played as midwife and nurse to OSS.

Philby gave a Soviet propaganda version. Hoover and the FBI actually provided Stephenson with enormous help during these frantic months. Russian agents, even after the Soviet Union was forced into alliance by German invaders, never ceased their efforts to sow distrust between the FBI and the British.

"Hoover is a man of great singleness of purpose, and his purpose is the welfare of the Federal Bureau of Investigation," Stephenson told Churchill. "The FBI was in existence when Hoover, at 29, took over; but the Bureau was a slovenly outfit. Hoover insisted that if he took the job, it would have to be completely divorced from politics and the civil service. He established absolute authority from the start. In the course of almost a quarter-century he has made it a national institution. As a result, the FBI does not have to endure the newspaper sniping to which other federal agencies, almost without exception, are periodically subjected. Its record is above criticism." Hoover's job was both his pride and his vanity. He was the son of a Washington civil servant and he had taken night courses in law while working as a library clerk. The facts of his personal life were emphasized because Stephenson "regarded them as fundamental to any understanding in London of a relationship that does not always run smoothly."

The BSC Papers commented: "Hoover needed courage and foresight to cooperate so wholeheartedly. His insistence that the liaison be kept secret is proof of his awareness that he was running a considerable risk that his connection with British Intelligence would be exposed and embroil him in a major political upheaval, with every isolationist and non-interventionist in the country after his blood."

Stephenson won over Hoover by assuring him that a time would come when the American public could be told of FBI accomplishments. The British desired neither recognition nor credit. The BSC Papers commented: "The truth was that internal security and for-

176

eign intelligence do not mix well. The FBI had to be flanked with teams of experts from different backgrounds."

Hoover had been outflanked already. FDR's private presidential intelligence service was introduced on the day Roosevelt wrote the letter to Churchill inviting the confidences that burgeoned into the momentous correspondence between Naval Person and POTUS. On September 8, 1939, after Hitler's armored columns charged deep into Poland, a "Limited Emergency" was proclaimed which covered the reorganization of the President's Executive Office. The Bureau of the Budget was transferred from the Treasury Department to this reorganized Executive Office. The Bureau's agents went into every branch of government, and their reports came directly back to the President. His special aide, Harry Hopkins, became a civilian chief of staff, with no legal authority and nothing more than a card table for a desk. Hopkins was, in Stephenson's words, "the President's own private Foreign Office." As the European war gathered momentum, more had to be done to protect the legitimate but clandestine intercourse between London and Washington. The President required an aide similar to Hopkins in the new sphere of secret warfare. Anyone who functioned as the President's secret-intelligence aide had to be willing to make decisions and risk being disowned. His patriotism and personal integrity had to be beyond dispute. Nobody seemed better fitted for that thankless task than Bill Donovan.

"For this reason," recorded the BSC diarists, Stephenson "worked to build up Donovan's authority while preserving his special relationship with J. Edgar Hoover. This became increasingly difficult. From time to time, the FBI actively tried to suppress BSC activities."

Hoover, sensing a decline in his own prospects, fell back on legalities. He said BSC was breaking American laws, besides contributing to what some historians would later describe as Roosevelt's autocracy in the field of foreign relations. Hoover's dangerous hostility was overcome, but there were occasions when London rekindled his jealousy by withholding information for bureaucratic reasons—but, from Hoover's viewpoint, seemingly out of distrust. Some idea of the tightrope Stephenson walked is conveyed in the BSC Papers: "Stephenson needed something in the United States which did not exist at the time he founded BSC . . . an agency with which he could collaborate fully by virtue of its being patterned, in the matter of coordinated functions, exactly after his own organization. He needed as its chief a man less rigid and sensitive to potential rivals."

Yet Hoover could be a good man to have on your side. "He was protective of Stephenson's position, on the principle of Better-the-Devil-You-Know," said Ian Fleming, who flew over with the British Director of Naval Intelligence in 1941 to a cool reception. He found Hoover to be "a chunky enigmatic man with slow eyes and a trap of a mouth who received us graciously, listened with close attention (and a witness) to our exposé of certain security problems, and expressed himself firmly but politely as being uninterested in our mission." Hoover made it clear that it would be foolish to develop separate channels with London that would bypass Stephenson or the Office of U.S. Naval Intelligence. The brush-off was conducted with a certain courtesy. "Hoover's negative response was soft as a cat's paw. With the air of doing us a favor, he had us piloted through the FBI Laboratory and Record Department and down to the basement shooting range," Fleming said later. "Even now I can hear the shattering roar of the Thompsons in the big dark cellar as the instructor demonstrated on the trick targets. Then with a firm, dry handclasp we were shown the door."

22

THE NEED FOR cross-Atlantic consultations rose with the tempo of Anglo-American secret warfare. Stephenson flew at least once a month to London to unscramble problems. Again he needed Hoover's good will, because the traffic in agents and couriers could have been so easily interrupted by FBI hair-splitting.

There were two fast routes between Washington and London. One required crossing the border into Canada, incognito, with help from the FBI and Canadian authorities forewarned by BSC. The traveler then joined a Ferry Command flight from Montreal by way of Labrador to Scotland. Couriers, atomic scientists, even spy masters went this way in extreme discomfort aboard bombers stripped of nonessentials. Passengers squeezed into gun turrets, and confidential mail was stuffed into bomb bays. The dangers varied. A famous magician, Jasper Maskelyne, whose talents were required for creating illusionary weapons, almost died from oxygen starvation. The song writer Eric Maschwitz, hired to direct the fabrication of documents, nearly froze to death when his transport was forced down in Iceland. A four-engined British plane loaded with VIPs was mistaken for a Focke-Wulf Kurier shadowing a convoy; a British carrier pilot was vectored onto the plane and, coming upon it in clouds, shot it down, with the resultant loss of all aboard. Flights were surrounded by such secrecy that the sudden appearance of large unidentified aircraft, observing radio silence, easily triggered such fatal reactions.

The southern route was just as dangerous. A doubly tragic incident was the killing of Leslie Howard, the British actor known to thousands of Americans as the harmless Ashley Wilkes in *Gone With the Wind*. He boarded an aircraft on a secret mission for Stephenson. The Germans knew about it and shot down the unarmed plane. The British knew beforehand that the Germans knew, but to protect the secret of how they knew, Bletchley, which had monitored the German Air Force orders, let the plane go down. The secret was so well preserved that this account of the true background to what was vaguely known to be a story of espionage never came before the public. In the skies over the Bay of Biscay, where Howard was shot down, Churchill was intercepted on another occasion by British fighters who were told the "unidentified object" was "hostile." Fortunately, Churchill's flying boat eluded the hunters by flying into thick cloud—or Britain might have been robbed of its chief inspiration at a critical moment in the war. Six RAF Hurricanes pursued the Prime Minister on the last leg of his flight back from Bermuda to deal with parliamentary accusations of bungling and mismanaging military affairs in the winter of 1941. History did not record Churchill's comments on this unsuccessful attempt to shoot him down.

The southerly route across the Atlantic was flown mostly by British Imperial Airways, whose Clippers took twenty-one hours to cross from New York, by way of Bermuda and Lisbon, to southern England. The Pan-American Boeing 314 flying boats were rated as merchant vessels and could not land in belligerent countries. One covert flight taken by Harry Hopkins left him too fatigued to unfasten his safety belt after landing. Nor was his ordeal at an end. German bombs followed his train to London. Within minutes of his arrival at Waterloo Station, hundreds of incendiaries blocked the tracks he recently had rolled over.

As a roving ambassador, Hopkins saw the need for a diplomatic repair job when he confronted Churchill on a bleak January day in 1941. He arrived at 10 Downing Street and found most of the windows blown out by bomb blast. He was led down to the basement, where "a rotund—smiling—red faced gentleman appeared—extended a fat but convincing hand and wished me welcome to England." The first meeting went smoothly, the Prime Minister concerned that Hopkins ate so frugally at lunch and expressing delight at the prospect of an "accidental" encounter with the President in Bermuda. But when Hopkins said there was a feeling in some quarters that Churchill did not like America or Roosevelt, the jolly gentleman's jaw stiffened and he went into a bitter attack on Ambassador Kennedy for misrepresenting so much and for creating so many false impressions.

The fascination of secret intelligence was, in Churchill, never-ending but seldom openly disclosed. He sensed Donovan's instinct for the work and encouraged Stephenson to "fly him over" whenever possible. A glimpse of these "illicit trysts" came from the American intelligence agent Ernest Cuneo, who in those days was called the President's special liaison officer. He had flown over with Stephenson and Donovan, and confided his secret ambition to meet the Prime Minister. He had to visit a base next day. The two Bills reported to 10 Downing Street. They were walking back to the hotel, Claridge's, in the early hours when they saw Cuneo at the corner of Grosvenor Square and Brooke Street.

"Come along, Ernie. We're going to see the PM."

"Good God . . . it's four o'clock in the morning!"

He was taken firmly by the elbow and told: "Yes, Ernie. The darkest hour before the dawn. The best time of all—"

Cuneo found Churchill in a romper suit, looking like a chubby spy waiting to drop into Europe. He was impressed by the Prime Minister's nonchalant greeting when he answered their knocking at the door. "Your name's Cuneo? Any relation to Cuneo the navigator who served with Columbus?"

"A direct descendant," Cuneo replied.

"Jolly good," said Churchill. "Let's drink to. . . ."

Churchill was impetuous and kept grueling hours. Roosevelt was predictable and went to bed early. Moving between them, one had to shift mental gears. There were all kinds of peculiar differences. When the moon was full and bright, Churchill did not go to Chequers for the weekend; the house was known to the Germans and provided a conspicuous target. When he did follow the traditional weekend ritual, Churchill carried with

181

him into retreat an umbilical cord of telephone lines and cables linking him to the world at war. He believed the enemy chose weekends for major operations, hoping to catch his War Cabinet napping. Consequently, weekends with Churchill were turmoil. When, in his own dramatic phrase, "the moon was high," he switched to Ditchley, near Oxford. There were three stately rooms on the ground floor of this seventeenth-century mansion equipped with all the electronics needed to conduct war from a distance. "Wherever he was, there was the battle front," said Stephenson. "Churchill was always at the command post, firing off memos like bullets. Roosevelt wrapped himself in tranquillity at regular intervals. Churchill required little sleep. He'd start revving up as midnight approached. Roosevelt worked in concentrated periods throughout the day and was ready for bed by ten."

Stephenson recalls one conference with Donovan in the Prime Minister's bathroom. Churchill was draped in a large bath towel, which he discarded to dress, revealing himself as an outsize cherub. They were joined by General Alan Brooke, the Chief of Staff, and perched themselves along the edge of the tub and on the toilet while the War Lord fought with a shirt that refused to join at the neck. He plodded up and down the room like a giant Humpty Dumpty and delivered his opinion on how Donovan might use his neutrality to get into a Nazi-run part of Europe to stir up a diversion. Stephenson reminded him that this should be discussed first with the President. The remonstrance was meekly accepted. "I've got it!" cried Churchill, succeeding at last in holding the shirt together with a bowtie. They dined amiably on plovers' eggs, chicken pie, and chocolate pudding, with champagne, port, and brandy and with whiskies to top things off. Donovan noted that Churchill heeded those who stood up to him and held in contempt those who felt intimidated by personal friendship. "War is a business of terrible pressures and persons who take part in it must fail if they are not strong enough to withstand them," Churchill had written in *The World Crisis*, and he continued to dispense with anyone who broke under the strain of his own pressure.

The President's style was more relaxed, spiced with good humor, and his conduct "never less than heroic," Stephenson told Churchill, who was growing more impatient by the day for a first meeting with Roosevelt. Stephenson described that moment when Roosevelt left his bedroom to begin the day's business: "Signal bells ring. Aides stand back. He sails by, chin up, cigaret holder tilted high, radiating confidence and energy. Yet he sits in an uncomfortable wheelchair without cushions or armrests, and depends upon a Negro valet to push him along at a good pace, followed by Secret Service men with wire baskets of papers."

Churchill confided in a letter to Field Marshal J. C. Smuts, then Prime Minister of South Africa: "I do not think it would be any use to make a personal appeal to Roosevelt at this juncture to enter war. . . . We must not underrate his constitutional difficulties. He may take action as Chief Executive, but only Congress can declare war. He went so far as to say to me, 'I may never declare war; I may make war. . . .' Public opinion in the United States has advanced lately, but with Congress it is all a matter of counting heads. Naturally, if I saw any way of helping to lift this situation on to a higher plane I would do so."

A graphic account of how Stephenson and BSC operated in this sensitive period was given by one of his staff. Roald Dahl was introduced into the Roosevelt family circle. A tall young man, he had been badly injured as a fighter pilot and was first sent to Washington as a British air attaché. The prospect of going back to peacetime conditions appalled him. "I said to the Under-Secretary for Air 'O no, sir, please, sir—anything but that, sir!' But he said it was an order, the job was jolly important. I found it was a most ungodly unimportant job. I'd just come from the war. People were getting killed. I had been flying around, seeing horrible things. Now, almost instantly, I found myself in the middle of a pre-war cocktail mob in America. I had to dress up in ghastly gold braid and tassles. The result was, I became rather outspoken and brash. The senior people decided I wasn't a very good fellow to have around. An RAF Air Chief Marshal there arranged that I get the sack and be sent home to England."

Dahl was, in effect, a misplaced Battle of Britain pilot. He could hardly help make the comparison between his comrades still fighting desperately to blunt the renewed German bomber offensive and the "whiskey warriors" in Washington. But his failure as a diplomat was his strength, too. Americans who considered that Britain was playing at war (strengthened in that impression by the more unctuous representatives sent out from London because they were of little use elsewhere) found Dahl more to their liking. They talked to him frankly about how they would invigorate the British war effort if allowed to cut through red tape; and before he left, his reputation as an outspoken voice for the ordinary British fighting man had reached Stephenson. "He sent word: 'Go home, you'll be contacted, and you'll come back for me.' So I went to London as a squadron leader and I was back in a week as a wing commander. I went to a party, and at the other end of the room was the Air Chief Marshal who'd kicked me out. He strode across and said, 'What the hell are you doing here?'

"I said, 'I'm afraid, sir, you'll have to ask Bill Stephenson.' And he went even darker purple and walked away. It showed Stephenson's power. The Air Chief Marshal was struck absolutely dumb. Couldn't say a word. Couldn't do a thing about it."

Eleanor Roosevelt had been reading *The Gremlins,* one of Dahl's many successful children's books, to her grandchildren. When she heard that the author was in Washington, she invited him to dinner with the President.

"I was working entirely for Bill Stephenson then," Dahl later said. "My job was to try and oil the wheels between the British and the Americans. After that first dinner with the President, I used to go out to Hyde Park at weekends. There were always Roosevelts there, and people like Henry Morgenthau. I was able to ask pointed questions and get equally pointed replies because, theoretically, I was a nobody.

"For instance, there might be some argument officially between London and Washington about future operations. I could ask FDR over lunch what he thought, and he could tell me quite openly, far more than he could say in a formal way. Bleeding this information on the highest level from the Americans was not for nefarious purposes, but for the war effort. That's why Bill planted fellows like us."

Roosevelt knew that the young RAF officer was yet another informal channel to Stephenson. It was part of the game never to make formal acknowledgment of this. "I'd walk into FDR's little side room on a Sunday morning in Hyde Park and he'd be making Martinis, as he always did. And I would say 'Good morning, Mr. President' and we'd pass the time of day. He treated me as just a friend of Eleanor. And he'd say, naïvely, as if I was nobody much and he was making idle gossip, 'I had an interesting communication from Winston today. . . .' "

In this way, questions were posed and answered that, officially raised, might cause trouble. None doubted the absolute security of Stephenson's communications. They were, as Donovan was to say, the only communications for a time that were as leakproof as human endeavor could make them. It was for this reason that Donovan himself played the game and became in his turn a man "put in place" by the unseen coordinator of intelligence in New York, knowing that the President himself approved.

23

BIG AS THE INTREPID network in Manhattan had grown by 1941, Stephenson needed satellite bases to support his operations and, in an emergency, to which he could retreat. At least one had to be controllable from London. The choice fell upon islands scattered in the Atlantic and the Caribbean. The handiest was

Bermuda. In the front line of the critical war at sea, the Bermuda Station became an extension of BSC. Flying there from New York, one sensed a promise of entry into enemy lines.

Years later, Ian Fleming wove Bermuda into the James Bond novels, where it obviously belonged. After Fleming died, a book, John Pearson's *007-James Bond: The Authorized Biography,* serialized in the London *Sunday Telegraph* in 1974, claimed Commander Bond really did exist and was turned into fiction to deceive his enemies. The alleged Bond was "unmasked" in one of Bermuda's oldest and poshest hotels, the Hamilton Princess, where he was said to occupy a private suite belonging to Sir William Stephenson, his chief. The book became a lively topic of talk in the hotel's Gazebo Bar, where one wall consists of a giant fish tank reminiscent of the glass wall that separated 007 from Dr. No's sharks. Tourists inquired about the private elevator to Stephenson's penthouse and watched for the gold-plated Cadillac in which he was said to glide. It was true that the name INTREPID BERMUDA was registered with cable companies around the world; Stephenson kept the code name Churchill gave him, and Bermuda was indeed where Stephenson lived—but modestly. Otherwise this entirely fictitious story fell short of a much more tantalizing reality. Bermuda had once been a center for intense intelligence operations, and the Hamilton Princess did once buzz with Allied secret agents.

The offshore island intercepted postal, telegraph, and radio traffic between the Western Hemisphere and enemy-occupied Europe. It was an exotic satellite of the ULTRA establishment at Bletchley. Under the pink colonial-style Princess Hotel, 1,200 British experts worked in dungeonlike cellars, unknown to the American public. The growth of these facilities had been forced by the official ban, at the outbreak of Britain's war, on co-operation between the FBI and British intelligence. Within months, Hoover was beginning to benefit from Bermuda's study of clandestine radio stations serving Axis espionage.

The men and women at "Bletchley-in-the-Tropics"

became almost as skilled in reading orders to Nazi secret-warfare units as the ULTRA teams. During the ups and downs of FBI relations with BSC, Hoover was always mindful of this early assistance and the probability that operations would continually improve. He was also aware that if co-operation broke down, Stephenson had this large island organization to fall back on from New York. He knew enough about the Bermuda operation to believe that he might need it more than BSC needed him. Moreover, Roosevelt had told the FBI that overseas communications were to be nudged through the British screen established on these offshore islands.

Bermuda was a crossroads of communication, a center for the interception of other people's messages. There, the material was sifted and transmitted to Stephenson in New York. "One of the best results of collaboration between Stephenson and Hoover," the BSC Papers recorded, "was in this field. . . . BSC began early to provide the FBI with material from its various sources—in particular correspondence intercepted and studied by Imperial Postal and Telegraph Censorship stations in Bermuda, Trinidad and Jamaica without which the FBI would have been severely handicapped, for there was no postal censorship in the United States. . . . For their successful prosecution of several espionage cases during 1940 and 1941 the FBI owed obligation to BSC. They reciprocated generously. . . ."

There was nothing colonial about Bermuda despite the use of the word "Imperial." The islands boasted the oldest parliament outside London, and volunteered their loyalty to the monarch. The people were descended from settlers who, among thousands who paused to search for fresh water and food, remained there instead of continuing 500 miles farther west to what is now North Carolina. By the 1930s Bermuda was a refueling base for air and sea transport. Stephenson saw it as a main artery in the circulation of transatlantic traffic, and in 1940 applied the tourniquet. Americans found their correspondence with Europe mysteriously delayed. Others, gradually aware of what was happening, protested at this inspection of personal and private affairs. But the FBI backed Stephenson when Hoover began to haul in a rich harvest of agents and smugglers.

Bermuda was also an outstation for British agents operating the South America Network. Their routine radio traffic was always in danger of interruptions. Their low-power transmitters were inadequate for direct communication with London. Much of their intelligence was of direct concern to the United States, and presidential statements reflected the growing volume of intelligence from this source. To a pro-Nazi ambassador who scoffed at any suggestion of Nazi expansion into the Americas, Roosevelt said: "Hitler is the most devastating and all-pervading conqueror and destroyer in the last thousand years. We believe there is no geographic limit whatsoever to his infamous plans." He spoke to the Senate of the vast proportions of the Führer's program and "the savagery of his unlimited objectives." He pictured Hitler's "march of invasion across the earth with ten million soldiers and thirty thousand planes." He produced maps taken from German agents showing a Nazified Latin America, indicating how the Panama Canal was to be captured and how German bombers would be within striking range of U.S. cities.

The raw material for these declarations filtered through the Bermuda station, which expanded when Stephenson was still unsure that Americans would tolerate large operations on U.S. soil.

Laboratories were buried under several Bermuda hotels, with the Princess as headquarters. Teams of experts read the microdot messages sent by German spies, extracted letters from tightly sealed envelopes and put them back again without leaving a trace, developed the secret inks that in staggering variety were the staple of Axis espionage, and in other ways helped to trap agents and frustrate operations against British life lines. Since Bermuda straddled the transatlantic routes, Flying Clippers refueled there en route to Lisbon, which was the largest neutral hotbed of spies. Diplomatic bags passed that way under the protection of international agreements on the sanctity of ambassadorial mail—but the sealed bags were not immune to the fingers of skilled investigators. To make sure that even more diplomatic bags passed through these interception points, Stephenson awarded the FBI with continuous pertinent information.

Stephenson picked up one of Pierre Laval's couriers there in November 1940. Any Vichy-sponsored traveler could be carrying confidential papers between Nazi-occupied France and the United States, papers that foreshadowed the role of pro-Nazi French collaborators in the Americas. Asked what made him suspect the courier, Stephenson pointed out that Laval had been mentioned to him before the war as a potential friend of Germany by SS General Alfred Rosenberg.

Donovan used Bermuda for stopovers during his frequent journeys across the Atlantic. In the winter of 1940 he was shown "something of singular importance." The case stuck in his mind as an example of what could be accomplished by those with prodigious memories who could leap to conclusions with an agility that was incomprehensible to more pedestrian minds.

A young English girl, Nadya Gardner, had fished in the stream of letters and caught one from New York to the cover name used by Reinhard Heydrich. "Heydrich was that most sinister chief of the most vicious of Hitler's terrorist agencies," Stephenson said later. "Heydrich's power as an opponent in the secret wars had been underestimated. He was the monster who outgrew his masters—'The Prince of Shadow,' Admiral Canaris, and 'The Crown Prince of the Order of the SS,' Heinrich Himmler. He was not known at the time of Donovan's visit to be dabbling in foreign intelligence, although his path had crossed mine on prewar missions into the Ruhr."

The discovery of his real activities was to prove illuminating, the final results devastating. Heydrich was actually spying on Germany's own spies.

"After we had exposed his agent Dr. Westrick, Heydrich became uneasy," said Stephenson. "We made him more uneasy by planting evidence that suggested Westrick had been betrayed by other Nazi agents in the United States."

The intercepted letter, to "Lothar Frederick, I, Helgolaender Ufer, Berlin," had been submitted to normal chemical tests in the hotel's basement. These failed to confirm the presence of any secret ink. Yet there was something about the typewritten letter that aroused Nadya Gardner's suspicions. She knew nothing about Heydrich's cover name and address. She did have an instinct for the stilted phrases and odd sentence structures that frequently betray a spy.

The girl pointed out these oddities. The letter was in English. Here and there, words were used that translated directly from the German, as if the writer absent-mindedly slipped into native habits of thought. He had signed himself "Joe K." He sounded like an ordinary American, except for this peculiarity of expression and his interest in the movements of Allied shipping.

Joe K.'s handwriting was studied by the Bermuda teams. More letters were intercepted, addressed more often to Spain and Portugal than to Berlin, with return addresses to nonexistent New York commercial houses. The chemists still failed to develop any secret writing. Gardner, believing the letters contained something, persisted in her search for invisible inks. The chemical team was led by Dr. Enrique Dent, who finally tried an old iodine-vapor test that was now almost forgotten. The mysterious Joe K. was indeed employing one of the oldest invisible inks, made from powdered pyramidon, which was sold by druggists as a simple painkiller. In March 1941, another Joe K. letter, to a cover address in Portugal, was intercepted, with details of American aircraft supplied to Britain. The secret writing disclosed that a duplicate letter had been sent through China by way of "Smith." The FBI managed to intercept just such a letter and another for Mr. Smith in China with a precise plan of U.S. defenses at Pearl Harbor.* Still nobody knew who Joe K. was

* This was not the Pearl Harbor questionnaire disclosed by double agent TRICYCLE to the FBI on behalf of his British masters, and which led to false accusations that President Roosevelt knew beforehand about the planned Japanese attack. TRICYCLE's story comes later.

A letter dated April 15, 1941, addressed to Manuel Alonso in Madrid, carried two pages of shipping reports in secret ink, and seemed to come from the same source. Another letter the following week reported 70,000 British troops in Iceland and thanked the unknown recipient for sinking the S.S. *Ville de Liege*. It listed types of U.S. aircraft now going to England and spoke of convoy systems from Halifax in Canada.

The FBI, working on a different series of Bermuda intercepts, concentrated on a letter written March 20, 1941, reporting that someone called "Phil" had been knocked down by a taxi while trying to cross Broadway at Times Square. Another car had then run over him. The visible part of the letter sounded matter-of-fact. The secret writing between the lines conveyed a note of panic.

Meanwhile, the manager of the Hotel Taft in New York had reported curious circumstances surrounding the traffic death of a certain Julio Lopez Lido. Police were puzzled by the suggestion that Lido had been run down deliberately. The hotel register showed that Lido claimed Shanghai as his place of residence, and Spain as his native land. Supplied with information from the Bermuda intercepts, the investigators put facts together but succeeded only in producing more questions. Was the dead man "Mr. Smith of China"? Or was he Joe K. himself? And was the death car driven by a British agent?

Rather reluctantly, BSC indicated that Lido was known as a German agent using the cover name "Phil." The spy had been "removed from circulation." The FBI asked to see the file on the dead agent. He was Ulrich von der Osten, a captain in German military intelligence. He had a brother in Denver, Colorado, who was put under FBI surveillance. The dead man's luggage had contained a notebook, and in it was the phone number of a New York shop. Investigators learned that the shop had been recently sold, and recalled a phrase, "My aunt sold her store," in the Joe K. letter reporting Lido's accident. The letter had warned the recipient that "it is not advisable to send her any more mail but my other friends and relatives are still in business."

There was still no link with Joe K. The most the FBI could learn was that the "aunt" who "sold her store" had a nephew named Fred Ludwig. But where was he? The phone directories were full of Ludwigs. Then a German agent in Lisbon cabled in code to FOUZIE NEW YORK. A BSC contact in the New York cable office obtained the address of FOUZIE. He was Fred Ludwig—aged forty-eight, born in Fremont, Ohio, educated in Germany, and returned to New York in March 1940 to organize a Nazi spy ring. He recruited subagents through the German-American Bund and drew expenses from the German Consulate through an intermediary whom he met usually at Child's Restaurant on 34th Street. His director was the dead von der Osten. Joe K. was Ludwig.

Someone had disposed of von der Osten, a native-born American traitor who had become an officer and secret agent for a foreign government. In this period of neutrality, however, deeper FBI probing would have led to acute embarrassment. The case, coming early in FBI-BSC collaboration, became a textbook example of manipulative techniques. The British knew more than they dared tell about the German Consulate's internal business. There was a limit to what they could do about a spy ring themselves. They neither wished to compromise their sources inside German organizations nor could they afford to be caught trespassing on American tolerance to the point where it might lead to a public outcry. Von der Osten's death and the alert minds in Bermuda were enough to propel the FBI into action.

Bermuda could examine 200,000 letters during a singler stopover of a westbound Clipper; another 15,-000 letters on the same flight could be subjected to clinical tests. All trace of examination had, of course, to be eliminated. The whole object would have been defeated if the enemy guessed that this clandestine traffic was being examined. It was a curious game, because one-half of the correspondence, that from enemy territory, was not always available.

Analysis of the case confirmed SS General Reinhard Heydrich's overriding authority in all branches of German intelligence, secret police work, and the Nazi party's internal security. He now dominated Admiral Canaris, the man assumed to be running Germany's professional intelligence organization. Canaris was eventually hanged for allegedly taking part in an assassination attempt against his Führer. But he had by then lost real power. It was in Heydrich's hands. This vital piece of information was to prove particularly hazardous to Heydrich.

24

BERMUDA WAS THRUST politically into the war at sea when U.S. and British Naval Intelligence officers met there in early 1941 to fight the U-boats lurking under the sun-glazed mirror of the Atlantic. The devastating submarine attacks on supply convoys threatened to break Britain before she could become the springboard for invading Fortress Europe as projected by ABC. Eleven months before official U.S. entry into the war, American naval chiefs were seeking further ways to give discreet support to their secret allies.

The Battle of the Atlantic meant life or death to the British, still recovering from the narrow squeak of the Battle of Britain. The life lines from America were almost severed. The crusty U.S. Chief of Naval Operations, Admiral Ernest J. King, was torn between sympathy and his own responsibility in the Pacific, where the Japanese seemed to be preparing for aggression.

The British knew that if they seemed on the verge of collapse from starvation, any responsible American strategist would be justified in tossing ABC-1 overboard. It was therefore a time for frank disclosures.

The meeting in Bermuda, at the Royal Navy base near the ancient town of St. George's, was held under the old fort whose cannon still faced toward traditional enemies in Europe. The British sought to demonstrate that behind the grim headlines a successful campaign was being fought in secret. They revealed their machinery for decoding German signals gathered by radio nets directed from Bermuda, having already received from the U.S. Army's Signal Intelligence Service a model of the Japanese version of Enigma. This had been sent aboard Britain's newest and most powerful battleship, *King George V*, in January 1941, for final installation at Bletchley.

The smaller version of Bletchley buried under Bermuda's hotels was visited by the American cryptologist William Friedman on his way back to the United States. Friedman had collapsed from mental strain, and in January 1941, he was ordered home to rest in Walter Reed General Hospital. But he made use of this temporary setback; and reports of his nervous breakdown allowed him to work quietly behind the scenes for closer collaboration between the ULTRA organization and the still understaffed and ill-equipped U.S. service agencies. A month after the secret ABC-1 talks, Friedman went to Bermuda.

He had seen in Bletchley how the U-boat campaign might be defeated by intelligence. With his uncanny sense of how situations might develop, he was sure that the German submarine menace was mounting. In the following year, 1942, the figures proved him right when 1,644 vessels sailing on Britain's account were sunk. In a catastrophic engagement lasting one night, twenty-one merchantmen went down. These losses would have been much greater if U.S. cooperation had not begun so much sooner. In February 1941, Bermuda began to weave together the intelligence gathered by U.S. radio monitors and those of the British, between them covering the U-boat fleets.

German U-boats were controlled from a central operational base to which reports on British convoys were radioed. These reports, from Nazi agents and observation posts, were analyzed and the U-boats instructed accordingly. The development of radio made the U-boats more flexible. But radio also gave the eavesdroppers a picture of their movements. U-boat commanders were careless in using radio, pinning their faith on the Enigma coding machines that each submarine carried. Even if a submarine were captured with its Enigma intact, the Germans assumed that nobody could work out how the coding-machine drums were constantly changed.

In addition to some decoding of Enigma signals, the British were locating submarine positions by taking bearings on their radio transmissions. This coverage was immensely increased when U.S. stations began to feed information through BSC and Bermuda.

In order to make captured German seamen talk, they were shown details of their own service records, bits of gossip, the names of their friends, details of their training, and even their domestic problems. The British interrogators supposed that this mass of detailed background—surely the most thorough reconstruction of an enemy's routine affairs—was due to a complex system of indexing, interrogation of earlier prisoners, and intelligence from spies inside the German Navy. There was such an index, intended to duplicate the German U-boat command's documentation center. Much of the information, however, was recovered through ULTRA and the substation in Bermuda. The seeming strength of the U-boats—their use of radio —had become a major weakness. Whereas German land and air forces could switch to landlines and couriers to reduce the mass of signals on the eve of a major operation, naval forces had to depend on radio links. The seemingly trivial details of, say, Torpedoman Schmidt's two-day training pause at Brest, would be filed away for the time when a member of an ULTRA Watch recalled this item and put it together with a new signal recording Schmidt's transfer to a supply ship in mid-Atlantic. Schmidt's expertise in a particular type of torpedo, plus the presence of the "milch cow" supplying U-boats at sea, and other bits of information would produce an updated picture of German intentions.

Stephenson realized that it was not enough to disclose the product of these deductions. American "clients" might justifiably show skepticism unless they knew how this material was obtained. The answer was to let Bill Donovan and high-ranking U.S. officers see the system at work. In this way, it was possible to circumvent a rule that there should be no "trading" of naval intelligence by British officers. Those responsible for passing intelligence to their American colleagues were not supposed to receive information in return because competitive methods might have disastrous effects on security. "Security was directed at keeping Anglo-American cooperation out of the newspapers," wrote Donald McLachlan, who was on the personal staff of the British Director of Naval Intelligence. "Publicity, which might alert the rivals and critics of Roosevelt could mean disaster."

In essence, Bermuda's methods were those of Bletchley. The requirements were first to hear the enemy U-boat traffic, then unscramble the gobbledygook, and finally analyze and distill information from the terse messages. The three functions were separate: signals, cryptography, intelligence. There was an additional absolute requirement that whenever intercepted information was acted upon, there must be a cover story to account for the acquisition of the knowledge. The Germans must not guess that the movements of the U-boat packs could be closely followed and even anticipated. If an enemy submarine surfaced under a waiting bomber, there had to be some acceptable explanation, however false, that would fool the enemy.

The basic work was done by Admiralty experts in London. The Watch there was kept twenty-four hours a day, every day, by specialists sitting in a horseshoe around the Watch Keeper. The British Navy also kept its own experts at Bermuda and Bletchley, because it was felt that significant items in enemy traffic might escape the notice of landlubbers. Significant naval material was selected and the most important went straight to London.

In Bermuda, a Special Liaison Unit, trained at Bletchley, rephrased information so that it bore no resemblance to the original signals. The SLU leader was the only man empowered to convey this distilled information to British or American service units. Once it had been demonstrated to the satisfaction of

Admiral King that these rephrased intelligence messages were obtained directly from German headquarters, it became possible to get fast U.S. Navy action, in close harmony with British warships.

One of the world's great secret-ink experts, Dr. Stanley W. Collins, of London, set up an operation in Bermuda's hot and humid vaults, where the pace of work was such that English girls fainted from a combination of fatigue and heat. So discreetly were these arrangements handled that it was more than three decades before it was partly acknowledged: "Britain's decision to intercept traffic from the United States to Europe brought the first big change here," wrote Bermuda's official historian and editor of the *Royal Gazette*, W. S. Zuill, in 1973. "Ships were herded into port. Aircraft waited while the mails were examined. Large numbers of experts and linguists moved into the Princess and Bermudiana hotels and their work exposed German spies already 'in place' in the United States. Art treasures stolen by the Nazis in France and shipped through neutral ports to be sold in New York for Hitler's war machine were confiscated. In one case, the American Export Lines' ship *Excalibur* carried valuable paintings in a sealed strong-room. When the captain refused to open it, the British burned it open like safecrackers, took the paintings and stored them in the Bank of Bermuda vaults until they could be returned to the Paris owner who got all 270 of these Impressionist works back intact, to his own considerable astonishment."

The commercial transatlantic airline route was Pan American's service of Boeing 314 flying boats, whose cargoes and passengers were discreetly screened while the planes refueled on the island. Sometimes a Clipper's entire cargo had to be hastily examined while the crew were entertained in the yacht club. While "trappers" moved at high speed through the mail, one excuse followed another for delaying the flying boat.

The techniques of prying open sealed envelopes without leaving a trace required practice. The most skillful trappers were women. And by some quirk in the law of averages, the girls who shone in this work had well-turned ankles. "It was fairly certain that a girl with unshapely legs would make a bad trapper and become a square peg in a round hole," one BSC medical officer wrote in a solemn memo. "Nobody has discovered what part the leg plays. There is here the basis for some fundamental research." The author was an athletic young doctor. BSC decided he was trying to create a new and rewarding department for himself. But would-be trappers continued to be baffled by requests to display their ankles.

Some of the girls came from MI-5. Postings to Bermuda sounded romantic. They proved dull and demanding. The girls outnumbered the men, who were, in any case, mostly married, middle-aged, or buried in work. Among the more printable comments was this verse from *The Virgin's Lament*:

> *I'm just a girl at MI 5*
> *and heading for a virgin's grave—*
> *My legs it was wot got me in—*
> *Still I wait for my bit of sin.*

Long ears, sharp eyes, and well-turned ankles were hardly a match for the enemy's more subtle methods of communication. "Duff," the microdot method of slipping information through the mail, involved photographically shrinking a typed page to the size of an ordinary typewritten punctuation mark. To recover the message, a 200-power microscope was required. The punctuation dots were scattered through a letter like raisins in the suet puddings called in the British Army "plum duff," hence the nickname.

The microdot was heralded by Hoover as "the enemy's masterpiece of espionage." Bermuda disclosed to the FBI the hypermicrophotographic dots and the method of their preparation by nonportable apparatus. The FBI, to protect British sources, gave the credit elsewhere. The Bermuda trappers could not hope to find the microdots by random search. They needed to be kept informed of suspects whose letters should be inspected, of addresses that BSC and the FBI felt uneasy about, and of the categories of correspondence that seemed to be destined for German intelligence fronts. Information gained through Bermuda led to the unmasking of clandestine German activities in Latin America, where British agents could then produce even more knowledge for the compilers of dossiers in New York. These compilations by BSC scholars were the basis of research and analysis, which became vital to special intelligence operations.

The procedure during U.S. neutrality was for Bermuda to pass to BSC in New York the essence of intercepted enemy intelligence messages, with additional details culled from the researchers' files. Inquiries could be made among London and European intelligence stations for further information concerning the addressee. The result, whether a fat dossier or a single sheet of paper, was passed to the FBI, whose outstanding work was in investigation and analysis. The identification of handwriting and typing was made by scanning thousands upon thousands of documents in which a suspect's script might pop up again, using composite cards displaying ten or more highly characteristic alphabetical letters originally found in the intercepted missive.

An intensive analysis was made of the information derived from the letters of known agents. Here the FBI threw into the pot whatever material BSC could provide. For instance, if an agent was using secret ink, he would have had to write visibly some kind of a letter that could withstand routine examination by inquisitive eyes. It is difficult to compose an open letter that makes sense, appears innocent, and deals with small details of business or domestic life without occasionally revealing some pertinent fact about the author's personal life. Where there is no secret ink, and the real message has to be buried in a seemingly innocent letter, the writer's task is harder. The greater the number of messages intercepted in connection with a single investigation, the better chance the FBI had of discovering a clue.

"Early cooperation in the field made it possible to keep pace with German improvements in technology," the BSC Papers noted. "We were ready when Professor Zapp's Cabinet appeared upon the scene! There really was a German professor of that name who simplified the process of microphotography."

This advance enabled German agents to send huge quantitites of technical information by airmail. Trade and technical journals, economic reports and other printed matter were smuggled over the border into Mexico, where they were microphotographed and sent to the European cover addresses in the form of dots. Even diagrams and chemical formulas traveled this way, twenty or more dots to an air letter. "Professor Zapp's Cabinet" was a compact folding laboratory. Microphotography had previously involved two stages: making a postage-stamp photograph of the material, then photographing this "stamp" through a reversed microscope. The resultant negative was lifted out of the emulsion with a modified hypodermic needle and cemented into a letter with collodion. Zapp's Cabinet mechanized an operation in which the microdots were consequently transparent negatives and could be stuck onto the gummed part of an envelope. The emulsion used in this process was an aniline dye instead of a silver compound, and an image could be resolved in very fine detail. Once the searchers became aware, they paid even closer attention to the mails.

Bermuda was thus more than a backstop to BSC operations in New York. It played an aggressive role against enemy operations in the Americas when few took the threat of a Nazi fifth column seriously. A British field organization for counterespionage in the United States itself was precluded for many reasons. Employment of agents would have violated the McKellar Act. Better results were to be won by the close and informal liaison nourished by Stephenson. This was helped by the legitimate co-operation between the U.S and Canadian peacekeeping agencies whereby covert co-operation on anti-Nazi intelligence was disguised as routine police work.

It suited Hoover to let Bermuda continue as an offshore catchall. There his agents could participate in British intelligence operations without having to answer awkward questions from the State Department, jealously resisting FBI expansion into foreign fields. After Stephenson's main base in Rockefeller Center grew to the point where it was difficult to disguise, Bermuda's machinery changed. The advantages of transferring activities to Bermuda became apparent. Hoover was given FDR's personal encouragement to collect secret intelligence concerning German subversion all through the Western Hemisphere. The President instructed him to prepare measures against any such operations at home if war should come. But Hoover was trapped between the President's determination to prepare for war and Congress's almost fanatic insistence upon guarding neutrality. When he realized that Stephenson not only would help him but also would one day give the FBI all the credit, he jumped at the chance to acquire knowledge and experience in a field new to him.

On his other doorstep was Camp X.

25

BLETCHLEY AND BERMUDA were important to BSC for detection. Camp X gave BSC its punch. These closely guarded acres of Canadian farmland were separated from the United States by a stretch of some of the blackest, coldest lake water in the world, a dramatic contrast with Bermuda, thrust far forward into a sea surrounded by war action, but lapped by warm waters.

"Here was the coiled strength, building toward aggressive intelligence operations," said the BSC Papers of Camp X.

Here agents trained, guerrilla devices were tested, and Hollywood-style dummy buildings were constructed "in imitation of important Nazi hide-outs to be invaded by the parachutist collectors of Nazi vermin," in Stephenson's more forceful words. "If Bermuda was the outthrust defensive arm, Camp X was the clenched fist preparing for the knockout."

This linkage of Camp X with Bermuda was typified by the case of SS General Heydrich. It was clear by the end of 1940 that Heydrich hoped to achieve power subordinate only to Hitler. Evidence of his designs upon the United States had been retrieved by Bermuda's trappers. His operations were analyzed by BSC in New York. Preparations for his execution were undertaken at Camp X; these involved a film producer, a set designer from Hollywood, and a French actress whose lover was a German double agent.

Camp X was near the Toronto-Kingston highway along the north shore of Lake Ontario, about 300 miles northwest of Manhattan. It was chosen in part because it could be reached easily by FBI agents and Donovan's men. Equipment and recruits could cross the border without attracting attention, but unauthorized visitors found it hard to reach. It was guarded on the south by forty miles of lake water and on the north by a dense, deep strip of bushland. The approaches from east and west were under constant scrutiny. The privileged few on special missions went to Roosevelt Beach, just east of Niagara Falls on the U.S. side and crossed the dark lake waters at night, glimpsing only briefly the blackened faces of British commandos in the gloom. These veterans of raids along the enemy coasts in Europe, now the protectors of Camp X, were skilled in the use of the hatpin, the thin copper wire, and other homely, silent, lethal weapons that would not needlessly alarm the local inhabitants or draw the unwelcome attentions of the local constabulary.

"The land was purchased in small lots in the best spy-story tradition," said Ian Fleming, who trained there. "That is, Stephenson's money was used, and the title transferred to a Crown company later. He and Bill Donovan figured the location was ideal for their purposes. Even in those days, Big Bill reckoned he'd be sending his own trainees up there before long."

Like its parent in Manhattan, the base kept growing. Station M, an important component of Camp X, faked documents, passing itself off as a radio relay transmitter. The Norman Rogers Airfield, a hundred miles to the east, trained British naval pilots and therefore had an excuse for heavily guarded hangars. One-man submarines and underwater demolition devices were tested in the lake. Buried underground was Hydra, the transmitter that linked Camp X with British secret-intelligence stations around the world. Aspidistra, the biggest radio-communication unit in the world, was added in 1943. It took its name from a London music-hall song about "the biggest aspidistra in the world." The Canadian Broadcasting Corporation told the townspeople of neighboring Oshawa that it was putting up radio aerials, this to explain some of the strange activities that began in 1940 when the general manager of CBC, Stephenson's old friend Gladstone Murray, the former fighter pilot, became a Baker Street Irregular.

"Despite its Boys-Own-Adventure tone, the complex had a deadly purpose," Murray said later. "When the British withdrew from continental Europe, their regular secret service was cut off. . . . A whole new system had to be created. . . . The nerve center for this work had to be far removed from enemy eyes, yet close to the over-all operational center of BSC in New York. It had to be able to work with U.S. citizens without contravening U.S. laws, to meet a rising demand for those with firsthand knowledge of Europe. There had to be space. Large-scale terrain maps, reproductions of buildings and targets and training grounds for para-troopers demanded room for maneuver. Obviously, we were talking about somewhere in Canada."

Colin Gubbins, the chief Baker Street Irregular, had pointed out to Murray: "The first men into occupied countries must be parachuted 'blind,' and this will continue to be the most efficient method of insertion. The coasts are guarded, the waters mined, and landing agents by sea results in high losses. We prefer to drop them in. And this requires highly specialized training in the air, for both pilots and agents."

"Factories" grew for production of false documents, camouflaged explosives, and all the paraphernalia of the spy trade that were life-and-death equipment, not romantic toys, to these silent invaders. The "ungentlemanly warfare boys" were conscious of the savage, terrifying aspects of their work, while convinced that it was the only way to undermine the new totalitarians. In Canada, experts could draw upon U.S. resources. These experts came from all levels of society. Some were men and women of such distinction in public life that their involvement is unmentionable to this day. Others were safe-crackers, forgers, and professional bank robbers whose expertise could not be duplicated by legitimate entrepreneurs. A compiler for a prewar directory of German companies could make swift associations between odd items of information, as if he carried a cross index in his head. A typewriter manufacturer could duplicate any patented machine in the world. A refugee from Europe haunted pawnshops for battered suitcases made and used on the Continent. A man on the FBI's wanted list was moved into Canada and protected a few miles north of the border as he devoted his extraordinary talent to the manufacture of counterfeit European currency.

British censorship stations provided material and information to Station M, where forged material was inserted into diplomatic bags as well as into "ordinary" parcels en route to Europe. This alone required a great many workers with the necessary skill to unseal and reseal mail without leaving a trace. "The cost of a criminal organisation devoted to similar ends, and obliged to make it all worthwhile, would be quite uneconomic," warned Eric Maschwitz. This composer of lyrics and musical comedies wrote, in typically cautious terms, in his autobiography: "The operations with which I was concerned under a genius known as 'Little Bill' were many and curious . . . I was associated with an industrial chemist and two ruffians who could reproduce faultlessly the imprint of any typewriter on earth. I controlled a chemical laboratory in one place, a photographic studio in another. My travels took me to Canada, Brazil and Bermuda."

The "M" in Station M was said to stand for Magic and Jasper Maskelyne, a hero to British schoolboys before the war, one of the great magicians of all time and a master at the art of deception. His section at Camp X was known as the "Magic Group"; it conjured up illusions and laid false trails.

Maskelyne was a genius at make-believe. During an early visit to the camp by Hoover, the FBI director was astonished to see what appeared to be several warships on Lake Ontario. He was standing in a hut, and Maskelyne had rigged mirrors to produce a magnified effect with toy German battle cruisers.

"He put the conjuring arts into battle," said Murray. "The trick was to make the enemy see what he had been led to expect." Maskelyne flew from Camp X to all corners of the world, creating nonexistent armies, dummy cannon, trick air bases, false fleets.

The Travellers Censorship, a division of BSC, sent Toronto special items needed for agents. Somewhere near the immigration wickets of American seaports and airfields, innocent-looking girls and men watched each pilgrim. They wanted clothes bearing the telltale stitching and labels of European tailors. They sought pens and pencils made in towns now under German occupation. They needed samples of "epistolary paraphernalia," in the jargon of officialdom—notepaper, rubber stamps, and stationery still in use behind Hitler's wall.

A traveler from Europe might be invited to step aside. Trembling, if his conscience was troubled, the newcomer would go to a cubicle, where his bags and clothing underwent a thorough search. Fearing the worst, the victim would be relieved when the official passed him through—so relieved he might not notice some small personal item had been removed, or, noticing, would prefer to make no fuss. In the United States, there was co-operation from all government departments. If the traveler happened to wear clothing needed for agents, he or she might be followed. Later, the clothing would vanish from a laundry or a secondhand shop. One way or another, it was paid for. A girl arrived in New York with a wardrobe of good-quality clothes tailored in Berlin. She passed through Customs and took the train to Chicago. Along the way, her baggage was lost. She was astonished by the generous settlement made instantly and without question by the railroad. Her clothes were in Toronto a week later, and were forwarded on a Ferry Command Liberator, together with a Jewish girl who had spent the previous three months in Camp X studying the new Reich Chancellery in Berlin. This girl was dropped into France, took the train from Paris to Berlin, and was in the heart of the Third Reich, complete with "authentic" documents and clothes, within a month.

The United States had been designated since 1939 "the largest potential source of agents because of the many Americans whose origins are European, who are fluent in European languages, and who will wish to fight oppression from within," according to the BSC Papers. For two years, 1940 and 1941, the U.S. government was officially opposed to potential agents being drawn from foreign or foreign-descended minorities, and could make its policy effective through the State and Justice departments and the Immigration Service, without whose permission a recruit found it theoretically impossible to leave the country. Despite this, some of the best agents were recruited in the U.S. for Toronto. Their acquisition had to be handled delicately when the recruit came from across the border. In exceptional cases, if bureaucracy threatened to frustrate matters, President Roosevelt was asked through Donovan to intervene. A sea captain with special knowledge of enemy waters was "sprung" in this way and then "lent" to frogman saboteurs requiring his navigational advice. None of this was ever admitted; nothing concerning the real purpose was ever entered into the record.

This meant high-level clearances. A future prime minister of Canada and secretary-general of the United Nations, Lester B. Pearson, was a humble diplomat when Stephenson asked him to become "a King's messenger," conveying secret documents. Orders had to be coordinated between London, BSC in New York, and Camp X. Pearson had spent the hard winter of 1940 in London. Then he was asked to carry top-secret material across the Atlantic. He later wrote in his autobiography:

I shall always remember this journey. I was flying from the war to peaceful unharmed Canada; from battered and beleaguered London in the hour of her agony and honour to the safe faraway city on the Ottawa River. . . .

I was asked to carry the top secret brown envelope to a certain floor of a building in New York, the headquarters of British Security Coordination. I agreed.

I left London the day after the heaviest and most damaging air raid of the war. When I drove to the airport fires were still burning fiercely and some buildings which had been hit were only a few yards from Canada House. . . . The contrast between that last night in London and my first exposure to a city not at war was staggering. As we flew over Lisbon, there were lights, actually lights! As we landed, we saw German and Italian planes. We went through, not military, but civilian inspection. The shops, gaily decorated, displayed fruit and flowers and candies. Very strange! I had been met by a secretary of the British Embassy who warned me that my hotel was the centre of Nazi and Fascist espionage. This made me very conscious of my brown envelope. I became more anxious after an experience on entering the hotel. The first person I saw looked familiar. With a start I recognized him as a German whom I had known in Geneva during the disarmament conferences. He was a very friendly fellow. I was impulsively about to say 'hello' and he seemed to share the same impulse, when suddenly I realized, as he may have too, who we were and where and when.

We turned away, and it was just as well because my British escort, who knew his way around Lisbon, pointed him out to me later as one of the principals in the German intelligence services in Spain and Portugal.

My career as a courier was off to a shaky start, but there were no further incidents. No Mata Hari dropped her handkerchief before me in the diningroom or at the casino. Nobody tried to snatch my brown envelope from under my pillow that night. I guarded it carefully during our stops at the Azores and Bermuda. On landing in New York I took a taxi at once to my destination and rode an elevator to the appointed floor of British Security Coordination. As I got out of the elevator

I expected to be stopped and asked to produce my credentials; or, if not there, certainly outside the particular room where I was to hand over my envelope. Nobody bothered me. There was indeed a New York policeman in a chair outside the door of the office I was seeking. But he was dozing and ignored my entrance over his outstretched legs. Within the office a receptionist glanced at my credentials, signed for my envelope, thanked me, and said goodbye. This all seemed very casual for a secret service, a first impression of carelessness which I later found to be deceptive.

Such enlightenment quickly followed. Before he reached his home town of Toronto, forty miles from Camp X, he was collected by British interrogators who had a complete file on the German he had encountered in Lisbon. "They were alarmed," he said later, "by the possibility that one name contained in my package could have been identified. I said the German intelligence chief would have to be not only telepathic but also a codebreaker and miracle-worker. One name was a cover for myself: MIKE."

Pearson went on to serve in Washington. His wry memoirs, *Mike*, reveal a good-humored tolerance of the sillier aspects of espionage. During his wartime career, however, he was as dedicated and tight-lipped as any, but what he could not know was that the name so closely guarded was that of a girl, not his own.

He wrote: "The need was for unconventional men and women who understood that the Second World War was ideological and fought against political terrorists. The guerilla and the agent had to forego the certainty and tradition of regimental life—the external marks of respect, uniforms and unquestioning obedience."

The Royal Canadian Mounted Police provided facilities and manpower without asking questions. Ernest W. Bavin, a fifth senior superintendent attached to Canadian intelligence headquarters, for instance, was swept in mid-career into adventures unforeseen even by a Mountie. He said later: "Recruits might be picked out by talent spotters as they passed through Bermuda en route from Europe to the United States, or identified in American trade unions as activists. A batch of Peruvian airmen in New York, on their way home from Italian flying schools, provided one recruit. Another was a Yugoslav-born American official of the United Mine, Mill, and Smelter Workers Union. What seemed like faults to rigid disciplinarians of the regular services often appealed to Stephenson as evidence of strong will power and an independent cast of mind."

The chances of fulfilling a mission had been worked out statistically and were known to many recruits: three chances in a hundred that the recruit would be incapacitated before going into action; three chances in a hundred of capture; one chance in three that if captured, he or she would be interrogated by the Gestapo. The situation was far worse in reality. Of 250 agents who left for the relatively quiet region of Belgium, 105 were arrested, of whom only forty survived. The life expectancy of the "pianists," or radio operators, they were warned, was six months in most areas. The casualties in training, of course, thinned out the ranks. The character and intelligence of the would-be agent were tested day and night. Ian Fleming took one course. "Ian was exceptionally good at underwater demolition, which we carried out in Lake Ontario," said Stephenson. "The water there is ice cold even in summer. Ian had a flair for the work. He had to deal with his own vivid imagination though.

"He went through an exercise called 'disposal of the tail,' the enemy agent on the trail of our man. He was told that the supposed agent had returned to a room in a hotel. This was a mock-up hotel near Toronto used for these exercises. Ian was to push open the door fast and shoot the alleged agent, actually a former Shanghai policeman, name of Fairbairn, one of our instructors. Ian walked along the corridor, and I loaded a Smith and Wesson 45 and handed it over. I said: 'It's all checked out. I tested it on the range yesterday. Now, you've got to take this seriously. Kick open that door and shoot the guy before he can possibly draw. Otherwise you're going to be a dead Ian.' He went up to the door, put his hand on the knob, and stopped dead. I asked, 'What's wrong?' He said: 'Bill, you know I can't shoot a man in cold blood.' He had too much imagination. A *good* imagination. He thought of the other fella lying in a pool of blood while he was alive and well, even though he knew it was all a game. . . ."

Churchill's term for the specialists in unarmed combat was "leopards," the word he had first used to describe Canadians evolving commando-type operations in World War I when he first met Stephenson. The leopards taught silent methods of killing, from the karate chop to slipping an ordinary needle into a part of the neck where it produced instant death. They put recruits through commando training; parachuting, handling of weapons and explosives, mountain climbing. The training was directed by Colonel John Skinner Wilson, transferred from Military Intelligence. His staff included "Mad Mike" Calvert, who later fought in the jungle with Orde Wingate, having spent his life between the ages of twenty-one and twenty-five virtually learning, teaching, or practicing these deadly skills.

The girls were taken into FANY, the First Aid Nursing Yeomanry, which gave them an innocent look. They seemed cheerful and harmless, putting up with the charge of being "a posh but idle corps." Their specialty was radio work. They were later attached to the secret armies. The "executions" of top Nazis were carried out, for example, because these girls provided close and continuous communication between clandestine transmitters and London.

Every agent received training in Morse code. "I dreamed in Morse," said one girl destined for France. "I even knitted in Morse."

Some agents with special knowledge were needed by SIS for intelligence-gathering missions. This did not always mean stealing enemy secrets. William Deakin was a professor who quit BSC in New York to command a partisan mission. Deakin had been literary assistant to Churchill, and an Oxford tutor in modern history. Why was an obviously valuable man like this dropped into an almost suicidal mission? The reason was that British scholars were needed in the field for tasks requiring particular qualities of intellect, filling gaps in the knowledge of the secret armies. "Many of the scholars who fled from Europe were not capable of decisive action despite their vehement declarations of hostility to Hitler," said an official account of recruitment problems. "Anti-Fascist intellectuals from Europe who sought sanctuary in the Western Hemisphere were in general not of tough enough fibre." Some European academics thought the work distasteful and displayed a misunderstanding of its purpose. The pseudo-scientific definition of "the ideal agent," given later by an American psychiatrist, conveys some of the misconceptions regarding agents. They were "men who plunge headlong into an undertaking of fast change and danger because they are discontented," he wrote. "They want to give worth and meaning to their otherwise futile lives."

The British approach was fundamentally different. Harold Macmillan, the publisher who became a prime minister, summed it up when describing a comrade's ordeal under German fire. "If he had fallen, later, into a psychiatrist's hands, he would have been sent to a mental home as insane. Instead, he was back in action next day." Many of Macmillan's literary colleagues worked in intelligence and took the same view: it was work where common sense counted more than pseudo-scientific claptrap. Stephenson looked for agents who believed in human decency and then found the job to fit their talent. He saw nothing wrong with "a love of productive peril" or a certain flamboyance if there was a moral force behind it. Years later, he gave this formula: "Some of the best agents are those who in peacetime make good bankers, physicians, or creative artists. Their response to danger is positive. In modern terms, they belong to the Type-A personality who has full control of himself although driven by great energy. The good agent starts out as a man who chose action over inaction but who learns to control his impulses and detach himself from a temporary reality in order to resume abstract thought."

A Personality Structure of the Ideal Agent was later drafted by American intelligence specialists in an attempt to systematize what had been informal and imprecise. American mass-production methods seemed to require a more definitive approach, with everything spelled out. They pinpointed, unconsciously, subtle differences between Americans and British that served as mild irritants. Some British concealed character under a veneer of dandyism. Their high-pitched nasal mumblings, passing for conversation, were useful for evading precise conversation on delicate issues. Young veterans from Britain had to be warned that outspoken FBI and U.S. intelligence officers who trained at Camp X were underestimated if their cousins thought all Americans were loud-mouthed and shallow.

Even at the top, differences in national character caused tension. It was one reason Canada and Canadians provided such a singular service, being part of both worlds. Even senior officers at Anglo-American staff talks were not above fisticuffs. The Anglo-American Chiefs of Staff still irritated each other. "Brooke got nasty and King got good and sore. King almost climbed over the table at Brooke. God, he was mad! I wish he had socked him," commented General "Vinegar Joe" Stilwell. He was describing, not two groups of schoolboys challenging one another, but a British general and an American admiral whose tempers were worn thin by personal idiosyncrasies that grew out of totally different backgrounds.

At Camp X, the only enemy was in Europe, and the trainees were taught that if a fight was inevitable, it was often better to "put a German in hospital. That ties up other Germans. A dead one is buried and out of the way." Students were taught leverage in attacking a man hand to hand; and they were taught the vulnerable parts of the body, rather more than most would suppose. "You've always got a weapon in your pockets: a nail file, a pin, a fountain pen." A box of matches could be thrown blazing into the face of a sudden attacker, blinding him; but there was a right and a wrong way of exploding the matches.

Scotland Yard detectives found themselves apprehensively teaching the gentle art of smuggling. A girl learned she had more places of concealment in her body than a man. She should take advantage of the reluctance of police to search the more intimate parts. With practice and regular exercise of the vaginal muscles, a woman could carry objects of considerable size.

The L pill could be carried in the mouth. The capsule's skin was insoluble. If the pill was swallowed by accident, it passed through the body without causing harm. If crushed between the teeth, the contents of potassium cyanide brought quick death.

The first agents into Europe found their forged papers outdated or badly faked. A routine inspection quickly betrayed them. Part of these troubles stemmed from wartime Britain's lack of materials. The documentation centers in Canada could draw on limitless reserves in the Western Hemisphere. Samples of German-occupation forms, rubber stamps, and inks were obtained through the BSC network, along with domestic articles that civilians were using under Nazi occupation: battered suitcases, ersatz toothpaste, cheap caps—and all providing possible places of concealment. A bewildered arrival from Genoa would wonder why his spectacles were borrowed by immigration authorities in New York. They were copied and sent up to Toronto for mass production, so that at some time in the future a bespectacled agent could carry a microdot in the form of a speck of dust on a lens.

The traffic in eccentric bits of equipment across the U.S.-Canada border was continuous. Some had to be smuggled. This gave trainees a mild taste of reality. When BSC was preparing agents in New York for an assignment, they might suddenly be required to smuggle medical drugs across the border because of a provision in regulations; the smuggling was safer than confiding to Customs men the reason for the drugs.

The time approached when Americans would call on stations like Camp X for instructors, equipment, and handbooks. An American officer inspecting sabotage devices, developed by the BSC Scientific Research Section, said, "I don't see any article of everyday use that's safe to touch," looking at explosive loaves of bread, fountain pens that squirted cyanide, artificial logs that would blow up when tossed on a fire, and booby traps that ranged from incendiary cigarets to animal droppings. The manure heaps were made of explosive plastic and painted to resemble the excrement found in different parts of the world, after consultation with Professor Julian Huxley, who ran the London Zoo. There was a particular demand for elephant droppings for use in Asia, where the plastic dung could be placed alongside the real faeces on trails used by the enemy. "It was one time," said Elder Wills, "when bullshit really did more than baffle brains. It blew 'em up." He was improvising on the unofficial Camp X slogan, camouflaged in the acronym BBB: Bullshit Baffles Brains.

Elder Wills was a former scenic artist from London's Drury Lane who became a camouflage expert. He was the friendly rival of Alexander Korda, who, with his brother Zoltan, reproduced locales in Nazi territories so that missions could be rehearsed as if enacting the scenarios for movies. Wills had escaped from Dunkirk and spent the following weeks frantically building cardboard tanks and wooden aircraft to distort enemy reconnaissance reports and discourage those contemplating invasion. He was a master of disguise and make-believe. Some of his prewar film sets were made for Stephenson in the Shepperton studios. He had no difficulty creating bogus airfields and camouflaging the real ones. Then he was plunged into the more complex BSC world of deception, where he was horrified to learn that agents were equipped in the beginning with radio transmitters straight from Army stores. He launched the search for European refugee suitcases in which miniaturized sets could be squeezed and camouflaged. He produced a secret ink that showed only under infrared light, and then designed pocket flashlights with infrared discs by which to read the secret ink. His first workshop was in the Victoria and Albert Museum in London.

As business grew, new quarters were sought in North America. Make-up artists, wardrobe mistresses, magicians, and comedians began to trek to New York or followed the Korda brothers to Camp X. One recruit was the husband of actress Constance Cummings. "I was given a code name and a phone number to call when I reached New York. By the time I reached New York I remembered the number but forgot my name. I dialed the number and then my mind went blank. There was an ugly pause. I said,

'Half a minute, I'll try to think.' Eventually the girl at the other end said, 'Well, never mind, because I know who you are anyway.'" He was Benn Levy, the playwright.

Even the pilots who flew some of these exotic creatures had the smell of grease paint on them. A captain ferrying planes through Montreal was Hughie Green, who had toured the music halls at the age of thirteen with his own road show and shared star billing in prewar movies with Freddie Bartholomew, and who would become one of Britain's best-known television personalities in the 1970s. As a young pilot attached to the Royal Canadian Air Force, he recognized some of his bomb-bay and gun-turret passengers despite their padded overalls and helmets. When he saw one of his old film producers, it was difficult pretending they had never met—especially someone like Carol Reed, who starred him when he was fifteen in his first movie, *Mr. Midshipman Easy*. It was pretty bizarre. A few years earlier, Green might have done almost anything to catch the attention of these movie moguls. Now he was the pipsqueak pilot taking their lives in his hands and they couldn't even admit knowing him, ex-star or not.

Noel Coward was sent to join Stephenson in New York after the French debacle. "I was awfully bewildered," he later said. "I thought it would be more Mata Hari—and then I told myself, 'Well, hardly that. I couldn't wear a jewel in my navel, which I believe she was given to doing.'

"I'd had a confusing talk with Winston Churchill before I left. He knew I'd done something in France for intelligence but he couldn't get it in his head that what I wanted was to *use* my intelligence— I kept saying, 'Winston, they want to use my *creative* intelligence.' But he'd got it in his head that Bill Stephenson was aiming for Mata Hari and he kept saying, 'No use, you'd be no good—too well known.'

"I said, 'That's the whole point. I'll be so well known nobody will think I'm doing anything special.' And Winston just kept shaking his head and insisting I'd never make a spy.

"Eventually I got it through to him—I was fluent

in Spanish and could do the whole of Latin America, where the Germans were very active preparing their campaigns in the United States. And so that's where I started."

Coward's career in secret intelligence must have been one of the best-kept secrets involving internationally known entertainers who reported to Stephenson and then were shot off into the unknown. He was knighted years later. As Sir Noel, on the eve of his death in 1973, he discussed that career for the first time and conveyed the flavor, the mixture of mock bravado, self-deriding, and understatement that characterized these talented amateurs.*

"My celebrity value was wonderful cover," he recalled. "So many career intelligence officers went around looking terribly mysterious—long black boots and sinister smiles. Nobody ever issued me with a false beard. And invisible ink—? I can't read my own writing when it's supposed to be visible. My disguise was my own reputation as a bit of an idiot.

"In the United States I just talked about Britain under bombing. Some of those senators—one or two who thought we were finished—did accuse me of being a spy. I said I would hardly be spying on my own people. It didn't make sense. But then in Latin America, I reported directly to Bill Stephenson while I sang my songs and spoke nicely to my hosts. A whole lot of tiny things are the stuff of intelligence. Smallest details fit into a big picture, and sometimes you repeat things and wonder if it's worth it. I traveled wherever I could go—Asia and what was left of Europe. And I ridiculed the whole business of intelligence, because that's the best way to get on with it—ridicule and belittle ourselves, and say what an awful lot of duffers we are, can't get the facts straight, all that sort of thing.

"Americans *are* my own people, speak the same language, believe in the same things. But I don't think they ever understood my own approach. I learned a lot from their technical people, became expert, could

---

* In these taped conversations with the author, Noel Coward anticipated his approaching death and wished to put his recollections on record.

have made a career in espionage, except my life's been full enough of intrigue as it is. All that technical expertise isn't worth a damn if you don't get the best out of people, though. Winston did understand *that*—and so did Roosevelt. I'd have done anything for Roosevelt. As for Bill Stephenson, if he was against you, there wasn't a chance for you—but if he was for you, Little Bill was for you until the last shot! These were leaders who saw the strength in ordinary people. Camp X did that—took ordinary people and showed them how to break tyranny."

Noel Coward was one of hundreds who had direct access to influential figures in "neutral" countries. Stephenson picked them to collect opinions, catch a whiff of political bonfires, plant rumors, and help fit the pieces into a mosaic of undercover Nazi activities. But the main thrust of operations was directed toward building popular resistance to the oppressors in occupied countries. "The wars of people will be more terrible than those of kings," Churchill had warned the House of Commons way back in 1901. His premonition shaped itself forty years later.

26

"THE PEOPLE'S WARS began in Yugoslavia. Tito's Communist armies fought guerrilla campaigns and humiliated what Churchill called 'the dulled, drilled, docile, brutish masses of the Hun soldiery plodding on like a swarm of crawling locusts.' Hitler thought himself Barbarossa, the great medieval conqueror. When he named his invasion of Russia BARBAROSSA, we calculated that his superstitious mind could be unbalanced by its failure," said Stephenson.

He was commenting on what Churchill called "the single outstanding intelligence coup of any war." This was to create the diversion that delayed BARBAROSSA, trapped the German armies, and brought them defeat.

The BSC Papers record: "Mr. Churchill had requested Mr. Donovan to visit the Balkans in Britain's behalf. The general pattern of future German aggression was already apparent, and what Mr. Churchill wanted was some upset in Hitler's timetable to delay his contemplated attack on Russia. In this way, it was thought Hitler would face defeat."

When President Roosevelt sunned himself in the Caribbean that winter of 1940, observers feared he had forgotten the war. He had in fact dispatched Big Bill Donovan with Little Bill Stephenson to Bermuda. Only Donovan was seen to go. He flew from Baltimore under the name of Donald Williams. Yet his bags bore the telltale initials WJD, so that within hours the New York newspapers bore headlines such as AMERICA'S SECRET ENVOY FLIES ON MYSTERY MISSION. Then he vanished for two weeks, delayed by diplomatically bad weather in Bermuda. While he was there, ULTRA'S recovery of Hitler's fateful Directive 21: Operation Barbarossa was submitted for analysis. It confirmed what had been anticipated for a long time. Germany would turn east against Russia.

Donovan resumed his journey and the intended security leaks began again. "Don't make me mysterious or important," he pleaded with reporters in London. Naturally, this had the effect of redoubling the speculation. It diverted attention from the little man never far away, springy of step, looking a great deal younger than middle age, a small man who said nothing and escaped through the port security net by a side exit, helped by two Scotland Yard men.

Donovan was teased by the newsmen for carrying false identity papers and leaving his initials on his bags. "FDR's enigmatic agent" wasn't so very enigmatic after all. Arthur Krock, of the New York *Times*, aired a State Department gripe: "Donovan is the kind of foreign emissary who causes difficulties for the foreign service." The columnist Westbrook Pegler sneered that "our Colonel Wild Bill Donovan seems to have a 50-ticket Pan-Am Clipper voucher to be used up within a certain time or he will forfeit the rest."

The Germans learned through their New York press-clipping service that the presidential agent was on another mission. They had a code name for him at the Intelligence Overseas Message Center, near Hamburg, which had him tagged as Roosevelt's eyes and ears since 1937, after journeys he had made abroad. In a rare exercise of humor, they called him MARY. Their jargon for a "tail" trained to follow suspects was *Lamm*. From now on, everywhere that MARY went, *Lamm* was sure to go. He went, they followed, and Hitler was led into a trap.

Donovan scattered clues right and left; Stephenson left no clues at all. When Little Bill later reported to Churchill, he received a wintry smile. "You have all the fun, Bill."

The real fun, if that was a fair description, was Donovan's. He never revealed this particular bit of deliberate clowning. Later, he told the story of his own initialed bags as a warning to young U.S. intelligence agents in training, and did not confess that the mistake had been calculated.

This first combined Anglo-American intelligence operation began a year before the United States entered the war. Donovan's overt mission was to seek proof for Roosevelt that Britain could survive long enough to benefit from more aid. This required a visit to the Middle East, where the threat to British naval power was acute.

When Charles Lindbergh told an America First rally that Britain's shipping losses placed her in danger of starvation, that her cities were "devastated by bombing," that her situation was desperate, and that America should have a separate destiny from Europe's, the papers reported that "he got furious applause." The President's strategy now was to demonstrate that America's first line of defense was overseas. Donovan's accepted purpose was to confirm the practical value of strengthening the British in the Mediterranean. This mission was the cover for an enterprise more delicate.

While Donovan talked with Churchill about "upsetting Hitler's timetable for the attack on Russia," Stephenson prepared a secondary cover story that would also explain Donovan's use of British facilities and his appearance at the eastern end of the Mediterranean. It was an investigation of the kind Donovan had conducted often for the President. It was opportune for disguising, even to service intelligence organizations, his political role.

Stephenson dictated a signal. It went through British Naval Intelligence channels, never hinting at the deeper secret. His message read:

FROM BRITISH DIRECTOR OF NAVAL INTELLIGENCE TO COMMANDER-IN-CHIEF MEDITERRANEAN FLEET . . . DONOVAN GOT US BOMBSIGHTS CMA DESTROYERS AND OTHER URGENT REQUIREMENTS. . . . WE CAN ACHIEVE MORE THROUGH DONOVAN THAN ANY OTHER INDIVIDUAL. . . . HE CAN BE TRUSTED TO REPRESENT OUR NEEDS IN THE RIGHT QUARTERS AND IN THE RIGHT WAY IN USA. . . .

This guaranteed help of a practical kind. Donovan would need it when he moved around the war zones. There were none of the facilities taken for granted today: no large, self-contained U.S. fleet within which Donovan could disappear, no fast forms of transport by which passage could be arranged at a moment's notice. He would have to depend on British bombers and base facilities. The message was just enough to explain an important American civilian's requirements to the operational intelligence echelons who would be nervous about a neutral moving freely through their most secret camps.

Churchill, meanwhile, had been following the redeployment of Panzer divisions. The movement orders for supply units and dive-bomber squadrons convinced him that Hitler would move in May 1941. The British Joint Intelligence Committee and the chiefs of the Imperial General Staff held firmly to the view that Hitler would not be so reckless as to attack Russia before polishing off Britain. Where all agreed was in regarding a Russo-German war as inevitable, in view of Hitler's ideological view of Bolshevism as the final enemy.

All evidence gathered by the INTREPID apparatus led to Churchill's conclusion. On this issue, Stephenson and he were in complete agreement. They knew Hitler planned to invade Russia. They had the text of what Hitler called *"the greatest deception plan in the history of war"* to disguise his preparations. But they could not convince Stalin. Was it because Hitler's deception plan was working? It seemed so. In that case, it was necessary to save Stalin from his own folly.

Churchill threw himself into this task unreservedly, although Russia would later allege that the Allies deliberately pushed Germany into conflict with the Soviet Union. "If Hitler invaded Hell, I should make at least a friendly reference to the Devil in the House of Commons" was Churchill's philosophy. His prime concern was to win time for the Russians to recover from the first surprise attack. The place to do it was the Balkans. Someone was needed who could speak with authority to the leaders of nations who were tempted by Hitler's most recent gambit, a tripartite pact that would bring East Europe into line with Germany. Donovan was the right man. His actual objective was Belgrade. There, Yugoslav rebels might draw German strength into a quagmire. It seemed a forlorn hope. Marshall Tito, the Communist Partisan leader, was to write later: "Hitler attempted to gain control over the south-eastern part of Europe with the help of pro-fascist regimes in the Balkans and thereby to protect the southern flank of his forces before they went into battle against the Soviet Union. In November 1940 the Tri-Partite Pact was joined by Hungary and Rumania, and later Bulgaria. Thus we found ourselves surrounded." Tito was then underground and his name unknown. The Yugoslav monarchy still ruled.

The German plans had been known through ULTRA for some time. The British were in the infuriating position of being unable to disclose sources, and therefore they could not do more than warn Stalin and make whatever moves they could in the Balkans. Anything that revealed ULTRA meant abandoning the critical advantage it gave, and would continue to give, British forces in the field and in secret. The full recovery of Hitler's directive on BARBAROSSA, issued on December 18, 1940, could not be disclosed to the Russians or to the leaders of the threatened countries in southeast Europe.

Hitler was preparing a complete strategic surprise. Stalin was unwittingly a collaborator. If the Russians were to be taken this way, then, Churchill argued, let the Nazi blitzkrieg bog down in the same Russian snows that defeated Napoleon. As it turned out, Donovan's intervention succeeded. Hitler was forced to postpone the attack until the very anniversary of Napoleon's own catastrophic invasion—to the very day and hour—an ill omen that nobody, least of all Hitler, should have ignored.

President Roosevelt had advance warning of Hitler's plans for invading Russia from an unexpected quarter. The Führer's companion between the wars had become the German Consul-General in San Francisco, and he informed British contacts there of the Nazi strategy. He was Captain Fritz Wiedemann. According to the BSC Papers, Wiedemann "was Hitler's commanding officer at the end of the first world war and became his right-hand man until the outbreak of the second." In April 1940, he had approached fellow diplomats in San Francisco with a request to be allowed to go to Britain. He claimed to be disenchanted with Hitler and opposed to Nazism.

But Wiedemann's record was not reassuring. Hitler had sent him to the United States in 1937 to report on the possibilities of spreading Nazi influence. His appointment to the consular post in San Francisco placed him in a good position to co-ordinate Nazi intelligence with that of the Japanese in the Pacific. The FBI had copies of his reports to Berlin in which he described Roosevelt as the Führer's "most dangerous opponent."

This complex man had, however, provided the British Joint Intelligence Committee with a summary of the conference on August 22, 1939, at which Hitler explained "the historical necessity to conquer Russia." How Wiedemann obtained this was almost as much of a mystery as his reasons for collaboration. The FBI leaned to the view that he was deliberately feeding reports to the West of Hitler's anti-Bolshevik policy in order to make Nazism palatable to those who feared Russia. But if he was actually still Hitler's stooge, why should he talk about plots to overthrow Hitler?

The FBI's puzzlement was increased after a self-styled "princess" joined Wiedemann in San Francisco. She called herself Her Serene Highness the Princess Hohenlohe-Waldenberg-Schillingsfurst, but she was in reality Steffi Richter, daughter of an undistinguished Viennese lawyer. She had been living in London until she was publicly denounced as "a notorious member of the Hitler spy-ring." Then she moved to the United States and became Wiedemann's mistress. When British agents in San Francisco reported that Wiedemann was frightened of returning to Germany, the FBI confirmed that he seemed to be at swords' points with good Nazis, but expressed misgivings about his alliance with this notoriously pro-Nazi "princess."

Something mind-boggling then happened. The man who had played a role similar to that of Stephenson in World War I, Sir William Wiseman, was asked to make discreet contact with this possible defector in October 1940. Negotiations were conducted by the Princess in the Mark Hopkins Hotel, Room 1026, a number now embalmed in FBI files along with transcripts of the conversations, recorded with Wiseman's knowledge. Her Serene Highness suggested that she should go to Berlin to persuade Hitler that lasting peace could be achieved through an alignment with England.

Then the State Department shook everyone by requesting Wiseman's deportation to Britain for abuse of American neutrality. There was a long incredulous silence on the British side. Wiseman had played an essential role as a trouble shooter in Anglo-American relations during World War I. Now, suddenly, Washington threatened to deport this top-level personal agent for abusing U.S. neutrality to negotiate with a belligerent.

Stephenson appealed to J. Edgar Hoover, who testified that the German Consul-General's meetings with the British were made with FBI knowledge and approval. This intensified State Department hostility. But the friction was more than mere bureaucratic discomfort. Hitler's former adjutant, in conversation with Wiseman, had specifically named members of influential Anglo-American groups who did not think Hitler was too bad if he could get rid of the Jews and destroy Communist Russia.

Neither Stephenson nor Wiseman had official recognition. The case had to be presented directly to President Roosevelt, who put a stop to the deportation proceedings.

Wiedemann's explanation for talking so freely in America was that he represented a monarchist German movement that wished to overthrow Hitler. This tallied with reports from a German informant known as "Johnny Herwarth," still described in some postwar histories as a mysterious figure who cannot be identified for security reasons. He was in fact Hans Heinrich Herwarth von Bittenfeld, a career German diplomat who later became West German ambassador in postwar London. He first began to keep the United States government informed on the Führer's plans for Russia in 1936, when he was stationed in Moscow. By 1940, he was in Berlin and communicating through the remarkable Texan Sam Edison Woods, who passed his information to FDR. Johnny provided collateral for Wiedemann, who was eventually given safe-conduct from the United States to the place where it seemed he could do least harm—China.

In one of his last disclosures, dated November 3, 1940, Wiedemann outlined what he said were Hitler's plans for closing the Mediterranean at both ends. He was specific in describing how German forces would move into the Balkans as a preliminary to the invasion of Russia. A possible obstacle was Yugoslavia, whose armed forces were the largest and best equipped in what was left of "neutral" Europe.

Fortunately, in this matter, Wiedemann was taken

seriously. He had indicated a potential military trap. If the Nazis met resistance in the Balkans, a long-drawn-out guerrilla war would bleed Germany. The possibilities were examined by British secret intelligence in Belgrade in that same month of November. By the end of the year, the President had agreed to put Bill Donovan at Churchill's disposal "to upset Hitler's timetable."

Before leaving London for East Europe, Donovan had encouraged the impression that his purpose was to look into British problems in the eastern Mediterranean. Knowing that German intelligence watched his movements, he once again skillfully misdirected newspaper speculation. Drew Pearson announced in his column that Donovan's real mission was to confer with French commanders in North Africa. The New York *Post* offered the "exclusive" revelation that he was seeking a new understanding with Vichy France. He told the New York *Times:* "I said I found the British 'resolute and courageous' in August. Now I would add 'confident.' " The fiction that he was only measuring British resolve on behalf of the Roosevelt administration was maintained. The Anglo-American deception plan was underway. Like all good cover stories, it closely resembled the truth.

Donovan began with a tour of the battle fronts where Mussolini's forces were calling for German help in Greece and Albania, and then left suddenly for Sofia. He carried with him secret documents purporting to be a combination of British military plans to support resistance to a Nazi invasion of Bulgaria and draft plans for American military aid. He was surprisingly open in cabling President Roosevelt that he was having talks with King Boris of Bulgaria, who was anxious to avoid any head-on collision with Germany.

BSC historians reported: "He did not dissuade the Bulgarian leaders from their pro-German policy, but he did implant in their minds a measure of doubt as to the wisdom of that policy. In result, they hesitated before implementing their proposed intervention on Germany's side, which would have allowed German

225

troops unrestricted passage through their country. Mr. Churchill had intimated that he would be content with a delay of twenty-four hours. Donovan secured a delay of eight days." He did this by suggesting that King Boris think twice about letting German forces pass through to attack British troops trying to safeguard Greece. "If the United States comes into the war, we will be guided in policy toward Bulgaria by what you do now," he said. King Boris hesitated—not long, but long enough.

Nazi agents kept hard on Donovan's heels in Sofia. Publicity was handled in such a way that newsmen still thought they were penetrating a security blackout. In Berlin, the Nazi propaganda mills spoke of Donovan abusing his status as the representative of a neutral power. During a final audience with Boris, Donovan's clothes were rifled by German agents in the Royal Palace. Documents were taken. Among them were "highly confidential" notes on American proposals for military intervention in the Balkans if Hitler went too far. Later it was reported that Donovan "got himself into a state of complete drunkenness." The canard came from Dr. Joseph Goebbels, the Nazi propaganda minister. The implication was that Donovan lost some personal papers through carelessness. The truth was that Donovan, who was a teetotaler, pretended to accept royal alcoholic hospitality out of courtesy. The "notes on military intervention" were for *German* eyes.

The personal documents that Donovan had been carrying since his departure from New York were skillful forgeries from a small unit Stephenson had organized in Toronto. It occupied the basements of the ramshackle houses adjoining the Canadian Broadcasting Corporation's headquarters on Jarvis Street, at the heart of the red-light district, where prostitutes and bootleggers had been joined by black-market traders in rationed commodities. The false papers appeared to be joint Anglo-American notes for East European leaders in addition to purely American military contingency plans. The net effect was to convince the German High Command that the United States was conspiring with "the British Secret Service," the phrase by which German leaders knew British Intelligence. The Secret Service was regarded with a mixture of fear and hatred by Hitler, impressed by grossly exaggerated accounts of British genius in espionage. The forged documents seemed to prove that Donovan was stirring up trouble on a British Secret Service mission that combined a survey of the political and military conditions that might await any American intervention with an Anglo-American diplomatic offensive in the area.

The success of Donovan's mission could be followed step by step by Churchill, reading the exchanges between the German High Command and German diplomats, between German intelligence and Hitler. Most of this material came through Bletchley, and the highlights were read to him directly by telephone. Another source was also being tapped: a Communist international radio network run from Moscow, in which some material came from Yugoslavia.

When Donovan arrived in Belgrade he found Prince-Regent Paul preparing to join the Axis, after being summoned to Hitler's presence. Hitler had imposed upon Paul the full force of the intimidating Nazi presence, subjecting the Prince to a display of military power, totalitarian efficiency, and the whole range of the Führer's histrionic talents.

Churchill, reading the blow-by-blow reports of Nazi leaders, including Hitler himself, commented to Roosevelt that "Prince Paul's attitude looks like that of an unfortunate man in a cage with a tiger, hoping not to provoke him while steadily dinnertime approaches."

The President replied through INTREPID that he would apply what counterpressure he could. Perhaps Yugoslavia would dig in her heels? Deliberately using the commercial cables that he knew the Germans tapped, Roosevelt wired Donovan: "Any nation which tamely submits will be regarded less sympathetically when the United States comes to settle accounts than any nation resisting the Nazis." Informed of this, Prince Paul told Donovan that any German move into Yugoslavia would be merely to secure Hitler's flank for an imminent attack on Russia. Hitler had told him so.

This was the kind of reasoning that Churchill most feared. Prince Paul was anti-Bolshevik. "Patriots may be robbed of any reason to rally to a resistance army," Churchill had already warned Donovan. "A mass uprising can result only from some violent Nazi action."

There was one group in Yugoslavia capable of resistance: Tito's Communists. Tito was then only a name. Some said he did not exist at all. He had returned from the Soviet Union a year earlier, disguised as Spiridon Mekas and carrying a British passport issued in Canada. How this came about is still classified information. Tito had been deeply disturbed by Stalin's treatment of other East European Communist leaders. ("When I went to Moscow I never knew whether I would come back alive," he said later.) While other Communist leaders followed Moscow's policy of placating Hitler, Tito had spent the past few months preparing for war. He was getting no guidance from Stalin. He did get guidance through intermediaries from Donovan. Regardless of political allegiances, said Donovan, anyone resisting fascism would get outside support. Yugoslavia must not collaborate with the Nazis. A sellout would relieve Hitler of the need to tie down security forces in the Balkans, and thus both the Balkans and Russia would be lost. The message was quite clear: "If Prince Paul kneels to the Nazis, revolt."

By the time Donovan left, the Germans were nervous and trigger-happy. In this uncertain atmosphere, British intelligence put pressure on the Yugoslav Air Force chief, General Dušan Simović, also secretly visited by Donovan.

On Saturday, March 22, a German ultimatum was presented to the Yugoslav government. Hitler had followed the softening-up process with a touch of the lash. During the next two days, while Prince Paul and his advisers rationalized surrender, senior officers mounted a short-lived palace revolt. In the background, lacking arms and unable to bring his extensive organization into the open, Tito had to bide his time. "But the detonator," he said later, "had been exploded." The officers' rebellion overthrew the Prince-Regent.

Donovan had flown back to Washington, where he added fuel to the fire. In a nationwide broadcast on March 25, 1941, cast in the form of a report on his mission, he talked of the courage of those resisting Nazi aggression in the eastern Mediterranean.

The speech was guaranteed to throw Hitler into an angry fit. The Führer was known to blunder when his tantrums were unpremeditated, and not staged for effect. The Donovan speech was filmed, appeared on newsreels all over Britain as well as the United States, and received unprecedented publicity, considering Donovan's officially modest role. It was produced a week after an early-morning breakfast with Roosevelt and Stephenson, following a message from Churchill thanking FDR "for the magnificent work done by Donovan in the Balkans." The President at once arranged that U.S. Navy warships would protect British supply ships sailing into this theater. He proclaimed the Red Sea and Persian Gulf to be no longer combat zones from which American vessels were excluded by the Neutrality Act. Stephenson was credited with accomplishing this significant step by suggesting it could be taken legally, while Roosevelt was still enjoying the success of Donovan's mission. The new U.S. Navy duties were tremendously important to the British, but it was Donovan's speech that inflamed Hitler. Its provocative nature makes it worth quoting at some length, as it appeared in a newsreel transcript distributed from London:

"I have been given an opportunity to study at first hand these great battles going on in the Atlantic and in the Mediterranean, in Africa, in Greece and in Albania. From my observations I have been able to form my conclusions on the basis of full information. These conclusions I will submit to my country for its use in furtherance of our national defence, an essential part of which is our policy of aid to Great Britain.

We have no choice as to whether or not we will be attacked. That choice is Hitler's: & he has already made it . . . not for Europe alone, but for Africa, Asia & the world. Our only choice is to decide whether or not we will resist it. And to choose in time: while resistance is still possible, while others are still alive to stand beside us.

Let us keep this in mind—Germany is a formidable, a resourceful, & a ruthless foe. Do not underrate her. If we do—we deceive ourselves. Her victories have brought her new military & industrial strength. . . . She got the jump at the start of the war and has kept it; but not yet has she made a full test. And until this test comes, it is better . . . not to overrate her But her greatest gains have been made through fear. Fear of the might of her war machine. So she has played upon that fear, & her recent diplomatic victories are the product.

But we must remember that there is a moral force in wars, that in the long run is stronger than any machine. And I say to you, my fellow citizens, all that Mr. Churchill has told you on the resolution & determination and valour and confidence of his people, is true.

The speech reached Hitler and, as intended, sent him into a dangerous and this time uncalculated rage. A week later, on April 6, the Orthodox Good Friday, German bombers began to raze Belgrade. It had been declared an open city. There was no declaration of war. The bombers destroyed the Palace, the university, hospitals, churches, schools, and most dwelling places. After four days of what the Germans codenamed OPERATION PUNISHMENT, some 24,000 corpses had been recovered from the ruins. Untold numbers were never found.

The devastation was a consequence of intelligence operations in which long-term advantages had to be weighed against short-term losses. After the war, Belgrade—though separated by the Iron Curtain between Communist and capitalist worlds—was "twinned" with Coventry. The public explanation was that the citizens of these cities had suffered and should work together in peace to prevent a recurrence, despite political differences. The real explanation was never publicized: each city had suffered from secret-warfare dilemmas to which there seemed no solution free from human sacrifice.

On April 7, with the bombing of Belgrade in full swing, the German Foreign Office announced in its usual self-pitying way that German troops had crossed the frontier to defend German civilians. Thereafter all happened as Roosevelt and Churchill had foreseen. ULTRA signals revealed how Nazi forces closed in upon Yugoslavia. German commanders announced that the Yugoslav Army had capitulated, then shot every Yugoslav soldier who surrendered.

"The news that Hitler had been defied by Yugoslavia travelled like sunshine over the countries which he had devoured and humiliated," wrote the English author Rebecca West at the time. It was the first wave of hope, the first promise that Nazi supermen were fallible, even though the price of this defiance was human suffering on an unprecedented scale.

The resistance of Yugoslavia, unexpected by the Germans, diverted Nazi forces and prolonged their advance through Greece. They had meant to use their divisions in Bulgaria against Turkey as a preliminary move before the attack on Russia. "OPERATION BARBAROSSA will have to be postponed up to four weeks," complained Field Marshal Wilhelm Keitel, the German Chief of Supreme Command. In reality, the delay was six weeks, and Hitler's order to launch OPERATION PUNISHMENT with "merciless harshness" against the Yugoslavs led him into a four-year quagmire of guerrilla warfare.

Churchill was emphatic that the fatal delay in Hitler's invasion of Russia resulted from this. The United States had employed operational intelligence to destroy an unwelcome political situation abroad—a successful essay in what would be called later "destabilizing" a foreign country. British intelligence had considered overthrowing Prince Paul's regime five months earlier, but could not.

The Nazi operation MARITA against Greece, was overshadowed by the fearful onslaught against Yugoslavia. The British also paid dearly. When Greek

231

resistance to the German armies collapsed, 62,000 British troops were trapped. Exactly three weeks after the Belgrade revolt, fewer than 50,000 men of this expeditionary force could be evacuated; all their guns, tanks, and transport were left behind. Coming on top of defeats and confusions in the desert, the seemingly ill-conceived attempt to rescue Greece helped diminish confidence in Britain among her critics in Washington. Unfortunately, they could not be told the facts, about either the ULTRA warnings or the grim calculation that even if British intervention failed, it would nonetheless help provoke Hitler's angry and ill-considered plunge into the Balkan quagmire.

Tito's handwritten order at the height of Yugoslavian resistance to the German invasion and during a series of bloody engagements known as "The Battle for the Wounded." The message reads:

Division I

The wounded must not be left there. We will be going far. They must be transferred through Mliniše and Glamočko Polje, and they'll go on from there. Issue orders that this be done immediately. *Speed up your march.* Koča should come here first for a consultation. I am close by.

TITO

February 3, 1943

"Churchill's decision to reinforce Greece was not the romantic gamble of an amateur," Stephenson said later. "It was essential that Britain demonstrate undiluted loyalty to her allies. The effect on American public opinion would have been worse if we had failed to make the effort."

FDR signaled Churchill: "You have done not only heroic but very useful work in Greece. The territorial loss is more than compensated for by the necessity for an enormous German concentration and resulting enormous German losses in men and material. . . . You have fought a wholly justifiable action."

Donovan and Stephenson were together in Washington when the vast diversion of Nazi forces began. They felt no sense of triumph. There was no sign that Stalin yet understood he had been given only a brief reprieve. On the contrary, the Soviet Union continued to disbelieve the warnings.

Hitler, who talked of winning a tactical surprise against Russia, achieved both this and total *strategic* surprise—the hobgoblin of all intelligence services. At first light on Sunday morning, June 22, 1941, his warplanes caught 1,400 Russian aircraft dozing on the ground. This Nazi aerial artillery rolled forward, clearing the way for German troops to advance 400 miles in four weeks. What saved the Russians was the fact that the first strike failed to reach its distant goal before the onset of winter.

Tito later wrote: "Hitler's Command was forced to postpone the attack on Russia by 38 days. . . . Every ninth Yugoslav lost his life fighting the enemy in the aftermath." This estimate of thirty-eight days falls modestly short of the U.S. and British intelligence estimates at the end of the war.

In *The Goebbels Diaries,* the Nazi Propaganda Minister unconsciously confirmed the success of

233

Donovan's mission when he blamed the Balkans bloodbath on "the notorious Colonel Donovan who later created the infamous OSS spy-ring. He brought disaster to Yugoslavia in order to pull other countries like Greece into the war. That was Donovan's mission. All was ready for the pacification of the Balkans with our troops when the secret Presidential agent came on the scene.

"Adolf Hitler ordered the swift and merciless destruction of Yugoslavia. He could do no less. 'Operation Punishment' was a lesson to the Balkans that nobody could defy our Fuehrer. The Wehrmacht conquered Yugoslavia in eleven days. The most vile canard of our enemies is that the Fuehrer is losing the Second World War because of personal rage and spite, delaying the attack on Russia to wreak vengeance on a small and harmless neighbor. The Fuehrer was simply impressing on his generals the need to exert themselves."

They had exerted themselves so well that Belgrade was a pile of rubble. President Roosevelt knew now the burdens of secret intelligence. He now had his own Coventry.

"Roosevelt could no more calculate German terrorist reprisals against Yugoslavia than the Prime Minister," Stephenson noted later. "Terrorism was a new weapon. We had to fight it with improvised weapons."

Nobody could foretell each consequence of BSC's improvisations, and the pressures were too great for hesitation. Stephenson was bringing into operation a fake astrologer to help irritate Hitler still more. If Hitler thought himself to be the German Emperor of the Holy Roman Empire, Barbarossa, then his superstitions might as well be fed by fortunetellers and rumor mills. The Nazis would soon be locked in a titanic struggle with the Soviets, and new weapons of psychological and political warfare were being forged to demoralize the enemy or provoke him into still further folly. Stephenson recalled Alexander Pope's poem in which someone might someday tamper with events and observe

234

> with equal eye, as God of all
> A hero perish, or a sparrow fall
> Atoms or systems into ruin hurl'd
> And now a bubble burst, and now a world

One sparrow was a young woman, one of the solitary agents whose work could result in harsh enemy reactions involving the lives of thousands. She was typical of those individual acts of self-sacrifice that could never be publicized then, but now help to explain what motivated the directors of secret intelligence, compelled to watch with equal eye the ruin of cities and of a single life. Her name was in the envelope carried by Lester Pearson when he served BSC as a King's Messenger. German intelligence never did discover her identity. The most dangerous post in Nazi-occupied France would become associated with her cover name: MADELEINE.

27

MADELEINE WAS A young woman of haunting beauty, the center of cruel controversy after her death. "She should never have been sent to France," declared a fellow agent, quoted in the official British history of these operations.* "She was a splendid, vague, dreamy creature, far too conspicuous—twice seen, never forgotten—and she had *no* sense of security. . . ." An attempt was made to stop her mission when spy-school

---

* Efforts to publish any account of Baker Street's work were blocked by the British government until, finally, in 1966, Her Majesty's Stationery Office produced a *History of Special Operations Executive in France,* by the Cambridge historian M. R. D. Foot. Even this lifted only a corner of the curtain and was restricted to that one region. Foot was obliged to state that he had been forbidden personal contact with survivors.

instructors said nothing could hide her striking appearance. She would certainly attract German officers, which was not the idea.

A writer of children's books, she had lived in a fairy world that left no room for cynicism or distrust. Her cover name was taken from one of her stories— the last that she read over Radio Paris to French children in freedom.

She was born in the Kremlin, incredibly enough, a descendant of the Tiger of Mysore, the last Muslim ruler in South India. Her father had been invited to teach Sufism to the Tsar in 1912. Her real name was Noor Inayat Khan, "Light of Womanhood." Her American mother was the niece of the founder of Christian Science. She had been raised by her father, the leader of an Islamic religious movement, to believe that love and tolerance were the only weapons against inhumanity. This doctrine—Sufism, which was to become fashionable in the West during the 1970's—had been banned in Germany as "alien to German culture." She still believed Sufism would overcome Nazism, just as nonviolence in India must overthrow British imperialism. Stephenson, who had met her in India before the war, sensed steel within her seemingly timid personality. At one time the family had moved to France, and Noor was working in Paris when the Germans invaded.

After the invasion, Noor's publisher in London helped her escape. She was then twenty-five years old, and intrigued by the pragmatism of the British in September of 1940, when they had a new medal struck to recognize the changed nature of war. It was the George Cross, valued above all orders of knighthood, awarded sparingly to civilians now drawn into frontline emergencies caused by German terror bombing, and given "for the most conspicuous courage in circumstances of extreme danger." The citation would become her epitaph.

Noor volunteered for the RAF. She was quick, intelligent, and dependable. She would have made a good officer. Instead, she was groomed for something else. In early 1941, such women were needed as radio operators to work with small guerrilla groups. The radio war, symbolized by ULTRA, was not only defensive. There was a need to build up circuits of agents and networks of saboteurs and partisans, providing them with radio contacts that would integrate their efforts. Nothing like this had been attempted in the history of war. The system would be so extensive that it would obviously be vulnerable to German counterespionage. The British had experience in breaking enemy radio security. They knew that thousands of their own agents reporting to a central control, risked the penetration of their circuits by their German counterparts. To escape detection, therefore, each network had its own transmitters, its own codes and controllers at Bletchley, and little or no contact with similar groups unless this was necessary.

The radio war conducted from Bletchley swung onto the offensive in early 1941, when Noor was being trained in telegraphy. Her story ended in the darkest hour before Europe was liberated in 1944. To make her an example of the harsh decision forced upon BSC and the American secret-warfare chiefs, it is useful to detour around the chronology of INTREPID operations. What happened to Noor was typical, even in 1941, of heroism that placed heavy moral responsibilities on Roosevelt, Churchill, and Stephenson.

Noor's international background, her familiarity with strange places and foreign languages encouraged BSC's attention—that and the girl's frankness.

She was recruited in London. There was no money for spies in wartime, and hiring an agent was a delicate affair. The French Section of the Baker Street Irregulars was wary of recruits with a taste for austerity; they were liable to be fanatics, dangerous to themselves and to their comrades. The French Section was also skeptical about romantics; secret dreams of glory would include martyrdom for the operator and also for the rest of the network. The first approach to a potential agent required finesse. If that person proved unsuitable, he or she must never know an interview had taken place; nor must he or she be in a position to recognize interviewing officers, or even the buildings that housed the secret agencies.

One of Noor's stories, "The Fairy and the Hare,"

was broadcast by the BBC about the time that she was accepted by the RAF as a radio telegraphist. She completed her training and was offered a commission. But in April 1942, she was asked, unexpectedly, to report to a room at the Hotel Victoria, on Northumberland Avenue, a dreary corner of central London. There she met an Army captain who represented, she thought, the War Office. The conversation covered a lot of ground, and she said at one point she felt rootless, being in some ways an American, though a product of a Russian childhood and a French adolescence, and yet had strong emotional ties to India.

The interviewing officer, Selwin Jepson, normally took his time in getting to the point. In Noor's case, he decided at once to trust her. She told him that she would struggle for India's freedom from British rule. It happened to be the right answer to his question about her loyalty, for she had demonstrated integrity, the most highly prized quality of all. He stressed that if she agreed to his proposal, she would not have the protection of a uniform, and that in the event of capture, she would be interrogated by the Gestapo— "something no human being could face with anything but terror."

Jepson was always reluctant to take on a girl who accepted such a prospect too readily. He suggested that, as a writer and broadcaster, she might be useful to humanity again after the war. She was in contact with the minds of children who would have to live in a partially destroyed world. "It might seem academic, considering our desperate situation right now, but you should consider if you might be better employed rebuilding society."

Noor rejected the idea. She would be more useful now, in Paris, the most dangerous part of Occupied Europe. Jepson agreed to let her start training, "with rather more of the bleak distress which I never failed to feel at this point in these interviews."

Noor knew more about the work ahead than Jepson could possibly guess. She had first met Bill Stephenson during one of her family journeys back to India. She was nineteen years old then, stunningly pretty, gifted with an innocence which he judged could never be cor-

238

rupted. He was leading a mission of technical experts that in 1934 studied India's resources and potential for self-development. He met her on a tiger shoot arranged by her father's fellow Muslim Air Vice-Marshal Nawab Haji Khan, chief of the Chamber of Princes and Nawab of Bhopal. The pomp and ceremony of the jungle *shikaris* amused both the girl and Stephenson. They talked about a future India where the gap between rich and poor might be narrowed through love and compassion. The Nawab was a close friend of Stephenson's and later, on active service with the RAF, he learned that the Canadian kept a fatherly eye on the girl. It was in this way that Noor entered the world of Baker Street armed with credentials. She could not remain in the RAF, however. The regular services had a regulation against women taking part in military operations.

Women agents had to wear some kind of uniform during training. Plain clothes would excite curiosity. Curiosity led to questions. For women who did take part in military operations, therefore, the tiresome ban was circumvented by that antiquated organization, which oddly enough was not stuffy about these things, the First Aid Nursing Yeomanry, FANY. Women agents could wear its khaki uniform in training. They continued as FANYs after going into action with the secret armies, plus holding an honorary commission granted to women agents by the RAF. This was supposed to make the Germans think twice about executing a captured agent, since a woman could claim to be in the armed forces and entitled to treatment as a prisoner of war, an improvisation of legalities that did not impress the enemy.

The two girls who went into final training with her were also doomed to die. One was Yolande Beekman. The last time they met before leaving for France was at a mock Gestapo interrogation. The next time they met was as real Gestapo prisoners on the dark journey to Dachau. The third girl, Cecily Lefort, was captured after distinguished work under the cover name ALICE.

Noor was provided with a new identity that fitted her personality and resembled her true background.

She became Jeanne-Marie Regnier, a children's nurse, known henceforth to Baker Street as MADELEINE. She needed ration books and identity papers. These were manufactured by the forgery experts in Toronto. She required a wardrobe of essential clothing from Paris. This was assembled by a Jewish "manufacturer" who, having escaped himself from Europe, managed an establishment in Montreal of expert tailors and seamstresses, who worked for purely nominal wages, had been enrolled in the armed forces, and were sworn to secrecy. Their skill lay in doctoring refugee clothing. There were, for example, a half-dozen different ways that a button might be stitched onto a coat, depending on where it was tailored in Europe. A wrongly sewn button could dispatch agents to death.

MADELEINE required pills. Some, slipped into an enemy's coffee, induced sleep of up to six hours. Others, self-administered, would keep her awake in an emergency. A third group would make her sick if she wished to fake illness. The fourth was the L pill, if she chose death rather than face Gestapo interrogation. She also needed a compact transmitter. She was a small girl, five feet three inches, and weighed 108 pounds. As a telegraphist, or "pianist," she needed lightweight equipment. There was a chronic shortage of transmitters, and each had to be ordered from U.S. manufacturers and then adapted for installation in a suitcase. Her job was central to the liaison team in a guerrilla group: an organizer, a courier, and the pianist. As the networks grew, the pianists suffered the highest casualties and had to be replaced most often.

MADELEINE learned what was in store. She was destined to join the biggest, busiest, and most hazardous of the networks, PROSPER, covering a vast part of France with headquarters in Paris. Its demands were insatiable. Its rural circuits were disrupting lines of communication by sabotage. Its guerrillas were arming for the day of liberation. It needed guns, explosives, booby traps, and money in an unending stream. PROSPER's prosperity depended on intimate daily contact with Bletchley, which in turn passed the shopping list to Baker Street and BSC And what PROSPER needed urgently was a new pianist.

The girl's cover story was tested by her instructors in fake Gestapo interrogations under blazing lights, accompanied with snarled commands. Her reactions were noted by a FANY conducting officer whose job was to watch for slips and continually review the trainee's mental fitness. The girl never deviated from her story, but her conducting officer reported later that the "Gestapo" found their task almost unbearable because of her terrified reactions.

She learned that her transmitter would be tuned permanently to a particular reception station. She memorized the schedules and coded abbreviations for commonly used signals. Thus QRB meant "Your message regarding broadcast received and understood"; QRM: "Interference is bad"; QSLIMI: "Please acknowledge receipt of message number—"; IMI: "Note of interrogation"; GRIMI: "Repeat group indicated." There were dozens of these groups, of which the least forgettable was QUO: "I am forced to stop transmitting because of imminent danger. If possible, I will try to make contact on next schedule." The code letters were part of elaborate arrangements to reduce transmissions and diminish the period of exposure to detection gear or detectives. The methods of making contact with another agent, with circuits, with cutouts, or with home base were all governed by rules that she had to stick with, or chaos would ensue. The rules had to be memorized, like everything else. Memories were tested while the trainee agent was under stress. The girl would return from strenuous field exercises to be asked to list the many procedures for making radio contact, of which this is only one: "If both stations have a message to send as soon as contact is made, the OUT STATION will send its message first unless the HOME STATION ends QSP, when the HOME STATION will then transmit first."

She was taught that "a knife should be used delicately as a paint brush." If unarmed, she should use the heel of her hand upward to smash an assailant's jaw or "knee him in the groin." She was taken to the pistol range every day, but warned not to carry arms except at vulnerable moments like dropping from a plane or during an emergency transmission in case she ran into a routine search.

She was taught simple coding. Letters of a message were systematically interchanged by "Key numbers." Her own codes could be concealed in several ways. (The one-time pad printed on ultra-thin paper was not feasible in the field, and microdotted codes had obvious limitations.) She was taught to write the codes on her underwear or conceal them on her body. There were ways of conveying a new code by radio transmission which she must memorize.

She was warned that interrogation was impossible to resist if the torturers knew their business and were willing to be patient. Agents, deprived of their L pills, sometimes broke down and revealed their security checks. These included meaningless questions from Bletchley to which should be given meaningless answers. Thus, to the challenge "Have you washed?" the correct answer would be "The trees blossom." There was an additional and simple safety device. If the agent was in captivity and forced to transmit under German supervision, she need only omit a meaningless letter or number that was regularly included in her transmissions while at liberty. MADELEINE might be given the group YB4, for instance, which she would insert after each five groups in a message. If YB4 was missing, the reception station would know something was wrong.

The dangers were not minimized. The German radio direction-finding service could latch onto a transmission with remarkable speed. From all over Europe two million words were processed every week in England. This meant that inevitably there must be foulups. Bletchley could not save agents from their own follies. If she became flustered or gave way to fatigue, she might make a mistake in transmission that would lead to greater and more tragic errors. There were cases of complete networks being "burned" or "blown." But she would have a distant "god-mother" a FANY telegraphist back in England familiar with her Morse style, which was as unmistakable as her signature. It would be an additional safeguard against any German attempt to take over her transmissions.

She was released officially from the RAF and then given the honorary commission that would guarantee an accumulation of salary while she was in enemy territory. As a FANY, she was a volunteer who received nothing but living expenses.

Vera Atkins took over as her CO, or conducting officer. Vera, the heart and brain of the Baker Street Irregulars' French Section, was a young and highly organized woman with a misleadingly innocent smile and an eagle eye for detail. She had an encyclopedic memory for local regulations in odd corners of Europe and subtleties of behavior that a stranger might fatally ignore. She had private sources of "bits of theater" that reinforced an agent's cover; tram tickets from the region where the agent was going, concert programs, crumpled French cigaret packs. She checked the agent in these last remaining days, at meals, in conversation, at work, and even while sleeping. A slip in the pouring of tea, the wrong use of jargon, a sudden reaction to the sound of the agent's real name—these she caught. Like other COs, she nursed the agent through final briefings in a cozy apartment at Orchard Court, near Baker Street.

The men at Orchard Court were informal and genial. They had a butler-doorman known as Park, who had been a messenger in the prewar Paris branch of the Westminster Bank. Park had a memory for faces and the quiet efficiency of Jeeves, whose creator, P. G. Wodehouse, was in Nazi hands and pretending to collaborate. It was one of the small ironies of the situation that the atmosphere in the Orchard Court flat resembled the Wodehouse parodies of English society, with all its eccentricities. But afternoon tea and cucumber sandwiches in that place covered a deadlier purpose.

Questions had been raised about employing MADELEINE. Fellow trainees had written confidentially to Vera Atkins, suggesting that the girl was unfit for the ordeals ahead; she was "emotionally fragile and in many ways too innocent." The girls who made these well-meaning pleas, reminiscent of a petition to save

243

a prisoner from the gallows, only reinforced the judgment of those who considered MADELEINE ideal for the task ahead. Atkins and MADELEINE convinced the men in Orchard Court that she should go.

On one of those June days in England when the quiet country roads are heavy with the scent of dog rose and honeysuckle, both girls, in civilian clothes, were driving an open car so old that it attracted no attention even in this austere time of severe gas rationing. They arrived that evening at a thatched Sussex cottage. Atkins led the way into a cramped hall and up a narrow flight of stairs. There was a ground-floor room from which MADELEINE could hear men's voices. She was rushed past. One of the CO's duties was to make sure the agent did not accidentally run into anyone, including the airmen of Special Duties 161 Squadron.

MADELEINE was to be delivered straight to a reception committee after flying in a Westland Lysander that would land in a field marked out by a prearranged pattern of lights. The signal of departure beamed to French listeners would be given at the very last moment in the middle of a routine BBC entertainment program: "Jasmine is playing her flute."

There now began the customary nerve-shattering delay. The moon was right, the weather was good, the receptions committee had reported that a field had been prepared. But no aircraft was available. There was a persistent struggle to get aircraft for these operations. The Baker Street Irregulars had to fight the regular armed forces for machines. They had to fight the regular intelligence services for priorities. The Air Ministry had to be placated when valuable planes and crews were lost in what seemed like foolhardy expeditions for which explanations were seldom, if ever, forthcoming. It was possible to jump the chain of command but not advisable: a short-circuited air marshal or general might prove resentful some other way—on some other day. When the bureaucracy became insupportable, Stephenson could be called upon to talk directly with Churchill. He could do this because all of them recognized that in the last resort, Stephenson was getting the weapons they needed. The situation eased later when Baker Street operated directly under SHAEF and its commander, General Dwight Eisenhower.

In day-to-day operations, not even the resourceful Vera Atkins would interfere. If she were told planes were busy elsewhere, that was it. She settled down in patient resignation. Some agents were not only put through the test of waiting, hour by hour, never knowing why, but also flew out to the drop zone or airstrip and came back again, sometimes three or four times. Their training taught them to make decisions, keep command of situations, seek positive solutions. It was difficult to submit unquestioningly to the dictates of others. MADELEINE had this submissive quality. Her attitude was expressed in her story of the river that reached the sea by going around obstacles instead of attacking head on. She liked and she wrote about gentle animals. She meditated a great deal on metaphysical matters. Her childhood friends remembered that she peopled her garden with small figures of her own imagination and was in despair when told there was no world of small benevolent spirits. She described her philosophy as oriental. She saw action and inaction intertwined in the Buddhist circle of life.

She checked her things again. Her transmitter and clothes were to be dropped by parachute later. She wore a simple dress and scuffed shoes. She carried in her handbag a small .38 pistol in case the reception committee should be ambushed. The pistol she would bury later, together with her parachute if she were obliged to drop instead of land. Atkins searched her once again, seeking some overlooked detail—a broken match that might be recognized as non-European, or even a piece of English gravel stuck in the sole of a shoe. Agents had been caught because they screwed up a London theater stub and absentmindedly left it in a pocket. There were small things that could never be explained during a surprise search in the middle of wartime Paris: a bobby pin, a strange piece of thread in a darned jacket, or a stale fragment of Virginia tobacco.

At two o'clock in the morning there was a clatter

on the stairs. A muffled figure knocked on the door and peered inside. "Time to go."

The Lysander was silhouetted against a moonlit sky. It was a high-wing monoplane with a fixed undercarriage and capable of 200 miles an hour, half the speed of German fighter aircraft. It relied on a single engine and it would hedge-hop low and slow. It was black like a winged hearse. The pilot looked about twenty years old. Nobody spoke. Mechanics moved in darkness through the prescribed drill. But when the Lysander rose heavily toward the near-full moon, MADELEINE was heading for certain execution.

Less than a hundred hours before her departure, the reception committee had radioed Bletchley that Nazi security forces were swarming through the reception area near Le Mans, and requested that all air operations be suspended. This was June 12, 1943. Yet supplies and agents continued to be dropped. On the sixteenth, two Canadian agents were parachuted into the district: John McAlister and Frank Pickersgill.

Why were the warnings ignored? Why was MADELEINE permitted to continue the mission? Investigations since then have failed to produce satisfactory answers. Perhaps there never can be logical explanations for tragedies in secret warfare. MADELEINE was picked in response to an urgent appeal for an operator from the PROSPER network. Yet there was already some evidence that the network had been betrayed. When her Lysander landed, there was no reception committee to ease her passage through the first awful hours in hostile country. Why did the pilot not bring her back to England? The trouble with secret operations was that the tight security, intended to protect agents, could work against them. The pilot was one link in a tenuous chain of men and women, each expected to follow orders and listen only to whatever information was relevant to the job. One hundred hours after PROSPER transmitted danger signals, those signals were still being evaluated while the machinery of secret operations ticked on.

MADELEINE had scrambled out of the Lysander, saw it roll forward and soar back into the air, and then she began walking to the railroad station at Le

Mans, confident that her "luggage" would be delivered by a later flight. She arrived by train in Paris late on Thursday, June 17, and went straight to her first contact, at 40 rue Erlanger: Emile Garry. He was a secret-army sector chief for the department of which Le Mans was the capital, commuting between there and Paris under cover of a fake work permit. He took her next day to Professor Alfred Serge Balachowsky, of the Pasteur Institute, a distinguished biologist who was also chief of the Versailles section of PROSPER. She reported to Baker Street over the section's transmitter, concealed in a greenhouse, less than forty-eight hours after her departure. Thus she became the first woman radio operator to transmit for the French secret armies.

The following Monday, Balachowsky drove to a farm where supplies had been dropped, including three transmitters for MADELEINE. He did not know it, but on this day the two Canadians, McAlister and Pickersgill, had just been caught. By a tragic coincidence, they were with the first woman agent ever sent into France by Baker Street, an elegant forty-seven-year-old Kensington interior decorator named Yvonne Rudelatt. She had come alone by boat, a *felucca* that had landed her on the Côte d'Azur. There she had reported to Peter Churchill as a courier. She had been in full operation for many months. Now she collected the Canadians and was on her way to Paris when they ran into a roadblock. They seemed to pass the brief interrogation. But an SS officer asked to see the Canadians' false papers again. The driver, scenting disaster, pushed hard on the accelerator of the tiny battered Citröen. There was a car chase, and the Citroën was gunned to a stop. Yvonne Rudelatt fell from the car, wounded. Before she lost consciousness, she shot and wounded two German guards who were beating her with rifle butts. For this she was to perish, after the agony of many jails, in a Belsen gas chamber at the age of fifty-two. McAlister and Pickersgill survived months of torture and a year in one death camp before being executed at Buchenwald; they were hung from butcher's hooks and allowed to die by slow strangulation against the crematorium wall. Before that horror, Pickersgill was to have a taste of freedom, only to refuse it when he saw what it entailed for MADELEINE.

Ten days after Professor Balachowsky retrieved her luggage on a peaceful June night, he was arrested. During the following week, dozens of French agents were rounded up. In London, a signal was delivered to Maurice Buckmaster at Baker Street. It reported the destruction of the PROSPER network. All the leaders and their equipment had been captured, and only one transmitter remained in operation. That was MADELEINE, whose call sign ended the message.

Buckmaster surveyed the area of disaster. He was to say later that Berlin security headquarters regarded the French network as the heart of the secret army that was most dangerous to the Third Reich. Now it was smashed. Buckmaster told MADELEINE to get out of Paris; an aircraft would be sent to pick her up. The girl replied no. She was the only operator left in the Paris region. Without her, all communication would be lost. She could pick up some threads and reconstruct at least one circuit, if not more.

Buckmaster made a hard decision. If the girl stayed, it could be only a matter of time before she was caught. Yet the catastrophe had left her as the most important "station" in France. He signaled approval, but warned her not to transmit. All Gestapo detection gear would be trained on her transmitter now that the rest had been wiped out.

The girl, on her own now, moved about Paris looking for old school friends. She found her former music teacher, Henriette Renie, for instance. One contact led to another. She stayed briefly in different parts of the city, trying not to compromise those who showed hospitality. She had a bicycle and carried the transmitter with her. Despite Buckmaster's warnings, she began regular transmissions from the first week of July and she continued until October, when she was caught and taken to Gestapo headquarters.

MADELEINE took frightful risks. This became clear after the war when the story was pieced together. But unwittingly she compromised a number of agents. Nobody could be blamed. She was not aware of other factions within the secret army. London was not aware, until too late, of who had been caught and who remained at liberty. Nor did Baker Street know of a so-called pact between the Gestapo and hapless French civilians on whose land the police had found British parachutes and containers. The pact was widely proclaimed in rural areas. It guaranteed that members of the Resistance would be treated as soldiers, not as traitors liable to execution. In the confusion, many farmers and laborers, believing they were going to be discovered anyway, collaborated. When the Gestapo had all the evidence it needed, the pact was predictably broken. Thus the smashing of one network led to the infiltration of others. The Gestapo was expert in bluff and counterbluff. For instance, only two weeks after MADELEINE's flight from England, a leader of the PROSPER network was lying in a Paris jail staring in horror at an old Michelin map marked with secret dropping zones. The map had been presented by SS Hauptscharführer Karl Langer, who followed this up with a file of photostats covering the previous five months: they were copies of reports to London of sabotage operations. Langer recited the dates and locations of parachute drops and then added: "We know that your network has just received someone called MADELEINE. We have not found her yet. We will."

What seems incredible is that the girl continued to function for so long after this. She took a few precautions: dyed her hair, made use of a dozen apartments scattered around Paris from which she could transmit. She picked up such invaluable contacts as the peacetime director of the French Société Radio Electrique, who serviced her transmitter, and a Paris businessman who had enrolled members of the secret army on his staff to provide them with cover. She had been taught to convert a cramped bathroom into a radio station: the French toilet bowls were worked by a chain to the water cistern, and this chain provided an aerial, while the current code could be read from one's underwear on the floor. Her "safe house" was 3 Boulevard Richard Wallace, the home of a doctor. At the beginning of October, the Gestapo had intercepted certain phone calls from Sablons 88.04 that indicated an agent at work. This was the telephone number of MADELEINE's safe house. She was working with a rebuilt circuit, a group of saboteurs, when arrested. The group had traced underground sewers in which the Germans stored torpedoes to be shipped to the U-boat pens at Brest, and MADELEINE had just conveyed their request to London for the new explosive known as marzipan because of its sweet smell resembling that of almonds.

She was taken to the top floor of the five-story Gestapo headquarters at 84 Avenue Foch, where cells were reserved for important agents. The two Canadians, McAlister and Pickersgill, had been removed to torture chambers at 13-bis, Place des Etats-Unis, where they continued to resist efforts to make them play back their own radio transmitters under Gestapo guidance, until finally they were shipped to extermination camps.

Her interrogations are now a matter of record, in evidence given at war-crime trials and in postwar questioning of German officers. She was almost killed in one attempt to escape. Her interrogators faced her with information suggesting that her colleagues had already confessed. The Gestapo knew about Buckmaster. They showed her details of Baker Street operations that made her wonder if a traitor existed at the head of the organization.

Baker Street began to fence in the dark with the Germans, a dangerous duel when invisible weapons sliced across a pitch-black stage. Whoever won, some agents must lose. On the German side, small bits of information gleaned from different prisoners gave MADELEINE an impression that the Nazi counterespionage authorities already knew everything. London, trying to confuse the enemy, had to be wary of being itself confused. Some of the stations, like Pickersgill's BERTRAND, were being played back under German control. Was MADELEINE under German control? Could she be persuaded to work for the enemy if confronted with evidence of "betrayal" by her colleagues? These anxieties plagued Baker Street, and the Germans knew it. But Baker Street knew German anxieties and transmitted personal messages to Pickersgill to see if he was working his post under German control, or had resumed working in freedom, or was not working it at all. The questions for Pickersgill could not be answered by the Germans operating BERTRAND, so they dredged him out of the cesspool of Rawicz concentration camp. He was brought back to Avenue Foch, sick and emaciated and reduced to that state of physical degradation when the mind functions badly. The Gestapo stood aside. Smooth young German officers offered Pickersgill good food, clean clothes, the prospect of an end to the nightmare. He refused. They proposed a small excursion into some of the more amusing quarters of Paris as proof of their good will. He refused. But he was a Canadian, a soldier, and, like themselves, a man with his life still ahead of him—surely he must recognize their good will, their intervention on his behalf, their outrage at the way he had been treated?

Pickersgill must have guessed what they were after. The tough training that seemed to have been all wasted when he was captured now did prevent a worse catastrophe. Bloodied, half-starved, aware of what awaited him back in Rawicz, he responded to the discipline of his own beliefs and the warnings of instructors: "If you are caught, they will try every trick. Say nothing beyond your cover story. Stick to it. Never stray from it. They will try kindness alternating with savagery. During the sunny periods, you will be tempted. . . ."

If Pickersgill had weakened, he might have talked about himself. He did not know that Bletchley, trying to check if he was still operational, was signaling him with stray personal references to which he alone could reply; therefore he could not know what personal matters were of interest to the Gestapo in its attempt to deceive Bletchley. These might have been the most innocent details of family life. He might have accepted the invitation to a decent dinner in a black-market Paris restaurant and inadvertently he might have mentioned in the atmosphere of false *bonhomie* that he liked porridge at breakfast or once bicycled to school or had a mother in Ottawa. He had no means of judging what was, and what was not, likely to help counterespionage experts maintain London's confidence in BERTRAND's transmissions. He did not even know if BERTRAND was transmitting under German guidance. Knowing nothing he refused to take any risk, yield any ground, or drop his guard in any way. He was aware of other prisoners, but were their messages, tapped on the water pipes, yet another trick? He knew there was a girl under interrogation. MADELEINE? What had she said? How did the Germans know about this or that aspect of the circuits into which Pickersgill had been inserted? Too many questions and no answers.

During one session, he grabbed a bottle, broke the neck, jabbed it into the face of an SS guard, and jumped from the second-floor window. He was running for the Bois de Boulogne when he was brought down by a hail of bullets. But his early training had paid off in one other respect: he had cut the jugular of the guard and killed him. Pickersgill was given the best German hospital treatment for his serious bullet wounds, was invited again to co-operate, again refused, and was finally tagged for *Nacht und Nebel— Rueckkehr Unerwuenscht* (Night and Fog—Return Not Required).

MADELEINE herself made another attempt to escape, together with two other agents held in Avenue Foch. They succeeded in breaking out of the top of the old building and jumping to flat roofs below in the dead of night. Their plans had been carefully prepared, but security was too much for them. This time, when the girl was marched back, SS Sturmbannführer Hans Kieffer* telegraphed Berlin that she was a desperado, and he could not remain responsible for her safe custody. She was dispatched to the Black Forest prison of Pforzheim.

Her requiem did not appear until four years after the end of the war. Even then, it broke the tradition that British secret operations remain a closed book. MADELEINE was one of the exceptions made when parts of a story become public and may lead to false con-

---

* Kieffer was executed by the British three years later, convicted of shooting prisoners in uniform who had been captured during the D-day landings.

clusions. On April 5, 1949, the long silence was ended by this notice that she had been awarded the highest honor the British could pay—the George Cross:

CHANCERY OF THE ORDERS OF KNIGHTHOOD
. . . Following her arrival the Gestapo made mass arrests in the Paris Resistance groups to which she had been detailed. She refused to abandon what had become the principal and most dangerous post in France, although given the opportunity to return to England. She did not wish to leave her French comrades without communications and she hoped also to rebuild her group.

The Gestapo had a full description of her but knew only her code name MADELEINE. They deployed considerable forces in their effort to catch her and so break the last remaining link with London. After 3½ months she was betrayed to the Gestapo and taken to their HQ in the Avenue Foch. The Gestapo had found her codes and messages and were in a position to work back to London. They asked her to cooperate, but she refused and gave them no information of any kind. . . .

The citation described her as the first Baker Street agent to be sent by the Nazis to a German camp. There she was labeled "particularly dangerous" and handcuffed and chained day and night in a crouching position so that she depended upon male jailers to deal with her sanitary and feeding problems. In this manner, chained like a vicious animal in total isolation, she was held for ten months. Despite this, she still refused to give any information about her work or her colleagues.

"She was taken with three others to Dachau Camp on the 12th September, 1944," concluded the notice outside St. James's Palace. "On arrival, she was taken to the crematorium and shot."

"At least 24,000 members of the French secret army were executed. Of 115,000 deported to death camps, some 40,000 returned in various stages of emaciation," Stephenson reported later. Of those who fought pitched battles with the enemy, another 30,000 were killed: These appalling losses were suffered in darkness, to become known only after the war. The diaries of Pickersgill helped his brother Jack, a Canadian cabinet minister, reconstruct that whole tragedy. The girls who became agents were many, ranging from HANNA, who parachuted into Tito's zone to bring out fellow Jewish survivors, to ODETTE, the young mother who left her children in Kensington to wind up in a Gestapo torture chamber. "The dimensions of the coming ordeal for such girls were dimly perceived in early 1941," Stephenson said. "President Roosevelt's 'arsenal of democracy' did more than give heart to those like Madeleine who defied the torturers until death brought welcome oblivion. In judging his deep involvement and personal risks, you must consider these individual acts of courage, which matched his own. Because he knew of these lonely acts of heroism, he felt he could do no less."

Part Three

IMPEACHABLE OFFENSES

"I am becoming more and more convinced that the British face imminent defeat unless they are given immediate aid by the United States in the matter of getting an adequate amount of shipping into United Kingdom ports. . . ."

—Frank Knox, U.S. Secretary of the Navy, in a note to President Roosevelt, April 1941

"We will want to be notified by you in great secrecy of movements of convoys so that our patrol units can seek out the ship of an aggressor nation. . . ."

—Franklin Roosevelt, in a note to INTREPID and Winston Churchill, April 1941

Although *INTREPID'S* headquarters were in New York, he traveled frequently and to far places. He virtually commuted to London by military aircraft to see Churchill and others involved in his secret operations. Churchill here broods among the bombed ruins of the Houses of Parliament. The dark figure silhouetted in the foreground is *INTREPID*.

This photograph of General William "Wild Bill" Donovan, founder and chief of the Office of Strategic Services was presented by him to *INTREPID*. The Inscription reads: "To Bill Stephenson whose friendship, knowledge and continuing assistance contributed so richly to the establishment and the maintenance of an American intelligence service in World War II—Bill Donovan"

Kim Philby, the Soviet superspy who tried covertly to undermine the Anglo-American wartime intelligence alliance, had earlier followed his masters' directives by openly expressing pro-Hitler views. Here (marked by arrow) he sits at a dinner, held by the Anglo-German Fellowship on July 14, 1936 in London, soon after Hitler proclaimed his anti-Jewish "Nuremberg Laws." Another member of the Fellowship was Geoffrey Dawson, editor of the London *Times,* who was "doing my utmost, night after night, to keep out of the paper anything that might hurt their [the Germans'] susceptibilities." The Nazi Foreign Minister, Joachim von Ribbentrop, was Ambassador to Great Britain when he harangued this gathering on the need to fight "Bolsheviks."

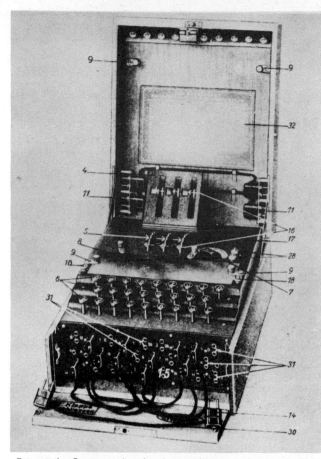

Enigma, the German coding-decoding machine, posed a seemingly in-soluble puzzle to the British. This version of Enigma was photographed directly from the operational manual issued by the German Army. (Other branches of the armed forces and the government used different versions of the device.) A huge variety of code wheels, called rotors, each wired differently from any other, and used in combinations of three, provided the enciphering-deciphering variable of the system. Three rotors are visible at the left rear of the machine illustrated. Not only did a letter or number entered emerge as a different unit, but also after each entry the rotors automatically turned; thus, the identical letter entered in im-mediate succession would not emerge as a coded duplicate. Decoding depended on precise knowledge of how the rotors were set for each specific encoding. The wire cables on the front of the machine permitted many additional changes in the circuitry and thereby provided even more individual code patterns. With so complex—yet fast and portable—a system, the Nazis quite naturally believed their Enigma communica-tions were unbreakable.

Photograph by David Kahn

Outside the town of Bletchley, a rail and industrial hub in the heart of England, stands a Victorian mansion on an estate called Bletchley Park. The mansion housed replicas of the German Enigma coding-decoding machines. Nearby buildings provided operational facilities and housing for the remarkable group that gradually broke the Enigma code system. That, in company with other deciphering and analysis of radio communications, was given the highest classification—"Top-secret Ultra"— and as ULTRA the Enigma decoding is now popularly known. The Bletchley operations permitted INTREPID to give President Roosevelt secret access to Hitler's intentions and plans.

Ian Fleming, creator of the James Bond intrigues, was an aide to the chief of British Naval Intelligence. He worked closely with INTREPID and received much of his training at BSC's secret establishment outside Toronto, in Canada, some phases from Stephenson personally. Many of the techniques and devices later portrayed in his fiction were derived, according to Fleming, from INTREPID's operations. Here Fleming is seen in Room 40 at Royal Navy headquarters in London.

INTREPID's communications required absolute security. He employed special ciphers developed by *SOE* and *SIS*. He frequently carried his highest-priority communications personally and sometimes sent them by hand of his most trusted couriers. ''With a price on his head, Eric Bailey outwitted the Soviet Security Police,'' wrote *INTREPID* of Bailey's youthful service. In World War II, he appointed this fabled British agent, by then close to sixty, a King's Messenger, to carry *ULTRA* intelligence too vital for transmission even in code. Here is Bailey in three of his many manifestations:

a. as a Tibetan, near Lhasa, in 1904;
b. as an Uzbek in an Asian corner of the Soviet Union, in 1920;
c. as a Russian (seated) in Tashkent, in 1919.

"Hitler has often protested that his plans for conquest do not extend across the Atlantic," President Roosevelt announced in a nationwide address on October 27, 1941. "...I have in my possession a secret map...[that] makes clear the Nazi design, not only against South America, but against the United States as well." This map was taken from a German agent and delivered to *INTREPID* by Ian Fleming. It showed the continent divided into five German-dominated regions. The handwritten notes concern queries about "fuel depots for overseas transports" and financial matters regarding their establishment, expansion, and supply.

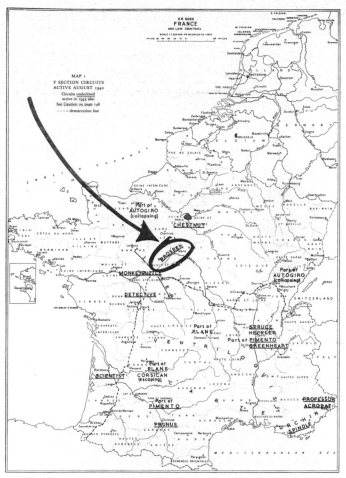

SOE (Special Operations Executive) was a vital branch of British intelligence entrusted with executing covert operations of an extraordinary range. Planning for these hazardous actions was intricate and had to consider every possibility from success to failure. SOE regularly produced for highly limited distribution updated maps locating, by code name only, its intelligence and resistance networks in enemy territory. This SOE map of Occupied France indicates (by superimposed arrow) *PROSPER*, "the biggest, busiest, and most hazardous of the networks." It was to *PROSPER* that a young British agent code-named *MADELEINE* was assigned only a short time, as it turned out, before the network was betrayed.

MADELEINE shortly before she was flown into Nazi territory to join the *PROSPER* network as a "pianist," the slang designation for a radio-telegraphy operator. She became the sole communication link between her unit of the French underground and London after the other agents attached to *PROSPER* were captured.

All British agents were volunteers. Each was thoroughly investigated, interviewed many times to determine psychological and intellectual motivation and fitness, and, if finally accepted, subjected to a rigorous course of training. Here *MADELEINE* is practicing "blind drops," parachuting from a moving aircraft at night. The figure behind her is the jump master.

Continuous conditioning and practice in parachute jumping and landing were possible through the use of take-offs from a stationary balloon. *MADELEINE* said of such drops: "It was more frightening to step cold-bloodedly into space without the comforting roar of aero-engines."

Agents were frequently given training in a specialty. *MADELEINE*, the first woman to be assigned as a radio-telegraphist in Occupied France, had to become fast and accurate in key transmission. Such facility was essential, but only a preliminary. Codes and their meanings had to be learned and then the operator had to demonstrate ability to work under extreme pressure. Speed and brevity were required to avoid German detection devices.

Every contingency that might arise was brought into the training program. A working knowledge and proficiency with firearms, particularly handguns, made up an important part of the agent's rigid schedule.

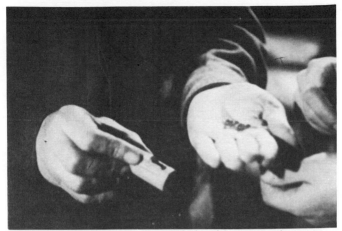

Because capture was not only possible, but also a statistical certainty among so large a group of individuals thrust into unpredictable and hazardous situations, and since the Nazis' effective use of physical and psychological torture was grimly known, all agents were supplied with an L pill. If captured, the agent could place the pill under the tongue, ready to crunch if conditions became unbearable. If a pill was swallowed unbroken, it would have no effect; if it was crushed by the teeth, certain death would follow within a matter of minutes.

Special circumstances might make landing from an aircraft preferable to a parachute drop, provided the plane was almost undetectable, could land in a limited space, and could accomplish its task quickly and then disappear. To this end, so-called Moon planes were designed. They were frequently made with plywood bodies, painted a dull black, to be almost invisible against a night sky, and designed for low flight, to permit hedge-hopping and landing in small fields. Here is a Moon plane, hardly visible against a night sky.

MADELEINE was sent into France by Moon plane. This aspect of an agent's training was also a subject of practice, the goal being to allow no more than one minute for the aircraft to land, the agent to disembark, and the plane to take off from the "reception field." An agent is here practicing scrambling from a Moon plane.

MADELEINE's last glimpse of England was this old farmhouse disguising one of numerous take-off points for agents.

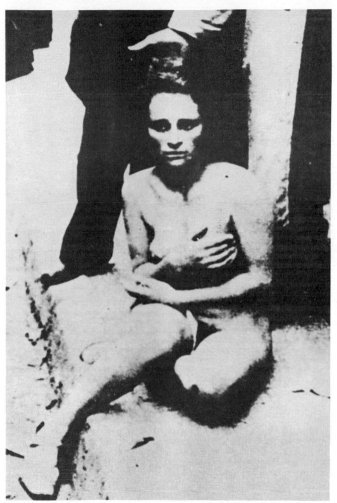

The methodical Gestapo took photographs of their victims before execution. Whenever possible, such pictures were copied or stolen and smuggled to Britain in the attempt to learn the fate of captured or missing agents. This photograph of a pathetic, emaciated, and defenseless agent, prior to execution, was stolen during the time when *MADELEINE* was a prisoner of the Gestapo, having been held continuously in hand and leg chains for many months. There is no record of a positive identification.

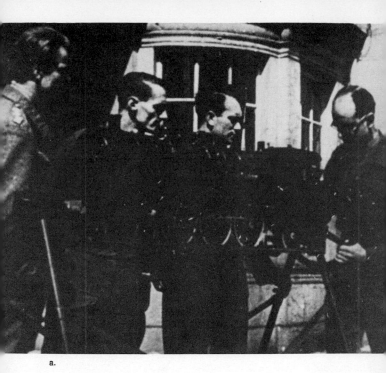

a.

a. Camp X, one of *INTREPID*'s concealed training centers in Canada, given cover by the Canadian Broadcasting Corporation, was an extraordinarily busy place. Among its subjects for study was guerrilla warfare. Great damage could be inflicted upon enemy industry and transportation by putting a single locomotive, strategically placed, out of action. Here agents are instructed in that art.

b. Small plastic charges could be placed at the most vulnerable points of a locomotive even under watchful eyes. Agents were carefully rehearsed in these procedures.

c. Another of Camp X's specialties was the disruption of power sources. Breaking cables was only a temporary deterrent, but the blowing up of a generator created a major problem. Destruction of generators was a standard part of the course.

b.

c.

Seer Sees Nazi Doom if U. S. Acts in 8 Months

CLEVELAND NEWS, Aug. 6 1941.
Voluntary Entrance Into War Would Hasten End, Hungarian Here for Astrologer Session Says

BY WALLACE R. KATZ

Stars Carry No Encouragement For Der Fuehrer

Astrologers Hold Hitler Is on Downgrade and Certain To Lose

Astrologers Predict Hitler's Star Is About to Set; Czechoslovakia Invasion Was His Turning Point

Hitler Isn't Getting Many Breaks From Students Of Stars

Astrologer Links His Downfall With F. D. R. Birth Date

Astrology
HITLER ILL-FATED
Stars Against Red War

Astrologers See Hitler's Star Setting

Hitler's Star Is Setting,
Astrologers Say, Seeing His Downfall In Roosevelt's "Beautiful Horoscope."

Astrologers List Errors Stargazer Hitler Made
Fuehrer Is on the Downgrade, They Claim; Criticize Attack on Russia

Astrologers See Feuhrer's Star Sinking In West

Hitler's Star Setting, Astrologers Agree
FDR Horoscope 'Perfectly Beautiful,' Says Noted Astro-Philosopher

Roosevelt's Star Shadows Hitler's

Astrologer Says Star of Adolf Hitler Setting; Roosevelt 'Towers Above Others' in Horoscope

Louis de Wohl, "the famous Hungarian astrologer," visited the United States in 1941, and his predictions, foreseeing disaster for certain high-ranking Nazis, received huge press coverage and worldwide circulation. Hitler was a believer in astrology and these predictions provoked the downfall of several of his henchmen. "Mr. de Wohl" was actually a captain in the British Army, detached to work for *INTREPID*. His "predictions" had snippets of accuracy to bolster his credibility. His horoscopes were supplied by the staff of BSC in New York.

LINEE AEREE TRANSCONTINENTALI
ITALIANE S.A.

Roma, 30 ottobre 1941 XX

IL PRESIDENTE

Caro Camerata,

ho ricevuto la Vostra relazione che è
giunta cinque giorni dopo essere stata spedita.

La relazione è stata portata subito a
conoscenza degl' interessati i quali la considera-
no di grande importanza. L' abbiamo confrontata con
altra ricevuta dal Fraça Del Prete. Le due relazio-
ni presentano un quadro analogo della situazione
che esiste laggiù ma la Vostra è più dettagliata.
Desidero esprimerVi il mio compiacimento. Il fatto
che, in questa occasione, noi abbiamo ottenuto infor-
mazioni più complete di quelle che abbiamo S. ed i
suoi, mi ha riempito di soddisfazione.

Non vi è dubbio che il grassoccio sta
cedendo alle lusinghe degli Americani e che soltan-
to un intervento violento da parte dei nostri
amici verdi può salvare il paese. I nostri collaboratori di Berlino, in seguito alle conversazioni
avute con il rappresentante a Lisbona, hanno deciso
che tale intervento deve aver luogo al più presto.
Ma Voi conoscete la situazione. Il giorno in cui si
verificherà il cambiamento, i nostri collaboratori
si preoccuperanno assai poco dei nostri interessi e
la Lufthansa raccoglierà tutti i vantaggi. Per impedire
che questo si verifichi dobbiamo procurarci al più
presto altri amici influenti tra i verdi. Fatelo senza
indugio. Lascio a Voi di decidere quali sarebbero le
persone più adatte: forse Fadilha o E.F. de Andrade

Comandante
Vicenzo COLHOLA
Linee Aeree Transcontinentali Italiane S.A.
RIO DE JANEIRO (Brasile)

Camp X contained a subsection designated Station M, which included
forgery as one of its special skills. Here is a letter so perfectly forged
by matching the imperfections of typewriter keys, the inks employed,
and the paper that it caused the removal of certain key pro-Nazis in
South America.

This passport gave protection to a naturalized Canadian citizen, Spiridon Mekas, who was able to travel in non-Occupied Europe and to enter Yugoslavia just before the Nazi invasion. This passport was a forgery. Its subject was a resistance leader, then hardly known, but now familiar as Tito.

Camp X became the staging for Heydrich's assassination. Every available detail of his habits, daily schedule, and surroundings was studied. His regular routes were photographed, built into three-dimensional scale models, and in critical places actually constructed full size. This photograph shows the castle in Prague where he lived.

Reinhard Tristam Eugen Heydrich, justifiably known as "the Butcher of Prague," was Hitler's chief executioner and master of terror. *INTREPID* and his advisers believed that Heydrich was quite possibly Hitler's choice as his successor, an event that would sink the monstrosity of the Third Reich to even more horrible depths. But the proposed assassination of Heydrich raised the grim specter of Nazi retaliation. The decision to proceed was soul-searing, but it was made. The retaliation was even more atrocious than could have been predicted, but it fanned the fires of resistance to unquenchable fury.

The assassins, volunteers from the Czech secret resistance army, slipped out of their occupied homeland, were flown to Camp X, and there prepared for their mission. Here is a scale model of the Prague area used in the planning and training.

An agent's photograph of the assassination scene, taken shortly after the action, shows why this hairpin bend was chosen for the attack. Heydrich's bomb-shattered car is at the lower left.

Heydrich's car close-up after the Reich Protector's fatally injured body had been removed.

The operations room of a Moon plane base that secretly brought the assassins out of Czechoslovakia and, when they were ready, returned them.

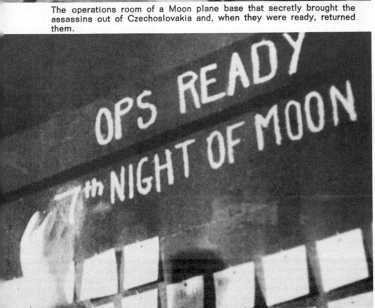

Close-up of the operations board announcing "ready" condition for dropping Heydrich's assassins into their action area.

S.6278

18 II 42

19 JUIN 20 F ABFAHRT TRANSPORTER MIT 9000 MANN ANGEBL.
AUSTRALIEN WEILL 2 WEITERE 2800 MANN U 24/26.F. 2~3000 MANN
ZWISCHEN 19 U. 6.25 U IM GANZEN 48.000 MANN. 1 FRACHTER
STW 8000 T. LADET EASCH TERMINAL BROOKLYN STURZFLUG-
ZEUGE SCHWERE BOMBER U FLUGZ CPN.GESCH. ZOLL 2 F. AU-
MUNIT. MIDRANGE + HALSCHITE POSM 04 F. LIEGT BROOKLYN
KRIEGSHAFEN WIRD AUSGERUESTET MINEN MUNITAS HIFE

New York,N.Y., 18th of Febr.1942

s 6278.

Dear Jose:-

It is almost a year, since I have seen you last,
and it now does not look as if we are going to meet again
for some time to come. Too bad that we had to get into this
war. I figured that it probably would not take more than
a few months to lick the Germans, with the Russians apparently making a good job of it, but now that Japan has come
into this fracass, it seems that it will take a least another year before we shall be able to lick the Germans as
well as the Japs. How I would love to roam again in Lisbon
and its beautiful surroundings, especially at this time of
the year, but that will simply have to wait now for the
duration of the war.

Since writing you last, my health has constantly
improved, so much so that I do not have to stay indoors any
longer, but again can go out any time during the day, and
in all kinds of weather, and again attend to my business,
which I had been forced to neglect for quite some time.
Nothing more aggravating than being ill, but once you are
entirely over it, you look at the world again through rose
colored glasses, and nature, even with its bare trees at
present, looks beautiful, a thing that cannot appeal to you
unless you have passed through a severe illness, after that

By design, Bermuda became a filter point for mail between the Americas
and Europe. Much German intelligence was smuggled out in innocent-
looking letters like this, part of the infamous "Fred Lewis" correspondence. Intercepted at Bermuda and tested for invisible inks, the letters
revealed hidden handwritten messages giving military information on the
same sheets containing the innocuous typed letter. Nazi spy rings were
uncovered through FBI persistance and BSC Bermuda staff's hunches.

you feel like hugging the whole cockeyed world. But that does not say that, in order for anyone to enjoy such feelings, I should wish him to go through what I had to go through. But it seems the good Lord sees to it that trees do not grow into heaven, and whenever in His belief it is best to visit a severe illness on anyone, who, like me, has not been too good, he does so in order to try to make us better human beings. Whether, in my case, my really good intentions will materialize for any great duration, I cannot vouch for, but let's hope so

How is your family now getting along on foodstuffs? Do you have any rationing at present or is everything still plentyful ? As it was at the time I saw you last ? That is on thing we do not have to worry about in this country. You can get everything, even sugar, which up to now has not yet been rationed, and if it actually should come to pass, we will still get enough to go around, and as for me I hardly need any. It would be a good lesson for many people, if rationing of sugar would come, in order to stop some people needlessly squandering same.

I do hope that you and all of your family are enjoying the best of health. When you see Alonso please give him my kindest regards. And don't forget to write from time to time.

With all good wishes and best regards to you and yours from my wife and myself,

Your friend

Z 6272.

Lewis

DOUGLAS-BUFFALO ADRBY JAPANK ALNGESTELLT.
60% ALLER GEWEHR-LOEWFE UNBRAUCHBAR VER-
WORFEN, URSACHE MANGEL AN BES. GEHOERT. WERK-
ZEUGSTAHL. PHILIPPINEN VERLUSTE TONNE EXILIPUR.
8-9000 MANN. LETZTE BRIEFE HOCH, BEIDE SEITE-
MIT GEHEIM- U. MASCH. SCHRIFT DA EINSEITIG
MASCH. SCHRIFT VERDRECHTIG LT. SPIONAGE PRO-
ZESS LUDWIG ET AL. KANN ENTWICKELT GUT LESER-
LICH T NOCHMALS ERBITTE KASSENUEBERWEISUNG.

HEIL HITLER!
FRED LEWIS.

German intelligence developed a new and ingenious method of using innocent-appearing mail to carry concealed messages. This was the microdot, a tiny speck of film that, by photographic reduction through a microscope, could carry a whole page of writing or drawing. Thus a comma in a typed letter might have a minute piece of film glued over it. Upon removal and enlargement, that film would produce extensive writing or graphics. An envelope, addressed to Lisbon from Mexico City, contained on its flap some small black spots that would hardly warrant attention at all.

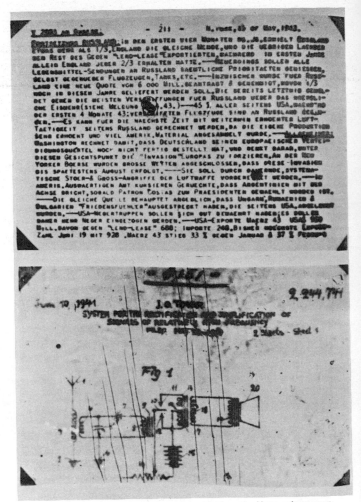

Microdots were discovered among those black spots. Upon enlargement, they were found to disclose military secrets. Thus the work of the Bermuda station of BSC again proved invaluable.

The woman code-named *CYNTHIA* was an American, the daughter of a U.S. Marine Corps major. She first served as a British agent in Poland during the search for the secrets of the Enigma coding machine. Courageous, daring, and ingenious, *CYNTHIA* exploited her beauty and undeniable sexual attraction with breathtaking success.

Vichy French diplomatic ciphers, obtained by *CYNTHIA* in an adventure that would seem incredible in a novel of intrigue, helped develop *ULTRA* solutions to Enigma codes.

Ministère de la Marine

Etat Major Général

SECRET

DICTIONNAIRE R.D. 36

pour la

Correspondance chiffrée avec les autorités

diplomatiques Consulaires et Coloniales

1939

DIPLOMATIE - VICHY

No. 1236 - 1237.

No. 282-283

De l'Attaché Naval à l'Amirauté Française.

J'ai appris de bonne source présence:

1). A Norfolk de l'"Illustrious";

2). A Philadelphia du "Repulse".

3). A New York de un ou deux croiseurs en plus du "Malaya" déjà signalé.

Tous ces bâtiments subissent des reparations de longue durée, le premier prêt sera sans doute le "Malaya" qui est immobilisé encore au moins pour un mois.

Ceci répond à votre télégramme No. 4093./.

HENRY-HAYE.

Among the sensitive and vital intelligence secured by *CYNTHIA* was the decoded telegram from Vichy requesting its Washington embassy to transmit for German intelligence information on British warships undergoing repairs in U.S. ports.

TO: PETER.

From: JARLEN.

MOST IMPORTANT

We intend sending to JUSTITSRAADEN in the near future a bunch of keys which contain a very important message from the British Government to Professor Niels Bohr. We would be very grateful if you could see that Professor BOHR gets the keys and also if you or someone appointed by you would explain to him how to find the message.

The following diagram shows the position in keys A. and A.1. of the message which has to be extracted. Key A.1. is the one with number 229 on it and Key A. is the long key next to it

A small hole to a depth of 4 mm. has been bored in the two keys. The holes were plugged up and concealed after the message was inserted. Professor Bohr should gently file the keys at the point indicated until the hole appears. The message can then be syringed or floated out on to a micro-glide. The message is a very very small micro film and is repeated in duplicate in each key. It should be handled very delicately.

I do not myself know the contents of the message except that I do know it is very important. Will you kindly warn JUSTITSRAADEN and tell him to expect the bunch of keys. We will send the keys through to him by seperate courier as soon as we know that this sending has reached you and that you have had time to warn Justitsraaden.

No operation conducted by *INTREPID* during the war was more crucial than his efforts to impede the Nazi pursuit of an atomic explosive and his strategy to aid the Anglo-American development of one. One of the most dramatic incidents in his career came about through his plan to free the brilliant physicist Niels Bohr from German custody. After his escape, Bohr became a vital member of the Manhattan Project, the supersecret Allied operation that did produce an atom bomb and thus opened a new era in weaponry. Microdot messages concealed in the keys shown here instructed Bohr on the details of his escape.

William Stephenson, the man called *INTREPID*, never sought public attention during his busy and productive life. He was rarely photographed. Once he accepted his role as Churchill's secret envoy and chief of what was to become the largest intelligence operation in history, he assumed the highest degree of anonymity. He is seen here at his New York home in 1954. Behind him stands the United Nations, a most appropriate background, for without him and those of his dedication and integrity the United Nations would not stand at all.

All photographs, except those of William Stephenson, William Donovan, the Enigma machine, and the mansion at Bletchley Park, are from the BSC Papers, Station M Archives.

28

"SUPPOSE THE *Bismarck* does show up in the Caribbean? We have some submarines down there. Suppose we order them to attack her and attempt to sink her? Do you think the people would demand to have me impeached?" These words by President Roosevelt were said on May 24, 1941, as reported by Robert Sherwood. The BSC Papers recorded the substance of the same conversation with the observation that U.S. opinion had become highly critical of Britain's poor performance against the enemy during this period, making it harder again for Roosevelt to display too much open support.

The President kept secret a flagrant breach of the Neutrality Act that led to the most celebrated victory in modern British naval annals. Bismarck, the most powerful warship then in existence, pride of the German Navy, was sunk after the longest running fight in naval history. The action brought into play every facet of warfare, from secret agents to aerial torpedoes. Every contemporary electronic device was used. What caused the President to brood before *Bismarck* met her fate was that the greatest sea epic in history might end in a terrible, perhaps fatal, British defeat. *Bismarck* had taken to sea and disappeared. Britain's future hinged dramatically on one final despairing air search.

Roosevelt was drawn into the drama from the moment the monster *Bismarck* broke out of the Baltic Sea and began a wild rampage by destroying the most famous warship in the world, "Britain's mighty *Hood*," as it was then known. *Hood* went down with 90 officers and 1,400 men near the pack ice northwest of Iceland, victim of a plunging shell that struck her magazines. In the several masterly accounts of the epic engagements that followed, the key role of American naval and intelligence missions has been unacknowledged, for officially it did not exist. Nonetheless, the United States was essential to the avenging of *Hood* and stemming a disaster so great that its effects are even now incalculable.

The first hint of the crisis to come reached the President in a signal relayed through INTREPID from a Baker Street Irregular, Odd Starheim. The son of a Norwegian shipowner in business with Stephenson, Starheim had escaped the Nazi occupation and was an active and daring member of the Norwegian resistance force. He was primarily engaged with a group working to destroy Germany's source of heavy water for atomic research. But on May 21, 1941, he spotted two German warships in the Sperr Zone of the Norwegian coast, an area forbidden to all vessels not involved in transporting atomic materials. He took the risk of transmitting a warning to the Norwegian Section of BSC. His brief description, "Two large enemy warships," was sufficient to tell the Admiralty in London that the two missing giants, *Bismarck* and *Prinz Eugen*, were preparing to make a run for the Atlantic. If they succeeded in joining the battle cruisers *Scharnhorst* and *Gneisenau*, Churchill immediately informed Roosevelt, "they could alter the whole course of the war." The two battle cruisers alone had already accounted for 115,622 tons of shipping sunk in two months' raiding. These losses were such that Churchill feared the fatal cutting of Britain's arteries. On that Wednesday morning, the peril became far more than doubled. The two newly loosed leviathans cast an immediate threat upon eleven British convoys then at sea and a future threat upon Britain's life line.

The following day a signal from Hitler to Admiral Erich Raeder was intercepted and decoded by ULTRA. The German Navy was to shatter British sea links. The Führer could not know that already the new battleship *Prince of Wales, Hood,* and six destroyers were making full speed to join the two British cruisers already in the vicinity of the Norwegian fjord where the two massive German warships had been seen. Before this sweeping action was over, the British would commit to it eight battleships, two aircraft carriers, eleven cruisers, twenty-one destroyers, six submarines, several squadrons of aircraft—and a U.S. Navy ensign, Leonard Smith.

Ensign Smith, a young man from Missouri farm country, was one of eighty U.S. Navy airmen lent, together with PBY Catalina amphibians, in response to Stephenson's urgent request for help from the President. The long-range multipurpose planes were then the most effective aerial counterweapon to German raids. Britian had nothing like them, or their radio equipment, or their crews. Smith's part in sinking the *Bismarck* was interred in official files.

In the afternoon of Hitler's signal, a Royal Navy aircraft flew through thick weather to penetrate the fjord where *Bismarck* and *Prinz Eugen* were thought to be hiding. The pilot risked piling into precipitous cliffs and mountains, his vision frequently reduced to zero by fog, sleet, and thunderclouds. He returned with devastating news. Both German warships had vanished.

On Thursday, May 22, Roosevelt was informed that Churchill was spending all his time in the Admiralty War Room directing the hunt for *Bismarck,* the more dangerous of the two raiders. But his full attention could be focused on this new threat only at intervals. In the Mediterranean, heavy Royal Navy losses, including the destroyer *Kelly,* whose captain, Lord Louis Mountbatten, had just been rescued from the sea, threatened the slippery British grasp of territory around Cairo.

At Scapa Flow, east of Scotland's aptly named Cape Wrath, the commander of the Home Fleet now decided to move out a powerful force to block the Germans' likeliest exits. Admiral Sir John Tovey, small and sharp-witted, who loved Americans and hated "yes men," had known Roosevelt from World War I, when he commanded a destroyer at Jutland. Now he was flying his flag in the new battleship *King George V.*

"It is likely to be an anxious weekend," signaled Churchill. For him, that most anxious weekend in naval history began early on Saturday. Of the widely spread net of warships, it was *Hood* and *Prince of Wales* that intercepted and engaged *Bismarck*. At 3:52 A.M., *Hood* fired her first salvo. *Bismarck* replied. Suddenly the *Hood* was bracketed by tall columns of fifteen-inch-shell splashes. The enemy's shooting was astonishingly accurate. Then a direct hit plunged through the *Hood*'s armor and penetrated a magazine. A violent explosion tore the ship apart. Within three minutes nothing was left of her except some debris and three survivors. *Prince of Wales* was hit, and crippled so badly she had to retire from action to avoid annihilation. *Bismarck* was not unscathed, but her wounds were not disabling. The news of the engagement was so shocking that all over the world, from Berlin to Washington, there were requests for the message to be repeated. *"Hood* sunk?" Roosevelt was supposed to have cried. "It's the end of Rule Britannia."

Bismarck was loose in the Atlantic, and *Prinz Eugen,* too. Moreover, gloomy news was coming from all the war fronts. Churchill heard "situation hopeless" from one commander in the Middle East; from another, an estimate that two-thirds of the Mediterranean Fleet had been damaged by a merciless Axis pounding during operations around Crete. Then Tovey reported that *Bismarck* had again given her pursuers the slip and was vanishing into a screen of foul weather. The War Cabinet atmosphere was foul, too, reported Foreign Office Under-Secretary Alexander Cadogan. "Winston almost threw his hand in. . . . But there is a bit of the histrionic in *that!"*

Histrionics had their place in the White House, too. "There was all sorts of speculation," said Stephenson. "Some thought the Germans would even shell New York and then sail into South American ports to make propaganda. Roosevelt thought the *Bismarck* might make a grab for Martinique, the Vichy French island in the Caribbean. That was when the President speculated about ordering American submarines to sink her."

Robert Sherwood described the moment in his *Roosevelt and Hopkins:*

Roosevelt was speaking in such a detached, even casual manner that one might have supposed he was playing with some time-machine fantasy, such as "Suppose you found yourself living in the middle of the thirteenth century. . . ." Yet here was the reality of one murderous ship, off on some wild, unpredictable career, guided by the will of one man who might be a maniac or a genius or both, capable of converting one inexplicable impulse into a turning point of history. And here was the President of the United States, sitting in the White House in an atmosphere of oppressive calm, wondering what the next naval dispatch would tell him, wondering what he would be able to do about it. He was behind his desk in the Oval Study, and he had his coat off. It was a very hot day. . . . The windows were open. Outside, to the southwest, was a big magnolia tree supposedly planted by Andrew Jackson. It was covered with big white blooms and their lemony scent drifted into the Study. You could look from these windows across to Virginia, which, when Lincoln lived in this house, was enemy territory. But Roosevelt was wondering whether he'd be impeached.

The U.S. role in what then happened is missing from contemporary accounts. Even long after the war, the British still felt that any American administration would be loath to collaborate in secret intelligence if that collaboration seemed in danger of being revealed later. The Royal Navy broke with its tradition as the Silent Service to give unusually full details of the running battle—in order to hide a deeper truth.

By Sunday, May 25, 1941, the British Admiralty had gathered forces from all over the Atlantic to weave a net that was intended to entangle *Bismarck* whichever way she turned. From Gibraltar came Force H, under Vice-Admiral Sir James Somerville

261

in the battle cruiser *Renown,* and comprising the aircraft carrier *Ark Royal,* a cruiser, and six destroyers. The battleships *Rodney* and *Ramillies* left the convoy they were escorting and converged south of Iceland. Out of Canadian and U.S. ports sailed additional warships. And hard on *Bismarck*'s heels came the carrier *Victorious,* with lumbering old Swordfish torpedo planes. The Swordfish were astonishing combinations of wood and fabric, open cockpits, twanging wires, and fixed undercarriages—and the first airborne radar, about which the enemy knew nothing. But although these elements were at the disposal of British naval commanders gathered in London like chess players, and although their every move on the big charts was immediately translated into action far away, *Bismarck* was still unfound.

Bismarck was lost to these forces for thirty hours. Early in this period, however, she transmitted a thirty-minute report to Germany. By then, Roosevelt had asked that all U.S. radio direction-finding stations should watch out for such a signal. These listening posts, as the BSC Papers noted, were extremely good at locating the source of transmissions. The stations included those of the Radio Intelligence Division of the Federal Communications Commission, whose primary duty was to run to earth unlicensed broadcasters. But they were also unofficially intercepting signals from Europe, and the information was passed along to BSC. When *Bismarck* broke radio silence, these stations took bearings. A stream of information came to the Admiralty in London from such sources and from teleprinters and telephones at British listening posts. By 8:30 on Sunday morning, *Bismarck*'s thirty-minute indiscretion made it possible to calculate that she had gone southeastward since last seen.

But an error in plotting these bearings when they were fed to *King George V* led the British Home Fleet to suppose the enemy was heading the other way, back toward the North Sea. By Sunday evening, the mistake was rectified, and the pursuers realized that *Bismarck* was making for a French port in the Bay of Biscay.

The British mistake was a costly one. The Home

Fleet, searching in the wrong direction, ran low on fuel. What helped to save the day was the U.S. Coast Guard cutter *Modoc*.

Modoc was supposed to be on weather-reporting duties. In the Bay of Biscay? Well, that was the story her crew would have given an inquisitive German. *Modoc* was also carrying out Roosevelt's order to all U.S. vessels to search the seas for survivors from German attacks. On Sunday evening, the Americans had the extraordinary experience of seeing *Bismarck*'s fighting tops rise over the horizon and then slowly recede. *Modoc* got off a signal.

Soon after midnight, a long-range Catalina lent by the United States to British Coastal Command left the Northern Ireland port of Londonderry to join the search. This unarmed patrol bomber was piloted by Ensign Smith and manned by a mixed British and U.S. Navy crew. They droned steadily south through foul weather, and six hours later arrived in the general area of the *Modoc*.

By this time, *Bismarck* had confused the Admiralty War Room and shaken off her pursuers so successfully that she seemed certain to come soon under the protection of German land-based warplanes. The shelter of heavily defended French ports was within her reach.

At 8:30 on Monday morning, exactly twenty-four hours after *Bismarck*'s ill-conceived signal had given the British an opportunity to find her, Ensign Smith thought he glimpsed a warship through a break in the dense cloud cover. Piloting his Catalina above the rough seas, he swung around. The light was bad, the clouds intermittent at several levels. He could either fly higher to try to catch sight again of the distant vessel, or drop closer to the sea, where his range of vision would be greatly reduced. He chose to descend through the rain clouds, and had to concentrate on his instruments while flying blind. Suddenly he was in clear air again. Almost dead ahead, horrifyingly close, was *Bismarck*. Her gunners opened fire. Their aim was good, their reactions swift, because they had earlier fought off attacks by Swordfish torpedo planes in the savage encounters immediately following *Hood*'s destruction. The Swordfish were so slow that German gunners overestimated their speed, never believing warplanes would fly at less than a hundred knots as these did. Thus, though surprised after eluding the hunt for so long, *Bismarck* was ready. The Catalina, also relatively slow, shuddered under the impact of explosions and flying shrapnel.

Smith made a tight 180-degree turn into the cloud. His message, sealing *Bismarck*'s fate, was in the Operational Intelligence Center in London within seconds:

BATTLESHIP BEARING 240 DEGREES DISTANCE FIVE MILES COURSE 150 DEGREES MY POSITION 49:33 N, 21.47 W. . . .

Fifteen clumsy-looking Swordfish were armed and fueled on the British carrier *Ark Royal*. They staggered off the heaving deck at lunchtime and were lost at once in driving rain, low cloud, and mist. They flew for what seemed the right length of time, and a contact appeared on their primitive radar. The first flight dived, and pilots cursed when they saw their torpedoes explode on hitting the water. The second flight wheeled to attack. Some torpedoes ran true. But the pilots saw with horror that they had struck at one of their own ships—the cruiser *Sheffield,* which luckily saw the torpedoes and took evasive action.

"The hunt for *Bismarck* was a series of catastrophes, mistakes, and errors," said one of the pilots later. "The near-disaster with *Sheffield* exposed the danger of relying on that early kind of radar equipment and revealed a defect in the magnetic pistols with which some torpedoes had been armed. The Home Fleet had dashed off in the wrong direction for so long that all ships, except *Sheffield* and *King George V,* were out of fuel and out of the fight. I remember thinking there was going to be one hell of a row back at the Operational Intelligence Center."

The Center in London was, however, too busy. Bletchley had reported a volume of sudden and unusual traffic on the German naval network of Group West in France. This, with all the other intelligence, indicated *Bismarck*'s intentions. She was seeking safe haven in France because she was leaking oil from damage previously not suspected. German radio traffic disclosed the preparations to help *Bismarck* by German air and naval forces on the French coast.

Ensign Smith's report of *Bismarck*'s position was intercepted by the 4th Destroyer Flotilla, escorting a British troop convoy. Destroyers *Cossack, Maori, Zulu, Sikh,* and the Polish *Piorun* swung to intercept, spreading out as they plowed into a gale and towering seas. Far astern of *Bismarck* was *King George V,* the remaining vessel in the Home Fleet still able to give chase, but forced to tell London that unless the enemy's speed could be reduced by midnight, she would have to break away for lack of fuel.

Ark Royal's Swordfish were launched again toward evening. They picked up *Sheffield,* which was now twelve miles astern of *Bismarck,* and were redirected toward the enemy. Gale-force winds and poor visibility made it impossible for the torpedo bombers to work as a pack. They were known fondly as "Stringbags" because they did indeed seem to be held together by string. They were also, however, remarkably sturdy. Each came separately upon *Bismarck* and delivered an independent attack at a stately speed of somewhat more than ninety miles an hour, reduced by head winds and the German battleship's own speed so that each aircraft at some stage in its attack kept pace with *Bismarck*'s fearsome guns. One torpedo jammed the battleship's two giant rudders, damaged her propellers, and put the steering gear out of action. Three hours before his self-imposed deadline, Admiral Tovey got what he wanted—a reduction in *Bismarck*'s speed. As darkness fell, the 4th Destroyer Flotilla made contact with the crippled battleship. In darkness and heavy seas, the destroyers stationed themselves around the doomed giant and crept in to launch torpedoes. Throughout that dreadful night, *Bismarck* was caught in the grip of the northwesterly gale and swung helplessly into it. By daybreak, *King George V* was on the scene. Tovey saw once again that the Germans could build warships that were almost indestructible by gunfire. *Bismarck*'s guns were silenced one by one and still she floated. Anxious to make an end, Tovey signaled for any ships with torpedoes unexpended to close and sink the battleship.

The task fell to another beneficiary of Ensign Smith's brief signal. The cruiser *Dorsetshire* had been escorting a convoy from West Africa when she picked up the Catalina's sighting report. She had turned at once toward the position, 600 miles to the northward, for it was the unwritten privilege of a warship's captain to "steer for the sound of the guns."

At 8:40 on the morning of Tuesday, May 27, *Bismarck* slowly capsized from *Dorsetshire*'s *coup de grâce*. There were 107 survivors out of the great battleship's company of 2,000; and a total of 4,100 sailors had drowned during the eight days' hunt from the Baltic to the Arctic and down to Biscay.

Churchill meanwhile prepared Parliament for news that land and sea battles were going badly everywhere. He had entered the House knowing only that *Bismarck* might be trapped. "It is . . . thought that there cannot be any lengthy delay in disposing of this vessel," he was saying when someone waved a piece of paper. The Prime Minister stopped and sank heavily to his seat. There was a sense of doom around him. The paper was thrust into his hand. He rose again. "I crave your indulgence, Mr. Speaker. I have just received news that the *Bismarck* is sunk." A sigh like a fresh wind swept through the Commons.

Roosevelt signaled his congratulations from "one former naval person to another former naval person" through BSC, adding a somber note of regret that such a notable victory was won while America remained officially frozen in peaceful and uncomprehending immobility.

The battle was described by Admiral Raeder as having "a decisive effect on the war at sea." Not only that—the battle had a decisive effect on President Roosevelt, psychologically. He made a speech that seemed to guarantee American action in the North Atlantic against German attempts to break the supply line, and proclaimed an "Unlimited National Emergency." When public reaction persuaded Roosevelt that he ran the risk again of getting too far ahead of opinion, he shifted to clandestine support through BSC channels. An invasion of Americans into Britain began: the build-up of "advisers," who were the nucleus of expeditionary forces yet to come.

The secrets of Ensign Smith's assignment and quick action were sealed in the Public Record Office, which has housed, since the eleventh century, "all documents relating to the actions of the central government and the courts of law of England and Wales," and were not made public for thirty-two years. Only then did scholars find the clue to Smith's role in a characteristically mild note. It mentions the vital moment when the *Bismarck* was found again, and the courage of the American PBY's crew. The public historian knew nothing about the secret arrangement whereby members of the U.S. armed forces participated in British operations, traveling abroad at U.S. government expense to join British organizations. He wrote the dry comment: "I am not quite clear why these American officers were in the aircraft. However, I suggest it would be a good thing if the Admiralty were to recognize their services."

But no recognition was given to Ensign Smith, and other Americans assigned to the British services, for the reason that, technically speaking, they had broken the law, aided and abetted by their president. The strain on U.S. Navy personnel engaged in "short of war" operations was noted by the American naval historian Samuel Eliot Morison: "They were forbidden to tell of their experiences. . . . The fact that morale remained high throughout this period of bitter warfare that was not yet war attests the intelligence, the discipline, and the fortitude of the United States Navy."

Stephenson recalled that shortly before FDR made his decision to give the British as much naval support as he could get away with, he sent for the musty documents concerning the torpedoing of the passenger liner *Lusitania,* in May 1915. That event played a major role in bringing the United States into World War I. There had long been a question about whether Churchill, then also First Lord of the Admiralty, maneuvered the situation so that the Germans would seem coldbloodedly to have preyed upon a neutral passenger ship. The suspicion was that the *Lusitania*'s cargo included arms and ammunition.

The original cargo manifest went down with the ship. But carbon copies had been obtained by Woodrow Wilson, who sealed the documents and marked them TO BE OPENED ONLY BY THE PRESIDENT OF THE UNITED STATES. They revealed an additional cargo of 200 tons of munitions, enough to make her the legitimate target of an enemy U-boat attack. This controversial manifest was put away with Roosevelt's personal papers. If it was a true copy of the original cargo list, then the official version of the sinking of the *Lusitania* had been negligent in failing to mention her service as a munitions ship. Furthermore, the Admiralty on Churchill's behalf had advised British ships to paint out their port of registry. The owners of the *Lusitania* had gone so far as to sail her under an American flag, posing therefore as neutral. The suppression of her true manifest would appear to have been an attempt to diminish the opposition of those Americans who did not wish the sinking to be made an excuse for war.

Whatever the truth about the *Lusitania,* there was never much doubt about Churchill's approach to the U-boat menace. In his book *The World Crisis,* he had written that in the 1914–18 submarine war there was always the possibility Germany would become embroiled with other Great Powers because the U-boat relied increasingly on underwater attack, which risked sinking neutral ships and drowning neutral crews. Clearly, he thought Germany deserved whatever she got by taking this risk.

What did President Roosevelt think of all this when he reviewed the case on the twenty-sixth anniversary of the *Lusitania*'s sinking? What did he have in mind? "We shall never know," Stephenson said. "The *Bismarck* drove all else from our minds, and the *Lusitania* papers were put away again. But for a moment one president glimpsed something which had guided the hand of another president, and those old documents bridged the truce between the wars."

Bismarck's end marked the beginning of closer U.S. radio-intelligence aid in British war operations. Pedestrians on New York's Fifth Avenue who had read in their morning newspapers of the great naval battle were actually closer than they knew to a most vital part of the conflict. A Traffic Exchange Section of BSC gathered threads from U.S. Coast Guard and Navy stations through the FBI's channels and sent them to the Radio Security Service in England. A rough-and-ready form of co-operation was clearly not good enough. The tracking and sinking of the German battleship had been marred by failures and misjudgments, but it had also shown the possibilities in the systematic analysis of radio traffic collected by U.S. and British listening posts around the globe. "Traffic analysis" became an important job of coordination for BSC, whose historians recorded that "deciphering signals is not the only way to discover what the enemy has in mind. . . . Intelligence can be extracted from external features of a message by means of 'traffic analysis.' "

The hunt for the *Bismarck* made the U.S. Navy chiefs aware that the British still possessed ingenuity even if they lacked time and equipment. The war at sea was especially influenced, they could see, by the skill of the traffic analysts, though they needed masses of material on which to work. The U.S. Navy, watching the looming threat from Japan, felt that whatever could be collected by British listening posts scattered around the Pacific was well worth getting. Since monitors in Canada gathered large quantities of coded Japanese transmissions, it made good sense to Washington to have the Navy help the Canadians build up their own naval forces in exchange for information.

German U-boat commanders were puzzled by a sudden expansion in antisubmarine patrols by the Canadian Navy around the strategic Gulf of St. Lawrence. The truth was that it was a makeshift fleet consisting of large U.S. seagoing craft purchased by Canadian civilians. Their own yachts had been requisitioned. In this way, U.S. legislation against the sale of arms to belligerents had been circumvented in early stages of the war; and it continued to be a useful way to transfer equipment from the U.S. to Canadian and British forces. The Germans were never sure how strong the North American coastal defenses might prove to be. Even when a U-boat torpedoed the Canadian naval vessel *Raccoon,* one of the guardians of the gulf, the Germans did not discover that it actually was a converted American luxury yacht.

Sometimes the new Canadian "owners" were themselves puzzled. They were allowed to operate the U.S. vessels for a while, "for the sake of artistic verisimilitude," before they were stripped and armed. The story was told of one red-faced Canadian on a shakedown cruise who complained, "M'damn captain kicked m'off m'own bridge!" Thirteen of these American vessels were purchased before U.S. bureaucracy intervened.

The fourteenth yacht was bought through President Roosevelt after a personal appeal from Hugh Keenlyside, a Canadian representative on the Canada –U.S. Permanent Joint Board on Defense.

The INTREPID organization had discovered German plans for using two French islands off the coast of Canada and seizing bases in the Gulf of St. Lawrence. The Royal Canadian Navy was officially equipped with only ten effective vessels. It more than doubled its strength overnight. The new ships' luxury fittings were replaced by detection gear and communications equipment for calling "real" warships whenever they located U-boats. Some of these American yachts, in their original form, seemed singularly unfitted for war. One had an eight-foot circular bed, the removal of which left sufficient space for radio direction-finding gear. The large seagoing yachts were inspected by Canadians dressed in civilian clothes who visited American marinas in the guise of wealthy businessmen—"cloak-and-dagger stuff" that aroused much huffing and puffing among bluff Canadian Navy types. They got their reward: before the war's end, the Canadian Navy had become the third largest in the world. Such a fleet, in the hands of a friendly neighbor, was in the United States's interest. The *quid pro quo* basis of these arrangements was well understood.

The most delicate field of co-operation was communications intelligence, because it necessitated a disclosure of each country's apparatus for eavesdropping upon the coded radio traffic of other nations, an activity to which nobody wished to confess. When the Canadians were building their makeshift navy, they offered through BSC communications intelligence their own intercepts of Japanese radio traffic. From as far away as Australia, New Guinea, and Singapore, units that specialized in plucking messages out of the ether directed their material to London with copies for Washington.

Stephenson had asked early in the game if American high-frequency direction-finding stations along the eastern seaboard would work with his people in locating enemy submarines. The Battle of the Atlantic has been described by naval historians as essentially a duel between Allied and Axis "wireless intelligence." It was an endless battle never decisively won or lost, reaching peaks of crisis at regular intervals, conducted in eerie circumstances.

The skippers of German U-boats, under the direct tactical control of Admiral Karl Doenitz, were encouraged to pour information by radio into his headquarters. Their talkative transmissions were easy prey for radio direction-finders, which worked on a simple principle. A sensitive directional antenna, swinging until it brought in the signal at the highest volume, was the accusing finger. Two widely spaced direction-finders, each pointing at the same transmitter, provided the bearings; where the lines crossed lay the transmitter. It was not difficult to keep track of garrulous U-boats, but catching them was another matter. The "fixes" had to be conveyed to the U-boat killers with great speed, and the more the better.

When the U-boat war reached one of its successful peaks in the fall of 1940, the United States possessed an arc of land-based stations equipped to locate the German submarines. This net, known as Huffduff (H/F D/F, from high-frequency direction-finding), reported to a central control in Maryland, which passed the information along to the U.S. Navy communications-intelligence headquarters in Washington. Its occupants, housed at 3801 Nebraska Avenue, Northwest, knew from the flood of radio traffic the extent of the catastrophes suffered by each British convoy, but they also realized that the British were introducing something new—shipborne Huffduff, so that escorts could pinpoint U-boats locally. A British scientific mission that had visited Washington earlier had provided information on the cavity magnetron, which would make shipborne radar more flexible. Now the Americans were anxious to see what was being done to develop a better system of Huffduff and to equip escorts with better communications, which were needed for the teamwork that alone would defeat the U-boat wolf packs.

And so, in another sphere the United States got into the war unnoticed. Communications intelligence did more than anything to break the U-boats' stranglehold. British Huffduff stations worked closely with American ships, aircraft, and shore-based Atlantic seaboard stations, as well as with their own British naval vessels. When, for instance, U-158 chatted with its German control center, having "nothing better to report," Huffduff stations in the British-held islands of the Caribbean and American locators at Georgetown fixed her position and got the information to an antisubmarine U.S. naval aircraft VP-74, already flying in the vicinity. Within minutes of U-158's imprudent gossip, she was caught on the surface and sunk west of Bermuda.

Americans who made the big decisions on defense were, by mid-1941, filling the Washington air with muted cries of concern that the British were taking unjustified risks by fighting the enemy wherever they could make contact with him. Harry Hopkins told Churchill: "[We] believe the British Empire is making too many sacrifices in trying to maintain an indefensible position in the Middle East. At any moment the Germans might take Gibraltar and seal up the Western Mediterranean. They might block the Suez Canal. They might overwhelm the British Armies in the Middle East. Our Chiefs of Staff believe that the Battle of the Atlantic is the final, decisive battle. . . ."

Churchill's reaction was recorded in the BSC Pa-

272

pers. "The Prime Minister felt there was insufficient understanding of the spirit that moved the British who had to fight in the Middle East and had to go to the aid of Greece in response to their obligations to friends and dependencies. The diversion of substantial numbers of men and arms to the Middle East when all might be needed for the desperate defense of the United Kingdom was a decision dictated by an age-old tradition. During the past eight months nearly half Britain's war production has been sent to the Middle East as a matter of calculated policy. It would be unfortunate if the British people were made to feel that the United States was more concerned with securing their islands as a launching-platform against Germany in the event of war than with helping those nations already at war to destroy Nazi tyranny." Finally, Churchill suggested that if the United States should be drawn into the war, "North and West Africa might well prove the areas most favourable for the operation of American forces." The Prime Minister's remark foreshadowed TORCH, the first combined Anglo-American intelligence and military operation, which was to be, as the BSC Papers later noted, the first light at the end of the tunnel, "when we could go over from the defensive to the offensive, that is to say to secure full American participation in secret activities directed against the enemy."

29

BEFORE THE HUNT for the *Bismarck,* Stephenson had cabled Churchill:

I HAVE BEEN ATTEMPTING TO MANEUVER DONOVAN INTO JOB OF COORDINATING ALL UNITED STATES INTELLIGENCE.

A few days after the *Bismarck* was sunk, he signaled:

DONOVAN SAW PRESIDENT TODAY AND AFTER LONG DISCUSSION WHEREIN ALL POINTS AGREED CMA HE ACCEPTED APPOINTMENT COORDINATION ALL FORMS INTELLIGENCE INCLUDING OFFENSIVE OPERATIONS. . . . HE WILL HOLD RANK OF MAJOR GENERAL AND WILL BE RESPONSIBLE ONLY REPEAT ONLY TO PRESIDENT. . . . DONOVAN ACCUSES ME OF HAVING INTRIGUED AND DRIVEN HIM INTO APPOINTMENT. . . . YOU CAN IMAGINE HOW RELIEVED I AM AFTER MONTHS OF BATTLE AND JOCKEYING IN WASHINGTON THAT OUR MAN IS IN POSITION.

Hitler's postponed invasion of Russia was now at hand—and so was the next phase of Donovan's unofficial partnership with INTREPID. The plan was to exploit their foreknowledge of Germany's intentions. This conflicted with Hoover's pursuit of publicity.

The British had learned that it paid to keep an intelligence coup to themselves—even to the extent of not making immediate use of the information. One master of dirty tricks and just moved into INTREPID's New York headquarters: Lieutenant-Commander Ewen Montagu,* a brilliant young barrister who knew how to deceive the enemy by making use of German intelligence networks rather than breaking them up. Hoover tended to break them up and tell the world. "He wanted to publicize everything to enhance the FBI's reputation," Montagu said later. "We dared not confide to him certain plans for fear of leaks. Our methods depended on concealment. This made Hoover more distrustful. A ghastly period began. . . ."

Montagu could not know that the real culprits were agents seeking to poison Anglo-American intelligence relations on behalf of the Soviet Union. Yet it was

* Montagu became Judge Advocate of the British fleet, but postwar fame came to him as the author of a scheme to float a corpse into German hands complete with bogus plans for the invasion of Sardinia—a cover for the planned and eventual invasion of Sicily—told in *The Man Who Never Was.*

Stalin, fearful of this alliance, who was about to become the chief beneficiary.

On Sunday, June 1, 1941, Stephenson walked into his office in Room 3553 at 630 Fifth Avenue. His organization was now spread through two floors of Rockefeller Center. His staff was accustomed to his seeming omnipresence. On this occasion he walked straight through his office and out by way of a rear exit concealed by bookcases. Back on the street, he was picked up by Donovan. They drove north, crossing unseen into Canada, and that night were cocooned in the gun turrets of a bomber being ferried to Scotland. The last part of the journey was made by night express from Glasgow to London. Air-raid alarms forced the train to stop frequently. They reached the blacked-out capital with their lightweight suits impregnated by the smell of locomotive smoke. They were greeted with news of a tremendous German success in using airborne invasion forces. They had captured the Mediterranean island of Crete, after the British again suffered high casualties. Hitler declared that the battle proved "no island is impregnable," a statement interpreted by the Joint Intelligence Committee to mean that their own islands must prepare for this new kind of assault from the skies.

ULTRA had a different story. On Friday, June 6, Stephenson and Donovan were driven to Woburn Abbey, on the Duke of Bedford's estate. This pleasantly rolling countryside was a favorite spot for young lovers, who knew a score of public footpaths where nobody would disturb them for hours. Now the woodlands were stiff with security men dressed as gamekeepers. Commandos in patched coveralls bicycled the narrow lanes or stood behind the ancient oaks fringing the wheat fields that stretched to the gates of Bletchley Park and the huts inside. Between there and the venerable abbey bicycled a few eccentric figures. Donovan recognized some as specialists in psychological warfare, then a new branch of aggressive intelligence operations. Without knowing about the gigantic bugging of the Nazi High Command, they received some of ULTRA's processed information for "black propaganda" broadcasts designed to mislead or demoralize the enemy.

The chief of British Political Intelligence, Reginald Leeper, addressed this curious collection of what appeared to be dissipated schoolmasters. "Gentlemen, I have been authorized by the Prime Minister to reveal to you a piece of secret information which has been known to Mr. Churchill and the Chiefs of Staff for several weeks. He permits me to tell you—and you only—in order that we may concert our plans, that Hitler is to attack Soviet Russia. The actual invasion is expected around the middle of June. The estimate is Sunday the twenty-second, which is to say two weeks and two days from now. You will not make notes of what I tell you, nor can you prepare any specific action until the day itself. You are each responsible for sections that will come into play when the Germans move. We have identified twenty-nine divisions under von Leeb in East Prussia who will advance from the north; fifty divisions under von Bock to the south on either side of the Minsk-Smolensk-Moscow line, forty-two divisions under von Rundstedt to move from Lublin towards Kiev. . . ."

The days slipped by. Donovan felt the Germans would achieve complete surprise. The British could not divulge to Stalin the unimpeachable sources of their information. Instead, they tried to convince the Russians of the impending attack on the basis of a multiplicity of leaks from other quarters. "If the British had sent the Kremlin the precise German military orders as they were intercepted," Donovan reported later to Roosevelt, "Stalin might have faced reality. But the British regard the whole Bletchley apparatus as far too secret. They feel they can use their information to gain advantage in other ways."

On Friday, June 20, two days before the Wehrmacht moved, Churchill worked on a speech to be broadcast to the world when the attacking forces rolled into Russia. It was to be one of the most politically significant declarations of his life. Postwar historians would be puzzled by the amount of time the Prime Minister spent on it, unaware as they were of Bletchley and Churchill's foreknowledge. It seemed as if he squandered precious hours fussing about the possibility of some German offensive in the east when he should have been dealing with actual events and real crises closer to home. Hitler had that very day proclaimed that "the siege of England" would be intensified. The War Cabinet was worrying about the new German techniques of invasion from the air, so devastatingly demonstrated in Crete. British forces in the Middle East were suffering new setbacks. In the Battle of the Atlantic, a record number of ships had been sunk that week. Warships that should have been available for escort duties were spread thin—eleven had been sunk during the disastrous Crete campaign. Yet here was Churchill pondering a new policy on Russia, a nation still officially opposed to Britain's continuation of the war. The historians did not know, of course, that the Prime Minister already had the date and time of attack.

The speech was long and carefully composed, full of grave themes and weighty arguments. It was written before even the Russians themselves knew about the German betrayal of their pact. Churchill polished the phrases that summer's day in his Elizabethan manor at Chequers, using that curious dithyrambic style that fascinated Roosevelt when Stephenson showed him the draft:

I see the Russian soldiers standing on the
threshold of their native land,
guarding the fields which
their forefathers tilled from time immemorial.
I see them guarding their homes where mothers
and wives pray—
Ah, yes, for there are times when all pray—
for the safety of their loved ones, the return of
the bread-winner, of their champion, of their
protector. . . .
I see advancing on all this in hideous onslaught
the Nazi war-machine, with its clanking,
heel-clicking, dandified Prussian officers, its
crafty expert agents fresh from the cowing and
tying-down of a dozen countries.
I see also the dulled, drilled, docile, brutish

masses of the Hun soldiery plodding on like a swarm of crawling locusts. . . .

Behind all this glare, behind all this storm, I see that small group of villainous men who plan, organize and launch this cataract of horrors upon mankind.

The following Sunday, these words flew around the globe, broadcast in every language, as quickly as the Kremlin learned that it had been taken by surprise. Next day, Churchill had to face his War Cabinet. To protect his sources, he apologized for having acted so swiftly on news of the invasion and said that he would have consulted his colleagues if there had been time. He knew, of course, that consultation would have meant delay and possibly worse. "He held it back from his political advisors lest it be toned down," reported his personal secretary, Jock Colville. Churchill wanted maximum impact for his declaration that "any man or state who fights on against Nazidom will have our aid" on the very day that the German war machine charged across the Soviet border.

The most remarkable aspect of this coup was that Stalin slept in his summer house on the Black Sea when Churchill spoke. The Russian leader apparently refused to believe the news. For eleven days, nothing was heard from Stalin. Finally, a recording of his voice was broadcast. He did not take full charge of the Russian war effort until the middle of the following month.

Meanwhile, Bletchley identified every one of the 200 BARBAROSSA generals, their 115 German divisions, eighteen Finnish, fourteen Italian, plus Rumanian, Slovak, Spanish, and Hungarian units. Hitler informed his war chiefs, and thus also Bletchley: "The name of Moscow will vanish forever." The conquest of all Russia was to take twenty weeks.

British and American military advisers forecast that Hitler would crush what he called "this brainless clay colossus" before winter. Stephenson disagreed and assured Roosevelt that the diversion of German forces into Yugoslavia had won the precious time required. "It was the Prime Minister's own inspiration to seize the moment and put heart in the Russians," Stephenson wrote in a memo to the White House. "Stalin has been shocked into temporary silence by events, and it is our belief that he has suffered a form of nervous breakdown. Mr. Churchill's prompt offer of all aid is immensely important in winning support from communist partisans already fighting in Nazi-occupied Europe and already unhappy at the Soviet failure to give them support."

"In weight of armour, firepower, flexibility and sheer momentum, the Wehrmacht is tuned to a pitch of perfection," Stephenson reported when he returned to Washington with Donovan that week. "But the German generals are still spellbound by Hitler. If he has miscalculated, as we think, the superstitious Nazi faith in the Fuehrer's infallibility will be destroyed. The psychological collapse that follows will break German morale."

On Roosevelt's own doorstep was an about-face of Communists in the United States, who had previously resisted aid-to-Britain movements. Stephenson's men had organized a Fight for Freedom rally in the Golden Gate ballroom in Harlem on the day Russia was attacked. Not having heard yet about BARBAROSSA, a Communist picket line outside waved placards condemning the tools of British and Wall Street imperialism. The black population in the neighborhood was urged to march in protest to Washington. When the Fight for Freedom speakers left the ballroom two hours later, they were astonished to find the pickets gone, the posters down, the protest march canceled. By the following day, all Communist publications and publicists were suddenly pro-British, pro-intervention, and, for the first time, unequivocally pro-Roosevelt.

"The President now fully accepted the concept of *offensive* intelligence," Stephenson said later. "The attack on Russia made it politically possible for him to declare Bill Donovan his Coordinator of Information 'to collect and analyze all information and data which may bear upon national security.'"

The Executive Order of July 11, 1941, made official a situation that was fundamentally irregular. "As much as six months before Pearl Harbor," the BSC Papers recorded, "we had secured full American participation and collaboration in secret activities directed against the enemy throughout the world."

Robert Sherwood, who was a liaison officer between Roosevelt and BSC at this time, noted to Stephenson: "FDR never for a moment overlooked the fact that his actions might lead to his immediate or eventual impeachment. He knew by heart that he was sworn to *defend* as well as uphold the Constitution. He had the right to judge *how* to defend. He could take advice, but he was getting into an irregular position in the way he took advice from and through you. Still he had this independent responsibility which devolves upon the Chief Executive to defend the nation in the way he thinks best. Each time he regularized one of his actions though, events forced him into yet another action that might result in impeachment."

The state of Roosevelt's mind was masked by his jaunty public image. The real turmoil in the man was seen by Stephenson in moments when the President aired his frustration. It had happened earlier that year during the uproar over military aid to Britain. Lend-Lease gave the President the power to extend aid to any country whose fate he felt was vital to American defense. His enemies called him a would-be dictator for assuming such power. Critics like Robert Hutchins declared that "we are about to commit national suicide," because of this new surrender of democratic rights in the name of national security. When the Lend-Lease bill finally passed into law in March 1941, the President indulged in an outburst that stunned his aides. "He said he was going to get tough," Stephenson recalled later. "So many lies had got around, so many attempts had been made to scare the people that the main issues got confused. He couldn't answer the lies until the bill was passed. Now he was going to dish out some medicine. He dictated for more than an hour a scathing and vindictive reply to the vicious attacks of senators, commentators, and propagandists. His staff were tremendously distressed. What they didn't realize was that the President had to get the poison out of his system. He never gave the speech."

Operation BARBAROSSA was preceded by a Nazi deception plan whose import was not understood until later. Hitler had "Guidelines for the Deception of the Enemy" distributed by hand—fifteen numbered copies labeled MATTER FOR CHIEFS!, the most highly secret category. The contents escaped Bletchley Park. The full picture was assembled after a BSC analysis of indirect references to the original order.

Hitler's deception plan confirmed the view that the policeman's straightforward approach to counterespionage was not good enough. This was bad luck for Hoover and the FBI, but a brief glance at the "Guidelines for Deception" revealed the sophisticated and ingenious techniques by which Hitler and his followers had tricked even the Soviet Union. False rumors, "disinformation" released through known Anglo-American intelligence and diplomatic channels, downright lies, and misleading military deployments took their place in a meticulous program to mislead and demoralize the target. A primary aim was to convince Stalin that a German attack would be preceded by an ultimatum, hence the Russian leader's refusal to heed Anglo-American warnings.

If Nazi deception had worked so well against the Russian colossus, what chance had the United States? The USSR was steeped in intrigue and armored against foreign propaganda. The U.S. believed in free speech and opened its windows to all political winds. The USSR was sealed tight against false alarms from abroad, and yet Hitler had penetrated the Kremlin with his lies. The U.S. still allowed Axis embassies to function freely and German propaganda agencies to spread Nazi versions of events. Big American corporations were interlocked with Axis commercial enterprise. There seemed no end to the opportunities for Nazi infiltration.

The British had learned to make use of these German channels instead of arresting the agents of propaganda and espionage. Wrong information was fed back to Berlin. Roosevelt saw that counterespionage could be handled as an offensive weapon. The FBI's chief was stubborn, though, in resisting the use of double agents. J. Edgar Hoover now made an error that, according to Hoover's enemies, led to the Japanese success at Pearl Harbor.

TRICYCLE, one of the double agents supposedly under British control, arrived in Stephenson's New York office fresh from talking with his German spy masters about Pearl Harbor six months before the Japanese struck there. Hoover refused to believe his extraordinary story. When Commander Montagu later spoke of the "ghastly period" when the FBI became obstructive, he was still sick with dismay over TRICYCLE's inability to get through to Hoover the significance of his Pearl Harbor reports.

The incident is significant for another reason. It offers an important lesson to those who would revise history long after the event. At any given time, the intelligence signals foreshadowing a move by the enemy are part of the general uproar of information, some true, but much of it possibly false, including deception material deliberately planted by the enemy or (even more effectively) by the enemy's secret friends. In hindsight, it may seem that the true warnings should have stood out like beacons. A distant observer, looking back, is unaware of all the other distractions, some of them contradictory, that at the time seemed equally important. The lesson applies as much to the varied evaluations of ULTRA as it does to the particular case of Pearl Harbor.

30

TRICYCLE WAS THE British code name for a Yugoslav patriot named Dusko Popov, pronounced Popoff (which resulted in his being given the password *Scoot!*). Among his many peculiarities that offended J. Edgar Hoover was the role he played of double agent. Though first recruited by German intelligence, he volunteered to report to the British Secret Intelligence Service and to feed the Germans "controlled" information—apparently valuable but approved first by SIS. In this way, he could extract information from the Germans, usually by a careful study of the questions for which they required answers.

In June 1941, having thrilled his German masters with his seemingly brilliant exploits in England, he was told to move to the United States. On the way, he held meetings in Lisbon with his German handlers. They told him the Japanese were studying a method of using carrier-borne torpedo bombers against Pearl Harbor, something along the lines of a British operation against the Italian fleet a few months earlier. Using a new kind of aerial torpedo, the British had sunk half the enemy fleet in the shallow waters of Taranto in southern Italy. The German Air Attaché in Tokyo, Baron Gronau, had flown to Taranto specifically to carry out research on the whole operation. The Japanese Foreign Minister, Yosuke Matsuoka, had gone to Berlin with a team of specialists to secure details. TRICYCLE was told all this and then given a questionnaire that focused on Pearl Harbor defenses.

He dutifully reported the German view that Japanese naval units for the first time seemed to think they could knock out a major portion of the American Pacific Fleet by using the tactics employed by the British Fleet Air Arm at Taranto—especially because the British had improvised aerial torpedoes for shallow water and launched them in the face of seemingly impenetrable defenses, anticipating the very conditions at Pearl Harbor. Stephenson, as an aviator, was outraged by the evidence of how Britain starved its Navy pilots of modern warplanes; their torpedoes were launched from obsolescent Swordfish biplanes. He redoubled his campaign to secure aircraft from the U.S. Navy, which had wisely preserved its own air service during the lean years. Many British naval fliers owed their survival to the subsequent adoption of U.S. carrier equipment, then far in advance of British designs. The swift American response to these British naval needs meant the transfer of weapons from the Pacific, where Japan's formidable carrier forces outmatched the Allies'. Perhaps this was a major result of Taranto. The clues it gave to the coming disaster of Pearl Harbor were lost in the daily accumulation of more immediate alarms.

Since TRICYCLE was now on American soil, he must be handed over to the FBI and Hoover, who would be quick to protest if he thought information was being withheld. But TRICYCLE's personality clashed violently with Hoover's; even his code name was an affront. "It arose from his sexual athleticism," Hoover later wrote caustically. "He had a liking for bedding two girls at one time." One of his mistresses, according to Hoover, left her home and work to be with him whenever possible. "He was a Balkan playboy with orders to investigate our atomic energy project and report monthly on our aid to Britain."

TRICYCLE's high-level contacts, exotic tastes, and extravagant style provided, he thought, perfect cover. The FBI took a dim view of all this, disregarding the justification of his British defenders that he had done excellent and dangerous work, which had placed him in high regard among German intelligence chiefs. Berlin had dispatched him to the United States to build his own espionage network, complete with radio station. The FBI did set up a transmitter and worked it back to Germany, but the enemy smelled a rat and broke off contact. TRICYCLE was never allowed near it.

This was disappointing to London. Even the British admitted later that they failed to put enough emphasis on the Pearl Harbor clues. The conversations TRICYCLE had with his Nazi contacts in Lisbon included one with a German intelligence officer who had gone to Taranto to make a report on the British attack there. "Their torpedo planes flew through a barrier of balloon cables and a massive volume of gunfire from six battleships, nine cruisers and a score of destroyers and escorts," he confided to TRICYCLE. "The British planes were launched from a carrier and in a single blow crippled the Italian fleet. The date November 11, 1940 must go down in history as the end of the battleship era in naval warfare."

The major lesson of Taranto was lost on Americans and acted on by the Japanese at Pearl Harbor.

If the British could manage aerial torpedoes with ancient aircraft operating in the teeth of the enemy, the Japanese should have no trouble with their superior torpedo planes and carriers.

TRICYCLE's efforts to arouse Americans through the FBI did not get far. He had brought with him specimens of German espionage equipment, but most important of all was the questionnaire and the section headed "Naval Strong Point Pearl Harbor." This requested:

1. Exact details and sketch about the situation of the state wharf, of the pier installations, situations of dry dock No. 1 and of the new dry dock which is being built.
2. Details about the submarine station (plan of situation). What land installations are in existence?
3. Where is the station for mine search formations? How far has the dredger work progressed at the entrance and in the east and southeast lock? Depths of water?
4. Number of anchorages?
5. Is there a floating dock in Pearl Harbor or is the transfer of such a dock to this place intended? Special Tasks—Reports about torpedo protection nets newly introduced in the British and U.S.A. navy. How far are they already in existence in the merchant and naval fleet? Use during voyage? Average speed reduction when in use. Details of construction and others.

This was passed along to Hoover. But when it became evident that the Director's seeming dislike of the newcomer's flamboyance would jeopardize mutual co-operation, Ewen Montagu flew over from London on behalf of the Twenty Committee, which took its name from the Roman numerals for 20—XX—symbolizing the double cross. He tried in vain to persuade the FBI to feed information to TRICYCLE so that he could satisfy his German spy masters. Though a craftsman in the difficult work of misleading the enemy's own agents, with Hoover, Montagu got nowhere.

The chief of the Twenty Committee, long associated as student and academic with Oxford University, was Sir John Masterman, who wrote of this episode, in *The Double-Cross System:* "It is noticeable that TRICYCLE's German questionnaire was more or less general or statistical, except the questions concerning Pearl Harbor which were specialised and detailed. It is therefore surely a fair deduction that the questionnaire indicated very clearly that in the event of the United States being at war, Pearl Harbor would be the first point attacked and that plans for this attack were at an advanced stage in the summer of 1941. Obviously it was for the Americans to make their appreciation and to draw their deductions from the questionnaire rather than for us to do so. Nonetheless, with our fuller knowledge of the case and of the man, we ought to have stressed its importance more than we did. With the greater experience of a few more years' work, we should certainly have risked a snub and pointed out to our friends in the United States what the significance of the document might be; but in 1941 we were still a little chary of expressing opinions and a little mistrustful of our own judgment."

TRICYCLE was never accepted by the FBI. He later moved to Camp X in Canada. His German spy masters kept up a flow of instructions through other Nazi networks. Their comments were ribald as well as revelatory. He had invented for the Germans an excuse they could understand for moving to Canada: a rendezvous with a woman of unusual beauty. A signal went out from Germany that revealed how closely and intimately informed the Nazis were on individual foibles. The lady in question, they had established through their other agents, had been treated for venereal disease. They suggested that the enterprising TRICYCLE take appropriate precautions, and even offered him the drug prescription for countering infection.

Secret-warfare chiefs strained at the leash, demanding to go over to the offensive, but they were restrained by their dependence on American material support. The U.S. regular forces, ill-prepared for war, begrudged the transfer of weapons even though there was sympathy—especially among U.S. Navy chiefs—for Britain's plight. Admiral Richmond Kelly Turner reflected this concern in a memo to Roosevelt: "Because of the tragic situation of the British Government, I do not recommend troubling them further as to our opinion on the seriousness of the situation. . . . They realize it pretty well themselves. . . ." The chief of the Maritime Commission, Admiral Emory S. Land, observed with salty brevity that "if we do not watch our step we shall find the White House enroute to England with the Washington Monument for a steering oar."

The Washington Monument stayed in place. President Roosevelt did, however, put to sea, and, on August 9, 1941, in a first dramatic meeting with Prime Minister Churchill was further distracted from danger in the Pacific. The leaders met on the ill-fated battleship *Prince of Wales,* which was sunk by Japanese torpedo-bombers exactly four months later, a few days after Pearl Harbor, and on the U.S. Navy Cruiser *Augusta* in Placentia Bay, Newfoundland. Their shipboard talks led to the Atlantic Charter, which not only had the immediate effect of boosting British morale, but became a cornerstone of the future United Nations. It had no teeth, however. The President wanted nothing that would sound remotely like a treaty, for then it would have to go to the Senate, where it might founder.

"That was how fragile Roosevelt's position really was," Stephenson observed. "Public-opinion polls had revealed a *decrease* in support for aid to Britain, despite rising expectations of war with Germany. A vast majority of Americans thought sending war matériel to Britain was pouring it down the sink. Europe was lost anyway."

In counteracting, the British stressed the poisonous effects of Nazi fifth columnists, their dupes and commercial allies. Hitler gave priority to corroding the will power of his intended victims, and subsequent frontal German assaults were merely the follow-through. The British arguments again forced the President's attention to the dangers of subversion at home and the need to build the spirit of resistance against Nazism. "Oppressed peoples of Europe were promised sovereignty and self-government," Stephenson wrote later. "We sought to unify resistance among those already under the Nazi yoke, and unite those still free."

The concrete results of the Atlantic conference were to take the form of further British help in fighting Nazi influence in the Americas. From the British viewpoint, of course, it was indeed the case that political opponents of Roosevelt were as deadly an enemy as Nazi Germany.

Churchill cabled the War Cabinet in London:

PRESIDENT OBVIOUSLY DETERMINED THAT THE AMERICANS SHOULD COME IN. BUT CLEARLY HE SKATES ON VERY THIN ICE IN RELATIONS WITH CONGRESS WHICH, HOWEVER, HE DOES NOT REGARD AS TRULY REPRESENTATIVE OF THE COUNTRY.

In an even franker report, so secret that it had to be divulged verbally at a closed session with his colleagues, Churchill added that "the President said he wanted war with Germany, but that he would not declare it. He would instead become more and more provocative. Mr. Roosevelt said he could look for an incident which would justify him in opening hostilities."

Churchill, sailing back from the talks, had taken delight in the protection provided part of the way by U.S. destroyers. Here were the seeds of just such a provocative incident. He made a broadcast talk to the people of Europe as well as Britain, blending implication with fact, hoping to stir Hitler into another frenzy by the suggestion of Anglo-American intimacies and brotherly good will. "And so we came back," he intoned. "Uplifted in spirit, fortified in resolve. Some American destroyers happened to be going the same way too, so we made a goodly company at sea together."

The mention of the American destroyers was made casually, as if this kind of happy accident could be taken for granted. The tone was part of a general air of good spirits between the two comrades. Noel Coward, waiting to go on a mission for INTREPID to South America, described the President and Prime Minister arguing over the words to one of his lyrics when "they should have been solving the world's woes." Such stories created an impression of common resolve and lighthearted confidence. In fact, the British felt they were getting less than Churchill had led them to expect, while American isolationists feared that secret protocols would commit the United States to more than was being admitted.

It seemed to that other playwright observer, Robert Sherwood, that Roosevelt came away more keenly aware of the threats posed by Axis bases in the Western Hemisphere. "The President had been reminded that Hitler's philosophy was highly unconventional," Sherwood said later. "The Nazi leader jeered at generals who wished to behave like chivalrous knights, and all rigid military thinkers. *'I have no use for knights,'* Hitler had written, adding: *'I need revolutions.'* He was looking for revolutions now in South America with a view to creeping into the United States through the back door.

"The British justifiably pressed their case and the need to prevent further Nazi encroachment in the Americas. The worst disaster to hit the whole human race had struck in Europe, and Churchill had once again reminded Roosevelt that in his small islands the defense of vital bases was in the hands of 150,000 men and women armed with pikes, maces, and grenades. With such emotional tugs, Roosevelt inevitably played down problems in the Pacific.

"The American destroyers going Churchill's way home meant that our Atlantic Fleet was now operating twenty-four hours a day under battle conditions.

"Our Fleet in the Pacific was paralyzed with the obsession of neutrality."

And so TRICYCLE's preview of Pearl Harbor passed into oblivion. Churchill had been too successful in distracting the President's attention from the East and focusing it instead upon Britain's own immediate worries.

Part
Four

CRY, "HAVOC!"

"Cry, 'Havoc!' and let slip the dogs of war."
—Shakespeare, *Julius Caesar*

31

THE ROOSEVELT-CHURCHILL meeting at sea four months before Pearl Harbor was their expression of hope for freedom's future. To defend what was still left of freedom, joint intelligence operations were intensified even as the American public seemed more anxious to keep out of the war. Hoover, who had theretofore been helpful about forgetting rules that limited FBI activities in order to preserve individual rights, was now uneasy. Stephenson had to cope with this, remembering the jealous concern of Americans to protect their freedoms, while at the same time he waded through a daily flood of horror stories out of Europe's nightmare.

An urgent request from British Naval Intelligence presented him with a typical dilemma. London wanted immediate disruption of links between Europe and South America, which was becoming dangerously generous in aiding the enemy. From London's viewpoint, any methods were justified provided they did not jeopardize BSC's use of New York. Stephenson had to choose the least bloody course of action.

The most troublesome base at the moment was Brazil, where the government was helping Nazi operations against the United States. The best solutions seemed to be either to frighten the leaders into cutting their ties with the enemy or to overthrow them. One way to accomplish either was to plant fake documents on the offending Brazilians and discredit them. Stephenson consulted his expert, the Canadian President of the Newsprint Association Charles Vining, who ran many of BSC's operations in Canada.

"Can you get straw pulp like this?" Stephenson asked, displaying a sheet of stationery.

Vining held the paper to the light. "Perhaps."

"And the letterhead?"

"The forgery department won't have much difficulty."

"How about the typewriter?"

Vining examined the type face. "Italian machine?"

"Right. And ancient."

"We'll have to rebuild one, with all the imperfections." Vining handed back the paper. "This the only copy?"

"Don't worry." Stephenson grinned lopsidedly. "We'll get the original."

"Facilities in the United States would be greater."

"Not while the kid gloves are still on."

From Rockefeller Center a coded message went out to the British secret intelligence chief in Brazil: "We propose to convey to the Brazilian Government a letter purporting to be written by someone in authority in Italy to an executive in Brazil. Purpose is to compromise the Italian transatlantic air services which provide safe passage for enemy agents, intelligence documents and strategic materials. We would welcome details and specimen Head Office letter of the LATI airline."

A letter stolen from General Aurelio Liotta, president of the airline, in Rome, was duly sent by safe-hand courier. It was a specimen of his personal letterhead. A follow-up signal from Rio de Janeiro advised INTREPID that any forged letters would be best addressed to Commandante Vicenzo Coppola, the regional manager in Brazil. A fake letter was in production by late September. The notepaper was produced by Station M, using the straw pulp normally found only in Europe. The engraved letterhead of Italy's state-owned Linnee Aeree Transcontinentali Italiane was copied by counterfeiters. A typewriter that precisely duplicated the machine in Rome had been constructed. The letter was addressed to Coppola and was "signed" by LATI's president. It said:

Dear Friend:
Thank you for your letter and for the report en-
closed. . . . I discussed your report immediately
with our friends. They regard it as being of the
highest importance. They compared it in my pres-
ence with certain information that had already
been received from the Prace del Prete. The two
reports coincided almost exactly. . . . It made me
feel proud. . . . There can be no doubt the "little
fat man" is falling into the pocket of the Ameri-
cans, and that only violent action on the part of
the "green gentlemen" can save the country. I
understand such action has been arranged for by
our respected collaborators in Berlin. . . .

This cunning forgery appeared to be part of a
fascist-inspired plot against President Getulio Vargas,
the "little fat man." The "green gentlemen" were notorious in Brazil as the revolutionary Integralists who
had tried to bring down the Vargas regime. A final
insult was the last line: "The Brazilians may be, as
you said, a 'nation of monkeys,' but they are monkeys
who will dance for anyone who can pull the string!
Saluti fascisti. . . ."

One of President Vargas's sons-in-law was chief
technical director of the airline. Other prominent Brazilians had an interest in its operations. Micropix of
the letter were smuggled to Rio and blowups eventually leaked to Vargas's cronies. The President flew
into a rage, canceled LATI's landing rights, and ordered Coppola's arrest. The Commandante, one step
ahead, had drawn the equivalent of a million dollars
in LATI funds and was caught on his way to the
Argentine border.

At that, he was lucky. A plan to blow up one of
his airliners in which he happened to be traveling,
along with a cargo of industrial diamonds, was stopped
by Stephenson. "I couldn't bring myself to destroy a
commercial plane. And being an airman myself, the
prospect of killing the crew was anathema."

President Vargas, enraged by the Italians and
antagonized by the Germans, moved under the Anglo-
American umbrella. This was to have far-reaching

effects when the United States needed Brazil's bases and ports for launching operations in Africa.

The FBI later claimed, in good faith, that the coup was theirs. The forged evidence was so well planted that copies reached the U.S. Embassy in Rio independently through one of Hoover's agents, and the documents fabricated in Canada were taken as genuine. BSC destroyed the original forgeries, and also the rebuilt Italian typewriter, which was taken apart and dropped into the lake.

There were such strong reasons for withholding information on British operations that it was a long time before Hoover learned the facts. "The trouble at this stage," noted the BSC Papers, "was that Americans handled some information with reckless disregard for consequences. By trumpeting successes, they tipped off the enemy." Though this problem was being tackled by Donovan's new intelligence agency, Hoover became increasingly agitated by BSC operations. Forged documents and their use, aimed at Nazis and governments hostile to British interests, were planned and organized in New York. Such operations might be "papered," equipped, and executed from Canada, but they were directed from Rockefeller Center by an organization that seemed immune to precautions that American citizens properly insisted upon to prevent foreign agencies from exploiting American freedom of movement and speech. There were moral and legalistic grounds for Hoover's objections. When he could be persuaded that some infringement of civil rights was necessary to prevent a greater danger, however, he still fell back upon the policy of maximum publicity for bureau success. The FBI had been turned into an incorruptible agency because Hoover made his agents feel part of an elite. Stephenson understood this, but it was difficult to convince London that FBI self-publicity was justifiable when the war against the Third Reich and its fifth columnists required the very antithesis of self-promotion. The price of Hoover's support seemed high when publicity could destroy a clandestine operation. Yet the cost of Hoover's hostility was unacceptable, too.

Ian Fleming, during one of his missions for British

Naval Intelligence in that summer of 1941, had a ringside view of an incident that typified Stephenson's dilemma. Being permanently silenced by British secrecy laws, Fleming described it later in fictional terms when he wrote about the two "justified killings" that earned James Bond his official double-O classification, which gave him a license to kill.

The first was in New York—a Japanese cipher expert cracking our codes on the thirty-sixth floor of the R. C. A. building in the Rockefeller Center, where the Japs had their consulate. I took a room on the fortieth floor of the next-door skyscraper and I could look across the street into his room and see him working. Then I got a colleague from our organization in New York and a couple of Remington thirty-thirtys with telescopic sights and silencers. . . . His job was only to blast a hole through the window so that I could shoot the Jap through it. They have tough windows at the Rockefeller Center to keep the noise out. It worked very well. . . . I got the Jap in the mouth as he turned to gape. . . .*

"The truth was," Stephenson commented later, "Fleming was always fascinated by gadgets. We were building up our mechanical coding equipment. One floor down was the Japanese Consul-General. We knew he was sending coded messages by short-wave radio to Tokyo. With two of my assistants, I broke into the Japanese consular offices at three in the morning. Fleming came as an onlooker. We cracked the safe and borrowed the code books long enough to microfilm them."

To Stephenson, it was straightforward counterespionage. To Fleming, it was "the spectacle of the greatest of secret agents at work." To Hoover, it was permissible only so long as he was taken fully into INTREPID's confidence. Now, logic and caution decreed that the FBI should become part of an over-all system, not dominate it. Roosevelt wanted an end

* _Casino Royale_, the first James Bond thriller, was seen by Stephenson in manuscript. "It will never sell, Ian," he told Fleming. "Truth is always less believable. . . ."

to fratricidal rivalries between the Army's G-1, the Navy's ONI, the State Department, Immigration and Customs' security, and the Treasury's Secret Service. There had been no central agency to survey all their work. Even the Federal Communications Commission, monitoring foreign broadcasts, frequently failed to reach those who would benefit from its recoveries. Bill Donovan took over, and tried to bring order out of this chaos, first as head of the Office of the Coordinator of Information, which later became the Office of Strategic Services, OSS.

"Hoover keenly resented Donovan's organization when it was established in July 1941," observed the BSC Papers. "He feared it would hurt the authority of the FBI, particularly in South America. . . . Realizing he could attack Donovan's agency most effectively by attacking what was then its mainstay, INTREPID, he began to treat it with hostility and his purpose was to suppress the British operations. He had the backing in the Roosevelt Administration of those who were latently anti-British and with the help of the Assistant Secretary of State, Adolf Berle, he worked toward a legal method of dissolving BSC and thus ending Donovan's fledgling agency."

The conflict began to hamper INTREPID's operations in mid-1941, a crucial time. Hoover decided to force disclosure of BSC operations and began to seek legal ways of doing so. He did not know what he was asking, for he was not conscious of the full extent of the training and build-up of secret armies in Europe, or of ULTRA, whose reports of enemy intentions did not reveal the source. He knew many channels had now opened between Washington and London, and that BSC's functions had changed and expanded. The British fear was that by sticking to the letter of the law he would require them to put on paper a full account of their activities, which would inevitably get into the enemy's hands, or to shift intelligence headquarters elsewhere—an almost impossible task, for by now Rockefeller Center was employing 2,000 full-time specialists at the hub of global networks.

There was a third alternative. Stephenson could recapture Hoover's good will by confiding more British secrets orally, on a personal basis. This was not easy. Within the British intelligence establishment in London were not only those who feared American indiscretions. There were also Soviet agents, or their pawns, who regarded Hoover as an anti-Communist zealot to be secretly undermined. When Soviet agents moved into key posts in London, they began the deliberate sabotage of Anglo-American intelligence collaboration—a campaign that never ceased, and a situation never fully exposed until long after the war, when two British diplomats, Guy Burgess and Donald Maclean, defected to Russia and thereby started investigations that reached back to wartime espionage.*

The secret-warfare chiefs in London were themselves fearful of too full and frank disclosures to their American colleagues, still poised between peace and war. Stephenson presented the arguments for action at the top on both sides of the Atlantic. President Roosevelt was persuaded that intelligence was the front line of U.S. defense and that the U.S. would depend for some time on British expertise. Churchill was persuaded that the FBI had been invaluable in fighting pro-Nazi forces in the Americas and must be kept friendly. Hoover had gone far beyond his duties to wrestle with the Third Reich. To judge what it would cost Britain to have Hoover as an enemy, it was necessary to see what he had done as a friend.

The first big FBI-BSC operation had been to knock out the key German intelligence outpost in Mexico, which directed Nazi subversion and espionage in the United States and co-ordinated these activities with similar campaigns in Latin America.

---

* Donald Maclean was a senior British diplomat who passed atom secrets to the Russians and was whisked out from under British security noses in 1951. He then went to work for the Soviet Foreign Service, taking Guy Burgess with him to Moscow. Twelve years later, Kim Philby escaped to Moscow after being exposed as a Russian agent inside British intelligence. The dreadful irony is that Hoover, between 1941 and 1945, several times requested investigation of British intelligence officers associated with Philby, on the grounds that they seemed determined to damage Anglo-American co-operation.

32

AS IT HAD been in World War I, the Latin-American republic of Mexico was, in the summer of 1940, once again a springboard for troublemakers instructed from Berlin. Unfortunately for the German spy masters, there were more instructions than money. The outpost had run out of hard currency.

"It seems funny in retrospect," Stephenson said later. "But the Mexican operations were not at all funny at the time, because German agents were breaking the economic blockade, smuggling thousands of tons of oil through Mexican ports, and directing a formidable network of clandestine radios. Their field officer was a big monocled Junker, a relative of that pretentious ass Franz von Papen, the dilettante politician who was also a failure as spy master, soldier, and diplomat. Von Papen directed spies and saboteurs in the U.S. and Canada during the First World War and now he was intriguing against the oldest of German intelligence chiefs, Admiral Canaris.* It was Canaris who sent von Papen's cousin to Mexico. Colonel Friedrich Karl von Schleebruegge moved into a posh house at 142 Donata Guerra in Mexico City. He knew how to spend funds—for his own amusement.

---

* Admiral Canaris was known as K within the British Foreign Office. His attempts to change sides once Hitler was doomed were treated with contempt by INTREPID, who remembered that Canaris's agents had posed as peacemakers or anti-Nazi Germans to disarm influential British and American personalities before the war. K was executed on Hitler's orders, giving rise to speculation long afterward that he was never fully committed in the secret war against the West. Yet, until the tide turned against Nazi Germany and he fell from Hitler's favor, K was never regarded as less than a most cunning and formidable foe.

His staff were experts but they needed a hell of a lot of money, which they weren't getting. Joachim Hertslet worked out of the German Legation, arranging oil for Germany by way of Japan and Siberia, and also through the blockade to Italy before she came into the war.

"Hertslet was a real problem to us before the cash ran out. He set up secret U-boat refueling bases in the Caribbean. He had influential friends. When I looked into his barter agreements, dating back to early 1938, I was impressed by his commercial ingenuity. He'd been swapping German industrial products for oil for two years.

"Then there was a sabotage expert who moved to Mexico after working for the New York company of H. Bischoll. While in New York, he taught Irish workers to damage docks and factories supplying Britain. His name was Karl Rekowski, and he needed hard cash to pay saboteurs inside the States.

"We'd set up a currency blockade. The Mexican outpost couldn't operate unless it had local currency for places like Colombia, Ecuador, Nicaragua. Hoover and I pooled our information. A lot came from intercepted wireless traffic codes we'd broken. The so-called 'Bolivar' net, for instance, transmitted to Germany such perishable intelligence as ship movements. It was tantamount to the German U-boats being directed onto target. . . .

"There's always two sides to secret radio transmissions. If the enemy doesn't know you're listening, he gives things away. What he was telling us now was that for all the success of their Mexican station, the Germans there were going bankrupt."

The German director turned for help to the Washington embassy of the Fascist Italian government, which in October 1940 was still enjoying a "correct" relationship with the State Department. The news was brought by Hoover, who dropped into the Stork Club one evening. He seldom drank more than a single shot of Jack Daniel's, usually with a close and trustworthy friend like Walter Winchell. This night he sat alone until one of Stephenson's go-betweens turned up. "Tell Bill we've got something for him," said Hoover.

The FBI had noticed money being withdrawn from New York banks by Italian diplomats. Now it appeared that a total of $3,850,000 had been collected for transfer across the Mexican border in small bills.

Hoover was powerless to interfere legally. Any action he took would have to be behind official backs. Could he tail the Italian Embassy couriers who were picking up the money, on the grounds that he suspected the funds were to finance subversive activities? "Yes," said presidential adviser Ernest Cuneo. "If the Italians move the money physically to Mexico, it can be confiscated by Stephenson's men once it crosses the border."

This was more than relaying a presidential view. Cuneo was an international lawyer and knew how far the rules could be stretched.

Three couriers were to carry the money in diplomatic bags, the FBI reported. An Italian Embassy secretary would take $1,400,000 to Mexico City. Two consuls would proceed with the rest to New Orleans. If the consuls took ship south, there was nothing to be done. The Italian government had a perfect right to transfer funds in case of a possible U.S. government freeze. The President wanted the move frustrated but he could not be publicly associated with a breach of diplomatic niceties. The British Embassy was afraid of repercussions, too. So the FBI went quietly about its business of watching the Italian Embassy, and BSC warned its agents in Latin America to stand by.

The three Italian couriers traveled to Brownsville, Texas, followed by FBI agents. The secretary took the train to Mexico City. Stephenson warned his man inside the Mexican Police Intelligence Department to have the single courier interrogated the moment he stepped over the border. The secretary cheerfully exploited his diplomatic privileges. His outraged cries when the police defiled the sanctity of his diplomatic pouch were heard as far away as Rome. The Mexican government blamed the inexperience of a clerk and put the money into a blocked account. With that, the German network centered on Mexico City collapsed.

One-third of Nazi espionage funds for Mexico thus vanished. The sums involved were exceedingly large for that period and in that part of the world. Stephenson waited to pounce on the remaining $2,450,000, carried by the two consuls, who had boarded a ship for Rio de Janeiro. His man in Rio extracted from the Brazilian foreign minister a promise that the money would be given "special protection." But just in case, a pair of Stephenson's agents raced to the east Brazilian port of Recife, then known as Pernambuco, where the ship was expected to pick up cargo.

"Both agents were keen types," Stephenson recalled. "Their job was quite simple. Steal the money. Nobody doubted they would faithfully make the dangerous journey home, turn in the money, and then itemize every cent in their own expense accounts. When you select an agent, you pick him first for his integrity. You're operating in a lawless underworld. But you trust your men. Every detail of the operation was worked out for these two. They planned to slip aboard the ship at Pernambuco, grab the diplomatic bags, and make a run for it. But the Brazilian foreign minister double-crossed us. A request was issued to the ship's agent in Rio to reroute her. She never stopped at Pernambuco. Instead, the Italian couriers were met at Rio and escorted to their embassy. A couple of million dollars slipped through our fingers. Such hard currency would buy the Nazis an awful lot in those days—not just the vital commodities which we were trying to stop from reaching German industry, but propaganda and informers. A police chief could be had for a few hundred dollars."

From this first FBI collaboration abroad with British intelligence, Hoover concluded that he could dominate the over-all U.S. intelligence effort. He liked to be responsible for delivering to U.S. armed forces' intelligence units any material obtained from Stephenson. With the FBI stamp of approval, it was more readily accepted—which in those early days was all that Stephenson wanted. "Hoover was in the war from the beginning," Stephenson said later. "He planted British deception material among Washington officials who talked too much. London would ask me to ask Hoover to palm off some rumor like the one about glass balls to be dropped from bombers. The balls supposedly contained a new explosive of tremendous heat which could not be extinguished. This eventually reached the Germans and may have discouraged plans to use poison gas on London. There were, of course, no glass balls."

In this crucial period, the war at sea was going so badly that sixteen Axis vessels sheltering in Mexican ports were far more of a potential threat than might appear to Washington's detached observers.

"The survival of Axis freighters making blatant use of Mexican ports might encourage a belief that Britain is powerless in the area," reported INTREPID. "The Royal Navy cannot patrol Mexico's territorial waters. Enemy ships stand a good chance of slipping through our blockade, scoring a moral victory that might influence fence-sitters. Four of the ships are German and twelve are Italian. The vessels are tied up in Vera Cruz and Tampico. This would be a bad time for them to break out. We got a lot of information out of friends in Mexico who sympathize with Britain. Mexico provides good coverage of the pro-Axis leaders in Latin America. If the ships escape, our stock in Mexico goes down and certain facilities will be discontinued."

"Take appropriate action," replied London.

A couple of Canadians appeared in BSC's Broadway office, having crossed into the U.S. by way of the International Bridge near Watertown, New York, where American border officials turned a blind eye to bits of metal and plastic explosives in the trunk of their car. The metal was magnetized, and the plastic was made in the "spy factory" near Toronto. When assembled, the frames and plastic became limpet mines, which would cling to the steel plates of a ship's hull. The two Canadians, underwater demolition men, began their journey to Mexico with a briefing from Stephenson, who had spoken directly with President Roosevelt, convincing him that the State Department's fear of diplomatic scandal was outweighed by America's need to impress the Mexicans with American strength in the event of war in the Pacific. It was then arranged that a British "naval adviser" should go to the U.S. Office of Naval Intelligence with a formal request that U.S. destroyers help prevent the Axis

304

vessels from escaping. Roosevelt's part was kept out of it; instead, Secretary of the Navy Frank Knox appeared to respond to Navy recommendation that four destroyers patrol the area.

On the night of November 15, 1940, the four German ships attempted to slip out through the Gulf of Mexico. They were confronted with blinding searchlights directed from what they took to be hostile warships. One German vessel, the *Phrygia,* caught fire and sank. The crews of the other three ships, back in Tampico next day, claimed they had been intercepted by British warships. Just what did happen to the *Phrygia* was never made clear. There were no other warships in the region except the U.S. destroyers. It was their searchlights that surprised the fleeing Germans. The Mexicans drew the conclusion that the United States was fighting alongside Britain, but not openly. It was a conclusion not displeasing to Roosevelt. He was alarmed by Nazi propaganda that the United States would never resist attack or help South American countries in danger. The incident conveyed its message to Berlin while escaping the attention of most Americans, still fighting shy of involvement.

Two of the remaining German ships tried to break out again a month later. German intelligence had identified the U.S. destroyers, and Berlin wished to demonstrate that the United States feared an open confrontation. The German ships were ordered to sail in broad daylight. This time, the U.S. destroyers merely shadowed them, transmitting their position hourly until British warships could be directed from operations elsewhere. The British made the capture, and the Americans remained ostensibly neutral. The Mexican government expropriated the remaining thirteen Axis vessels so fast that the Canadian team of saboteurs had no need to carry out their own orders.

Hoover was disappointed about the saboteurs, whose passage through the United States was made under FBI protection. His uneasiness about ONI working directly through Stephenson with the Royal Navy was tempered by the fact that he had been kept fully informed. The FBI's counterespionage tentacles were creeping into South America, even though the State Department was not happy about it.

Stephenson had created a Ship's Observer network in which one member of every crew sailing out of Western Hemisphere ports reported to INTREPID when anything suspicious occurred. These reports were shared with the FBI and added to Hoover's prestige. The FBI director was given credit for the arrest and execution of the first British traitor caught in a U.S. port. He was George Thomas Armstrong, a thirty-two-year-old sailor who sold convoy information to the German consul in New York. Part of his price was that German U-boats did not torpedo *him*. Armstrong was an ardent Communist, and in this period before Russia was attacked, he had followed the Communist line of opposing his native England's continuance of the war. He was allowed to sail back to England, where Scotland Yard picked him up. He was hanged in Wandsworth Jail on July 9, 1941.

The British did not want publicity given to their vast counter-spy network, which existed not only to expose traitors, but also to prevent the smuggling of enemy documents and special cargoes. Thus, Hoover, having established Armstrong's method of conveying sailing schedules through New York by radio and cable to Nazi submarine-information centers in South America and Spain, was flattered by recognition from Scotland Yard.

Others of Armstrong's persuasion were left to roam free in the United States until they had unwittingly given away their collaborators, whereupon they met with "accidents." For this, however, the FBI did not get the credit. BSC had its own disposal squads to handle such disagreeable duties. The normal formula was that the victim "has departed for Canada," a fate more final than it seemed when written on a police blotter.

33

IN HIS ACCOUNT of Nazi strategy in the United States, Stephenson prefaced a report to President Roosevelt with the comment: "Never did a man of immense ambition such as Hitler so clearly disclose beforehand the general process and particular methods by which he fulfils his plans for conquest. The Nazi program for the moral disintegration of ideological enemies regards the Americas as the last and largest enemy."

For many years before the war, German industrial organizations such as I.G. Farben and Schering A.G. had been methodically consolidating their interest in the United States according to a plan for German infiltration in the Americas through U.S. subsidiaries of German-owned companies. The subsidiaries were camouflaged by dummy neutral ownership in Sweden or Switzerland or by secret cartel agreements between them and the German parent companies.

When Germany went to war, this intricate network of companies supported German intelligence and propaganda systems in the Western Hemisphere. "To combat and liquidate this threat is one of BSC's chief objectives," Stephenson wrote in 1940. "BSC has to achieve its objective without offending sensitive U.S. public opinion, particularly as represented in Congress. A false step may create revulsion against Britain. . . ."

The plan Stephenson formulated included turning over to the FBI all evidence providing legal grounds for action against German-controlled businesses on technical grounds such as the infraction of antitrust laws. Hoover would be receptive to the plan. Any sign of immorality in Big Business bothered his conscience, which may come as a surprise to those who think of him as so devoutly anti-Communist that he was blind to capitalist sins.

"The Secret Intelligence Division first had to obtain absolute proof of the existence of direct connections between Germany and German firms operating under cover in the United States," stated the BSC Papers. "The Special Operations Division would then expose these connections by powerful propaganda campaigns to persuade public opinion that American/German firms menaced the security of the United States. This would bring pressure on the U.S. Government and facilitate the President's own desires. The FBI would provide the Treasury and the Anti-Trust Division of the Department of Justice with grounds for action . . . all these U.S. agencies, though anxious to cooperate, never commanded enough public support to buck Big Business. . . ."

Stephenson went after the offenders with the ferocity of a fox terrier and quickly found himself hanging on to his own landlord, Nelson Rockefeller.

The Standard Oil Company of New Jersey was discovered to be maintaining close relations with Nazi Germany and especially with I. G. Farben, which, apart from its involvement with concentration camps and mass-extermination techniques, had a special intelligence section known as NW7 working hand-in-glove with the economic section of German intelligence. Standard Oil's relationships went back to 1927, when it began a series of agreements with Farben. The Standard Oil description of the basic agreement was: "The I. G. are going to stay out of the oil business and we are going to stay out of the chemical business." In 1929, they consummated what each corporation called "a full marriage": Standard had a free hand in oil anywhere in the world in exchange for giving Farben no global competition in the chemical industry.

Nelson Rockefeller worked in the Standard Oil offices at 26 Broadway as a young man, before he turned his full attention to leasing offices in the family complex at Rockefeller Center. Though he wrote off BSC's rentals as a nonrepayable loan to Britain, his good will was more than financial. He lacked the power to pick apart Standard Oil's international knitting, but he could make the details of its more questionable activities available. A vice-president of the corporation, for instance, negotiated, after the war in Europe broke out, a method of operation that would, as he wrote in a memo, "allow us to continue in partnership with the Germans whether or not the United States comes into the war. I. G. assigned to me some 2,000 foreign patents, and in three days of negotiations in Holland we worked out a *modus vivendi.*"

Rockefeller agreed with Stephenson that the best possible weapon against this "business-as-usual" mentality would be publicity. He goaded and persuaded other oil executives to recognize their social and political responsibilities and worked with BSC in pinning down precisely how involved Standard Oil and other U.S. corporations were with Axis commerce. After Roosevelt made him Co-ordinator of Inter-American Affairs in 1940, he began countering the Nazis with BSC's methods: controlling U.S. newsprint exports to South America, for instance, thus influencing an estimated 1,200 newspapers in the republics.

The joke was that Standard Oil executives offered a considerable fortune in hard cash, no questions asked, to anyone who would identify the source of a book called *Sequel to the Apocalypse: How Your Dimes Pay for Hitler's War.* Nobody ever claimed the reward. The book, detailing I. G. Farben–Standard Oil collaboration, was printed on Camp X presses and smuggled from Canada into the United States by BSC. It exposed "the tangled nature of the corporate structure" and charted the links from Germany to dozens of dummy companies in the Americas and with big U.S. corporations, including Ford. What it did not mention was that I. G. Farben had a significant interest in German atomic-bomb research and was the principal shareholder in a Norwegian plant producing ingredients for German atomic projects.

Rockefeller had the book distributed by U.S. embassies in South America even as executives of his family's company muttered about lawsuits. The Stephenson view of corporation ethics was colored by the June 1940 German-sponsored victory celebration in the Waldorf Astoria, when American tycoons were told not to waste time on Britain, whose armies had just been chased out of France.

A typical INTREPID signal on the problem was this one of April 14, 1941:

> THE STANDARD OIL COMPANY IS PLAYING THIS WAR AT BOTH ENDS AND IN THE MIDDLE. THEIR TANKERS OPERATING UNDER THE PANAMANIAN FLAG PLY BETWEEN GULF OF MEXICO PORTS AND TENERIFE OSTENSIBLY TO SUPPLY THE SPANISH REFINERY BUT IN FACT TO SUPPLY ENEMY VESSELS.

This ran parallel to Stephenson's charges against the International Telephone and Telegraph Corporation—that it was associated with Hitler's SS and war industries like Focke-Wulff, which built bombers. He was trying, too, to put an end to a situation in which ITT carried messages from the United States to the enemy by way of its own cables and those of its subsidiaries in South America: Chile, Cuba, Colombia, and Ecuador. The piquancy of the situation was that ITT also owned a British company, Standard Telephones and Cables. When the supreme boss, the notorious Sosthenes Behn, visited his English workers after the fall of France, none knew about his German activities across the Channel. Yet it was this very situation that had allowed ITT engineers to draw Stephenson's attention to the Enigma coding machine, whose solution was vital to ULTRA.

"If the Nazis won, some of these business realists would have been impeccably Nazi," Stephenson said of them. "If the Nazis lost, the same businessmen were impeccably American."

This upset the Ministry of Economic Warfare, worried about offending U.S. financiers, for British international commerce did not always bear close inspection earlier. To INTREPID's Standard Oil messages of April 1941, one reply from London read:

> MEW SUSPECT ATTEMPT CREATE BAD BLOOD BETWEEN YOUR INFORMANTS AND STANDARD. REGARDING ALLEGED SUPPLY TO ENEMY SHIPS OF

STANDARD OIL THIS REPORT WITHOUT FOUNDA-
TON. . . .

INTREPID's answer was a mass of details. He kept up similar barrages until finally a senatorial investigating committee headed by Harry Truman reviewed the evidence. Standard Oil's record was then set forth, from its continuing sale of fuel to Axis airlines, despite State Department protests, to its providing German companies with strategic materials. In Venezuela, where Rockefeller checked out his family oil holdings, it was established that Standard Oil gave Germans preference in supervising the development of oil fields. The BSC Papers declared: "Standard Oil could be scarcely regarded as an American business machine. It was a hostile and dangerous agency of the enemy."

Early in 1941, after Roosevelt's re-election but before his inauguration, Stephenson turned over to Hoover and the FBI a 400-page report, one of many produced by the men who were forming the nucleus of the new Political-Warfare Division within British Security Coordination. For Hoover, it came as a shock. Among disclosures about the links between Nazi corporations and American businessmen were the names of British collaborators. The report recounted the experience of "The Worried German" awaiting American naturalization who had gone to a State Department official to offer information on Nazi activities. The official was not much interested. Eventually a confidential report was written by Assistant Secretary of State Adolf Berle, beginning: "From a source—the reliability of which is not confirmed—I have learned the following . . ." In effect, as Stephenson pointed out, the State Department was saying it could not care less. Berle was a loyal American, but his approach to foreign affairs was "schoolmasterish and rigidly opposed to British manipulations and secret British police and espionage agencies in Washington." He clashed later with Stephenson over BSC's activities, until eventually he had to accept the President's ruling that "for the sake of our own national survival, you must cooperate."

The report opened the door to further action against Nazi organizations working under commercial cover.

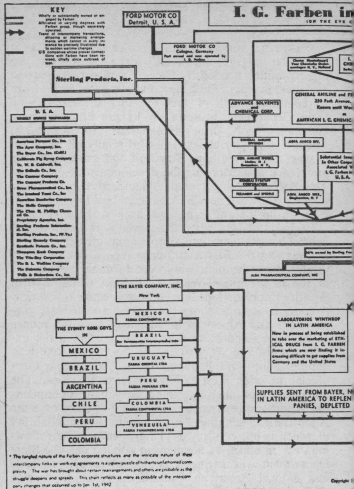

I. G. Farben in

*The tangled nature of the Farben corporate structures and the intricate nature of these intercompany links or working agreements is a jigsaw puzzle of hitherto unfathomed complexity. The war has brought about certain rearrangements and others are probable as the struggle deepens and spreads. This chart reflects as many as possible of the intercompany changes that occurred up to Jan 1st, 1942.

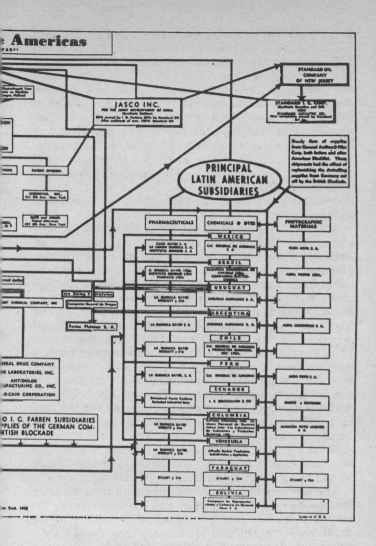

e Americas

STANDARD OIL
COMPANY
OF NEW JERSEY

JASCO INC.
FOR THE JOINT DEVELOPMENT OF BUNA
(Synthetic Rubber)
50% owned by I. G. Farben; 50% by Standard Oil
After outbreak of war, 100% Standard Oil

STANDARD I. G. CORP.
(Synthetic Gasoline and Oil)
now
STANDARD CATALYTIC CO.
Now completely owned by Standard
Oil Co.

Steady flow of supplies
from General Aniline & Film
Corp. both before and after
American Blacklist. Those
shipments had the effect of
replenishing the dwindling
supplies from Germany cut
off by the British Blockade.

PATENT DIVISION

CHEMNYCO, INC.
521 5th Ave. New York

RUFF and JOHLIN
Patent Attorneys
521 5th Ave. New York

PRINCIPAL LATIN AMERICAN SUBSIDIARIES

PHARMACEUTICALS	CHEMICALS & DYES	PHOTOGRAPHIC MATERIALS
	MEXICO	
CASA BAYER S. A. LA UNION QUIMICA S. A. INSTITUTO BEHRING S A	CIA GENERAL DE ANILINAS S A	CASA AGFA S. A.
	BRAZIL	
A. QUIMICA BAYER LTDA INSTITUTO BEHRING LTDA FARMACO LTDA	INSTITUTO QUIMICO DE ANILINAS LTDA COMPANHIA ELECTRO QUIMICA	AGFA PHOTO LTDA.
	URUGUAY	
LA QUIMICA BAYER WERBOTT y CIA	ANILINAS ALEMANAS S. A.	
	ARGENTINA	
LA QUIMICA BAYER S A	ANILINAS ALEMANAS S. A.	AGFA ARGENTINA S. A.
	CHILE	
LA QUIMICA BAYER WERBOTT y CIA	CIA GENERAL DE ANILINAS y PRODUCTOS QUIMICOS, SOC LTDA.	
	PERU	
LA QUIMICA BAYER, S. A.	CIA GENERAL DE ANILINAS	AGFA FOTO S. A.
	ECUADOR	
Droguería Punto Carbone Sociedad Industrial Saxo	L. E. BOUCKMANN & CO	QUIST y SCHRÄDER
	COLUMBIA	
LA QUIMICA BAYER WERBOTT y CIA	Anilinas Alemanas Ltda. La Union Nacional de Anilinas Induco Ltda. Cia. Colombiana de Colorantes y Productos Quimicos Ltda.	ALMACEN FOTO LINDNER S A
	VENEZUELA	
LA QUIMICA BAYER WERBOTT y CIA	Alfredo Sacker Productos Industriales y Agricolas	
	PARAGUAY	
STAUDT y CIA	STAUDT y CIA	STAUDT y CIA
	BOLIVIA	
	Compania de Representantes y Comercio en General Hans S A	

merced Aniline

..OP CHEMICAL COMPANY, INC

Farma Platanos S. A.

..ERAL DRUG COMPANY

..HK LABORATORIES, INC.

ANTIDOLOR
..UFACTURING CO., INC.

..O-CAIN CORPORATION

**..O I. G. FARBEN SUBSIDIARIES
..PPLIES OF THE GERMAN COM-
..NTISH BLOCKADE**

H'g Bering F' & S.Farben
Compania General de Drogas

..w York 1943

Litho in U S A

It analyzed the fifteen big German trusts that provided the social base for Hitler. The most interesting was I. G. Farben, whose directors endorsed the Nazi party because it opposed free enterprise, and who encouraged the building of slave-labor camps in order to make production more "efficient." Few in the West wanted to believe reports of Nazi mass-murder programs. Stephenson had blueprints of the mobile gas chambers and a Farben report on experiments with the prussic-acid derivative later known as Zyklon-B, which would exterminate "sub-humans" on an assembly-line basis with speed, dispatch, and little fuss in the chambers that became notorious in their guise as communal showers.

INTREPID's report went on to describe what happened when "The Worried German" was turned away by Berle, who saw him on behalf of the State Department. The man was an executive of Schering A. G., a chemical firm in Bloomfield, New Jersey. Its Swiss "ownership" was camouflage for a subsidiary of Schering/ Berlin, which had built up a network of neutral holding companies and dummies from Scandinavia to South America. Known in BSC records as The Bloomfield Man, the disenchanted German executive made contact with Stephenson's organization. It was still unregistered with the United States government and the informant was in a precarious position. Despite his honorable motives, he could be deported to Germany for working on behalf of a foreign secret agency. If he kept quiet, his application to become an American citizen could be rejected if the United States came into the war and he was seen as part of a Nazi conspiracy. For this reason he was never identified by name in official papers.

The Bloomfield Man collaborated with British agents for several months. Material was removed from the corporation's files and photographed in a suite at the St. Regis Hotel, in mid-Manhattan, then owned by a friend of Stephenson working for BSC. Schering worked for Berlin, and was a source of hard currency and cargoes regarded by the British as contraband.

A section of the State Department was angered by a public statement from London that certain American companies were "trading with the enemy." The

Ministry of Economic Warfare, responding to the 400-page report, tried to pressure Washington to "freeze enemy assets, cooperate in black-listing enemy commercial firms and deny fuel to vessels serving enemy interests." The Secretary of State, Cordell Hull, expressed outrage at British accusations.

BSC decided to "find" evidence that would reach the FBI and eventually the State Department. Suspicious material netted in the Bermuda censorship station from outgoing mails was normally shared with the FBI. Letters on Schering/USA stationery that compromised the company were faked and sent back from Bermuda. One FBI man who was not surprised by the letters was J. Edgar Hoover. He had agreed this was the way to jolt the Justice Department into action. Investigators who reported their discovery of the Schering conspiracy were perfectly spontaneous in their reaction. They *were* surprised, and angry.

The Bloomfield Man had also written an extensive account of the Schering corporation's activities. Some of this material was leaked to the Washington bureau of International News Service, including photostats of forged Schering letters "proving" the firm was breaking the Sherman Anti-Trust Act. Joseph Borkin, of the Department of Justice, was approached by INS, which undertook to sit on the story provided the Anti-Trust Division began legal proceedings and gave the news agency the first break when action was taken.

This strengthened Borkin's hand. He was one of many middle-level officials who had trouble getting action against German and other foreign cartels, although he was convinced this was morally the proper course of action. Opposition to these troubled souls, and to the FBI, seemed to come from the State Department and its friends in higher business levels.

"President Roosevelt himself proposed in his Fireside Chat after re-election in 1941 to say that American citizens in high places were aiding and abetting the work of Nazi agents," the BSC Papers noted. "The President sent a draft of the speech to the State Department. It was returned with the words 'in high places' ringed in red. When Roosevelt asked who was responsible, he was told 'State—they think the words dangerous.' The President said sharply, then let's change the sentence to read—'There are also American citizens, many of them in high places, *especially in the State Department. . . .'*

"This gives a taste of circumstances even this late in time," the BSC Papers continued. "Borkin was one of many frustrated men who ran into mysterious resistance at higher levels. The Schering/USA reports on subversion could not be totally ignored. But the State Department was conducting its own feud with Hoover and the FBI, and accused them and the Justice Department of intruding into State's preserves. It was recognized by BSC that the threatened press campaign, proceeding through INS and other media, would have to go ahead."

During preparations for this, Stephenson applied another form of polite pressure on a Swiss bank, which professed to control Schering/USA. The managing director later recalled being reached by "Mr. Samuel of General Trust of London." He thought he would hear some proposition for laundering currency through the Swiss bank. Instead, over massive Martinis, he heard that Schering/USA was about to have its properties seized by the U.S. government. The gossip was mentioned in passing. The managing director hastily drew Mr. Samuel back to this topic. Why, yes, said Mr. Samuel, surprised. Surely the Swiss banker did not think U.S. authorities were as innocent as they appeared? Come to think of it—suppose Schering/ USA were expropriated? Where would this leave the Swiss bank? The conversation passed on to the subject of Mr. Samuel's interest in meeting Swiss businessmen in Geneva. . . .

A few days later the banker called Samuel, who seemed to be Canadian. Did Mr. Samuel know much about business in Canada? Indeed Samuel did. The two met again. Mr. Samuel suggested a way out of the banker's difficulties—form a Canadian holding company to take over the Schering/USA share certificates. There would be no loss of profit, the U.S. authorities would be satisfied that the Canadian government exercised proper supervision, and the Swiss banker would be relieved to know he was on the right side of the fence.

This game distracted the banker while German ownership through his bank was documented. "On April 10, 1941 a superbly orchestrated press campaign was launched, exposing the scandal of the New Jersey firm under disguised Nazi control," Cuneo said years later "A series of carefully timed leaks to friendly newsmen and broadcasters ensured that the media pursued these news stories."

Schering's operations came to a standstill. The U.S. Treasury took over. The Swiss bank was ordered to divest itself of all stock held in the chemical company. The managing director never discovered that helpful cozy Mr. Samuel was chief of British intelligence.

"A new attitude of suspicion surrounded and embarrassed Standard Oil," the BSC Papers recorded. "The U.S. Economic Defense Board was now compelled to put a stop to another deal under which Standard would have sold Germany its Hungarian oil interests." This economic warfare against the enemy in the Western Hemisphere was waged against many commercial enterprises. Stephenson became expert in unexpected areas like the smuggling of diamonds, through which Germany could beat the economic blockade. Strategic goods were purchased by Nazi collaborators in black markets where the currency might be gold, precious stones, or other "light-weight, high-value" commodities whose origin could be disguised. The case of Standard Oil underlined the relentless nature of the pursuit of Nazi dupes by Stephenson, and his disregard for special interests. When BSC's detective work exposed offenders like Standard Oil, whose ultimate ownership rested with the Rockefellers, no favors were asked and no quarter was given. In files labeled "The Campaign Against German Business," a BSC historian comments: "We helped create an atmosphere in which the President could act and issue orders to seize companies or suspend their activities. The American people, persuaded by disclosures in the Press that German commercial machinations were a menace to their own security, accepted these orders as essential. American Big

Business, conscious of public sentiment, did not dare oppose them."

A curious alliance between business, labor, and pro-Nazi groups was uncovered. John L. Lewis, president of both the United Mine Workers of America and the Congress of Industrial Organizations, was involved with the "oilies," the big oil companies trading with the Axis powers. His activities drew attention first of all because, in the words of the BSC Papers, he "nursed a personal hatred of President Roosevelt, was violently isolationist so long as Russia was allied with Germany, and had a virulent loathing for Britain."

BSC created societies to discredit enemies in the U.S., "spontaneous" and seemingly home-grown agencies such as the American Labor Committee to Aid British Labor, the Fight-for-Freedom Committee, and subcommittees within the American Federation of Labor. In the course of plotting the downfall of Lewis as dictator of the American labor movement, BSC prepared a report on "the American working class" that reached Hoover. He read with some interest that "the American working class is uninformed and politically disorganised. Many of the workers came from the uneducated foreign-born population, which having no political tradition (and often a good deal of language difficulty) is confused and easily swayed by mass emotional appeals of the crudest character. . . . As the majority of unions in the vital defense industries are affiliated with the CIO, Lewis's prejudices are a menace to Britain."

Hoover had to swallow this judgment, and the FBI checked out the reported dealings between the labor leader and an American oilman, registered with German intelligence as a subagent. The name of this oddly placed oilman was William Rhodes Davis. He worked from the 34th floor of 630 Fifth Avenue, sandwiched between Stephenson's Economic Intelligence Division and his coding machines.

Davis was a railroad engineer from Alabama who got into oil in his mid-twenties. He had been an independent operator in the Oklahoma oil fields for fifteen years when he was dazzled by the possibilities of Nazi commercial cartels by the son of a German immigrant

318

to the United States, Dr. Horace Greeley Hjalmar Schacht, regarded as the Third Reich's financial genius. The man who was named after Horace Greeley proved a popular salesman for Hitler because he made Nazism sound like American-style enterprise. Schacht talked of a great economic union with the Anglophile world, and his expansionist philosophy appealed to the rock-fisted oilman. Davis also saw that in the coming war Germany would need huge reserves of oil to fuel its U-boats and commerce raiders. By 1936, when Davis was forty-seven years old, he was on intimate terms with the Nazi Ministry of Economic Affairs and German industrial cartels involved in Hitler's fortunes. He built a refinery at Hamburg, using blocked assets that the First National Bank of New York had in Germany, and then arranged to ship crude oil there from the Americas by a route that would circumvent British blockades. His company and its subsidiaries began shipping to the oil terminal at Malmö, in Sweden, which had attracted Stephenson's interest in early 1939. Five days after war in Europe broke out, word leaked to London that William Rhodes Davis was on a "peace mission" in Berlin, and claimed to represent President Roosevelt.

Roosevelt had indeed talked with Davis, at John L. Lewis's request. He listened to Davis and agreed "it would be tragic if the war should spread." By the time Davis reached Berlin, this brief conversation had been enlarged in his own imagination. He met several times with Göring. Reports duly filtered back to Washington that Davis had described the President as being under the control of John L. Lewis, who "in turn controls a block of fourteen million votes." Lewis was said to have dropped his opposition to the Nazis since the Nazi-Soviet Pact of 1939 and to be willing to pressure Roosevelt into stopping the war. If the British persisted in their "aggressive war" with the President's support, Lewis intended, provided he had sufficient funds, to bring about Roosevelt's downfall.

Behind all this was Davis's anger that the British had stopped shipments of oil to Germany after he sold the first 400,000 tons from his Mexican refineries. Another 33,000 tons of crude oil had been confiscated on its way to the Swedish terminal for redistribution to Germany.

When Davis left Berlin, he was given a German military intelligence number—Agent C 80—and he traveled in the company of the well-known Nazi economic expert Dr. Joachim Hertslet. They were intercepted by SIS in Lisbon. Hertslet was using a Swedish passport in the name of Carl Bluecher, and the British exposed the fraud, preventing Hertslet from continuing his journey to South America, where his job was to have been the penetration of commercial interests. Later, he assumed another false identity and flew first to New York, unaware that he had been allowed deliberately to slip through so that the FBI could tail him.

This was the period when the German Air Force chief was active in putting out "peace feelers." Göring, by promising to get rid of the fanatic elements in the Nazi leadership, hoped to confuse and divide British and Americans. He readily believed that the American presidency was at the mercy of John L. Lewis, who was in effect boss of the Confederation of Mexico Workers, and that Lewis had pressured the Mexican government into guaranteeing oil supplies for the German Luftwaffe. Thus Lewis was entered in German military files as a subagent. In due course, he appeared in the BSC Papers as "a menace to be liquidated"—although direct action against the labor leader had to be postponed until after the crucial third-term election. The covert war against John L. Lewis began early in 1940 and was waged by the British on U.S. soil. The danger was that it might seem to be a campaign against the workers of America

"The miners, who carried Lewis to power, were an incredibly neglected and oppressed group in 1940," Stephenson later commented. "In that year alone, nearly 1,300 American miners were killed on the job and thousands more suffered permanent injury without compensation.

"Their greater enemy in the long run was the enemy we were fighting and which many American labor organizations were, in some cases unknowingly, helping. Lewis was their symbol."

The somersaults performed by international Communism after the Nazi-Soviet Pact of 1939 were repeated by Lewis. A political and subversive campaign to stop supplies to Britain continued from the time Soviet leaders accused Britain of provoking and prolonging the war with Hitler until the Führer invaded Russia. Labor strikes hit U.S. ports where ships waited to run the gantlet of Nazi submarines with vital cargoes. The details of sailing schedules were passed by Communist informers to German agents. It was this devotion to alien dogma that so shook Eleanor Roosevelt. She had tried to work with "liberal" youth movements, which served as Communist fronts, but by the third-term election she was saying that John L. Lewis seemed to be indistinguishable from either Communist or Nazi propagandists. "This fearsome labor leader says that he and millions of workers who obey him will vote against Franklin," she wrote in October 1940 to Stephenson. "The so-called Lewis Hymn of Hate turns the election into a personal battle between the labor leader and the President."

President Roosevelt said a few days later in a Brooklyn speech: "We must remember what the collaborative understanding between Communism and Nazism has done to the process of democracy abroad. Something evil is happening to this country. . . ."

The German Embassy reported to Berlin a confident assertion that Lewis could swing the workers' vote. The chargé d'affaires, Hans Thomsen, wrote those dispatches, which were read by Roosevelt as quickly as by Berlin. Thomsen's resident spy master worked with Hertslet; that enterprising gentleman was now directing Nazi subversion in the Western Hemisphere. Meetings between Hertslet and his agent C 80, William Rhodes Davis, took place in the oilman's Rockefeller Center office, as well as in his Scarsdale home, with John L. Lewis, in April 1940. Then Hertslet moved to Mexico City and instructed Lewis to begin inciting the strikes that would hit those industries that represented life lines to Britain. His instructions were synchronized with the German campaign to convince American industrialists that Britain was already defeated.

There were several ways to get at John L. Lewis. An overt attack might play into the hands of those who could block Roosevelt's measures; and so it seemed best to have BSC agents destroy the credibility of smaller men who buttressed Lewis or who were supported by Lewis in opposition to Roosevelt. Such an opponent of the President was Senator Burton K. Wheeler.

Wheeler, regarded with favor by the Nazi leaders, was an America Firster and proclaimed his belief that aid to Britain meant "plowing under every fourth American boy in foreign battlefields for the benefit of a decayed British Empire."

At that time the American First group was only one result of a massive German propaganda effort. BSC recorded: "When Britain was on the ropes and needed every kind of assistance, the enemy redoubled his efforts to swing American public opinion against Britain. Isolationist anti-British propaganda was splashed over the newspapers, shouted at mass meetings, disseminated through special societies and proclaimed in the Senate and in the House of Representatives. . . . Paralleling the tactics used by the NSDAP [National Socialist German Workers' Party] in Germany, the pro-Nazi forces within the United States formed 'patriotic societies' devoted ostensibly to serving the interests of 'Americanism.' There were a great many such organizations, from the ridiculous little imitations of Fascism like William Dudley Pelley's Silver Shirts to the wealthy and powerful, like the America First Committee. The dozens of interlocking isolationist organizations held mass meetings, issued pamphlets, trained street-corner rabble-rousers and organized 'educational' meetings. Their effectiveness grew so that by 1941 the temper of the people became difficult to assess. It gave the impression of being unstable and dangerous."

The German propaganda machine was working with economy and skill even after Roosevelt was re-elected. Americans who feared for their nation's security thought it was imperiled by surrender to the totalitarian propaganda of Lewis and Wheeler. A stream of messages from the German Embassy in Washington referred to both men in connection with reports on American production capacity and readiness for war. The messages were intercepted by the British, who concluded that Wheeler had access to secret U.S. military contingency plans, including the politically explosive ABC-1 "Germany First" blueprint.

While the FBI tried to prove that military secrets were getting into wrong hands, Stephenson looked for other ways to limit Wheeler's influence. He found one in what BSC called "The Congressional Franking Case."

"It is a long-standing privilege of Senators and Representatives to send letters without paying postage, using envelopes which are 'franked' with the signature of the sender," Stephenson noted. "Certain Congressmen were using the 'frank' for distributing free through the mails not only their own isolationist speeches but the work of Nazi hacks. Moreover, this went to people throughout the United States and not just to the Congressman's own constituents. Congress was converted into a distributing house for enemy propaganda."

His agents drew up a list of the recipients of this curious mail. They ran into thousands of names. The same names were on the distribution list of the German Library of Information in New York. BSC inserted extra names and addresses into the German Library list. Within days, these names began to appear on franked pro-Nazi mail from Congressmen. British agents examined envelopes franked by Senator Wheeler. They were found to have addresses stenciled by a distinctive addressing machine, an out-of-date Elliott. The German Steuben Society, a "cultural" organization that sent out confidential bulletins, still used an Elliott. The Society's confidential bulletins were intercepted. The envelopes were found to have been stenciled in a particular ink matching that used on the franked envelopes. The address plate carried the same coded number as the one used on Wheeler's outgoing mail.

Senator Wheeler was accused of abusing his Congressional privilege. He replied in the Senate in such an evasive way that he received hostile press comment and lost a good deal of prestige. He was forced to admit America First had purchased a million of his franked envelopes. A month later, in June 1941, all German consulates and agencies were closed by executive order. BSC ended a period during which 1,173,000 copies of Axis propaganda had been mailed at the expense of the American taxpayer through twenty-four members of Congress. It was not, however, the end of Senator Wheeler just yet; the BSC would have further use for him.

John L. Lewis was in difficulty that same June of 1941 as the result of Hitler's invasion of Russia. Suddenly, American Communists were in favor of war. Lewis himself was never a Communist. He pandered to Communist sympathizers for reasons of political expediency.

Stephenson mounted a campaign to discredit Lewis with the Kremlin. His agents in Moscow openly discussed the need to separate Lewis from the labor unions, arguing that it was now in Russia's interest to stop further labor troubles in the war industries. The Soviet press declared that the U.S. labor movement as represented by John L. Lewis was "a racket run by racketeers." Within weeks, BSC reported: "The isolationist faction within the American Communist Party has been bludgeoned into line by the Party Executive . . . a belated flip-flop among union leaders, made all the more painful for those who denied they were members of the Party. But all are now opposed to Lewis."

Other influential figures inside the CIO did not subscribe to Communist policies or to Lewis's isolationism. Now, for the first time, they felt stronger. BSC gave them extra courage through the Fight-for-Freedom Committee, taking care to conceal the British connection. Agents were sent to the CIO National Convention in Detroit the following November. The results were summarized in the BSC Papers:

"Fight-for-Freedom conducted a public opinion poll of the delegates. Great care was taken beforehand to make certain the poll results would turn out as desired. The questions were . . . to steer the delegates' opinion toward support of Britain and the war. . . . 96 per cent thought defeating Hitler was more important than keeping the USA out of the war; 95 per cent said they would advocate keeping the Japanese out of British possessions in Asia; 90 per cent said they would fight at once if it seemed certain Hitler would defeat Britain. Lindbergh was voted U.S. Fascist Number One and Senator Wheeler was U.S. Fascist Number Two. . . . BSC agents met union leaders and explained the purpose of Fight-for-Freedom and the poll. . . . The campaign was particularly appreciated by some representatives of the Roosevelt Administration who attended the convention as observers."

Public opinion had been manipulated through what seemed an objective poll. This was a resounding defeat for Lewis. Before Senator Wheeler could mobilize his remaining resources, another member of the trio met an untimely end. William Rhodes Davis had placed his business at the disposal of German friends. Nazi spy networks meshed with Davis's trading agencies in neutral countries like Spain. His vice-president in charge of foreign operations, Henry Warren Wilson, carried information from London to German military-intelligence intermediaries in neutral centers like Madrid and Mexico. Davis himself had excellent contacts inside England, including Lord Inverforth, whose knowledge of the munitions industry was voluminous. Inverforth fed Davis information that was distinctively misleading. When this "tagged information" turned up in intercepted German radio traffic, the source was unmistakable. In May 1940, for instance, Wilson had been informed at Inverforth's home in Hampstead that the Royal Navy had developed a device to detect submarines between the surface and a depth of fifty feet. This was a flight of imagination, confided to nobody else. Soon afterward, ULTRA recoverd German Navy instructions that U-boats should keep below fifty feet while submerged to avoid British sub killers equipped with new detection gear. The inference was obvious.

Even inferences were no longer necessary by the

summer of 1941. The Davis organization had been under prolonged scrutiny wherever in the world its employees showed their faces. It had become deeply involved in German plans for air and naval bases within striking distance of American shores. Davis himself had received large sums of money for political campaigns to keep America out of the war.

In the prime of life, at the age of fifty-two, William Rhodes Davis died unexpectedly. The cause of death was given as "a sudden seizure of the heart," and further police inquiries were discouraged by the FBI, at BSC's request. There were even reports of foul play. The BSC Papers merely record that among Davis's many business deals with Nazi Germany was "a project to ship oil through Mexican charter vessels to hidden fuel depots in the Atlantic and Caribbean among lesser-known islands where the German U-boats could prey upon merchant vessels along the American Eastern seaboard without the need to return to Europe to refuel. The swiftest way to put a stop to this scheme was to remove Davis from the scene."

34

SENATOR WHEELER WAS uneasy. He was sure British intelligence was manipulating the new U.S. intelligence agency under Donovan, and, further, that both were operating extensively behind various American front organizations.

On October 27, 1941, President Roosevelt made a speech that deepened the Senator's suspicions: ". . . Hitler has often protested that his plans for conquest do not extend across the Atlantic Ocean. . . . I have in my possession a secret map, made in Germany by Hitler's government—by planners of the New World Order. . . . It is a map of South America as

Hitler proposes to reorganize it. . . . Today in this area there are 14 separate countries. . . . The geographical experts of Berlin, however, have ruthlessly obliterated all the existing boundary lines, bringing the whole continent under their domination. . . . This map makes clear the Nazi design, not only against South America but against the United States as well. . . ."

The map showed the continent divided into four German-governed regions and one German colony. Axis strategy was to break one of the few remaining reservoirs of British economic strength by plunging South America into Nazi or pro-Axis revolutions. Stephenson noted: "The prizes in oil and other raw material seemed huge. The United States was the ultimate target."

Wheeler discovered that the map had been passed by Stephenson to Roosevelt. Previously, the Senator had somehow suspected the fabrication of documents to topple Britain's enemies. With this in mind, he told friends that the German map was a forgery.

In fact, the map had been taken from a German courier by British agents organizing groups in South America to form the nucleus of an anti-Nazi resistance wherever enemy influence predominated. A former attaché in the German Embassy in Argentina, Gottfried Sandstede, had made a copy of the original in the possession of his ambassador. Ordinarily, details of this sort would not have been passed along, but in this instance, because it was thought necessary to quell doubts about the authenticity of the map, Roosevelt was informed. This had unfortunate results for Sandstede. His identity as the source of information found its way back to German Gestapo agents in Buenos Aires. They had Sandstede killed, in yet another of the many "accidents" that marked this secret battle.

Twelve days after the President had produced the map at the Navy Day banquet, Wheeler asked the Senate: "Where did this originate? It originated in the office of Colonel Donovan, in the office of the Coordinator of Information of the United States Government. Perhaps I should say it originated in New York,

327

in the minds of gentlemen closely associated with the British Government. . . ."

Determined to denounce undercover operations by a foreign power, Wheeler seized upon a War Department report, some 350 pages in length and clearly stamped TOP SECRET, which came his way in circumstances that should have aroused his suspicions. It was called *Victory Program* and purported to forecast U.S. government plans to enter the war. The "Germany First" thesis was set forth, with an estimate of the numbers of troops and equipment required to launch offensives in Europe and Africa.

Wheeler passed this report to the Chicago *Tribune,* which splashed it under banner headlines and a lead paragraph: "A confidential report prepared by the joint Army and Navy high command by direction of President Roosevelt . . . is a blueprint for total war."

The leak reached the anti-Roosevelt press in the final days of peace. By December 3, 1941, a copy had reached the German Embassy. A summary was dispatched by radio to Berlin and was duly decoded in England. The German High Command celebrated "this fantastic intelligence coup." The fact was that the *Victory Program* was a plant.

Senator Wheeler had been watched by FBI counterespionage agents as a politician who thought preparation for war ran counter to the people's will. The Political-Warfare Division of BSC concocted the *Victory Program* out of material already known to have reached the enemy in dribs and drabs, and added some misleading information. The moment for bringing the Senator and the report together had come into sight the previous month. Stephenson had men inside Japanese diplomatic and commercial agencies in the United States. One agent was in the "peace mission" of Saburo Kurusu, in Washington to negotiate. Kurusu's real feelings were reported daily by the British to Roosevelt, who used his son James as the courier between BSC and the White House to guarantee security. On November 26, Colonel James Roosevelt had informed Stephenson that negotiations with the Japanese were regarded by the President as leading nowhere. A cable went to Churchill and the London headquarters of the Baker Street Irregulars from INTREPID:

JAPANESE NEGOTIATIONS OFF. SERVICES EXPECT ACTION WITHIN TWO WEEKS.

This historic message was delivered in London on November 27, ten days before Pearl Harbor.

It was then that the deception of Wheeler went into effect. A young U.S. Army captain delivered the bogus *Victory Program* to the Senator, claiming he did this out of concern for the American people, who should be warned against the President's duplicity.

The primary aim of this deception was to use isolationist channels as a means of revealing to Hitler a "secret plan" calculated to provoke him into a declaration of war. Even if the Japanese attacked British and American bases without warning, the British feared that the United States still would not declare war on Germany.

The secondary aim was to plant the notion that Anglo-American planners of a massive assault upon Europe had set Invasion Day for July 1, 1943. The date confronted the Germans with a credible military threat that would force them to maintain large forces along the Western wall and reduce pressure against Russia.

The attack on Pearl Harbor gave the United States no option about war with Japan. But Hitler had been persuaded by his military and political advisers that even Japanese aggression would not budge the Americans into a voluntary declaration of war against Germany.

The Führer abruptly changed policy when the *Victory Program* reached him, supposedly as a major revelation of American intent. Hitler declared war on the United States on December 11, a sudden decision that shocked Nazi diplomats. "The Führer felt that he alone had the right to plan surprise attacks against unsuspecting victims," Stephenson commented. "Here the United States had arrogantly used his own tactics against him. Angered, giddy with visions, Hitler gloried in beating Roosevelt to the punch.

"Hitler helped us achieve what Congress might have prevented or delayed. Under the U.S. Constitution, only Congress could declare war. And Roosevelt, with all his enormous personal influence and prestige as President, had failed to move the large isolationist block in Congress."

The most awkward of isolationists, Senator Wheeler —crony of Davis the oilman and Lewis the labor leader—had been made an instrument of justice. By leaking supposedly secret war plans, he tripped a wire in the minefield of Hitler's mind.

Those fateful days in December 1941 were recalled many years later by Stephenson. He wrote:

"Triple Priority and *Most Urgent* and finally *Personal and Secret to the President* were the warnings preceding a message from London on the day before Pearl Harbor. It read: 'British Admiralty reports that at 0300 hours London time this morning two Japanese groups seen off Cambodia Point sailing westward toward Malaya and Thailand. . . . First group twenty-five transports, six cruisers, ten destroyers. Second group ten transports, two cruisers, ten destroyers. . . .'

"This did no more than confirm what American code breakers had suspected for some time—that the Japanese were preparing aggression. The U.S. Navy's Bainbridge Island intercept station in Puget Sound read the coded traffic transmitted by the Japanese Embassy and the radio messages received from Tokyo. At 0128 on the morning of December 7, 1941, Tokyo instructed its Ambassador to tell the United States that negotiations were to be broken off an hour after midday, Washington time. The actual text meant little, unless seen within the frame of previous messages. Lieutenant-Commander Alwin D. Kramer, the duty Japanese-language expert at the Navy Department, was familiar with those messages, and when he saw the latest he ran the eight blocks down Constitution Avenue to the State Department to report his conviction that the Pacific war was about to begin.

"The Americans knew they were about to be attacked, but they did not know where. The sighting of heavy Japanese forces around Indochina strengthened the general opinion that Imperial Japan would seek easy prey among the colonies of the European powers now under the Nazi jackboot or close to it. The task force of Japanese aircraft carriers that waited to strike Pearl Harbor had sheltered in the cold and secret rendezvous of the Kurile Islands until late November. When the carriers positioned themselves to attack, they had escaped detection by keeping radio silence. It was an ironical twist of fate that gave them this unexpected advantage. Those Americans intercepting the Tokyo-Washington diplomatic traffic, and an unusual amount of Japanese radio transmissions from naval ships in Southeast Asia, were distracted from the biggest threat of all. The Japanese took Pearl Harbor by surprise and in two hours disposed of 349 U.S. aircraft, 3,700 American servicemen and damaged or sank eighteen U.S. Navy warships.

"This stunning blow stamped the name and date indelibly upon the history of conventional warfare. But in secret warfare, the boundaries were blurred between tension and outright hostilities.

"Pearl Harbor, December 7, 1941, is a signpost. Before that day of infamy, President Roosevelt had let slip the dogs of war in less spectacular fashion.

"Postwar historians felt that Hitler acted foolishly when he declared war on America, because the U.S. Congress was not at the time committed to fight the Nazis. Distinguished Americans like George Ball, later a presidential adviser himself, said: 'If Hitler had not made this decision and if he had simply done nothing, there would have been an enormous sentiment in the United States . . . that the Pacific was now our war and the European war was for the Europeans and we Americans should concentrate all our efforts on Japan.'

"But of course Hitler had long before declared war unofficially and secretly against America, his ultimate target. He had written: 'Our strategy is to destroy the enemy from within. Our aim is to conquer the enemy through himself.'

"This was, and still is, the most difficult challenge

to meet. It threatens national security when there is no evident state of war.

"In the worst possible sense, it does 'Cry, Havoc!' "

Three days after the Führer's unnecessary declaration of war, Churchill bustled aboard the battleship *Duke of York* complete with chiefs of staff and a series of proposals to be submitted to the first war council with the Americans. He had been prepared for Hitler's tantrum and its consequences. The display of power (a great battleship), flexibility (the swift passage through North Atlantic gales and U-boats), and the seizing of the initiative in Washington formed part of a careful campaign, executed by a veteran of foreign wars and political battles. Churchill pounced upon Washington, ready armed with a grand design to win the war.

"Unprepared for detailed argument while the shock of Pearl Harbor was still wearing off, the U.S. War Department had no time to combine forces to resist this sudden onslaught which it vaguely suspected to be designed to serve British interests first," the BSC Papers commented later. In fairness, on the night the Japanese made their fatal move, and *before* Hitler reacted in the way Stephenson hoped he would, the British showed no hesitation in jumping to America's side. "We shall declare war on Japan," Churchill said to U.S. Ambassador John G. Winant, who replied, "Good God, you can't declare war on a radio announcement." The BBC announcer was still delivering the first details of Pearl Harbor. Churchill signaled INTREPID and Roosevelt that "His Majesty's Ambassador at Tokyo has been instructed to inform the Imperial Japanese Government in the name of His Majesty's Government in the United Kingdom that a state of war exists between our two countries." Churchill sent a similar message to the Japanese Ambassador in London, ending: "I have the honour to be, with high consideration, Sir, Your obedient servant, Winston S. Churchill."

The Prime Minister commented: "When you have to kill a man it costs nothing to be polite." He had no obvious reason to display puckish good humor. Europe had entered the new Dark Age. Russia was in retreat. In all the vast expanse of waters from the Indian Ocean to the Pacific, Japan was supreme. Churchill's first military priority was still "the defence of this Island and the U-boat war," despite the fact that a large part of his first-line forces were fighting in the Middle East. Yet he displayed rising good spirits because the greatest burden had been lifted from his mind. The United States would be fully committed as Britain's ally on terms almost beyond belief—agreement on the policy of dealing with *Germany First*—terms that might have been greatly altered if President Roosevelt had been obliged to plead and bargain with Congress to get a declaration of war. Hitler, by seizing that initiative, had vindicated Roosevelt in all his preparations. As Ball commented, without the Nazis' impulsive and militarily useless announcement, Americans would have voted overwhelmingly to fight the Japanese and leave Europe for others to handle.

"Instinct warned Churchill that his friend the President would turn his attention and energies to the Pacific," commented a BSC historian. "How much the *Victory Program* tilted the balance the other way, I suppose we can only guess."

Churchill had a powerful inkling. "The manoeuvre which brings an ally into the field is as serviceable as that which wins a great battle," he had written long before, and the remark bears repetition. After Hitler's reckless and impassioned attack on the United States, and despite all the gloomy war news, he confided to his diary: "So we had won after all! . . . I had studied the American Civil War. . . . American blood flowed in my veins. I thought of a remark . . . that the United States is like 'a gigantic boiler. Once the fire is lighted under it there is no limit to the power it can generate.' Being saturated and satiated with emotion and sensation, I went to bed and slept the sleep of the saved and thankful."

There was little sleep for Stephenson. The underground wars merely intensified. For regular soldiers, the enemy could be spotted by their uniform and insignia. But for guerrilla leaders, the enemy might appear in the guise of a friend.

"We have always looked on this war as global and maritime," he told a small group at Camp X that included Donovan's hand-picked Americans, who would become leaders of OSS.

He turned to a map display in the blacked-out hut. "Now the whole of North America is officially in the conflict and we can fight more openly. . . . The enemy is loose throughout the ocean depths, and also within the land mass of the Western Hemisphere. His U-boats we can sink. His allies here in the Americas are more difficult to identify. The worst are the Vichy French. If we stop them here, we rob the enemy of eyes and ears. . . ." His pointer moved to small dots marking French colonial possessions in the Caribbean and west Atlantic.

"The Vichy French in continental America, however, provide channels through which we can feed false information back to the enemy. . . . When they lose this limited usefulness, when we finally destroy the Nazis among Frenchmen on this continent, it will be time to move into French possessions here. . . ." The pointer swept from North America across to Africa, paused, then moved up the western Mediterranean. "We can unite patriotic Frenchmen everywhere, once we're in French North Africa. Then France itself will revolt. The corrosion will spread."

Churchill, in Washington with his blueprint for action, spoke of preparing "for the liberation of the captive countries . . . to enable the conquered populations to revolt . . . to release the fury of rebellion."

A few blocks from Churchill in the White House, preparations were already underway. A BSC pawn inside the French Embassy had started a process of corrosion that would eat into Fortress Europe.

Part Five

AN ORIGINAL AND SINISTER TOUCH

"There is required for the composition of the great commander not only massive commonsense and reasoning power, not only imagination, but also an element of legerdemain, an original and sinister touch, which leaves the enemy puzzled as well as beaten. There are many kinds of maneuvers in war, some only of which take place upon the battlefield."

—Winston S. Churchill, *The World Crisis*
(written between World Wars I and II)

"In the high ranges of Secret Service work the actual facts in many cases were in every respect equal to the most fantastic inventions of romance and melodrama. Tangle within tangle, plot and counter-plot, ruse and treachery, cross and double-cross, true agent, false agent, double agent, gold and steel, the bomb, the dagger and the firing party, were interwoven in many a texture so intricate as to be incredible and yet true."

—Winston S. Churchill, as quoted by Ian Fleming
in a letter to Sir William Stephenson

35

THE VICHY FRENCH ran their own Gestapo and intelligence services from the embassy in Washington, demonstrating how the Nazis were most effective in disguise. The French offshore islands were used to refuel enemy submarines roaming the Atlantic in search of unarmed merchantmen. In December 1941, the French Gestapo was blackmailing a technician to tap the vital cable from the United States to Britain that passed through the fishing islands of St. Pierre and Miquelon. These islands inside the Gulf of St. Lawrence were linked physically with Canada. They took dictation, legally, from Vichy France. Plans were afoot to transmit from the islands the latest details on the big convoys that assembled nearby at Halifax.

Stephenson's agents reported that the majority of islanders were anti-Nazi supporters of the Free French led by General Charles de Gaulle. Ten days after Pearl Harbor, the Free French gathered a small invasion fleet—against the wishes of Canadian and U.S. diplomats. On Christmas Eve they occupied the two islands. There was an uproar. Cordell Hull took the same legalistic view as Ottawa: Hitler could use De Gaulle's action to justify overt German moves against other French territories.

"We had heard such cries of alarm before," said Stephenson. "Before the Germans took Austria, the Sudetenland, Poland . . . It was the same old fear of provoking Hitler, and the same old delusion that if you placate a tyrant he'll leave you be."

The hidden cause of the diplomatic uproar was the realization by the Canadian Prime Minister, Mackenzie King, and by the U.S. State Department that clandestine forces were making policies that might affect foreign relations—and in Canada could cause a political crisis between the French-speaking population and the rest of the country. President Roosevelt called the incident a teapot tempest. Secretly, he approved. He had made the calculated but controversial decision to recognize Vichy France because it provided a window into Nazi Europe. He had received from Stephenson a report on the Vichy Embassy, the suspicion being that members of the staff could be assigned to Washington to serve Germany, not France. One BSC undercover agent, who had successfully infiltrated the Embassy, reported a new arrival from Vichy as confiding: "Our prime objective is to establish the fact that Britain betrayed France and is therefore the real enemy. Every means at our disposal must be used to convince American officialdom and the American public that this is true."

Vichy began with certain advantages. "There already existed a secret police body in the United States and Canada whose duty was to report on supporters of General de Gaulle or the former French Government," noted the BSC Papers. "These Vichy agents burgled offices and homes where they might find lists of anti-Nazis, and used every means to prevent their countrymen from helping build the secret armies. In Nazi fashion, they threatened reprisals against relatives in both German-occupied France and the Vichy zone. They shanghaied French sailors trying to join Free French forces. They met all new French arrivals in North America with threats tailored to the occasion. . . . Penetration of the Embassy itself by BSC agents helped weaken the effectiveness of this formidable Fifth Column."

The full extent of Vichy French activity on Nazi Germany's behalf has been documented. The Vichy Government was believed to be using as couriers to Washington certain diplomats, officials, envoys, and members of their families. They could claim diplomatic immunity when passing through control points, which meant their baggage was not searched. Such a distinction held certain obvious advantages for the traditionally inviolable transmission of documents.

Vichy had created a French intelligence service with links in Canada. In November 1940, one of the couriers traveled to New York and boarded a Pan Am 314 flying boat. As the Clipper lumbered into the air, BSC signaled Bermuda that the courier was carrying papers inside wrappers still stamped with the old French Foreign Office identification. This economy cost Vichy dearly.

In Bermuda, the courier was invited to join passengers ashore while the plane refueled. British investigators extracted the packages and claimed that since they were destined for Paris, an enemy-occupied city, they must be confiscated. The courier protested: the parcels were destined for Vichy.

"But the Quai d'Orsay is in Paris," said one of the control officers, displaying an envelope with the French Quai d'Orsay Foreign Office label.

"Do you know who I am?" demanded the courier.

"Yes."

"This is an outrage against diplomatic protocol. . . ."

While the argument proceeded, the Clipper's cargo was ransacked. The courier's diplomatic papers were opened and photographed, then replaced. The flying boat was delayed overnight. When it left the next day, the courier had his paperss and an official apology, but Bermuda had all the evidence Stephenson needed of Vichy duplicity.

"Vichy was proposing methods by which the French people would join Germany to share the spoils, being convinced Britain was finished and American Big Business ready to work with German cartels in exploiting the vast new European markets in prospect," said Stephenson. "Vichy offered Germany the French colonies as sources of raw materials and as military bases. French industry would be geared to the Ruhr's war machine.

"French power and influence, thrown into the German side of the scales, could fatally damage us. Pragmatic Americans might see the second-largest fleet in Europe, the military and industrial resources, the considerable numbers of airmen and machines, and the rich colonies that stretched from Africa to Saigon as a French contribution to a German empire with which it would be wise to do business. Vichy proposed that French airmen fly alongside Germans in the assaults upon Britain. The French had already carried out bombing raids against British bases at Gibraltar. Enormous reserves of gold—the bulk of the French Treasury, worth in today's terms $150 billion—were stowed in the island of Martinique off the American coast and might be used to purchase American goods on Germany's behalf."

Vichy's commercial attractions had been presented to influential Americans, according to the reports carried by the courier. If France joined Germany in a purely economic sense, the possibilities for American business were staggering. "In aluminum alone," stated one of the reports, "France is the major supplier for aircraft production."

Vichy's courier also carried a letter from Jean-Louis Musa, a citizen of the United States, to the most powerful German in Paris, Otto Abetz, who had been Ribbentrop's spy there before the occupation and was attached to the staff of the German military authority. Abetz had been insinuated into the Paris situation to save Vichy's pride by providing a means of negotiating on a quasi-diplomatic level, as if between equals, rather than as conqueror and victim.

Musa was working for Abetz. One of his jobs in Washington was that of aide to a Vichy Envoy. The other was director of the French intelligence service. His American citizenship enabled him to move around North America with a freedom denied the diplomat. He supervised erection of powerful transmitters on the French island of St. Pierre, supposedly as a business enterprise. A BSC investigation disclosed that he had returned to the United States just before the Nazi conquest of Paris to perform such transactions on behalf of French firms run, behind the scenes, by German cartels. He reported to Abetz on the preparation of American opinion for French entry into a "consolidated Europe," the euphemism for a fascist union.

The Vichy French were a formidable threat in the Western Hemisphere. Distinguished French intellectuals argued the German case cleverly and confusingly. German commercial propositions were given polish by Vichy financiers, which helped diminish American confidence in the small and shrinking British market. A sizable part of Canada's population was French. Some already resented "fighting the war for Britain."

The subtle dangers were exemplified by André Maurois, one of many who turned upon their former friends. The BSC Papers put the situation bluntly: "His sojourn in the United States was distinguished for his systematic and subtle attempts to sabotage American good will toward Britain. His previous record gave him a ready-made and receptive public. He had protested his undying devotion to Britain to the Queen before his departure for America where he thereupon told all who would listen that Britain had no chance of survival whatsoever, that assisting her was tantamount to handing the Nazis those arms required for defense against Japan. He arrived in New York in the autumn of 1940 and lived lavishly at the Ritz Towers. He was later accused by de Gaulle of being a deserter and Maurois wisely decided to remain in the United States. . . . It is to be hoped that his record will not be forgotten in the years to come."

"A woman agent under the direction of BSC in New York accomplished the most important work that opened the way back into France and ultimately into Germany," noted the BSC Papers. "She had a soft soothing voice which doubtless in itself inspired confidences. Her appeal to her victims was in the first place intellectual. The discovery of her physical attraction came later as an intoxicating realization.

"The powerful hold she exercised over the worldly wise men whose secrets she sought was based on sex. But she had many other qualities. She was widely travelled and understood well the psychology of Europeans. She had a keen incisive brain and was an accurate reporter. She was extremely courageous,

341

often asking to run risks we could not allow. She was paid little more than her living expenses although her value to Britain and ultimately to her native America is incalculable. Her cover name of CYNTHIA was known to perhaps three persons at most."

This most exotic of lady spies, Minneapolis-born daughter of a U.S. Marine Corps major and Cora Wells, whose father was a Minnesota state senator, first attracted the close attention of Stephenson in the winter of 1937. CYNTHIA was twenty-seven and married to a British diplomat, Arthur Pack, who had been transferred to Warsaw. In the year that followed, CYNTHIA formed a series of liaisons with top-ranking members of Poland's Foreign Service. Her husband was away a great deal and he was frequently ill. Any young wife in Poland on the eve of war was never lacking for distraction. This one could hardly fail to win lovers. She was a striking girl: bright auburn hair, large green eyes, one brow arched in challenge, a stubborn cleft in her chin, and a slender yet voluptuous figure. Polish officers who met her at parties spoke of that high-spirited American girl who found her English husband dull and boring. She was said to have shown great bravery in the Spanish Civil War, helping political refugees from both sides to escape. The gossips claimed that she required the most exquisite food and wine, followed by several hours of intense intellectual intercourse before she could be lured into bed, where she would make it all worthwhile.

What the gossips did not suspect was that British intelligence was the chief beneficiary of her charms. She was in a position to help the understaffed SIS at a crucial moment in history. Poland's Secret Service was preparing for a war that its politicians felt they could avoid. The future manipulators of ULTRA were looking for details of the Enigma coding machine adapted for Nazi security services. Polish engineers worked on the new Enigma models, in which the Polish Foreign Minister, Jozef Beck, was thought to be interested. Colonel Beck was on good terms with Nazis in Berlin. Beck's confidential aide was one of CYNTHIA's lovers.

Following a procedure that was to become familiar, she persuaded him first to talk and later to give her documents from Beck's office, which were copied and returned. CYNTHIA never knew the contribution they made to success in the search for the ULTRA secret. In fact, she died knowing nothing of the vast ULTRA establishment at Bletchley. She once remarked: "I discovered how easy it was to make highly trained, professionally close-mouthed patriots give away secrets in bed, and I swore to close my ears to everything confidential on our side. The greatest joy is a man and a woman together. Making love allows a discharge of all those private innermost thoughts that have accumulated. In this sudden flood, everything is released. Everything. I just never dared to learn our own secrets. . . ."

Foreign Minister Beck's aide took CYNTHIA with him on confidential missions to Prague and Berlin. She learned that the Polish Biuro Szyfrow (cipher bureau) had possession of some keys to German Army cryptograms. This reinforced earlier information that three Polish mathematicians in the bureau, Jerzy Rozycki, Henryk Zygalski, and Mademoiselle Marian Rejewski had been working on the Heydrich-Enigmas. Some of her material doubtless duplicated details from other sources, but Stephenson always felt that she contributed a great deal to the vital statistics that were required for a machine that later, as part of the ULTRA system, became the first modern computer, nicknamed "Colossus." Being an electronics breakthrough, it came within Stephenson's own scientific sphere. By the time the future chief cryptologist of Bletchley flew to Warsaw for a sample of the Heydrich-Enigma, in the summer of 1939, CYNTHIA had been moved out of harm's way. Her affairs were coming to light, and the British had to stop any investigation, however private and personal. Rumors were deliberately circulated that she had been sent back to London because the British Ambassador thought she leaked British secrets to pro-Nazi diplomats.

Foreign affairs of a sexual nature were the rule in Europe. Her husband was attached to another woman, and was posted to South America. If he guessed that

343

it was more on account of his wife's usefulness than his, he never acknowledged it. The year war broke out in Europe, CYNTHIA was needed to work among pro-Nazi politicians in the Western Hemisphere. The weightiest German influence was in Chile. CYNTHIA had lived there four years as a young girl. She was fluent in Spanish and in the local dialects, as, indeed, she was fluent in German and French. David Kahn, in *The Codebreakers,* later said that "she reestablished contact with British intelligence on arrival in South America and shortly before the war broke out in Europe."* In fact, she had been under Stephenson's direction since the Enigma coup. Her complaisant husband made no secret of regarding her as useful to his own career. The British Foreign Office was never comfortable in the company of SIS, or, later, the Baker Street Irregulars, but when higher authority intervened, the dullest diplomat could find himself shuffled into an agreeable position where his other talents or connections served an unexpected purpose. So it was with Arthur Pack. He faded gracefully from the scene. The fall of France in the summer of 1940 made survival more important than saving face. CYNTHIA was told to report to New York.

Stephenson needed someone to work on Italian and French diplomats in Washington. He had the power to bring in the best agents from anywhere, and he did. His preference was for enthusiastic amateurs. They were unlikely to be on enemy files. They were free from careerist timidity. CYNTHIA's work in Warsaw had been brilliant. She displayed good sense in heeding a recall before she was found out—which indicated a strong feeling of confidence, since many agents are afraid of being thought afraid, and consequently take needless risks. She had a spectacular

---

* David Kahn, who describes himself as an "amateur cryptologist," holds a Ph.D. degree from Oxford, was a newspaperman, and is an associate professor of journalism at New York University. He is a past president of the American Cryptogram Association and of the New York Cipher Society. He has written numerous articles and a celebrated book. "Kahn's *The Codebreakers* is indispensable to the serious student of cryptology," INTREPID wrote in 1975.

record of seductions among well-placed men, including an admiral who was now in Washington as Italian naval attaché. She could move easily in the unreal atmosphere of Washington at peace. Embassies faced each other across neutral streets while their denizens reported back to chieftains confronting each other as enemies. Cocktail parties were miniature battle-fields. Dining rooms became hotbeds of intrigue. CYNTHIA was writing for British publications, she said, calling herself Elizabeth Thorpe and making no secret of her sympathies. It was known that she had left Chile in August 1940 and that her widowed mother lived in Washington. Elizabeth Thorpe was intended to lure both enemies and potential defectors.

CYNTHIA was established in a discreet two-story house rented for her by BSC through a third party. She had chosen 3327 O Street, in fashionable George-town, because it combined charm and a suggestion of wealth without being manifestly beyond the means of a free-lance reporter. She had "tried finger exercises" on a few nondescript local politicians and then snared her old admirer, Admiral Alberto Lais, whom she had known in prewar Paris.

Lais was a short, handsome, middle-aged man with a large family, diminishing hopes of making new conquests, and an expanding desire to make the best of what little time was left him. When CYNTHIA first called, reminding him of their previous friendship, he seemed alarmed. But, perhaps reacting to her per-suasive, almost hypnotic voice, he called her back a few days later. He was clearly under the spell. They began meeting in secret. She told him that she was separated from her English husband and had resumed using her family name. He confided that he was the custodian of a complete set of Italian naval ciphers, and doubted Italy's future in the Axis. She said frankly that she had close friends in U.S. Naval Intelligence and told him of plans for an Anglo-American liber-ation of Europe. Incredibly, Lais let her persuade him to have the cipher and code books removed for micro-filming—an act for which, he was assured, the U.S. Navy would be forever grateful. Even the stolid BSC historians, participants in many of these operations, uttered a stiff cry of outrage. "It seems fantastic that a man of his experience and seniority who was by instinct, training and conviction a patriotic officer, should have been so enfeebled by passion. . . ."

The Italian ciphers helped the British Navy outfox and eventually dominate the much superior Italian Navy in the Mediterranean. Admiral Lais having served his purpose, CYNTHIA disposed of him; he was declared *persona non grata* and sent home. Details of the Italian Embassy's direction of pro-Nazi subversive activities in U.S. ports, she gave to the FBI.

CYNTHIA was resting one afternoon in May 1941 when the maid announced a caller. She found the visitor standing at a window in her library, staring down onto O Street. He was a small man with a dry and surprisingly powerful hand-clasp. "He introduced himself as Mister Williams," she recalled later. "He sat and watched me make the martinis. . . . I glanced at him once or twice. He had remarkable eyes that seemed to change color. I tried to make light conversation. He hardly replied. . . . His movements were all economical. He gave me an odd sense of enormous power lurking behind the polite smile. For the very first time in my life, I was not altogether self-assured in the presence of a man.

"He had said he was 'from the New York office.' This put me on guard. I used to go to New York once a week. The routine never varied. I stayed at the same hotel on Madison and awaited MARION or MISTER HOWARD. They debriefed me, and gave me assignments, and acted as paymasters. They were my only contacts. So I had no way of telling who this 'Mister Williams' might be.

"I was worried about agents-provocateurs. The FBI was becoming troublesome and was now trying to figure out my game. I knew nothing then about squabbles and lines of command. I didn't want to know. It was enough to be told to deal with the two BSC contacts and—from time to time—anyone to whom they referred me.

"It became obvious that Mister Williams was no ordinary man. He looked about forty-five, with the rugged handsomeness which is improved by a small flaw—in his case, what seemed a scar that pulled up one corner of his mouth. This gave him a lopsided grin.

"He didn't waste time. He referred to a couple of things I'd done, in a way that told me he *must* be from the New York office. He dropped a couple of remarks that indicated he knew *all* my background—one I remember was a reference to when Cora, my mother, studied at the Sorbonne in Paris. It was a discreet little warning that I had been thoroughly investigated.

"You know the first time as a child that you suspect the man behind the Father Christmas beard is your father? That's how I felt that wet afternoon as darkness fell. I began to tease a little. When he said my work had been appreciated, I asked if that was his opinion—or the Chief's. 'Oh, the Chief,' he said, twinkling. 'What's he like, the Chief?' 'Terrible chap.'

"And you know how, for a while after you've guessed who Father Christmas really is, you go on playing the game. Well . . . he knew that I knew that he guessed that I had guessed 'Mister Williams' was Bill Stephenson. But part of the game is never to verbalize delicate matters. If it hasn't been said, the pretense can be maintained. This may sound kindergarten stuff. But it has real value, psychologically. For instance, most agents are highly motivated and honest. It makes their lives easier if they can to some extent deceive themselves.

"He was a master at this avoidance of embarrassing you with too much knowledge. And yet, when he did tell you something, you knew it was for a purpose—and, perhaps more important, it was a token of confidence in you.

"He said he had an extremely difficult job for me. . . . 'The New York office needs certain things' was the way he put it. And I knew he meant London, Churchill, the secret armies needed them. And what they needed was all correspondence, personal letters, and plain-text cables between the Vichy French and Europe.

"He acknowledged the impossibility while he made

it seem possible. This is a quality in him, I realize now, which frightens the timid and challenges the bold. It filters out the recruits who would never make it. You either respond to him, or you sense the dangers implicit in pursuing the conversation and you back off. He gives you that option. No melodramatic statement of mission and a call for volunteers—none of that stuff. Just a quiet, calm voice talking so indirectly that if anyone listens, they have nothing concrete to quote in court. And you let him know if you're willing to go ahead by simply continuing the conversation. And if you're scared and want out—you have a dozen opportunities to pick up a thread that leads you out of the conversational maze."

Stephenson had come to satisfy himself that CYNTHIA could pursue a prolonged assignment in gossip-ridden Washington. He found a young American matron who had developed her talents. Her personal standards were above reproach. She was what is known as a self-starter, able to drive herself without orders from above, willing to risk sudden improvisations, resourceful and ingenious. She had none of the hangups usual among intelligent young women in a male-dominated city. Her critics, scornful of her promiscuity, would have been surprised by her personal code of honor. She had a powerful devotion to the cause, and she needed it. In May 1941, when she began to work on the Vichy French, the hazards were many. She was an American. Her homeland was not at war. She could hardly claim police protection if her enemies tried to kill her.

The two critical issues on which she would have to focus were the fate of the Vichy fleet, which could drastically change the balance of naval power, and secret French funds that helped finance Nazi operations in the Americas. She began by requesting an interview with a senior diplomat. The press officer was a former naval fighter pilot, Captain Charles Brousse, who suggested a preliminary meeting. Obviously, this was to screen CYNTHIA. She found Brousse amiable and *simpático*. He told her straight away, almost in self-defense, that he had served on the joint

348

Anglo-French Air Intelligence Board prior to the German conquest.

She had the perception to pick out this item from the odds and ends Brousse revealed about himself, and on her next weekly "shopping trip" to New York, passed the information through MARION to Stephenson. Within twenty-four hours, it was established that Brousse had been with Air Intelligence in Paris. It would be useful to learn if he retained his old friendliness for British airmen.

CYNTHIA saw a Vichy spokesman after he returned from an interview at the State Department. CYNTHIA reported to BSC. "He was full of contempt for American vulgarity and lack of civilized manners. Americans did not comprehend the subtleties of European politics. How dare they judge France when they themselves had never suffered invasion?"

Vichy's man appeared to find his visitor disarming. She was American, without doubt, but she had been exposed to French culture in France itself. She would understand the sophistication of Vichy policy. It was not *collaboration*. It was survival.

"If your car is in the ditch, you turn to the person who can help you put it back on the road. Our future requires that sort of cooperation with Germany." The man warmed to his theme. France, after all, was a nation governed by intellect, not by crude emotions. Her accommodation with Germany was not surrender. A great consolidation of Europe was in progress. Naturally, some of the baser elements would suffer. Of course, the British were jealous. They continued the war to spite France and to protect their empire.

He continued in this vein for two and a half hours. When CYNTHIA left, her respondent expressed a desire to see her again. She flirted a little. With elegant courtesy he escorted her through the courtyard. Captain Brousse became competitive, lingered on the Embassy steps, and outdid his superior in flattery.

The next day CYNTHIA received red roses from

Brousse and a discreet little card from her respondent. The flowers paved the way for lunch. The card was an invitation to an Embassy party.

Lunch was a long affair and ended in the house on O Street. Charles Brousse had been married three times, and the proximity of his latest wife gave piquancy to the affair—and protective secrecy for CYNTHIA.

She played the role of mistress so well that Brousse paid her the highest compliment. She would have been the ideal wife of an ambassador, provided he was the ambassador. He had social and cultural attributes far superior to his official seniors, did she not agree? CYNTHIA agreed.

36

CAPTAIN BROUSSE WAS understandably bitter about the British preventive attack on the French fleet at Oran in 1940. Admiral Sir James Somerville, commanding Force H, which sank the French warships, wrote later: "It was the biggest political blunder of modern times. . . . The French were furious that we did not trust them to prevent the ships falling into German hands. . . . I'd sooner that happened than we should have to kill a lot of our former allies. We all feel thoroughly dirty and ashamed. . . ."

What had led to this drastic action? CYNTHIA, trying to coax Brousse into co-operation, felt she needed some answers and asked for a briefing. In her personal notes, which became part of the BSC Papers, she wrote:

"I had been in South America when France fell. Naturally I knew the general course of events. I never understood, until BSC briefed me, how desperately hard Churchill struggled to keep the French fighting. He had just become Prime Minister when the Germans swarmed across the French frontiers. In War Cabinet sessions on May 27 and 28, 1940, he learned that Lord Halifax, then still foreign minister, was *exploring the possibilities of peace through Italian mediation.** This persistent stupidity terrified Churchill and Stephenson more than anything. This had been their chief enemy for so long—this pathetic belief that somehow you could negotiate peace with Hitler. A puppet French state would deceive Britishers and Americans into thinking you could collaborate with a German empire.

"There was a frantic period when Churchill tried everything to stop France making a separate peace, even to manipulating President Roosevelt and presenting his statements as evidence of imminent American intervention.

"There was one exchange, when Stephenson got from the President a guarded message that he was impressed by the French declarations of their intent to continue fighting (this was just before Premier Paul Reynaud packed in). Churchill seized on this, wanted to publish it, called the French and said it was close to an American declaration of war. He signalled Roosevelt his belief that 'this magnificent message might play a decisive part in turning the course of history.'

"The President backed off, knowing Churchill's impetuosity could ruin everything—unseat the President, fuel up the isolationists. He wired Churchill specifically refusing to grant him the right to publish anything with regard to his private communications. This

---

* Churchill has been accused of employing the devices of *suggestio falsi* and *suppressio veri* in his history of World War II to enhance his own standing. On the contrary, he concealed information that might redound to his own credit in order to protect those who might be considered his enemies. He carefully omitted reference to Lord Halifax's near-sabotage of the war effort, which became apparent to the public many years later with the opening of the Public Record Office archive. The BSC Papers and Stephenson's files and recollections make clear the size of the appeasement movement in Britain. Halifax replaced Lothian as ambassador to the United States in 1941, and gave Stephenson his full support once the die was cast.

caused consternation in the War Cabinet. Stephenson had to explain the complexities of American politics while Europe fell around British ears. It can't have been easy.

"It didn't help to have the American Ambassador in France, Bill Bullitt, reporting to Washington that the British were holding back help in order to improve their own bargaining position [and after the armistice that] 'the physical and moral defeat of the new French leaders is so complete that they accept the fate of becoming a province of Nazi Germany. . . . They hope England will be rapidly and completely defeated.'

"This inside knowledge of Vichy French hatred was what powered Bill Stephenson, of course. He had heard Churchill imploring Marshal Pétain not to hand over the French fleet to the Germans. It was the most violent conversation Churchill ever conducted. Defeated, he told Stephenson 'We are faced with total French collapse. The total collapse of civilization is inevitable unless we put up a successful defense of these islands.'

"But that defense could be undermined by appeasement. This was what he wanted to make Americans understand. The Vichy French could destroy us all by encouraging the peace-chasers—what Churchill called the damned benighted bishops and Quakers, capitalists and communists, cowards and cranks, peers and plain dyspeptics. . . ."

Captain Brousse seemed convinced by the skillful arguments of his new mistress—yes, he agreed, the British did have justification for attacking the French warships. Even now, the French fleet could become a German instrument of war. It was no coincidence that a French admiral, Georges Robert, governed the island of Martinique in Vichy's name. The island lay off the northeast shoulder of Latin America, on the outer perimeter of the Caribbean. Quite apart from its usefulness to German U-boats, and as a relay station for German intelligence, it served agents of the Foreign Organization of the German National Socialist Party (Ausland Organization NSDAP) under Gauleiter

Ernst Wilhelm Bohle, whose principal work was conducted now among Germans in South America.

And Brousse revealed another reason why Martinique was so handy: there were fifty million ounces of French gold hidden in an old fort there, gold that belonged rightfully to the French people but could be spent, if Vichy continued to dictate what was right for the people, to promote pro-Nazi interests in the Americas.

The gold could also buy the necessary raw materials for war weapons. If Gauleiter Bohle got his hands on it, he would have the means to tap the rich mineral resources of South America. The secret armies and their suppliers needed large sums of foreign currency. Often it had to be delivered in small-denomination American dollars. These had to be purchased in the United States. But with what? Martinique's gold offered an obvious solution to the bankrupt British.

A coded signal left New York for London:

OPPORTUNITY ARISES OF ORGANIZING REVISED SCHEME TO RELEASE VICHY GOLD. OKAY?

The reply was equally terse:

PROCEED PROVIDED BRITISH CONNECTION DISAVOWED.

Goldfinger told James Bond about his plans to rob Fort Knox:

Mr. Bond, all my life I have been in love. I have been in love with gold. I love its color, its brilliance, its divine heaviness. I love the texture of gold, that soft slimness that I have learned to gauge so accurately by touch that I can estimate the fineness of a bar within one karat. And I love the warm tang it exudes when I melt it down into a true golden syrup. But above all, Mr. Bond, I love the power that gold alone gives to its owner—the magic of controlling energy, exacting labor, fulfilling one's every wish and whim and, when need be, purchasing bodies, minds, even souls.

Goldfinger, like much of Ian Fleming's writing, was not pure invention. It was inspired by Stephenson's plan to rob Martinique of the gold that could give BSC the power to energize the revolution in Europe.

A loyal Frenchman swam the channel, thick with barracuda, between Martinique and the British-held island of St. Lucia with the intention of eventually joining the Free French of General de Gaulle. He gave an astonishing account of how the gold had been delivered by the French naval cruiser *Emile Bertin* to the capital, Fort-de-France, was loaded onto the ammunition hoists of the old fort nearby and lowered into vaults for storing shells. The stronghold was familiar to the British, who had fought back and forth with the French for control of these islands, so strategically located, in earlier wars for America's riches.

A scheme was devised for stealing the gold. A Martiniquais, Jacques Vauzanges, of the French Deuxième Bureau (Military Intelligence) had joined BSC in New York. He was a swashbuckling figure who proposed that he return to Martinique and lead a rebellion against Vichy. The British equipped him with radio and codes. The Vichy French issued him with travel papers on the strength of his past loyalties and his present claim to have become a businessman.

Stephenson had strong arguments for backing a coup. The island harbored a squadron of the French fleet, the aircraft carrier *Béarn* and some 120 planes—a dangerously unknown quantity and the largest combined fighting force in the region. Even without help from these Vichy units, the Germans made good use of Martinique. In a single month, twenty British-run ships were sunk by U-boats around the island. If Germany took over completely, there was also the gold waiting to finance Nazi operations and buy strategic goods in South America.

Vauzanges had some support among French naval commanders in Martinique. He persuaded other Frenchmen to join them in escaping with naval units to the Canadian port of Halifax. The gold would be carried in one of the warships. But the fall in British fortunes, coupled with resentment over the British attack on French warships at Oran, sapped the plotters' resolve. By mid-1941, Martinique was firmly committed to Vichy French policies, and Vauzanges abandoned his schemes after a row with the potential rebels, who feared that they might be guilty of betrayal and desertion.

Churchill queried BSC: Was the whole fifty million ounces of gold still there?

One of Stephenson's experts made an assessment. He was Colonel Louis Franck, one of the world's leading specialists in bullion and arbitrage, and descended from a long line of Belgian government bankers. From New York he followed every financial transaction that might benefit his enemies. He could see no proof that the Martinique gold was yet infiltrating the open markets. But he also reckoned it had the purchasing power of something like one hundred times the fixed price that kept the book value down to $3 billion, an unreal figure.

Was there some way of getting the gold out? It alone was enough to finance the secret armies that would some day overthrow the occupiers of his homeland.

Franck suggested an alternative: "Take custody of it, then use it against loans to buy American arms."

"That's the general idea," said Stephenson. "There's a small problem of taking custody."

They were sitting in his office high above Manhattan. In that remote setting, any idea seemed possible.

"Neutralize the governor of the French West Indies," said Franck. "Then prevent any movement out of Martinique. In effect, that puts the gold under our control." He ended reasonably, "You don't ask to see each bar of gold in Fort Knox each time you buy U.S. dollars."

Stephenson leaned forward suddenly. "I think you've got something. We make sure the gold stays in Martinique, but demonstrate we've got the power to take it. In those circumstances they might even pay us in the State Department *not* to take it. . . ." He pressed a buzzer. "Slip out the back," he told Franck. "I've someone I can use for this—best you don't meet."

The newcomer was the astrologer Louis de Wohl, shipped over from London to become a BSC "magician" in the Jasper Maskelyne world of illusions. Built up in the press by news stories and a "Stars Foretell" column, he was fed enough accurate information so that his prophecies about the course of the war were validated. An ever-growing audience was becoming convinced of his supernatural powers. He had been touring American cities as "the famous Hungarian astrologer" and was now back in New York.

"Cancel further engagements," Stephenson told this stout little man with the high-domed head and heavy-frame glasses. "Do a bit of honest fortune telling. We'll be in touch."

CYNTHIA's reports from Washington were examined with renewed care, especially those in which the Vichy Embassy commented on the West Indies. Then Wohl wrote in his syndicated column that a prominent Vichy collaborator serving in some ramshackle tropical island would shortly suffer a "stroke of the sun" and go *maboul*.

A week later, a senior French naval officer escaped from Martinique and told reporters in Miami that Admiral Robert had gone mad. The French Governor was indeed ill with sunstroke. Wohl's credibility rose; the BSC rumor factories found a receptive audience for gossip that the Free French might take over the island. These hints and rumors unnerved the garrison. Policy became less pro-German. The gold was as good as in British custody, because the island was now under constant British naval and BSC surveillance. Adding to the pressure, U.S. Admiral John W. Greenslade flew over to see Robert. While the United States would never dream of interfering, Washington was watching the fate of the base and its warships and warplanes. Back at the White House, Greenslade reported that even if the Bank of England went "bust" the British could pay their debts "one way or another."

It occasionally happened that a Washington bureaucrat inquired about how exactly the British proposed to cover their borrowings. Stephenson had prepared for just such an inquiry by drawing up detailed and convincing plans for seizing Martinique with the help of agents he had placed there. Whenever the possibility of such an operation was mentioned, the State Department raised violent objections, remembering de Gaulle's seizure of the islands of St. Pierre and Miquelon and the subsequent furore. Then BSC gracefully withdrew, a fresh loan in hand. "It was," commented a BSC historian, "an exercise in constructive blackmail."

37

THE MARTINIQUE MANEUVERS were helped by CYNTHIA's service of Vichy plain-text telegrams. Captain Charles Brousse, her source, must have been in an agony of indecision. Having worked with Anglo-French Air Intelligence before France collapsed, and being an admirer of British resistance, his emotions were not hard to imagine when he handled Telegram 4093, of June 15, 1941, from Admiral François Darlan, Vichy's Minister of Marine. The telegram required details of repairs performed on British ships in U.S. dockyards; it was one of hundreds inspired by German intelligence.

Vichy diplomats were in a position to sink great battleships. Although in peacetime they might have no more naval influence than a market-town mayor rowing across *le petit lac* for the annual gala, they now could inflict destruction almost as effectively as Darlan, who passed on information from Embassy sources in Washington to the Germans and was more passionately anti-British than most collaborators. Telegrams 1236-1237 from Vichy's embassy in Washington disclosed that the British carrier *Illustrious* was at Norfolk for repair, the battleship *Repulse* at Philadelphia, and the cruiser *Malaya* at New York. The subsequent sinking of the *Repulse* was, said Churchill, "the most direct shock I ever suffered."

The telegrams must have seemed revolting enough at the time to Captain Brousse. His tortured conscience displayed to Stephenson the kind of psychological disturbance that would soon shake all Europe despite the dictators' controls. Was Brousse a traitor for resisting Vichy's requests for information? He suffered from the same confusions of loyalty that perplexed the French garrison in Martinique. Fortress Europe was full of such people, reconsidering their loyalties.

Vichy decided in July to dispense with the services of Captain Brousse as press officer but keep him as an aide paid from secret funds. This meant a cut in Brousse's salary. It was a good time for CYNTHIA to suggest she might find ways to augment it. Brousse agreed to take a weekly fee for *daily* reports on events inside Vichy's embassy. This produced a multitude of new leads. BSC in New York found itself with more investigations than it could manage. One example indicates the sudden snowballing of work.

Vichy's funds were closely watched, since they worked for Nazi purposes. The Embassy's financial staff and other commercial posts in the United States were outlets for money to pay agents, and inlets for economic intelligence useful to Berlin. In the French Consulate in New York, the financial attaché was particularly active. His secretary was a bright young woman, married but not without outside interests. Because she is still alive, still married, and with a large family, she remains Mme. Cadet, the name used in the BSC Papers. A BSC agent was given the agreeable task of having an affair with her. Soon she was bringing him copies of correspondence that confirmed that Nazi sympathizers existed in Quebec. This was explosive stuff in Canada, where the federal government was touchy about its independence of Britain— and often went to ludicrous lengths to demonstrate it. A direct appeal to the government in Ottawa was likely to be neglected. Like Roosevelt, the Canadian Prime Minister had to put national unity first. A separate section of BSC was created to work with Canadian security on the threat posed by this fifth column. Mme. Cadet was later transferred to Washington, where she provided another BSC agent with documents, rubber stamps, and blank passports, invaluable in "papering" agents. She saved many lives by disclosing that secret marks were made on Vichy visas, indicating their validity and the degree of reliability of the holder. Station M's forgery experts in Toronto were duly grateful.

CYNTHIA had now moved out of the Georgetown house into a room at the Wardman Park Hotel, where Brousse lived with his wife. "It made things tidier all around," she wrote later. "Also, this was a period when the FBI were becoming altogether too curious about me. Quite unconsciously, because they knew nothing of my work for BSC, they could foul my lines. . . ."

She had to drop one of her contacts, the French-American controlling the Vichy Gestapo, Jean-Louis Musa; a warning had been passed along that Musa was already under the surveillance of the FBI. Hoover's men knew nothing about CYNTHIA's true role, and they might regard her as another Nazi agent.

Musa was being paid $300 a month plus $200 for expenses by the Vichy embassy—a lot of money in those days, though not a princely sum. His business activities were also primed by Nazi funds. A French BSC agent was put to work, equipped with an international-trading corporation in New York, a cramped office and a brass plaque, and an impressive file of correspondence, all of it painstakingly composed and counterfeited by Station M. An accidental encounter with Musa, a couple of drinks in a bar, a few indiscretions, and he was suddenly alert and interested in the prospect of a little private enterprise. The BSC man in a burst of "drunken" candor confided that he loathed Americans, loved Germans, and wished to hell he'd stayed in France to serve the new fascist union. Musa confessed himself pleased to hear these sentiments. In that case, said the BSC agent, would Musa like to go into business with him? He could provide an office and secretarial help—both scarce in New York. Musa agreed. It seemed an opportunity to enlarge his undercover activities.

Musa, vain as well as greedy, believed the BSC agent's expressions of delight upon acquiring such a resourceful partner. Musa talked to him about Vichy;

about the necessity to be realistic with regard to Hitler; about the importance of remembering he was a Frenchman. "After all," said Musa, "I may be an American citizen but I am French at heart." He was flattered but not surprised when this new friend declared that Musa had helped him straighten out his own thinking and that he would like to be in on spreading the Vichy gospel. Musa thus unknowingly recruited a BSC man into his camp, with results that were catastrophic for Musa. His office was bugged from top to bottom. His phone calls, correspondence, conversations, and contacts were under twenty-four-hour-a-day scrutiny—which, among other things, produced the details of a Vichy proposal to make use of St. Pierre.

It looked like a simple commercial enterprise. Western Union was to receive from the French government a long-term concession and sufficient ground in the French colony of St. Pierre to put up a radio station with transmitters powerful enough to reach anywhere in the world. Western Union's 34,000 offices in the United States would be linked by cable with the station. This meant Western Union could offer a worldwide service without depending upon rival overseas-cable companies. However, it meant a great deal more to the Nazi controllers of Europe, as Stephenson soon explained to Vincent Astor, who had been appointed a special BSC liaison officer by President Roosevelt. His special value was that the family's business interests extended into fields that provided the British with covert aid and cover. They held a controlling interest, for instance, in the St. Regis Hotel, which became the Manhattan rendezvous for Stephenson and distinguished figures like Albert Einstein, whose connection with British intelligence at that time, however peripheral, could not be advertised. (There was a certain irony in the role Lady Astor, on the British side of the family, had played as a leader of the Cliveden Set of appeasement-minded influences. Vincent directed certain British antisabotage operations and later became a captain in the U.S. Navy.)

Vincent Astor was also a director of Western Union, and in April 1941, he recommended that the seemingly harmless deal be called off. His fellow directors knew he was a confidential adviser to Roosevelt and accepted assurances that the decision was a matter of national security. The decision cost Western Union an opportunity to expand its services and greatly expand its profits. But Stephenson had produced evidence that the St. Pierre station would be used by Nazi agents to communicate through Vichy without censorship. Musa's own correspondence betrayed the real purpose of the station.

Musa tried to buy into the U.S. manufacture of the Bren submachine gun with German money. He bought forged passports and visas for German agents. He hired a defector from the British Purchasing Commission, Paul Seguin, to run a pro-Nazi newssheet. He set up the Vichy French news service, *Havas,* which distributed thinly disguised Nazi propaganda throughout the Western Hemisphere. His efforts to influence the media reached as far as Montreal, where French-language newspapers were discouraged from hiring refugee French journalists with anti-Nazi views. He was an operator whose amorality happened to find a satisfactory sponsor in fascism. He knew how to get around currency control. He did a little pimping on the side and found himself working with French girls willing to pass along information useful to Vichy's economic-intelligence unit. He had a scheme for chartering ships that would carry refugees from Europe to Mexico, returning to ports in Unoccupied France with cargoes that could not be shipped directly to Germany because of trade controls. The trouble with Musa was that he proved to be too clever by half.

Armed with evidence against him, and copies of several thousand incriminating documents on Vichy operations from other sources, Stephenson put an argument to Churchill that summer of 1941. Surely it was time to expose Vichy's perfidy? American rearmament was still halfhearted. The country was badly prepared for war, and likely to become FDR's Arsenal of Democracy too late. War-aid charities gave well-meaning Americans a comfortable sense of doing something while doing nothing. The war production program was in chaos. The U.S. armed forces lacked equipment. The troops felt futile. If the Vichy embassy was revealed as the cover for large-scale Nazi efforts to subvert the United States, Americans might be shocked into a more warlike mood.

This was fine with Churchill, then sharpening his wits for the Atlantic Charter conference with the President. The Prime Minister thought "it might be well if the President saw photostats and transcripts of documents in the case." Roosevelt duly got them. He told Stephenson: "Publicity should help our people see the danger in our midst."

Stephenson's Political-Warfare Division was preparing the publicity campaign when the Free French created a diversion. General Charles de Gaulle had been in Cairo during the Roosevelt-Churchill meeting at sea. His pride wounded, and suspicious of decisions being made behind his back, he apparently concluded that the British were about to barter away French possessions. He threatened to withdraw his Free French fighting forces from British command. Once again the French islands along America's eastern seaboard stirred controversy.

A week after Roosevelt returned from signing the Atlantic Charter with Churchill, British intelligence reports on Vichy France were leaked to the New York *Herald Tribune* and distributed through the BSC-subsidized Overseas News Agency (originally a branch of the Jewish Telegraph Agency), which serviced forty-five U.S. newspapers and a significant percentage of the U.S. ethnic press.* The series of

* The Overseas News Agency, after Stephenson's negotiations with the New York owners in April 1941, dispatched fifteen newly recruited correspondents to key foreign posts. They were all BSC agents. Another agency, Overseas Features, set up office in Rockefeller Center, complete with ticker tapes. Britanova, another news agency covering these operations, disseminated stories planted by BSC in U.S. newspapers. Czech, Italian, Polish, and Spanish foreign-language bureaus supplied news to the dozens of foreign-language newspapers published in the United States and South America. These overseas bureaus, while providing cover for BSC agents, were instructed to file for publication.

exposés accused the French Embassy in Washington of conspiracies against the nation's well-being and in support of Nazi Germany's ambitions. Although this was a well-orchestrated propaganda campaign, the facts were indisputable. They stirred a nationwide furore. VICHY AGENTS SOUGHT PLANS ran a September 4, 1941 headline in the *Herald Tribune*. TRIED TO GET BLUE-PRINTS OF WEAPON DEFENDING BRITAIN FROM INVASION. A Vichy spokesman was stung into charging that the whole affair was a "de Gaullist-Jewish-FBI-British intrigue."

If events in the Pacific had not been approaching their climax at Pearl Harbor, this might have proved to be the incident that Roosevelt told Churchill he was seeking "to get America into the war openly."

38

CYNTHIA CONTINUED HER work. The exposés did not cause any break in Washington's diplomatic relations with Vichy. Jean-Louis Musa was arrested by the FBI for failing to register as a foreign agent. BSC agents reported a curtailment of covert activities at the French Embassy. Captain Charles Brousse continued to confide to his mistress its secrets.

The climate of American public opinion had been changed dramatically by Pearl Harbor, but the Vichy French survived in Washington. CYNTHIA was told to fly to New York in March of 1942. She checked into the Ritz-Carlton Hotel, then on Madison Avenue, and was unpacking when someone knocked on the door. It was HOWARD. His request was brief: Can you get the new Vichy French naval crypto-system?

It seemed a staggering challenge: steal ciphers, code books, and superenciphering equipment from an embassy safe in a code room to which only the chief cipher officer and his assistant had access. The Vichy Foreign Ministry's orders were that the room be kept under guard night and day. Even if she broke through the security measures, somehow unlocked the code room, and finally cracked the safe, she would have to find a way of removing the bulky cipher books. It all seemed impossible. And surely the ciphers were not more important than preserving her ability to keep BSC informed on the daily traffic of telegrams to Vichy?

What CYNTHIA could not be told was that the ciphers seemed essential for the success of the plan for clearing North Africa of Axis forces in preparation for the assault on Europe. This meant intervention in French North Africa. To the British, this appeared as almost the only effective demonstration of military competence and resolve open to them in a period of disasters in every theater of the war.

She was aware of the possible moves the Nazis could make to complete their stranglehold on British marine life lines. The German Navy hoped to acquire U-boat bases in the Vichy ports of Casablanca and Dakar, on the West African coast, and to expand into the Indian Ocean through Vichy-controlled Madagascar, seriously considered by Hitler as a place to confine Europe's Jews, before he decided to liquidate them instead. Finally, the Vichy French proposed to close the Mediterranean to democratic forces by a move through Spain. She was aware, too, of Churchill's personal appeal to Roosevelt for help: "When I reflect how I have longed and prayed for the entry of the United States into the war, I find it difficult to realize how gravely our British affairs have deteriorated." Her new assignment might lift a burden from the Prime Minister, whose man at the Foreign Office, Alexander Cadogan, had written Stephenson: "Poor old Winston, feeling deeply the present situation. . . . Outlook pretty bloody."

CYNTHIA left New York with her new orders on March 10. Admiral Harold Stark, U.S. Chief of Naval Operations, had just swung his powerful support behind the proposed operation in North Africa, because French Navy forces loyal to Vichy, and secure in the

French colonies there, could be neutralized. Here, thought Stark, was the key to the Middle East, "the loss of which would be much more serious to the United States than the loss of the Far East."

CYNTHIA called Brousse when she arrived back in Washington. They met in her hotel room. She came straight to the point. "I want the naval ciphers."

The French diplomat slumped into a chair. "It's impossible."

"Perhaps. You'll have to try."

"Me?" Brousse lifted his head.

"With my help."

"But the only member of the Embassy with access to the code room is the chief cipher officer, old Benoit. He has the civil-service disease of loyalty in all circumstances."

"Let me work on him."

Brousse laughed. "On Benoit? He's forgotten what it's for. Even you could never excite him to forget his damned duty."

She went, nonetheless, to visit the chief cipher officer at home. He talked like the patriotic Frenchmen typical of the times: Marshal Pétain was chief of state, no matter what wrongs were done by Laval. It was not Benoit's job to judge policies or question superiors. Benoit was in the service of the government. Perhaps he was old-fashioned, but if governments could not depend upon total loyalty, where would it all end? In anarchy, without a doubt.

CYNTHIA nodded. She had a loyalty, too—to a principle of justice that transcended nationalism and narrow codes of discipline. She was not, she said, asking him to betray his country. On the contrary, she was appealing to his humanity. Good French patriots were dying every day fighting with the secret armies. Benoit listened courteously and then gave his answer: "The ciphers have been my responsibility. On principle, I cannot betray them. This is not a question of larger issues. My job is to protect Embassy secrets. I quarrel with the policies that the Embassy serves. But my first and only obligation is to myself as a man of honor. I cannot now give away what I protected before."

CYNTHIA put more pressure on Brousse, who fell

back on his original excuse. He was not entitled to go into the code room. Why not forget this insane scheme? CYNTHIA said no more. There was always a danger that Brousse, despite his professed disenchantment with Vichy, might alert his ambassador to this sudden interest in naval ciphers, from which the French government might reach conclusions.

Old Benoit was retired soon afterward. He was replaced by the Comte de la Grandville. CYNTHIA found that the Comte was poorly paid as a junior diplomat. His funds in France were cut off. His wife was about to produce their second child. She was a petulant young woman, aggrieved because the Comte had failed to win the rank or salary she had anticipated when marrying him. Madame sounded pragmatic. Money would take priority over fidelity: status was more important than sex on the side. On a weekend when this potentially compliant wife was away, CYNTHIA called the Comte at his home. Speaking French, she said that she had something to discuss. Her voice stroked his ego. The Comte suggested she come and talk more. She arrived within the hour. The Comte, resigned to a boring evening alone, brightened at the sight of this stunning lady in distress. When she said she would be brief, he assured her that he had all the time in the world.

CYNTHIA hung her head. "I feel ashamed. It seems so trivial . . ."

"Nothing is trivial when one is young."

"You do not remember me?"

He was mixing a drink and paused in surprise. *"Mais non . . ."*

"I called at your Embassy once. We discussed Vichy. I am disturbed by Vichy's policies—"

"Who is not?" The Comte de la Grandville sat beside her.

"Then how do you justify your job?"

"I am a career diplomat. One learns to perform one's duties. Not question one's masters."

"But your duties are performed for France."

He gave her a long look. "Is this why you came?"

She shook her head. "You know Washington is full

366

of Free French, loyal to de Gaulle. They have a great deal of money to buy help for the Resistance. I don't want their money but I would like to help."

"How?"

"They would train me and then I would be ready to parachute into Occupied France—"

"That's suicide." He rested a hand on her arm. "You would achieve nothing. Nothing."

"You think so?"

"I'm sure of it. You mustn't do it. Not because you would be on the wrong side. Because it would be the waste of a beautiful and intelligent woman."

She looked around. "You must find it difficult to lead an exciting life on a small salary."

"Ah . . ." He smiled. "Money is not important. There is an intensity of the mind, of intellect, of love."

That night he walked her back to her hotel. The subject of money came up again, casually and briefly, as a consideration to be dismissed.

She had to fly to New York next day with her regular weekly collection of stolen Embassy telegrams. When she returned that evening, the Comte de la Grandville was waiting at her hotel. This worried CYNTHIA. The FBI was probably still watching her, and this new friend was not displaying much discretion. Then, too, Charles Brousse might see them together, and she had not told him about approaching the assistant cipher officer. There was the danger that if Brousse bumped into her, the Comte would realize she had a more intimate relationship with the French Embassy than that of a confused young woman who once visited there for an interview. She decided it best to invite the Comte to her room.

The phone rang. It was Brousse, on his way up. She made the Comte leave at once. Brousse arrived a few minutes later in a fury, having watched, unseen, his rival. There was a fight. Later, when he was in a mood to listen, she told him that he was to blame. "If you had co-operated in the first place, I would not have tried to win the Comte's favor."

"I can forgive you but I can't help you," Brousse insisted.

"Why not? I'm going to tell him that I work for

367

American Naval Intelligence. I'll offer him money and say it's from the Free French, who are sponsored by the Americans. He'll probably tell your superior."

"Oh, God!" groaned Brousse.

"Leave it to me. I know his type. He wants to keep in with the boss. He'd rather win approval and promotion than sacrifice his career for a cause."

The Comte de la Grandville announced with a virtuous smirk a week later that the had rejected a large bribe and the charms of a beautiful spy who wanted him to desert Vichy. By then, Brousse was briefed to play his part. He took his supervisor aside and confided that the Comte was spreading gossip of this sort all over the capital. Even gossip about a senior diplomat's affair with a prominent Washington hostess.

The Embassy official was startled. He *was* having an affair, but thought it secret. He was not to know that CYNTHIA, having got the necessary details, was the author of the Comte's gossip. Comte de la Grandville now appeared in the eyes of his master as an ambitious intriguer. His superior's first act was to suspend him from code-room duties.

CYNTHIA reported to BSC that the Embassy could now be burgled. The guardian of the code room had been neutralized.

"What about Brousse?" she was asked by HOWARD.

"I can use him. But only for cover. I'll have to break into the Embassy, remove the ciphers, and have someone wait outside to take them to a lab. They'll have about an hour to photograph several hundred pages. Is it possible?"

"That part is. What worries me is you. There are locks to be broken, a safe to be cracked. What do you know about burglaries and safecracking?"

"I can learn. Look! I made a ground plan of the Embassy chancery."

She was recalled to New York a week later and introduced to "Mr. Hunter," lent by OSS. He would be her liaison officer. This meant that, if CYNTHIA was caught, he would talk her way out of any legal difficulties, and that the FBI was out of the picture.

She met another OSS man: The Exterminator. She said later she assumed the worst when he called at her hotel room and announced: "I'm the exterminator." It was actually a common role to play in Washington at the time. Cockroaches and rodents were providing pest-control companies with a roaring trade —and the OSS Exterminators with a valid reason for scarching behind wall panels, undcr floor boards, and in every nook and cranny for bugs of another variety. After declaring the room bug-free, Mr. Hunter moved in with the Cracker.

The Cracker was a Canadian, one of several professional crooks allowed to leave jail after volunteering for dangerous assignments. Some, expert in the handling of explosives, were sent to Nazi-held Europe. The Cracker was a peteman, a safecracker with an encyclopedic knowledge of locks. While he studied the Embassy layout, CYNTHIA worked on Brousse, so far into conspiracy now that he could hardly back out. He was to confide to the Embassy night guard that he had a problem about his girl: it was dangerous to take her to a hotel and dangerous to be away from home without reason. He proposed to "work" late at the Embassy. If his wife phoned, she would find him there. Would the night guard help by letting the girl through? The watchman's co-operation was clinched with a bribe. For several nights he turned a blind eye while Brousse and his girl spent the hours on an elegant sofa in the reception hall. When the watchman had been conditioned to this illicit affair, CYNTHIA brought along a BSC drug, a mild and undetectable soporific that left no aftereffects. Brousse usually had a drink with the guard; one evening, he encouraged the victim to have a couple of extra shots, which would later explain his falling asleep.

The Cracker slipped into the Embassy. An hour later he was still operating on the safe, grumbling that it was so old that the combination lock was hard to break. Just before dawn, the perspiring peteman swung open the safe. The large metalbound cipher books were there all right, but it was too late to deal with

369

them. The Cracker wrote the combination on a card for CYNTHIA and closed the safe again.

The group left as daylight stained the sky. Brousse, reporting to work as usual, found nothing untoward. The Naval Attaché went that afternoon to the code room, used the cipher books, and emerged unruffled. No suspicions had been aroused. But Brousse told CYNTHIA it would be pressing their luck to try to drug the watchman a second time.

"I've got the combination of the safe," said CYNTHIA. "And the Cracker's made duplicate keys for the code room. We can repeat the lovemaking routine, and if the watchman does happen to make his rounds and finds me missing, say I've gone to the bathroom."

That in fact is what happened. But then CYNTHIA was not able to release the lock. She checked and double-checked the combination just as the Georgia Cracker had written it down, to no avail. Hot and annoyed, she collected poor Brousse, sweating it out alone on the sofa, and they left empty-handed. What now?

BSC patiently invited her to catch the next plane to New York. She met HOWARD, and they took a cab through Manhattan, driving to the foot of Wall Street and then back to Broadway. Opposite the 55th Street intersection, he made the cab stop. "See the black Ford over there? Get into it. When you're finished, come back to my place."

CYNTHIA crossed over, slipped into the car, and found the Cracker at the wheel. "Stuck, eh?" He slipped into gear. "Them old locks ain't easy."

"You sure I got the right combination?"

"Sure. All you need's practice."

The practice took place in the back of the car, away from crowds. The girl and the peteman crouched under a spread of newspapers, fumbling with the combination lock on a safe duplicating the one in the Embassy. "Do what you did the other night," said the peteman, laughing. "With the lock, that is." She went through the numbers again. The door opened.

"What happened before?"

The Cracker shrugged. "Maybe you were nervous."

"I doubt it."

"They coulda changed the lock?"

"I don't think so."

"Well, practice some more."

Back in Washington, CYNTHIA made another attempt. Despite the expert tuition, she failed again to open the safe.

Brousse was in a state of nervous and physical exhaustion.

"One more time," she pleaded when they left the Embassy at dawn.

"Making love, yes," said Brousse. "But not on a sofa. Not with burglary on my mind."

"We must try. I'll bring the Cracker. . . ."

"No. We had him around before."

"Leave him outside. If anything goes wrong, bring him in. Please, Charles?"

"I feel as if I'm having an affair with a damned safe," he grumbled. CYNTHIA quickly demonstrated that he was wrong.

Two nights later, Brousse took her back to the Embassy. They parked in the next street, leaving the Cracker in the car. CYNTHIA noticed a black sedan at the next corner with two men sitting inside.

The night watchman was nowhere to be seen. Brousse let himself into the chancery. They spread out on the sofa. "Darling," said Brousse, "I can't continue this way—"

Suddenly the girl jumped to her feet. Brousse protested, and she shushed him. In the light from outside, he saw that she was tearing off her clothes at a furious speed, tossing them around the floor. She fell back naked beside him and whispered, "Your turn."

"What—?"

"Take your clothes off." When he hesitated, she hissed. "We're supposed to be making love. This time we'd better be seen."

Brousse, damp with anxiety, began to strip. He was interrupted by footsteps. A beam of light shot across the hall and focused on the naked girl. It caressed her body and moved over to Brousse, bare-legged and clutching at his shirt.

371

"A thousand apologies, *m'sieu*." The flashlight was switched off. They heard the familiar voice of the watchman. "I—I was worried—please forgive me." He stumbled away in confusion.

Brousse collapsed on the sofa. "Jesu!"

"I think the FBI was outside. Stay here. The way you are."

"And you—?"

She wriggled into her slip. "I'll let the Cracker in."

The peteman was stationed outside a window in the Embassy courtyard. CYNTHIA helped him through. "There was a car outside," he told her. "It drove off after the watchman talked to one of the guys."

"Good." To CYNTHIA it could only mean the FBI was satisfied with the story of a lovers' tryst. She wondered what kind of report they would add to her file.

The Cracker was back at work on the safe. "They never changed the lock," he muttered. "They just never greased it." The tumblers fell into place and the door swung open.

It took five hours to remove the cipher books, pass them to another BSC man outside the Embassy walls, remove each page for photographing in a studio, and return the reassembled books to the safe without leaving a trace. By noon that same day, copies of the cipher were ready for transfer by courier to Bletchley, where they would provide the keys to a new version of the enemy's coding machinery. The ULTRA service would now have additional insights into Fortress Europe by matching decoded Vichy messages with those same messages transmitted through German Enigmas working with a new cipher system.

This was the real significance of CYNTHIA's coup —one that few outside ULTRA's most senior guardians could comprehend. ULTRA teams faced a continuously changing challenge because, though they had their own duplicate Enigmas and batteries of computers, they still had to cope with the sudden adoption of new guidebooks by which German operators set the Enigma drums. Each new guide had to be painstakingly reconstructed at Bletchley from scraps of fresh information. The Vichy codes were a windfall.

A few weeks later, in Stalin's study on August 12, 1942, Churchill unrolled a map of southern France and French North Africa. He sketched a Nazi crocodile overlapping Occupied Europe and said it would be attacked "in the soft underbelly and on the hard snout" by Allied Forces.

He was talking abut what would be the first Anglo-American amphibious operations, which would secure bases for the return into Fortress Europe—code-named TORCH—made possible through CYNTHIA's acquisition of the Vichy cryptosystem. TORCH would "set Europe ablaze." A lot of mistakes would be made; the co-ordination of regular and guerrilla forces would entail unsuspected difficulties. But it gave the French an opportunity to regain their self-respect.

CYNTHIA remained in Washington. While the FBI still regarded her with cold reserve, they had been assured that her British diplomat husband, Arthur Pack, was giving her a divorce. So she stayed Elizabeth Thorpe, and she stayed on the merry-go-round. She helped visiting BSC agents to cope with what was to them a frighteningly open society after their missions in secret-police states. One Englishman jumped like a shot rabbit when he saw the sign SECRET SERVICE. CYNTHIA explained that on this side of the Atlantic, it referred only to protection of the President.

One baffled expert on war production was described in her notes:

The FBI's reputation for efficiency had already intimidated those whose business in the United States was not for public advertisement. Professor R. H. Tawney had been sent from London as a link on the question of labor relations. Tawney was impressed by the need for discretion. He kept no diary and memorized his engagements. One was lunch with a millionaire in Washington. He arrived on the wrong day. The host, with typical American courtesy, greeted him as if he had come on the right day. During lunch, the host indicated a painting on the wall: "Professor, I think you will find that is the finest Manet to have crossed the Atlantic." Next day, Tawney was reminded that he was to have lunch with a prominent businessman. Tawney was driven off to the same millionaire. The host again displayed tact. Nothing was said about yesterday's lunch. The same ritual was observed with regard to the Manet painting: "the finest to have crossed the Atlantic." Professor Tawney paused with his fork in midair, thought carefully, and said: "Oh no, I'm afraid you're wrong. I was shown the finest Manet in America by my host at lunch yesterday."

Nevertheless, CYNTHIA hungered for action. She had a clear picture of conditions in Europe under Hitler's decree of *Nacht und Nebel,* which caused victims to vanish without trace. All identity was erased. Relatives knew nothing. The victim disappeared, perhaps to jail, perhaps to the gallows, perhaps to slave-labor camps. The cruelty was in the uncertainty. It applied to victims and to surviving families alike. For those taken away, there was the agony of doubt because no further communication was possible with loved ones. For those left behind, there was the nightmare of unending speculation.

"Hitler knew very well what he was doing," CYNTHIA wrote later. "This was psychological terrorism with a vengeance. All Europe was sinking into this night and fog which paralysed the will."

To reactivate the will power of those who were able-bodied, acts of violence were necessary. TORCH was still a long way off; full-scale invasion of Europe could not be carried out unless the secret armies grew in numbers and resolve. In 1942, most of the people under Hitler's and Mussolini's tyranny were so bullied and worn down by lack of food and shelter that resistance was beyond their energies. They were easy prey for Nazi vultures, like Dr. Gerhard Alois Westrick.

Westrick had been expelled from the United States after Stephenson exposed his attempts to enlarge American entanglement with Nazi cartels. His activities dated back to ITT's partnership with Hitler's industrial supporters in the 1930s. Now he operated among French industrialists in the same way. CYNTHIA had seen references to him in Vichy telegrams.

Assassination teams were being sent into Europe. Why not Westrick as a target? She took the proposal to Stephenson. She knew Westrick had gone to Langenstein Castle, in Germany, owned by a Swedish industrialist. And who was the Swede? None other than Birger Dahlerus, who once had British and American statesmen chasing his rainbows of peace. What was the castle for? Nothing less than a meeting ground where Westrick wined and dined the nobility and rich hangers-on from Vichy France and other "neutral" regions whose treasures were needed by Nazi industry.

The proposal to execute Westrick as a warning was tempting. But was Westrick important enough to be made a public example? Yes or no, CYNTHIA nevertheless went to Canada, where she was instructed in the skills of the assassin. She was flown to London. There she passed through a modest terrace house at 1 Dorset Square, Marylebone, which in peacetime ran the affairs of an institution famed throughout Europe: the Bertram Mills Circus. With its extensive and unorthodox knowledge of Europe, the Circus was now a reservoir of experts to whom hand-picked Baker Street Irregulars came for information.

She studied the files on prominent Vichy French collaborators, comparing them with knowledge she had gained in Washington. She reported to BSC that when Westrick caught Stephenson's attention in the 1930s, he was already employed in reality by Hitler's favorite intelligence chief, Heydrich.

She left Dorset Square persuaded that it might be better to keep Westrick under secret observation until France was liberated. Such men would be needed to reconstruct the shameful story of collaboration at the top. The need to clarify that story was officially recognized when the house in Marylebone was identified by a plaque after the war—an exceptional breach of security:

> TO COMMEMORATE
> THE DEEDS OF THE MEN AND WOMEN
> OF THE FREE FRENCH FORCES. . . .
> WHO LEFT FROM THIS HOUSE
> ON SPECIAL MISSIONS
> TO ENEMY-OCCUPIED FRANCE
> AND TO HONOR
> THOSE WHO DID NOT RETURN.

CYNTHIA might have become one who did not return, had Stephenson not convinced her to devote her ingenious mind to research, instead of risking recognition by pursuing the assassination plan.

39

"THE SATANIC FORCES which were Nazism constructed their own instruments of rule with thoroughness and cunning. Heydrich was the fiendish brain of the Party and the State." These were words in the case for the prosecution by the State of Israel of Reinhard Heydrich's director for Jewish Emigration (meaning extermination), Karl Adolf Eichmann.

Plans for the assassination of this man Heydrich were begun in New York, at the beginning of August 1941. They were carried out when the aftermath of Pearl Harbor was distracting attention from the fate of helpless civilians.

The intended slaughter of innocents was revealed to BSC in an ULTRA recovery of an order by Reich Commissioner for Jewish Affairs, Hermann Göring. Stripped of its superencipherment, decoded, and dispatched to BSC in New York in that last summer of peace for the United States, it instructed Heydrich "to complete the mission imposed upon you [to] make all the organizational, practical and material preparations for a comprehensive solution of the Jewish question."

The specialists called to a conference in Room 3553 knew nothing of the order, or of the Heydrich file in front of Stephenson. They were men and women of varied talents, including Alexander Korda, his brother Zoltan, Louis de Wohl, an Oxford don who specialized in recreating the sights and sounds of Ancient Rome, and assorted eccentrics, including a linguist whose current field of research, West Slavic, might have been guessed from his costume—a long black leather coat and beard.

Papers and drawings were distributed singly. Each contained separate information. It was the job of Stephenson's chief administrator, Captain Herbert Rowland, to make sure they did not compare notes. This Canadian officer, BISON, had also to arrange the passage through U.S. Customs of a batch of yellow-fever serum.

Rowland was asked to remain when the others withdrew.

"Stephenson sat through the conference, saying little," Rowland recalled. "The organization had been growing rapidly. The pressures had multiplied and become enormous—but you'd never suspect it. He was always elegantly dressed, clean-shaven, though he never seemed to sleep. His head was half-turning as a new man came through the sidedoor. He was a professor-type, shaggy gray hair, old country jacket with baggy pockets and corduroy trousers still smeared with what I'd swear was the clay of Bletchley Park. He sat down and reeled off figures. It dawned on me that he was talking of human beings and slave camps."

Stephenson asked: "What are the arguments for getting rid of Heydrich now?"

"It will warn the slave-masters. Give the people hope," replied the visitor.

"Hitler will strike back at the very people whose support we need."

"The time will come when we'll have to take the risk," said the professor with flowing locks. "Fight terror with terror."

Stephenson stared through him.

"We have to become monsters to destroy monsters," said the visitor.

Stephenson shook his head. "No—" He seemed to be miles away. Suddenly the eyes snapped. Rowland had the familiar experience of sensing the sudden flow of energy. "Take care of our guest."

Rowland nodded. He was skilled in tucking visitors into quiet backwaters. His new charge was "the mumbly kind of English agent, disinclined to move their lips or project their voices. German counter-intelligence used deaf-and-dumb lip-readers to watch suspects from a distance. The lip-readers would be driven crazy by these English types. Swallowing their words came naturally to them. But in New York, inarticulate strangers attracted attention. We had to hide them."

The mumbly professor was introducing an intelligence technique that became a feature of the OSS Research and Analysis Branch.* It was a fine weapon, properly handled. The technique pulled together all the small details about an absent person until you could make him seem to speak and move before your eyes. Heydrich, its first victim, had been known to Stephenson, of course, since before the war. Later, Bermuda intercepts of the "Joe K" spy letters disclosed that Heydrich was responsible not only for Nazi party internal security, but for party intelligence abroad as well. "He now combines the Gestapo and the SS into a single office," Stephenson had reported. "He controls all the powers of spying and intelligence, interrogation and execution."

Captain Rowland, in trying not to abuse U.S. hospitality, resorted to many stratagems. This is how

---

* R & A was later described as "the first concerted effort on the part of any world power to apply the talents of its academic community to official analysis of foreign affairs," by a former CIA officer, R. Harris Smith, in *OSS: The Secret History of America's First Central Intelligence Agency*. Smith, writing in 1972, presumably was denied access to British records at that time still classified.

it happened that shortly after the conference, his brother William, a young doctor at Polyclinic, near Madison Square Garden, found himself walking along a grimy street until he came to a certain store, where he stopped in accordance with instructions and gazed into the darkened window. It was a hot summer's night in Hell's Kitchen, and Dr. Rowland had seen too many victims of muggings dumped into his emergency ward to relish this business. A shadow loomed alongside. Had the doctor brought his bag? Well, of course he had, he replied impatiently. Then would he come this way?

The doctor followed his scruffy guide. As a Canadian resident physician in a New York hospital, the less he knew about cloak-and-dagger the better. He trusted his brother, and did not need to know BSC's purpose. He looked after the Canadian secretaries when they became sick, wondering sometimes at the way their numbers proliferated. If called to the bedside of a "businessman," he would ask no questions about the emaciated body or fresh scars or an exotic fever. It did seem faintly ridiculous now to go to an apartment obviously rented for the occasion, at an address he must forget, to meet nine ruffians standing in an unlit room, faces averted while he went down the line giving each a yellow-fever shot. He knew the serum must have been flown down from the Connaught Laboratories in Toronto, because this was the only source at that time. He guessed his "patients" must be leaving for enemy territory. But why yellow-fever protection? Dr. Rowland was not to know that the Nazis often proclaimed "widespread plague" as an excuse for rounding up families for the death camps. The plagues might or might not be real. BSC could take no chances.

"All agents were put through Canadian military books to give some protection if they were caught," said Captain Rowland later. "They could claim to be officers entitled to treatment according to international law."

A way around the U.S. Neutrality Act was pioneered by New York artist Clayton Knight, who had flown with Stephenson in World War I. In 1940, he had organized a committee to help young Americans get to Canada to join the Canadian and British air forces. Another of Knight's comrades in the first war had been Captain Fiorello La Guardia, who was Mayor of New York City during BSC's residence there. La Guardia gave BSC protection by suspending the routine inquiries that would have revealed its true purpose—the regular fire and elevator inspections, for instance. La Guardia's former legal adviser, Ernest Cunco, was now on loan to President Roosevelt as a liaison officer with BSC. One of Cuneo's jobs was to get the astrologer Louis de Wohl launched on his new career. The BSC Papers note that "his mission was to shake public confidence in the invincibility of Adolf Hitler and terrorists like Heydrich."

At a press conference on his arrival in New York, de Wohl said Hitler's horoscope showed the planet Neptune in the house of death. Days later, a Cairo newspaper dutifully carried a statement by the prominent soothsayer Sheikh Youssef Afifi: "Four months hence a red planet will appear in the eastern horizon. A dangerous evildoer who had drenched the world in blood will die." The report was widely syndicated as part of BSC's scheme. A Nigerian priest conveniently saw a vision: "A group of five men on a rock . . . One short with long hair, one fat like breadfruit, the third monkey-faced and crippled. . . ." The five were recognized by newspaper readers around the world as representing Hitler and his chiefs. The priest predicted the sudden fall from the rock of the tall fair-haired blue-eyed one in jackboots.

Such stories were echoed by muezzins from their minarets in Malaya, the Chinese in their temples in Hong Kong, and wherever else British propaganda warfare could orchestrate prophecies that would confirm de Wohl's eminence in his field. In September 1941, the Associated Press carried reports of the annual convention in Cleveland of the American Federation of Scientific Astrologers. They agreed that the Führer's star was setting. It would have been odd if they said anything else, since the Federation was a BSC creation. Its headliner was the "distinguished Hungarian astro-philosopher Louis de Wohl." The

Cleveland *News* ran a series of photographs of de Wohl with a banner line: ASTROLOGY HAS TOO MANY QUACKS, HE SAYS.

Indeed it had. The greatest of them all was now established in a modest Manhattan hotel. Benn Levy, the British playwright, had the job of climbing the fire escape each week to deliver the Hungarian quack's salary in untraceable greenbacks through a back window, together with any advance information that de Wohl could drop into his now widely read column. The only stars de Wohl ever consulted were in BSC.

While de Wohl, actually a captain in the British Army, prepared for one of his more devastating prophecies, Station M, near Toronto, was forging necessary documents and Camp X was reproducing conditions in which Heydrich was said to live. But in September 1941, his wife, Lina, and their three children turned Castle Hradcany in Prague into home when Hitler named him Reich Protector of Bohemia-Moravia. Here the doomed man held boozy parties and reminded his minions of Hitler's tribute: "You have all the makings of a Führer of the Third Reich."

Hitler wrote to the Reich Protector: "I have accepted your plan for destroying the Czech nation. Basically it will cover three points: the Germanization of as great a proportion of the Czechs as possible; the deportation or extermination of those Czechs who cannot be absorbed and of the intelligentsia hostile to the Reich; and resettlement of the space freed by these measures with good German blood. To that basis I add my decree: that Czechs about whom there exists doubt from the racial standpoint—or who are antagonistic toward the Reich—must be excluded from assimilation. *This category*," Hitler underlined, "*must be exterminated.*" The Bletchley transmission of this grim message confirmed the decision of Heydrich's distant judges in New York, where star-gazing de Wohl had already written the death sentence in his syndicated column: "Hitler's chief jackal is moving into the house of violence."

With a portfolio of plans for the execution of Hitler's mass-extermination orders, Heydrich would set forth for Berlin on Wednesday morning, May 27,

1942, stopping as usual at his office. Waiting for him at the hairpin bend in the road leading down the valley of the Vltava from the village of Jungfern-Breschen to the bridge over the river in Prague would be four of the nine "ruffians," Boy Scout whistles in their pockets, one carrying a Sten gun, another a hand grenade. Their Baker Street instructor, ICICLE, had warned them: "It'll seem a long wait, however short. Remember what George Jean Nathan said about *Parsifal*? It is an opera that begins at five-thirty. Three hours later you look at your watch. And it's only twenty to six."

A different kind of wait had been long and frustrating for the brothers Korda, Zoltan and Alexander.

Zoltan specialized in re-creating Nazi targets in the Canadian wilderness at Camp X. He would study plans and photographs, and then duplicate the key points of exit and entry. On these scale models, BSC agents could practice their burglary skills. But Zoltan was more at home in Hollywood. There he reproduced battles, and the cameras made them life-size. His patient and painstaking work at the isolated camp east of Toronto was even more illusionary. It could be destroyed on an order from some unseen authority. And there were no movie producers for Zoltan to bully.

"He looked like Groucho Marx," said Stephenson. "When some job was aborted, he'd pace up and down, shoulders hunched, peering at me over his enormous moustache, speechless because of course there was no tantrum he could throw that would change the decision."

Alexander knew every nook and cranny of Europe and had an incredible talent for discovering bits of old movies and newsreels that might help to visualize a place now under enemy control.

"We never knew officially what we were doing," Zoltan said later. "But—" shrug—"I wasn't a middle-European for nothing. I knew the locality pretty well. It was one of many jobs, of course. Some of them work. Some you never hear of again. This one—well, it was special. I knew where, but I was very very curious about *who*. For months I would listen to the radio bulletins, waiting to find out. . . ."

In Montreal, his brother waited for the plane that would carry him back to London. Alexander had finished the movie *Lady Hamilton* in six weeks. Its propaganda value was high. It made Churchill weep each time he saw it, and he saw it eight times. When Korda was not making films, "he would hop back and forth in unheated Liberator bombers cooking things up with Bill Stephenson," said Korda's wife, Merle Oberon, years later. Now he was being shown how to wear a life jacket for the umpteenth time. The pilot said it would keep him afloat for twenty hours. Korda said plaintively: "But I do not wish to float for twenty hours." Someone called him to the airfield scrambler phone. It was Zoltan from Camp X. "You heard? It was Heydrich. . . ."

"Who?"

"The Butcher of Prague."

Korda put down the phone. Why Heydrich?

BSC had developed a technique for synthesizing a psychological-behavioral pattern from random information gathered about a subject. Stephenson called these unconventional analyses Proso-Profiles. Prosopography was described after the war by Gilbert Highet,* one of Stephenson's BSC men in New York, as being based upon Professor Ronald Syme's work on the Roman Revolution. "You ask what was the Roman Revolution? It was the one in which Augustus, heir to Julius Caesar, took over and established himself and his family as the new monarchy. What Syme did was analyze Augustus's henchmen, their families and background and social type. Then he demonstrated that in fact Augustus replaced the old senators and businessmen with hand-picked supporters to form a new ruling class. In modern times, you can do this with a dictator, examine his personality and friends, and make deductions from all the facts you've been able to learn."

* Gilbert Highet, a Scot, was a professor of classics at Columbia University when he joined BSC in 1941. In 1943, he was commissioned in the British Army, left as a lieutenant-colonel in 1946 to resume his academic career at Columbia, and achieved pre-eminence as an educator, scholar, author, translator, and poet. He became a U.S. citizen in 1951.

Few knew about Heydrich when the BSC went to work on him. The final analysis said this about him:

He was the protégé of Heinrich Himmler, Reich Commissioner for Consolidation of German Racial Stock. Heydrich was fanatical in his hatred of Jews, having himself some Jewish blood. For this reason, Himmler considered him safe. It was always useful to have the means of blackmailing one's colleagues. . . . "Nobody," Heydrich declared in his anxiety to reach the top, "has greater contempt for Jews than myself. I intend to eliminate the strain."

The fate of "sub-humans" herded into Germany's new mercy-killing centers to be executed on the strength of a physician's oath that the victim was no use to society, the preparations that moved inexorably forward to redesign Europe's entire railroad system to serve the future death camps, all such obscenities before the war were made tolerable by the pretence that if you could not actually see them, they could not be happening. In this atmosphere, Heydrich moved with single-minded purpose to a position so close to the Fuehrer that none dared touch him except perhaps Admiral Canaris, who directed the German High Command intelligence service (HICOMINTEL). But even Canaris lost control over young Heydrich. The Admiral had a dossier on Heydrich's homosexual activities after he had been cashiered from the navy, but Heydrich had also become expert at ferreting out embarrassing information about colleagues and superiors, forging evidence for one end: the satisfaction of Hitler's fantasies. Heydrich manufactured the evidence against the Soviet Russian generals that resulted in the great Stalinist purge of military forces. He produced counterfeit evidence against the German army's commander-in-chief Werner von Fritsch who stood in the way of nazification, in a fashion that again touched Hitler's sickly fancies, bringing the victim down with charges of sexual perversion.

In November 1938,* the SS newspaper *The Black Corps* called for "the extermination with fire and sword, the actual and final end of Jewry in Germany." Hitler made speeches in that month attacking Jewry, prophesying the annihilation of the Jewish race. On the night of the 9th, synagogues went up in flames all over Germany. Jewish homes were burned, Jewish stores pillaged, and some 20,000 Jews were arrested. The pretext for this wave of terror was the shooting of a German Embassy official in Paris, Ernst von Rath, shot by a young Jewish exile grieving for his victimised family in Germany. Hitler blew up the incident, decreed nationwide memorial services, and began systematically whipping an entire nation into a frenzy of hatred against "world Jewry."

The stage-manager of this pogrom was Heydrich. His instructions were distributed by teleprinter to all secret police groups:

1. Only such measures are to be taken which do not involve danger to German life or property. . . . Synagogues to be burned down only when there is no danger of fire to the surroundings.

2. Business and private apartments of Jews may be destroyed but not looted.

3. The demonstrations which are going to take place must not be hindered by the civil police.

4. As many Jews, especially rich ones, are to be arrested as can be accommodated in the existing prisons. Upon their arrest, the appropriate concentration camps should be contacted immediately in order to confine them in these camps as soon as possible.

Hitler described him as "the genius of all the police and security forces of the Reich" for this "triumph of organisation and cunning" and con-

---

* The year is significant. The fact of the systematic extermination of Jews was public knowledge in Germany, in the democracies of Europe and America, and in the Soviet Union. As Stephenson later commented: "It is impossible to deny that Hitler's actual liquidation policies were known to have started even while Western and Russian leaders appeased him."

sidered that he should be given governorship of an entire satellite state. What seemed to pleasure the *Fuehrer* was the way Heydrich organised The Night of Broken Glass, down to the bothersome aftermath like insurance claims. "Settle the Jews' claims in full," Heydrich advised in his report of November 11, 1938, to Hitler. "Then confiscate the money. Claims for broken glass alone will amount to some five million marks. . . . As for the practical matter of clearing up the destruction, Jews will be released from the concentration camps to clear up their own mess under supervision and the courts will impose upon them a fine of a billion marks to be paid out of the proceeds of their confiscated property. Heil Hitler!" One year before Heydrich started the Second World War with the simulated attack on the Polish border on August 10, 1939, he had already launched the first large scale operations to destroy "the racial vermin" as Hitler planned.

His power was total by mid-1941. He was the symbol of Hitler's "new kind of ruler, youthful, self-assured, untrammeled by tradition, and so brutal that the world shrinks back in horror . . . ruling by terror, eye gleaming with pride and the merciless independence of the beast of prey."

The size of Heydrich's empire of horror could be measured by the lengths to which BSC agents went to travel around it. The file on Heydrich included information from SIS stations the world over. One of the busiest was Stockholm, run by Ronald Turnbull. To get from London to Sweden in 1941, he traveled to South Africa, flew to Cairo, sailed to Turkey, and took a train through Moscow to Leningrad, where he proceeded by ferry to Finland and thus slipped into Stockholm by the back door. He covered 10,000 miles to reach a city some 900 miles from his point of departure.

Inside the perimeter of Turnbull's travels lay Heydrich's wasteland. From end to end, the traffic of death moved toward the new camps "built with all possible speed," said Heydrich, "to receive all who misunderstand the aim of the Third Reich which is on a far higher plane than any religious doctrine." Trains rolled across Europe with their human cargoes. Guards chanted monotonously, *"Schnell! Schnell!"* The victims marched in orderly groups, often into the gas chambers. The direction of the Final Solution remained Heydrich's responsibility until the end of his life.

Heydrich's predecessor in governing Occupied Czechoslovakia had won the friendship of local leaders. Czech exiles in London, in daily touch with Czech intelligence circuits, such as Sparta I and Sparta II, and the Czech secret army, UVOD, the Central Committee for Internal Resistance, feared that resistance to the Nazis was being undermined by the collaborators.

When Heydrich issued a public announcement that he had taken control, the secret-army chiefs had already decided to arrange the death of a prominent collaborator, a Czech code-named JUDAS.

Three JUDAS letters had been forged at Station M, using information culled from a Proso-Profile. The letters were hand-carried from Canada to Chile, from where they were mailed at intervals to JUDAS in Prague. Chile, dominated by German economic and political agents, was the logical place for a mistress of JUDAS to go, and the fake letters were signed by that mistress—"Anna." She was in fact a product of BSC's imagination.

The JUDAS letters were copied from drafts prepared by a girl in New York with a Slovakian background. The dictation of the draft letters was carried out by a BSC expert who knew nothing about the intended victim in Prague. All he had was the study written by a professor who analyzed enemy personalities. Enough was known about JUDAS to formulate a convincing series of letters that made Anna seem familiar with his personal life. The paper on which the letters were written had been prepared by experts in the Canadian pulp-and-paper industry, working from samples of stationery used in Chile. They, too, had been given no more information than was necessary to carry out their

387

part of the job. The forgers were equipped with ink, pens, and envelopes consistent with the false story that JUDAS was in communication with someone in Santiago.

JUDAS's real name was Alois Elias; the General was Prime Minister of the puppet government in Prague. It is doubtful if more than three men involved in his overthrow through the JUDAS letters were aware of his identity.

German censors, examining these fabricated letters as they came drifting in from Santiago, became convinced that General Elias must be in secret communication with enemies of Nazism. The letters contained phrases and figures that read like code. For instance: "Father caught 75 fish on Wednesday the 17th. Brother was not well but caught 82."

When Elias was questioned by the Gestapo, he could not explain mysterious sentences like "Look after the marks and do nothing with the Polish zlotys." The letters struck out of a clear blue sky. They were proof, said the Germans, that he was communicating in plain-language code. What, otherwise, was the meaning of "I knitted Karl a sweater using 14 skeins of wool each 60 feet long although two were only 28 feet"?

Elias had no answer. When he denied knowledge of Anna, the Gestapo pointed out, not unreasonably, that she seemed to know all about *him*. How else could she write about the habits of his former wife or the circumstances of his brother's unusual death?

The trial of Prime Minister Elias marked Heydrich's actual assumption of supreme power in the conquered land. Elias was charged in Division I of the People's Court on October 1, 1941. He was then tried, sentenced, and, on the morning of October 2, executed for action in aid of the enemy.

The Butcher of Prague thus began a reign of terror by destroying the one man who might have helped him survive. "The day of parliamentary decisions which only hinder the practical measures of government has gone," Heydrich told the Prague government. "Get out of your heads that you can continue the tricks of the democratic party politicians." He purged

388

the administration and then announced: "Accounts with the Czech Resistance Movement will also be settled." And so they were. He sat in the tapestry room of the castle to watch the mass execution of "intellectuals" in the courtyard below.

Heydrich had been maneuvered into one self-defeating act; could he be manipulated further? He wielded great power outside his satrapy. Shuttling between Prague and Berlin, he tended his other allotments. In December, he summoned a high-level meeting of Nazi party officials to discuss the Final Solution and practical methods for "raking Europe from East to West." The conference was to be held at the International Criminal Police Commission in Berlin. Using this ambitious institution, Heydrich, already seeking prospective victims in the next phase of Hitler's purification of the human race, extended his probing fingers into North and South America.

It was in this December of Pearl Harbor that the final decision was made to eliminate Heydrich. The case against him was bolstered by a legal justification volunteered by a courageous German Catholic, Clemens Count von Galen, Bishop of Münster. In a sermon aimed at Nazi leaders now conducting massacres in their respective regions, the Bishop reminded the authorities that the German legal code still authorized the punishment by death of "any individual who kills." In London, the exiled Beneš government agreed that Heydrich deserved the death sentence as "the pivot around which the Nazi regime revolves and as the designer of the mechanism for mass murder."

Heydrich's conference took place on January 20, 1942. It boiled down to a simple order: All opponents of German occupation troops should be banished into Night and Fog.

Heydrich had conceived this method of reinforcing Nazi propaganda after the capture of Warsaw. The German authorities published a version of why they had occupied new territory. This claimed that National Socialism was the solution to economic chaos. The victims of economic chaos were the people. Therefore, anyone opposing Nazism must be an enemy of the people. Wherever Hitler governed, the Gestapo could recruit helpers by putting this gloss on reality. Traitors came forward: Quisling in Norway, Clausen in Denmark, Mussert in Holland, Sima in Rumania, Szalassy in Hungary, and Pavelič in Crotia. The Grand Mufti of Jerusalem could enthusiastically issue calls to nationalists from Berlin, for he had brainwashed himself with Nazi claims to be helping other victims of Jewish, American, or some other imperialism. Those who opposed these Nazi collaborators masquerading as "nationalists" were *ipso facto* enemies of the people and joined Jews, gypsies, and Slavs in the catalogue of the condemned.

Now the Gestapo and the SS were authorized to go beyond the mass extermination of inferior races. "After lengthy consideration the Führer has decided that measures taken against those guilty of offenses against the Reich or against the occupation forces in the occupied areas must be changed," Heydrich announced. "The Führer is of the opinion that in such cases penal servitude or a sentence of hard labor for life will be regarded as a sign of weakness. A more effective and lasting deterrent can be achieved only by the death penalty or by taking measures that will leave the family and population uncertain as to the fate of the offender. . . ."

Night and Fog came one year after the first Baker Street agent was parachuted into enemy territory: eighteen months after Stephenson organized the supply of American equipment to the secret armies. Night and Fog was a response to underground warfare. It was Heydrich responding defensively to something he did not yet understand.

He soon would. Josef Gabcik and Jan Kubris were two of the agents selected to kill Heydrich. Nine men had gone through training before the final decision was taken, each expert in his field. At first, like the forgers who destroyed JUDAS, they were unaware of their target. But there came a point when they knew the nature of their mission. Gabcik carried a Sten under the raincoat draped over his arm as he stood waiting at the hairpin bend outside Prague on the morning of May 27. Kubris had a grenade in the deep poacher's pocket of his jacket. One hundred yards away, up the hill toward the village of Jungfern-Breschen, stood a third man, known as Valcik. And another two hundred yards farther on, the man called Jemelik waited on the opposite side of the road. He would be the first to see the open green Mercedes in which the Protector rode to his office.

Getting the assassins into position required a more intricate series of maneuvers than putting men on the moon. At least the moon follows a set course. Heydrich did not. The four agents had parachuted near the Polish border from an aircraft whose crewmen were constantly adjusting to conditions in enemy skies, so that until the last moment nobody could be sure where the men would be dropped. Since it had been decided that the difficulties were too great for penetrating Heydrich's castle, at Camp X a replica was made of the green Mercedes he used when not piloting himself to Berlin. But who could be sure that the car had not been changed, the route altered?

The hairpin bend where Gabcik stood with the Sten was a sharp one. Streetcars, two trolleys hitched together and taking power from overhead cables, screeched agonizingly as they turned. The street was busy. German soldiers drilled in the woods nearby. The two lookouts, Valcik and Jemelik, had difficulty keeping each other and the two assassins in view, what with passing German military vehicles and trucks, and the need to avoid attracting attention. For fifty-five minutes, this painful wait continued—painful and dangerous. At any moment some sharp-eyed German might well have wondered why four able-bodied men were loitering.

At ten-twenty-five Gabcik heard four sharp whistles —H in Morse code—the signal. A moment later an open Mercedes swept down the hill. Klein, the chauffeur, changed gear to take the turn. Beside him sat Heydrich, in the silver-trimmed SS uniform with wings on the arms and braided cords on the shoulders, a target so naked that Gabcik caught his breath. Heydrich was leafing through papers, and his head was down. Klein was concentrating on the road. A pair of trolleys came grinding down the hill behind; and another streetcar hauled its way up from the opposite direction. Gabcik dropped his coat, just as he had done a dozen times in training. The coat carried misleading documents and false labels. He brought up the Sten and squeezed the trigger. Nothing happened. The Sten was something you did not aim so much as spray, but now no stream of bullets emerged. Heydrich, fifty feet away, looked up, saw the light machine gun pointing at him, drew his revolver, and shouted something. Klein threw the Mercedes into a skid.

The car screeched to a stop across the tram tracks. The following trolleys slid, with metal brakes throwing sparks, to within a few feet of the stalled Mercedes. Heydrich was standing, trying to force his door. The uphill streetcar rattled into the bend. Kubris, seeing his companion trying to clear the Sten, tossed his grenade against the side of the victim's car. There was an explosion. Out of the billowing smoke emerged Heydrich, vaulting over the stuck door, firing at the assassins caught between the two stalled trams. They began to run.

Heydrich staggered to the sidewalk. Passengers from the trams climbed down, puzzled more than frightened. "Fetch an ambulance," said a woman. "It's the Protector."

An hour later, Heydrich was delivered in a commandeered baker's van to Bulovka Hospital, where the medical director tried to reach Hradcany Castle, official headquarters of the Protectorate as well as Heydrich's family residence. Nobody at the Castle seemed to comprehend what had happened. The Protector was on his way to Berlin. No, there was no way Secretary of State Dr. Karl Frank would come to the phone. "Too bad," said the medical director. "Tell him we have the Obergruppenführer here and he is unlikely to live. He's full of holes."

The subsequent events are known from reports made by the assassins to the Czech secret army before they were trapped and killed, by Dr. Frank and witnesses, and by the surgeon Dietrich Hohlbaum, who was faced with the impossible task of trying to remove from Heydrich's vital organs the pieces of metal, wire, glass, leather, and horsehair distributed by the exploding grenade. The surgeon went to work while the hospital was surrounded by SS troops. Patients were bundled out. During the following week, Hitler telegraphed around Europe for the best physicians. Specialists flew in from a half-dozen capitals. The Führer, from his headquarters on the Russian front, ordered "a stamping out of the whole canker at the heart of the Protectorate."

The scale of retribution was to be extended to the very limit possible without harming war production, a prudent recognition of Germany's reliance upon factories like that of the huge Skoda munitions complex. Karl Frank, as chief of the Protectorate police forces, blocked all roads into the city, stopped all public transport, and permitted the passage only of trains bringing reinforcements of SS from other corners of Eastern Europe and from Berlin. Every public place was closed. Every citizen was ordered to go home and await the Gestapo unless he or she could prove to be engaged in essential war work. A reward of a million crowns was announced by loudspeaker vans touring the city.

An escape plan had been worked out beforehand with local guerrillas. The assassins were taken to the crypt of the Karl Borromaeus church. A change of clothing and fresh documents transformed them into barge workers plying the Vltava river, and it was intended that they should travel downstream out of danger when the hue and cry subsided. Meanwhile, they hid in the crypt, which was entered through a removable slab that appeared to commemorate a Bohemian knight. The church was Greek Orthodox, and the SS and Gestapo were under instruction to avoid provoking members of that faith for political reasons. The church, like all buildings, was put under guard but not searched. The priests smuggled into the crypt during the next few days more than eighty members of the Resistance, while outside 10,000 hostages were herded to places of execution. From the day of the attack, 100 Czechs were shot each evening. Thirteen days after the attack, Frank announced that the assassins had been parachuted by the British into the village of Lidice, twenty miles northwest of Prague.

On the night of June 8, special squads from Heydrich's Main Security Office surrounded the village. Every house was emptied of occupants. When workers from the local mines came off shift, they were pushed into the village square to join women and children. Babies had been torn from their mothers' arms and thrown into cattle troughs to drown. During the night, fathers were separated from their families. Wives were locked into the village school. Children were pushed into the village hall. At dawn, the men were brought out in groups of ten and shot against the wall of the village café, watched by their relatives. When 189 had been executed, Captain Max Rostock, in charge of the operation, decided it was taking too long. The remaining men and youths were marched into a farmer's barn; the barn was set alight, and those inside burned to death. All the women except those who were pregnant were sent to the gas chambers of Ravensbrück. The pregnant women were sent to Bulovka Hospital, where Heydrich had died a full week after the attack on him, and there their babies were aborted by the same doctors who had tried to save the Protector. Then the women were sent to Berlin to be experimented upon by "racial experts." Finally, Lidice was burned to the ground with flame-throwers.

The punishment was filmed. A medal was struck for the film makers; it bore Heydrich's profile and the word *Rache* (Revenge). All over Europe, revenge was taken in a similar fashion. From a village in Norway to Oradour-sur-Glane in France, families were either incinerated within burning barns or machine-gunned as they tried to get away.

As for the assassins, their escape plan was never completed. The SS division Das Reich, acting on an informer's tip, tore down the church where they had taken refuge. Inevitably, they found the false tomb. Two machine guns were lowered into the crypt, and everyone inside was killed either by bullets or by a subsequent fire caused by setting alight gasoline poured on the bodies.

Hitler flew to the funeral of the Protector. "He was

one of the greatest defenders of our greater German concept," he proclaimed.

In Stern Park Gardens, Illinois, and in Bohemia, Long Island, the citizens voted to change the names of their communities to "Lidice."

The Destroyer of Lidice, Karl Frank, was eventually hanged. After the war, a socialist member of the British Parliament questioned the wisdom of provoking such killers. The MP, Robert Paget, challenged the Baker Street concept of sending agents on missions that stung the Nazis into reprisals that in turn created more civilian hatred against the occupiers. "This was our general idea when we flew in a party to murder Heydrich," Paget protested. "The main Czech resistance movement was a direct consequence of SS reprisals."

Was it worth the loss of so many innocent lives? That was Paget's question. A voice from the past replied: "The killing of Heydrich was an act of justice that lightened our darkness and gave us hope."

The surprise witness had been working for the Destroyer of Lidice as a gardener. He was a Baker Street Irregular, an Englishman named Richard Pinder.

Pinder put aside his anonymity to defend wartime actions because the MP's questions had started a discreet parliamentary inquiry. Otherwise, like so many others, he would have taken his particular secret to the grave. He had been training guerrillas in sabotage when caught in a German drive to round up men for forced labor. Pinder's fake papers were made out in the name of a Frenchman whose occupation was given as *horticulteur*. Frank, as Deputy Protector of Czechoslovakia, had taken over the big estates of a wealthy Jewish family and had applied for a professional landscape gardener. Pinder wangled the job. Thereafter, he was the silent witness of Frank's career as a gangster-tyrant.

"It is true Frank avenged Heydrich's murder," he said years later. "But in all the occupied countries, the Nazis were liquidating communities once they had served their purpose. Czechoslovakia was industrially very important to the German war machine. The people fed the guns until it came their turn to die."

A new and more ghastly form of warfare had overtaken the world. For the sake of individual survival, millions died. Was it worth it? "The question never arose in stark terms," Stephenson once commented. "Mankind created the conditions. Mankind reacted to terrors of its own making. We were on a course dictated by our own inventiveness.

"In mid-1942, on the day Heydrich died, the Soviet Union put pressure on Roosevelt to launch an invasion across the English Channel. The British War Cabinet that day was forced to say that opening a Second Front now would be suicidal. Civilian morale inside Fortress Europe had to be prepared, and our guerrilla forces had to be supported by most of the population. There was only one way to mobilize popular support for the secret armies, and that was to stage more dramatic acts of resistance and counterterrorism."

40

WHILE THREE DEADLY campaigns were waged in Europe, Stephenson had to play politics. It was a foretaste of the problems that face an intelligence service in free societies. Matters of life and death on the perimeter of a network tend to lose urgency at the center. In order simply to survive, the directors of the agency have to be vigilant against attacks from within the society they defend.

A future chief of the Central Intelligence Agency, Allen W. Dulles, moved into Room 3663 at Rockefeller Center a month after Pearl Harbor. American academics began to be seen in English country lanes around Bletchley, so that in time ULTRA was served by Telford Taylor, the future distinguished Columbia University professor; William Bundy, future Assistant

Secretary of State and editor of the influential *Foreign Affairs;* Lewis Powell, who would sit on the Supreme Court.

Slowly, reluctantly, the British were disclosing more about their secret agencies. Just as hesitantly, Americans entered an underworld that in peacetime would offend upholders of free speech and an open society.

By the time Dulles occupied quarters there, BSC realized it would have to fight for its survival in New York. Its relationship with Americans was becoming as intricate as the tangle of pneumatic tubes winding through 630 Fifth Avenue from one BSC office to another, speeding canisters between the message centers that kept the secret of who worked where. Dulles eventually left for a key intelligence post in Switzerland. He wanted an expansion of co-ordinated U.S. intelligence and he had known Donovan since he was Assistant Attorney-General in Washington. If anyone could overtake the British, it was Donovan, he felt.

Attached to Dulles at BSC were prominent Germans snatched out of Gestapo hands by the British—a former chancellor and leader of the German Catholic Center party, a former Prussian cabinet minister, an assortment of diplomats. They made an odd group, but they had a common purpose in briefing Dulles for his mission to make use of anti-Hitler forces inside Germany. *Their* political fight for survival was directed against professional British intelligence officers who refused to believe their reports of a German resistance movement.

The British had become cynical about German reports of opposition to Hitler. Admiral Canaris, Germany's most professional intelligence chief, had earlier divided European governments by floating these deceptive reports. By the time Canaris genuinely sought an escape hatch from a collapsing Nazi empire, his record in the British file marked "K" made London feel an obligation to let him stew in his own juice. This resulted in quarrels with Dulles and OSS, who felt an equal obligation to pursue such contacts. "The Atlantic divided both sides in time as well as space," Stephenson commented later. "Each side had arrived at a different stage in experience."

New York was an unreal environment for anyone trying to visualize anti-Nazi groups in Europe. Allied intelligence agents who were superb in the field tended to become churlish, quarrelsome, and neurotic at New York headquarters, where the staff seemed far removed from the bloody struggle. Hardship was a relative term. There, the need for parachutes was associated with a shortage of nylon stockings. The secretaries walking through the portals of Rockefeller Center wore short skirts or slacks for the sake of economy, but they could still get the fruit and candy that children in Britain either had forgotten or never knew.

The realities were plainer in the ciphers flowing through Rockefeller Center. When the SS commander in Warsaw, General Franz Kutschera, was sentenced to death by the guerrilla Polish Home Army, the policy aspects had to be studied in New York. Details of his quarters, his appearance, and his habits were assembled at Camp X, using information supplied by Baker Street, including timetables radioed by three girls who had studied the victim's movements. In Poland, the secret army's police was to strike at the Germans responsible for terror in as public a manner as possible. Kutschera was killed by nine executioners armed with light machine guns and grenades in an operation that lasted sixty seconds. Stephenson said later: "If the Warsaw rebels had received no encouragement, the city would have been razed anyway. The hardest decisions were made by those enemies of the Third Reich who slipped out of the occupied territories to help plan secret operations that must endanger their own comrades."

The mathematics of secret warfare were unknown to the Allied military establishment. The lesson had yet to be learned that apparently primitive methods of warfare can be combined with the most modern techniques; that if the regular armies have been defeated, guerrillas can play a major part in defensive strategy until the regular armies can be reconstituted, whereupon the guerrillas assist in offensive operations.

"We could argue that a brigade of guerrillas was worth thirty regular army brigades but it made no dent on conventional military minds," recalled Bickham

Sweet-Escott, the Baker Street Irregular drafted from the higher financial realms of the oil industry. Furthermore, any such argument was hampered by the obsession with secrecy. This made the companionship of Dulles important to BSC.

Dulles and his colleagues were under as much political pressure as Roosevelt. And the President was in turn feeling the formidable pressure of the Soviet Union by mid-1942 when he was visited by the drab little Commissar of Foreign Affairs, Vyacheslav Molotov, sent by Stalin to demand an early invasion of Europe. Molotov had been told in London that the cross-Channel invasion was not possible that year. But Stephenson was shaken to learn, on the last day of May 1942, that Roosevelt unthinkingly had speculated to Molotov that "we expect the development of a Second Front this year."

Molotov treated this as a formal commitment. It put Britain on the spot. Small-scale intelligence raids, scattered guerrilla operations, did not impress the politicians, the press, or the conventional militarists, who were looking for spectacular battlefield victories, big naval engagements, and the mass bombings of enemy cities. The last came under a portentous title: the Strategic Air Offensive. Stephenson opposed mass bombing. He felt vindicated when the Strategic Air Offensive results demonstrated that there were more Allied airmen lost in the first year of mass bombing raids than there were German casualties. Stephenson's instinct was for guerrilla warfare, which gave priority to individual leadership, inventiveness, and lonely courage.

Secret warfare did not make headlines, however. It produced no glamorous young heroes for front-page treatment. BSC's difficulties in paying agents and armies increased just when Hoover and the FBI became less sympathetic, and misunderstandings began to arise between British secret-warfare planners in London and the new foreign-intelligence organization run by Bill Donovan.

The BSC Papers recorded: "Hoover keenly resented Donovan's organization when it was first established, because he feared that its interests would clash with the authority of the FBI, particularly in Latin America. His resentment extended to BSC. Indeed, realizing that he could attack Donovan's organization most effectively by attacking what was then its mainstay, he began shortly before Pearl Harbor to treat BSC with ill-concealed hostility, and his purpose was quite evidently to suppress its activities if he could. In that purpose, he had the backing, among others in the administration who were latently anti-British, of Adolf Berle, Assistant Secretary of State.

"Immediately after January 1942 [when Allen Dulles moved into BSC quarters] a joint committee was set up to coordinate all Anglo-American intelligence activities. At its first meeting, which was attended by Hoover, Berle and Stephenson among others, Berle proposed that BSC should maintain liaison with no other agency than the FBI. Stephenson resisted the proposal and went on to refer to the pending McKellar bill [which would prevent all foreign intelligence agencies from operating within the United States] pointing out that in its present form it would mean the end of his organization inasmuch as the bill stipulated 'all records used by foreign agencies would be liable to inspection by U.S. government authorities at any time.'

"Berle replied with a smile that this was regrettable but that it was too late to effect any modification since the bill was already on the President's desk awaiting signature.

"Stephenson left the meeting before it was over. With Donovan's help, he persuaded President Roosevelt not to sign the bill unless and until it was modified to allow adequate safeguard of BSC's legitimate interests."

Sweet-Escott reckoned "I spent forty per cent of my time fighting the enemy and sixty per cent of my time fighting our friends."

The biggest challenge was to meet the rapidly rising costs of BSC operations. Payment in full had to be made for American services at the same time that the secret armies had to be paid in Nazi territory—not wages, but money to buy food, bribe officials, travel, and purchase goods. BSC was forking out cash in both directions. If cash was unavailable, BSC offered services. There was always the collateral of the French gold in Martinique. This concept by which secret-warfare loans could be raised in the United States was extended to cover whatever natural wealth was locked behind the British economic blockade. It became increasingly important for BSC to keep redramatizing its usefulness to the United States.

Fortunately, it could do this in economic terms in South America, where the dangers from both Nazi and Japanese conspiracies were only now disturbing American complacency about the area; and where it was suddenly evident that the British could sabotage the sources of wealth and raw materials.

Buried in Latin America were the metals of war and those minerals and exotica for which there was a demand created by new and sophisticated weapons: vanadium, mercury, tungsten, and tin; mica, bauxite, chromium, and antimony. BSC had thrown a noose around the source of these materials. Specialists on this vast region drew up estimates of the riches stored behind the blockade. Some treasures were not immediately recognizable as such. The cinchona bark of German-dominated Bolivia, for instance, was required for a variety of medicines and drugs wanted by the secret armies.

Ecuador's balsa wood was needed in large and continuous quantities for the nonmetal Baker Street spy planes. If German-influenced suppliers or middlemen tried to sabotage the supply, the way to strike back— as specified in BSC guidebooks—was to cause damage by fire at the strategic locations or foment labor troubles through BSC-run union organizers.

The treasures locked in the "vaults" of Latin America were like stocks and bonds held in the BSC "bank" as collateral against loans. The banker might be small and weak but he had the unusual advantage of directing potential bank robbers. BSC's sections were run by economic-warfare experts. One section was called "The Physical Security of Strategic Raw Material Supplies from Latin America" and contained six separate Security Zones. In each Zone, BSC controlled an apparatus neatly dovetailed into the existing police system.

Generations of British explorers contributed to the BSC files in New York. They catalogued methods by which British agents and their friends could damage the economies or manipulate the politics of ten supposedly neutral countries in Latin America. Neat files labeled "Vulnerability to Sabotage," for instance, were specific in analyzing the weak points in each republic's socioeconomic structure so that agents might know where to strike if a government or an industry failed to fall into line with British policies.

Senior American officials were shocked before Pearl Harbor to discover that a foreign intelligence agency on American soil was cold-bloodedly examining ways to change or overthrow neighboring governments. After the U.S.'s entry into the war, BSC's conspiracies began to seem more like prudent safeguards.

British strength lay in precision of knowledge, which ranged from the personal records of influential Axis-directed Japanese and Germans in key industrial areas to the development of knockout drops made from poisons even more inaccessible than the Venezuelan curare that was in such demand among agents in Europe. William Rowland, the Canadian doctor whose brother was Stephenson's aide, experimented in New York with new drugs. He sought a mix that would escape the notice of someone drinking at a bar. Strychnine is easily detected. Gallamine, though hard to find, is smoother than curare. Herb and Bill Rowland spent many happy hours sipping alcoholic concoctions in the quest. Their final formula, far superior to the usual knockout mixture called "Mickey Finn," was passed to U.S. agents.

The secret armies needed foreign currency, which Stephenson bought through New York bankers or through Donovan. Millions of dollars' worth of funds were shipped to London for parachuting into Europe. But the basic currency was not dollars or pounds sterling; it was a currency of trust, which ran the length of the chain, from Americans made privy to why the cash was required suddenly to guerrilla leaders whose word was as good as their bond. Sackloads of francs, zlotys, guilders, kroner, and lire were smuggled up to Canada for transfer by air.

The Baker Street financial section arranged barter deals whereby wealthy businessmen and bankers in the occupied zones lent cash on the promise it would be repaid after the war. This took a lot of arranging. The leader of a Paris network, in urgent need of money, called on a French banker for help. How was the banker to know the agent was genuine, The banker was told to make up any phrase. This phrase the agent then radioed to London. When the phrase was broadcast in a regular BBC program to occupied Europe, the financier knew his visitor was not a criminal exploiting the strange situation. Large sums were handed over by other anti-Nazi businessmen, who required no receipts and took everything on trust.

The New York banking house of Ladenburg, Thalman & Co. worked directly with Stephenson. Any leakage of information could place an agent or an army in peril. Deals had to be made on a personal basis, Donovan stepping into the picture when necessary. On one occasion, a fortune in American dollars was required for operations so secret that Donovan himself could not be told their purpose. A cold-eyed official of the U.S. Treasury came unwittingly close to sabotaging the transaction, which involved large guerrilla forces. The money was transferred in large denominations, in a series of maneuvers known only to Stephenson, a Baker Street paymaster, Donovan, and two of his top men. The President and the Prime Minister were aware only that secret funds were being handled on a very large scale. A BSC report summarized the difficulties: "The dollars will be used in occupied Europe and must fall into German hands eventually, which the U.S. Treasury and the Federal Reserve Bank both disallow. The dollar notes cannot be purchased from the U.S. Treasury by the British Treasury against a check, because the telltale check will go through the American financial machine, leaking its tale of conspiracy."

Donovan drew an initial three million dollars from the U.S. Treasury in large notes. The bigger denominations, handiest in German zones, were sent to London. In time, the money would come back in the small bills still rustled up in Britain. Small notes required an enormous number of bags to carry them. This meant a lot of cargo space when space was at a premium. So the repayments were delayed. Donovan tried to draw another two million dollars. The U.S. Treasury inquired when he planned to pay back the earlier amount. There was no quick answer. Yet Baker Street was pressing Stephenson for the next shipment before the winter's last lunar period, during which aircraft could exploit long hours of darkness to make the dangerous "paymaster" flights into the Third Reich.

Stephenson had to draw on his own reserves of cash and good will. He gave his word that the debt would be covered, and told the President the gist of the problem. FDR discussed it with Henry Morgenthau, Jr., the Secretary of the Treasury. Another two million dollars were released. This particular sum was flown to a field prepared by the Polish secret army, the RAF Moon Squadron STS Mosquito landing at the center of a triangle made by three hooded lanterns.

Nobody anticipated a statistical problem. A million in hundred-dollar bills fitted inside a single bag and could be flown eastward over the Atlantic. The small bills coming back from Britain filled, for the initial five million, nearly 200 bags. They did arrive, after an agonizing pause that prompted more embarrrassing questions from Treasury watchdogs. The final shipment was almost sabotaged by Donovan's own financial man. He wondered, in the politest way, if Donovan could tell him how the money was being spent. Or was it being hoarded? Donovan replied that "U.S. 100 and 50 dollar bills were needed in large quantities by those secret armies built up by Baker Street and that the guerrilla chiefs in the field depended upon London revealing nothing. The huge sums were required to finance preparations for the final uprising against Hitler."

The American financial genius needed to help Stephenson out of these embarrassments was Henry Morgenthau, Jr. Hitler, back in the spring of 1939, had said "Roosevelt and his Jewish treasurer, Morgenthau," were so fully absorbed in domestic politics that

404

Germany could always count on a seven months' time lag before American industry could be mobilized or an expeditionary force launched. To maintain this period of grace, Hitler ordered propagandists to show moderation in supporting American isolationists. But the success of the first blitzkrieg, the conquest of Poland, went to Nazi heads. The archives of the Polish Foreign Ministry were rifled and the contents falsified to show how prominent Americans had conspired against the Reich along with "Jews and sinister ambassadors." In New York, the German Library released documents that told in revolting detail of Polish atrocities against Germans. Photographs "too horrible for public dissemination" might be viewed in the privacy of the Library's premises at 17 Battery Place. "Murder, mutilation and scenes of mass killing and rape" were offered, in which the Germans appeared as victims.

Morgenthau's personal outrage was widely shared. As the war in Europe spread, he campaigned quietly on Britain's behalf. His influence with the President often resulted in his getting blamed for inconvenient military situations. When the U.S. Army found that the rounds of ammunition fired by recruits had been cut by forty percent to release supplies to Britain, it blamed Morgenthau.

By 1942, even gentle Henry Morgenthau had ventured a long way into clandestine operations. Fake as well as real money was being used by guerrillas in Europe. The counterfeit currency was purchased by the U.S. government on Britain's behalf. "The law forbade its manufacture on American soil," said Ernest Cuneo. "So we had BSC manufacture the stuff through private commercial printing-works specializing in this sort of thing. These were British firms geared for maximum security. In peacetime they manufactured the currencies of foreign governments, so they were trained in special protective measures. We had to pay them a hell of a price—about sixty percent of the real value. So I said Christ Almighty—how about *us* paying *you* off in phoney British pounds?

"And they said, thanks, we've got all the fake pounds we need."

These technical breaches of the law became less amusing after Hoover began trying to suppress BSC activities. It became necessary to call a Western Hemisphere Intelligence Conference in April 1942. Stephenson wanted to impress on Hoover and U.S. service chiefs the consequences of losing BSC's cooperation. American suspicion persisted, nonetheless, that BSC was no less efficient in manipulating the White House than it was the Axis. Stephenson replied with examples of the ghastly results of separate efforts in the field.

British policy was to guard against the enemy guessing that his secret radio traffic was being read. The British would not make available to their own SIS representatives in Latin America the deciphered versions of this German traffic, in case of leaks that could endanger Bletchley.

American procedure, however, was to distribute transcripts of monitored traffic in all directions. The State Department's own monitor reports might go to the American Ambassador in Uruguay, for instance; the War Department's product to the military attaché in Venezuela; the Navy's to naval observers in Brazil. Even the Associated Press filed material leaked to it by the American Embassy in Rio, based on deciphered material, and once used a complete sentence from the original transcript.

Things had come to a head when the Brazilian police rounded up dozens of Germans in March 1942. All were known to Stephenson as members of separate espionage rings. Their identification had been made through British analysis of deciphered German signals. To preserve the secret, and to continue listening to these enemy spies, the British had taken no action. Yet Brazil clearly received a summary of BSC investigations. Nobody under Stephenson's direction had provided it. That left, as suspects, the recipients of BSC reports in Washington. Once again, Stephenson went to the White House. He had staked his personal reputation, his credibility in London, upon his trust in American judiciousness; but an incident of this kind would make it harder than ever to argue with Churchill's intelligence chiefs that information should be freely shared. FDR agreed, pressed for an inquiry, and had to confess that the innocent culprit was his own Ambassador in Brazil, who had presented a note requesting the arrest of German agents. His list of names and supporting quotations from intercepted messages were placed in the hands of the Brazilian police, who quoted them during legal proceedings. Only luck prevented Berlin from receiving word of the broken ciphers.

Stephenson's aim at the conference—attended by representatives of BSC, the FBI, the State Department, and the U.S. armed forces—was to heal wounds and bring about the smoothest possible working partnership. He was up against Hoover's legalistic mind, however, when he tried again to preach the double-cross system of letting enemy agents continue their work if this would expose others. Hoover did not take kindly to suppression of evidence. Stephenson wanted to delay justice until the suspect's sources, his paymaster and accomplices and communications, had all been disinterred. He quoted the case of an intercepted letter from a German agent in Colombia: "The German wrote that his radio receiver had been confiscated by the Ministry of Communications. The identity of the writer was hidden under a false name but the Colombian government obligingly consulted the records and found that only two Germans had been required to surrender their radios. It was easy from this to pin down the agent. A skilled spy had slipped up while composing a letter. But by leaving him in place, a great deal more was learned about shipment of platinum badly needed for aircraft-engine magnetos in Germany. Agents were paying from three to ten times the official American market price for platinum and then smuggling it either through Italian LATI airliners or by sea to Lisbon. This led to new operations against supplies from Latin America to Germany."

The penalties of secrecy were evident in the simultaneous discussions in Washington between U.S. and British representatives on routine communications intelligence. Their knowledge of BSC operations was

407

scanty. Few realized how much ULTRA information had been disclosed to the White House. "Cryptographic liaison with the United States," reported the BSC Papers, "had previously been restricted and *sub rosa*. It could now become open and complete in regard to both operational and diplomatic codes and ciphers."

This optimistic observation glossed over the frictions between U.S. services. "Amity between the U.S. War and Navy Departments," BSC conceded discreetly, "was not at that time remarkable. The Office of Naval Communications regarded itself as a professional agency, able to perform its duties without outside help. The Army Signal Corps, faced with a program of vast and rapid expansion, was both conscious of its own temporary shortcomings and resentful of the professed self-sufficiency of the Navy."

Fascinating questions were discussed finally; for instance, the technique of "radio finger-printing," by which individual telegraphists could be identified. A smooth exchange of radio intelligence between the Allies was the goal. As the talks progressed, the service delegates showed an increasing, though grudging, respect for each other.

BSC was vaguely known to senior officers as an amateur organization. The British Admiralty representative was warned, before he left London, that Stephenson was "out of bounds . . . off limits" because of the sensitive role he was playing on U.S. soil. But it was impossible to conceal INTREPID's communications system. It carried more and more inter-Allied service traffic on an informal and temporary basis that became formal and permanent.

It seemed incredible that one group of intelligence specialists could be often unaware of the work conducted by another group. But BSC had been born in a period when its presence had to be kept utterly secret. It's relations with U.S. agencies may have seemed casual. They resulted from long and careful diplomacy. In this situation, the normal compartmentalization of secret agencies could only add to the general ignorance of BSC's purpose. This, of course, was the most persuasive reason for keeping on good terms with the FBI and Hoover.

When Hoover and Stephenson worked in tandem, operations often went smoothly indeed—inevitably to the annoyance of some State Department officials guarding national sovereignty. Each case presented Stephenson with a difficult choice: to tread on someone's corns or to let the real enemy slip out of reach.

The case of double agent William Sebold created a scandal, disclosed the loss of major military secrets to Germany, put thirty-three members of a Nazi spy ring in an American court, and established Hoover's authority in intelligence operations—at least in the public mind, though not in that of the State Department. But it made possible the open transfer of a secret weapon to the RAF when Washington was embarrassed to discover that the blueprints had been smuggled out to the Nazis while the British were refused it on grounds of security.

Sebold was a naturalized American of German birth. German intelligence trained him in 1939 in code and cipher work, the use of secret radio transmitters, and microphotography. He reported all this to the American authorities. Under FBI instruction, he established his German intelligence headquarters under cover of the Deisel Research Company in the Knickerbocker Building on 42nd Street in Manhattan, and a radio transmitter at Centerport, Long Island. He was put in touch with other German agents. When the FBI felt that his usefulness was ending, he was instructed to fold up. When he next appeared, it was to give evidence for the prosecution against other German-Americans who betrayed secrets, including the Norden bombsight.

The bombsight was described as "this country's most jealously guarded air defense weapon" by the prosecuting attorney at the subsequent trial. Stephenson had petitioned FDR for it. Now it could be acknowledged that Germany had been provided with vital bits of information on the bombsight back in 1938, enabling the Germans to reconstruct a model like the original.

What was never revealed, at the trial or later, was that secret transmissions to Germany had been intercepted and decoded more than a year earlier by the British. Stephenson had gone to the White House with evidence that the Norden and Sperry navigation and bomb aids had been betrayed already to the Germans. He said, three decades later: "The President ruled that the vital units should be released to the RAF during the Battle of Britain—a brave and lonely decision, unrecognized to this day."

By using Sebold's transmitter, and continuing to work the German intelligence channel, the FBI solved the mystery of another new Nazi microdot system. As early as November 1941, Bermuda had been warned to test for microdots in intercepted mail. In the following months, ironically the period when Hoover was personally still feuding with the British, twenty-one letters sprinkled with the deadly dots were picked up from mail traveling to and from Mexico.

By staying in the background but throwing all BSC's resources behind the FBI investigations that followed, Stephenson convinced Hoover again that he stood to lose by closing down British operations. BSC's man in Mexico persuaded the local police to arrest several "undesirable aliens," all Germans. All were to be repatriated by way of the United States. Thus they could be scrutinized at leisure by the FBI. The State Department, scrupulous about international law, had agreed to give them safe conduct to the repatriation ship in New York. Before the ship sailed, one of the Germans was found to be carrying microfilms on U.S. war production concealed in his shoes. The German, Georg Nicolaus, was thereupon interned.

More microdots were later detected in a letter intercepted by Bermuda. This one contained thirty dots addressed to Guseck/Berlin from Y2983. An investigation of Nicolaus's accounts in Mexico showed payments to a certain Y2983. Perhaps Nicolaus could be questioned in his place of internment?

But the State Department honored its word to the Mexicans that Nicolaus would be treated as an alien. Thus he remained safely out of reach behind the wired fence. The one person who would know the real identity of Y2983 was guarded against his FBI enemies by the U.S. State Department.

Seven more dotted letters were intercepted from Y2983. By this time, the United States was at war. U.S. service censors refused to release the letters, because nobody knew the code used in the dotted material.

"But by holding them," Stephenson argued, "you will warn the Germans that Y2983 is under observation."

A few letters were released after the dots were smudged and made indecipherable. Then Bermuda stumbled across a letter from Europe to a Mexico City post box. Hidden in the letter were instructions in microdots. SIS/Mexico rummaged through the suburban post office and came up with the name Joachim Ruge. The FBI found that a letter written by someone called Joachim Ruge had been posted in Honolulu more than two years earlier. The letter was addressed to Clara Ruge, Schaeferstrasse 22, Wannsee, Berlin, and began, "My dear Mother." The Y2983 letters already indicated that the writer knew Clara at Schaeferstrasse 22. Old street directories were consulted in London. The address was identified as a boardinghouse run by Clara Ruge, who had a son named Joachim.

Y2983 had been unmasked. The original Mexican spy ring had transmitted messages to New York for relay to Hamburg. The relay was operated by Sebold, the double agent. Once the Sebold connection was uncovered, the rest was simple. All the relevant information was passed to Stephenson's willing ally, the Mexican Prosecutor-General. With this, and a forty-seven-page FBI report, the Mexicans cleaned up. The FBI checked back through old messages and sent copies to BSC. Some referred to the mysterious company of Franco, Saunders and Fernandez. Fernandez was the new cover name for a resurrected German agent, Edgar Hilgert, who had come by way of Japan. Rereading the old messages, the examiners realized that the FBI had mistranslated after decoding the material recovered from Sebold, their double agent. The spy ring that everyone thought had been

411

smashed was still operating, with new code names for the survivors. In fact, German agents never ceased to be a problem in Mexico, despite the claim of one resounding and finalizing success from Hoover's publicity machine.

"He lived by publicity," commented BSC's Herbert Rowland. "Stephenson avoided publicity at all costs. Inevitably, the FBI got the credit. We never minded this. The FBI, in day-to-day working relations, were always superbly helpful. Hoover only began ordering his department heads to cut us off after he saw Roosevelt had bought Stephenson's arguments for an independent and co-ordinated intelligence agency."

The tension was made worse by skepticism about some British claims that the Second Front was established *behind* enemy lines because the secret armies already tied down German forces. Churchill told both the Russians and Roosevelt that in 1942 the choice of a conventional cross-Channel target was restricted to the few areas where the RAF could provide cover. Plans were being studied for landing successive waves of assault troops to bring about air battles that would result in the virtual destruction of enemy air power over Europe and further relief for the Russians. But, Churchill insisted, these plans must not be allowed to go off at half-cock.

"You are fighting the ghosts of the Somme," Stephenson told General George C. Marshall, the U.S. Army Chief of Staff, when Marshall wondered out loud why the British hesitated to launch the mass invasion of Europe. The Somme was synonymous with the slaughter of World War I, and Churchill never rid himself of the fear that it might be repeated.

"Churchill approached with dread the final reckoning," said Stephenson. "He loved action, mobility, swift moves and countermoves. A premature invasion could end in another slogging match and open-ended massacre."

There was always this hope that the tyrants could be destroyed without wholesale slaughter; that small

412

intelligence operations, selective assassination, and sabotage would corrode the foundations of Fortress Europe.

"Even if we had foreseen where this all might lead, there was no possible alternative response," said Stephenson. "Dirty tricks were like dirty atom bombs . . . you could not undo them. Passive resistance might work for Gandhi against the British. It could never work for French peasants against the Gestapo. The story of secret warfare was that of proceeding from one extreme to another—a steady escalation."

The most ambitious secret-intelligence operation, JUBILEE, dramatized his point. It was forced on the British by the need to convince allies as well as the enemy that a Second Front could not be opened across the English Channel yet. JUBILEE was a deliberate sacrifice, designed to save many more lives when the dreaded D day finally arrived. Making the best of things, the intelligence chiefs utilized it as cover for sixteen special operations. Americans, preparing at Camp X to take part for the first time in "offensive intelligence," rubbed shoulders with a Jewish refugee returning voluntarily to the nightmare. He was earmarked for a mission camouflaged by this strangest of invasions—one that was never intended to succeed.

41

OPERATION JUBILEE DECEIVED the enemy into thinking the slaves of Nazidom were about to be freed. When it seemed to fail, JUBILEE deceived the enemy about how the Second Front would be created. Canadian troops, who suffered the bulk of the casualties, thought it was a horrible mistake. Sergeant Peretz Rose saw it as a classic guerrilla operation that served political and military ends.

One of the many mysteries that JUBILEE was intended to solve was: How good is German radar?

Part of the answer was provided by Rose, an expert on communications for the Jewish Agency and its own secret army. Of German origin, he had debriefed a captured German radio-detection specialist and concluded from this and other evidence that the latest enemy radar units were scattered along the western wall of Fortress Europe. The most up-to-date was at the French port of Dieppe, seventy miles across the English Channel from Newhaven. The Newhaven-Dieppe cross-Channel ferry had been a prewar tourist route into Europe; now it might be possible to persuade the Germans that it was the future route of Allied invasion.

Two British radar experts were brought for special training to Camp X. They were introduced to the FBI man who would go with them to examine the enemy radar at Dieppe. The FBI man's job would be to shoot either or both of them dead if there was any danger of their being captured. Sergeant Rose would go along to demolish the enemy radar after the two British scientists had removed key pieces from the unit. The men would have an air umbrella and a rag-taggle fleet of more than 230 ships, with 16,000 soldiers, sailors, and airmen. Many would be slaughtered in what seemed a reckless and mismanaged attempt to invade Europe. Long afterwards although the real purpose of the raid remained obscure, Churchill wrote: "Dieppe occupys a place of its own in the story of the war, and the grim casualty figures must not class it as a failure." Lord Louis Mountbatten, who had then been the Chief of Combined Operations disclosed thirty-two years later that "Dieppe was one of the most vital operations of the whole Second World War. . . . It was The Great Deception."

All that Sergeant Rose ever said, when he retired to an Israeli settlement near Haifa, was: "Nobody was told the real reason for it, but the code name JUBILEE came out of a discussion with Stephenson, Chaim Weizmann, and other Jewish leaders.

"Weizmann, as a scientist, was in touch with Germans on matters like the atomic bomb and so on. I regarded him as the man working for a Jewish national home. Somehow we got talking about Jewish biblical traditions. If ever Hitler were destroyed and Europe liberated, it would be like that biblical period when slaves are freed and the land restored to its rightful owners—the period that Jews traditionally call Jubilee."

The FBI had been sending agents to Camp X in anticipation of setting up similar facilities in the United States for training men and women in foreign-intelligence operations. OSS, Bill Donovan's new organization, took over the responsibility in 1942.

Former FBI man James Callaghan, now working for Donovan, regarded himself as practically a Canadian. His parents had been born just across the Michigan border in Windsor, Ontario. He had worked closely with the Royal Canadian Mounted Police in helping cut the bureaucratic red tape when Stephenson needed to move bodies and equipment between Canada and New York. He was a first-class gunman, thirty years old in 1942, mature, stable, and accustomed to thinking for himself. He began working with the Toronto police in April, helping to test Camp X trainees. Some of them were assigned to "raid" targets in the city, eluding police "guards" who were playing the role of German sentries and counterespionage squads. None knew they were rehearsing the theft of Nazi military secrets.

Twelve French Resistance leaders were taken to the Gestapo headquarters at Dieppe that same April.

In BSC's Research and Analysis Division in New York, one of the German political refugees discussed with Allen Dulles the possibility of a military revolt against Hitler. The prospects were not good, he said. Not unless direct contact could be made with certain German officers. It would be dangerous for a German-born agent to try to return to the Fatherland through normal ports of entry. Trains, roads, and commercial airlines into German territory were too carefully scrutinized. To go in by parachute was risky, and capture would jeopardize others in the German forces who were interested in killing Hitler. One means of entry might be to land on the coast somewhere, under cover of a raid.

Baker Street was collecting information on German defenses and the number and quality of troops in the Dieppe area. Young women in civilian clothes traveled around Britain with prewar lists of visitors to France. They knocked on doors and asked surprised householders if they had taken photographs in tourist resorts. A snap of Ma or Pa playing on a beach with the kids would help to build up an estimate of the beach gradient; the density of pebbles would give a clue to capacity to take the weight of a tank. At Danesfield Hall in Buckinghamshire, not far from Bletchley Park, a young RAF Wing Commander, Douglas Kendall, supervised the analysis of aerial pictures taken by Spitfires emptied of guns and stuffed with cameras. A book was being compiled by Combined Operations Intelligence to guide a new kind of armed tourist.

The idea of a raid in force had been raised early in 1942 with a few limited intelligence objectives in view. Then in April of that year the U.S. Navy bounced back from disaster at Pearl Harbor with remarkable resilience. For the first time in history, heavy bombers designed for land-based operations were launched from a pitching carrier; they struck Tokyo, a display of American fighting spirit that made the British feel suddenly spiritless and slow. Churchill ordered a series of lightning raids against the enemy coast, but nothing faintly approaching the massive assault that many Americans seemed to regard as possible and necessary to relieve German pressure on Russia. The first six months of 1942 had been the most disastrous for Britain. The Royal Navy failed to communicate its faith in its highly developed convoy system, so that the U.S. Navy did not take advantage of freely offered experience. "We were woefully unprepared," commented the American naval historian Samuel Eliot Morison, "both materially and mentally." He was writing about the Atlantic. In the Pacific, the Americans were building up a powerful head of steam. They might still switch to a Japan First policy if the British seemed to hang back.

Dieppe began to evolve into the Great Deception.

France and all her overseas territories had been blacked out, so far as British diplomacy was concerned. American diplomats had become London's eyes and ears in France since the fall of Paris, piping intelligence to Washington, which passed it along to Stephenson for London.

For six months before Pearl Harbor, and right up until the late spring of 1942, American intelligence specialists under Donovan had been preparing for the invasion by Anglo-American forces into French North Africa: TORCH. But now the U.S. service chiefs wanted a direct assault into France, immediately.

A top-level strategy meeting between the President's military advisers and the British Chief of Combined Operations, Mountbatten, took place in Washington in June 1942 and brought the conflict into focus. "I faced my most important task of the whole war," Mountbatten said later. "I had to persuade Roosevelt's Service chiefs that our entire strategy needed rethinking." He carried the unwelcome news that the British were not confident about a frontal assault into France that year or even possibly the next. Every effort should be concentrated upon TORCH.

The prelude to TORCH would be the Dieppe raid—OPERATION JUBILEE. The British had not even told their own First Lord of the Admiralty about the Dieppe plan—nor would they, until it was all over, for security reasons. With each passing day, Dieppe's importance seemed to grow. President Roosevelt understood this, but he felt in no position to disclose to his own service chiefs a British-run operation so secret that even their own top men were not being informed unless they were directly involved.

"Mountbatten put one over the President" was the verdict of Henry Stimson, the Secretary of War, when it became known that the big invasion had been put off. The U.S. Joint Chiefs shared his anger. Roosevelt was backing TORCH again, apparently for no reason other than the slippery-tongued persuasiveness of a forty-year-old cousin to King George VI.

Lord Mountbatten was a great deal more than the King's cousin, of course. He had been fighting at sea for two years, rising up through the demanding ranks of the Royal Navy, which gave no quarter to a man because of his landlubber relatives. The degree of ignorance in Washington about the British, however, was startling. Part of it was Britain's own fault —caused by trying to do too much in too many places, and neglecting the need to explain herself to anybody.

Stephenson flew to London to discuss the dangers with Churchill, perching himself on the edge of the Prime Minister's bed the next morning. There he heard of more trouble with the Russians. Soviet Foreign Minister Molotov had produced the text of an unpublished communiqué drafted by the British Prime Minister that said "full understanding has been reached with regard to the urgent task of creating a Second Front in Europe in 1942." Churchill was nailed by his own vague promise. The Russians were publicizing it in a way he had not authorized. Now he must agree or else comfort the enemy with a conflicting announcement. He gave Molotov an *aide-mémoire* stating that although preparations were being made for cross-Channel landings in August or September, the size would be limited by landing-craft shortages. ". . . it would not further either the Russian cause or that of the Allies as a whole," Churchill stated flatly, "if, for the sake of action at any price, we embarked on some operation which ended in disaster. . . ."

What prompted this statement? JUBILEE seemed to be planned to fail, as if to prove the truth of Churchill's warnings. Indeed, JUBILEE's critics later used the statement as proof of a British intention to discourage further Russian demands for a Second Front that year.

There was a compelling reason for Churchill's concern to convince the Soviet Union that a cross-Channel invasion in 1942 would be suicidal. He wished to prevent Russia from deserting her allies. ULTRA and other Bletchley code-breaking teams were watching Russia flirt with the possibility of a negotiated peace. Germany dangled tempting bait. If the Soviet Union agreed to an armistice, Germany would be content with the land already captured. The Russians might take the bait if they believed Anglo-American strategy was to let Hitler and Stalin destroy one another, delaying a Second Front for this reason only. Churchill's fears were well founded, as ULTRA subsequently proved when it retrieved messages concerning the unprecedented journey that Molotov made, 200 miles into German-occupied territory, to discuss a separate peace with the Nazis in June 1943, an astonishing episode never officially made public.*

In the atmosphere of distrust already evident in mid-1942, Stephenson suggested it might be time for Churchill to talk directly with the President. The Prime Minister, in one of his glummer moods, was cheered by the prospect of action and agreed to go to Washington. The War Cabinet had gone through a depressing session on June 15, after the Germans had launched renewed offensives in Russia that synchronized with General Erwin Rommel's mysterious string of victories in North Africa. In Europe, retaliation for the assassination of Heydrich had gathered momentum, and Churchill listened to reports of children sent to camps for experimental purposes.

On June 17, Churchill penned a note to his King: "Sir, In case of my death on this journey I am about to undertake, I avail myself of Your Majesty's gracious permission to advise that you should entrust the formation of a new Government to Mr. Anthony Eden. . . ."

He traveled in the co-pilot's seat of a flying boat, wearing his siren suit, a black Homburg tilted on the back of his head, his hands resting on his gold-topped malacca cane. Stephenson had flown ahead with du-

* The Molotov peace mission was wrapped in mystery until ULTRA's story became known thirty-one years later. One reference to it appeared briefly in Sir Basil Liddell Hart's *History of the Second World War*.

plicates of secret documents dealing with the development of nuclear weapons and the Dieppe raid.

Churchill still seemed laden with doom when he sat with Roosevelt in the days that followed, either talking in a tiny sweltering room at Hyde Park or in their quarters at the White House. "He looked rather crumpled in his rompers, with a face of gloomy thunder," reported one of his air marshals. "Mr. Roosevelt also looked rather dishevelled." Neither seemed much interested in crucial matters of logistics. And little wonder. The President on June 21 handed the Prime Minister a pink slip, which stated simply: "Tobruk has fallen."

The fall of Tobruk was a disaster of the first magnitude. The seaport had symbolic importance in the great desert battles swirling west of Cairo. The Germans had launched an advance through the Crimea that would link them with their Afrika Korps under Rommel in the Middle East. From England, reinforcements were rushed by the long route around the far southern tip of South Africa.

The unadvertised tragedy in the loss of Tobruk was the innocent help given Rommel by the U.S. Military Attaché in Cairo, Colonel Bonner Fellers. Every detail of British operations had been radioed by Fellers to the Military Intelligence in Washington—and, because they had broken the State Department's Black code, which he was using, to the Germans as well. Every morning at breakfast, General Rommel had been presented with a concise appreciation of his opponent's plans, location of units, strength, and morale. Since January 1942, Rommel had been receiving the very information needed to reverse his fortunes. The Afrika Korps had been driven back during the previous year, but on January 21, 1942, Rommel rebounded with such elasticity that he had the British on the run for seventeen consecutive days. Churchill was thunderstruck. The Desert Fox seemed to anticipate each change in British tactics. By May 1942, he was driving to isolate Tobruk with a confidence that seemed born of foreknowledge. Tobruk, which had previously withstood a siege of 230 days, and appeared to be a tough nut to crack, was actually in

420

bad shape, for reasons Rommel ought not to have known. British traffic analysis of enemy transmissions concluded that Rommel was getting advance information from inside the British camp at Cairo.

Meanwhile, Rommel's thrusts could be throttled down by squeezing his fuel lines, which had to cross the Mediterranean in convoys vulnerable to attack from the island bastion of Malta. Malta alone had the capacity to slow Rommel; so Axis bombers and submarines struck the island time and time again, trying to prevent British ships from supplying the island. To hobble Axis attackers, a large-scale British operation was to go into effect on June 12 and 13. Paratroopers and strike forces would knock out nine Axis bases from which the raids on Malta were being launched. On June 11, Colonel Fellers obtained the details and in good faith filed them in the Black code to Washington through the Egyptian Telegraph Company in Cairo. A few hours later, the details were in enemy hands. The British sabotage units and supporting strike forces ran into the waiting arms of the Germans. Next day, the Axis bombers that should have been destroyed were launched instead against a British supply convoy. The convoy suffered such damage that it was forced to turn back. It would be months before another convoy broke through.

At the moment of disaster, the British were tracing the leaks back to the U.S. Military Attaché in Cairo, who was relying on the supposed impenetrability of the Black code.

Churchill wept over American criticism of Britain after she had fought steadily for nearly three years around the globe. Before the discovery of the Cairo leak, the Prime Minister burst out when told of yet another defeat in the desert: "Defeat is one thing. Disgrace is another." Now some of the disgrace was found to be shared with Americans, and Churchill seized his advantage. He asked for tanks and self-propelled guns for British forces in North Africa. He pressed Roosevelt to agree once more to the TORCH invasion of French North Africa. And he unfolded the substitute plan that would postpone the full-scale

421

crossing of the English Channel. The pendulum had swung back in favor of irregular operations.

JUBILEE had secret objectives. Its stated objectives sounded tiny and timid to the regular warfare chiefs. When Chief of U.S. Naval Operations Ernest King heard of it, he said: "I don't give a damn what the British do, so long as I get my battleships back into the Pacific."

A rehearsal for JUBILEE was slated for early July. Stephenson proposed flying back with Churchill, taking Bill Donovan along. "It would help," he wrote, "if Donovan might have some of his own men attached to the operation to convey what this is really all about."

Roosevelt had just issued the Military Order establishing the Office of Strategic Services. Stephenson's recommendation was the first routine reference to OSS. In this casual way, the forerunner of the Central Intelligence Agency popped into history. The date of the President's order, June 13, 1942, coincided with the British discovery of the Cairo leak, which underscored the need to co-ordinate intelligence.

On July 7, Donovan and Stephenson witnessed the German destruction of a British naval force probing across the Channel in an attempt to feel out the western wall of Fortress Europe. German planes spotted the small fleet before it got underway. The subsequent bombing forced cancellation of the raid. A profound depression descended upon the newly formed Hunting Groups, so named after an order Churchill issued for striking back at the enemy. The leaders met at their informal headquarters in London's bomb-scarred Richmond Terrace.

"They felt thwarted," Donovan reported later. "They were literally hunters, and they thirsted for action. They stood in the bare room of the bomb-blasted house, a youthful elite which had proved itself in battle, eating their hearts out."

The Great Deception would have to be built into something bigger than a coastal raid, and the Germans had just demonstrated how ill-equipped the British were to launch any raid at all. The Prime

Minister had issued a defiant order after the fall of France and he could not retreat: "Self-contained, thoroughly equipped raiding units . . . with specially trained troops of the hunter class must develop a reign of terror down the enemy coasts." He had foreseen that these raids would gather experience for the final invasion; and out of his order emerged Combined Operations, with Lord Mountbatten as its chief, charged with the special task of "devising the techniques of amphibious landings and designing and acquiring the appurtenances and appliances."

Appurtenances and appliances were being invented in Britain but their mass production would have to be left to the Americans. The Americans were not in the mood to supply arms until they saw evidence of British resolve. In mid-July, the President dispatched both Admiral King and the Army Chief of Staff, George Marshall, to London to fight out the argument for themselves with Churchill. They still insisted upon a cross-Channel invasion of substance. Churchill stalled. Two weeks later, JUBILEE forces began to gather.

On August 12, Churchill flew to Moscow, where he listened to an extended insult from Stalin about British fighting qualities. Stalin kept his face averted from Churchill, whose own expression darkened. Stalin spoke softly and deliberately. Suddenly Churchill crashed his fist on the table and unleashed on the Soviet leader a five-minute explosion of angry words. "I do not understand what you say," Stalin interrupted. "But by God, I like your spirit."

A message to Stephenson, back in New York, followed: "I think Stalin's Council of Commissars did not take the news I brought as well as he did. In his heart, so far as he has one, Stalin knows we are right."

Churchill had stated that there was nothing wrong with British courage but there was everything wrong about attempting to open the Second Front in France now. A week later, JUBILEE proved him right.

Sergeant Rose, the chubby-cheeked specialist from the Jewish Agency, had been flown from Camp X to the English county of Sussex, where Canadian troops were supposedly defending that part of the countryside against invaders. In fact, they were preparing for JU-BILEE. With Rose came the former FBI agent, Jim Callaghan. Both men had to be inserted into regular army units without arousing any suspicion that they were "funnies."

The two radar experts who were to go to Dieppe with them spent the final days studying relief maps and timing each phase of their own task. They carried slips of paper ordering the "beachmasters" to give them absolute priority to commandeer transport. A Canadian Field Security sergeant had been secretly ordered to back up Callaghan. He would act ostensibly as the scientists' bodyguard. In reality, he was to kill either or both if Callaghan failed to prevent them falling into enemy hands alive.

A team of Baker Street Irregulars was split up, each member attached to one of the regular Canadian military units. The Irregulars carried in their heads the details of the Gestapo jail where French Resistance leaders were being held. They carried with them new radiophones using a special wave length code-named PHANTOM. Their relay station would be a large new mobile transmitter. All this equipment had been wheedled out of United States Army supplies through Donovan, who, rather than jeopardize the expedition, said it was needed by his own men. In fact, two OSS men went along as observers, attaching themselves temporarily to an American unit—the now famous 1st United States Ranger Battalion, which had been training in the heart of the Scottish highlands. These were the first Rangers to be put through the British Commando battle drill, and from them were selected six officers and forty-four men.

At 10:00 A.M. on Tuesday, August 18, JUBILEE commanders sent a curt message crackling across southeastern England: "The show is on—*Now!*" Thousands of men in army camps and embarkation ports from Southampton to Newhaven were galvanized into chaotic action. Six hours later, the last battalions were aboard and the ships sealed. The largest British fleet to sail the Channel since the outbreak of war prepared to leave under cover of darkness. The statistics seemed impressive: 5,000 crack Canadian troops would carry the brunt of the fighting, supported by naval craft and planes handled by 10,000 sailors and airmen. Separate forces of Commandos would strike the coast on either side of the main target: Dieppe.

But the "invasion fleet" consisted of lightly armed small craft, including four river gunboats and a 700-ton sloop with one four-inch gun. During the night crossing, some of the 237 vessels ran into enemy torpedo boats. When the first troops and tanks hit the beaches early Wednesday morning, the Germans were waiting. Among the Canadians, three out of four were doomed the moment they left the landing barges.

The first official versions of the raid made it out to be a successful probing action to "unlock the priceless secret to victory" by showing the way back into Fortress Europe. This idea was later expanded into the terse statement: *No raid—no invasion,* meaning that the massive assault of D day nearly two years later was planned on the basis of JUBILEE, and could not have been planned in any other way. All this was true enough. American service chiefs saw the consequences of inadequate forces and hasty improvisations. The U.S. Rangers who saw the carnage summed up the reasons for failure: "Lack of equipment."

A handwritten note dispatched by carrier pigeon from one of the ships underlined the lesson.

To 1st Canadian Corps

From HMS Fernie

Date: 19 August 1942

Recording opinion now in case of trouble later. Surprise probably lost when naval encounter early A.M. *Strength of enemy:* seems to have been increased. Basic view of all officers . . . bomber command must provide really heavy support in future combined operations.

Troops seem to have behaved magnificently— never a trace of panic on radio . . . getting reports of casualties by lamp.

Sorry we failed. . . .

425

Almost all the survivors thought of the Dieppe raid as a failure. The hard decision had been made that they could not be told otherwise—but it had been a tremendous, if extravagant, success.

Frank Koons, from Iowa, was one who thought it a success. He was the first American soldier to kill a German in World War II and to earn the British Military Medal for bravery. He went ashore with the fixed bayonets of No. 4 Commando under the chief of the Scottish Clan of Fraser, Lord Lovat, a lanky figure in corduroy slacks and a knitted sweater, his gaunt face (like the rest of his 250 men) smeared with boot blacking. Koons was one of six American Rangers who were dropped in pitch darkness at a point some distance from Dieppe beneath the formidable Hess Battery of guns perched on high and seemingly unscalable cliffs. A German pillbox opened fire at the withdrawing landing craft, and the Commando went into action with clockwork precision. One group rushed the pillbox with hand grenades. Another hurled grappling irons and raised scaling ladders. The gully at the top of the beach was mined. Lovat led the men through the mine field by lamplight, following signposts planted by the Germans for themselves. A battery of Bangalore torpedo carriers crept across open ground to the Hess Battery perimeter wire and waited for the air strike, which should come within seconds, delivered by Hawker Hurricanes screaming flat over the water from England.

Koons saw a German sentry emerge from the dimly lit interior of a house. He raised his rifle and fired, and with four other Rangers rushed the house. They fought their way to the roof, and were rewarded with a bird's-eye view of the battery pits as the early light flooded this peaceful corner of France.

The Commandos around the battery fixed bayonets. The Hurricanes swept out of the dawn, their cannon and rockets firing, and were gone in seconds. Koons heard the wail of a hunting horn. It was Lovat's signal for the bayonet charge. They had to cover 250 yards at a run into enemy machine guns firing from behind concrete emplacements. As they leapt through gaps cut in the wire, some fell and the rest plunged on over their bodies. Once through the wire, they were frozen briefly by the sight of a jackbooted German officer stomping on the head of a prostrate and wounded Commando. Then bayonets and knives slashed limbs, bellies, and throats. Only four of the 112 Germans in the big guns' crews were left alive.

Other Commandos carried out similar assaults along the coast. Some, like Lovat's, had the dual purpose of dividing enemy defenses and diverting attention from groups of agents now at work. For them, too, the operation seemed a success.

Rose and Callaghan reached the big radio-detection station above the harbor, together with the radar scientists and the Canadian Field Security sergeant. By then, Canadian tanks had broken into the streets of Dieppe. "How they got there, God knows," said Callaghan later. He had been listening on the PHANTOM intelligence net and knew that most of the central assault force was pinned down, dying on the main beach. He carried no arms aside from the pistol for shooting the scientists if they were in danger of being captured alive. He packed, instead, the single very-high-frequency radiophone that linked his group with Baker Street by way of the big American Motorola, then the most advanced mobile radio in existence, aboard a ship standing off the coast.

"Thanks to the briefings from Watson-Watt, our own objective was like an open book," said Rose. The inventor of radar had wanted to go on the raid himself. His two substitutes were preceded by two of Callaghan's colleagues from Camp X. They took the guards by surprise, slitting their throats with knives and thin copper wire. Rose dived for the small hut where he expected to find certain radar controls.

Meanwhile, one of the scientists scrambled toward the big radar station overlooking the beach. He was Jack Nissenthall, one of Watson-Watt's young colleagues, temporarily attached to the RAF as a sergeant, selected because he combined the qualities of a good combat soldier and knowledge of what to look for inside an enemy radar station. He was the son of a Jewish tailor who had settled in London after escaping from Poland. With Sergeant Nissenthall were nine sharpshooters of the South Saskatchewan Regiment. Nissenthall's task was to search for signs of a German equivalent to the British cavity magnetron, the "magic black box" that made radar more flexible. The Canadians' job was to kill Nissenthall if he, too, seemed in danger of being captured alive.

Nissenthall found the main defenses of the German radar station impregnable. He was searching for a way inside when the first Hurricane air strikes burst around him. These were timed to cover the work of Rose, blowing up the radar control hut with plastic explosives after removing instruments. The RAF bombing made it unlikely that the Germans would realize their radar had been inspected and robbed of vital equipment.

Nissenthall picked himself up after the bombing, then cut the land-lines connecting the main radar station with Dieppe. The Germans would now have to send information by radio once they had the radar back in operation. And across the English Channel, monitors would retrieve the signals and other scientists could compare German data with that of British radar. It would give further insight into the progress of enemy research.*

On the other side of town, men of Special Operations Executive broke into the local jail, which had been converted into a Gestapo interrogation center, and collected the French Resistance leaders. Three Sudeten Germans in Nazi uniforms briefly shook hands with the Baker Street representatives before disappearing into the interior, doubtless relieved that the Irregulars had not found it necessary to shoot them.

Lord Lovat's timetable, to which he adhered with cold precision, required him to be back for reembarkation at 7:30 A.M. With seconds in hand, he surveyed the carnage at Battery Hess. With his Winchester sporting rifle now tucked under one arm, he suggested a laird on a grouse shoot. The big enemy

* The men on Baker Street Special Operations were not awarded medals, nor was their work disclosed after the war. Nissenthall was advised to change his name, for fear of German reprisals. He later settled in South Africa, where he ran an electronics company in Johannesburg.

guns had been spiked. Around lay the Commando dead. "Burn 'em," said Lovat. "Set fire to the lot." The Battery buildings were set alight, and the corpses piled around the blackened guns.

When they regained the boats, Lovat broke radio silence: "Every one of gun crews finished with the bayonet. Okay by you?"

A series of air battles began overhead. Under cover of this, and the fighting withdrawal of U.S. Rangers, British Commandos, and Canadian troops, the Baker Street teams escaped to the fast motor-torpedo-boat that would carry them and information on new German radar back to Newhaven. Their biggest achievement was the theft of equipment that would reveal details of enemy coastal radar and lead to countermeasures that would ease the path of Allied bombers into the Third Reich. The recovery of French intelligence chiefs and the insertion of anti-Nazi German agents would have long-term results. Even Canadians who were captured found the means to continue fighting. Among those who later escaped was a French-Canadian, Lucien Dumais. With his fluent French, he worked his way through Occupied France back to London, where he was asked to undertake "service out of this world." He duly returned to run the SHERIDAN network that helped 307 Allied fliers escape from Nazi hands after being downed in combat.

It was essential, however, that the Germans should believe JUBILEE had failed. This myth was so scrupulously preserved that even Mountbatten—who had at least defended the raid as a dummy run and the Great Deception—was unaware of all the secret operations it covered. Thirty years later, he met with Canadian survivors and relatives to reassure them that there had been no irresponsible sacrifice of life. Asked about the orders to shoot the scientists, rather than let them be captured, he said: "If I had known of those orders . . . I would immediately have canceled them." (Here can be briefly glimpsed the tension between regular service chiefs and the Baker Street Irregulars, who could not play by the accepted rules.) The men who carried out the secret mission all vanished, unrewarded, into anonymity. The commanding officer of the South Saskatchewans, Cecil Merritt, received the highest award for valor—the Victoria Cross. He, as a regular service officer, could receive it publicly, but he made it known that he regarded the medal as being for men whose courage could not be acknowledged.

A confidential briefing of newsmen in London at the conclusion of the raid was accompanied by a warning note: "This must not be quoted as coming from official sources. . . . Certain factors which for obvious reasons could not be previously disclosed are given for your guidance. The Combined Operations raid on Dieppe marks an important step forward in the planned program of our agreed offensive policy. . . ."

The over-all aim of JUBILEE had been, as Churchill later proposed to tell Parliament, "to deceive the enemy." The Prime Minister's statement was never made public, because the deception kept on working; by the end of 1942, Hitler held at least thirty-three German divisions along the Atlantic wall to protect primarily the small ports in the Calais-Boulogne area, in the belief that it was here the British intended to strike again. The statement, finally made to a secret session of Parliament, was conveyed through BSC to the President: "The attack which will be made in due course across the Channel or the North Sea requires an immense degree of preparation, vast numbers of special landing-craft and a great army trained, division by division, in amphibious warfare. . . . It would have been most improvident of us to attempt such an enterprise before all our preparations were ready. . . . A joint communiqué spoke of a Second Front in Europe in 1942 [because] it was of the utmost consequence to Russia that the enemy should believe we were so prepared and so resolved."

The injuries sustained by the raiders were analyzed. Out of 4,963 Canadians who fought on the beaches, 3,367 were casualties. Most were hit during landing or re-embarkation. Troops were most likely to be wounded in the lower limbs, then the upper limbs, thorax, neck and head, and, finally, abdomen —in that order.

These grisly studies led to development of the armor, craft, and techniques finally employed on D day to cut down casualties. JUBILEE proved the need for overwhelming bomber and fire support. New landing craft, the LCT(R)s, were devised to fire 1,080 heavy rockets on a single patch of beach in twenty-six seconds—matching the bombardment that would ensue if eighty naval cruisers shelled simultaneously. The island-hopping campaign through the Pacific by U.S. amphibious forces was based on equipment and lessons arising from the ashes of Dieppe.

During the raid, more than 1,000 messages were exchanged with radio operators in Occupied France. From these, BSC, in a combined operation with the research and analysis section of OSS, demonstrated that the secret armies of Europe were not yet ready. "The sea of people in which the guerrillas could swim like fish was still missing," said Stephenson, paraphrasing Mao.

Both Admiral King and General Marshall, such bitter and impatient critics, would eventually put their signatures to a letter to Mountbatten written on the final D day:

Today we visited the British and American armies on the soil of France. We sailed through vast fleets of ships with landing-craft of many types pouring men, vehicles and stores ashore. . . . We have shared our secrets in common and helped each other all we could. We wish to tell you at this moment that we realize that much of this remarkable technique, and therefore the success of the venture, has its origins in developments effected by you and your staff of Combined Operations.

JUBILEE's secrets were so well kept that long after the war, a famous libel action was fought over a report by the author Quentin Reynolds that "a scientist known as Professor Wendell" went to Dieppe on a suicide mission. The columnist Westbrook Pegler called Reynolds a liar, braggart, and absentee war correspondent, arguing that the story of "a mad scientist" was woven out of Reynolds's imagination.

Reynolds sued, and in 1955 the libel case was heard. A member of Lord Mountbatten's staff, Jock Laurence, testified that Quentin Reynolds had reported accurately the presence of scientists on a dangerous mission. But details could not be released from secret files, even after so long a period. The judge agreed to treat the information as confidential if the witness would write names on a piece of paper which was later destroyed. Reynolds won the libel action and was awarded $175,000. Another twenty years passed before Mountbatten, speaking as the Chief of Combined Operations, made further disclosures.

JUBILEE, said Mountbatten in 1974, convinced the Germans that the full-scale invasion could not be conducted over open beaches. "We came firmly to the conclusion that we could invade the open beaches with prefabricated mobile ports," said Mountbatten. "MULBERRIES were developed—the ports we floated across the Channel to produce sheltered water off those open beaches that the enemy had been deceived into lightly defending. So JUBILEE became the Great Deception."

Mountbatten knew nothing about the prizes won by Allied intelligence, except where these affected his own forward planning. Among the agents brought out for BSC was one whose report, sealed and stamped THIS IS OF PARTICULAR SECRECY, told of "liquid air bombs being developed in Germany . . . of terrific destructive power." Stephenson noted that these were likely to be rockets with atomic warheads.

The report began a chain of events, obscured in the months immediately ahead by preparations for the next big amphibious operation—TORCH—on the road to D day.

432

Part
Six

THE END OF
THE BEGINNING

"Now this is not the end.
It is not even the beginning of the end.
But it is, perhaps, the end of the beginning."

—Winston Churchill, at a meeting
in the City of London on the final day
of fighting in OPERATION TORCH

42

September 5, 1942: Roosevelt to Churchill: "Hurrah!"
September 6, 1942: Former Naval Person to Roosevelt: "O.K., full blast."

LOTS OF THINGS would go wrong with TORCH, the mass onslaught against French North Africa heralded by the brief exchange of hurrahs. Even FDR and Churchill were premature in congratulating each other on the decision to go ahead, made in the face of opposition from some of their own commanders. TORCH was delayed by one unforeseen obstacle after another. Mistakes were made. But the infant OSS was ready to slide into harness within three weeks of Dieppe. Ahead was complete U.S. entry into the type of conflict that would produce the gigantic organizations with their unaccountable budgets known today as the Central Intelligence Agency and the National Security Agency. History must judge if TORCH also marked a fatal division between British and U.S. intelligence systems—shattering Stephenson's dream of one coordinated agency, democratically monitored without being exposed to subversion.

TORCH, made possible by BSC's acquisition of the French codes, signified the final spark that would fulfill Churchill's vision of "Europe ablaze." After TORCH, BSC became the junior partner. The partnership worked well enough in completing an atomic bomb. In secret warfare, it depended more and more upon personal friendship between men like Stephenson and Donovan. Sometimes they just could not paper over the cracks, especially in the early days of OSS in England. Miles Copeland, a future CIA case officer, unconsciously annoyed the British from the moment he arrived in mid-1942.

He described the OSS mood as one of "we have to show these British how to clean up their mess." When security was finally lifted in 1974, he wrote in the *Spectator:* "We Americans bumbled about Britain launching out on what we thought were new tacks, only to have it brought home to us that the British had been there first and we were muddying the waters. . . . There was our *gaming* by which carefully briefed American officers imagined themselves in the shoes of the German General Staff and *gamed out* how they would react to the various alternative moves [the British] General Staff were contemplating. For not always acting on our results, we thought our commanders fools and incompetents. Eventually we were told that they knew exactly what intelligence the Germans were acting upon—for the simple reason that it was they who had furnished it through the 'double X' operation which John Masterman revealed thirty years later. We were *not* told that [the British] General Staff also knew what counter-moves the Germans were about to make, because they were reading the Germans' top secret orders—often before [German] commanders in the field were receiving them. Only some twenty-odd American officers had access to ULTRA. The rest of us, despite our 'top secret' security clearances, went through the war judging our commanders as we saw them—usually with not very flattering conclusions."

Copeland in July 1942 had arrested a German suspect in London. He was helped by Frank Kearns, who later became a well-known CBS newscaster. They marched their captive to Grosvenor Square and what was then U.S. military headquarters, where they were stopped by a very angry British colonel.

"Our agent was already under Scotland Yard's surveillance," Copeland related. "He was to have been turned into a controlled double-agent sending his spymasters in Berlin only what the British High Command wanted them to have. . . . There were several such incidents at God-knows-what cost to 'Deception.' . . ."

There was only so much Stephenson could do to persuade London to stop treating the OSS like an infant. Finally he sent Donovan a note, quoting *Hamlet*:

> *"To thine own self be true,*
> *And it must follow, as the night the day,*
> *Thou canst not then be false to any man."*

This, said Stephenson, was the philosophy at the top in Britain, as it was that of Donovan and his colleagues. If they could all remember this, and treat one another as honorable men, a fatal rift could be avoided.

The basic argument arose during preparations for TORCH. The Anglo-American invasion of French North Africa was preceded by large-scale OSS operations. Bill Donovan and BSC were agreed on extending coordination to the Mediterranean area.

But from London came word that secret operations must be kept separate. This "seeming perfidy" sent Donovan into "a towering rage," according to Bickham Sweet-Escott, who was then the senior Baker Street Irregular in Washington. "Donovan was convinced he had been double-crossed."

The cause of Donovan's distress was troublemaking by Russian agents who had infiltrated London. One was Kim Philby, holding a key desk job in British Secret Intelligence. He was in the best possible position to help his real masters, the Soviet Secret Service. Philby, as he wrote later in his memoirs, published in Moscow, was keenly aware that "Stephenson offered all help in the early stages in order to earn the right to receive from the Americans the intelligence that might be expected to flow from deployment of the far greater American resources." In the long run, any partnership between American and British intelligence agencies was a threat to Russia. Philby had access to the top professionals in British intelligence and easily persuaded them that OSS would introduce blundering or ambitious American interference into their tidy arrangements. After that, efforts were made constantly to sabotage the Stephenson-Donovan partnership. This did not tax the integrity of specialists in dirty tricks. Orders could be mislaid, messages overlooked. Hoover glimpsed what was going on when he requested certain British files on Communist subversion which had a direct bearing on the U.S. war effort. Philby sidetracked the FBI's inquiries, then withheld some files and redirected others. Hoover became rightly convinced that somewhere in the pipelines were operatives working against his country's interests, but the proof itself was under Philby's control until he finally scampered off to Moscow twenty years later.

The rush of events in the fall of 1942 kept Stephenson and Donovan in control of what might have proved a disintegrating alliance. Donovan had proposed to the President that preparatory work in the French colonies be speeded up so that "the aid of native chiefs might be obtained, the loyalty of the inhabitants cultivated, fifth columnists organized and placed, demolition materials cached and secret armies of bold and daring men installed." All this would fall upon OSS shoulders. The British had been expelled from French territories overseas, and were diplomatically "blind" there. To the Soviet-directed traitors within British intelligence, these proposals added to the threat of OSS dominance in a strategically important region.

While the bickering went on, the commander of the U.S. Fifth Army, General Mark Clark, code-named MARK, and a Baker Street Irregular were in the British submarine *Seraph*, nosing its way along the Mediterranean sea bed for a rendezvous in enemy waters. The crew was skilled in clandestine operations. Awaiting MARK on a beach seventy-five miles from Algiers was the same Robert Murphy who had been the U.S. Embassy Counsellor at Vichy, lending an attentive ear to the pro-Nazi French leader, Pierre Laval.

"This was the kind of co-ordination we were aiming

for," commented Stephenson later. "Huge armies waited in the wings to sail through hostile waters to the French colonies. The British were in no position to judge the temper of French commanders in Morocco and Algeria. The Americans had been doing that. General Clark was now heading for the most delicate talks to discover how much resistance there might be to the landings. We wanted the French empire to re-enter the war against the Axis. TORCH would open the road back."

Clark's submarine surfaced at 2100 hours on October 22. Ridgeway Knight, an OSS agent, had been feeling his way back and forth across the empty beach for nearly three hours. Behind him, Murphy watched from a villa where he had slung a naked light bulb in the window. With him in the villa was the French General Charles Mast.

At midnight a rubber raft paddled by a British Commando sniffed along the sands. Three more rafts followed, with Clark and his staff officers. The *Seraph*, sank to the sea floor and would not surface again until the following night. In between, French and American generals conferred.

This last-minute reconnaissance was intended to convince French military leaders that TORCH was underway; that France itself would be liberated if this operation was successful; and that the American government guaranteed the honesty of British intent.

The commander of French troops in Algeria was General Alphonse Juin, who had negotiated with Göring in Berlin only eleven months earlier on the use of French African territory by German troops under Rommel. On the day of Clark's meeting, the battles raging in the deserts east of the French colonies were still apparently inflicting defeat on the British. The French under Juin—who knew nothing of Rommel's moral defeat—thought the Germans were heading beyond the Pyramids for a link-up with German forces striking out of the Russian Caucasus. Juin and his cronies were unlikely to come off the fence for the sake of an ill-favored Anglo-American expedition. Also, Juin was on close terms with the chief of the German military mission in Casablanca, General

Theodor Auer, and his fluctuating neutrality might become TORCH's death knell. There were now 107,000 Allied troops preparing to land along 2,000 miles of North African coast. Outside Cairo, the British 8th Army was standing its ground at last and would soon move onto the offensive. All this was at risk. By nightfall, Clark had concluded his talks with the French. The meeting was about to break up. A local coast watcher bicycled over with a warning that a police search had just started and was approaching the villa.

"We dived into the wine cellar as if fifty skunks had been tossed into the room," Clark said later. The French general and his staff officers hunkered down with the Americans while Murphy and Knight slid a table over the trap door, rolled back their sleeves, and began a game of poker. The police duly arrived, inspected Murphy's diplomatic credentials, and Knight's vice-consular papers, apologized, and left.

General Clark left *Seraph* at Gibraltar on Monday after a weekend of terrifying possibilities. Churchill cabled Cairo:

CLARK HAS VISITED "TORCH" AREA AND HELD LONG CONFERENCE WITH FRIENDLY FRENCH GENERALS. WE HAVE REASON TO BELIEVE THAT NOT ONLY WILL LITTLE OPPOSITION BE ENCOUNTERED, BUT THAT POWERFUL ASSISTANCE WILL BE FORTHCOMING. EVENTS MAY THEREFORE MOVE MORE QUICKLY, PERHAPS CONSIDERABLY MORE QUICKLY, THAN HAD BEEN PLANNED. . . .

Clark's accomplishment was a climax to months of preparations. CYNTHIA had secured the code books that unlocked Vichy's naval mysteries and allowed ULTRA to break the new German-French codes and so gain insight into plans to resist any landings. The Dieppe raid provided practical information. Donovan's research and analysis teams studied French North African shipping and railroads, cargo capacities, terrain maps, tidal tables, and charts of reefs and channels. Two U.S. vice-consuls smuggled out of Casablanca a French marine pilot who could navigate an armada through sunken ships and reefs.

A clandestine network of radio stations was strung across North Africa: LINCOLN at Casablanca, FRANKLIN at Oran, YANKEE at Algiers, PILGRIM at Tunis. Tribal chiefs were enlisted to enter enemy fortifications, provide escorts for agents, and carry plastic explosives, guns, and other equipment inland. Fishermen located U-boat hideouts. Cable offices were infiltrated. Airline and shipping clerks were bribed for information on the movements of senior Axis officials. The center of the web was Tangier International Zone, where contact was possible between the Americans and the British, who maintained there a solitary legation in an ocean of enemies.

ULTRA played little part at this stage. General Clark gave it equal value to the field intelligence so patiently gathered. U.S. service chiefs in general were still not fully informed of the range of Bletchley's work in retrieving, decoding, and analyzing all German signals. Apart from President Roosevelt and Bill Donovan, Americans were told only as much as the British felt they needed to know, on the same basis as their own commanders. The Americans at Bletchley had a severely restricted view of the vast operations there. One result was that American commanders, like many of their British colleagues, did not exploit ULTRA situation reports. Perhaps this was just as well. The special ULTRA liaison unit shipped to Gibraltar prior to TORCH distilled little useful information from German traffic. Later, General Clark declared that ULTRA became the vital intelligence weapon once it's value was understood. The problem persisted of when to risk losing a battle to protect the secret.

General Dwight D. Eisenhower became Supreme Commander Allied Expeditionary Force a week after Dieppe, and moved into London's drab Norfolk House, a battered building near The Hole. He plunged into plans for the amphibious operation that would make Dieppe seem like child's play. One TORCH force with 35,000 troops under General George S. Patton would invade Africa, 3,000 miles from the point of embarkation at Norfolk, Virginia. Another 39,000 U.S. Army troops would sail from England. Yet another force embarked in England would consist of British and American troops totaling 33,000 men. These forces had to hit widely separated beaches in French North Africa within narrow time slots.

Even in peacetime, the synchronization of such mixed groups of sea, land, and air units would have been a triumph. Eisenhower had good reason for misgivings. There were the same difficulties encountered at Dieppe: shortages of shipping, lack of escorts, and inadequate landing craft. And what if intelligence proved as faulty?

On August 23, Eisenhower warned the Chiefs of Staff: "It is my opinion that this expedition . . . is not sufficiently powerful to accomplish against the potential opposition . . . the purpose prescribed."

The Casablanca landings struck him as presenting the gravest risks. Divisions of troops would be sailing directly from the United States, unblooded in war, exposed to U-boat attack, many of them unfit for action after riding heavy Atlantic swells, and with the imponderables greatly enlarged by distance and time. The other targets, at Bône, Algiers, and Oran, would have to be hit simultaneously; and the whole combination, depending as it did upon lack of organized French and German resistance, seemed fraught with uncertainties.

"TORCH was one of the most momentous decisions. It would eventually pull more than a million Americans into the Mediterranean theater," Stephenson later noted in BSC records. "This was the first amphibious operation conducted by the United States in forty-five years except for the landings at Guadalcanal. By any yardstick, it was the boldest. And it presented the most formidable security problems. There would have to be two refuelings at sea. Nobody on board the American vessels had ever seen such an operation and very few had seen combat. The USN Air Group of five carriers alone had to sortie out of Bermuda, only one of hundreds of movements that required co-ordination while being concealed from an enemy who had listened for weeks to the preliminary volume of radio traffic." London was worried and Stephenson reported that Washington had become equally cautious. There were renewed doubts about

British ability to hold Egypt; a German victory there would raise the odds against TORCH.

"If 'Torch' collapses or is cut down," Churchill signaled, "I should feel my position painfully affected in view of my promises made to Stalin with the President's approval."

Admiral King in Washington said it was the British now who made light of the hazards after dramatizing the dangers of a cross-Channel invasion. The Americans, who thought the risks worth taking in the Channel, now suffered a fit of nerves about North Africa.

Churchill called it "a formidable moment in Anglo-American-Soviet affairs." He was under heavy strain and had to be protected by Stephenson, who knew Roosevelt thought the Prime Minister's judgment was disturbed by the insistent Russian demand for more supplies and more action. The PQ convoys* from Britain to Russia were threatened by TORCH itself. PQ 18 had sailed after Russian protests against suspension of these suicidal supply runs through northern waters. On September 14 the War Cabinet in London learned that although no previous convoy had been subjected to such repeated German air attacks "twenty-seven ships out of the forty in convoy have arrived in Archangel." The yardstick was that the PQ convoys should continue provided half the ships got through. By those standards, as Stalin well knew, the British must continue their PQ convoys. But delays with TORCH meant that the next PQ sailing would have to be put back: the British simply did not have enough ships and escorts for both.

In the middle of dealing with this crisis, Churchill had to cope with a domestic political challenge. Its nature was disclosed to the President by Stephenson because the crux of the matter was a War Cabinet minute labeled *Confidential Record: Not for Circulation.*

"The challenge comes from the former British Am-

---

* PQ supply convoys were coded by BSC, which reported to Roosevelt that the last to get through had lost twenty-five out of thirty-six British merchantmen, together with cargoes of 430 tanks, 210 aircraft, and 3,350 vehicles for the hard-pressed Russians.

bassador to Moscow, enthroned as Lord Privy Seal: Stafford Cripps. Cripps is regarded with a jaundiced eye by Churchill. He was a pacifist until Russia was invaded. As a socialist, he is entitled to a position within the all-party Cabinet. Cripps expressed dissatisfaction with the machinery for central direction of the war and threatened to resign. This could spell disaster. Churchill has written to Stafford Cripps: 'Great operations impend which are in full accordance with your own conceptions and on which we are all agreed. . . . We must have fibre and fortitude.' "

The Lord Privy Seal still kept running interference. Churchill, weary and sick, wondered if there was something Machiavellian about Cripps's behavior. Finally, Cripps was warned that his actions were dangerously distracting. "If TORCH fails," Churchill repeated, "we are all sunk."

Fears for Churchill's health mounted with the suspense. "Winston's very low," Stephenson told Roosevelt.

"He finds it harder to wait for action than I do," said Roosevelt, glancing at his useless legs.

But now even the President was betraying impatience. American equipment and troops were in some cases to be transported by British ships diverted from the Russian convoys. These ships could not be ready before November 8. Roosevelt wanted the ships for TORCH but he also wanted a resumption of the convoys to Russia—a contradictory request, received with silence in London. The calculations there had been narrowed down to a simple proposition: if the Soviet Union was to get relief from enemy pressure, it must choose between short-term aid in the form of supplies or long-term benefits from TORCH special-intelligence operations, which were the dry run for mass uprisings planned throughout Europe. If TORCH worked, a start would be made in undermining the enemy. The trouble was that TORCH was running behind schedule.

On Wednesday, September 23, ULTRA picked up German signals disclosing that Rommel had quit the desert to be treated for nasal diphtheria, chronic stomach ailments, and poor blood circulation. Mussolini saw him in Rome next day and expressed the view that Rommel's ailments were psychological. ULTRA took note. All was reported through Stephenson to Roosevelt. The President commented that Rommel must have suffered a demoralization more severe because he had been accustomed to a diet of victories "based on intelligence from inside the British camp which, thank God, we have now terminated."

Roosevelt's remarks were passed along with another request for Churchill to reconsider the PQ convoys. The President noted that since the Russians were just now performing so splendidly at Stalingrad, it seemed wrong to tell Stalin that the British convoys could not sail. Roosevelt signaled: "I would like to suggest a different approach in which PQ 19 would sail in successive groups."

Churchill's reply was terse: "The convoy is *not* sailing and there is no way to conceal this from the Russians. We are preparing to sail ten ships individually during the October twilight. They are all British ships for which the crews will have to volunteer, the danger being terrible and their sole hope if sunk being Arctic clothing. The chance of crews from sunken ships surviving in open boats is very remote."

Now the Russians again accused Britain of secretly conspiring with the Nazis; this was why convoys to Russia were being suspended. The accusations were based on the strange flight of Deputy Führer Rudolf Hess to England. A statement was issued from London on October 21, flatly denying any conspiracy. Roosevelt asked Stephenson if any more was known about Hess. "Only that he's quite mad," Stephenson replied. "Unfortunately, we can't convince Moscow."

General Mark Clark made his secret journey to North Africa the next day. Eisenhower moved his headquarters to Gibraltar, adopting the code name HOWE. Fast troopships began to assemble for the dash to TORCH beaches. Stephenson again called on Roosevelt before flying to London. The President said gleefully that he was glad to recognize the old firm of MARK, HOWE & TORCH was setting up shop on the Rock, "for wasn't Gibraltar the symbol of permanence for some well-known American insurance company?"

Less than 200 miles from TORCH, the British 8th

Army began to sweep forward. "The battle which is now about to begin will be one of the decisive battles of history," declared General Bernard Montgomery in Cairo.

In restaurants and bars from Marseilles to Casablanca, a campaign of misinformation got underway. Rumors were leaked by Allied agents that an Allied invasion fleet was moving toward Dakar on the South Atlantic coast of French Africa. Murphy's spadework now yielded results. He had used his diplomatic window into the Third Reich to study Nazi espionage. The Germans ran spy schools, using instructors from the Vichy French, to produce experts in African tribal languages and customs. Murphy had pretty well pinpointed the enemy's agents. A flood of "security leaks" and gossip was directed toward them. The Nazi command headquarters at Wiesbaden, analyzing the false reports, concluded that the Allied armada was heading for Dakar, some 2,000 miles from the impending action. The German Mediterranean fleet, long-range aircraft, U-boat wolf packs and raiders were thus misdirected, away from the scene of action. Even the passage of 151 Allied ships through the narrow Gibraltar strait was misinterpreted with the help of planted reports: double agents told their German contacts that the ships were rushing aid to starving Malta.

On November 5, when small boys in England celebrate the Gunpowder Plot to blow up Parliament, Churchill wrote a message for the men already fighting west of Cairo: "I propose to ring the bells all over Britain for the first time this war. Try to give me the moment to do this in the next few days. At least 20,000 prisoners would be necessary."

To Roosevelt, a personal message was sent that scarcely concealed Churchill's pride. "He had been pricked for too long by sniping critics," Stephenson recalled. "He found these the most trying weeks of the entire war. He hated to have it thought that he, or his people, lacked guts or stamina because he knew how untrue it was. Now he began to see daylight. He asked me to convey to the President the news that after twelve days of heavy and violent fighting, his

446

troops in the desert were inflicting a severe defeat on the enemy. It was his answer to suggestions of reluctance to fight. And the British 8th Army had done it *before* relief came."

The TORCH armada slid through hostile waters untouched. At each of the landing areas, secret-army radio transmitters were now in contact with troopships and escorts, reporting the disposition of pro-Nazi French units of the three fighting services. Guerrillas began a series of sabotage operations timed to diminish any resistance. In London, SIS men moved into the studios of the British Broadcasting Corporation with copies of a message to be inserted into regular programs beamed to enemy-held territories. "Robert has arrived."

That Thursday, children in the Strand were singing "Remember, remember, the fifth of November . . . Gunpowder, treason and plot" as Stephenson walked toward Downing Street. There were none of the usual bonfires except those lit by German bombers, no firecrackers except those of antiaircraft red tracers. But there were young urchins with straw-stuffed dummies depicting Guy Fawkes, the man who had failed to destroy the Mother of Parliaments. At five minutes to midnight, sitting with Churchill, he heard a BBC piano recital interrupted by a communiqué from Cairo: "The Germans are in full retreat." And still, miraculously, TORCH went unreported.

On Friday the key installations in Algiers were quietly surrounded by young guerrillas. Elsewhere, post offices and prefectures, radio stations and police posts, government quarters and transport centers were infiltrated by those Frenchmen loyal to General Charles Mast, on whom authority would legally devolve. Mast, once the very model of a proper St. Cyr military graduate, had become a convert to the rough guerrilla style on the night he dived with General Clark into a wine cellar.

Saturday passed. Churchill mulled over a message from Cairo: "Ring out the bells . . . 8th Army advancing." But Churchill wanted confirmation about the 20,-000 prisoners.

Early Sunday, the then-secret War Cabinet minutes

recorded: "24 hours ending 0700—November 8, 1942—French North Africa. Operations commenced early this morning to occupy French Morocco and Algeria to provide base for advance on Tunisia."

In the White House, the President received the message that signaled the closing of the first phase in the history of British Security Co-ordination. "Landings taking place at Algiers and Oran. . . . Landings at Casablanca . . . Reports received from American and British forces indicate early success . . . In Egypt the pursuit of the enemy continues."

Sitting in the U.S. consulate at Gibraltar, Generals Clark and Eisenhower listened to the chorus of radio announcements to the waiting armies in the shadows, and the repeated BBC call: "Listen Yankee Pilgrim Franklin Lincoln . . . Robert has arrived. Robert has arrived."

Stephenson flew back to New York by the usual route with reports from TORCH and El Alamein. BSC had achieved the purpose implicit in its title: co-ordination of security. Little Bill would present an even lower profile now. Big Bill Donovan's future rested upon convincing the Joint Chiefs of Staff that co-operation and integration of intelligence did work; that the British had something of value to offer; that rag-tag-bobble mobs of rebels were worth more than their lack of arms would indicate.

Hard times lay ahead. Nobody pretended guerrilla warfare could do more than prepare the way for regular armies. There would be arguments about the secret operations in North Africa and revived doubts about the President's cozy relationship through unorthodox channels with the Prime Minister. But it could never be denied that American losses in TORCH were light because at El Alamein the British had finally destroyed "nine-tenths of the enemy's tanks and three-quarters of their guns." Nor could it be doubted that intelligence operations at Dieppe had made this possible, or that already a fresh wave of hope lifted the spirits of the resisters in Europe as the code sentence was finally heard: "Robert has arrived."

It was eighteen months since Stephenson had signaled Churchill: "I have been attempting maneuver Donovan into co-ordinating all United States intelligence." Now Donovan was to get overriding authority to operate in the fields of intelligence, sabotage and counterespionage, and to conduct guerrilla operations.

On Sunday, November 15, 1942, it was confirmed to Churchill that 40,000 prisoners had been taken, double the number he requested. For the first time in more than three years of war, the church bells pealed across Britain.

"Now this is not the end," the Prime Minister signaled INTREPID and FDR. "It is not even the beginning of the end. But it is the end of the beginning."

For both Churchill and Roosevelt, it was the end of the beginning in two fields of warfare that could not be discussed openly. "Atomic bombs and guerrillas seemed at opposite ends of a spectrum ranging from sophisticated to primitive," said Stephenson. "This was really not so. Each agent, saboteur, and partisan had to be brought together in a most intricate design to create the final war-winning explosion just as much as atomic particles had to be properly juggled. Nuclear warfare and the Baker Street Irregulars intertwined, and for the balance of the twentieth century, the world would be changed by this bizarre relationship between the physicist and the guerrilla."

Communist agents within the Allied intelligence agencies saw this, too.

43

NEW AND EVEN more mysterious misunderstandings bedeviled American and British intelligence agencies after TORCH. Signals went astray. Questions went unanswered.

Stephenson was notorious for catching small imperfections in his far-flung enterprises. Now time was against him. He was reading through the night, as reports and signals piled into BSC. They arrived according to priority, a system far from foolproof. A significant action might start so modestly that early reports went to the bottom of the pile.

A seemingly routine request from Hoover was given a low priority. "The FBI director asked for information only available in London," recorded the BSC Papers. "The response was insufficient in speed, quantity and quality."

Hoover had asked for further data on subversion. He told Stephenson in late 1942 that he suspected Communist sympathizers had buried his request.

Stephenson was in the thick of a dozen battles. His grueling schedules averaged out at twenty working hours each day of the war. More than 30,000 experts, engaged in communications-intelligence throughout the world, were linked by invisible threads to BSC in New York. Each fresh crisis was analyzed by Stephenson and, when feasible, turned over to an officer who had both the freedom to act and the responsibility of reporting only when the case was resolved. A familiar spectacle was the expressionless face bent over documents, digesting each page in what seemed like split seconds. Now, hearing Hoover's concern, he shot off a signal. Dated November 9, 1942, it went to C, the chief of the British establishment Secret Intelligence Service:

> I have arranged, on my personal word to Hoover, the appointment to us of a trusted FBI representative as liaison with us on Communist activities exclusively. . . . If I am not to be accused once again by Hoover of withholding relevant material from London, it will be essential that you personally instruct that I be promptly supplied with all available material so I may implement our promises and so that it will not be necessary for Hoover to turn elsewhere. . . .

Despite sharply worded reminders, C's reply came after Christmas: "My officers are already engaged in careful and exhaustive survey of Communist material. . . ."

C at the time was General Sir Stewart Menzies, who had been in intelligence since 1915. He was an honest soldier but quite at sea with men like Hoover. His career and background exemplified the narrow confines of regular British secret agencies. He had grown up among men who "played the game," never cheated, consequently (this is hard to imagine today) never dreamed of distrusting a colleague.

The colleague whom C should have distrusted was Kim Philby, the Soviet spy, handling routine INTREPID traffic. After the Japanese surrender, Hoover had discussed his own confusions with Stephenson. He sensed something wrong, could not put his finger on it, and for a time withheld co-operation. This gave way to his feeling that INTREPID's expulsion might be precisely what the Soviet Union sought. Stalin did not want strong and independent revolutionary armies that would challenge his authority in postwar Europe. Thus he would be accused by Tito of depriving the Yugoslav secret armies of help, even though they held down a significant part of the German Army and relieved pressure on Russia.

The covert diplomatic policy of INTREPID in the latter half of World War II was designed to keep the Americans involved in the secret wars while managing the rapidly expanding resistance movements against Axis tyranny. The prefabricated suburbs of Bletchley Park to take care of expanding ULTRA teams exemplified the magnitude of secret warfare and the methods by which Stephenson bartered for U.S. support. Seven thousand "boffins"—experts in a variety of recondite skills—poured out vital intelligence, which continued to reach Roosevelt and impress him with British work in this field and the need to keep on getting it. Brilliant men served ULTRA: sharp-witted dons, wayward professors, eccentrics who hated the dreary routine and the heavy secrecy that fettered their freewheeling intellects. Felix Fetterlein, once cryptographer to the czars of Russia, decorated one end of the spectrum of talent. At the other end was a former Merchant Navy radio operator who seemed telepathic in his ability to read the weak and distorted signals of a distant agent.

Meanwhile, the regular service intelligence agencies charted future postwar policy, reverting to their old preoccupation with rank, salary, advancement and the comforts of the club. The Baker Street amateurs bore the load and the Kim Philbys burrowed away unnoticed.

The twenty-three-year-old Philby, recruited into the Russian secret service in 1935, had become, shortly before the TORCH landings, the key man in Section Five of the British Secret Intelligence Service. This dealt with counterespionage. Philby was perfectly placed to do mischief to the Anglo-American alliance in "the first intelligence operation we'd planned together," as Sweet-Escott described it.

Caught in the middle was Bill Stephenson. All he knew in November 1942 was that understandings between himself and Bill Donovan had been sabotaged in London. The plans to conduct secret warfare as one team had been somehow sidetracked.

"For this to go wrong left an appalling taste," said Sweet-Escott later. "Donovan lost all confidence in us. We could have postponed the evil day, for instance, when OSS and ourselves went separate ways. We would have had joint operations instead of each side jealous of the other."

The split began in the Middle East and extended to the Far East. In Europe, Stephenson was able to preserve the BSC-OSS partnership at the top. In the race to build an atomic bomb, the partnership was compulsive. The Soviet Union was treated as an honest ally, and the full extent of subversive activities by Russian agents against the Western alliance was only vaguely understood. In 1942, Kim Philby's authority allowed him to work through the British establishment. He played on the rivalries of professionals in London, who not only bickered among themselves but resented and resisted the arrival of Americans on their scene.

Before and during the North African landings, Philby was flying busily between Cairo, Gibraltar, Lisbon, and London headquarters. He seemed to some colleagues to be shrewdly outmaneuvering an American threat to British domination of espionage in the region. The French had shown unexpected resistance to American landings in their North African colonies. Philby blamed the failure on U.S. intelligence, with sneers that seemed consistent with his air of English superiority. But what he was doing was pursuing the Soviet aim of driving a wedge between U.S. and British agencies.

"Stephenson thought he'd killed the worms of doubt," Donovan said later. "And so he had, within our limited circle. David Bruce* was sent over to run OSS/London and smooth things over. At such levels, and between President and Prime Minister, the co-operation went on. But if Hoover's personal friendship with Stephenson had been less secure, he might have withdrawn the co-operation he was giving with a good heart again."

A compelling reason to continue sharing secrets was that the British had under their control in 1942 the dean of nuclear physicists, Niels Bohr, and access to the best source of heavy water for atomic experiments. The trouble was that Bohr and the heavy water were inside Nazi territory. It was touch and go whether or not Hitler would exploit his advantage. He had the pieces to put together a nuclear bomb. The British thought they could remove the pieces, with American help.

During the talks prior to TORCH, Churchill and Roosevelt discussed TUBE ALLOYS, the code name for British work on nuclear fission. Churchill's Scientific Advisory Committee recommended a plant in

---

* David Bruce, after distinguished service with OSS, became chief of the Marshall Plan mission to postwar France, and later U.S. Ambassador to Paris and then to London. He was U.S. delegate to the Vietnam peace conference and subsequently became the first U.S. diplomat to head a permanent diplomatic mission to China under Mao Tse-tung's chairmanship. He returned to Europe as U.S. Permanent Representative on the North Atlantic Council. "He was the perfect example of all that was best in U.S. intelligence," wrote the British veteran diplomat and intelligence expert Charles Ellis. "His postwar career was devoted to making intelligence work for peace."

Canada to construct an atomic bomb of colossal destructive power. Stephenson sketched the problems to Churchill and Roosevelt together.

"You keep abreast of atomic science," Roosevelt commented.

"I keep in touch with those who do," Stephenson corrected him. "The most important is Doctor Bohr in Denmark."

Churchill took a sudden interest in the tip of his cigar.

"Is he a danger to us?" asked Roosevelt.

"Unwittingly."

"Can you get him out?"

"We have several plans under review," replied Stephenson.

Anglo-American co-operation in this enterprise was harassed by Communist mischief-making and later betrayed by Soviet spies. There was plenty of material on which troublemakers could seize. There was resentment among British intellectuals, voiced later by the economist John Maynard Keynes, who wrote: "To secure American support, without which the atomic bomb could not be built, we were stripped of all gold reserves and overseas investment. But we saved ourselves and we saved the world."

Because of the secrecy surrounding TUBE ALLOYS and later American work on the bomb, the resentment festered unseen. Lies and half-truths distorted the picture, and came to the surface too late to be corrected. Thus a distinguished British historian, A. J. P. Taylor, was still repeating a negative version in 1974 when he wrote in the New York *Times* (April 28): "Churchill received from Roosevelt a formal promise that Great Britain, having revealed how to make a controlled nuclear explosion should share equally in all further nuclear discoveries. The promise was subsequently evaded by President Roosevelt. . . . Churchill counted on 'the special relationship' and put his trust in American generosity. The trust was misplaced."

Stephenson played a key role throughout the struggle to possess and protect nuclear secrets right up to his own intervention in a Russian spy-ring crisis in Canada that led to the discovery of secrets stolen

454

from the American atomic-bomb project.* He never doubted that Churchill and Roosevelt understood exactly what was involved in Anglo-American cooperation. "Roosevelt's decisiveness saved us all," he said later. "Work on the atomic bomb was proceeding in every part of the world. We had a head start. We could have done the job in the Canadian wilderness . . . It was sensible to seek American cooperation from the start. Without it, we might have been too late. . . . The Germans were already in the race."

This was the awesome and apocalyptic secret knowledge Churchill shared with Roosevelt from the day Stephenson had first flown from London to Washington. On June 15, 1940, President Roosevelt signed a private letter on "the possible relationship to national defense of recent discoveries in the field of atomistics. . . . The methods and mechanisms of warfare have altered radically. . . ."† In this way, he carried the ball thrown him by Stephenson, during the Dunkirk drama when the British were driven from continental Europe and it seemed that civilization was coming to an end.

The chain reaction of events showed that "the methods and mechanisms of warfare" had indeed changed. The dilemmas created by the explosion of guerrilla bands and atomic bombs were much the same. The clandestine struggle to capture secrets of nuclear warfare involved all branches of the INTREPID organization. Typical of the hard decisions taken by

---

* A Russian cipher clerk, Igor Gouzenko, defected in Ottawa in September 1945. The Soviet Union pressed the Canadian government to return him. Stephenson took over, hiding Gouzenko from his pursuers, a group of KGB thugs who would have killed him. The Canadian Prime Minister, Mackenzie King, was anxious to avoid offending Russia and initially wanted to surrender Gouzenko. A subsequent inquiry by a Royal commission exposed Soviet espionage within U.S., Canadian, and British atomic projects. It was INTREPID's last big case.

† The letter was to Dr. Vannevar Bush, President of the Carnegie Institution in Washington, requesting that his fellow scientists review work on the fission of uranium. The text was released by Robert Sherwood after he took charge of the U.S. Foreign Information Service.

men like Stephenson was Churchill's when Herbert Morrison made strong objections to the measures to meet a supposed threat from atom-tipped German rockets.

German "flying bombs" finally did strike southern England, but the enemy could calculate precisely only the arrival *time,* not the *place* for each missile. The deception plan was to report hits west of London at the time when others struck inside the city or to the east and send these reports to Germany through double agents. The Germans kept correcting their aim. The mean point of impact was thus moved eastward about two miles a week, redirecting the rockets beyond the London region to less densely populated areas.

Morrison, a socialist member of the British War Cabinet, protested against secret-warfare experts deciding that citizens of Kent or Essex should be killed instead of Londoners.

"War is an evil thing," Churchill said in a secret War Cabinet session. "Do you wish us to surrender, Mr. Morrison?"

Morrison shook his head angrily.

"Then I greatly fear, sir, that in order to live," replied Churchill, lowering his head, "we must play God."

44

"THE GREATEST INTELLIGENCE enterprise was the battle for control of the first atomic bomb," the BSC Papers reported. "The Germans had the man whose theoretical work was the basis of the bomb. We had the eccentricity to make it. A thousand secret threads were drawn together to prevent the Germans developing atomic warheads for the rockets they began to rain on London. . . ." And Churchill said, in 1945: "By

God's mercy, British and American science outpaced all German efforts."

The man who lectured at a British university on the theory of atomic constitution during World War I was unconsciously pointing the way to nuclear weapons when the Nazis occupied his native Denmark. Niels Bohr was a brilliant scientist, but he had a dangerous passion to share knowledge.* The Gestapo let him proceed with his research. German physicists called upon him, breathing good fellowship, to be led to the solution of their problems, having already captured in Norway a source of heavy water—the peculiar substance with the doubled hydrogen nucleus that acts as a neutron brake in uranium fission. They ordered the Kaiser Wilhelm Institute to work exclusively on the German discovery of the explosive properties of the isotope U-235. They guessed the U-235 bomb would be possible, and they suspected that Bohr was working toward a controlled chain reaction of uranium fission that would make conventional bloodletting shrink in significance. When Hitler marched into Russia, Stephenson knew that the Führer's generals had a more concrete cause for confidence than Nazi claims to mystic infallibility. They felt certain their country could build an atomic bomb.

Stephenson became interested in Niels Bohr in 1922 when the Danish physicist won a Nobel Prize for his pioneer research. Among the brilliant physicists working along similar lines were Steinmetz, who eventually went to Stephenson's research labs, and the Polish scientist Stefan Rozental, who was also forced by political reasons to leave his native Cracow; he joined Bohr in Copenhagen. Steiny had worked closely with Rozental, and he alerted Stephenson to the significance of the Copenhagen research. Inter-

---

* Bohr's conviction that nuclear physicists should share all secrets was expressed in his appeal for an *"Open World . . .* where each nation can assert itself solely by the extent to which it can help others with experience and resources . . . [with] free access to information and unhampered opportunity for exchange of ideas." It was addressed to the United Nations in 1950, long after Bohr had contributed to the development of atomic weapons. His philosophy had not changed.

national co-operation revolved around Einstein and Chaim Weizmann. Weizmann's services to Britain and the Allied cause in World War I as a defense scientist gave him freedom to move in these European circles, and he, too, shared news of developments with Stephenson. In 1932, the neutron was discovered by James Chadwick, whose lifelong friendship with Bohr played a vital part in frustrating German progress toward the bomb.

Churchill, of course, had this information, provided by Stephenson and other members of the scientific team formed when Frederick Lindemann first became concerned about German weapons research in the 1920s. They had watched silently while some of the beneficiaries of British scientific institutions were whisked away—kidnapped, in the case of Peter Kapitsa, who had worked from 1921 with atomic scientist Lord Rutherford and then disappeared into the Soviet Union to work under duress on a project to smash the atom. Outside Russia and Germany, the scientific community was slow to recognize the point when work with the nucleus of the atom passed from the theoretical to the practical, and military, stage.

"The year war broke out in Europe happened to be a turning point in atomic research everywhere," said Stephenson. "The embryo of the atom bomb was concealed in the brains of physicists in the United States, Britain, Russia, and Europe. In the military field, the view prevailed in 1939 that the country with the greatest chance of bringing together the pieces was Germany. Hitler could decree the necessary discipline, sacrifice, and mobilization of resources, including slave labor. Otto Hahn, who had made the decisive German discovery about chain reaction, considered that smashing the atomic nucleus could be done at the cost of enormous effort. This was true. At that time, the prime requirement was a totalitarian state run by a dictator who could demand without explanation the diversion of the major part of society's power and wealth into the vast machinery then necessary to produce the bomb. There was a slim chance Hitler, who best met the qualifications, might miss his opportunity."

British attention focused on Bohr and the Norsk Hydro heavy-water plant in Norway. The danger in doing anything about either, then, Stephenson said, was that Hitler might be directed to the very target that everyone hoped he would overlook.

German scientists had *not* overlooked it; but Hitler was giving their efforts a lower priority than he might have if he had been aware of his enemies' rivalry. Hans Suess, a German physicist, needed a moderator to control an atomic reaction. Heavy water was tried successfully in small-scale experiments. The German War Office estimated that five tons of it would be required to moderate a practical reactor. In early 1939, Norsk Hydro was the only production center in the world for heavy water in any quantity, and its output was a comparative dribble of ten kilograms a month.

In a study of I. G. Farben interests that same year, Stephenson noted that the German chemical combine had quietly invested in the Norwegian plant, with the requirements of exclusive purchasing rights for an open-ended period and a thousand-percent increase in production. One month after Farben formally submitted this significant demand, in December 1939, the French Secret Service sent Jacques Allier, an international banker and friend of Stephenson, to tell Norsk Hydro's managing director, Dr. Axel Aubert, that the French were testing an atomic pile under the direction of Frédéric Joilot-Curie. The first delivery of heavy water to Paris followed, in February 1940. When the Germans captured the plant three months later, they discovered that Norsk Hydro's entire supply had vanished.

Stephenson had inspected Barren Mountain, in Norway, which offered a natural barrier against intruders, just before the German occupation. He had recommended an escape route to link London and friendly Norsk Hydro personnel, including Professor Leif Tronstad, the thirty-six-year-old chemist who was to become the key Baker Street Irregular in future atomic missions. Tronstad knew the layout of the heavy-water plant.

In this nervous period prior to the German invasion

of Norway, another visitor arrived at Norsk Hydro. This was Dr. Bohr, seeking supplies for his own experiments. On his way back to Denmark, Bohr talked with King Haakon about the correct policy to be followed by neutrals threatened by German occupation. There was an unworldly style in Bohr's approach to politics. He believed in Gandhi's nonviolent methods of fighting oppression. His return to Copenhagen in April coincided with German bombers, which put an end to academic discussions about passive resistance. Denmark and Norway were occupied. Suddenly the Uranium Intelligence Committee in London was confronted with two crises. One of the world's great atomic scientists was lost inside the German fortress, and production of heavy water at the newly captured Norsk plant was to be increased to 3,000 pounds a year, the amount required for "atomistics," according to captured German military orders. The Norwegian Section of Baker Street kept under lock and key a scientific paper prophesying that it would take a full two years before atomic weapons, if developed, could be brought into military operation. With a great many other pressing problems clamoring for attention, the Irregulars were not in a good position to demand aircraft and equipment to knock out the heavy-water plant in Norway and rescue Niels Bohr from Denmark.

Meanwhile, the theory of nuclear fission was discussed openly by Bohr in Nazi-occupied Denmark. "He needed to talk with others to develop his ideas," said Stephenson. "Unfortunately, we couldn't control the people he talked with." His listeners included German physicists, who heard him define the liberation of nuclear energy during the fission process, and what he regarded as the horrible possibilities of its use for destructive purposes. In a spirit of scientific inquiry, Bohr was discussing the atomic bomb with those who wanted to use it to conquer the world. His practice of dictating most of his work, a fact known to his old colleagues in Britain, added to the risk that he might unwittingly help the Third Reich.

Under the false cover of TUBE ALLOYS, the British had now started the first intensive search for an atomic

460

weapon in laboratories scattered around the country-side and co-ordinated from a Dickensian office on Old Queen Street, near Whitehall. The fruits of these labors were passed along to the United States after it became clear that the development work required immense resources—20,000 workers, half a million kilowatts of electricity, and some $150 million to produce one kilogram of Uranium-235 a day, and absolute security. The British concluded that such an independent effort was beyond the reach of a small democracy. It could be tried by a dictatorship like Nazi Germany. The British drew no comfort from the knowledge that each stage of Bohr's progress in this direction was available to the Germans. Veiled warnings were sent to Bohr through Danish underground channels, and the results of his dictation were duly concealed among folders and files, misleadingly inscribed to foil German investigators. This schoolboyish attempt to hide the work typified Bohr's frighteningly simple view of the world outside. In London, a good many people held their breath.

So, too, in Washington, where FDR had independent sources. His earliest intelligence on German use of heavy water came from Sam Woods, whose contacts inside the German hierarchy were maintained after he moved from Berlin to Zurich to become U.S. consul-general there until the war's end. Through him, Chaim Weizmann was able to talk with a dissident German physicist, Professor Willstatter, on neutral Swiss territory. Willstatter feared Hitler might be galvanized into action if the British intervened, but he feared British inaction even more.

Weizmann later confided to Stephenson his fear that the threat was not taken seriously enough. "The two men would take long walks through Central Park," said Herb Rowland. "They were lost in the Manhattan crowds and used to cut across to watch the squirrels, or so we thought. We'd never heard, never suspected, that an ultimate weapon hung over us."

Weizmann recalled stopping at Schwarz's toyshop on Fifth Avenue one crisp spring day. "There was a construction kit on display for schoolboys. Bill said, 'Once the Germans know how to do it, they'll put it together like one of those toy cranes, patiently screwing the nuts and bolts together until they've completed it, totally absorbed in the task, like children indifferent to the pain they cause.'

"I had to point out that not all German scientists were insensitive. I quoted Professor Willstatter, who, although the leading German chemist of his time, refused to be involved.

"Stephenson peered into Schwarz's window and shrugged. 'He did not refuse. He ran off. That leaves the rest free to play.' "

It was harsh but true. Hitler had boasted of a secret weapon against which there was no defense: a weapon his enemies did not have. German scientists who rebelled against this perversion of their work were obliged to escape or lose their positions. Some who might have put up a dumb resistance, including Werner Heisenberg and C. F. von Weizsacker, were among Bohr's visitors in Copenhagen. It was said that they submitted a secret plan to prevent the development of the bomb—an underground agreement with Allied physicists. "These stories were untrue," said Aage Bohr. "Every contact with German scientists strengthened the impression that the German authorities attached great military importance to atomic energy."[*]

So many reports of German secret weapons had been floated by Hitler that it was difficult to assign a priority to this one. Shortly after the outbreak of war in Europe, the Führer had said, "Do not deceive yourselves. The moment may come when we shall use a weapon which is not yet known and with which we ourselves could not be attacked." The British Foreign Secretary at that time, Lord Halifax, noted: "The implication is that . . . Hitler is determined to resort to frightfulness." In the following month, October

---

[*] Bohr denied any such "ban-the-bomb" plan, although Robert Jungk, in *Brighter Than a Thousand Suns,* later asserted that Heisenberg and Weizsacker submitted a proposal that German and British scientists should agree to ban the bomb's development. German physicist Hans Jensen was said to have made a similar proposal, but this, too, was denied by Bohr.

1939, the British Joint Intelligence Sub-Committee considered a list of "weapons with which Germany has been experimenting," from gliding torpedoes to rockets and "the use of atomic energy as high explosive." The intelligence chiefs decided that Hitler meant that he would break Britain by the use of air power and "possibly bombs containing a new and secret explosive."

When the first conventional bombs fell on London, the British Chiefs of Staff received a report that heavy-water production was being increased again in Norway. Leif Tronstad, destined to die at the hands of a traitor, began seriously to plan Norsk Hydro's destruction. Many others were to die in the repeated attempts to sabotage this seemingly inaccessible plant.

There were several secret projects in hand. In Copenhagen, under German eyes, Bohr was swept forward by his own enthusiasm toward a goal that for him meant unlocking fresh mysteries; whereas for the Nazis it meant the key to atomic power. In Stockholm, a Baker Street/SIS station gathered information from Bohr and from Norsk Hydro. Copies of Stockholm bulletins went to Stephenson, who had started the training of agents and a new "school of danger" in the Canadian wilderness, where saboteurs could prepare for a suicidal mission.

"The western coast of Norway, because of its many indentations, was hard to guard," said Stephenson later. "Thousands of fjords made the actual length ten thousand miles and so the Germans threw a cordon around the coastal waters. I was looking for American speedboats to run the blockade—eventually they ran with clockwork efficiency between enemy territory and the Shetland Isles, where an uncle of Robert Louis Stevenson had built the lighthouse from which the boats now took bearings. They were so regular, we called the service 'The Shetland Bus.' "

Odd Starheim, a Norwegian shipowner's son, escaped to Scotland in a small boat and returned to Norway as a trained agent before the Shetland Bus went into operation. His mission was code-named CHEESE. He began transmitting reports on enemy naval operations while waiting for the moment when he could break through Nazi security around the Norsk Hydro plant. The Gestapo's radio detectors began closing in on Starheim after he had located the German warships *Bismarck* and *Prinz Eugen,* waiting to sail into the Atlantic as fast raiders. His hide-out in a farmhouse sixty miles from the German naval base at Kristiansand was surrounded. His courier, a striking girl, Sofie Rorvig, slipped through SS patrols to warn him, then ran the double risk of passing through the patrols again with him, their arms entwined. As young lovers, they passed unmolested among SS troops probing haystacks and barns. Starheim continued the long and dangerous journey alone to neutral Sweden, where he reported to Stephenson's friends. Sofie stayed behind with the CHEESE network, which was expanded in preparation for the major task to come.

Starheim was parachuted back into Norway after reporting new details of German security to London, which now wanted him to fetch out one of the Norsk Hydro engineers. Before he could begin work again, he was trapped by the Gestapo in the parlor of a friend's house. He fought his way into a passage and bolted across the grandmother's bedroom, leaping through the window before the old lady's astonished eyes. He scrambled into a truck and was gone before his pursuers recovered their wits. The next day, he reported to the former CHEESE radio center. By the end of 1941, he was installed in an abandoned hut overlooking the factories and laboratories of Norsk Hydro on Barren Mountain. Then, on March 10, 1942, Bletchley received a message: HAVE STOLEN BOAT AND MAKING FOR SCOTLAND PLEASE GIVE AIR PROTECTION CHEESE. He had come down the 6,000-foot glacier with Einar Skinnarland, the engineer most familiar with the plant's layout, and hijacked the 620-ton coastal steamer *Galtesund.* A week later they were being escorted by an RAF bomber into the east Scotland port of Aberdeen. They continued immediately on to London, where Skinnarland went promptly into consultation with intelligence chiefs and atomic scientists.

After an eleven-day crash course in secret warfare, Skinnarland parachuted back onto Barren Mountain—just three weeks after he had disappeared from the plant. The German managers accepted his explanation that he had been ill. "This was the quickest turnaround and the most vital bit of training we'd ever achieved," reported the chief of Baker Street's Norwegian Section, John Skinner Wilson. "No more than three people in London knew the real reason."

Skinnarland's job now at Barren Mountain was to prepare for a sabotage operation so secret that his reports could not be entrusted to radio transmission but had to go through elaborate coding and microdot reduction by way of Sweden. A typical report: "The Germans depend too much on natural defences. . . . Change of guard inside the plant is at 1800 hours. . . . Sentries on suspension bridge between Vemork and Rjukan . . . only approach road can be flood-lit on alarm . . . guards billeted between electrolysis plant and engine halls . . ."

Terrifying risks were run. "Our orders were to—uh—eliminate the place," said the Baker Street chief, Colin Gubbins. "It was our top priority."

Urgency had been given to the enterprise by that hazardous 4,000-mile journey by flying boat made by Churchill in June 1942 to discuss with Roosevelt the future of atomic weaponry. "The British uranium bomb was within reach," said Stephenson. "But for many reasons, the construction had to be undertaken in Canada or the United States. A pilot plant had been recommended in Britain by the scientific-advisory committee, with a full-scale plant to be built in Canada. But this meant a duplication of effort. FDR proposed a joint development, with atomic plants sited in the United States. Everything on the basis of fully sharing the results as equal partners. The President and the Prime Minister studied the scientific papers, and concluded everything must be done to delay the Germans. There was a high concentration of physicists from Germany at work on our own atomic programs. Parallel progress inside the Third Reich could not be ruled out."

Stephenson flew to Canada, where agents of the Norwegian secret army were now in training. Here he linked up with Gubbins and John Wilson, whose position as director and camp chief of the Boy Scouts

International gave him an excuse to build up certain informal contacts. They began scouring a region near Toronto known as "Little Norway," where hundreds of young men and women learned about airborne warfare. Out of these trainees, a tiny handful were to be inserted onto Barren Mountain. The smaller the team, the less risk of detection.

Wilson had no illusions about the dangers. "Weather is appalling most of the time," he wrote. "Sudden fogs, unpredictable gales, swift upward air currents. The terrain is mountain peaks with hundreds of dangerous glaciers and precipices, marshes, swamps and impassable streams." It was not the place for paratroopers or gliders. Wilson had the job of selecting the men who would undertake an impossible mission. "I knew that any qualified Norwegian I approached would agree to carry it out." The four who did, graduates of the spy school, underwent additional hardening with British Commando instructors. Special ski equipment was hand-crafted in Canada. In September 1942, the men were ready. Twice they were flown from eastern Scotland to the drop zone. Twice they returned because of foul weather. The third time, they landed on a mountain plateau separated by peaks and glaciers from the Norsk Hydro plant. A few days later CHEESE signaled:

GERMANS TO SHIP ENTIRE STOCK OF HEAVY WATER STOP QUANTITY BELIEVED SUFFICIENT TO SATISFY PRESENT DEMANDS FROM BERLIN.

This created a mild panic. Time was running out. Stephenson was again summoned for urgent talks in London. The War Cabinet met in emergency session. There were arguments between Baker Street Irregulars and military planners with a traditional dislike of unconventional warfare.

"The fate of the world seemed to hang on those four young agents," said Stephenson. "The Germans were using all heavy-water stocks. They must be close to a solution. It was decided to mount a full-scale armed attack by gliding into the area a force of regular commandos."

He flew back to New York unconvinced that a commando operation had a fighting chance, and began hunting for new American equipment in another irregular mission. In November another terse message was received from Norway: THREE PINK ELEPHANTS. It meant the four agents were in sight of their target. Meanwhile, the crews of two bombers left the big special operations base at Wick, on the northeast coast of Scotland, to tow thirty-four British commandos across the North Sea in two Horsa gliders.

Twenty-four hours later, a local German communiqué was intercepted by Bletchley. "Two British bombers, towing gliders loaded with saboteurs, flew yesterday over southern Norway and were forced down by fighter aircraft of the Luftwaffe. The crews of the enemy bombers and gliders were annihilated to the last man in the air fight."

This was a lie. One glider crashed when the tow broke under the weight of ice. Eight of the seventeen uniformed commandos crawled out of the wreck alive. Four were killed by the injection of air bubbles into their veins at a German field hospital. The remaining four were executed. The second glider crashlanded after the towing bomber flew into a mountain. The fourteen survivors were shot, starting with the wounded, who were propped in front of their comrades against a wall.

Another nineteen agents were now in the field, dispatched by Baker Street by air and sea. One, Arne Vaerum, code-named PENGUIN, was part of a radio net busily transmitting back to base. PENGUIN was still at his transmitter key when SS troops caught him. The message he was sending came stuttering through the night to a girl telegraphist in England who not only knew his "fist," but also was a close friend. The girl belonged to the First Aid Nursing Yeomanry. On the night PENGUIN died, another FANY heroine was born. She knew what the interrupted message meant and asked to be dropped into enemy territory, where she could relieve her mental pain in physical action. She was trained for special duties in Denmark, and became the courier who was known as TRUDI in the subsequent escape of Niels Bohr.

The winter of late 1942 was the worst any Norwegian could remember. The four "pink elephants," codenamed SWALLOW, were still in position on the mountain above the target, half starved and suffering from prolonged exposure. A new operation was mounted to reinforce them with six more Baker Street Irregulars, who had gone through even more ruthless training at a so-called gangster school near Southampton. One of them was Knut Haukelid, twin brother of the actress and film star Sigrid Gurie.

"Knut is first and foremost a hunter," wrote Gubbins. "He is also a philosopher with a sense of values. . . . I spent two days with Knut in the valley in Barren Mountain: a ravine so deep and precipitous that in winter the sun never touches its depths and workers must be taken by cable car to the peaks to get their daily ration of light."

While Haukelid prepared to go back to Norway, new assessments were made in America. "Manhattan Engineer District. Priority: AAA" covered the combined effort of scientist-refugees from Europe and United States and British atomic scientists to build the bomb first. Atomic fission had already been started under the football stands of Stagg Field at the University of Chicago. Physicists had mastered a swiftly multiplying chain reaction that would be placed in a weapon of incredible powers.

The gigantic Manhattan Project had been pulled together by Roosevelt. He knew that far away in Hitler's Europe, the greatest potential menace was Niels Bohr. In his Denmark labs, Bohr had split the uranium atom with a release of energy calculated to be a million times as powerful as that from an equal amount of high explosive.

"Could Bohr be whisked out from under Nazi noses and brought to the Manhattan Project?" Roosevelt asked Stephenson.

"It will have to be a British mission," Stephenson replied. "Niels Bohr is a stubborn pacifist. He does not believe his work in Copenhagen will benefit the German military caste. Nor is he likely to join an American enterprise which has as its sole objective the construction of a bomb. But he is in constant touch with old colleagues in England whose integrity he respects."

From this point, Roosevelt was kept informed on each development of the unfolding drama as it was reported to BSC in New York.

Knut Haukelid and five companions were parachuted into Norway on February 16, 1943. A carefully phrased message was meanwhile composed by James Chadwick to Niels Bohr, inviting him to England, where "no scientist in the world would be more acceptable." Chadwick could only hint at "special problems" in which Bohr's co-operation would be welcome. The letter was reduced to microfilm and concealed in a bunch of keys.

On February 23, SWALLOW was reinforced by Haukelid's party. All were partly disabled by frostbite. The ten agents had enough explosives to destroy the Barren Mountain plant but little food and fewer medical aids. They drew up a final operational order: "All men to wear uniform. Positions will be taken at midnight 500 metres from perimeter fence. Attack at 0030 hours after guards change. If alarm is sounded, covering party to attack guards immediately while demolition party is to proceed. Demolition party to destroy high-concentration plant in cellar of electrolysis hall. Each demolition expert is to be covered by one man with a .45 pistol. If fighting starts before the target is reached, men in the covering party will take over, where necessary, to place explosives. Two 'L' pills of potassium cyanide are to be carried by each man. Any man about to be taken prisoner will take his own life."

The grim order was written in desolation on a wind-swept glacier during an ice storm. The destruction of the plant had been decided almost a year before. One attempt after another had failed. "If the Germans capture the SWALLOW team alive, they may well deduce that such a suicidal attack has been launched only because the allies have now proved an atom bomb is a practical proposition," INTREPID informed Roosevelt.

Two months after the American atomic breakthrough in Chicago, the SWALLOWS descended into that forbidding ravine whose depths were never touched by the winter sun. They knew each detail of the Norsk Hydro complex from a new model built under the direction of the former chief engineer, Professor Jonar Brun, who had escaped to Britain with the plans. They crept like creatures of the night through the cable-intake tunnel leading to the electrolysis cellar, negotiating a tangle of ice-sheathed pipes in total darkness. They had decided upon passwords taken from the soldiers' song, "It's a long way to Tipperary." If attacked or lost in confusion, the challenge was "Piccadilly" and the reply "Leicester Square," an ironic extract from the music-hall lines.

An hour later, the demolition team returned. The charges were laid, the fuses lit. Haukelid took six grenades from his jacket and guarded the withdrawal. Minutes later a soft whistling sound emerged from the main seven-story building, followed by a deep and muted rumble. "An insignificant little bang," Haukelid called it. Hours later, back in their mountain hide-out, they mourned the failure of the mission. It was a long time before they learned that the high-concentration installations had been totally destroyed. By then, five of the agents, in full British uniform, had traveled 350 miles across peaks and valleys to Sweden. The rest remained in Norway to continue operations in an area to which the Germans in their rage sent ski squads— Gestapo and SS forces and Quisling's *Hird* storm troopers.

When the plant was back in production again, the RAF tried to bomb it. A series of heavy raids failed to make much impression. The cost was high in bomber crews and Norwegian civilian casualties. The U.S. Air Force tried, with similar results. SWALLOW had demonstrated the value of guerrilla warfare but Allied military leaders were reluctant to draw the lesson. A year after SWALLOW sabotaged the plant, the supply of heavy water had been resumed. This time Knut Haukelid advised against another attempt at sabotage. Instead, he proposed striking at the supply lines. A consignment of some 5,000 pounds of heavy water, about six months' production, was to be transported to Germany. The weakest point along the route was the train ferry. Haukelid and two members of the secret army boarded the ferry and placed charges set to explode the following noon when the vessel would be in deep water. The ferry and its vital cargo blew up on time, killing four of the Norwegian crew. There was no consolation for Haukelid in this; it was one of many cruel decisions. Against the loss of his compatriots had to be weighed the deaths of eighty-three Allied servicemen in previous operations. He wrote modestly after the war: "Heavy water was not itself part of the atom bomb but it was an important factor in experiments with substances required for use in the bomb." It had taken three years to destroy finally this source of Nazi atomic-research material—three years since Stephenson first scouted the Norwegian supply lines. President Roosevelt's backing of secret warfare had been based in part on Stephenson's report in April 1940 on heavy water and the conclusion that an atom bomb was now in the realm of possibility.

Stephenson's only comment, in the BSC Papers, was: "If it had not been for Haukelid's resolve, the Germans would have had the opportunity to devastate the civilized world. We would be either dead or living under Hitler's zealots."

45

DR. BOHR PLUGGED away in Copenhagen, watched by Danish secret-army chiefs. King Christian X and his philosopher-scientist still hoped to save other people by avoiding an open confrontation with the Gestapo. But Bohr's zeal was carrying him toward a success that must benefit Germany's search for an atomic bomb. His labs at the Institute for Theoretical Physics grew by a sort of gemmation, putting forth new buds as space was acquired for new experiments and as new sources of finance mysteriously appeared. Underneath the labs, in the sewers binding the heavy-water cyclotron, Danish saboteurs quietly laid explosive charges, just in case.

"Barren Mountain and other Norwegian operations divert the enemy from what worries us more than anything—Niels Bohr, whose work is dangerously like atomic projects underway in the United States," Stephenson told Roosevelt. "The risk of atomic information falling into German hands has to be weighed against the danger of reprisals following destruction of Bohr's cyclotron."

Best able to weigh the dangers was Sven Truelsen, a Danish military intelligence chief who shuttled between Nazi Europe and London. His couriers carried an explosive correspondence between Baker Street and Bohr.

From that most eminent and unflappable of physicists Sir James Chadwick went a veiled appeal, preceded by these instructions:

To: 'Peter'
From: Jarlen

We intend sending to JUSTITSRAADEN in the near future a bunch of keys which contain a very important message from the British Government to Professor Niels Bohr. We would be very grateful if you could see that Professor BOHR gets the keys and also if you or someone appointed by you would explain to him how to find the message.

The following diagram shows the position in keys A. and A.1. of the message which has to be extracted. Key A.1. is the one with number 229 on it and Key A. is the *long* key next to it.

A small hole to a depth of 4 mm has been bored in the two keys. The holes were plugged up and concealed after the message was inserted. Professor Bohr should gently file the keys at the point indicated until the hole appears. The message can then be syringed or floated out on to a microslide. The message is a very very small micro film and is repeated in duplicate in each key. It should be handled very delicately.

I do not myself know the contents of the message except that I do know it is *very important*. Will you kindly warn JUSTITSRAADEN and tell him to expect the bunch of keys. We will send the keys through to him by separate courier as soon as we know that this sending has reached you and that you have had time to warn JUSTITS-RAADEN.

The keys arrived while the SWALLOWS were actually destroying the Norsk Hydro heavy-water plant in that harsh winter of 1942. Bohr locked himself in his lab and floated out the pinhead communications. His reply was read by BSC in New York with dismay: "I feel it my duty in our desperate situation to help resist the threat against freedom of our institutions and to assist in the protection of the exiled scientists who sought refuge here. . . . Any immediate use of the latest marvellous discoveries of atomic physics is impracticable."

He was rejecting the delicately phrased invitation to stop work, and declining to continue his research in England. Chadwick did not dare mention that Bohr was needed for Anglo-American work on the bomb. Bohr disapproved of violence. In Denmark he had immense prestige. He was president of the Royal Danish Academy and close to the King, who was seventy-three years old and ailing. Both men were handled with kid gloves by the Nazis in the early days. The King sat in his castle, trying to protect his people. The Professor discharged his responsibility, as he saw it, to science and humanity. He continued his dangerous correspondence with Chadwick in England and early in the spring of 1943 he warned that the Germans were looking for more of the metallic uranium and heavy water that could be used to produce atomic bombs.

There were urgent conferences in London and New York. BSC had profiles in Rockefeller Center on Bohr and the refugee scientists he was trying to protect.

Stephenson understood Niels Bohr and the ticklish problem of persuading him to escape. Churchill was impatient of scientists like Bohr and thought he came "very near the edge of mortal crimes." Professor Lindemann, pursuing an almost personal vendetta against the Germans, thought in the last resort that Danish saboteurs should trigger the explosive devices under Bohr's Institute, for Germany "already increases its demands for heavy water and metallic uranium and German scientists now submit proposals for the use of chain reactions with slow neutrons for producing bombs."

Stephenson flew over for discussions and argued for getting Bohr out. "Germany is getting immense profit from an avoidance of conflict between occupiers and occupied in Denmark, but it cannot last. The Fuehrer's Special Plenipotentiary in Denmark is Dr. Werner Best who puts his faith in talking softly and carrying a big stick. But once terror is let loose in Copenhagen, we can rely on Bohr to do the right thing. What's important now is to organise his escape."*

The Germans deliberately confused those they con-

---

* A rare glimpse of Churchill's ruthless approach to secret warfare was given by General Alan Brooke after one of these discussions. A diversionary raid had been proposed. "Churchill shoved his chin out in his aggressive way and said: 'I had instructed you to prepare a detailed plan. . . . What have you done? You have submitted instead a masterly treatise on all the difficulties. . . .' He then cross-examined me for nearly two hours on most of the minor points." The chief reason for rejecting the proposed operation was lack of air support. Churchill avoided this issue and selected his own arguments: "You state that you will be confronted by thaws and frosts which will render mobility difficult. How can you account for such a statement?" Brooke said this was a trivial matter but in any case the statement came from The Climate Book. The Climate Book, an essential part of intelligence, was duly produced. It exactly supported the objection. Churchill shifted his attack: "You state it will take you some twenty-four hours to cover the ground between A and B. Explain to me exactly how every hour of those twenty-four will be occupied? "It was no easy matter to give a detailed picture of every hour, since the twenty-four-hour period allowed for overcoming enemy resistance, removal of roadblocks, repair of bridges and culverts. Brooke did his best: "This led to a series of more questions, interspersed with sarcasm and criticism. A very unpleasant gruelling to stand up to in a full room, but excellent training. . . ."

quered. The paramilitary force of dedicated Nazis, the Schutzstaffeln, or SS, operated in Denmark alongside the Reich Commissar. Local officials were unsure about who was the real master, and tended to cooperate with the soft-spoken German administrators and close their eyes to the purpose of the SS until the paramilitary emerged as the iron fist inside the velvet glove. The showdown came in August with King Christian, who suddenly resolved the conflicts of his friend Niels Bohr.

"There are no Danish Nazis," the King once told Berlin, replying to a suggestion that local Nazi party leaders should help govern the country. Hitler missed the veiled insult but SS Ober-Führer Werner Best did not. Now he suggested to Berlin that the King be neutered and Professor Bohr's project brought under German direction. SS kangaroo courts began summary trials of "terrorists." The King was forced into a corner by a request that the Danish police help the Gestapo. The King replied: "Never." A few days later the palace was stormed by German troops led by a general who was received by Christian X with the sarcastic words: "Good morning, my brave general. You have won a splendid victory." It had taken a thousand storm troopers armed with machine guns and grenades to overpower the fifty-man Royal Guards, whose weapons were swords and staves. The General, angered by this sudden display of royal contempt, clattered back to his armored car, which was what the King wanted. He scribbled a note advising Bohr to go; nothing more could be done to stave off disaster. Bohr should instruct Princess Ingeborg in Sweden to plead with King Gustaf to intervene on behalf of thousands of Danish citizens.

The first roundup of Jews began. The protection of scientists like Stefan Rozental, a former colleague of Stephenson's friend Steinmetz, now working with Bohr on atomic research, was no longer an issue. "Bohr called me to his home at Carlsberg," said Rozental later. "He told me what I must do to escape to England and gave me all his papers on the passage of charged particles through matter, a manuscript that must not fall into Nazi hands. He gave me money and said we should meet again soon. He was privately convinced he would be sent to Germany before he could himself escape, and gave me messages for King Christian's sister and the King of Sweden."

Copies of all Bohr's communications with the free world, including his messages regarding German preparations for expanding production of uranium and heavy water, were sealed into a metal tube and buried in the garden of his residence at Carlsberg as proof of his true loyalties. Some trace of civilized German behavior, Bohr had always argued, might be maintained if one conducted oneself as though other human beings were rational in their behavior. He had been proved wrong.

Escape routes were established to Sweden, refugees crossing the narrow waters of the Øresund between Copenhagen and the neutral Swedish port of Landskrona. It was now mid-September, the order for Bohr's arrest sat on a desk at Gestapo headquarters, and Rozental was making his way by rowboat to safety. In the confusion of leaving the Danish shore, he lost the manuscript containing Bohr's theories. The papers were never found.

A wave of terror swept Denmark in the days that followed, beginning with the mass deportation of Jews. It seemed to Stephenson that Niels Bohr had left things too late. It was five months since Stephenson had asked if Washington could supply three fast ships for clandestine operations between Scandinavia and Britain. The specifications had been spelled out in precise terms: minimum range of 3,000 miles, maximum speed of sixteen knots, four tons of cargo space and adequate guns. By September, three sub-chasers were delivered by the U.S. Navy through Bill Donovan who said nothing about their ultimate destination. The vessels were to carry strategic materials and VIPs from Sweden; one of the passengers was expected to be Professor Bohr.

On the last day of September, shortly before the Gestapo launched a series of widespread arrests, Bohr landed on the Swedish coast. During the night he sought out Princess Ingeborg, King Christian's sister, a fascinating woman who had joined Stephenson's service.

Bohr pleaded with the Princess for swift action on behalf of the Jews left in Denmark, who that morning were being scooped up and put aboard cattle ships for Germany. She took him to King Gustaf, who seemed dubious. Bohr wanted the King to have Germany redirect the shiploads of Jewish prisoners to Sweden. King Gustaf replied that he had made such a proposal when the deportation of Jews from Norway began. He was humiliatingly rejected. Bohr pressed his arguments. The King agreed to try a personal appeal to Hitler.

"You are very much out of touch with reality," Princess Ingeborg told Bohr sadly. "You lived in the Third Reich but you never understood it."

They were on their way out of the royal palace. Bohr glanced at her in astonishment. "Surely an appeal to Hitler—?"

"Dear God!" the Princess burst out. "An appeal to Hitler is an appeal to the Devil. If we draw attention to those Jews, he could kill every one of them just to spite us. . . . Your laboratory has been a fool's paradise."

Without knowing it, Bohr had enjoyed special dispensation. Even when the first order was signed for his arrest, higher authority in Berlin intervened. He had been insulated against the daily practice of evil. Now that he was truly free, he was tortured by what he learned.

The Swedish King finally broadcast an offer to Denmark to give refuge to fugitives. Swedish ships were sent to the limit of territorial waters to embark those who could escape. As a result, among the countries under SS control, Denmark suffered fewer casualties in the death camps.

Bohr was asked by Baker Street bodyguards if he would undertake the dangerous journey through the winter blockade to London. He guessed now that the British were building the bomb as part of some vast American project. He shrank from the thought of atomic arms but it was becoming obvious that if one side should end the war with a vast incineration, it had better be the side opposed to the dictators. Yes, he would go. But how?

Baker Street decided against sub-chasers slipping through the long northern nights, missing German interception by inches. It seemed too risky a method of extracting the Dane. Would Bohr ride in the bomb bay of an unarmed Moon aircraft of a Special Duties Squadron?

The flight at great altitude was dangerous. So were the alternatives. Bohr asked only one question: What kind of aircraft?

Great secrecy surrounded these Moon flights. It still does. The planes used neutral fields with the help of government officials whose action had no formal sanction. Countries like Sweden were on a tight-rope. The smallest sign of favoring the Allies would invite Nazi reprisal.

Professor Bohr's question about the type of plane could be answered only by taking him to an apparently abandoned airstrip near Stockholm. There he saw what was known as the "Termite's Delight" or the "Wooden Wonder," a plywood aircraft, brutish engines still grumbling from the long, frightening flight from Britain, piloted by an anonymous black-suited figure from a Moon squadron.

Moon squadrons were now running the enemy gantlet as far afield as northern Russia. The favored aircraft was the twin-engined Mosquito, made mostly of wood to baffle enemy radar. These fighter-bombers had been modified to carry agents instead of bombs. No flight was ever wasted; this one had brought a girl, who stood mummified in hooded coveralls.

Bohr understood the implications of being carried in a Mosquito's belly. He listened politely to the briefing given him by the young woman who had just come out from England. Her code name was TRUDI. A former telegraphist with the FANY communications section, she was a cousin of King George VI. There were serious objections to her being exposed to possible capture by the enemy, since it was thought she might be used as a hostage. Nobody was happy about the political repercussions if she were tortured and the facts became known later. Her true identity remains secret. She was caught in Denmark, a country she knew well, and was last seen in Gestapo headquarters at Copenhagen, where she presumably killed herself with the regulation-issue L pill while under interrogation.

TRUDI was blunt with the atomic scientist. He would be cut off from the Mosquito's skipper and could expect no help if the unarmed and unprotected plane were attacked. If he should be wounded, he would have to hang on until the Mosquito reached Britain. He would have morphine and pain-killing tablets in a small hand-held kit, but his quarters would allow him practically no room to move, being molded to fit the human body. If the plane ditched in the North Sea he would be trapped in water so cold that pilots expected no more than ninety seconds' grace before dying from exposure.

Bohr glanced at the Mosquito, painted entirely black and without identification markings of any sort. "My wife and children?"

"They'll be taken care of—here, in Sweden. . . . We—someone will always be watching them. There is no danger."

"Can they follow me later?"

The girl shook her head. "That *is* dangerous. Their movements will be known to the enemy. Here we can keep a tight guard. Between here and England, we are naked."

Bohr followed her gesture toward the northern sky. TRUDI peeled off the padded suit in which she had traveled. "This is yours now." She paused. "If you still want to go."

"Yes," said Bohr. "I have no choice."

Thus, a few days after his fifty-eighth birthday, on October 7, 1943, Professor Niels Bohr, one of the world's great nuclear physicists, was fitted into a kind of snowsuit still warm from the body of a young woman agent, was helmeted, masked, and strapped into the bomb bay between two massive Rolls-Royce engines hanging from a plywood air frame, to begin the long journey to the birth of the atomic age.

The bomb-bay doors hissed shut like clamshells. The ground party ducked out of the way and retreated to the hedgerows. They waited long enough to hear the shattering roar of engines being run up and the final squeal of brakes as the Moon plane jockeyed for position. They watched the great blue sheets of flame flung back as it pulled into the night sky, and then they ran to the baker's van that would take them to Stockholm and other problems. Professor Bohr was in the lap of the gods. So, possibly, was the future of atomic science.

The Mosquito climbed beyond the height where oxygen is needed. The pilot spoke over the intercom: "You should be getting oxygen now."

There was no response. The pilot checked instruments that told him if oxygen was flowing into the passenger's mask. The black-and-white-checkerboard dial showed no response. He tried the intercom again. Still no reply.

Two hours' flying still lay ahead. The Mosquito's only protection was extremely high altitude, where enemy interception was difficult. If they stayed at that height, Bohr would die. Already he seemed to have lost consciousness. If they dropped height, he might recover only to be killed by night fighters.

Turning back would mean internment. The base from which they had taken off was already once again abandoned. If Bohr was to get medical aid in a hurry, they should land at Stockholm. The Swedes, under Nazi pressure, would never let him out of their sight again.

The pilot shrugged and pushed the nose down. If he must risk low altitude, the quicker the better. Holding the plane at maximum speed, despite a warning sign against exceeding a diving velocity that could tear off the wings. He headed for the sea, turning gently northward at the same time. One eye on the panel, he went to work on the Dalton computer strapped to one thigh. At sea level, flying flat out, he had fuel enough to sweep farther north and approach Scotland along a route beyond the range of German fighters. It would mean a careful juggling of speed at the cost of high fuel consumption, and the risk of a landfall with near-empty tanks.

Northeast of the bleak Orkney Islands, he switched

on the Iffy—Identification/Friend or Foe—device that told Britain's radar guardians he was harmless. Ten miles from Scapa Flow he broke radio silence to request emergency landing. There was no sign of life from Professor Bohr.

46

WAITING ON A desolate Moon squadron base near Edinburgh was the man who could persuade Professor Bohr to join the Allied attempt to build an atomic bomb—Bill Stephenson.

A small RAF van sped across the field to meet the Mosquito. Ambulance men raced with mechanics to the sealed belly of the gaunt aircraft as the blue flame of the exhausts stabbed the darkness for the last time. Bomb-bay doors hissed open. The limp form of Professor Bohr was lowered to the waiting stretcher.

The Mosquito pilot slid down the wing. "Not much I could do—"

His arm was squeezed by the small man in nondescript clothes. "We'll take care of this."

The pilot glanced at the ring of silent civilians. "Well—"

"It's okay." The commanding voice cut through the gloom. "You did your job."

The pilot nodded. In this strange work, you said nothing and you asked nothing. He slung his parachute over one shoulder and moved out of the circle of emergency lights. For him, a dangerous and solitary mission would be fixed in memory as a disaster.

Stephenson turned back to the Baker Street doctor. "Any chance?"

The younger man fiddled with needles and tubes. "Pulse a bit weak. But we'll pull him through."

Stephenson suppressed an urge to say "You'd

481

better." He turned and walked over to the flight shack. Across the fields, lanterns glowed in the village of Elmdon, where farm workers prepared for another day. "We'll need to airlift his son," Stephenson told the young officer who joined him. "Aage Bohr—he's familiar with Professor Bohr's work."

"Yes, sir."

Aage Bohr was brought out of Sweden a few days later. By then, his father had recovered. Professor Bohr's intercom plug had been jerked out of its jack during the take-off. Unable to see, scarcely able to move, he was unable to trace the problem. His oxygen mask was unclipped, and he had heard nothing of the pilot's instruction to seal it over his mouth and regulate the oxygen flow. He was lucky to be alive.

Father and son were installed briefly in a drab Westminster hotel and given an office on Old Queen Street, headquarters of the British atomic project, TUBE ALLOYS. "We were baffled by the mob of eccentrics who came to see us," Aage wrote later. "We were staggered by the information they had. . . . In Copenhagen we had viewed Europe through a tiny slit in the wall."

"Professor Bohr was a gentle soul," said Stephenson. "He genuinely believed in Gandhi's philosophy of opposing evil with humility, of resisting violence with intellectual weapons. He had to come out of Nazi surroundings to comprehend the scale of wickedness we were dealing with."

Five days after the atomic scientist's strange flight to England, he met Churchill, whose Foreign Office adviser, Alexander Cadogan, wrote in his diary: "Nils [sic] Bohr. What a man! He talked, quite inaudibly, for three-quarters of an hour—about what, I haven't the faintest idea. . . . It's a growing, lazy habit to mutter away a jumble of ill-arranged thoughts." Cadogan knew nothing of how Bohr had arrived. Churchill, better informed, still had little time to waste on formality.

Bohr was questioned about Hitler's plan to shower London with 5,000 *Vergeltung* (Vengeance) V-1 rockets a day. How did this dovetail into reports of atomic rockets? Could an atomic warhead be carried by these German rockets already in existence?

He was shown details of rockets that he never knew existed. He was told that experiments with these long-range Vengeance weapons had been conducted only 120 miles from his labs, at a place called Peenemünde, in such secrecy that for each of 40,000 inhabitants there was one SS guard.

Finally, he was told that he was needed in the United States "to work on the bomb."

Bohr objected. "We cannot fight one barbarism with another barbarism."

"We won't survive to fight for anything if we neglect this new weapon," argued one of the chief researchers.

"I cannot subscribe to violence," said Bohr.

"If you don't resist violence, you'll surrender to a violent ideology all the values of our civilization, built up by generations of struggle."

"But civilized behaviour calls for non-violence."

"The freedom to behave in a civilized way must be defended, and sometimes that means using violence. . . ."

It was the old dilemma. Bohr, the theoretician, was being talked down from his ivory tower. He agreed to join the team racing against time to produce the bomb. He still insisted, however, on his right to climb back later to a higher view of mankind. As Britain entered her fourth winter of war, Bohr in late 1943 traveled with his son to New York. They were provided with false identity papers in the name of Baker—it was the one name that Bohr seemed able to remember at all times. Baker of Baker Street. In Stockholm and in London, he had been given other false names and always forgot them, often answering the telephone with the familiar "Bohr here. . . ." Now he was a Baker Street Irregular, and in the guise of "Uncle Nick" Baker and young Jim Baker, father and son were absorbed into the Manhattan Project. They would have sixteen months' intensive work before "the design of the weapon was finally frozen (March 1945)," according to the BSC Papers, "and even then, feverish activity was necessary at Los Alamos to get the weapon ready." How close Bohr came to helping the wrong side, at least in Churchill's view, was betrayed in the memo written to his scientific adviser, Professor Lindemann, by then Lord Cherwell: "It seems to me that Bohr ought to be confined or at any rate made to see that he is very near to mortal crimes."

Aage Bohr described his father returning from an encounter with Churchill "downcast. . . . He had been scolded and immediately began to dictate a letter and a description of the atomic energy project and of the arguments against the bomb."

Roosevelt actually dispatched Bohr back to London, bearing messages reflecting the concern of prominent scientists who feared Russia's exclusion from atomic secrets. But the President, for once, failed to read the Prime Minister's mood. Churchill's doubts and suspicions were based on hard experience. He felt that Nazism and other forms of tyranny were possible because men like Bohr clung blindly to their belief that reason is the strongest force in human beings. Because of this belief, Bohr had been vulnerable to German blandishments. The SS tore away the wraps of self-deception. Yet Bohr continued to preach his faith in men, arguing that atomic secrets must be shared to prevent another fatal arms race.

Bohr may have been right. But Churchill did not think so. He had only to cast his mind back to Munich in 1938, when he had met with the Focus group at the Savoy to compose a telegram warning Chamberlain not to make more concessions. One by one, the members of the small circle confessed they saw no way to make appeasement-minded men face reality. "Winston sat alone with tears in his eyes," Stephenson recalled. "The iron entered his soul. His attempt to salvage what was left of honor and good faith had failed. . . .

"The lesson of Munich was that free men should stand together. Churchill had not hesitated to share secrets with the United States from 1940 onwards because Americans shared the same traditions of freedom. He had no reason to believe the Soviet Union would repay any such gesture. His experience of Russian leaders was that they behaved like other leaders of totalitarian states. They understood only one thing —power. This may have been a glum conclusion compared with Bohr's idealism. But that was what Churchill had learned from his own position in history."

Four years after Britain's gamble in dispatching scientific secrets to Washington in 1940, Stephenson felt vindicated. His faith in the triumph of the individual over the state was being tested in Europe. In occupied Paris, the German directorate of the flying-bomb organization played a war game. Rockets and flying bombs would be launched during that summer of 1944 in a series of six-hour salvos on London, with between 672 and 840 winged bombs in each salvo. The commander of the flying-bomb regiment, Colonel Ulrich Wachtel, was not to know that the Americans had developed the first effective antiaircraft radar system, repayment for the "boxes of tricks" protected by Stephenson after his original talk with Roosevelt. The British cavity magnetron tube and the proximity fuse, among the gifts delivered by Sir Henry Tizard, led to the American SCR 584, which linked radar with predictor and gun, and came into action in time to help counter the frightening V-1 attacks.

Less than a hundred miles from London, 5,000 German engineers worked on a vast concrete structure concealing batteries of guns with barrels each 416 feet long to pump shells at the rate of one every ten seconds into Whitehall and Westminster. Launch sites for missiles were scattered just inside Fortress Europe's wall. The potential scale of the assault was daunting.

"It failed because of individuals who never met, who played no direct part, and yet were bound in a symbiotic union the implications of which we would do well to heed," Stephenson wrote in a subsequent assessment. The V-1 and V-2 rockets were defused by American knowhow and by Baker Street's skillful use of the secret armies.

"The counter-offensive to mass raids by German Vengeance rockets saw the dawn of missile strategies in a world balanced on the edge of nuclear death," he said later. "German work on 'atomistics' and rockets was thwarted by us before it could mature—but it was thwarted through thousands of individuals, scattered from Poland where one secret army reassembled bits of German rockets to ship to London and New York, to Paris where Jewish scientists took terrible risks getting data on electronic brains to steer the new weapons onto London."

Each group worked independently and thought itself alone responsible for the defeat of Hitler's V plan to atomize the little English donkey.

47

ALL THROUGH NAZI Europe, the individual was pitted against technology and the totalitarian machine. The resistance armies were highly independent, without uniforms half the time, seldom in awe of rank, and always ready to question orders. Vital undertakings depended on single acts of courage that brought neither praise nor military awards.

They had turned to London as the source of hope. Now, London was threatened by V bombs. London had become General Eisenhower's headquarters; and British secret operations came under American command. London had become the forward base of OSS, whose American agents parachuted into enemy territory to make contact with the secret armies. But London, for the irregular forces who recognized no single direction, was still an emotional symbol. In groups of two or three—Norwegian, French, Belgian, Dutch, elderly ladies in Pomerania and teen-age girls in Zagreb—they worked to lift the threat hanging over the city that many had never seen but all knew as a voice out of the darkness: "This is London calling," followed by those opening bars from Beethoven that spelled out V for Victory.

Agents in Denmark sent back photographs of rockets

and control mechanisms. In Poland a team collected the pieces of a smashed V-1 and managed to ship it over to London. None could be told of the work of others. Each group, with understandable pride, thought it had solved the scientific riddle that loomed before the war when Stephenson received hints of it through the secret Jewish agency FRIENDS, whose members were in the defense-research branch of the French General Staff. One was Dr. Alfred Eskenazy, a specialist in the new science of electronic controls for pilotless aircraft. Another was Professor André Heilbronner, an expert on rocket fuels. Both, being Jews, ran a terrible risk by remaining in Paris after the German occupation. They became part of the MARCO POLO group, whose members took code names from science fiction. VERNE, one of the leaders, reported to London that German experiments with Hitler's promised "atomic rockets" were centered on Peenemünde, in Pomeranian Bay, a secluded part of the Baltic coast. The rockets, shooting out to sea, appeared to be controlled by radio from an island belonging to Denmark and only twenty-five miles from Sweden. Some test rockets were falling into nearby Poland. Many separate and independent networks became involved when the German experiments spread from one occupied country to another.

"The first incredible play of chance was Hitler's decision to launch the rockets against London," Stephenson recalled. "He named them Vengeance weapons. The concerted attacks took place after the D-day invasion of France. He should have aimed his rockets at the English Channel ports, to stop reinforcements from relieving Allied armies establishing a foothold in Normandy. Instead, he vented his spleen on civilian targets."

The German rockets had been strategically delayed by co-ordinated secret Allied operations separately performed. At Bletchley Park, the ULTRA teams sat at the hub of underground radio traffic. The demand for radio units from the United States fell upon the INTREPID organization in New York, which had to convey to American manufacturers the urgency of new and intricate orders without revealing the purpose of

487

their use. The special teams inside Nazi territory often depended on these slender threads—radio contact with Bletchley and thus to BSC in New York. Bill Donovan, who knew the real reasons behind the seemingly excessive demands, was beset by so much interference that the BSC Papers contain a section called "The Menace of U.S. Inter-Departmental Strife."

When American air intelligence began to designate Peenemünde for reconnaissance and strikes, an acceptable story had to be issued by the British to explain how the secret weapons had been located. A pretty WAAF officer, Constance Babington-Smith, was said to have been studying aerial photographs in May 1943 when she recognized what appeared to be rocket launch ramps. By that time, MARCO POLO in Paris and other secret networks had provided a great deal of related information. Babington-Smith was young and photogenic, and she had indeed spotted in hundreds of aerial pictures the T-shaped ramps. She was skilled at estimating the dimensions of objects by relating such factors as the length of shadows to the time of day when each picture was taken. More important, the publicity about her exploits misdirected the Germans about how the Allies were getting information.

Babington-Smith had to compete with headline events around the world. Gory battles raged from China to Italy. The chief of OSS in Switzerland, Allen Dulles, was negotiating the surrender of German armies in one theater. In the Pacific, OSS was using Australia as the springboard for operations against Japanese garrisons from Singapore to Shanghai. In Washington, careerists peered ahead, sensing the danger OSS presented to the traditional service intelligence establishment. A permanent, central intelligence agency might deprive service chiefs of some instruments of power and rob diplomats of their full authority.

The English, under the threat of direct annihilation, could think only of today. Death plunged out of the sky, unheralded. London's vulnerability was an urgent problem for Americans whose headquarters were there. Technical experts in the United States thought they could perfect a counterweapon, given more information. But even the most primitive of the new Nazi weapons—nicknamed the "doodle-bug" by Londoners—had 25,000 parts. And when this particular rocket exploded, away went all the parts. Stephenson, having persuaded Washington that this threat was real and could still influence the outcome of the war, now had to persuade London to secure a complete rocket, undamaged, for Americans to study. A request was radioed to the Polish secret army and instructions were sent by courier for interfering with the radio guidance system of some German rockets. Shortly afterward, a V-1 swerved off course from Peenemünde and fell in the marshes beside the River Bug in Poland. Local farmers hid the stubby wings in mud. German search parties failed to spot the buried weapon.

The Polish partisans informed London that the rocket was being dismantled. Tantalizing reports followed. One signal read: REGRET WARHEAD GONE. There was a thoughtful silence in London. Had it exploded? Was it mislaid? A later signal was more explicit. The live warhead was in deep water, making it hard to locate. These operations were taking place under the most brutal Nazi occupation forces in Europe. Despite this, the entire V-1, warhead and all, was reassembled, and an aircraft was sent to pick it up. The twin-engined DC-3 Dakota landed safely enough. On the night of July 25, 1944, it waddled across the "reception field" in occupied Poland with the rocket on board. The gamble almost failed when the plane swerved and became stuck in the rain-sodden ground. The small partisan group, anxious to leave the scene, heaved and tugged; the plane's engines roared until it seemed impossible that German security forces had not heard the racket. But shortly before dawn the Moon plane got away. "Sure that we could now quickly find a countermeasure, Churchill announced next day the extent of V-1 damage," Stephenson recalled later. "People had to know, but until this moment, we could promise no relief. For every rocket that fell in London or southern England, there was one civilian casualty. Churchill gave the figures —the number launched to July 26 was 2,754 V-1s, and the number of casualties was 2,752. Two hundred V-1s fell on London within a single day. The rockets seemed unaffected by anything—fog, moon, light, or dark—and people felt helpless. The moment we saw the possibility of stopping them, the facts were made public. During the following month of August, only one in six V-1s got through the new defenses. By September 7, London was told the danger had passed. Then the big V-2s began to fall. . . ."

The secret army's risks, taken to save London, were closely held secrets. An anonymous Polish partisan experimented with signal equipment to check the report that some rockets could be diverted off course by radio signals on an assigned wave length. He confirmed that they could by doing it, landing the V-1 in the River Bug. He worked in an attic above a German Luftwaffe billet. An engineer inside the German military construction organization copied plans of a launching ramp. Agents secured speed and range figures that instructed RAF interceptors, enabling the pilots to work out a technique for tipping the unmanned V-1s by sliding a wing under one of the rocket stabilizers and gently lifting it into a steep descending turn. The larger V-2s dropped almost vertically out of the sky from a great height. There was one final answer to them—mass bombing raids against their bases and launch ramps. The raids were executed by American and British fliers utilizing the detailed information accumulated over a long period by Europe's guerrilla forces.

"So many different agencies and fighting units had a hand at the kill, each thought itself responsible for ending the threat," said Stephenson. "It was Allied armies crossing the Rhine that finally stopped the launchings.

"As to why the V weapons never fatally hurt us —one reason was that German double agents were fed false information on where the rockets fell. The Double Cross, or Twenty Committee, gradually moved the targets into the countryside by reporting a false position for each explosion through German intelligence channels under British control.

"Later came the accusation of 'playing God.' "

The miracle was that the rockets had only conventional warheads. Roosevelt received from INTREPID in late 1944 the studies made of the Vengeance weapons. The Germans had plans to launch bombers and rockets against American targets. BSC recovered plans to modify a U-boat to fire rockets into New York and to dispatch Focke-Wulf Condor aircraft on one-way bombing runs over the American eastern seaboard. Their scientists understood the theory of atomic bombs. If the Third Reich had survived, if Hitler had been replaced by an equally ruthless but less exhausted Führer, the new era of push-button warfare might have opened and closed with the destruction of Western civilization.

Nobody understood this better than the President. In the following April, he prepared a speech for delivery on Jefferson Day. A copy reached Stephenson, and he added his sad penciled comment in the margin: "A great speech, by the greatest President, never delivered—"

President Roosevelt died on April 12, 1945, on the brink of opening debate on the great moral issues that arose with the swift growth of all the weapons of secrecy. These issues haunted INTREPID. The uncontrolled release of atomic reaction was seen as being no less dangerous than the explosive force of individuals trained in new methods of terror through sabotage and assassination.

Roosevelt had intended to expose openly to the world "the danger that politicians will accept as inevitable the destruction of innocent people to achieve their goals and that scientists will concentrate on the means and ignore the ends of their research."

One symbol of the new power and responsibility awesomely placed in the hands of men was Bohr's heavy-water cyclotron left behind in Denmark.

The moral issues of such soul-searing concern to Roosevelt and Stephenson were dramatically exemplified in microcosm only three weeks before the President's death. By an irony of fate, Denmark again was the locale. This blazing event, hardly noticed by the rest of the world, its secret purpose known only to a few, became symbolic of the grim dilemma so perpetually to plague those who faced the making of deadly decisions. It was the RAF raid on Gestapo headquarters in Copenhagen.

48

"A CRUEL TIME comes," said Niels Bohr to Stephenson, "when to save a nation's deepest values, we have to disobey the state."

· Disobedience was forced on the Danes from the day Bohr vanished. They had been advised by their king to continue their daily routine when the Nazis invaded in 1940. If good citizens obeyed the law, they would keep both government and monarchy. Then the government found it could no longer submit to the Third Reich's imperial decrees. Thousands of Danes were rounded up by the Gestapo. The violence resolved conflicts of conscience. It had become necessary to disobey the state. The cruel time had come. It reached a peak of agony when Danish agents were obliged to request the destruction of Gestapo headquarters at the risk of killing chieftains of the secret army and hundreds of innocent children.

Bohr came to New York in November 1943 with more than atomic secrets locked in his head. He told BSC how the Gestapo operated behind a façade of "correct" German administrators and therefore confused the people. The German overlords identified with King Christian, who commanded the loyalty and devotion of his subjects. The King co-operated in the hope of preventing tragedy, unaware for a long time that many Danes who did actively resist Nazi pressures were taken to Aarhus University in Jutland, away from public view, to be tortured and killed. Bohr, aware now that this double-headed German administration had slowly undermined the nation's independence, helped to fill in the details of Nazi headquarters so that mock-ups could be built at Camp X for the training of guerrillas.

Bohr pleaded only for the preservation of his labs, and the Van de Graaff machine in which he had used heavy water in accelerating deuterons. He knew the Danish secret army had mined the labs, but he feared that blowing them up would confirm the view of those Germans who claimed that his atomic experiments were of practical value.

A curious controversy raged between scientists already involved in the Manhattan Project and those still in Copenhagen under Nazi control. Should the labs be destroyed? The argument was conducted through secret channels, in coded messages carried by couriers. Finally, a signal was sent to Copenhagen:

DO NOT—REPEAT NOT—ACTIVATE THE
DEMOLITION CHARGES.

The cyclotron was left unharmed. To sabotage it would alert Hitler to the significance of Bohr's work.

A more painful decision now had to be made. The Gestapo had captured Danish agents who knew of Denmark's secret army and its plans for industrial sabotage and the armed diversion of German forces in the path of an Allied invasion. The prisoners knew the importance of Bohr's work. It had been summarized in the manuscript lost during the escape of other scientists. The papers contained information that, properly interpreted, would help the German atomic project. Their importance, not apparent to German field police if they should stumble upon them, might be betrayed by prisoners under questioning. And Baker Street always had to assume that prisoners would talk—in the end.

The prisoners did not have suicide pills. They were local guerrilla chiefs with five regional headquarters who had been taking orders through neutral Stockholm from London. They were imprisoned in Gestapo headquarters in the heart of Copenhagen. Skillfully manipulated, they could help the Germans continue exploiting a country torn between self-preservation and outright rebellion. Those of Denmark's leaders under King Christian X who had obeyed enemy orders were condemned by the British Foreign Office. "Denmark is neither an ally nor even a belligerent but a nation accepting German dictates," wrote a diplomatic adviser. Churchill rebuked the man: "Danish administrators obviously have a first duty to their own people, when their conquerors are prepared to take hostages or punish whole communities in retaliation for disobedience. *Taking orders is not the same as collaboration but the borderline between the two activities can never be clear.*"

This was the agony shared by public servants in all the conquered territories when the Germans governed through local dignitaries. A mayor might be told to provide workers for German industry. He was not required to ask questions. A minister might be told to round up Jews. What happened to them might be, or might not be, his affair. A king could preside over the execution of his own people, believing he was protecting them.

Denmark was technically a neutral country under German occupation, but with King and Cabinet still in nominal control. Beside them was the double-headed monster: the "correct" governors from Berlin and the jackbooted SS silent in the shadows. There was the King. So long as he remained in position, loyal Danes were uncertain about helping the secret army. Christian was well aware of the borderline between submission and active help for the Nazi overlords. When pushed to the point of defiance, the old monarch understood what terrible consequences might flow from a self-indulgent display of anger. "It might satisfy his ego but it could cost lives" was the way Sven Truelsen had expressed it to Stephenson. "In this kind of warfare, the hardest role is that of the prominent figure who must risk having his actions misunderstood."

After the Allied invasion of Europe, King Christian faced the dreadful reality that if his people did not revolt against Nazi control, they would be slowly destroyed by the Germans becoming more desperate in defense. He sent word through Truelsen to Baker Street: "We have the German armies under a magnifying glass. We know the order of battle down to the last platoon. We know what German warships use which harbors and what guns they carry. We know the airfields, how many planes, which sort. . . . *We have also lost our best leaders who are now in Gestapo cells.*"

Truelsen turned up one day in London in his customary manner, casual and without warning. A raid had been conducted against a concentration camp and the RAF air crews were celebrating the release of Danish agents through the breached walls. "The party was in full swing," Stephenson recalled. "Suddenly this unassuming civilian walked in, fresh from a very different scene. It was Truelsen."

Air Chief Marshal Sir Basil Embry, who directed special air operations, said: "He asked me to knock out a reinforced concrete building in the center of Copenhagen. Considering the risks he'd taken to get to the party, I had to listen. Even so, the scheme sounded crazy."

The legendary Dane sought out the young RAF commander because his pilots had already disemboweled Gestapo headquarters in Jutland to release the prisoners held there. What Truelsen proposed now raised the hair on well-mannered heads in the British Air Ministry.

"Truelsen wanted a group of bombers to rupture the foundations of the Shell building in Copenhagen so that some forty Danish secret army chiefs in the top floor could escape," said Stephenson. "Gestapo files in the bottom part of the building had to be destroyed before interrogation began upstairs. The War Cabinet said it couldn't be done. I said the Americans had new radar equipment that OSS might get us. Even so, the target was at extreme range for Mosquitos carrying the special bombs required. Pilots would have to fly flat on the sea to get under German radar and then sweep into Copenhagen's streets at very high speed, weaving below the rooftops to get one-shot strikes. . . . Everyone turned thumbs down. Then Air Marshal Sir Basil Embry listened to the other side of the story. If the raid did *not* take place, Gestapo records, which had just been assembled, would be painstakingly examined along with the Danish resistance leaders, and it was a matter of time before the secret army was mopped up in one big German operation. So long as Danish patriots could undertake guerrilla operations, the Germans would be obliged to keep 200,000 troops in the country. If the Germans smashed the Danish resistance, those troops would be released for use against American forces. Sir Basil got the okay by telling Churchill privately that he would go with the raiders under an assumed name. So the operational order came down from on high."

Ted Sismore, an ace pathfinder for these tricky low-level raids, was selected to solve the navigational problems. He said to Truelsen: "It would be rather nice if someone could take a photograph of the damn building from the sea approach." Two weeks later Truelsen turned up in his office. "He had the very picture I wanted. Gone back, stolen a boat to photograph from the right angle, then scampered out again. The perfect target photograph, just as we would see it, sweeping in at wave-top level."

Old tourist postcards and travel brochures were dug up and a large model made of Copenhagen. Ted Sismore planned the route. "We set the model so all crews could look at it by crouching beside the table. They got the picture of the city as it would come up very suddenly—terribly fast."

There were arguments about the size of the force. The tactical leader of the operation, Group Captain Robert Bateson, figured six Mosquitos would do nicely. "The more aircraft, the less controllable they are."

Embry insisted on at least eighteen aircraft. "Once you're committed to an operation, you can't make a mistake and go back. The second time, the Germans are ready and waiting." Already the Gestapo had imprisoned more Danes in the sixth floor of the Shell building. A founding member of the Freedom Council, political chief of anti-Nazi operations, Dr. Mogens Fog, was held there. Another prisoner was Professor Brandt Rehberg, a scientist colleague of Bohr.

Could the raid on Shell House be justified when the lives of such men were at risk? There was a convent school adjoining it, crowded with children. Even if the Mosquitos hit the target, and even if none crashed into nearby streets, the RAF analysts estimated some Danish civilian lives must be lost.

What did Bohr think? Could he suggest the kind of decision that his old colleague Professor Rehberg would make? The questions were put to Bohr by Stephenson, who reported that Rehberg would likely consider the gamble worthwhile. But it would be wise to send a man into Denmark to make the fateful decision.

Ole Lippmann was the man most qualified, already a veteran at twenty-eight. "I had been away six months," he said later. "The Gestapo had accomplished a lot in my absence. I slipped back into Copenhagen and began calling members of our circuits. In every case, the Gestapo was at the other end of the phone. I took a train to Deer Park and went for a long walk. The situation was familiar. The time before, we tried to smuggle suicide L-pills to our comrades in the interrogation cells *as a favour to them*. I thought, well, if L-pills were regarded as a favour then, why not bombs now? There were three-dozen secret-army leaders in the Shell attic. I thought I knew how each must regard the prospect of further torture. They would do what their predecessors had done: appeal for death.

"I walked around Shell House again. The houses on either side, the school across the road, all would be hit. But irrespective of this, irrespective of my friends sitting up there behind bars, I concluded we must ask for the raid."

The decision was received by Basil Embry with horror. "But I said I'd carry it out if Lippmann said so."

Eighteen Mosquitos were diverted from the European battle fronts. "They and the crews could be spared for forty-eight hours, no more," said the leader of the raid, Bob Bateson. "The first briefing came the morning after the Mosquitos were transferred to a Special Duties field in Norfolk. Truelsen from Denmark was there. I wanted my crews to comprehend the problem in human terms. This wasn't just a question

497

of destroying Shell House. There were people in there who must be helped to escape."

Thirty-six young airmen watched the Dane with veiled curiosity. Sven Turelsen was something outside their experience. Secret wars were fought unseen, except when flying crews were required for special duties, about which they were told only as much as seemed necessary. Seldom did they glimpse a member of the European underground. Many suspected it did not exist. They disliked operations that produced no visible results but involved abnormal risks. Sitting on muddy fields behind enemy lines, they waited for ghostly figures who never spoke and sometimes failed to materialize. Hovering low over lakes that shimmered in the treacherous light of a full moon, they endured heavy ground fire to drop anonymous foreigners and mysterious bundles into limbo. Back from these exhausting and lonely flights, they had nothing to report and no tangible proof that their patience and skill hurt anyone but themselves. Here, at last, was a man speaking from the shadows, soon to return to a nether world that seemed at times mythological.

"I told them if the hostages were not killed in the raid, they were going to die slowly and more terribly anyway," said Truelsen. "I said if the hostages could escape, their value was enormous. And if the Gestapo files were destroyed, it meant there would be a secret army in Denmark that still evaded German detection."

Shortly before dawn on March 21, 1945, the Mosquitos took off across the English coast. They carried eleven-second-delay bombs. That meant eleven seconds' grace for each aircraft to get out of its own bomb blast, and a similar span of time between each attack. The first wave carried incendiaries, and so did the third, to make a bonfire of the wrecked building. In half a gale blowing across the North Sea, they flew just above the wave tops. "The pilots had trouble holding on course," said Sismore, master navigator for the raid. "I had difficulty holding the map, and I certainly couldn't calculate with pad and pencil. The windscreens were covered in salt from the sea and this was a serious hazard because in Mosquitos you have to navigate a great deal by visual checks."

Bateson had to control the formation without using radio, and this meant predetermined signals between aircraft in visual range of each other. Flying in number-three position on Bateson's port side was a certain "Smith." He was the commander of the special-duties group, Air Chief Marshal Sir Basil Embry. He had been forbidden to take part in such missions by his immediate superiors. His experience was too valuable. He would be irreplaceable if lost. He knew too much about ULTRA. Still, it was the kind of adventure Churchill would have insisted on joining, and the Prime Minister had given his approval. So Sir Basil was known as Smith. If he crashed and the Germans should identify him, there would be an interrogation accompanied by truth drugs, whose effects were thought impossible to fight. Smith therefore carried lethal tablets, too.

"He was absolutely insistent that he come on the raid," said Bateson. "One had to accept that, coming from a superior officer. But once in the air, he was under my command. I had to forget who he was, and not worry about his safety."

Embry planned the raid to hit Copenhagen when, according to Truelsen's intelligence reports, the maximum number of Gestapo would be inside Shell House. "I wanted to kill as many as I could."

The whole formation flew straight for Jutland, spread out in a single but manageable formation. They hit their first landmark on the coast of Denmark right on time. "It became very exhilarating," said Smith. "All the Danes along the flight path stood up and waved. We were weaving between trees, pulling up over power lines."

A protective force of thirty Mustangs provided escort under the command of the Belgian Baron Michel Donnet. "It was really rather a pleasant trip," he reported afterward. "Hopping over church steeples, one eye looking ahead so you didn't slice off a wing on a power line, one eye sideways watching for enemy fighters. We took Copenhagen completely by surprise."

The first wave was led by Bateson. Ironically, German efforts to hide Shell House made it stand out. It was the only building painted in green-and-brown camouflage. "It was a case of bowling right down the alley, releasing bombs at the last moment, and pulling away in a tight turn up a side street."

Behind him, Smith saw the first bombs go straight into the base of the building. He pulled up over the roof top and found himself staring into the belly of another Mosquito an arm's length above him. "I dived into a lane, terrified one of my wings would catch the side of a house."

The raid came on the eleventh day of interrogation inside Shell House for secret-army leader Paul Bruun. "I could not have held out much longer. Then from nowhere came this bang. Then another. A bit of ceiling came down. A big hole appeared. Walls tumbled in upon me."

Dr. Mogens Fog remembered later: "I was never so frightened in my life. The cell door fell in, and blocked my escape. The bombs came thudding in, one after another. There were actually thirty-eight hostages in the Gestapo cells. One of us got hold of some keys from a German warder who was stunned by the first blast."

The Mosquito piloted by Wing Commander Kleobo was caught in the sudden melee of aircraft when the second wave, confused by fires, decided to make another run at the target. Kleobo's wing struck a pole and his aircraft plunged into the Catholic school of Jeanne d'Arc, killing children and nuns.

Fog stumbled into the street dazedly aware that this miraculous escape was the result of pinpoint bombing, and then encountered a girl. "She was walking through the smoke across a yard and I thought the Gestapo had shot her in the back until she fell forward and I saw that the back of her head was torn open. Even then we never understood the price paid for our escape."

Across the yard, Sister Gertrud at first was shouting with excitement: "Look, children, the British." She saw the RAF markings very clearly, then realized that one of the machines was lurching toward the school. "It crashed and burst in flames."

The leader of the raid, Bob Bateson, pieced together the story later. "The unfortunate thing was Kleobo crashing. His bombs exploded with him, right on the

500

final run to target. Following pilots were not sure which fire was Shell House. Some had time to see the burning school, realized the smoke obscured the real target, and didn't bomb. Others did. They mistook the black column of smoke for a marker. Their bombs fell into the school."

The price for saving Denmark's secret army was ten airmen, twenty-seven teachers, and eighty-seven children killed, and many more civilians badly mutilated. For this, Gestapo files on Denmark's anti-Nazi forces were destroyed before they could be acted upon; thirty leading Danish guerrillas escaped from their interrogation cells.

President Roosevelt knew about the raid although the public did not. He recognized in it the moral questions that would plague his successors. He requested, through Stephenson, an assessment. The report never reached him because he was dead by the time it was ready.

Ted Sismore later made a lonely pilgrimage back to the bombed school to try to explain what had happened. The parents of the dead children, to his astonishment, gave him comfort. "They wanted me to know the raid was necessary."

Merete Jensen was a twelve-year-old girl at the time. "We were all so jubilant because at last here were our friends flying in from the sea. Then there was a terrible crash and everything went dark and it seemed as if after that there was just a long silence. I thought maybe I am dead. So I sat waiting. And then I heard children crying and praying and crying and then suddenly there was the smell again of Spring. It had been such a marvelous day, you know. The first day of Spring . . ."

Epilogue

A VIEW FROM ANOTHER ISLAND

"No man is an *Iland*, intire of it selfe;
every man is a peece of the *Continent*, a
part of the *maine*; if a *Clod* bee washed
away by the *sea*, *Europe* is the lesse, as
well as if a *Promontorie* were, as well as if
a *Mannor* of thy *friends* or of *thine owne*
were; any mans *death* diminishes *me*, because
I am involved in *Mankinde*; And therefore
never send to know for whom the *bell* tolls;
It tolls for thee."

—John Donne, *Devotions*

49

"DOES IT SEEM odd, to finish with a young girl's dream of spring shattered?" I asked.

"No." Stephenson was silent for a long moment. The manuscript lay on the table nearby. "No. It's a good place to break off—not finish. Wars are never really won. We still face the consequences of this one. The springtime of our hope was 1945. If the world had fully grasped the essence of the devastating experience we'd survived, we might by now have dispensed with secret intelligence and stopped the creation of terrifying weapons." He paused again, lost in thought, then continued. "Roosevelt saw the growing contradictions in the last year of his life. On the one hand, there was increasing reliance on technology, on scientific specialists. On the other, secret warfare, depending on intuition, on the individual. Both were essential to bring down the colossus. But intelligence was the key, the nervous system and brain of strength. Peace in the future would rely on the control of this combination.

"After Roosevelt died, the West invested heavily in technology. Mao and Ho applied the lessons of the guerrilla. And more recently the PLO learned how a terrorist could blackmail a government."

We sat in his study in Bermuda. He was Sir William now, his name on the Roll of Knights, originating a thousand years ago. The recommendation for this distinction, sent to his king from Churchill, carried an unusual, personal inscription: "This one is dear to my heart." President Harry Truman, making Stephenson the first non-American to receive the highest award for a civilian, the Presidential Medal of Merit, wrote: "Some day the story must be told."

Was it yet told? The full story could never be told. There were gaps that would always remain mysteries. And the story, even as it can be pieced together, is staggeringly huge. But I had made a beginning.

I thought back to OVERLORD—the final Allied invasion of Fortress Europe. Not even the most senior American and British military chiefs knew at the time how ULTRA was employed to protect the D-day armies. Only Churchill, Roosevelt, and the handful of intelligence chiefs directing these secret operations were aware of the critical deception made possible from intelligence gained through JUBILEE at Dieppe.

ULTRA, intercepting and studying each German reaction to the D-day invasion, was able to feed false information through the Bletchley transmission network to reinforce an error made by German General von Rundstedt. The German commander was persuaded by Dieppe, and by subsequent intelligence "leaks," that the Allied invasion of Europe would be launched across the narrowest part of the English Channel, at Calais. Even after the D-day landings in Normandy, the Germans did not commit all available forces to smashing the OVERLORD beachhead.

Hitler and his generals (except for Rommel, whose opinion was initially dismissed) thought Normandy was a diversion. Thirty divisions of Allied troops seemed poised to strike at Calais once the Germans were fully committed in Normandy. Those thirty divisions existed only in Bletchley's fertile imagination and in fake radio messages to Allied agents in Europe.

ULTRA revealed how Hitler vacillated between Rundstedt and those who, like Rommel, now began to suspect the truth. Acting with almost split-second precision, Bletchley redoubled the flood of false information that would back up Rundstedt's delusions. As a result, Hitler delayed the dispatch of reserves that might have driven the Allies back into the sea.

I thought back further, to the Quebec conference of 1943, when OVERLORD was agreed upon. Two of Stephenson's secretaries were there: Grace Garner and

Eleanor Fleming, young Canadian women who carried the tremendous secret in their heads for almost another year, until D day on June 6, 1944. Grace and Eleanor had a fiery chapter of history locked in their stenographic notebooks—and that was still only a microscopic fraction of the whole. A single drama was concealed in the word "Jedburgh," which appeared briefly among millions of coded messages. The name had been picked at random from a school textbook—it referred to an abbey that once sheltered Mary Queen of Scots. Its coded meaning covered teams of agents dropped behind German lines before the OVERLORD landings. Each team was known as a Jedburgh and marked a significant merging of American, British, and European intelligence groups in the new Special Forces Headquarters under General Eisenhower. Each team of three agents worked with the secret armies whose final upsurge was to clog the inner mechanism of Fortress Europe while OVERLORD vaulted the battlements.

Stephenson flew with the D-day armies as rear gunner in an Allied bomber and then returned to BSC, now dividing itself between Europe and the Pacific through the most sophisticated system of communications ever to support invisible armies. Its scope could one day be guessed by the Alsop brothers, the Washington newsmen who volunteered for secret operations. Stewart was dropped behind German lines. Joseph, partner of another BSC agent, the British banker John Keswick, was in China. It was years before the brothers pieced together the fragments of their own experiences and traced the links back to BSC in New York. There, too, was a book, but the Alsops never wrote it, out of regard for British intelligence sensitivities. (Though Stewart, with Thomas Braden, covered another facet in *Sub Rosa: The OSS and American Espionage*.) The British philosophy was "rather than have half the truth emerge, let it all be suppressed," this based on Lord Chancellor William Jowitt's theory that a biased history emerges unless every word of testimony is included. To achieve that ideal would require a multitude of books.

The day after the OVERLORD landings, a single German SS Armored Division was directed to counterattack in Normandy. Twenty-three days later, that division finally extricated itself from savage ambushes by DAVID, the network led by Claude de Baissac, who with his sister Lise had been parachuted into the region. Their particular contribution was noted eventually in a London *Times* obituary when Claude died in 1975. As the thirty-year ban on wartime secrecy ran out, the obituary columns became a major source of these new revelations.

The secrecy continued beyond all reason. One explanation offered was that the details could help hostile powers. DAVID was part of the plan covering Europe to provoke disorder. The instructions given to citizen armies for turning German-held towns overnight into jungles might prove useful to postwar enemies. What happened in Nazi-held territory, it was argued, could be made to happen by relatively small fanatical groups against established Western governments. When telephones suddenly go dead, trains are sidetracked, signposts turned awry, factories crippled by mass absenteeism, postal services rendered unreliable, then anarchy triumphs.

The obvious weakness in this argument for keeping the secret war secret was that some of the guerrillas trained in such methods were already and irreconcilably opposed to the restoration of the old order. Whom were the secrets kept from?

"The secret war was fought by amateurs," said Stephenson. "And the amateurs were being replaced by careerists with a vested interest in secrecy. And the conventional war had its generals and admirals with an eye to the future, and therefore good reason to downgrade or ignore the role of the resistance movements. They found security could be used to withhold information from the public."

Almost six months after D day, Stephenson and Donovan drafted an appeal to Roosevelt for the preservation of the partnership that crossed national boundaries. They were looking ahead, though not for themselves. Each had civilian interests to resume. They judged that Hitler's methods of aggression, the blitzkrieg wars of speed and surprise, could be vastly strengthened with the new weapons available. Even the declaration of wars had become an archaic formality. A future war might be launched and finished within a day or two—or less. The first line of the free world's defense was the free flow of information. Where this flow was impeded by the censorship and controls imposed within a totalitarian society, it became necessary to secure the information through secret intelligence and disseminate it as widely as possible. A world war had been started because of miscalculations based on lack of accurate and objective information on both sides. The dictators mistook for weakness the normal divisions within the democracies. Their intended victims were unprepared for the ruthless efficiency of the Axis military machines.

On November 18, 1944, Donovan signed the memo that resulted from these deliberations: "Once our enemies are defeated the demand will be equally pressing for information that will aid in solving the problems of peace. This requires that intelligence be returned to the President and a central authority established, reporting directly to you."

Addressed to President Roosevelt, this top-secret document was leaked to the press by critics of OSS and BSC. The Chicago *Tribune* published articles attacking "this super-spy plan . . . an all-powerful intelligence service to spy on the post-war world and to pry into the lives of citizens at home." For a time gossip was revived that Donovan was conspiring with the British in New York. When the fuss died down, Roosevelt prepared to act. It was April 1945. He died before he could put into effect a plan to carry into peacetime the knowledge and experience gained from Allied comradeship.

What Stephenson envisaged was "a worldwide intelligence service to maintain the security of the democracies in the critical years ahead with safeguards against abuse of power." The safeguards were to have taken the form of a central authority made up of responsible citizens working within the framework of democratic government. The safeguards were the most important feature of the proposals, anticipating the problems and moral dilemmas that would finally explode in the 1970s.

But a month after Roosevelt died, BSC was asked to leave American soil. INTREPID's wartime operations in Manhattan shrank as the military campaigns in Europe and Asia approached their climax. The sudden requirement to suspend operations might have excused bitterness, but Stephenson loyally refused to discuss the feuds between U.S. agencies that caused the break-up of his partnership with Donovan and OSS, and then even the demise of OSS. President Truman saw no further need for a co-ordinating intelligence agency duplicating what he was assured could be done by the military services, the State Department, and the FBI separately. Truman signed the fatal order disbanding the OSS on September 20, 1945. All BSC records were hauled away to Camp X, on the Canadian side of the border.

Secrecy had become the ally of rival professional intelligence services. Unfortunately, secrecy was also the ally of the Soviet Union, once again hostile, a massive totalitarian power sealed against outside inspection.

The electronic chatter of the Axis armies ceased, and ULTRA was dissolved. Silence fell over Bletchley Park. The secrecy there was so durable that when I returned thirty years later, the townspeople either knew nothing or would say nothing. The effect of such tight security was that a later crop of leaders knew little or nothing about the secret war. Some veterans, mainly for political purposes, occasionally cracked the silence. Richard Crossman, former deputy-director of British Psychological Warfare, wrote that intelligence agencies "appeal to those who revel in being mysterious men with secret knowledge, loving the moral twilight shrouding activities that by civilized standards are barbaric."

This was exactly what Stephenson had wanted to prevent by creating out of BSC experience a service that retained wartime integrity, staffed by civilians accountable to their elected representatives. He wrote from his New York office on the last day of 1945, when the last BSC cipher machines had been carted away: "The conception of coordinated operations in the field of secret activities, which BSC originally exemplified, was the basis upon which the Americans built, with astonishing speed, their own highly successful wartime Intelligence Service. It is, perhaps, not going too far to suggest that this conception may properly be regarded as essential to the maintenance of peace. . . ."

By 1947, INTREPID's secret war was buried under conventional accounts of military campaigns. The British contribution to the new weapons, both nuclear and guerrilla, was virtually forgotten. Congress, reacting to the rising hostility of the Soviet Union and the condition called the "Cold War," passed a hotly debated National Security Act that set up an information-gathering agency. On September 18, 1947, two years after the OSS was dissolved, the Central Intelligence Agency came into being. And so the peacetime alliance, so earnestly advocated by Stephenson and Donovan, slipped into oblivion.

Churchill let cities be mauled rather than expose those secrets on which the survival of democratic civilization might depend. There were no bloodless alternatives unless leaders were to retreat into self-righteous horror and refuse to make decisions at all.

"A similar situation exists today," said Stephenson. "The easy way out is to pretend there are no crises. That's the way to win elections. That's the way we stumbled into war in the first place—there were too many men in power who preferred to see no threat to freedom because to admit to such a threat implies a willingness to accept sacrifice to combat it. There's a considerable difference between being high-minded and soft-headed."

There was a long silence. Outside the study, the yellow-breasted kiskadees of Bermuda crowded the bird tables in the garden, their cries drifting through the window.

I broke the silence: "For the first time in history, we see everywhere the means of conveying informa-

511

tion—and everywhere we seem in greater darkness then before. Secrecy seems like a disease—"

"That might destroy us?"

"It seems a clear threat to the freedom we have."

"More than half the world is under dictatorship," said Stephenson. "Those people do not know what we call 'freedom.' Only sixty generations stretch back from you and me, here, to the dawn of Western history. Two world wars in this century remind us that 'civilized' Europe is the bat of an eye from the Dark Ages. We've sailed a long, stormy course to this small island of freedom. We had to endure the sacrifices of war, risk our lives daily, carry on despite the loss of those we love, and overcome statistically insuperable odds to preserve what we have. Are we now to admit that we can no longer find the means to control the weapons we create to defend ourselves? Or are we saying we can't control ourselves? For free people, the future is filled with hazard and challenge. When was that not so?"

Such a very small island, I thought, when measured against recorded history. Did living in Bermuda suggest the analogy to Stephenson? He had retired here for practical reasons to do with his own need for anonymity. And he had withdrawn here to reflect. His life had come briefly out of obscurity in 1962 when British author H. Montgomery Hyde published a revealing account of "The Quiet Canadian" in *Room 3603*. Ian Fleming wrote of it: "Bill Stephenson worked himself almost to death carrying out undercover operations and often dangerous assignments that can only be hinted at. . . ."

Stephenson was then living in an apartment overlooking the East River in New York. He withdrew when the last BSC papers were disposed of, making no comment about the brief biographical exposure. In Bermuda, he was left undisturbed to fight against severe physical handicaps caused by two wars. There are a few clues to Stephenson's character in his modest home there. The evidence would suggest a retired professor with an interest in wildlife. But one would search in vain for diaries, photographs, or souvenirs that reassure those who have retired. Stephenson discarded purely personal papers and memorabilia with the same ruthlessness that he destroyed his past in the mid-1930s. He had his phenomenal memory. And he had Mary, his wife, with her own amazing capacity for recall.

While writing this book, I regularly visited the Stephensons to check details. Mary would greet me and then "disappear into the wood-work," a trick she knew to perfection. Bill, dressed in casual slacks and a plaid shirt, would stand in his corner of that austere study and grasp my hand with a grip of iron.

"This is your book," he declared. "Write it the way you see it." But he struggled against this becoming his biography. He wanted it to give a fundamental understanding of the secret war. The time had come for the telling, and he was the custodian of the facts. He took quiet pride in his knighthood because it was recognition of public service. Otherwise, as I had learned from the wartime Minister of Economic Warfare, Hugh Dalton, he drew no salary throughout the war, and gave away much of his own resources to win it.

Mary and Bill whittled their lives down to a level of unostentatious comfort such as they had known in childhood. What retained importance in the study was the Morse key, worn and polished by his hand in periodic practice since he rigged it as a schoolboy.

"The totalitarian powers don't have to answer to their own people for the actions of their secret agencies," Stephenson said to me one day. "They don't have newspapers and television probing and watching constantly. Yet they have complete freedom to conduct campaigns in our own world. They have great advantages.

"Our primary defense is more than ever information. And it's in our interests to see that a potential aggressor is aware of our strength and resolve.

"We're still evolving democratic societies. If we want to continue this natural growth, we can't ignore ideological enemies who want to stunt it—or destroy it. By working through our own democratic institutions, they can disarm us. The campaigns against Western

513

intelligence agencies are fought often with unwitting help from our own citizens, honestly outraged by the excesses of huge sealed organizations with unaccountable budgets. The disclosed failures of these agencies are widely publicized. Their achievements have to be kept secret—or they cease to be effective. The same old rule applies as it did with ULTRA—better lose a battle than lose a secret that might win a war.

"How can the citizens of a free society exercise proper control without losing these defenses? Those responsible for intelligence feel that any public scrutiny is a danger to security. The citizen feels that secret power corrupts.

"Somewhere along the line, there has to be trust. The Second World War involved thousands of individuals who had to be trusted to carry out their missions in solitude, without acclaim, making decisions that could affect whole communities. These men and women, courageous, informed, but essentially ordinary people, not professional agents or intelligence careerists, proved they could be trusted. Perhaps we had better look for them and to them in these most sensitive and critical undertakings."

Stephenson felt that we had to get the priorities right. The greater danger to individual freedom comes from totalitarian regimes that regard any dissenting view as a threat to be destroyed—no matter if the threat comes from a lonely writer protesting against injustice or from another nation. One nation has the power to stop this obliteration of dissenting views—the United States.

"At the worst moment in Britain's resistance in 1940," he recalled, "John Buchan wrote: 'The United States is actually and potentially the most powerful State on the globe. She has much, I believe, to give the world; indeed, to her hands is chiefly entrusted the shaping of the future. If democracy in the broadest and truest sense is to survive, it will be mainly because of her guardianship. For, with all her imperfections, she has a clearer view than any other people of the democratic fundamentals.'

"Every word," said Stephenson, "is true today. Which is why our enemies would like to isolate the

United States and see her retreat from the confusion and the chaos as she did during the rise of the Third Reich.

"I believe Americans will resist the pressures and the propaganda to discard primary defenses. They'll find responsible ways to control the weapons of secrecy. I don't agree with that metaphor of Walter Lippmann that the people of the West, to stop their hands shaking, prepare to welcome manacles.

"It would be a great irony if, having proved to the would-be conquerors of the world that freedom will prevail, we cannot prove it to ourselves."

The most compelling reason for Stephenson's willingness to reopen a chapter of his life that he had hoped was closed forever is that BSC affords a glimpse of what can be done by the citizens of many nations when their freedoms have been savagely threatened or destroyed. Churchill, on being made an honorary citizen of the United States, drafted a letter to President John F. Kennedy. He broke the key sentences into blank verse, as was his habit, and caught the essence of Stephenson's own feelings:

> *Our comradeship*
> *and our brotherhood in war*
> *were unexampled.*
> *We stood together*
> *and because of that*
> *the free world now stands.*

Stephenson later wrote: "We learn from experience. The comradeship reveals itself whenever these dark forces try to reassert themselves. This brotherhood is a human response that grows within us. It cannot be legislated any more than can a mother's response to danger. It becomes a matter of courteous and concerned habit within our evolving civilization.

"What is often forgotten is that the worst abuses of power within our democratic societies are exposed by our own people. The spirit of resistance is opposed to all forms of tyranny. We purge ourselves while we

515

resist our enemies. This is the response of a concerned citizenry, knowing freedom is in danger, putting the responsibility for defending it squarely on individuals of honor and good intent. This is a sense of brotherhood that won't fit into rules and regulations. And so long as this holds true, there will always be struggle, but there will be no final defeat."

Once a year, those who worked with BSC and OSS exchange greetings on a card with the silhouette of a parachutist dropping into the arsenals of Hell. Printed on the bottom are the words *Spirit of Resistance*. The cards fly across national frontiers and political boundaries. A frequent inscription is taken from a French Resistance song:

> *When you fall, my friend,*
> *Another friend will emerge*
> *From the shadows*
> *To take your place.*

"That may seem a flimsy kind of mysticism to pin your faith on," said the man called INTREPID. "But it's all we've ever had in bad times.

"Abraham Lincoln captured its essence more than a century ago when he wrote: 'What constitutes the bulwark of our own liberty and independence? It is not our frowning battlements, or bristling seacoasts, our army and navy. . . . Our defense is in the spirit which prized liberty as the heritage of all men, in all lands everywhere.'

"Roosevelt understood that spirit, replaced the friends who fell, and gave us the means to salvage liberty again. Strong armies would have been useless without that deeper commitment to principles. The human race came very close to falling into a Dark Age.

"The same spirit still lives. Perhaps it only survives through struggle. It's needed now to re-create an alliance in defense of the main priorities of Western civilization. This is what we did then. This is what we can do now."

I listened to this valiant man and thought once again how superbly apt Winston Churchill had been in selecting his code name: INTREPID.

Valediction

BEFORE TAKING LEAVE of this book, which has occupied most of my working time for almost three years, I want to acknowledge those who have most particularly contributed to my efforts. INTREPID, as the reader will know, made many things possible and, because of them, this book as well. For that, and more, I tender him my boundless gratitude.

It must be evident that I owe a large debt to those who, through direct interviews with me or INTREPID, generously provided significant detail to certain events I selected to illustrate the vast scope of secret warfare. Many others entrusted to me personal and confidential documents. When possible, and only with their consent, I have identified such contributors in the appropriate place in the text. At times, however, the nature of the material or the structure of the narrative did not permit attribution. And in some instances, for compelling reasons, many confidants could not be openly identified. Rather than single out some and not others, I have refrained from appending here what would prove to be an imposing list in length as well as in content. I have privately expressed myself to these unnamed individuals and here remind each of my appreciation.

No one who served in the secret armies would begrudge special mention of that extraordinary and self-effacing man General Sir Colin Gubbins, who remained characteristically gentle but unswervingly resolute through the bitter years of suffering, and of his Norwegian wife, Tulla, who bore her share of hardship and loss with fortitude. They typify the irregulars —French, British, American, Dutch, Canadian, Belgian, whatever their nationality—those who fought as individuals against the mechanized juggernaut, who accepted anonymity in adversity, and thus did not receive the prayerful thanks they so richly deserved. I am particularly grateful to them.

Institutional sources I have acknowledged in the text. I hold a special obligation to the crown corporation that gave cover for such BSC operations as Camp X, Station M, and Hydra—the Canadian Broadcasting Corporation, which aided me by many indispensable services, including archival material and illustrations.

Herbert Rowland's integrity and loyalty during thirty-five years of devotion to INTREPID insured absolute discretion in the safekeeping and security of the BSC Papers and other records from which I drew so much material.

To save me from drowning in vast oceans of detail, Julian Muller, friend and editor, formerly of U.S. Naval Intelligence and with four years of wartime service at sea, helped launch this book and then navigate its course with what INTREPID himself described as "authoritative sorcery."

William Stevenson

Toronto, Canada

Index

Aarhus University, Jutland, 492

ABC-1, 170-72, 193-94, 323

Aberdeen, Scot., 464

Abetz, Otto, 340

Afifi, Sheikh Youssef, 380

Africa, 96, 230, 273, 296

Albania, 225, 229

Albert, Heinrich, 27

Algeria, 439, 448

Algiers, Alg., 441, 442, 447

Allied Committee of Resistance, 29

Allier, Jacques, 459

Allies: World War I, 6, 22, 37; World War II, 101, 125, 186, 190, 221, 363, 398, 429, 432, 440, 462, 470, 478, 488, 490, 506

Alonso, Manuel, 191

Alsop, Joseph, 507

Alsop, Stewart, 507; *Sub Rosa: The OSS and American Espionage* (with Braden), 507

America First Comm., 88, 143, 219, 322-24

American Committee for the Defense of British Homes, 128

American Export Lines, 197

American Federation of Labor, 318

American Federation of Scientific Astrologers, 380

American War Relief Comm., 5

Anderson, Rear Adm. Walter S., 34, 37

antiaircraft, 485

Archangel, U.S.S.R., 443

Argentina, 327

Ark Royal (Br. carrier), 262, 264-65

Armstrong, George R., 306

art treasures: recovery of, 197

asdic, 142

Asia, 33, 46, 52, 216

Aspidistra, 203

Associated Press, 380, 406

Astor, Lady Nancy, 360

Astor, Vincent, 360-61

Atkins, Vera, 243-45

Atlantic, Battle of, 72, 104, 110, 128, 136, 142, 147, 148, 193-97, 255, 257-73, 277, 337

Atlanic Charter, 287, 362

atomic research and weapons, xvi, 3, 82-83, 167, 415, 420, 435, 449, 452-86; Canada, 454-55, 455n., 465; England, 16, 82, 119, 155, 453-54, 461, 465, 468, 473, 477, 482-83, 511; Germany, 25, 45, 59-60, 65-66, 70, 82-83, 119, 171, 258, 309, 432, 453, 455, 456-75 *passim*, 485-86, 491, 493; Soviet Union, 59-60, 299n., 458, 484-85,; U.S., 455 and *n.*, 458, 461-62, 465, 468-69, 472-73, 478, 483-84, 493

Aubert, Dr. Axel, 459

Auer, Gen. Theodor, 439-40

Augusta (U.S. cruiser), 287

519

Chamberlain, Neville, 40, 47, 50, 55-61, 66, 68-71, 72-78, 86-87, 92, 96, 110, 137-38, 484

CHEESE, 464, 466

Chequers (estate), 181, 277

Chicago, Ill., 469

Chicago *Daily News*, 116, 132

Chicago *Tribune*, 88, 328, 509

Chile, 310, 344, 345, 387

China, 30, 88, 123, 190, 224, 507

Christian X, King of Denmark, 62, 471, 473, 475, 492, 494-95

Churchill, Mary, 50

Churchill, Peter, 247

Churchill, Randolph, 75

Churchill, Winston, xvi, xxii, xxiv, 3, 7, 17-26, 29, 33, 41, 43, 46-51, 56-57, 66, 67-68, 71, 73-74, 80-87, 93-95, 135, 162, 176, 210, 217-18, 267-68, 383, 515, 517; as Prime Minister, 89-91, 92, 96-97, 101-102, 106-109, 112-15, 122, 128-69 *passim*, 180-83, 220-22, 226-34 *passim*, 255, 258-66, 272-78 *passim*, 287-89, 293, 299, 329, 332-33, 350-64 *passim*, 373, 412, 415-23 *passim*, 430, 433, 435, 440-49 *passim*, 454-58, 465, 473-74 and *n.*, 482-85, 489, 494, 496, 499, 505, 506; and secret intelligence, xvi, 30-34, 41-42, 44-45, 51, 56-60, 67, 69-71, 73, 77, 83, 105, 164-65, 168, 181, 186, 215, 219, 237, 244, 335, 403, 406, 511; *World Crisis, The*, 182, 268, 335

Churchill, Mrs. Winston, 89

Cipher Machines, 24

Clark, Gen. Mark, 439-40, 441, 445, 447, 448

Clausen, Fritz, 390

Cleveland, Ohio, 381

Cleveland *News*, 381

Cockburn, Claud, 88

Cold War, 511

Collins, Dr. Stanley W., 197

Colombia, 301, 310, 407

Colville, Jock, 278

Combined Operations Intelligence, 416, 417, 423, 432

communications, 13-16, 507; interception of, 16, 20, 26-27, 32, 35, 39-40, 48, 54-55, 63, 85-86, 113, 157, 158, 185-200 *passim*, 270-72, 325-26; *see also* cryptology; individual means of

Communists, 131, 146, 217, 224, 228, 279, 306, 321, 324, 438, 449, 450, 454

concentration camps, 3, 49, 153, 253, 308, 314, 374, 384, 385-86, 419; *see also* individual camps

Condors (Ger. planes), 491

Confederation of Mexico Workers, 320

Congress of Industrial Organizations, 317-18, 324

Connaught Laboratories, 379

Copeland, Miles, 436

Copenhagen, Den., 59, 62, 66, 457-58, 460, 463, 468, 471, 474, 476, 482, 491-501 *passim*

Coppola, Vicenzo, 294-95

Cornelius, 103

Cossack (Br. destroyer), 265

Coughlin, Father Charles, 118, 144

523

Dorniers (Ger. bombers), 126

Dorsetshire (Br. cruiser), 266

Dover, Eng., 101, 110

Dowding, Air Marshal Hugh, 126, 166

Drew-Brook, Thomas, 6, 8-9

Driberg, Tom, 143

Dublin, Ire., 30

Duff Cooper, Alfred, 40-41

Duke of York (Br. battleship), 332

Dulles, Allen W., 396-400, 415, 488

Dumais, Lucien, 429

Dunkirk, Fr., 101-102, 109-10, 128, 139, 141, 145, 170

DYNAMO, *see* Dunkirk, Fr.

early-warning system, 19

Economic Pressure on Germany Comm., 57-58

Ecuador, 301, 310, 401

Eden, Anthony, 158, 419

Edinburgh, Scot., 129

Edward VIII, King of England, 62

Egypt, 443, 448

Eichmann, Karl Adolf, 376

Einstein, Albert, 17, 25, 60, 82, 360, 458

Eisenhower, Gen. Dwight D., 245, 441-42, 445, 448, 486, 507

El Alamein, 448

Electra, 30

Electric and General Industrial Trust, 28

Elias, Gen. Alois (JUDAS), 387-88

Elizabeth, Queen Consort of George VI, 71, 118, 121

Ellis, C. H. ("Dick"), xxvii, 52, 453 *n.*

Embry, Air Chief Marshal Sir Basil, 495-99

Emile Bertin (Fr. cruiser), 354

England, 6-16, 19, 20, 23, 25, 28-34, 38, 41, 45-55, 56-62, 66-97 *passim,* 101-109, 110-11, 118, 119-21, 124, 131, 135-38, 145-49, 154-56, 160-61, 167-68, 238, 261, 267-69, 271-72, 276-78, 306, 321, 332-33, 341, 349, 350-54, 360, 385 *n.,* 396, 420, 443-48, 453, 456, 459-68 *passim,* 473, 477, 482, 485, 496, 511; American aid for, 64, 83-84, 94-97, 102, 109, 121, 135, 138-51 *passim,* 155, 168, 171, 172, 191, 229, 255, 280, 288, 321-22, 353; Anglo-American cooperation, 167, 169-72, 177, 193-96, 212, 219, 269-73, 299 and *n.,* 400, 406-407, 416-17, 420-22, 435, 453-55, 465, 468-69, 507; Battle of Britain, xiv, 64, 70, 72, 73, 87, 94, 97, 109-69, 177-84, 193, 216, 219, 236, 277, 339, 488-90; *see also* BSC; Churchill, Winston; Hitler, Adolf, appeasement of; individual agencies and military forces

ENIGMA: of Germany, 24, 27-28, 32, 35-36, 38-39, 42, 45, 49, 52-56, 57, 60, 63, 67, 68-71, 72, 78-79, 85, 86, 91-92, 103-105, 120, 142, 157, 195, 311, 342-43, 372; of Japan, 30, 33, 35-36, 39, 157, 164, 194; stealing of, 45, 50-54; *see also* ULTRA

Eskenazy, Dr. Alfred, 487

espionage, 7, 46, 54, 151, 175,

French Navy, 147, 171, 340, 348, 350-54, 364; codes of, 363-73, 435, 440
French North Africa, 334, 364, 373, 417, 419-22, 435-48, 452
Freud, Dr. Sigmund, 25
Friedman, William, 164, 166, 194
Friendly, Alfred, 165
FRIENDS, 487
Frisch-Peierls paper, 82, 120
Fritsch, Gen. Werner von, 384

Gabcik, Josef, 390-92
Galen, Clemens Count von, 389
Galtesund (steamer), 464
Gandhi, Mohandas, 412, 460, 482
Garbo, Greta, 57, 62
Gardner, Nadya, 189-90
Garner, Grace, 506-507
Garry, Emile, 247
General Aircraft, 31
General Motors, 22, 114
General Radio company, 17
Genoa Conference, 36 n.
George V, King of England, 30
George VI, King of England, 47, 51, 61, 62, 71-72, 73, 76, 77, 118, 122, 419, 478
George Cross, 239, 253
German Air Force (Luftwaffe), 32-33, 55, 76, 88, 188, 207, 220, 230-31, 233, 275, 276, 320, 422, 460, 467; Battle of Britain, 79, 110-11, 113-15, 121, 123, 126-29, 133-35, 148-50, 156-58 and n., 162-66, 169, 179-80, 184, 216, 236, 340, 447, 463
German-American Bund, 192
German Army, 78-79, 92,

110-11, 121, 220, 230-31, 233, 343, 419, 420, 439-40, 451
German Library of Information, 323, 405
German Navy, 195, 257-69, 364, 446; see also submarine warfare
German Steuben Society, 323
German United Steel Works, 38, 61-62
Germany, xv, 5-11, 17, 18, 21-28, 34, 36-37 and n., 40-42, 44-51 passim, 56, 57-67, 69, 77-78, 79-83, 85-86, 94, 109-10, 118-19, 123, 124, 131, 136-37, 142, 153, 156-57, 158 n., 159, 164, 166, 171, 193, 194, 198-99, 218, 220-37 passim, 240, 242-43, 249-52, 258, 259, 268, 273-84, 287-88, 296, 300-305, 307-309, 318-21, 323-26, 329, 339-40, 348, 352, 354, 357, 378, 384, 385 n., 397, 401, 406-12, 414-19, 427-29, 432, 444, 446, 453, 455, 456-75 passim, 485-86, 488-94; and Balkans, 221, 225-34, 278; blitzkreig tactic of, 32, 38-39, 42, 44, 47, 48, 70, 79, 92, 111, 113, 156, 405, 509; military conquests of, xxiv, 40-43, 47-50, 53, 55, 58, 66, 67, 70, 73, 88, 89, 93-97, 101-102, 115, 128-29, 177, 307; see also ENIGMA; Hitler, Adolf; propaganda; terrorism; individual agencies and military forces
Gershwin, George, 22
Gertrud, Sister, 500
Gestapo, 27, 37, 122, 126, 209, 238-42, 249-53, 327,

337, 339, 340, 378, 389-90, 393, 397, 413, 415, 424, 428, 457, 464, 470, 471, 475, 476, 479, 491-501 *passim*
Gibraltar, 340, 441, 448, 452
Gneisenau (Ger. battle cruiser), 258
Goebbels, Dr. Joseph, 226, 233-34
Göring, Hermann, 68, 76, 77-78, 111, 115, 148, 320, 376, 439
Gouzenko, Igor, 455 *n.*
Government Code and Cipher School, 48, 50, 51, 56, 60, 85
Gowing, Margaret, 119 *n.*
Greece, 225, 226, 229, 231-34, 273
Green, Capt. Hughie, 215
Greenslade, Adm. John W., 356
Gronau, Baron, 283
Guadalcanal, 442
Gubbins, Col. Colin M., 46-48, 53, 54, 55, 58, 74, 76-77, 123, 131, 203, 465; books of, 46
Guernsey, 115, 129
guerrilla warfare, xviii, 46, 57, 73, 75, 91, 97, 106, 109, 123, 130, 135, 168, 208, 218, 225, 231, 237, 240, 334, 373, 396, 398-400, 403-404, 412, 414, 447-49, 456, 470, 490, 492, 505, 508, 516; *see also* occupied countries
guided missiles: Larynx, 18
Gurie, Sigrid, 468
Gustav V, King of Sweden, 62, 68, 77, 476, 477

Haakon VII, King of Norway, 460

Hahn, Otto, 82, 458
Haldane, J. B. S., 122
Halifax, Edward Wood, 1st Earl of, 62, 77, 95, 96, 110, 132, 161, 351 and *n.*, 462-63
Halifax, Can., 191, 337, 354
Hall, Adm. Sir Reginald ("Blinker"), 7-8, 12, 13-14, 15-16, 20, 29, 34, 37, 39-41, 51, 55, 81
Hamburg, Ger., 319, 411
Hamilton Princess Hotel, Bermuda, 186-88, 197
HANNA, 254
Harriman, Averell, 168
Hart, John, 154
Haukelid, Knut, 468-71
Havas news service, 361
Haw-Haw, Lord (William Joyce), 55, 94
Heilbroner, André, 487
Heisenberg, Werner, 462 and *n.*
Helsinki, Fin., 63
Hertslet, Dr. Joachim, 301, 320
Herwarth von Bittenfeld, Hans H., 224
Hess, Rudolf, 445
Heydrich, Reinhard T. E., 36-37 and *n.*, 38-39, 45, 48-49, 114, 189, 193, 202, 375-96 *passim*, 419
Highet, Gilbert, 383 and *n.*
Hilgert, Edgar, 411
Himmler, Heinrich, 189, 384
Hiroshima, Jap., xv
Hitler, Adolf, 18, 22-24, 25, 26, 29, 33-34, 40, 73, 81, 85, 129, and *n.*, 153, 157, 172, 217-18, 220-23, 226-31, 233-34, 281, 288-89, 307, 314, 319, 325, 329-32, 374, 377-96 *passim*, 404-405, 416,

302, 345-46; *see also* Mussolini, Benito

Jackson, Robert, 146
Jamaica, 187
Japan, xiii, xiv, 31, 34, 35, 39, 88, 131, 158, 164, 167, 170-71, 194, 222, 269, 271, 282-86, 290, 297, 301, 325, 329-33, 341, 401, 417, 488
Japanese Navy, 31, 147
Jemelik, 391
Jensen, Hans, 462 *n.*
Jensen, Merete, 501
Jepson, Selwin, 238
Jersey, 115, 129
Jerusalem, Grand Mufti of, 390
Jewish Agency, 414, 423
Jews, 18-19, 87-88, 144, 172-73, 486, 487; and Nazis, 22, 26, 37, 44, 77, 87, 93, 128, 224, 254, 364, 376-77, 384-85 and *n.*, 386, 404-405, 475-77, 494
Johnson, Axel Axelson, 61, 63
Johnson, Lyndon B., 162
Joliot-Curie, Frédéric, 459
Jowitt, William, 507
Juin, Gen. Alphonse, 439
Jungk, Robert, 462 *n.*

Kahn, David: *Codebreakers, The,* 344 and *n.*
Kaiser Wilhelm Institute, Berlin, 59
Kapitsa, Peter, 458
Kearns, Frank, 436
Keenlyside, Hugh, 270
Keitel, Field Marshal Wilhelm, 231
Kelly (Br. destroyer), 259
Kendall, Douglas, 416
Kennedy, John F., 162-63, 515
Kennedy, Joseph P., 50, 72, 75, 81, 85, 86-90, 93, 95-96, 117, 121, 132, 135-36, 137, 140, 143, 159-63, 181
Kent, Tyler G., 84-85, 92-96, 125
Kesselring, Albert, 32
Keswick, John, 507
Keynes, John Maynard, 454
Khan, Air Vice-Marshal Newab Haji, 239
Kieffer, Hans, 252 and *n.*
King, Adm. Ernest J., 193, 197, 212, 422, 423, 431, 443
King, Mackenzie, 42-43, 147, 338, 455 *n.*
King George V (Br. battleship), 194, 259, 262, 265
Kipling, Rudyard, 13
Kirk, Capt. Alan, 147
Kleobo, Wing Commander, 500
Knickebein beacons, 148 and *n.* 164
Knight, Clayton, 379-80
Knight, Ridgeway, 439-40
Knox, Frank, 116, 132, 255, 304
Koons, Frank, 426
Korda, Alexander, 214, 377, 382-83
Korda, Zoltan, 214, 377, 382-83
Kramer, Lt. Com. Alwin D., 330
Krock, Arthur, 218
Krupp firm, 37
Kubris, Jan, 390-91
Kurusu, Saburo, 328
Kutschera, Gen. Franz, 398

Labour party, 76, 89-90
Labrador, 179
Ladenburg, Thalman & Co., 403
La Grandville, Comte de, 366-68
La Guardia, Fiorello, 380
Lais, Adm. Alberto, 346

Manitoba Transvaal Contingent, 4
Mann, Thomas, 25
Mannerheim, Field Marshal Baron Carl, 63-64
Maori (Br. destroyer), 265
Mao Tse-tung, 46, 123, 431, 505
MARCO POLO, 487
MARION, 349
Mark Hopkins Hotel, San Francisco, 223
Marlborough, John Churchill, 1st Duke of, 90
Marshall, Gen. George C., 170-71, 412, 423, 431
Martin, John, 157
Martinique, 340, 352-57, 400
Maryland, 271
Masaryk, Jan, 87-88
Maschwitz, Eric, 90, 179, 204
Maskelyne, Jasper, 179, 205, 356
Mast, Gen. Charles, 439, 447
Masterman, Sir John: *Double-Cross System, The*, 286, 436
Matusoka, Yosuke, 283
Maurois, André, 341
McAlister, John, 246-47, 250
McLachlan, Donald, 196
Menzies, Stewart (C), 70, 450-51
Merritt, Cecil, 430
Messerschmitts (Ger. planes), 126
Metropolitan Museum of Art, N.Y.C., 130
Mexico, 8, 197, 299-306, 320, 325, 410-12
Mexico City, Mex., 299, 321, 410-11
Michelin firm, 12, 249
microphotography, 188, 198-200, 213, 242, 410, 465
Middle East, 96, 219, 260, 272-73, 277, 333, 365, 452

Mid-Pacific Strategic Direction-Finding Net, 33
Milch, Gen. Erhard, 32
Milwaukee, Wis., 10
Ministry of Economic Warfare, 30, 33, 58, 76, 90, 310, 315
Miquelon, 337, 357
Mitchell, Reginald, 28
Modoc (U.S. cutter), 263
Moffat, Jean, 4
Molotov, Vyacheslav, 131, 399, 419 and *n.*
Montagu, Lt. Com. Ewen, 274 and *n.*, 282, 285
Montgomery, Gen. Bernard, 446
Montreal, Can., 179, 240, 361
Mooney, James D. (STALLFORTH), 114-16
Moon squadrons, 478-81, 489
Morgenthau, Henry, Jr., 144, 184, 404
Morison, Samuel Eliot, 267, 417
Morocco, 439, 448
Morrison, Herbert, 456
Morse, Samuel F. B., 4
Morton, Maj. Desmond, 29-30, 58
Moscow, U.S.S.R., 156, 228, 423
Mosquitos (Br. planes), 404, 478-81, 495-500
Mountbatten, Lord Louis, 138, 259, 414, 417, 423, 429, 431
MULBERRIES, 432
Munich agreement, 40-42, 79, 86, 484
Murphy, Robert, 439-40, 446
Murray, Gladstone, 16, 203, 205
Musa, Jean-Louis, 340, 359-60, 363
Mussert, Anton, 390

Schleebruegge, Col. Friedrich K., 300-301
Schroeder, Kurt von, 27
Scotland, 66, 179, 275, 464, 480-81
Scotland Yard, 7, 47, 75, 82, 93, 212, 218, 306, 436
Sebold, William, 409-10, 441
Second Front, 396, 399, 413, 418, 423, 430
secrecy, xvii, xviii, xxii-xxiii, 109, 144-45, 152, 159, 180, 185, 407-408, 508, 510, 511, 514, 515
secret agents, xvii, 201-17, 234-54, 344-45, 402, 429-30, 446, 486-87; captured, 239-43, 247, 250-54; as radio operators, 209, 210, 214, 236-53; see also Camp X; espionage
secret intelligence, xiii-xiv, 15-16, 20, 21, 28, 30-35, 45-46, 51, 53-55, 105-106, 206-208, 338, 352, 356, 398-404, 506, 509-10, 514; double-cross system, 286, 406-407, 436, 490; see also BSC; communications; ULTRA
Security Executive, see BSC
Seguin, Paul, 361
Seraph (Br. submarine), 439-40
SHAEF, 245
Shakespeare, William, 122; King Henry V, 141
Shaw, George Bernard, 28
Sheffield (Br. cruiser), 264
Shepardson, Whitney, 5 n.
SHERIDAN, 429
Sherwood, Robert, 142-43, 155, 168 n., 170, 257, 280, 289, 455 n.; Roosevelt and Hopkins, 170, 261
Shetland Isles, 463
Siberia, 21, 301
Sikh (Br. destroyer), 265

Sima, Hora, 390
Simon, John, 89
Simović, Gen. Dušan, 228
Sinclair, Sir Hugh (C), 51, 70
Singapore, 271
Sismore, Ted, 496, 498, 501
Six, Dr. Franz, 128
Skinnarland, Einar, 464-65
Skoda firm, 42, 393
Smith, Francis O. J., 4
Smith, Ens. Leonard, 259, 263-67 passim
Smith, R. Harris, 378 n.
Smuts, Field Marshal J. C., 183
Sofia, Bulgaria, 225
Somerville, Adm. Sir James, 262, 350
South Africa, 3
South America, 115, 173, 188, 289, 293, 298, 305, 306, 309, 310, 314, 320, 326, 344, 353, 354, 389, 401
Southeast Asia, 172
Soviet Union, xxii, xxiii, 21, 22, 26, 34-40, 46, 48, 52, 59-60, 61, 63-64, 123, 131, 135, 146, 175-76, 228, 299 and n., 321, 384-85 and n., 396, 399, 412, 418-19, 430, 443-45, 457, 458, 510, 511; espionage of, xxiii-xxiv, 175-76, 299 n., 437-38, 449, 451-54, 455 n.; and Germany, 32, 36 and n., 48, 58-59, 64, 65, 66-67, 156, 171, 176, 218, 220-33 passim, 274-81, 320-21, 324, 329, 333, 416-19, 444-45; military conquest of, 61, 64, 67, 145; see also Stalin, Joseph
Spain, 38, 190, 207, 306, 325, 364; Civil War in, 93, 123, 342
Special Forces Headquarters, 507
Special Operations Executive,

537

386, 388-96, 398, 419, 451, 476; *see also* Gestapo; SS

Texaco, 115

Thomsen, Hans, 321

Thurloe, John, 13

Thyssen, Fritz, 38, 62

Tibet, 38, 52

Tito, Marshal, 217, 221, 228, 234, 254, 451

Tizard, Sir Henry, 154-55, 160, 485

Tobruk, Libya, 420-21

Toyko, Jap., 297, 330, 416

Toronto, Can., 208, 226, 240, 415

Toronto *Telegram,* 174

totalitarianism, 486, 509-15 *passim*

Tovey, Adm. Sir John, 259-60, 265-66

Travellers Censorship, 205

Treaty of Rapallo, 36 *n.*

Treaty of Versailles, 37

Trenchard, Air Marshal Hugh, 107-108

TRICYCLE (Dusko Popov), 175, 190 *n.*, 282-86, 290

Trinidad, 187

Tri-Partite Pact, 221

Tronstad, Leif, 65, 459, 463

TRUDI, 467, 478-79

Truelsen, Sven, 472, 494-95, 497-98, 499

Truman, Harry, xxiv, 311, 505-506, 511

TUBE ALLOYS, 155, 453-54, 460-61, 482

Tukhachevsky, Marshal Mikhail, 36-37

Tunis, Tun., 441

Tunisia, 448

Tunney, Gene, 11

Turkey, 231

Turnbull, Ronald, 380

Turner, Adm. Richmond K., 287

Tuscaloosa, U.S.S., 167

Tweedsmuir, Lord, *see* Buchan, John

Twenty Comm., 285-86, 490

ULTRA, 92, 103-105, 109-10, 142, 156, 173, 194, 195, 218, 221-22, 231, 237, 258, 275-76, 279, 282, 298, 310, 325, 342-43, 372, 376, 396-97, 408, 419, 436, 440, 441, 445, 451, 487, 499, 506, 510; Battle of Britain, 111-12, 113, 121, 127, 134, 138, 141, 149, 154-56, 158 *n.,* 163-67; secrecy of, 92, 105, 163-67, 180, 233, 234, 276, 510, 514

United Mine, Mill, and Smelter Workers Union, 209

United Mine Workers of America, 318

United Nations, xv, 287, 457 *n.*

United States, xiii-xiv, 5, 13-14, 21, 23, 26-28, 31, 33-35, 39-40, 44, 47, 54, 61, 64, 70-73, 75, 79, 80-90, 92-96, 102, 105-106, 111, 113-18, 120-21, 125, 131, 136-38, 143-45, 146, 153, 157, 158, 160, 162-63, 164-65, 168-74 *passim,* 193, 194, 200-201, 204-13 *passim,* 237, 257-58, 265-70, 273, 274, 278-89, 298, 303-304, 307-21, 324-25, 327-28, 330, 333, 340, 361-62, 375, 385 *n.,* 402, 406, 407-408, 410-11, 448-49, 455 and *n.,* 458, 461, 484, 491, 510, 514-15; Anglo-American cooperation, 167, 169-72, 177, 193-96, 212, 219, 269-73, 299 and *n.,* 400, 406-407, 435, 453-55, 465, 468-69, 507; fifth column in, 85, 111, 114-16, 135-37, 154-55, 189-92, 197, 200-201,

HISTORY COMES ALIVE

Bestselling and acclaimed true stories of war, peace, rebellion and intrigue.

Available at your bookstore or use this coupon.

___**A DISTANT MIRROR: THE CALAMITOUS 14th CENTURY**   29542 8.95
by Barbara W. Tuchman
The #1 bestseller by a Pulitzer Prize winning historian. "A beautiful, extraordinary book!"—*Wall Street Journal.*

___**A RUMOR OF WAR by Philip Caputo**   29070 2.50
A true story of Vietnam combat by one who was there. "Heartbreaking, terrifying and enraging!"—*Los Angeles Times*

___**FOUR DAYS OF NAPLES by Aubrey Menan**   28906 2.50
An army of children brings the Nazis to their knees in this "stirring story."
—*San Francisco Chronicle*

___**A MAN CALLED INTREPID by William Stevenson**   29352 3.50
Over 2 million copies sold! The authentic account of the war's boldest superspy!

___**RETURN FROM THE RIVER KWAI by John and Clay Blair, Jr.**   29007 2.75
The famous story continues in this book hailed as "magnificent!"—*Pittsburgh Press*

BB **BALLANTINE MAIL SALES**
Dept. AL, 201 E. 50th St., New York, N.Y. 10022

Please send me the BALLANTINE or DEL REY BOOKS I have checked above. I am enclosing $.......... (add 50¢ per copy to cover postage and handling). Send check or money order — no cash or C.O.D.'s please. Prices and numbers are subject to change without notice.

Name_____

Address_____

City_____ State_____ Zip Code_____
04   Allow at least 4 weeks for delivery.   AL-29

The most fascinating people and events of World War II

Available at your bookstore or use this coupon.

___**ADOLF HITLER, John Toland**   27533 3.95
Pulitzer Prize-winning author John Toland's bestselling biography of Hitler based on over 150 interviews with the numerous survivors of his circle of friends, servants and associates.

___**A MAN CALLED INTREPID, William Stevenson**   28124 2.50
The authentic account of the most decisive intelligence operations of World War II - and the superspy who controlled them.

___**CYNTHIA, H. Montgomery Hyde**   28197 1.95
The incredible, but fully-documented true story of a brave, shrewd sensual woman's contribution to the allied victory — in World War II's most unusual battlefield.

___**PIERCING THE REICH, Joseph E. Persico**   28280 2.50
After 35 years of silence, top-secret files have been opened to reveal the stupendous drama of the most perilous and heroic chapter of intelligence history.

BB **BALLANTINE MAIL SALES**
Dept. NE, 201 E. 50th St., New York, N.Y. 10022

Please send me the BALLANTINE or DEL REY BOOKS I have checked above. I am enclosing $.......... (add 50¢ per copy to cover postage and handling). Send check or money order — no cash or C.O.D.'s please. Prices and numbers are subject to change without notice.

Name_____

Address_____

City_____State_____Zip Code_____

Allow at least 4 weeks for delivery.

06   NE-13

Bestsellers from BALLANTINE

Available at your bookstore or use this coupon.

____**SHIBUMI by Trevanian**   28585   2.95
The battle lines are drawn: ruthless power and corruption on one side and on the other—SHIBUMI.

____**LAUREN BACALL; BY MYSELF by Lauren Bacall**   29216   2.95
She was Bogie's Baby, Sinatra's Lady, Robard's Wife. She lived every woman's fantasy. "Marvelous!"—**Cosmopolitan.** The #1 bestselling paperback!

____**HOW TO GET WHATEVER YOU WANT OUT OF LIFE**
by Dr. Joyce Brothers   28542   2.50
America's most trusted psychologist and advisor helps you find out what you really want and then outlines key psychological findings and techniques that can be used to attain your goals.

____**JACKIE OH! by Kitty Kelley**   28327   2.50
The outrageous, outspoken, controversial bestseller about the world's most famous woman.

____**FINAL PAYMENTS by Mary Gordon**   27909   2.50
The outstanding bestseller of a young woman's rites of passage by "one of the best writers in years."—N.Y. Times

____**CAPTIVE SPLENDORS by Fern Michaels**   28847   2.50
Innocent and torn, young lovers struggle to resist each other—envy and treachery threaten them forever...

BB   **BALLANTINE MAIL SALES**
Dept. LG, 201 E. 50th St., New York, N.Y. 10022

Please send me the BALLANTINE or DEL REY BOOKS I have checked above. I am enclosing $........ (add 50¢ per copy to cover postage and handling). Send check or money order — no cash or C.O.D.'s please. Prices and numbers are subject to change without notice.

Name_____

Address_____

City_____State_____Zip Code_____

Allow at least 4 weeks for delivery.